BRITISH BATTLES AND MEDALS

No. 40. The Naval General Service
Medal, 1793-1840.

No. 38. The Waterloo Medal, 1815.

No. 100. The Indian General Service Medal, 1908-1935.

The awards depicted above are individual to the Royal Navy, the Army, and the Royal Air Force.

BRITISH BATTLES AND MEDALS

by

MAJOR L.L. GORDON

FIFTH EDITION REVISED BY

EDWARD C. JOSLIN

*A description of every Campaign Medal and
Bar awarded since the Armada, with the
historical reasons for their award and the
names of the ships, regiments and squadrons
of the Royal Air Force whose personnel are
entitled to them*

SPINK & SON LTD.
LONDON
1979

By Appointment
To Her Majesty The Queen
Medallists

By Appointment
To H.R.H. The Duke of Edinburgh
Medallists

Originally published	1947
Second edition	1949
Third edition	1962
Fourth edition	1971
Fifth edition	1979

© Spink & Son Ltd.

PRINTED IN GREAT BRITAIN BY
ROBERT STOCKWELL LTD.
LONDON SE1 1YP

PREFACE

This book has been compiled in the hope that it may be useful in helping collec-. tors to ascertain which regiments and ships, and when present squadrons of the Royal Air Force, took part in the many campaigns and battles for which a medal or bar has been awarded.

No attempt has been made to encroach too much on the historical aspect of the campaigns. However, just sufficient detail has been given to enable the reader to see for what the medal, or bar, was awarded. The dates of the actions are included, as it is considered that this information is particularly useful to collectors to let them see what is the correct order for the bars.

Where reliable information as to the number of medals issued, either for the campaign as a whole or to individual units, is available. I have given it. In the case of individual units the number of medals claimed or issued will be found in brackets immediately after the unit concerned, except where it is obvious that the figure refers to the number present.

To save space I have, in most cases, given the regimental number of the battalion at the time. Where doubt might arise as to which batallion was present the number is in the form of a fraction. For instance, 1/6 signifies that the First Battalion of the Royal Warwickshire Regiment was present.

There is a complete list of all regimental numbers at the end of the book together with the 1970 revised list.

The term "bar" has been used throughout, though many will contend that I should have used the term "clasp". To those with this view I apologize, and can only say that from experience I have found that the former term is far more often used by both collectors and dealers. In this connection it is interesting to read the General Order which authorized the issue of the Sutlej Medal which was the first medal with bars to be issued alike to both officers and men. One sentence of this order reads, "If the individual is entitled to be decorated for two battles he will receive one silver medal bearing the name of the first battle in which he was engaged and a clasp, or bar, on which will be inscribed the name of the second battle."

Collectors will probably agree that it is absolutely impossible to give a comprehensive list of every man of every regiment or ship's company present. We all know of a few isolated cases where men such as gallopers and servants of senior officers have been present at battles, and in many cases campaigns, although their regiments as a whole were not. This also occurred when the shortage of men present necessitated the diverting of troopships to and from India, bearing men going on or returning from leave, or individual postings.

There were also several cases when composite units were formed and in these cases the medals were usually named with the man's parent unit.

Again, too, many colonial units had instructors from England, so that we find in the case of many campaigns in Africa a multiplicity of regimental medals.

Often only part of a regiment was present, and where it had been possible to obtain the exact numbers they have been given. In some cases I have had to resort to expressions such as "a Company of", "a Detachment of", or "part of". Sometimes I have been quite unable to find the exact military sub-divisions or actual numbers present.

Needless to say, I have made use of many books, especially historical ones. Whenever possible, the information has been cross-checked in more than one history, both English and French. These, strange to say, vary considerably, especially as regards to date.

Thanks are due to several friends for their help, but I would particularly like to acknowledge our indebtedness to Mr. James Barker, who has put in so much work in finding and verifying facts. His unstinted help throughout was a very great and pleasant encouragement. Both he and Mr. H.F. Phillips were kind enough to lend some of their valuable medals, of which photographs appear in the book.

I am aslo greatly indebted to the Rev. G. Hawkes Field, Mr. R.O. Gray of the Newcastle Public Libraries, Mr. R.E. Atkinson of Messrs. Baldwin & Sons, Mr. D.F. Spink of Messrs. Spink & Son, Mr. G.W. Harrison, and Lieutenant-Colonel B.K. Dymott for their spontaneous help at all times.

I must also thank the Chief Clerk of the Royal Mint for supplying the names of the designers of many of the medals, which was information of a sort that we were unable to obtain elsewhere.

I would like to record that Messrs. Baldwin & Sons and Messrs. Spink & Son went out of their way to give me any help I ever asked for. Nothing, whether the loan of a book, a medal or ribbons, was ever refused, and I greatly appreciate the way they placed their vast knowledge and facilities at my disposal.

The help afforded us by the Admiralty, India Office, the Air Ministry, and the London office of the Sudan Government is also appreciated.

Considerable praise, as well as thanks, are due to Colonel A.A. Duke for reading the whole of the manuscript and giving much valuable criticism and advice.

I acknowledge the kindness of the Curator of the Queen Victoria Memorial Museum, Salisbury, Southern Rhodesia, for permission to publish the photograph of the British South Africa Company's medal, with four bars, awarded to M.E. Weale, and also that of Lieutenant-General Sir George MacMunn for allowing me to copy the colouring of the ribbon to the Hunza Nagar Badge.

It was a great pleasure to correspond with the editor of *The Nongqai*, in Pretoria, and I thank him and Mr. H.H. Curson, the writer of several very interesting articles therein on campaigns in South Africa, for their great kindness and help.

There is one retired major, whose requests for anonymity I must respect, who had the faculty for producing the very information I was after on more occasions than can be counted. His help and good humour were infections and I have no hesitation in saying that without them I could never have hoped to cover so much ground. I am very grateful to him.

The same remarks apply to many others at home and overseas. I reluctantly respect their requests and would ask them all to accept my most sincere thanks.

Finally I would like to apologize to those who feel hurt that certain items are left out, and for any errors present. I welcome any corrections and suggestions for improvement, or additions.

May I ask that those who find errors, and I am sure there are some, will let me know where the correct information can be found, or the source of their knowledge which disagrees with mine?

FARNHAM.   L.L. GORDON
August, 1947

PREFACE TO THE SECOND EDITION

In submitting this second edition I should like to thank the many new friends that I have made for their help. I have been overwhelmed by the interest which my efforts have aroused.

vi

in this edition I have tried to include as many as possible of the suggestions that I have received and yet keep the book to a reasonable price. In spite of the many requests, I am unable to include Decorations, Long Service Medals and many others. I have, however, included many new items concerning campaign medals which I hope will be of interest and use.

I must be frank, and admit that I have had to completely reverse certain ideas which I had previously held. Much information about medals is not generally available, but now, thanks to the kindness of many collectors and others, I have been given an opportunity of reading original documents, etc.

I have, in places, had to continue to use the term "Foot" instead of giving the full terriotrial titles. This has been necessary in order to save space, especially in the case of the Queen's South Africa Medal.

The spelling of surnames varies on different rolls and, surprisingly often, the name on the medal is spelt differently from that given on any roll. This remark also applies to the ranks of the recipients which also vary on different rolls and sometimes on the medal. I can see no way of proving which are correct. When the name has been spelt the same way in more than one place I have used it, but I cannot vouch for the accuracy of many of the spellings in the case of the Naval General Service Medal.

Anyone who has been to India will realize how the spellings of place names vary. It should be realized that many of them have been altered during the last hundred or more years. It has been amusing to note how many of my friends who have queried my spellings have differed among themselves!

It would be wellnigh impossible for me to give the names of all those who have so kindly and spontaneously given me help and advice in compiling this edition. I would, however, particularly like to acknowledge my indebtedness to the Chief Clerk, the Royal Mint; the Historical Section of the Canadian Army; the High Commissioner for South Africa; the British North Borneo Company; the Royal Geographical Society; the Scott Polar Research Institute; Mr. R.E. Atkinson; Lieutenant-Colonel H.N. Cole, O.B.E., T.D.; Colonel K.O.N. Foster; Mr. G.N. Harding; the Rev. G. Hawkes Field; Mr. A.L. Kipling; Mr. D.F. Spink; and Sir Godfrey Dalrymple White, Bart.

I should like to record my sincere thanks to my publishers, Messrs. Gale & Polden Ltd., and to Messrs. Spink & Son Ltd., for allowing me to pool the knowledge that I have gained in writing for them. The pleasure of writing has been immeasurably increased by their great kindness to me at all times.

May I once again remind my readers that the figure given in brackets after a regiment represents, to the best of my knowledge, the number of medals awarded to that regiment and not the number of men present, though, of course, they often coincide. The same remarks apply to the figures given on pages 34-43.

I hope that I have eliminated many of my previous mistakes. *I can see no finality in the knowledge of the absorbing subject of medals. New facts keep cropping up which alter existing beliefs.*

It has been extremely difficult, especially in the case of some of the medals awarded for service in South Africa, to be consistent when referring to the regiment represents, to the best of my knowledge, the number of medals awarded time of the engagement or campaign for which they were awarded. If, however, I omitted to mention them, then collectors would wonder whey they were not included. Where, therefore, it is obvious that the regiment was not in existence, though included as one of those present, I must ask readers to understand the reason. A somewhat similar difficulty arises over the alteration of regimental titles. On one or two occasions I may have given the same unit twice under different titles, because I have an idea that when the medal rolls were being compiled and the men were asked the names of their units some gave the title at the time of the action or campaign, whereas others quoted the names of the units they were actually serving in at the time the question was asked.

It is an indisputable fact that all medal rolls are not accurate, so that in trying to be complete I have probably made some mistakes.

When I say that one unit changed its title three times during a campaign, I am sure my readers will appreciate my difficulties.

There were many occasions when units were divided and parts served with different brigades, especially in India. When this has happened, I have mentioned the unit twice, as for example the 1 Punjab Cavalry, squadrons of which served in both the 1st and 2nd Brigades during the operations in Waziristan 1894-95.

I have been both thanked and criticized for including the two pages of foreign medals and the illustrations of their ribbons. It seems that in pleasing Scylla I annoyed Charybdis, or *vice versa*.

It is to the good of the hobby that we hold different opinions about certain points, but may I ask those who find obvious errors to let me know of them?

I shall continue to welcome any corrections and suggestions for improvement, or additions.

FARNHAM.   L.L. GORDON
November, 1949

PREFACE TO THE THIRD EDITION

Once again it is my duty and pleasure to thank all those in many parts of the world who have written to me with corrections and suggestions for this edition. I must ask to be forgiven for not mentioning all of them by name, for, apart from anything else, it would necessitate sorting through an enormous amount of correspondence extending over the last twelve years.

Corrections are always welcome, but it is a great pity that so many of my correspondents do not differentiate between matters of opinion and fact. The two main contentions of those who consider that a medal must be genuine are either that they have one or know of a picture of someone wearing one. If I make a Bank of England note and then have my photograph taken wearing it, does that validate it? If I make several notes and pass them round, does that mean that they must all be genuine because a lot of people have one? If you answer both these questions in the negative, then what is the difference between my notes and unauthenticated medals?

As many beginners have asked my advice on collecting, I have considerably enlarged the notes on the subject and hope that they now cover all the questions asked.

If I may say so, I think that too many start off with the idea of collecting an awful lot of medals, and that is just about what they do! If a beginner is reading this, I would earnestly advise him to study the subject before he gets too expensively involved, and to always bear in mind that because a medal has a name on it, or a number of bars, it is no criterion at all that it is worth buying. It depends on the type of lettering, the titles and order of the bars, etc. Generally speaking, each series has its own peculiar type of lettering, whether engraved or impressed, and one should know what to expect to see on the edge of medals of that series. There are many bars to some series of medals, but in some cases it is not possible for two of them to be on the same genuine medal. A very simple example of this is the case of two battles miles apart having been fought on or about the same date, so that a man could not have been present at both.

Many have asked me where to look for medals. I found my first on a battlefield and others during the next forty years in all sorts of strange places, such as the junk box in a garage! Sometimes Orders and medals are found worn in strange places, too. I remember a little man, dressed in a combination of military and naval uniform of the Crimean period, who, at a South American function, had his breast covered with ribbons and Orders. When he turned round I was astonished to see a large jewelled affair immediately over his backside. I managed to get into conversation with him and asked about it. He immediately broke into a tirade of abuse. Pointing to the offending piece he informed me, almost bursting with anger, "That country no good, they just damned bunch of niggers!" After a while I discovered that he was a sort of major-domo responsible for organizing State functions and that it was usual for him to receive an order and a good tip. That country had forgotten the tip!

I disposed of all my medals and books in 1956, and therefore would like to take this opportunity of thanking all those who have helped me in the past and left me with so many pleasant memories. I am greatly indebted to dealers, collectors, librarians and many others, and I hope that this book, which in great measure is only a collation of their kindnesses, will be of use to them in return.

In conclusion, may I ask all those who have read thus far, and may risk going even farther, to confine their correspondence to matters dealing solely with this book and not, as previously, to any particular medal they may have and collecting generally. I am producing this edition entirely off my own bat in every respect, except for the actual printing, so, apart from reasons that should now be obvious, I simply shall not have the time to deal with other than essential correspondence.

I have, I believe and trust, answered every letter that I have rec eived from collectors — and they total many thousands — so now I must ask to be allowed out to graze!

GNOSALL,   L.L. GORDON
STAFFORD.
July, 1962

FOREWORD TO THE FOURTH EDITION
(Including a short history of Medal Collecting)

It would appear that the first work of note was Carter's "Medals of the British Army", first published in 1861 in three volumes. These were very early days for this particular collecting activity, but it was a notable and excellent achievement by the author, and was probably responsible for the great upsurge in collecting which began a few years later. Strangely enough, nothing further of importance appeared in print for another thirty years. But the eighteen nineties saw what was probably the heyday of medal collecting in the United Kingdom, and such household names as Day, Payne, Hastings Irwin, Gascoigne, Whittaker and Dalrymple White were all synonymous with collections of the highest importance.

The same period also produced quite a spate of good handbooks on the subject. Hastings Irwin published the first edition of his "War Medals and Decorations" in 1890, followed by Tancred's "Historical Record of Medals and Honorary Distinctions" in 1891 — a very interesting collection of miscellany — and a second edition of Carter's "Medals of the British Army", edited by W.H. Long in 1893, and now a very good book on the subject.

Long published his "Medals of the British Navy" in 1895, a fascinating and most readable book. My firm then issued "The War Medal Record" in monthly parts, starting in 1896. This resulted in two volumes containing much valuable information, including a complete list of the awards of the Peninsular Gold Crosses and Medals, the Naval Gold Medals, and the Military General Service medals awarded to officers. Perhaps the finest work of all, and a "must" for very student collector, was Mayo's "Medals and Decorations of the British Army and Navy". It was published in two volumes, beautifully illustrated and produced, and extremely well documented.

To conclude the period up to World War I, Hasting Irwin put out three more editions of his work, in 1898, 1904 and 1910. The last edition is a most useful book, with some information not found elsewhere. In addition mention should be made of the vast catalogue of Payne's collection, 1911, also with much valuable information on unusual and foreign pieces; and the catalogue of the Whittaker Collection, published in two volumes in 1890 and 1897. Both of these were privately printed.

The period of World War I saw the first edition of Taprell Dorling's handbook "Ribbons & Medals" which appeared in 1916. This was so popular that no less than nine further editions have been issued, the last in 1963. The coloured ribbon charts are extremely useful. Just previously, in 1915, W. August Steward had published "War Medals and their History", which included for the first time in a work of this kind a list of auction prices for a wide range of medals. Then in 1921 Stanley Johnson issued a rather more elementary but quite good book "The Medal Collector". Most of the books so far quoted are now out of print, though obtainable from time to time.

Twenty-six years were to pass before another authoritative handbook appeared in the form of L.L. Gordon's now widely known "British Battles and Medals". The first edition contained many — too many — errors of omission and commission. The author was either in too much of a hurry, or too shy, to consult other authorities and collectors. This state of affairs was largely remedied in the second edition in 1949, and still further improved by the third edition in 1962. This book has become by far the best handbook available and was a splendid effort in the right direction, but it still left room for improvement.

And now, after a further 20 years, I am glad to be able to commend to all collectors, whether beginners or advanced, the fourth edition of "British Battles and Medals". Several years ago we purchased the copyright from Major Gordon, and during the past year or more Mr. E.C. Joslin has spent a great deal of time and energy in revising it. Some irrelevant matter has been omitted. Changes and additions have been made in details concerning the units and numbers of men present at certain battles, campaigns or naval actions. Information on new medals or clasps, issued since 1950, has been added. Major Gordon himself supplied some of the addenda and corrigenda, and much has been collected and collated by us during the past 20 years. Many collectors, too, have sent in information for which we are grateful, but it is not possible to make acknowledgments individually to them all. However we do feel that we should make exceptions in the case of Captain W. Morgan and Dr. F.K. Mitchell. The former made available to us the formidable array of records which he had compiled over a long period of years. The latter placed at our disposal his unrivalled knowledge of medals relating to S. Africa. To both we record our appreciation. We do not claim this new edition to be either complete or perfect, but we shall welcome any information of value which readers are able to send to us in order to improve still further subsequent editions.

Finally, I would like to put on record that the original concept, compilation and publication of "British Battles and Medals" was entirely Major Gordon's, as well as the two subsequent editions, and medal collectors owe him a great debt of gratitude. Major Gordon however is not responsible for the present edition in any way, apart from the original material which has been incorporated, and which naturally forms the bulk of the book. Collectors are now indebted to Mr. Joslin for the knowledge, skill and immense amount of work which he has put into this revised, improved and enlarged edition, which I am sure will be welcomed all over the world by those who find their joy and relaxation in the fascinating study of British medals.

LONDON. *May, 1971*   DAVID F. SPINK

PREFACE TO THE FIFTH EDITION

In presenting the 5th Edition of this standard work, it would be very amiss if I did not first acknowledge that this improved edition could not have been prepared without the ready assistance and advice given by so many collectors. In particular, I wish to acknowledge contributions from the undermentioned collectors who have specialised in their own particular fields, namely:

Capt. K.J. Douglas-Morris, D.L., R.N., who has kindly placed his specialised knowlege of the First Naval General Service Medal at the disposal of the author. The majority of the bars appertaining to this medal now reflect the researches carried out by Capt. Douglas-Morris in preparation for his up to date N.G.S. Medal Roll which is in the process of being published. The remainder of the Naval Medals of the last century have also benefitted from the more general researches carried out by Capt. Douglas-Morris.

To Mr. D. Corbett for placing, at very short notice, his observations concerning the New Zealand series.

To Mr. H. William Neale of Salisbury, Rhodesia, for his kind comments regarding the British South Africa Medals etc.

To Mr. H.G. Hibbard of Cape Town for kindly allowing his rarity table covering single Queen South Africa Medals to be included, as well as his comments and corrections covering other medals relating to South Africa.

To Mr. D.R. Forsyth of Johannesburg for the help which he has been able to give following his particular study of the Cape of Good Hope General Service Medal, a roll of which he has recently prepared.

To Dr. Frank Mitchell the doyen of South African collectors, whose study of medals relating to South Africa goes back several decades.

To Mr. W.H. Fevyer for his analysis and summaries of the bars and medals relating to the Queen's South Africa Medals to the Royal Navy.

To Mr. C. Bacon for his considerable help with the current General Service Medal.

In addition numberous other collectors have contributed, thus making this volume a considerable improvement on the earlier volume. This particular edition could not have been produced without the assistance of specialists and even now the work does not claim to be perfect. In fact, I am inclined to remind readers of the comment made by the orginal author, Major Gordon, who stated in the preface to his 2nd Edition, almost thirty years ago, *"I can see no finality in the knowledge of the absorbing subject of medals, as new facts keep cropping up which alter existing beliefs"*. This is still happening today.

CONTENTS

LIST OF PLATES

BRITISH BATTLES
AND
MEDALS

1 ELIZABETHAN NAVAL MEDALS (1588)

These medals were probably instituted to commemorate the defeat of the Armada on 29th July, 1588. They are the first issued for service against a foreign foe and are allegorical in that they depict on their reverse sides either the island representing Great Britian or an ark undamaged by enemy action. There were three designs issued, which are generally divided into two types, known as Bay Tree Medals and the Ark in Flood Medal.*

BAY TREE MEDAL (1589)

Obverse   The bust of Queen Elizabeth with the legend "DITIOR · IN · TOTO · NON · ALTER · CIRCVLVS · ORBE."

Reverse   A bay tree standing on a small island surrounded by a rough sea. Beneath the tree is the legend, in two lines, "NON · IPSA · PERICVLA · TANGVNT."

There is a small ring for suspension attached direct on to the piece, which is oval, measuring about 1.75in. x 1.5in. It was struck in gold, silver and bronze.

SECOND TYPE

This medal is similar to the above except that the initials "E.R." appear one on either side of the bay tree. It was struck in gold, silver and copper.

ARK IN FLOOD MEDAL

Obverse   The Queen facing left and wearing a large ruff.

Reverse   A completely closed-in Ark, with smoke coming from the chimney, on a turbulent sea. Above the Ark is a heavy cloud. Surrounding the whole is the legend "PER : VNDAS : SERVAS : TRANQVILLA."

This medal is oval, somewhat larger than the above, and fitted with a ring for suspension. The ship represented is probably symbolic of the *Ark Royal*, which was the flagship of Lord Howard. Sir Francis Drake, the second-in-command, flew his flag in the *Revenge*, whilst Admiral Hawkins was in the *Victory*. This is the first record of a ship bearing this famous name.

2 CHARLES I MEDALS (1643)

Several medals were struck during this reign. The following Royal Warrant makes the purpose of the issue of one of them quite clear.

---

* There were about ten different medals struck to commemorate the defeat of the Armada, but it would be difficult to classify others than the above as naval awards.

"Charles R.

"Trusty and well beloved, we greet you well; Whereas we have received information that those soldiers which have been forward to serve us in the Forlorn-hope, are not looked upon according to their merited valour and loyal service. We do therefore require, that from henceforward the Commander-in-Chief, both of Horse and Foot, which lead up the Forlorn-hope, upon whom also we mean to bestow special tokens of our princely favour, do signify in writing the names of those soldiers whom they find most forward in serving us, their King and Country, that care may be taken to reward their deservings, and make them specially known to all our good subjects. For which end we have thought fit to require Sir William Parkhurst, Knight, and Thomas Bushell, Esquire, Wardens of our Mint, to provide from time to timer certain Badges of silver, containing our Royal image, and that of our dearest son, Prince Charles, to be delivered to wear on the breast of every man who shall be certified under the hands of their Commanders-in-Chief to have done us faithful service in the Forlorn-hope. And we do, therefore, most straitly command, that no soldier at any time do sell, nor any of our subjects presume to buy, or wear, any of those said Badges, other than they to whom we shall give the same, and that under such pain and punishment as our Council of War shall think fit to inflict, if any shall presume to offend against this our Royal command. And we further require the said Commanders, and Wardens of our Mint, to keep several Registers of the names of those and of their country, for whom they shall give their certificate.

"Given at our Court at Oxford, the eighteenth day of May, 1643. To Our trusty and well-beloved Sir William Parkhurst and Thomas Bushell, Esquire, Wardens of Our Mint at Oxford."

The Forlorn-hope party was that which led in an attack, and it is suggested that the word "forlorn" has been derived in some way or another from the German word *forloren*, which means lost.

It is interesting to note the regulations forbidding recipients to sell, or other persons to buy or wear these medals, which constitute the first issue of military awards that can be traced.

Mr. J.H. Mayo doubts whether any of these medals were ever issued. If they were not issued then one can only credit them with being the first military medals intended for issue and consider the Dunbar Medals which follow (No. 5) as being the first that were actually distributed.

A description of the medal, or badge, which was of silver-gilt, referred to in the Royal Warrant is as follows:

Obverse	Bust of Charles I, three-quarter view facing right, wearing a lace collar over a coat of armour. There is no legend.
Reverse	Bust of Prince Charles, facing left with long hair falling on his shoulder. There is no legend.
Size	Oval, 1.65in. x 1.3in.
Suspension	There is a small circular loop at both the top and bottom, but whether they were suspended from a chain or cord one cannot say.
Designer	Thomas Rawlins.

3 THE WELCH MEDAL

Obverse	Charles I and Prince Charles.
Reverse	Shows the standard recovered by Sir Robert Welch.

This gold medal is oval, measuring 1.7in. x 1.5in., and was specially struck for presentation to Sir Robert Welch for recapturing a standard at the Battle of Edge Hill on 23rd October, 1642. This was the first battle of the Civil War. As it was given to him for a particular act of gallantry, it may be considered as the forerunner of our Distinguished Service and Conduct Medals. The medal was designed by Thomas Rawlins.

4 COMMONWEALTH NAVAL MEDALS (1649)

Obverse   The House in Session.

Reverse   An anchor and two shields, one with the Cross of St. George and the other the Harp of Erin. The word "MERVISTI" is super-inscribed.

Designer   Thomas Simon.

These medals, which are oval (0.95in. x 0.85in.), were struck in gold and silver and were awarded after an Act of Parliament in 1649 had decreed that one-tenth of all prize-money should be set aside for the purpose of granting medals and rewards to officers and men who had performed "Extraordinary Service". As these medals all bore the inscription "MERVISTI" (Thou has deserved), they are obviously the first purely Naval medals awarded for particular acts of gallantry.

5 THE DUNBAR MEDAL (1650)

Obverse   The bust of Cromwell facing left, with legend, "THE LORD OF HOSTS · WORD AT DVNBAR · SEPTEM : Y. 3. 1650."

Reverse   A scene of the House of Commons in Session.

Designer   Thomas Simon.

The House voted that a medal should be struck for issue to all members of the Parliamentary Forces who took part in the victory at Dunbar on 3rd September, 1650. It is the first medal which was issued to both officers and men alike. Though the design was the same, the officers received gold medals (1in. x 0.85in.) and the men received silver ones (1.35in. x 1.15in.). Bronze medals of both sizes were also struck, but we have been unable to trace to whom they were to be awarded. The medals were, apparently, to have been worn suspended around the neck.

Later issues of these medals were made from a cracked die and consequently bear a scar right across.

The original dies were found at Hursley, near Winchester, in about 1760, and it is believed that several strikings were made from them.

The medals were apparently intended for award to both officers and men, but not to *all*. The first British medal awarded to *all* officers and men was the Waterloo Medal.

6 THE WYARD MEDAL (31st July, 1650)

Obverse   An anchor, suspended from which are the shields of St. George and Erin. Above is the inscription "MERVISTI".

Reverse   A naval action and inscription, in two lines, "SERVICE DON AGAINST SIX SHIPS, IVLY XXXI & AUGUST Y.I. 1650".

Designer   Thomas Simon.

This oval medal (1.6in. x 1.3in.) was especially voted by Parliament to be given in gold to Captain Wyard of the *Adventure* and in silver to his officers for the protection of a convoy when attacked by six Dutch frigates. The medals had a loop attached to the piece for suspension.

7 DUTCH WAR MEDALS (1653)

Four medals were awarded by Parliament in 1658 to be designed by Thomas Simon for issue to the Admirals, officers and men for services against the Dutch during 1653. One encounter was on 8th February, off Cape la Hogue, when Blake with his flag flown from the *Triumph* defeated Tromp. In this action Blake was wounded and had not recovered in time to take part in a second action fought on 31st July. Blake's second-in-command, during an earlier action fought on 9th December, 1652, was General Monk, later Duke of Albemarle, who had had no naval experience whatever! During the action of 8th February, Monk was in command of the troops attached to the fleet. In the second action he commanded the fleet and Tromp was killed. As a result of this battle the Dutch agreed to Cromwell's terms, one of which was that they had to salute the British Flag in the Channel.

In 1664, an Admiral's Regiment was raised and in 1684 received the title of "His Royal Highness the Duke of York and Albany's Maritime Regiment of Foot". The Marines were permanently constituted in 1755 and received the title of Royal Marines after their services at Copenhagen by a Royal Order dated 29th April, 1802, and divided into Infantry and Artillery on 18th August, 1804.

FIRST TYPE

Obverse   An anchor from which are suspended the three shields of England, Scotland and Ireland, surrounded by a cable.

Reverse   A naval engagement with the designer's name on the stern of one vessel and initials "T.S." on the prow of another.

These medals were of gold and fitted with a loop for suspension from gold chains. Four of them, measuring 2.2in. x 2in., were awarded. Generals Blake and Monk each received one with a chain worth £300 and Vice-Admiral Penn and Rear-Admiral Lawson were awarded them with chains valued at £100 each.

SECOND TYPE

The obverse and reverse were the same as the first type except for a different border and being slightly smaller (2in. x 1.8in.). These were awarded to four ships' captains and were of gold.

THIRD TYPE

The obverse and reverse were the same as for the first type without any ornamental borders. They were of gold and measured 1.6in. x 1.4in. and were given to selected junior officers. No chains were given for suspension though the pieces were fitted with rings.

FOURTH TYPE

Obverse   An anchor, suspended from the stock of which are the shields of England and Ireland, superinscribed "MERVISTI".

Reverse   The House in Session.

These oval silver medals, measuring about an inch by three-quarters, were awarded to seamen and were fitted with a ring on the piece for suspension.

Another medal was issued at this time to the crew of the *Triumph*, which caught fire during the action on 31st July, 1653. The design was the same as the first type referred to with the addition of an inscription on the obverse which reads "FOR EMINENT SERVICE IN SAVING Y TRIUMPH FIERED IN FIGHT WH Y DUTCH IN JULY, 1653".

8 CHARLES II MEDALS (1660-1685)

During this reign, several medals were struck for service at sea against the Dutch, but the records do not show which actions they were awarded for. One of the medals is a truly magnificent example of the engraver's art. It is a circular medal of 2.5in. diameter, by John Roettier, and is found in gold and silver.

Obverse   The laureated head of Charles II facing right with the legend "CAROLVS · SECVNDVS · DEI · GRATIA · MAG · BRIT · FRAN · ET · HIBER · REX."

Reverse   A view of the fleet with a wrecked ship in the left foreground. On the right foreground is the figure of the King holding a baton in his right hand. He is somewhat incongruously dressed as a Roman General. In the exergue is the inscription "PRO TALIBVS AVSIS" (For such enterprises).

The wording on the reverse would suggest that it was intended that it should be awarded for future meritorious service.

9 LA HOGUE (19th MAY, 1692)

To show her pleasure at the defeat of the French by the combined fleets of England and Holland, Queen Mary ordered medals to be struck for presentation to Admiral Russell and his officers. They were 1.95in. diameter. The Admiral and a Captain Tupper, who gave warning that the French fleet was in the Channel, received gold medals suspended from gold chains. As silver medals are also known, perhaps they were given to junior officers. The facts concerning their distribution are not known.

Obverse   The jugate heads of William and Mary facing to the right.

Reverse   A picture of the French flagship *Le Soleil Royal* on fire, super-scribed "NOX · NVLLA · SECTVA · EST." In the exergue is the legend "PVGN : NAV INT : ANG : ET FR : 21 MAY : 1692."

Engraver   James Roettier.

In 1692 an Act of Parliament authorized the granting of medals to "Officers, Marines and Seamen who shall be found to have done any signal or extraordinary service". These medals bore the same obverse as that just mentioned. The reverses were plain except for a description of the act for which the medal was awarded. They were of silver and fitted with a ring for suspension.

10 THE TOUBOCANTI MEDAL (8th February, 1700)

In 1695 a Scotsman, named William Paterson, received a charter from William III to start a colony on the Isthmus of Darien in Central America, on behalf of the African and Indian Company of Scotland.

Sailing from Leith on 26th July, 1698, he landed and found the settlement then known as New St. Andrews, now Acia.

These colonists, and those that followed soon afterwards, were continually attacked by the Spaniards. The Company sent out a Colonel Campbell, who arrived there just prior to an attack on a large scale. With a few men he advanced to attack the Spaniards, whom he met and routed at Toubocanti, but the forces at his disposal were not sufficient to hold the colony.

On the arrival of Spanish vessels in the harbour the colonists counselled surrender, but Campbell would not agree. With a few followers he set sail for Scotland.

To commemorate his services the Company awarded him a gold medal, whilst his followers received similar ones in silver.

The obverse illustrates a Highlander, sword in hand, with a decorated shield, attacking a fort. Above is the inscription "QUID NON PRO PATRIA". The reverse bears the armorial shield of the Company, with helmet, crest and supporters. Above these, on a scroll, is the inscription "QUA PANDITUR ORBIS"; below, "VIS UNITOR FORTIOR".

The medals, 2.2in. diameter, were designed by M. Smeltzing.

It was this William Paterson who, in conjunction with Michael Godfrey, Charles Montague and various merchants, raised £500,000 towards the £1,200,000 to be lent to the Government on condition that the subscribers formed a corporation. This became known as the Governor and Company of the Bank of England. With Sir John Houblon as the first Governor and Michael Godfrey as the first Deputy Governor, the bank commenced to operate on 1st January, 1695.

11 VIGO MEDAL (12th October, 1702)

Obverse   Bust of Queen Anne.

Reverse   A scene of the action and the date.

This medal was struck to commemorate the daring attack on Vigo Bay, where seventeen laden galleons from the West Indies were lying under the protection of French and Spanish warships. Sir George Rooke battered the forts guarding the harbour, and the *Torbay*, wearing the flag of Admiral Hopson, attacked the boom and in doing so was set on fire. Eventually all the fifteen French and three Spanish warships were either sunk or captured. Sir George Rooke entrusted Sir Cloudesley Shovel with the task of bringing home seventeen captured galleons, which were said to have contained over two and a half million pounds' worth of bullion and merchandise. It would appear that this issue of silver medals was only made to officers.

Two specially engraved gold medals were struck for issue to the master and boatswain of the *Torbay*.

12 LAMPRIERE GOLD MEDALS (1703)

Obverse   The Crowned Head of Queen Anne.

Reverse   The arms of Admiral Dilkes or the recipient, with the motto "TRUE TO MY TRUST".

These gold medals, 2.75in. in diameter, were personal awards from the Sovereign to Admiral Dilkes and his officers for the destruction of the French fleet off Jersey. We have been unable to ascertain why the medal has been named after Captain Lamprière, who was only one of the captains, instead of after the Admiral.

13 CAPTURE AND DEFENCE OF GIBRALTAR (1704-1705)

Obverse   Head of Queen Anne and inscription "ANNA DEI GRATIA. MAG.

BRITAN. FRA. ET HIB. REGINA."

Reverse   Neptune, seated in his chariot, presenting naval and mural crowns to Britannia, who is standing on the shore. Around the top is the inscription "VICTORIAE NAVALES". In the exergue is the inscription "CALPE EXPVG. ET GALL. VIT. MDCCIV."

A few of these medals were given for the capture of Gibraltar, which took place between 21st and 24th July, 1704, and for its subsequent defence against various attempts to recapture it that were made by France and Spain in the remainder of that year and in 1705.

After the death of Charles II of Spain on 1st November, 1700, Europe became involved in what was known as "The War of the Spanish Succession".

There were three claimants — Philip of Anjou, grandson of Louis XIV; Joseph, Electoral Prince of Bavaria; and Archduke Charles, son of the Emperor Leopold of Austria.

Though Joseph was selected, he died suddenly and then the British favoured Charles owing to the political and territorial advantages his accession would have, compared with those of Philip. The Spaniards, however, favoured Philip and the war started.

On 12th February, 1704, Admiral Sir George Rooke enbarked the Archduke Charles at Portsmouth and set sail for Lisbon and then to Barcelona, where he landed 2,000 men under the Prince of Hesse-Darmstadt. Finding that the populace was unsympathetic, he re-embarked the force and sailed to Lagos, where he was joined by Sir Cloudesley Shovel with more ships and men.

On 17th July, 1704, he called a council of war which decided to attack Gibraltar. With a fleet of sixty English and Dutch ships and an army of 1,800 men under the Prince of Hesse, he arrived off the Bay of Gibraltar on 21st July. As the Governor, Don Diego de Salinas, refused to surrender, the troops were disembarked on the isthmus. These consisted of the King's Own, East Lancashire, East Surrey Regiments, and the Duke of Cornwall's Light Infantry, which had accompanied the fleets as marines.

On the 22nd the fleet bombarded the forts and sent landing parties ashore from H.M.S. *Lennox* (Captain Jumper), *Yarmouth* (Captain Hicks) and *Nottingham* (Captain Whitaker).

The Governor surrendered the fortress on 24th July, 1704. British troops remained in occupation. Admiral Rooke revictualled his fleet at Tetuan and awaited the attack of the French fleet under the Count of Toulouse. With forty-one English and eleven Dutch ships he defeated the French off Malaga on 13th August, 1704.

The Spaniards tried to recapture Gibraltar from the landward side, assisted by a French fleet under Admiral de Pointis. Admiral Sir John Leake was ordered by Admiral Rooke to sail from Lisbon to assist the garrison, which he did by surprising the blockading French Squadron and landing 400 marines, on 29th October, 1704.

On 18th December reinforcements consisting of a composite battalion of Grenadier and Coldstream Guards, a battalion of the Somerset Light Infantry and a battalion of the Royal Sussex Regiment arrived to increase the strength of the garrison to 3,000 men.

In 1705, the Spaniards, this time under the French Marshal de Tesse, again attacked the fortress, but Sir John Leake when on his way from Lisbon encountered and defeated the French fleet, driving a part of it, including the flagship, ashore.

After this Marshal de Tesse raised the siege. Gibraltar was ceded to Britain by the Treaty of Utrecht signed on 11th April, 1713.

It was again attacked by the Spanish in 1720 and 1727, but, so far as we know, no medals or Battle Honours were awarded for these operations.

The major credit for the capture of Gibraltar belongs to the Navy, who not only protected and transported the troops and acted as marines, but fired over 15,000 projectiles into the defensive works and then manned their small boats and captured the key positions.

It was to Sir George Rooke that the Governor surrendered.

Credit for the subsequent defence is shared by both services.

The military units present at the capture and defence of Gibraltar between 1704 and 1705 were: 1, 2 Foot Guards; 4, 13, 30, 31, 32 and 35 Foot.

14 CULLODEN MEDAL (16th April, 1746)

Obverse	Gold medals. Bust of the Duke of Cumberland with the word "CUMBERLAND" superinscribed.
	Silver medals. Bust of the Duke of Cumberland and the legend "GUL : DUX : CUMBRIAE".
	Bronze medals. A scene of the battle with the Duke of Cumberland on horseback and the legend "GUL. AUG. DUX. CUM. TERROR. RIB."
Reverse	Gold medals. The standing figure of Apollo with a dragon pierced by an arrow at his feet. There is also the legend "ACTUM EST ILICET PERIIT." In the exergue is the wording "PROEL. COLOD. AP XVI MDCCXLVI."
	Silver medals. The Duke of Cumberland on horseback with a scene of the battle and the River Spey. There is also the inscription "HORAE MOMENTO".
	Bronze medals: Plain.
Size	The gold and silver medals are oval and measure 1.75in. x 1.45in.* The bronze medals are circular.
Ribbon	Crimson with green edges, 2.5in. wide.
Designer	Richard Yeo.

This medal is generally considered to have been given by George II to the senior officers who fought at the Battle of Culloden on 16th April, 1746.

The original Minutes Book of the Cumberland Society have been examined. The first meeting was held on 17th April, 1746, the day after the battle.

This book is in the possession of a descendant of Sir Adolphus Oughton, K.B., who served as secretary to the Society throughout its existence.

The first rule of the Society laid down that there should be twenty-seven members and that only one should be elected in each subsequent year. In some years, due no doubt to deaths and resignations two or three new members were elected.

*In addition to the above there are circular silver medals to be found. These are 2in. diameter and were designed by R. Yeo. On the obverse is the bust of George II facing right and wearing a breastplate. There is also the legend "GEOR II·R·FIL·DUX·CUMBRIAE." On the reverse the Duke of Cumberland is portrayed as Hercules trampling upon Discord and raising Britannia. In the exergue is the legend "PER DUELLIB·EX·FVGAT AD·CULLOD·DUBEL-LAT·16·APR·1746."

It should be noted that the "U" in FVGT is depicted as "V."

These medals must not be confused with the silver ones given for the capture of Carlisle by the Duke of Cumberland in 1745, which bear on the obverse the bust of the Duke of Cumberland in Armour and the legend "GVLIELMVS DVX·CVMBRIAE." On a truncation of the right arm is the designer's name T. PINGO. F. The reverse depicts a lion overcoming a wolf with the legend "INSTITIA·TRIVMPHANS."

If it is remembered that these medals were designed by T. Pingo and the silver so called Culloden medals by R. Yeo they will not be difficult to distinguish.

(Obverse)   (Reverse)

No. 1. The Elizabethan Naval Medal, 1588. Bay Tree Type.

(Reverse)

No. 14. The Culloden Medal, 1746.

 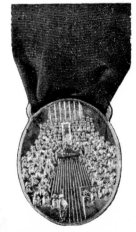

(Obverse)   (Reverse)

No. 5. The Dunbar Medal, 1650.

(Reverse)

No. 17. The German Town Medal, 1777.

(Obverse)

No. 18. General Eliott's Medal for the Defence
of Gibraltar. 1779-1783.

(Obverse)

No. 20. The Mysore Campaign Medal, 1790-92.

(Obverse)

No. 21. The Isle of St. Vincent Medal, 1795.

(Reverse)

No. 16. The Carib War Medal, 1773.

To face page 9

The first member elected was the Most Noble John Marquess of Granby. The last was Capt. Ross, of General Oughton's Regiment, who was elected on 27th April, 1766. There were only fifty-four members elected in all.

One rule stated that members "shall wear their medals openly in battle and should they be lost in action with the enemy a new one, to the value of ten guineas, is to be replaced at the cost of the Society."

There is only one entry to show that this was ever done. It was dated 1758 and reads "that a gold medal be granted to Captain William Sparkes, of Conway's Regiment, his having been lost at the Battle of Monongahela." This action, sometimes referred to as "Braddock's Defeat", was fought on the banks of the Monongahela river where it joins the Allegheny river to form the Ohio. The city of Pittsburg, Pennsylvania, now stands on the site.

There is no mention whatever of any silver or bronze medals, and the fact that the rule quoted states that lost medals will be replaced by the Society would show that the gold medals were *not* awarded by the Sovereign. The cost of the medals — ten guineas — would indicate that they were of gold.

It is probable that the silver and bronze medals to be found were struck and sold to commemorate the Battle of Culloden. They would also commemorate the overthrow of Jacobite cause, which was a matter of great rejoicing to many at the time.*

The gold medals were probably peculiar to the Cumberland Society and all the other so-called Culloden Medals are probably only tokens.

If there were any other official medals than the gold ones it seems extraordinary that they were not mentioned in the Minutes Book. It is difficult, if not impossible, to understand why a society with so few members should have had three different kinds of medals.

The gold medal was worn suspended from the neck on a crimson and green ribbon, 36in. long.

This is the first medal that can be traced with a definite coloured ribbon.

15 LOUISBOURG (27th July, 1758). GORÉE (29th December, 1758). GUADALOUPE (23rd January, 1759). MINDEN (31st July, 1759). QUEBEC (15th September, 1759)

The medal for Louisbourg, which was designed by T. Pingo, is 1.7in. diameter and was awarded in gold, silver and bronze. On the obverse is depicted a globe resting on the prone figure of France. On the globe are the words "CANADA AMERICA", whilst immediately above it is scroll bearing the legend "PARITER · IN · BELLA". Above this again is the flying figure of Victory and the Union Jack. To the right of the globe is a sailor with his hat raised in his left hand, on the left is a soldier with a musket in his right hand. The reverse gives a representation of the bombardment of Louisbourg, with the inscription "LOVIS-BOVRG · TAKEN · MDCCLVIII". Riband thought to have been half yellow and half blue. Awarded in gold to Sir Alexander Schomberg, Captain of the frigate *Diana*, Mid. Geo. Young, H.M.S. *York* and Capt. Buckler, Flag Captain to Admiral Boscawen. In addition two others are known.

16 CARIB WAR (1773)

Obverse   George III in armour, facing right, superinscribed "GEORGIVS . III . MB . REX."

*Silver and pewter medals were struck to commemorate the defeats of the German fleets at the battles of Heligoland Bight, 28th August, 1914, the Dogger Bank, 24th January, 1915, and the Battle of Jutland, 31st May, 1916. Anybody could buy them, so that they are no more than tokens or plaques. It is probable that the Culloden so-called medals of silver and bronze come into the same category.

Reverse	The helmeted and standing figure of Britannia offering an olive branch of peace to a defeated Carib. In the exergue is the date "MDCCLXXIII".
Engraver	C.M. Moser.
Ribbon	Red.

This medal was issued by the islanders of St. Vincent to those who took part in the suppression of the native rising. It is a large silver medal, measuring 2.2in. in diameter and fitted with a ring for suspension.

17 GERMAN TOWN MEDAL (4th October, 1777)

Obverse	Within a wreath is the inscription, on four lines, "40 Reg GERMAN TOWN Oct" . 4 . 1777."
Reverse	A picture of the attack on Chew's storehouse. In the sky is the inscription "Reward of Merit".
Size	1.75in. diameter.
Ribbon	Dark blue.
Suspension	A flattish loop is riveted through a hole at the top of the piece through which the ribbon is threaded.
Designer	Milton.
Naming	The medals are unnamed.

Three speciments of this medal are known: (1) with no inscription on the obverse, (2) with "Reward of Merit" only, and (3) with that and the recipient's name.

As the medal was subsequently used as a regimental one, it is thought regarding the foregoing that (1) is awarded to the defenders of Chew's storehouse, (2) was inscribed pending award during the period the medal was a regimental one, and (3) was awarded as a regimental medal for merit.

The supposition is strengthened by the fact that the recipient's name on the named medal is not among those given on the Muster Roll for German Town.

During the War of American Independence, George Washington, after his defeat at Brandywine on 11th September, 1777, by General Howe, advanced to German Town, now part of Philadelphia.

By a surprise night attack the British toops were forced to withdraw. Lieutenant-Colonel Musgrove, with six companies of the 40th Foot, held a large building known as Chew's storehouse until relieved.

The losses during the action were very heavy. The Americans said to have 1,000 and the British over 600 casualties.

To commemorate the action, Colonel Musgrove presented medals to the 40th Foot. They were awarded in both silver and bronze, though the latter are very rare. Also seen in gilt.

18 DEFENCE OF GIBRALTAR* (21st June, 1779-2nd February, 1783)

The two most common medals awarded for the Defence of Gibraltar are the silver ones which were presented by Generals Picton and Eliott at their own expense. There were, however, other medals given for the same event.

---

*In A.D. 711 the fortress was captured by the Saracens under Tarik, who called it Gibel-el-Tarik (Mountain, or Rock of Tarik), from whence it gets its present name of Gibraltar and its popular title The Rock.

GENERAL PICTON'S MEDAL

Obverse   View of Gibraltar and part of La Linea. On a scroll around the top is the legend "BATTERING SHIPS DESTROYED". At the bottom is the date "SEPTEMBER XIII MDCCLXXXII".

Reverse   An inscription which reads "BY ZEALOUS EXERTION OF PATIENCE PERSEVERANCE AND INTREPIDITY AFTER CONTENDING WITH AN UNPARALLELED SUCCESSION OF DANGERS AND DIFFICULTIES IN THE DEFENCE OF GIBRALTER DURING A BLOCKADE AND SIEGE OF ALMOST FOUR YEARS, THE GARRISON UNDER THE AUSPICES OF GEORGE III, TRIUMPHED OVER THE COMBINED POWERS OF FRANCE AND SPAIN." The dates of the siege are given in the exergue, thus: "BLOCKADE COMMENCED JUNE XXI. MDCCLXXIX : SIEGE TERMINATED FEBRUARY II. MDCCLXXXIII."

The medal is of silver and 2.25in. diameter.

GENERAL ELIOTT'S MEDAL

Obverse   View of Gibraltar. Above this view is the legend "PER TOT DIS-CRIMINA RERUM", and in the exergue is the date "XIII · SEPT · MDCCLXXXII".

Reverse   The names of four officers, "REDEN LAMOTTE SYDOW ELIOTT" one underneath the other in the centre surrounded by a laurel wreath. In large letters almost round the circumference the word "BRUDERSCHAFT". At the bottom in small lettering is the Designer's name L. PINGO F. The diameter of the medal, which is silver, is 1.95in. On some a loop 1½in. wide is fitted to the top of the piece whilst others have rings, etc., fitted.

Ribbon   As medals fitted with different methods of suspension are to be found, it is obvious that some of them must have been worn with a ribbon, but I have not been able to trace any mention of particulars concerning its colour or correct width. The riband usually seen fitted is dark blue although there does not appear to be any particular reason for this.

Naming   The medals were issued unnamed.

Designer   L. Pingo.

The latter medal was presented by General Eliott (sometimes incorrectly spelt Elliot) to his Hanoverian troops. The defence was carried out by 7,000 British and Hanoverian troops against French and Spanish forces.

The British garrison, composed of the following troops, appears to have gone unrewarded: Royal Artillery; Royal Marines; 12, 39, 56, 58 and 72 Foot.

RED HOT SHOT MEDAL

In addition to the Picton and Eliott medals there is one made of copper with a very home-made appearance. 1.5in. diameter.

The obverse depicts a closed-in ship with three fire bombs landing on the roof. The sea is portrayed by five straight lines, under which is inscribed in two lines "The *Pastora Batt!y Ship Admr̠* Morino". Under this is the recipient's name.

Named medals to T. Cole, J. Dodd, C. Hills, H. Hobbs, James Rogers and John Wells are known.

The reverse depicts a furnace with "Fur" on the left and "nace" on the right of it. Below this, in five lines, is the inscription *"Spaniards defeated by* RED hot SHOT *at* GIBRALTAR *Sep:ye* 13*th* 1782."

The medal has a flat suspender fitted to the top as part of the piece, with a hole in the centre through which either the cord or ribbon for suspension was threaded.

Both the obverse, reverse and suspender are edged with a cable border.

The grand attack, which started on 13th September, 1782, was opened by a cannonade from 200 pieces of heavy ordnance, followed by an assault of some 40,000 Frenchmen, under the Duc de Crillon, from the landward side.

The Bay was crowded with the combined French and Spanish fleets composed of forty-seven line-of-battle ships, numerous frigates, small armed vessels and ten battery ships which their designer, the French engineer Jean Claude d'Arcon, states in his book cost over half a million pounds apiece. They were converted line-of-battle ships from 600-1,400 tons, armed with from nine to twenty-one guns, with crews of from 250 to 760 men. The fronts of the batteries were protected by thick layers of square timber and covered with a sloping roof. The whole was lined with cordage and hides. In order to make them fireproof, a reservoir was installed in each battery from which, by means of hand pumps, hoses and buckets, every part of the fabric could be kept wet. Each battery had a single sail to enable it to take up its desired position, which was about four hundred yards offshore.

The fate of these batteries, in view of the high hopes that they raised, became comical. The wetting system was so efficient that not only did it keep the fabric wet but the powder as well, so that by the time the two leading and largest batteries, the *Talla Piedra* and *Pastora*, had got into position they were more soaking targets than fireproof batteries.

During the first evening of the attack a red-hot shot became lodged in and set alight to the roof of the *Talla Piedra*, on which D'Arcon was serving, but as the British fire was so severe it could not be removed. The sight of this vaunt incombustible vessel burning furiously was too much and orders were given to destroy and abandon the others. Why the remainder, which were functioning quite well, should have been sacrificied, D'Arcon at the time could not understand.

These vessels are particularly interesting in that they were probably the first to be built purely as floating gun platforms with no consideration whatever as to quarters for the crews. Similar ships, but without the water systems, were used by us up the Irawadi during the War in Ava, 1824-26, so that the rocket ships used during the second world war beach landings were only an improvement of an old idea.

19 DECCAN MEDAL (1778-1784)

Obverse   Britannia seated holding a wreath in her right hand. There is also a fort flying the Union Jack.

Reverse   Persian inscriptions.

The centre reading: "AS COINS ARE CURRENT IN THE WORLD, SO SHALL BE THE BRAVE AND EXPLOITS OF THOSE HEROES BY WHOM THE NAME OF THE VICTORIOUS ENGLISH NATION WAS CARRIED FROM BENGAL TO THE DECCAN." The surrounding inscription reads: "PRESENTED IN A.D. 1784 (HEGIRA 1199) BY THE EAST INDIA COMPANY'S CALCUTTA GOVERNMENT".

Designer   The dies were prepared and medals struck by the firm of Young & Shepperd of Calcutta.

This is an unusual medal, as the edge is milled like that of a coin. The medal was struck in two sizes, 1.6in. and 1.25in. diameter. The former, a few of which were issued in gold, were for officers, whilst the latter, which were of silver, were given to non-commissioned officers and natives in Bengal regiments. It is the first medal issued by the Honourable East India Company and was given for service in Gujerat, 1778-1784, and the Carnatic, 1780-1784. They are usually found with a piece of yellow cord attached, though there was no specified colour or material from which they whould be suspended.

20 MYSORE CAMPAIGN (1790-1792)

Obverse   A Sepoy holding the Union Jack in his right hand the flag of Mysore, which is upside down, in his left. In the background is the fortress of Seringapatam.

Reverse   The inscription "FOR SERVICES IN MYSORE A.D. 1791-1792". Surrounding this is a laurel wreath and around this again is a Persian inscription.

Suspension   A ring is affixed to the piece through which a cord of no specified colour is threaded although a yellow or sand coloured cord is frequently seen. The medal was worn round the neck.

Designer   The dies were prepared by Mr. Mair, a silversmith of Calcutta.

This medal was struck in two sizes, 1.7in. and 1.5in. diameter. The larger was issued in gold to Subadars. Two types and sizes of silver medals were struck. The larger ones of good quality were given to Jemadars and Serangs, whereas Havildars, Naiks, Tindals, etc., received the smaller and inferior specimens. There are two strikings, which vary in the number of cannon-balls shown on the obverse near the right foot of the Sepoy. On some medals there are two and on others five or seven. The medal illustrated has seven. This medal appears to have been a favourite with the fakers, presumably because the genuine specimens are in themselves somewhat crude. These fakes should not be difficult to detect if it is remembered that almost all faked pieces are slightly smaller than the originals. due to shrinkage when the metal cools. A rough-and-ready guide is to look for the gap which there should be between the top of the staff of the Union Jack n the rim of the piece. The surest way is to examine the piece carefully through a glass for a sort of blotchy look. Sometimes this has been reduced by careful polishing, but in the doing of this, the relief has suffered. These remarks refer to the examination for fakes in all pieces.

The medal was issued by the English Government to native troops who served under Abercromby and Cornwallis in the defeat of Tippoo Sahib.

21 ISLE OF ST. VINCENT (1795)

Obverse   A winged figure of Britannia holding out a sword in her right hand. Behind her is the figure of a native lying down and supporting himself on his right elbow. Round the edge is written "ST VINCENT'S BLACK CORPS".

Reverse   A native holding a musket and bayonet in his right hand. In the exergue is "H.G.FEC." Around the circumference is written "BOLD LOYAL OBEDIENT".

Designer   No information can be found as to who H.G. was.

This bronze medal, 1.9in. diameter and 0.19in. thick, was issued to native soldiers only. At the Treaty of Peace signed in Paris on 10th February, 1763, between Britain, France, Spain and Portugal, ending the Seven Years War, the island of St. Vincent was ceded to Britain by the French. The majority of the Caribs were not kindly disposed to us. In 1779 the French assisted the Caribs to revolt, and again in 1795. It was for the loyalty shown to us in this last attempted coercion on the part of the French that the medal was awarded.

22 NAVAL GOLD MEDALS

Obverse	A small figure of Victory standing on the prow of a galley is crowning Britannia with a wreath of laurel. Britannia's right foot is resting on a helmet and she is holding a spear in her left hand. Slightly behind her and to the right is an oval shield bearing the Union Jack.
Reverse	In the case of the larger medals, the rank and name of the recipient, the event and date for which the medal was awarded, all surrounded by a wreath of oak and laurel. In the case of the smaller medals the wreaths are omitted.
Sizes	Large medals 2in. diameter; small medals 1.3in. diameter.
Ribbon	1½in. wide, white with 3/8in. wide dark blue borders.
Suspensions	The large medals are fitted with a gold ring through which the ribbon is threaded. Admirals wore their medals suspended round their necks. Captains fastened their ribbons through the third or fourth button-hole on the left side.
	The small medals are fitted with a small ring to which is attached a straight gold wire suspender through which the ribbon is threaded. The medal is glazed on both sides.
Designer	R. Wood.
Naming	The recipient's name and the action for which he received the award are on the reverse.
No. of bars issued	Nil.

These medals are, of course, extremely rare and costly, as only twenty-two of unlike the Army Gold Medals did not prevent the recipients from receiving the Naval G.S. medal. They were originally struck for presentation to the Admirals and Captains of Lord Howe's fleet in the victory over the French generally referred to as "The Glorious First of June", which took place off Ushant on 1st June, 1794. Probably no victory has ever evoked such approbation from the Sovereign and the people, and awards, promotion and thanks were lavishly distributed by both Houses, Lloyd's, Trinity House, and citizens of all the large towns in Great Britain. It was also intended that these medals should be given to officers who especially distinguished themselves in the future, though the last one awarded was to Captain Hope of the *Endymion* for the capture of the *President* on 15th January, 1815.

These beautiful medals were instituted in 1795 and abolished 1815. These medals are, of course, extremely rare and costly, as only twenty-two of the larger (including six with gold chains) and one hundred and seventeen of the smaller were awarded being issued for: 1st June, 1794 (17/8), St. Vincent, 1797 (15/6); Camperdown 1797 (15/2); Nile 1798 (14/1); Recapture of *Hermione* 1799 (1/-); Trafalgar 1805 (27/3); 4th November, 1805 (4/-); St. Domingo 1806 (8/2); Curacoa 1807 (4/-); Capture of *Thetis* 1808 (1/-); Capture of *Badere Zaffer* 1808 (1/-); Capture of *Furiese* 1809 (1/-); Lissa 1811 (4/-); Banda Neira 1811 (1/-); Capture of *Rivoli* 1812 (1/-); Capture of *Chesapeake* 1813 (1/-); Capture of *L'Etoile* 1814 (1/-); *Endymion* with *President* 1815 (1/-);

Numbers in brackets indicate small and large medals awarded thus: Trafalgar 27 small and 3 large gold medals.

23 CAPTURE OF CEYLON (1795-1796)

Obverse   The legend "FOR SERVICES ON THE ISLAND OF CEYLON A.D. 1795/6".

Reverse   A Persian inscription.

Suspension   The medal was suspended from a cord of no specified colour worn round the neck. There is a loop riveted on to the piece through which the cord is threaded.

Size   2 in. diameter.

This medal was awarded in gold to Captains Barton and Clarke and in silver to 121 native gunners of the Bengal Artillery for their services during the capturing of the Island from the Dutch. The dies were engraved and the medals struck at the Calcutta Mint. This medal must not be confused with another issued in 1818 as a meritorious service medal for the Kandy Rebellion.

24 DAVISON'S NILE MEDAL (1st August 1798)

Obverse   The figure of Pax with an olive branch in her right hand. Under her left arm she is supporting a large shield bearing the head and waist figure of Lord Nelson, with the inscription "EUROPES HOPES AND BRITAINS GLORY". Around the circumference is the legend "REAR ADMIRAL LORD NELSON OF THE NILE".

Reverse   A view of the fleet sailing into Aboukir Bay with the inscription "ALMIGHTY GOD HAS BLESSED HIS MAJESTY'S ARMS". In the exergue is written "VICTORY OF THE NILE AUGUST 1 1798".

Suspension   A loop was fitted to the top of the piece through which passed the 1½ in. wide dark blue ribbon of various lengths, so there does not appear to have been any set way of wearing the medal.

Designer   C. H. Küchler.*

This medal was a personal award from Nelson's prize agent Mr. Davison, to the officers and men present. Admirals and Captains received it in gold, other officers in silver, petty officers in bronze gilt, and the remainder in bronze. All the medals were 1.85 in. diameter and bore the name of the donor impressed on the edge, The name of the recipient is sometimes found engraved on the face of the reverse, sometimes his initials. Engraved in large capitals around the edge is the wording "A TRIBUTE OF REGARD FROM ALEX^R DAVISON ESQ. ST. JAMES'S SQUARE." Many recipients appear to have left them as issued, that is, unnamed. For further particulars concerning the action see the appropriate bar of the Naval General Service Medal. It is also worth noting that, except for the issue of one large Naval Gold Medal and thirteen small, neither the Sovereign nor Parliament considered, at the time, that this award was granted, and by then only 351 officers and men who had taken part were alive, or at any rate claimed the bar.

---

*C H. Küchler was the designer of the firm of Boulton and Watt, Birmingham. Coin collectors will recognize his name as the designer of the Britannia and Trident series of the George III (1977) copper coinage.

The first copper coinage bearing the figure of Britannia (which was represented by a Miss Stewart) was struck in 1665. On these Britannia was shown holding a spear.

25 SERINGAPATAM MEDAL (4th May, 1799)

Obverse A fine picture of a fight between the British Lion and Tippoo Sahib's Tiger. In the exergue is the date "IV MAY MDCCXCIX".

Reverse A scene of the attack on the fortress of Seringapatam showing a breach in the wall and a scaling party.

Suspension The medals were issued in 1808 but it was not until 1815 that the British Army were permitted to wear them. They were issued without means of suspension but they are found with various types added subsequently. Controversy has arisen over the correct ribbon for this medal. The correct one appears to be a pale watered orange colour 1·5 in. wide, but it is found with the same ribbon as the Peninsular Gold Medal, and also suspended from a yellow cord passing through a slightly tubular ring fitted on to the piece by a pin passing through it (the piece).

Types Five types of the medal were issued in England and two in Calcutta, as follows:

	Gold	Silver Gilt	Silver	Bronze	Pewter
English Medals	30	185	850	5,000	45,000
Calcutta Medals	83	Nil	2,786	Nil	Nil

Designer C. H. Küchler.

Size and naming The English medals were 1·9 in. diameter and the Calcutta ones 1·8 in. diameter.* All were issued unnamed, although some were engraved by the recipients.

No. of bars issued Nil, though some had bars added which were inscribed "SERINGAPATAM".

This medal was awarded for the siege and capture of Seringapatam, which lasted from 17 April-4th May, 1799. To those of us who have served in both the European Wars of 1914 and 1939, the most interesting fact about Seringapatam is the value of the prize-money, which came to over £1,140,000, and was distributed roughly as follows: The Commander-in-Chief, £100,000; Generals, £10,000; Colonels, £4,300; Lieutenant-Colonels, £2,600; Majors, £1,700; Captains, £860; Lieutenants, £430; Warrant Officers, £105; Sergeants, £14; Privates £7. It would have been interesting to have heard the Commander-in-Chief and one of his men comparing notes on the siege!

The following regiments took part in the campaign which led to the capture of the fortress:

European 19, 22 Light Dragoons; 12, 33, 57, 73, 74, 75, 77, 102, 103 Foot; The Scots Brigade (94th); Regiment de Meuron.†

Native Detachment Bengal Artillery; Detachment Bombay Artillery; 1, 2 Madras Artillery; Coast Artillery; Madras Engineers; Pioneers; 1, 2, 3 Battalions Bengal Native Volunteers; 1/1, 2/2, 2/3, 2/5, 1/6, 2/7, 1/8, 2/9, 1/11, 2/11, 1/12, 2/12 Madras N.I.; 1/2, 2/2, 1/3, 2/3, 1/4, 1/5 Bombay N.I.

* It is quite easy to distinguish the medals without having to compare the sizes by examining the designer's initials which are found on the right immediately above the exergue. The medals struck at the Soho Mint, Birmingham, bear the initials C.H.K. Those struck by the Calcutta Mint have the initials in the wrong order and the letter "K" reversed, thus: C.Я.H.

† The Regiment de Meuron was composed of Swiss mercenaries.

(Obverse)

No. 23. The Medal for the Capture of Ceylon,
1795-6.

(Obverse)

No. 24. Mr. Davison's Nile Medal, 1st August,
1798.

(Obverse)

No. 25. The Seringapatam Medal, 4th May, 1799.

(Obverse)

No. 27. The Honourable East India Company's
Medal for Egypt, 1801.

To face page 16

(Obverse)

No. 30. Mr. Boulton's Trafalgar Medal, 1805.

(Obverse)

No. 31. Mr. Davison's Trafalgar Medal, 1805.

(Obverse)

No. 33. The medal for the capture of Rodrigues, Isle of Bourbon and Isle of France, 1809-10.

(Obverse)

(Reverse)

No. 36. The Military General Service Medal, 1793-1814.

To face page 17

26 EARL ST. VINCENT'S MEDAL (1800)

Obverse   The Earl in uniform and the legend "EARL ST. VINCENT'S TESTIMONY OF APPROBATION 1800".

Reverse   A sailor and a marine shaking hands and the legend "LOYAL AND TRUE".

These medals were given by the Earl to the crew of his ship, the *Ville de Paris*, which did not take part in the mutiny in the Mediterranean soon after the more famous one at the Nore in 1797. They were only given to petty officers and below. They are circular and measure 1·85 in. diameter. They are normally found in silver, though three or four are known in gold.

27 HONOURABLE EAST INDIA COMPANY'S EGYPT MEDAL (1801)

Obverse   A Sepoy with his left hand on his hip and holding a Union Jack in his right. There is a Persian inscription in the exergue.

Reverse   A ship in full sail, and the Pyramids. In the exergue is the date "MDCCCI".

Size   1·9 in. diameter.

Suspension   The medals are generally found suspended from a yellow, or buff-coloured, cord which passes through a loop fitted to the piece. There is, however, no specified colour for the cord.

Designer   The dies were engraved and the medals struck at the Calcutta Mint.

Sixteen gold medals and 2,199 silver medals* were issued to the troops from India who formed a division under Major-General Sir David Baird. Those who had received this medal did not get the bar for Egypt which was subsequently (1850) awarded with the Military General Service Medal. The 61st Foot sailed from the Cape of Good Hope and joined the division on 17th May, 1801, but did not qualify for this medal. The eligible British recipients were members of the following regiments: One Troop 8 Light Dragoons; 10, 80, 86, 88 Foot; and 450 Artillerymen.

28 THE SULTAN'S MEDAL FOR EGYPT (1801)

Obverse   Crescent and eight-pointed star.

Reverse   Turkish inscription and the date below.

Sizes   Four sizes of gold medals were issued, 2·1 in., 1·9 in., 1·7 in., and 1·4 in. diameter. The silver medals issued to N.C.Os. were 1·4 in. diameter.

Suspension   The plain gold medals were fitted with a chain and sharp-pointed hook. The jewel-studded gold medals were suspended from an orange ribbon which passed through a loop attached to the piece.

This medal was given by Sultan Selim III to officers and N.C.Os. who took part in the Egyptian Campaign, 1801. Officers received gold medals and N.C.Os. received silver ones. It is also referred to as the Order of the Crescent, which is its correct title.

These medals, which were both very thin, were each suspended from a fine gold chain 1½ in. long. At the end of each chain was a small and exceedingly sharp-pointed hook.

*Bronze and Bronze Gilt Medals are known but those are probably later strikings.

Before Napoleon finally decided to abandon all hopes of retaining Egypt he dispatched an army and a fleet, the latter under Admiral Gentheaume, to re-capture the country.

This fleet was sighted off the coast of Egypt by Admiral Warren, who sailed out to attack it, but before contact could be made the French turned and fled.

The fastest ship in the English squadron was the *Renown*, which continued to chase the French almost to Toulon.

The Sultan was so pleased with Admiral Warren and Captain White that he presented each of them with another gold medal!

When the news of Admiral Gentheaume's retreat reached Napoleon, who was at Fontainebleau at the time, he is said to have been so angry that he smashed a gilded chair. He certainly ruined Gentheaume's naval career by dismissing him!

29 THE HIGHLAND SOCIETY'S MEDAL (1804)

Obverse   Sir Ralph Abercromby and inscription "ABERCROMBIUS DUX IN EGYPTO CECIDIT VICTOR".

Reverse   A Highlander, the date "21 MAR. 1801" and "NA FIR A CHOISIN BUAIDH" In Gaelic (These are the heroes who achieved victory in Egypt).

Size   2 in. diameter.

Designer   The medal was designed by B. West and engraved by G. F. Pidgeon.

This medal, which was awarded in silver and bronze, was given by the Highland Society of London to the 42nd Highlanders (Black Watch) for their action at Alexandria on 21st March, 1801, where they captured a standard from Bonaparte's Invincible Legion. This is the first medal that can be traced as having been given to the nearest relatives of those killed in action.

30 MR. BOULTON'S TRAFALGAR MEDAL (1805)

Obverse   Bust of Nelson facing left, surrounded by the inscription "HORATIO VISCOUNT NELSON K·B· DUKE OF BRONTE . & ."

Reverse   A scene of the battle surmounted by Nelson's famous signal. In the exergue is "TRAFALGAR OCT^R 21. 1805."

Size   1·9 in. diameter.

Ribbon   Dark blue.

Suspension   The ribbon passes through a small ring which is fitted to another small one attached to the piece.

Designer   C. H. Küchler.

This medal was given by Mr. Boulton, a manufacturer of Birmingham, at his own expense to the survivors of the action. Around the edge is the inscription "FROM M. BOULTON TO THE HEROES OF TRAFALGAR." It was given in silver, bronze-gilt, bronze and white metal, according to the rank of the recipient. A gold medal was sold by auction in London in April 1965.

31 MR DAVISON'S TRAFALGAR MEDAL (1805)

Obverse   A small bust of Lord Nelson surmounting a shield, the garter of which is inscribed "TRIA JUNCTA IN UNO." On a scroll beneath the shield is the inscription "PALMAM QUI MERUIT FERAT." The small letters H.F. appear under the ME of MERUIT. Under

18

these, in three lines is the inscription "NATUS SEP. 29 1758, HOSTE DEVICTO REQUIEVIT, OCT 21 1805." Around the top in large lettering is the wording "ADMIRAL LORD NELSON D. OF BRONTE." Under this is his famous signal in small lettering.

Reverse	In the centre is a three-masted man-of-war facing to the right. Above is the inscription "THE LORD IS A MAN OF WAR, EXODUS C. 15. V. 3." Around the bottom half in four lines, is the wording "VICTORY OFF TRAFALGAR OVER THE COMBINED FLEETS OF FRANCE & SPAIN OCT. 21 1805."
Composition	The piece is of pewter sometimes surrounded by a thin copper ring.
Size	2·1 diameter and 0·2 in. thick.
Ribbon	Dark blue.
Suspension	A small loop is fitted to the copper rim through which there is a small ring. The ribbon passes through this ring.
Designer	Halliday.
Naming	Issued unnamed.

32 MAIDA (4th July, 1806). GOLD MEDALS

Obverse	Laureated head of George III and the inscription "GEORGIVS TERTIVS REX."
Reverse	The standing figure of Britannia facing left in the attitude of throwing a javelin. In her left hand she holds a shield bearing the Union banner. A small flying figure of Victory is crowning her with a laurel wreath. Behind Britannia is a trinacria* and in front of her is inscribed in large letters in two lines "MAI" and "DA", whilst the date also occupies a further two lines, "IVL.IV" and "MDCCCVI". In the exergue are crossed spears tied with a knot.
Size	1·5 in. diameter.
Ribbon	Red with blue edges, 1½ in. wide, fitted with a gold buckle.
Designer	G. F. Pidgeon.

Medals were issued to officers of the rank of Lieutenant-Colonel and above,† whose names were usually engraved around the edge.

Maida is a small village in the west-central part of Calabria on the toe of Italy. It was here that a small force under Major-General Sir John Stuart, who had landed in support of the King of Naples, defeated the French under General Regnier who were preparing to assault Sicily so as to complete the destruction of the Neapolitan forces.

The following regiments took part: 20 Light Dragoons; R.A.; R.E.; Sappers and Miners; Commissariat; Medical Staff; 20, 27, 35, 39 (1), 42 (1), 58, 61, 78, 81 Foot; Corsican Rangers; de Watteville's Regiment.

Recipients of the Gold Medal for Maida 1806

  1. Sir John Stuart, K.B., Major-General Commanding.
  2. Hon. Sir G. L. Cole, K.B., Brigadier-General.

* A Trinacria is the old symbol of Sicily which the ancients considered to be the island of Thrinacia referrred to by Homer. The island was variously called Thrinacia, Trinacia, Trinacris, and Triquetra by the Romans. All these names are, of course symbolical of its triangular shape.

† A silver medal was awarded to Lieutenant Pearce Lowen, 4 Foot, but the reason for this, apparently, unique award cannot be traced.

3. W. P. Acland, Brigadier-General.
4. John Oswald, Colonel, commanding a brigade.
5. James Kempt, Lieut-Colonel, commanding Light Infantry.
6. Haviland Smith, Lieut-Colonel, commanding 27th Foot.
7. Hon. R. W. O'Callaghan, Lieut-Colonel, Commanding Grenadiers
8. Robert Ross, Lieut-Colonel, commanding 20th Foot.
9. George Johnson, Lieut-Colonel, commanding 58th Foot.
10. Patrick McLeod, Lieut-Colonel, commanding 78th Foot.
11. Louis de Watteville, Lieut-Colonel, commanding Regiment de Watteville.
12. David Stewart, Major, commanding left battalion 78th Foot.
13. James Macdonnel, Major, commanding 78th Foot.
14. George D. Robertson, Major, commanding 35th Foot.
15. John M'Combe, Major, commanding Royal Corsican Rangers.
16. John Lemoine, Lieut-Colonel, commanding Royal Artillery.
17. H. E. Banbury, Dep. Quartermaster-General.

33 MEDALS FOR CAPTURE OF RODRIGUES, ISLE OF BOURBON AND ISLE OF FRANCE (1809-1810)

Obverse   A native holding a Union Jack whilst standing in front of a gun.

Reverse   A Persian inscription surrounded by a wreath and around this again the following in block lettering "RODRIGUES VI JULY MDCCCIX. BOURBON VIII JULY & ISLE OF FRANCE III DEC. MDCCCX."

Size   1·9 in. diameter.

Suspension   The medals are suspended by a cord of no specified colour.

Designer   The dies were engraved and the medals struck at the Calcutta Mint.

This medal was issued in gold and silver. Mr. Hastings Irwin quotes forty-five of the former and 2,156 of the latter as having been awarded. It was given by the Honourable East India Company to native troops from Bombay and Bengal for their services in the capture of these three islands. The British troops present did not receive any medals.

Re-strikes of this medal are to be found.

Rodrigues, 6th July, 1809.

Regiments present: 56 Foot (200 men), 2/2 Bombay Native Infantry (200 men).

Isle of Bourbon, 8th July, 1810.

This island, now known as Reunion, had already been invaded by Colonel Keatinge on 21st September, 1809. Owing to the small size of his force, he was unable to retain possession. A further attack became necessary, and so Colonel Keatinge was reinforced and, together with 236 seamen from the Squadron under Commodore Josias Rowley, of the *Raisonable*, a descent was made on 8th July, 1810.

Regiments present: 12, 33, 69, 86 Foot; 1/6, 2/22 Madras N.I.; 2/2 Bombay N.I.

H. M. Ships: *Nereide, Otter, Raisonable.*

Isle of France, 3rd December, 1810.

This island, now known as Mauritius, had for long been a nuisance, as it was the home of Corsairs who raided our merchantmen. A force 10,000 strong under

General Sir John Abercromby* was dispatched from India and together with a strong fleet, appeared off the island on 29th November, 1810. Several French ships were captured in the harbour of Port Louis, including the *Iphigenia*, which had recently been captured from us.

The British regiments present were the 22, 69 and 86 Foot.

34 MEDALS FOR BAGUR AND PALAMOS (10th-14th September, 1810)

Obverse	The shields of Britain and Spain.
Reverse	A Spanish inscription "GRATITUDE OF SPAIN TO THE BRAVE BRITISH AT BAGUR 10 SEPT. 1810, PALAMOS 14 SEPT. 1810."
Size	1·9 in. diameter approx.
Ribbon	Red with narrow yellow edges.
Designer	These medals were awarded by the Spanish Government and were designed by a Spaniard.
Naming	In the case of the silver medals, the recipient's name is sometimes engraved in script at the top of the reverse, with the name of his ship in capital letters at the bottom. On others the recipient's initials only are engraved on the reverse.

Eight of these medals were issued in gold to senior officers, and the remainder were of silver. They were given to the crews of the *Ajax*, *Cambrian* and *Kent*. It is difficult to understand why the name of Palamos should have been included as this was no victory. Here a party of 600 seamen and marines, under Captain Fane of the *Cambrian*, was landed to capture merchant-ships lying tied up to the quays. They were driven through the town and eventually managed to get back to their ships after suffering heavy casualties and losing two officers and eighty-four men prisoners. Though the records only mention the *Ajax, Cambrian* and *Kent* as receiving medals, the sloops *Minstrel* and *Sparrowhawk* also took part.

35 JAVA MEDAL (26th August 1811)

Obverse	A scene of the attack on Fort Cornelis with the inscription "CORNELIS" at the top.
Reverse	A Persian inscription and "JAVA CONQUERED XXVI AUGUST MDCCCXI".
Size	2 in. diameter.
Suspension	By a cord of no specified colour.
Designer	The medals were engraved and struck at the Calcutta Mint.

This medal was issued by the H.E.I.C. to the native troops of the 3rd, 4th, 5th and 6th Bengal Volunteers, Madras Pioneers and the Governor's Bodyguard. One hundred and thirty-three gold medals were issued; 5,761 natives received silver medals as well as about 750 Europeans. Only those in the service of the Company were allowed to wear their medals. For further particulars of the British troops and Naval ships present, the Military and Naval General Service Medals should be referred to.

*Son of Sir Ralph Abercromby, who died during the Egyptian Campaign, 1801.

36 MILITARY GENERAL SERVICE MEDAL (1793-1814)

Obverse   The diademed head of Queen Victoria and legend "VICTORIA REGINA" with the date "1848".

Reverse   Queen Victoria standing on a dais about to place a laurel wreath on the Duke of Wellington, who is kneeling on his left knee. Beside the dais is a diminutive representation of the British Lion dormant. Around the top half of the circumference is the inscription "TO THE BRITISH ARMY". In the exergue are the dates "1793-1814". It is difficult to understand how these dates were arrived at as the first bar, for "EGYPT", was not authorized until 1850, that is two years after the issue of the medal. I can only presume that the intention was to award the medal for earlier actions which were subsequently deleted after the medal had been struck, but it would be difficult to trace which actions could have been in mind. perhaps the idea was to make this medal the military equivalent of the Naval General Service Medal, which bears the date 1848.

Size   1·42 in. diameter.

Ribbon   1·25 in. wide crimson with 1/8 in. wide dark blue borders.

Suspension   By a plain straight swivelling suspender.

Designer   W. Wyon, R.A.

Naming   In indented large Roman capitals.

No. of bars issued   Twenty-nine.

This medal was authorized by a General Order dated 1st June, 1847,* and issued in 1848—thirty-four years after the last battle it commemorates. For some inexplicable reason the medal is often referred to as the Peninsular Medal, even though the medal commemorates such places as Egypt, the East and West Indies, U.S.A., etc. Personal application had to be made for the medal, and Mr. Carter, in his book *Medals of the British Army*, gives an amusing account of an old officer who had to refer to the records to see whether he was present at a particular action or not, "having been in so many at such a distant date".

There were about 25,650 applications for the medal, for which twenty-nine bars were awarded, fifteen being the most to any one recipient. The bars are fixed in multiples of three where applicable.

There were two recipients of the medal with fifteen bars and eleven with fourteen, though in the latter case the medal roll only gives nine.

15 Bars   James Talbot, 45th Foot.
Daniel Loochstadt, who appears on the roll of the 60th and King's German Legion.

14 Bars*   John Hughes, R.A.
George Legg, R.A., who is credited with only thirteen bars on the medal roll.
Sergt. John Hardy, 7th Foot, who received bars for Martinique, Talavera, Busaco, Albuhera, Ciudad Rodrigo, Badajoz, Salamanca, Vittoria, Pyrenees, St. Sebastian, Nivelle, Nive, Orthes, Toulouse. His brothers, Cpl. Peter Hardy and Pte. James Hardy, received the medal with thirteen bars. They were not present at the Battle of Talavera.

*Medals were awarded to the next-of-kin of those who applied for them but who died before the medals were issued.

**There is a medal with fourteen bars to Peter March, 95th Foot, which does not agree with the medal roll, but is said to be genuine.

14 Bars	Drum-Major John Green, 45th Foot.
	Edwin Kean, 45th Foot.
	James Nixon, 45th Foot.
	Major James Campbell, 50th Foot.
	Patrick Haggerty, 52nd Foot.
	James Morris, 52nd Foot.
	Lieut. Sir. J. A. Schoede, 60th Foot.
	Sergt. Joseph Hindle, 95th Foot.

The following table shows the approximate order of scarcity of the bars when awarded singly and in conjunction with others. The value of the medals is not, however, in the same order.

Single Bars	*With two or more Bars*
1 Benvente.	Benevente.
2 Roleia (10).	Sahagun.
3 Sahagun.	Chrystler's Farm.
4 Ciudad Rodrigo.	Chateauguay.
5 Nivelle.	Sahagun and Benevente.
6 Pyrenees.	Fort Detroit.
7 Sahagun and Benevente.	Java.
8 Orthes.	Guadaloupe.
9 St. Sebastian.	Maida.
10 Busaco.	Martinique.
11 Vimiera.	Barrosa.
12 Albuhera.	Roleia.
13 Fuentes d'Onor.	Egypt.
14 Badajoz.	Vimiera.
15 Nive.	Albuhera.
16 Guadaloupe.	St. Sebastian.
17 Chrystler's Farm.	Fuentes d'Onor.
18 Chateauguay.	Ciudad Rodrigo.
19 Martinique.	Talavera.
20 Fort Detroit.	Badajoz.
21 Barrosa.	Busaco.
22 Talavera.	Corunna.
23 Salamanca.	Nive.
24 Maida.	Nivelle.
25 Java.	Orthes.
26 Vittoria.	Salamanca.
27 Toulouse.	Pyrenees.
28 Egypt.	Toulouse.
29 Corunna.	Vittoria.

Officers and men received bars for actions when attached to other than their parent units, so that it is difficult to say to which the medal should be credited. The unit given on the medal is not consistently given as the first or last with which a man served although it is known for officers medals to contain up to three different units and more than one rank on a medal.

Several officers were attached to the Portuguese Forces and received medals with a greater number of bars than normally awarded to members of their regiments.

Though twenty-nine bars were issued with the Military General Service Medal, only twenty-one of them were awarded for service in the above mentioned wars. The historical reasons for the award of the other eight are given separately.

The cause of the wars is to be found in the discontent in Portugal and Spain in the year 1808 and the rising of the Spaniards caused by the dislike of Napoleon, especially by his transference of his brother Joseph from Naples to Madrid. This was done, of course, to give Napoleon control of the Iberian Peninsula. Portugal was to all intents and purposes under his control by virtue of the fact that a French army, under Marshal Junot, occupied the country in considerable strength.

Space will not allow me to give the reasons why British forces were sent out, so we must confine ourselves to a very brief statement of what happened after they arrived.

Two forces were dispatched under the supreme command of Sir Arthur Wellesley with a view to affording the Spanish and Portuguese nations every possible aid in "throwing off the yoke of France", to quote the instructions received by Sir Arthur from the Duke of York.

Before we go any farther we must realize that though the Spanish and Portuguese were of unreliable fighting value we were not alone. We had, in addition, a large number of German mercenaries known as the King's German Legion.

The troops sailed from Cork on 10th July, 1808, arrived off Mondego Bay, about ninety miles to the north-west of Lisbon, on the 26th and started disembarkation on 1st August. Further reinforcements were sent which arrived on 20th August.

As soon as possible the advance inland commenced. The first encounter with the French occurred on 15th August at Lourinha, where General Laborde, commanding the French, had sited his outpost line to guard Lisbon. On 17th August Wellesley fought his first battle against the French at Rolica, as a result of which they were driven back towards Lisbon.

As further reinforcements were due to arrive at Maceira, about thirty miles north-west of Lisbon, Wellesley decided to wait until they had joined him before continuing his advance.

Marshal Junot, who had taken over command from Laborde, attacked Wellesley in his position around Vimiera on 21st August, but was heavily defeated. During the action Lieutenant-General Sir Harry Burrard arrived, but did not take over command. The next day Sir Hew Dalrymple assumed command.

On 22nd August a treaty was signed with the French which was ratified on the 30th under the title of the Convention of Cintra, by the terms of which Junot and the French army were to be evacuated from Portugal in British ships.

It is hardly to be wondered at that the authorities at home were somewhat puzzled, to say the least, as to the reasons for such a pact so soon after two crushing defeats of the French, and Wellesley, Burrard and Dalrymple were ordered home to attend a court of inquiry. Sir John Moore was then given supreme command.

The French were evacuated from Portugal and landed in Brittany, whence they promptly crossed the Pyrenees and re-entered Spain from the north, having been rested and re-equipped and being resolved to do better next time!

Moore was left the almost impossible task of clearing the French out of Spain while having his hands tied by having to consider his forces "an Auxiliary to the Spanish Forces to support the Spanish Nation against the attempts of Napoleon to subjugate them, and should the Spanish Government appoint a Commander-in-Chief, he was to consider himself as under his command". The Spaniards never did make an appointment and Napoleon was able to give instructions for the destruction of the isolated forces piecemeal.

The Spaniards, flushed by a victory under Castanos, at Baylen on 22nd July, 1808, not only resented but were almost hostile to the presence of British troops.

General Baird was ordered to land at Corunna in the extreme north-west of Spain, with instructions to march towards Madrid to make a junction with Sir John, who was receiving the most encouraging reports concerning the results of actions between the Spanish and French. The truth was that the Spanish had been heavily defeated, and instead of an unharassed meeting between himself and Baird he found that his total force of about 25,000 men was opposed to some 300,000 Frenchmen, the rigours of winter, the embarrassing presence of Spanish troops, and the complete apathy of the local population and government.

Sir John, realizing that far from being able to clear the French out of Spain, he would be lucky if his armies escaped annihilation, ordered a retreat towards Corunna, from which place the army could be re-embarked.

We cannot go into the interesting details of Napoleon's attempt to entice Moore to Madrid, so must concentrate on the retreat to Corunna and the attempts of Napoleon to prevent it.

On 21st December, 1808, the army halted at Sahagun, where a cavalry charge was made. A few days later another was made at Benevente. Luckily for Moore, Marshal Soult, to whom Napoleon had delegated the task of driving the British into the sea, made no determined attack on the retreating army and allowed it to concentrate at Lugo, outside Corunna, between 6th and 16th January, 1809.

On the 14th the fleet had arrived at Corunna to embark the army, but on the 17th the French attacked (during which Lt. Gen. Sir John Moore was killed), so that it was not until the 18th that the embarkation was completed.

This ended the first phase. Though not devoid of military triumphs, the war bears a striking resemblance to our subsequent evacuations from Gallipoli, Dunkirk, Greece and Crete, in that it kindled the flame in the British character which has the extraordinary faculty for burning brightest after defeat.

The court of inquiry exonerated Wellesley and he was now appointed to command another army. This disembarked at Lisbon on 22nd April, 1809, and crossed the River Douro* on 12th May. Soult was driven out of Oporto and up the valley of the Tagus to Talavera, where the French grouped their forces under Marshal Victor.

On the evening of 27th July the French attacked, but were defeated on the 28th after severe fighting during which the touch of humanity, that even the heat of battle cannot obliterate, showed itself. Between the contending armies was a small stream to which both sides went to draw water for their wounded and themselves; yes, and to exchange remarks and souvenirs in much the same way as happened in the 1914-18 War for no other reason than physical exhaustion and the mutual realization of the horrors and futility of human slaughter.†

---

* This river is known as the Duero in Spain.

†After the sanguinary Battle of Fredericksburg, which was fought on 13th December, 1862, during the American Civil War, the Federals and Conferates faced each other across the Rappahannock river, barely one hundred yards wide at this place. A Federal band came down to the river bank and played popular and patriotic tunes. At a shout from some Confederates to "play some of ours" the band struck up with "Dixie", "My Maryland", and "The Bonnie Blue Flag". The concert ended with both sides singing "Home, Sweet Home". As the Confederate general, G. Moxley Sorrell, so delightfully quotes in his book *Recollections of a Confederate Staff Officer,.* "One touch of nature makes the whole world kin".

Since the dawn of history and the birth of war there has always been respect between chivalrous foes. As chivalry declines, hatred both during and after battle increases—a fact which is now only too plain for all to see.

After the battle of Talavera, Wellesley was created a peer with the style of Lord Wellington of Wellington, in Somerset, and Talavera. Marshal Victor was given the title of Duke of Talavera by the French. It is a strange if not unique occurrence for commanders to take their titles from the place where they were opposed to each other.

The exhaustion and losses were such that Wellington could not take immediate advantage of his victory; in fact, he had to withdraw into Portugal.

In May 1810, Napoleon ordered Masséna to drive Wellington out of Portugal, but he remained completely inactive for some months before besieging the frontier fortress of Almeida. He started his advance on 15th August and by a lucky chance exploded the defenders' ammunition store. Wellington, who had moved up to help the garrison, realized that nothing could be done, so retired to the valley of the Mondego. Masséna remained inactive till the 15th September, when he advanced down the right bank of the river to where Wellington had taken up a strong position along the high ridge of the Sierra de Busaco.

Though the action that followed was an allied victory, it was fought as a delaying action to give the Portuguese inhabitants of the area time to get behind the prepared defences of Torres Vedras.

Once again Masséna was slow to follow up, thus giving the allies time to make an unhurried withdrawal to behind these thirty miles of prepared positions, where they spent the period from September, 1810, to March, 1811, during which the weather and conditions in the area made all but a few sporadic engagements impossible.

The scene now shifts to the South of Spain to Barosa, which is a few miles south of Cadiz. Here General Graham, who had disembraked at Algeciras, on the other side of the bay from Gibraltar, joined forces with a Spanish army under General Lapena with a view to operating in the rear of the French. There appears to have been a certain amount of confusion between the two generals, and of this Marshal Victor was quick to take advantage. The Spaniards were no sooner attacked than defeated, leaving the British, not for the last time in war, alone. After two hours of heavy fighting the French retired, thus leaving open the way to Cadiz.

We must now return to the north, where Masséna had crossed the River Agueda at Ciudad Rodrigo on 2nd May, 1811, remembering that the battle to which this place gives its name was not fought until January of the next year. Masséna's movement was a continuation of the withdrawal forced on him by the approach of the Portuguese in his rear and the poor condition of his troops due to sickness and lack of supplies, not to mention the fact that he was also being closely pressed by Wellington. His reputation had suffered a severe blow as a result of this retreat, so he decided to draw Wellington away from Lisbon and then sidestep and get in behind him. His intentions were anticipated and the two forces met at Fuentes d'Onor, where Masséna's defeat was so decisive that he was relieved of his command and returned to France.

To the west and slightly north of Fuentes d'Onor is the town of Almeida, in which a French garrison under General Brennier was surrounded. Whether it was partly due to mistakes on our part or not, one cannot but admire the skill with which this garrison escaped and joined Marmont, who, having taken over command from Masséna, now withdrew towards Salamanca.

During the early part of May the British were also besieging Badajoz. Marshal Soult left Seville with strong forces to relieve it, but was intercepted at Albuhera on 16th May by Marshal Sir William Beresford.

Here it is well to remind the reader that our forces in the Peninsula were small compared with those opposing them. To operate with small forces of tired troops on long lines of communication which would only get longer as the French were driven back would have been the very acme of folly. We find, therefore, that after those two battles there was a lull in the operations as regards major battles. We had in 1809, as already explained, to withdraw from the Peninsula. The Spanish army and people were unreliable, so that defeat or another withdrawal might have had unpredictable consequences.

After the two major battles of Fuentes d'Onor and Albuhera the position was serious, and it was as well that Soult did not realize it or at any rate take advantage of it. Be that as it may, Wellington was given time to reorganize, so that by the beginning of January, 1812, he was ready to take the offensive again.

His first move was to capture Ciudad Rodrigo, the siege of which lasted from 8th to 10th January. For this action he was granted an earldom, and the Spanish Government conferred on him the title of Duke of Ciudad Rodrigo.

Before a general advance could begin, a further garrison fortress had to be captured for the third time during the campaign. This was Badajoz, which after a heroic defence by General Phillipon and terrible slaughter on both sides fell on 6th April, 1812.

There was another French garrison in Salamanca, after which the next battle is named. The town was surrounded by small forts, and these, though strong after the three weeks' work that had been spent on them, did not hold out so long as Marmont expected. His tactics here are extremely difficult to understand, because, though he had spent considerable time and labour in putting it in a strong state of defence, he withdrew all the garrison, except 800 men, as soon as Wellington approached on 16th June. The town was captured on the 17th.

Once again Marmont's tactics are hard to understand: though in the neighbourhood with large forces he appears to have made no effort to come to the assistance of the garrison.

As soon as he knew that Salamanca had fallen he withdrew behind the River Duero in two columns, both of which had to cross at least two rivers before they could get into their new positions. As it turned out it was a case of *reculer pour mieux sauter*. Wellington, for reasons which are not clear, was very slow in following up, thus giving Marmont the initiative. On 17th July he recrossed the Duero and from then onwards to the end of the battle a study of thrusts, parries and counter-thrusts of these two masters of war make fine reading.

In the end, all else being equal, victory goes to the general who makes the fewest mistakes. By the night of 22nd July the French were in full retreat. The British casualties had been in the region of 8,000, with those of the French about double.*

For this action Wellington was created a marquis and granted a bounty of £100,000.

The way to Madrid was now open, and the capital was entered by Wellington on 12th August, 1812. Here he halted and became involved in a certain amount of politics with the Spanish and Portuguese Governments. He was, however, appointed Commander-in-Chief of the Spanish forces, so that at last there was that essential to success where allies are concerned—a unified command.

On 14th September, 1812, Napoleon entered Moscow. In the following month began the world-famous retreat which frittered, or correctly speaking froze, away his Grande Armée and reputation.

From August, 1812, to May, 1813, Wellington reorganized the Spanish and Portuguese armies, the latter of which was commanded by British officers. By

The bar to the Military General Service Medal was awarded for the Battle of Salamanca and not for the capture of the town.

May the strengths of the opposing forces were about equal; perhaps we were slightly the stronger.

On 4th June, 1813, the advance towards the Pyrenees began. It was undertaken in three columns, the left under Graham and the right under Hill, with Wellington in the centre. On the 20th the French were encountered holding a position at Vittoria, on the River Zadora. Once again Wellington's brilliant tactics were too good for the French under Marshal Jourdan, who were forced to withdraw. Marshal Jourdan's baton was captured, together with the personal baggage of King Joseph Napoleon, in addition to the greater part of the French artillery, ammunition and wagons.

For this outstanding victory Wellington was made a Field Marshal. Napoleon now appointed Marshal Soult to command the French armies in Spain.

After the battle of Vittoria the French withdrew to the extreme north of Spain, leaving behind garrisons at Pampeluna and St. Sebastian. Wellington, however, pushed on. He left the Spaniards to deal with Pampeluna and Graham to attack St. Sebastian. When he reached the Pyrenees he was met and attacked by Soult. The battle which takes its name from the mountains was fought where they run down to the Bay of Biscay near Irun. It lasted for four days, but in the end the French were forced back on to their own soil.

St. Sebastian did not fall as soon as expected, so Wellington, considering it inadvisable to continue his advance into France, decided that the place had to be taken.

Weapons used in mobile warfare are not suitable for siege work, so there was some delay. Though the town was surrounded, one must remember that Soult was in considerable strength not far away and was obviously intent on relieving. This he tried to do by crossing the Badossa in force on 30th August.

Though the investment started on 17th July, the town did not fall until 31st August. The battle, to which the town gives its name, continued until 8th September.

Having found no evidence to the contrary, one presumes that the bar for St. Sebastian was awarded to those who had taken part in the siege and/or the subsequent battle which took place in the neighbourhood.* Pampeluna, for the capture of which no bars were awarded, did not fall until 31st October.

The losses on both sides were in and around St. Sebastian were considerable and once again a halt was made until reinforcements arrived. Meanwhile, Soult withdrew and took up a defensive position along the River Nivelle.

Whilst the events with which we have just been dealing were taking place even greater ones were happening, or were about to happen, elsewhere which, though outside the scope of this short account, had a very great bearing on those that follow. Between 16th and 19th October, 1813, there was fought the battle of Leipsic or "The Battle of the Nations" as it has been called, in which Napoleon with 160,000 men was decisively defeated by the combined armies of Austria, Russia and Prussia, numbering about 400,000. The French losses were tremendous in men, artillery and above all in morale. It was obvious that after this shattering blow the French forces opposing Wellington could not expect much in the way of reinforcements to make good subsequent losses and that if they were given one or two more hard knocks the war would be over. The fact that the fighting continued until the following April was due, so some say, to the personal vanity of Soult. The marshal should be given credit for his skill and to the bravery of his army which, though continually defeated and forced to withdraw for hundreds of miles, fought with a gallantry undiminished by events which

* The *London Gazette* of 1st June, 1847, quotes just "August and September ,1813." The days of the month are not stated.

they could see for themselves and those which they must have heard about through that most demoralizing of all methods, rumour.

If we refuse to give credit for the bravery and skill of our opponents in this campaign we automatically detract from the skill of Wellington and the value of the Battle Honours and awards which were awarded. We cannot have it both ways.

Further reinforcements having arrived from England, Wellington attacked and captured the mountain of La Rhune which overlooked the French position along the Nivelle. After this the French left wing, resting on Amotz, was attacked and turned on 10th November, 1813. Hill, who was now on our left, forded the river at its mouth just abouve St. Jean de Luz. These two movements "rolled up" the French army, which now withdrew to the River Nive, running almost parallel to the Nivelle at a distance varying from twelve to eight miles.

The weather at the end of November and in early December made futher military operations impossible, so that once again there was a hiatus, this time for a month.

On 9th December, 1813, the advance continued and the battle along the Nive commenced.

There were three crossings over the river, one at Cambo on the British right, one at Ustaritz in the centre, and another at Bayonne on the left. The battle raged from the 9th to the 13th December, when the French had their left flank turned and were compelled to withdraw, leaving a garrison in Bayonne which did not surrender until after the war was over.

After the fighting along the Nive the behaviour of the Spanish troops so annoyed the Basque peasants that they rose in revolt and formed, under the leadership of Harispe, what in the 1939-45 War would have been termed a Maquis. They caused considerable trouble and hindered the subsequent operations. Among the other things which they did was to gain time for Soult to take up another position on the high ground between St. Boes and Orthez, from which, after the battle of the latter name, he was forced to withdraw on 27th February, 1814. In this action Wellington was wounded, though not seriously, in the thigh.

After several further engagements which are not commemorated on the medals, Soult withdrew to his home town of Toulouse, on the River Garonne. Apart from the fact that he was fighting on his home ground, the site was well chosen, as it was a focal point of the roads leading into the heart of France. It is also located in an area traversed by many rivers. He could, if occasion arose, retire to the Lyons area.

Through good marching and local knowledge he withdrew his forces so expeditiously that he gained three days—three valuable days—in which to reorganize and prepare for the attack by the British forces which arrived in the neighbourhood on 8th April, 1814.

On the 10th the attack on Toulouse started. The town was surrounded by battlements and intersected by the Garonne. From the west to the south-east, about half a mile outside these battlements, was the Languedoc Canal. Beyond this again were a range of hills and a few isolated crests, all of which were strongly fortified. By some unaccountable failure Beresford was allowed to get into position to attack the outer ridge of high ground without being molested, with the result that after terrific fighting round the whole perimeter Soult was forced to evacuate the town on the 12th and retire on Villefranque.

Napoleon having abdicated on 31st March, the Peninsular War was now over.

This brief account of the campaign should show that the battles commemorated on the Military General Service Medal were not fought in a sequence as a result of one long advance. There were two distinct phases to the campaign, the first of which ended with our evacuation from Corunna.

During the campaign units known as "Battalions of Detachments" were formed from details of various strengths from many regiments. It is on account of this that medals are found to regiments which were not present as a whole, and it is also the reason why some men received many more bars than those normally gained by their regiment. Officers were attached to the Portuguese forces, so that they received bars not normally awarded to their parent units.

There is no finality in the compilation of statistics concerning the Military General Service Medal. Rolls obtained from different sources disagree as to the spelling of the names and, what is far more important, as to the title of the bars to which they quote the man as being eligible.

The following three examples will illustrate the difficulty of obtaining complete accuracy:

(1) Pte. R. Atkinson, 3 Foot Guards, received a medal with bars for Talavera, Ciudad Rodrigo, Salamanca and Vittoria, whereas the roll shows him as being entitled to bars for Busaco, Fuentes d'Onor, Nivelle and Nive in addition.

(2) Charles Shepperd, 29 Foot, received a medal with the single bar for Vimiera, though the roll shows him as being entitled to those for Vittoria, Talavera and Albuhera in addition.

(3) Wm. Chadwick, 12th Light Dragoons, received a medal with bars for Salamanca and Nivelle, though some rolls show him as entitled to those for Salamanca and Vittoria.

Egypt *(2nd March-2nd September, 1801)*

Napoleon, as everyone knows, had visions of world conquest, but before this could be achieved he, like Hitler after him, realized that Egypt was the stepping-stone to the East.

At the beginning of the year 1801 Egypt was occupied by Napoleon's "Army of the East" under General Menou.

An expedition to conquer the country was dispatched from England under General Sir Ralph Abercromby, and additional forces were sent from India and the Cape of Good Hope. These were commanded by Major-General Baird.

The troops from home assembled at Marmorice, in Asiatic Turkey. Sailing from thence on 2nd March, 1801, they arrived in Aboukir Bay during a heavy storm. A landing was made on the 8th, and the French were forced back towards Alexandria. They took up a position at Mandora (borne on the Colours of the 90th and 92nd Foot) which was attacked on the 13th. They were then driven back into Alexandria itself, which lies on a thin neck of land with the sea on the north and Lake Mareotis on the south.

The two armies faced each other on this strip from 13th to 21st March, on which latter day the French attacked our position and, led by the Invincible Legion, broke through. Wheeling left, it encircled the 28th Foot, which, attacked both in front and rear, earned its right to wear two badges on the headdress, one in front and one behind. After severe fighting, the Invincible Legion surrendered to Major Stirling of the 42nd Foot, and handed over their Standard.

General Abercromby was wounded in this battle and Lieutenant-General Hutchinson assumed command. He contained the French garrison in Alexandria and attacked Cairo, which surrendered on 27th June.

General Menou, now besieged in Alexandria, refused to surrender, so a landing was made by General Coote to the west of the town. The fort of Marabout, which stood on an island in the harbour, was attacked and captured by the 54th Foot, which is the only regiment to have this honour on its colours.

Severe fighting ensued both to the west and east of the town, which capitulated on 2nd September.

The Sultan of Egypt awarded the Order of the Crescent to the General Officers and large and small gold medals to the others. (See No. 28.)

The Highland Society presented medals to members of the 42nd Highlanders. (See No. 29)

Maida (4th July, 1806)

For further particulars of awards for Maida see No. 32.

Lieut. W. F. Carroll, R.N., received the M.G.S. medal with this bar.

Roleia (17th August, 1808)

This is the spelling used on the bar, though the correct one is Rolica as used on the regimental colours.

There were only eleven recipients of a medal with this as a single bar, They were:

Staff	Samuel Brown (who was carrying dispatches).
5th Foot	Adam Lloyd, Joseph Stevenson, Wm. Tollerday.
9th Foot	Capt. Samuel Sanky, Lieut. Samuel Nicholls, Thos. Fuller (on Muster Roll only).
29th Foot	Joseph Beer.
91st Foot	James Bennett.
95th Foot	Sergt. John Wheeler.
Medical Dept.	John Winter, Purveyor's Clerk.

Vimiera (21st August, 1808)

Sahagun (21st December, 1808)

Only twenty *single* bars were issued, all to 15th Hussars. The recipients were: Major F. Forrester; Capt. J. Broadhurst; Capt. A. Gordon; Paymaster E. P. Henstowe; Tp. Qr. Mr. T. Ledger; T. Bannister; J. Barnett; J. Bartholomew; J. Clarke; G. Edmonds; Sergt-Major R. Harvey; Sergt. B. Loach; F. May; J. Pluckett; W. Pontin; W. Skinner; S. Skuse; L. Taylor; Wm. Thackeray; J. Westcot.

Benevente (1st January, 1809)

Four single bars were awarded to 10th Hussars: Sergt. W. Ace; Jas. Foster; W. Humbert; Jas. Scrambler. Four bars were awarded to 7th Hussars: A. Barry; W. Lyne; J. Norse; Jonathon Brown and M. McCartney. 18th Lt. Dgns.

One medal with this single bar was awarded to the Royal Artillery: Capt. Henry Eveleigh, R.H.A.—a total of ten bars only.

Sahagun and Benevente

This bar was awarded to those present at both the battles of Sahagun and Benevente.

Corunna (16th January, 1809)

The recipients of this bar to the 45th Foot were James Talbot, Matthew Harris and William Smith.

Martinique (30th January—24th February, 1809)

This bar was awarded to members of the Expeditionary Force under Lieutenant-General Beckwith. The colours, or eagles as the French call them, of the French 62nd and 80th Regiments were captured. They were the first to arrive in England and now hang in the Royal Hospital, Chelsea.

Talavera (27th—28th July, 1809)

It will bear out the remarks made at the end of the historical detail to this medal concerning detachments or a few recipients of many regiments receiving bars for engagements at which the regiment was not present as whole, if we quote the following movements of regiments.

The 50th Foot left the Downs on 28th July, 1809, and disembarked on the island of Walcheren on 2nd August. Brigaded with them on landing were the 11th and 79th Foot and later the 6th and 91st Foot, and yet, as will be seen, three of these regiments received medals for Talvera.

There were two "Battalions of Detachments" formed from the detachments left in Portugal when Sir John Moore marched from Lisbon to Salamanca, hence the number of regiments awarded this and subsequent bars.

Guadaloupe (January—February, 1810)

For the historical detail see the bar for Guadaloupe awarded with the Naval General Service Medal (page 105).

Busaco (27th September, 1810)

A. Hobbs, John Jenkins, John Jones and George Waterman of the 9th Foot were the only members of the regiment to receive a medal with the single bar for Busaco.

Barrosa (5th March, 1811)

Fuentes d'Onor (5th May, 1811)

Albuhera (16th May, 1811)

The 57th; (The Diehards) had 415 casualties.

Java (14th—26th August 1811)

In order to prevent the East Indies from coming under the domination of Napoleon, who had already absorbed Holland, it was decided that the island should be captured.

The Governor-General of India, Lord Minto, organized an expedition. The naval forces were commanded by Rear-Admiral the Honourable Robert Stopford. Though Lord Minto accompanied the force, the command of the troops was given to Lieutenant-General Sir Samuel Auchmuty.

The first landing was made on 4th August, 1811, to the east of the capital, Batavia, which was captured on the 9th.

After the fall of the town the Gallo-Batavians, under General Jansen, took up a strong position at Cornelis from which they were driven out by the combined action of the two services on 26th August, on which day the island surrendered.

The 14th Foot remained to garrison the island, which was restored to Holland by the Treaty of Vienna, signed on 28th September, 1814.

Capt. George Sayer, R.N., and Capt. Richard Bunce, R.M., both received Army Gold Medals for their services during the capture of the island.

Ciudad Rodrigo *(8th—19th January, 1812)*

Only one medal with a single bar was awarded to the 45th Foot, and that was to John Bedford.

Badajoz *(17th March and 6th April, 1812)*

Salamanca *(22nd July, 1812)*

Fort Detroit *(16th August, 1812)**

Having declared war on Britain on 18th June, 1812, the United States intended to invade Upper Canada.

Fort Detroit was situated at the extreme north-western end of Lake Erie on the south bank of the Detroit river, on the opposite bank of which were the British garrisons of Sandwich and Amherstburg.

An American force, under Brigadier-General William Hull, reached Fort Detroit on 8th August and then crossed the river and occupied Sandwich without opposition. Instead of immediately continuing his advance to Amerherstburg, some twenty miles away, he decided to wait for heavy artillery. Whilst waiting he became overawed by the apparent magnitude of his task and withdrew his force to the American bank.

The Commander-in-Chief in Upper Canada was Brigadier-General Isaac Brock, who noticing the half-heartedness of the Americans, decided to cross the river and attack Fort Detroit. This he did on 16th August under cover of the fire of his artillery and the supporting fire from the *Queen Charlotte*. No sooner had his attackers got in position to start the assault when the garrison surrendered.

The units taking part in the capture of the fort were 30 men of the Royal Artillery, 250 men of the 41st Foot (Welch Regiment), 50 men of the Royal Newfoundland Regiment, and about 650 Indians.

The Welch Regiment also have the honour "Miami"† for the action fought on 23rd April, 1813. It is rather extraordinary that this action and those of Queenstown (26th October, 1813), Niagara (19th December, 1813), and Blandensburg (24th August, 1814) should have been considered as worthy of being given the status of battle honours, but not to warrant a bar to the Military General Service Medal.

The medal to J. B. Lapierre, Canadian Militia, is the only one awarded with the bars for Fort Detroit, Chateauguay and Chrystler's Farm.

*Fort Detroit was the original name of the present city of Detroit. The site was first visited by the French in 1610 and then again by them under Antoine de la Mothe Cadillac in 1701, when he founded Fort Detroit. It was ceded to the British in 1763. In the same year it was unsuccessfully besieged by Chief Pontiac with his Ottawa Indians. In 1783 it was given back to the United States, but was not occupied by them until 1796. It was captured again, as related, by the British on 16th August, 1812; and recovered by the United States in 1813.

†This was a small American post in the state of Ohio and so nothing whatever to do with the present town of that name in Florida which gives its name to the well-known pleasure beach.

	Egypt	Maida	Roleia	Vimiera	Sahagun	Benevente	Sahagun and Benevente	Corunna	Martinique	Talavera	Guadaloupe	Busaco	Barrosa	Fuentes d'Onor
1st Life Guards														
2nd Life Guards														
Royal Horse Guards														
3rd Dragoon Guards							1			97		2		
5th Dragoon Guards							1							79
1st Royal Dragoons							1							79
3rd Light Dragoons														
4th Dragoons										98		55		
6th Dragoons														
7th Light Dragoons						4	85	2						
8th Light Dragoons	7													
9th Light Dragoons														
10th Light Dragoons						4	93	1						
11th Light Dragoons	10							1						
12th Light Dragoons	48													
13th Light Dragoons														
14th Light Dragoons	1									102		53	1	79
15th Light Dragoons					99		1							
16th Light Dragoons										86		48		62
18th Light Dragoons						1	79			1				
20th Light Dragoons		4	17	33										
22nd Light Dragoons	46													
23rd Light Dragoons	34								1	60				
Royal Artillery	48	39	55	81	1	1	7*	433	48	168	21	216	147	181
Royal Engineers	3	3	3	2				6	5	3	3	2	5	
Royal Sappers and Miners	8							3	10	1	1		15	
1st Foot (Grenadiers) Guards								348					108	
2nd (Coldstream) Foot Guards	70									141		104	36	108
3rd Foot (Scots) Guards	63									164		119	73	139
LINE REGIMENTS														
1	29							74	2		7	114		38
2	28			74				67		18		1		2
3								5		130		64		
4				2				88		6				21
5			54	69				105		16		64		39
6			60	92				100		17	1			
7									111	100		179		2
8	42								113					
9	1		76	203				85				90	42	32
10	60													
11												71		1
12														

*The Army List quotes 8.

Albuhera	Java	Ciudad Rodrigo	Badajos	Salamanca	Fort Detroit	Chateauguay	Chrysler's Farm	Vittoria	Pyrenees	St. Sebastian	Nivelle	Nive	Orthes	Toulouse	Number of Medals	Maximum number of bars awarded to		
																Officers	Other Ranks	
							72							84	106	2	2	1st L.G.
				1				62						76	94	2	2	2nd L.G.
								121						116	158	2	2	R.H.G.
83								92	1					112	150	4	4	3rd Dgn.
				101				109						140	156	3	3	5th Dgn.
								113	3					105	151	4	3	1st R. Dgn.
			89					112						122	137	3	3	3rd Lt. Dgn.
81			92					95						99	131	7	6	4th Dgns.
									1					1	1	4	4	6th Dgns.
												18	145	116	206	4	4	7th Lt. Dgns.
		1													7		1	8th Lt. Dgns.
		1	1												2		1	9th Lt. Dgns.
								142					105	163	215	4	4	10th Lt. Dgns.
				87				1							98	2	2	11th Lt. Dgns.
1				86				104		1	28	30			128	5	4	12th Lt. Dgns.
90								92	3		16	22	53	85	124	7	6	13th Lt. Dgns.
			72	109				133	91		42	47	95	125	184	11	11	14th Lt. Dgns.
1								132					95	142	184	4	4	15th Lt. Dgns.
				71				80				30	2	3	126	6	6	16th Lt. Dgns.
								90			28	5	69	124	165	7	5	18th Lt. Dgns.
															36	3	2	20th Lt. Dgns.
	54														93	1	2	22nd Lt. Dgns.
			1												123	2	2	23rd Lt. Dgns.
133	10	308	382	582	6	3	4	1023	537	621	194	195	403	740	2134	12	14	R.A.
3		8	13	1				8	2	12	11	12	5	6	46	8	–	R.E.
3		9	29	1				28	13	56	56	46	33	33	118	–	7	R.S. & M.
										63	241	259			606	3	4	1st Ft. Gds.
		116		161				175		27	72	80			337	6	10	2nd Ft. Gds.
		169	1	109				239		42	105	155	1	1	425	6	9	3rd Ft. Gds.
		110		147				174		145	35	59			327	6	9	1st Ft.
1			1	76				90	66	13	30	9	11	68	163	6	10	2nd Ft.
165								2	164		88	87	62	125	281	7	8	3rd Ft.
1			106	217				154		171	38	62			321	6	7	4th Ft.
		65	73	195				145	96		87	44	127	154	322	12	11	5th Ft.
								255	195		107		217		337	7	8	6th Ft.
256		124	159	156				213	193	41	57	46	179	205	438	13	13	7th Ft.
															142	1	2	8th Ft.
			1	150				186		196	51	97			359	7	10	9th Ft.
															60	1	1	10th Ft.
		2	1	62				2	148	5	105	78	89	160	277	6	7	11th Ft.
																		12th Ft.

	Egypt	Maida	Roleia	Vimiera	Sahagun	Benevente	Sahagun and Benevente	Corunna	Martinique	Talavera	Guadaloupe	Busaco	Barrosa	Fuentes d'Onor
LINE REGIMENTS														
13	24								70		60			
14								79						
15									26		44			
16														
17												1		2
18	14													
19														
20	103	72	1	63				85		14				
21														
22														
23	31		1	1				68	77					
24	21									115		63		78
25	34								42		104			
26	12							162						
27	90	122						1		1		113	1	2
28	27							124		18		74	132	
29			90	88						103		65		
30	20													42
31	1									121		68		
32			77	109				126		4				
33														
34												78		
35	1	46												
36			33	87				72		6		1		2
37														
38			39	65				85		12		62		8
39		1										66		
40	25		51	114				1		135		101		1
41														
42	65	1						141		9		103		206
43				126				101		23		48		140
44	53													42
45	1		73	121				3		144		115		65
46									21		18			
47													51	
48										200		101		
49								1					1?	2
50	22		36	112				103		11		15		47
51								85						73
52			1	83				62		26		175	1	121
53										79		54		
54	47													
55														
56														
57												69		
58	24	102						1						

Maximum number of bars awarded to — given under the "Officers" and "Other Ranks" columns.

Albuhera	Java	Ciudad Rodrigo	Badajos	Salamanca	Fort Detroit	Chateauguay	Chrystler's Farm	Vittoria	Pyrenees	St. Sebastian	Nivelle	Nive	Orthes	Toulouse	Number of Medals	Officers	Other Ranks	Regiment
															88	2	2	13th Ft.
	74														149	2	2	14th Ft.
															47	2	2	15th Ft.
																		16th Ft.
		2	1	2							1	1		1	2	8	—	17th Ft.
															14			18th Ft.
																		19th Ft.
								164	124	18	28	29	110	90	269	10	11	20th Ft.
																		21st Ft.
																		22nd Ft.
121	84	120	118					117	107	30	53	37	130	140	295	10	12	23rd Ft.
	81	3	99					89	82		24		75	1	184	9	9	24th Ft.
					1		1								125	6	3	25th Ft.
				1					1		1	1	1		173	1	5	26th Ft.
55	2	165	132					146	126	28	81	47	113	144	445	9	13	27th Ft.
127	1	3	3					220	160	1	90	103	101	146	376	8	8	28th Ft.
114											1				150	8	5	29th Ft.
	11	102	77												136	4	7	30th Ft.
116		2						122	97		52	53	55	83	184	9	9	31st Ft.
	1	1	197					1	146		101	79	114	76	283	8	9	32nd Ft.
													1		1	1	1	33rd Ft.
145								162	134		49	70	70	112	198	8	2	34th Ft.
															46	1	2	35th Ft.
			113					2	112	10	68	55	69	121	212	9	10	36th Ft.
												1			1		1	37th Ft.
	67	165						119		134	23	38		12	243	7	9	38th Ft.
128								207	162		82	95	102	209	344	8	8	39th Ft.
35	126	116	137					210	146	8	83	27	125	176	373	10	13	40th Ft.
					52										62	1	1	41st Ft.
	90		248						224		166	162	228	252	448	7	10	42nd Ft.
	268	269	252					307	191	21	162	138	3	291	485	12	12	43rd Ft.
		93	80												153	3	4	44th Ft.
	140	143	142					170	129		76	43	145	155	278	11	15	45th Ft.
															23	2	2	46th Ft.
								90		90	29	41			108	4	5	47th Ft.
190	83	137	98					140	132	17	80	20	110	138	310	11	12	48th Ft.
	1	1	1		5		61								74	8	1	49th Ft.
		2						180	149		39	53	60	107	271	9	10	50th Ft.
			114					135	120	23	79	5	77		202	6	8	51st Ft.
	302	260	251					269	215	52	135	115	214	239	452	10	14	52nd Ft.
	1	1	75					61	50	11	18	12		80	129	6	9	53rd Ft.
															47	1	1	54th Ft.
																		55th Ft.
																		56th Ft.
122								172	131		86	80	51	125	237	7	8	57th Ft.
				52				35	29		13		23		173	5	5	58th Ft.

1608
12 10

	Egypt	Maida	Roleia	Vimiera	Sahagun	Benevente	Sahagun and Benevente	Corunna	Martinique	Talavera	Guadaloupe	Busaco	Barrosa	Fuentes d'Onor
LINE REGIMENTS														
59								78						
60	9		13	15				6	8	15	15	14		10
61	36	24						1		136		74		1
62														
63									46		39			
64														
65														
66										97		56		
67													67	
68														
69	2													
70									1		8			
71			104	147				131		3				123
72														
73												118		96
74														
75														
76								124						
77														
78		97						1						
79	58							146		12		149		182
80	7							1						
81		119						98						2
82			44	79				63		24			43	
83										117		72		79
84														
85												1		54
86	8													
87										86			110	
88	20									124		163		206
89	32													
90	44								98		120			
91			95	141				105		14				
92	79							140		11				130
93														
94												1		120
95			40	105				192	1	11	1	163	110	153
96											19			
97	7		2	69						70		63		
98														
Royal York Rangers									34		33			
Royal Staff Corps			3	5				17		6		1	10	3

Albuhera	Java	Ciudad Rodrigo	Badajos	Salamanca	Fort Detroit	Chateauguay	Chrystler's Farm	Vittoria	Pyrenees	St. Sebastian	Nivelle	Nive	Orthes	Toulouse	Number of Medals	Maximum number of bars awarded to		
																Officers	Other Ranks	
	104			1				120		115	17	37			275	5	4	59th Ft.
2	16	14	18					24	19	1	7	8	10	16	77	14	15	60th Ft.
			2	154				3	113	1	66	62	96	131	277	9	8	61st Ft.
											64	83			89	2	2	62nd Ft.
															59	2	2	63rd Ft.
																		64th Ft.
																		65th Ft.
99			1					110	104		37	43	52	92	172	8	9	66th Ft.
															67	1	1	67th Ft.
				96				136	94	18	45		93		151	5	6	68th Ft.
	105														105	2	1	69th Ft.
															9	1	1	70th Ft.
								237	182		90	131	141	182	388	8	10	71st Ft.
																		72nd Ft.
																		73rd Ft.
		111	90	113				142	124		69	35	129	141	223	11	11	74th Ft.
																		75th Ft.
											73	99		1	169	3	3	76th Ft.
		64	76					1	1			1	1	1	89	2	7	77th Ft.
	107							1							185	2	2	78th Ft.
				175					175		142	142		212	360	10	9	79th Ft.
															7			80th Ft.
				2											213	7	2	81st Ft.
								114	99	20	67		87	1	218	6	8	82nd Ft.
1		89	99	81				110	60		62	18	94	98	203	11	12	83rd Ft.
											88	151			155	2	2	84th Ft.
										86	89	96			146	3	4	85th Ft.
															8	1	1	86th Ft.
								102	57	5	59	22	72	70	173	7	8	87th Ft.
		200	195	162				229	173		153	121	201	220	408	10	13	88th Ft.
	41						80								150	1	2	89th Ft.
			1												176	2	3	90th Ft.
									195		141	132	161	177	283	8	8	91st Ft.
			2					193	168		64	103	116	131	310	7	9	92nd Ft.
																		93rd Ft.
		109	134	130				163	121		112	78	140	164	221	10	10	94th Ft.
		186	300	308				403	314	59	162	167	299	421	691	12	14	95th Ft.
															19	1	1	96th Ft.
36															88	4	6	97th Ft.
							1								1	1	1	98th Ft.
															47	2	2	R.Y.R.
3		16	25	21				22	11	1	14	12	5	34	60	8	8	R.S.C.

1621
1608
426
3655

39

	Egypt	Maida	Roleia	Vimiera	Sahagun	Benevente	Sahagun and Benevente	Corunna	Martinique	Talavera	Guadaloupe	Busaco	Barrosa	Fuentes d'Onor
Royal Waggon Train			3	7			2	36		15		13	2	3
Staff Officers	10	2	15	13	2		5	28	8	22	5	30	10	23
Chaplains								2						
Commissariat Dept. Officers		1	5	5			2	11		12	2	17	3	9
Medical Staff	3	2	6	6				7	3	2	4	4	3	3
Paymaster-General's Dept.	1	1	1	1						1		2		
Cavalry Staff Corps					1									
Civil Artificers														
Newfoundland Fencibles														
Canadian Militia (Upper & Lower)														
1st West India Regt.									25		6			
3rd West India Regt.									42		42			
6th West India Regt.											5			
8th West India Regt.									15		17			
Royal West India Rangers									3		9			
H.E.I. Coy.'s Service	5													
Chasseurs Britannique														2
Corsican Rangers	?	3												
4th Royal Veterans Bn.													1	
Indian Warriors (Canadian)														
York Lt. Inf.									1		1			
Indian Chiefs & Warriors														
KING'S GERMAN LEGION														
Staff Officers										1	1			1
Artillery Officers										3	3			
Artillery Other Ranks										58	51			4
1st Light Dragoons										3	1			1
2nd Light Dragoons													1	
1st Hussars										81	72		1	71
2nd Hussars													43	
3rd Hussars							96							
1st Light Battalion										4	5			5
2nd Light Battalion										6	7			9
1st Line Battalion							1			66	62		1	73
2nd Line Battalion										80	71			72
5th Line Battalion										78	71			60
7th Line Battalion										28	19			17
Duke of Brunswick Hussars														
Brunswick Oels Light Infantry			1	1										15
Officers Corps of Guides										3	3			2

																Maximum number of bars awarded to		
Albuhera	Java	Ciudad Rodrigo	Badajos	Salamanca	Fort Detroit	Chateauguay	Chrysler's Farm	Vittoria	Pyrenees	St. Sebastian	Nivelle	Nive	Orthes	Toulouse	Number of Medals	Officers	Other Ranks	
16		26	43	45				70	31	24	8	7	21	59	130	6	11	R.W.T.
7	4	29	32	29	1	2		38	31	16	33	23	21	24	127	12	12	S.O.
							1	1		1		2	2		3		4	Chaplains
6		8	4	27				46	19	3	29	26	27	32	85	11	11	C.D.O.
1	1	4	6	10			1	13	12	6	12	10	11	13	53	11	11	Med. St.
				1				5	3	1	1	1	3	8	14	7		P.G.D.
								5	12		10	8	10	15	19	7		C.S.C.
			2					1		2					2	3		C.A.
															3		3	N.F.
					3	224	250	67							533	1	1	C.M.
															25	2	2	1st WIR
															43	2	2	3rd WIR
															5			6th WIR
															17			8th WIR
															9			R.W.I.R.
	41														46			H.E.I. Co.
				3				2	1		1	1			4			C.B.
															?			C.R.
															1			4th R.V.
							?								?			Ind. Warr.
															?		?	York L.I.
					15	75	10								102			Ind. Chfs. & W.
																		K.G.L.
		1		2				1	1	1	2	2			3	8		Staff Ofr.
3		2	3	3				4	3	3	2	3	3	3	9	8		Arty Ofr.
53		23	9	48				52	32	32	11		45	50	82		12	Arty O.R.
			1												1	1		
		1		77				67			1		2	72	84	7	4	1st L.D.
				92				70					2	80	100			2nd L.D.
1		66		74				69	73	3	83	5	74	74	112	10	11	1st Huss.
		1		2				2	1		1	1	1	1	43	1	5	2nd Huss.
													1	1	96	1	3	3rd Huss.
111			3	108				124	1	115	114	116	1	1	137	7	9	1st L.B.
97		4	2	114				115	1	118	107	109	1	7	144	9	8	2nd L.B.
1		69	3	72				64		61	58	58		1	95	9	9	1st Line B.
1		70		78				76		74	72	74			101	9	9	2nd Line B.
		73		76				73		68	70	69			98	9	9	5th Line B.
															34	3	5	7th Line B.
				2				2							2	2	2	Bruns. Hrs.
1		10	11	24				27	8	5	10	11	5	1	39	9	6	Bruns. O.L.I.
			2	1				1				1	2	1	4	7		Ofr. C.G.

(handwritten annotations in lower margin: "126", "5", "533" (circled), "6", "3")

	Egypt	Maida	Roleia	Vimiera	Sahagun	Benevente	Sahagun and Benevente	Corunna	Martinique	Talavera	Guadaloupe	Busaco	Barrosa	Fuentes d'Onor
OTHER RECIPIENTS														
Royal Navy		1							6		2			
Royal Marines									3		4			
de Watteville's Regt.		?												
Dillon's Regiment	?													
de Rolle's Regiment	?													
Stuart's Regiment	?													
Ancient Irish Fencibles														
Maltese Pioneers	?													
Foreign Corps	?	·												
2nd Bombay N.I.	?													
13th Bombay N.I.	?													

MILITARY GENERAL SERVICE MEDALS TO NAVAL RECIPIENTS

Bars	Name		Rank	Ship
Maida	CARROLL	Wm. F.	Lieut. R.N.	*Flag Lt. To Sir S. Smith*
Martinique	BIGLAND	Wm. B.	Lieut.	*Pompee*
	BURDWOOD	Thos.	Lieut.	*Belle Isle*
	JACKSON	Chas. S.	Mid.	*Captain*
	RICHARDS	Edwin	Master's Mate	*Pompee*
	SCOTT	James	Master's Mate	*Pompee*
	WELLS	William	A.B.	*Amarouth*
Guadaloupe	NEILL	John	Surgeon	*Sceptre*
	PITT	E.W.	Lieut.	*Sceptre*
Java	CABBURN	John E.	Master's Mate	*Cornelia*
	DENNEHY	Lawrence	Master's Mate	*Illustrious*
	FESTING	Robert	Act. Captain	*Illustrious*
	LLOYD	Edward	Lieut.	*Vol. on Staff of Gen. Auchmuty*
	SIMMONS	Wm. C.	Mid.	*Illustrious*
	BIRTLES	Thomas	L.K.	*Scipion*
	NORRIS	John	Coxswain	*Leda*
	REYNOLDS	James	Seaman	

Henry Barrister, Ord., *Illustrious*, whose name does not appear in this list also received the medal. Possibly there are some others omitted.

St. Sebastian	COLEWELL	Thos.		
	COLVILLE	Thos.	Ord.	*Surveillante*

Albuhera	Java	Ciudad Rodrigo	Badajos	Salamanca	Fort Detroit	Chateauguay	Chrysler's Farm	Vittoria	Pyrenees	St. Sebastian	Nivelle	Nive	Orthes	Toulouse	Number of Medals	Maximum number of bars awarded to	
																Officers	Other Ranks
8										2							R. Navy
10																	R. Marines

ROYAL MARINES

Martinique	BALHETCHET	William	2nd Lieut.	*Neptune also Guadaloupe*
	HOOKEY	George	2nd Lieut.	*Acasta*
	ROBYNS	John	Captain	*Neptune*
Guadaloupe	ABBOTT	Christopher	Captain	*Pompee*
	BALHETCHET	William	2nd Lieut.	*Pompee*
	CLARKE	James	Lieut.	*Pompee*
	WESLEY	Samuel R.	2nd Lieut.	*Abercombie*
Java	CALAMY	William	2nd Lieut.	*Nisno*
	GARRISTON	Samuel	Lieut.	*Bucephalus*
	GILL	George	Lieut.	*Scipion*
	PASCOE	Richard W.	Lieut.	*Phoebe*
	STEELE	Matthew F.	2nd Lieut.	*Illustrious*
	CRESSLY	John	Sergt.	*President*
	FIELD	Francis	Pte.	*Presidn*
	FOX	Dennis	Pte.	*Scipion*
	MORGAN	William	Pte.	*Phoebe*
	PLATT	James	Pte.	*Scipion*

Vittoria *(21st June, 1813)**

Pyrenees *(28th July—2nd August, 1813)*

St. Sebastian *(17th July—8th September, 1813)**

Chateauguay *(26th October, 1813)†*

In September, 1813, the United States decided to capture Montreal, which lies on the St. Lawrence below where it is joined by the Chateauguay.

A force under Major-General Wade Hampton advanced down the left bank of the Chateauguay, whilst another, under Colonel Purdy, kept touch on the other.

The British, under Lieutenant-Colonel Charles de Salaberry, had taken up a defensive position near the mouth of the Chateauguay.

On 26th October the advanced elements of Colonel Purdy's force were surprised by fire from a well-concealed position which caused them to withdraw and then start a spirited action with the remainder of their comrades. When General Hampton heard of the confusion on the opposite bank he withdrew his own troops after only a few minutes' contact with the British on his side of the river.

Three British artillerymen received this bar; the remainder were awarded to Canadians and Indians. Lieutenant-Colonel Charles de Salaberry of the 1st Battalion the 60th Foot was awarded a gold medal for this action.

The three artillerymen were James Dougherty, John Gibson and John Purdie.

Nivelle *(10th November, 1813)*

Wellington mentions in his dispatch concerning this action that the bomb ketch *Vesuvius*, together with the *Challenger*, *Sparrow* and *Racer*, were sent up the River Nivelle to co-operate with the army although no medals were awarded to the Navy for this service.

Chrystler's Farm *(11th November, 1813)†*

After the American defeat at Chateauguay a further attempt was made by them to capture Montreal. On this occasion General James Wilkinson and Wade Hampton were to join forces at St. Regis, but Hampton, without informing his senior, withdrew to Lake Champlain.

The British Commander-in-Chief, Lieutenant-General Sir George Prevost, ordered Lieutenant-Colonel Morrison to leave Kingston and attack the Americans in the rear. To counter this move General Wilkinson ordered General Boyd to attack him. On hearing that the Americans were advancing, Colonel Morrison took up a position at Chrystler's Farm, where he was heavily attacked for over two hours. By the clever use of his reserves he forced the Americans to withdraw.

Soon after this defeat General Wilkinson learnt that General Hampton was taking no part in the advance. Being now on the Canadian bank and sandwiched between two advancing forces, he decided to return to the American side. Thus ended the American invasion of Lower Canada, though the war did not end until the signing of the Peace of Ghent on 24th December, 1814.

---

*A. Rea, R.M. Surveyor and Draftsman received the M.G.S. Medal with these two bars.

†The actions at Fort Detroit, Chateauguay and Chrystler's Farm were fought during the American War of 1812-1814.

The medals with this bar are to be found with additional unofficial bars for Stoney Creek, Fort George and Queenstown affixed to the ribbon.

Six artillerymen received this bar; they were John Boyle, Thomas Gosling, Dennis Martin, Samuel Nuttall, Joseph Sterling and Joseph Wells.

Nive *(9th—15th December, 1813)*

Orthes *(27th February, 1814)*

Toulouse *(10th April, 1814)*

It is interesting to note that of the thirteen recipients of the military General Service Medal with fourteen or more bars, whose names appear on pages 22 and 23, eleven of them received this bar, though it commemorates the last action fought in the Peninsular War. Ten of these men received the bars for Nive and Orthes; eight those for Nivelle, Nive and Orthes; whilst Haggerty and Nixon were not present at any of these four actions.

37 THE ARMY GOLD MEDALS AND PENINSULAR GOLD CROSSES

Gold Medals

Obverse	A seated and helmeted figure of Britannia, who holds a laurel wreath in her right hand and a palm branch in her left, which is resting on a shield bearing the Union Crosses.
Reverse	The name of the battle for which it was awarded is engraved in the centre and surrounded by a laurel wreath. The medal for Barrosa has the name of the battle embossed instead of engraved. The reason for this exception having been made cannot be traced.
Suspension	The medals were suspended from the buttonhole by a 1¾ in. wide ribbon, which was crimson with dark blue edges. The large medals are suspended by a ring, the small by means of a delicate gold triangular-shaped suspender which is occasionally found bent as that illustrated.
Bars	These are very heavy-looking and bear the name of the action in embossed lettering within an oval surrounded by a wreath of laurel. The bars themselves are rectangular and measure 1.7/8 in x 5/8 in. In addition to the bars, most of the small medals have a three-pointed gold buckle which is worn above the bars, which are affixed to the ribbon and not to the medal.
Designer	T. Wyon, Junior.
Size	The gold medals were of two sizes, 2·1 in. and 1·3 in. diameter, the larger for issue to general officers and the smaller to field officers. Their designs were the same.

The gold crosses are of the pattee and not Maltese design as so often described. They are 1½ in. diameter. Both sides are the same and bear a very fine relief of the British Lion facing to the right. The names of the actions for which the cross was awarded are inscribed one on each arm, but not all are consistent in the order according to the dates of the engagements. Around the edge of each arm is a wreath of laurel. The cross is suspended by an ornate ring which is joined to a plain gold ring which swivels from a straight suspender, which is ornamented on its bottom edge. If the recipient was present at more than four actions, each subsequent action is commemorated by a bar fixed to the ribbon. These bars are the same as those already described as worn with the gold medals. The three-pointed gold brooches are also found attached to the ribbons.

The names of the recipients of the medals and crosses were engraved around the edges in capital lettering. The Duke of Wellington received the gold cross with nine bars. Altogether 163 crosses, 88 large and 596 small gold medals were issued. Needless to say, these crosses and medals rarely come on the market, and rightly so too, but when they do they command high prices. Both the crosses and medals were awarded to officers of the King's German Legion.

The following extracts from the *London Gazette* dated 7th October, 1813, make the reason for, and descriptions as to their recipients, so clear that no further amplification is necessary.

"HORSE GUARDS, *7th Oct., 1813.*

"Whereas considerable inconvenience having been found to attend the increased number of medals that have been issued in commemoration of the brilliant and distinguished events ... the Prince Regent has been pleased to command, in the name and on the behalf of His Majesty, that the following regulations shall be adopted in the grant and circulation of such marks of distinction, namely:

1 That one medal only shall be borne by each officer recommended for such distinction.

2 That for the second and third events, which may be subsequently commemorated in like manner, each individual recommended to bear the distinction, shall carry a gold clasp attached to the ribbon to which the medal is suspended, and inscribed with the name of the battle, or siege, to which it relates.

3 That upon a claim being admitted to a fourth mark of distinction, a cross shall be borne by each officer, with the names of the four battles, or sieges, respectively inscribed thereupon; and to be worn in substitution of the distinctions previously granted to such individuals.

4 Upon each occasion of a similar nature, that may occur subsequently to the grant of a cross, the clasp shall again be issued to those who have a claim to the additional distinction, to be borne on the ribbon to which the cross is suspended, in the same manner as described in No. 2 of these regulations."

The regulations concerning the distribution of these medals were as follows:

"1 That no general, or other officer, shall be considered entitled to receive them, unless he has been personally and particularly engaged upon those occasions of great importance and peculiar brillancy, in commemoration of which the Prince Regent, in the name and on behalf of His Majesty, may be graciously pleased to bestow such marks of distinction.

2 That no officer shall be considered a candidate for the medal, or badge, except under the special selection and report of the Commander of the Forces on the spot, as having merited the distinction by conspicuous services.

3 That the Commander of the Forces shall transmit to the Commander-in-Chief returns signed by himself, specifying the names and ranks of those officers whom he shall have selected as particularly deserving.

4 The Commander of the Forces in making the selection, shall restrict his choice to the undermentioned ranks, namely: General Officers; Commanding Officers of Brigades; Commanding Officers of Artillery, or Engineers; Adjutant General, and Quartermaster General; Deputies of Adjutant General; and Quartermaster General having the rank of Field Officers; Assistants Adjutant and Quartermaster General, having the rank of Field Officers, and being at the head of the Staff with a detached corps, or distinct division of the army; Military Secretary, having the rank of Field Officer; Commanding Officers of

The undermentioned gold awards were authorised:

Action	Small Medal	Bars	Large Medal	Bars	Cross	Bars
Albuhera	29	3	6	2	23	—
Badajoz	28	13	1	3	48	3
Barrosa	15	—	1	—	9	—
Benevente	1	—	—	—	—	—
Busaco	22	6	2	3	32	2
Chateauguay	2	—	—	—	—	—
Chrystler's Farm	6	1	—	—	—	—
Corunna	20	4	10	1	22	—
Cuidad Rodrigo	11	5	1	2	22	1
Fort Detroit	10	—	1	—	—	—
Fuentes d'Onor	21	8	1	4	32	1
Guadaloupe	8	7	6	4	3	—
Java	27	1	5	—	—	—
Maida	11	—	2	—	4	—
Martinique	18	1	9	—	5	2
Nive	34	28	2	5	53	39
Nivelle	30	13	—	1	69	30
Orthes	32	36	—	1	38	47
Pyrenees	18	24	1	3	61	18
Roleia	2	—	—	—	—	—
Roleia & Vimiera	18	—	5	—	9	—
Sahagun & Benevente	4	—	1	—	2	—
Salamanca	73	18	11	2	81	11
St. Sebastian	17	10	1	3	19	11
Talavera	36	5	13	1	23	1
Toulouse	21	30	—	—	22	50
Vimiera	9	—	2	1	1	—
Vittoria	73	24	7	7	99	21

The small gold medals awarded for North America 18/2/14 were issued to:

FORT DETROIT
Major Peter Latouche Chambers 41st. Foot
Capt. Comm. Matthew Chas. Dixon R.E.
Capt. Adam Muir 41st. Foot
Capt. Joseph Tallon 41st. Foot
Lt. Felix Troughton R.A.

CHATEAUGUAY
Lt. Col. Chas. de Saluberry 60th. Foot

CHRYSTLER'S FARM
Major Miller Clifford 89th. Foot
Capt. Henry Geo. Jackson R.A.
Major Thos. Pearson 23rd. Foot (bar only)
Lt. Chas. Plenderleath 49th. Foot

Battalions, or corps equivalent thereto; and officers who may have succeeded to the actual command during the engagement in consequence of, the death or removal of the original commanding officer.

"The Prince Regent is therefore graciously pleased to command, in the name and on behalf of His Majesty, that in commemoration of the brilliant victories attained by His Majesty's arms in the battles of Roleia and Vimiera, Corunna, Talavera de la Reyna, Busaco, Barossa, Fuentes d'Onor, Albuhera, and Salamanca, and in the assaults and captures of Ciudad Rodrigo and Badajoz, the officers of the army, present on those occasions, shall enjoy the privilege of bearing badges of distinction and His Royal Highness having approved of the crosses, medals and clasps, which have been prepared, is pleased to command that they shall be worn by the general officers, suspended by a ribbon of colour of the sash, with a blue edge, round the neck; and by the commanding officers of battalions, or corps equivalent thereto, and officers who may have succeeded to the actual command during the engagement, the chiefs of miliatary departments and their deputies and assistants, (having the rank of field officers), and such other officers as may be specially recommended, attached by a ribbon of the same description to the buttonhole of their uniform.

"The Prince Regent is also pleased to command, in the name and on behalf of His Majesty, that those badges which would have been conferred upon the officers who have fallen at, or died since the above-named battles and sieges, shall, as a token of respect for their memories, be transmitted to their respective families."

The point to note is that the crosses were only issued to those who would normally have become entitled to a medal and three bars. This means that the maximum number of bars to the gold medals was two. It is also interesting to note that this is the first occasion on which clasps are mentioned. They were worn so that the first battle commemorated was farthest from the piece.

After the publication of the first edition several collectors wrote to point out that it was illogical to call a medal a Peninsular Gold Medal when it only has a single bar for Martinique. They suggested that the correct title should be Field Officers' Gold Medal.* I pointed out that this title is equally inaccurate because eleven of the small gold medals were awarded to captains of the English and Spanish Armies. As a matter of fact one small gold medal was awarded to a warrant officer — Sergeant-Major Don Santiago Ruiz of the Spanish Army.

The name of Army Gold Medals has therefore been adopted.

General Viscount Hill received a Gold Cross with *five* engagements on the Cross. The battles on the Cross are, reading clockwise from the top, Roleia; Vimiera; Corunna; Vittoria and Talavera. The bars, reading upwards are Pyrenees, Nivelle, Corunna, Talavera, Orthes and Nive. It should be noted that the bars are in the wrong order and that the battles of Talavera and Corunna are duplicated.

He also received a Gold Medal for Roleia, Vimiera, Corunna and Talavera, so that Corunna and Vimiera are mentioned three times on these two awards.

His twenty-seven decorations and medals together with his gold cornelian fob seal and silver watch sold for £1,010 on 19th April, 1910. This was the highest figure known to be obtained for a group of awards and medals till more recently.

After the termination of the Peninsular War the conditions governing the awarding of the Order of the Bath were revised. The awarding of Gold Crosses and Medals was discontinued and those who would have received either a Gold Medal or Cross received one of the three classes into which that Order was subdivided in 1815. Those awarded a Cross, Large or Small medal were not entitled to the appropriate bars on the Military G.S.

*The lowest rank of field officer is a major. .

48

38 WATERLOO MEDAL (18th June, 1815)

Obverse The laureated head of the Prince Regent with the legend "GEORGE P. REGENT."

Reverse The winged figure of Victory seated on a pedestal and holding a palm branch in her right hand and an olive branch in her left; below the pedestal is the word "WATERLOO" within a rectangle. The date "JUNE 18 1815" is in two lines underneath. The word "WELLINGTON" is above the seated figure.

Size 1.4in. diameter.

Ribbon 1.5in. crimson with ¼in. wide dark blue edges.

Suspension The medals were originally issued with a steel clip on the piece through which passed a steel ring 1.1in. diameter, through which the ribbon was threaded. Many recipients removed the method of suspension as issued and replaced it with designs of their own.

Designer T. Wyon.

Naming In large impressed Roman capitals.

Though styled the Waterloo Medal, it was awarded to anyone who had taken part in one or more of the following battles: Ligny, 16th June; Quatre Bras, 16th June; Waterloo, 18th June. Every soldier present at either of these battles was credited with two extra years' service, to count for all purposes.

By a General Order dated 29th July, 1815, the 1st Regiment of Foot Guards were granted the title of "Grenadiers" for their service during the battle of Waterloo.

This is the first medal issued by the British Government to *all* soldiers present. This statement must not be confused and read as if this were the first battle for which a general issue was made. The Dunbar Medal of 1650 was issued to both officers and men, but there is no verification of its having been given to *all* officers and men. The Military General Service Medal commemorates earlier battles, but was not issued until 1848.

It is also the first *campaign* medal awarded to the next-of-kin of men killed in action. (The Highland Society's medal of 1801 was not a campaign medal.)

It is not generally known that this medal also has another distinction in that it was the first on which the recipient's name was impressed around the edge by machine.

LIST OF REGIMENTS*

UNDER THE COMMAND OF

𝔉ield 𝔐arshal 𝔇uke of 𝔚ellington,

ON SUNDAY, JUNE 18, 1815;

AND THE

TOTAL LOSS

OF THE

BRITISH AND HANOVERIANS,

From June 16th, to 26th, 1815.

TO WHICH IS ADDED,

The computed Losses of the Dutch and Prussians,

DURING THE CAMPAIGN IN THE NETHERLANDS.

	OFFICERS			RANK AND FILE				Strength of unit	**Desir-ability
	Killed	Wounded	Missing	Killed	Wounded	Missing	Total		
General Staff	12	46	3				61	–	–
1st Life Guards	2	4		24	49	4	83	228	36%
2d Life Guards	1		1	16	40	97	155	231	67%
Royal Horse, Grds. Blue	1	4	1	19	61	20	106	237	45%
1st Dragoon Grds.	3	4	4	40	100	124	275	530	52%
1st, or Royal Dgns.	4	·9	1	86	88	9	197	394	50%
2d, or Royal N.B. Dgns.	6	9		96	89		199	391	51%
6th Dragoons	1	5	1	72	111	27	217	396	55%
7th Hussars		7	3	62	109	15	196	380	52%
10th Hussars	2	6		20	40	26	94	390	24%
11th Light Dragoons	2	5		10	34	25	76	390	19%
12th Light Dragoons	2	3		45	61		111	388	29%
13th Light Dragoons	1	9		11	69	19	109	390	28%
15th Hussars	2	3		21	48	5	79	392	20%
16th Light Dragoons	2	4		8	18		32	393	8%
18th Hussars		2		13	72	17	104	396	26%
23d Light Dragoons		5	1	14	26	33	79	387	20%
1st Light Dgns. K.G.L.	3	11		30	99	10	153	462	33%
2d Ditto	2	4		19	54	3	82	437	19%
1st Hussars, ditto		1		1	5	3	10	493	2%
2d Hussars, ditto							–	622	–
3d Hussars	4	8		40		78	130	622	21%
Royal Artillery	5	26		62	228	10	331	5030	7%
Ditto, K.G.L.							–	526	–
Royal Engineers		2					2	–	–
Royal Staff Corps		2					2	–	–

*Extract from the official 1815 reports.
**Based on strength of the unit and the percentage of casualties.

| | OFFICERS | | | RANK AND FILE | | | | | ** |
	Killed	Wounded	Missing	Killed	Wounded	Missing	Total	Strength of unit	Desirability
Royal Sappers and Miners		1			2		3	—	—
1st Foot Guards, 2d Battalion	3	9		73	353		438	967	45%
Ditto, 3d Battalion	4	12		101	487		604	1021	59%
2d Cold. Guards	1	7		54	242	4	308	1003	31%
3d Foot Grds, 2d Battalion	3	9		39	195		246	1061	23%
1st Foot, (Royal Scots) 3d Batt.	8	26		33	295		362	604	60%
4th Foot, 1st Batt.		9		12	113		134	669	20%
14th Ditto, 3d Batt.		3		7	26		36	571	6%
23d Ditto	5	6		13	80		104	647	16%
27th Ditto, 1st Batt.	2	13		103	360		478	698	68%
28th Ditto, ditto	1	19		29	203		252	557	45%
30th Ditto, ditto	6	14		51	181	27	279	615	45%
32d Ditto	1	30		49	290		370	662	56%
33d Ditto	5	17		49	162	58	291	561	52%
35th Ditto				5			5	570	1%
40th Ditto, 1st Batt.	2	10		30	159	18	219	761	29%
42d Ditto, 1st Batt.	3	21		47	266		337	526	64%
44th Ditto, 2nd Batt.	2	18		14	151	17	202	455	44%
51st Ditto		2		11	29		42	549	8%
52d Ditto, 1st Batt.	1	8		16	174		199	1038	19%
54th Ditto				2	2		4	541	1%
59th Ditto					2		2	461	2%
69th Ditto, 2d Batt.	4	7		51	162	15	240	516	46%
71st Ditto, 1st Batt.	1	14		24	160	3	202	810	25%
73d Ditto, 2d Batt.	6	16		54	219	41	336	563	60%
79th Ditto, 1st Batt.	3	27	1	57	390	1	479	703	68%
91st Ditto	4	2		1	6		13	824	2%
92d Ditto	2	27		49	322		402	588	68%
95th, 1st Batt.		15		28	175		220	604	36%
95th, 2d Ditto		14		34	178	20	246	585	42%
95th, 3d Ditto		4		3	36	7	50	188	27%
13th Veteran Batt.									
1st Lt. Infantry Batt. K.G.L.	4	9		37	82	13	145	423	34%
2d Ditto ditto	3	9	1	40	120	29	202	433	47%
1st Line Batt. K.G.L.	1	6		22	69	17	115	437	26%
2d Ditto ditto	1	2		18	79	7	107	437	24%
3d Ditto ditto	1	5		17	93	31	147	494	30%
4th Ditto ditto	1	7		13	77	15	113	416	27%
5th Ditto ditto	2	3		36	47	74	162	379	43%
8th Ditto ditto	3	4		44	80	16	147	388	38%
THE DUTCH LOSS	27	115	—	2058	1936	—	4136	—	—
THE PRUSSIAN LOSS	—	—	—	—	—	—	33120	—	—

**Based on the strength of the unit and the percentage of casualties in approximate terms.

Effective strength and composition of the Anglo-Allied Army under the command of the Duke of Wellington at Waterloo taken from the official 1815 returns.

FIRST CORPS   H.R.H. The Prince of Orange

1st Division   Maj.-Gen. Cooke

		MEN
1st British Brigade	{ 2nd Batt. 1st Guards	967
Maj.-Gen. Maitland	{ 3rd Batt. 1st Guards	1,021
2nd British Brigade	{ 2nd Batt. Coldsteam Guards	1,003
Maj.-Gen. Sir John Byng	{ 2nd Batt. 3rd Guards	1,061
Artillery	{ Capt. Sandhams British Foot Battery	
Lieut.-Col. Adye	{ Maj. Kuhlmann's Horse Battery	
	{ K.G.L.	

3rd Division   Lieut.-Gen. Sir Charles Alten

5th British Brigade	{ 2nd Batt. 30th Regiment	615
Maj.-Gen. Sir Colin Halkett	{ 33rd Regiment	561
	{ 2nd Batt. 69th Regiment	516
	{ 2nd Batt. 73rd Regiment	562
2nd Brigade, K.G.L.	{ 1st Light Batt. K.G.L.	423
Col. von Ompteda	{ 2nd Light Batt. K.G.L.	337
	{ 5th Line Batt. K.G.L.	379
	{ 8th Line Batt. K.G.L.	388
1st Hanoverian Brigade	{ Field Batt. Bremen	512
Maj.-Gen. Count Kielmansegge	{ Field Batt. Verden	533
	{ Field Batt. York	607
	{ Field Batt. Luneburg	595
	{ Field Batt. Grubenhagen	621
	{ Field Batt. Jager Corps	321
Artillery	{ Maj. Lloyd's British Foot Battery	
Lieut.-Col. Williamson	{ Capt. Cleev's Foot Battery, K.G.L.	

SECOND CORPS   Lieut-Gen. Lord Hill

2nd Division   Lieut.-Gen. Sir H. Clinton

3rd British Brigade	{ 1st Batt. 52nd Regiment	1,038
Maj.-Gen. Adam	{ 1st Batt. 71st Regiment	810
	{ 2nd Batt. 95th Regiment	585
	{ 3rd Batt. 95th Regiment	188
1st Brigade, K.G.L.	{ 1st Line Batt.	411
Col. du Plat	{ 2nd Line Batt.	437
	{ 3rd Line Batt.	494
	{ 4th Line Batt.	416
3rd Hanoverian Brigade	{ Landwehr Batt. Bremervorde	632
Col. Halkett	{ Landwehr Batt. Osnabruck	612
	{ Landwehr Batt. Quackenbruck	588
	{ Landwehr Batt. Salzgitter	622
Artillery	{ Capt. Bolton's British Foot Battery	
Lieut.-Col. Gold	{ Maj. Sympher's Horse Battery, K.G.L.	

4th Division   Lieut.-Gen. Sir Charles Colville   MEN

4th British Brigade Col. Mitchell	3rd Batt. 14th Regiment	571
	1st Batt. 23rd Regiment	647
	1st Batt. 51st Regiment	549
6th British Brigade Maj.-Gen. Johnstone	2nd Batt. 35th Regiment	570
	1st Batt. 54th Regiment	541
	2nd Batt. 59th Regiment	461
	1st Batt. 91st Regiment	824
6th Hanoverian Brigade Maj.-Gen. Sir James Lyon	Field Batt. Lauenburg	553
	Field Batt. Calenberg	634
	Landwehr Batt. Nienburg	625
	Landwehr Batt. Hoya	629
	Landwehr Batt. Betheim	608
Artillery Lieut.-Col. Hawker	Maj. Brome's British Foot Battery Capt. von Rettberg's Hanoverian Foot Battery	

RESERVE

5th Division   Lieut.-Gen. Sir Thomas Picton

8th British Brigade Maj.-Gen. Sir James Kemp	1st Batt. 28th Regiment	557
	1st Batt. 32nd Regiment	662
	1st Batt. 79th Regiment	703
	1st Batt. 95th Regiment	549
9th British Brigade Maj.-Gen. Sir Denis Pack	3rd Batt. 1st Regiment	604
	1st Batt. 42nd Regiment	526
	2nd Batt. 44th Regiment	455
	1st Batt. 92nd Regiment	588
5th Hanoverian Brigade Col. von Vinke	Landwehr Batt. Hamelm	669
	Landwehr Batt. Gifhorn	617
	Landwehr Batt. Hildesheim	617
	Landwehr Batt. Peine	611
Artillery Maj. Heisse	Maj. Roger's British Foot Battery Capt. Braun's Hanoverian Foot Battery	

6th Division
6th Division   Lieut.-Gen. Hon. Sir L. Cole

10th British Brigade Maj.-Gen. Sir John Lambert	1st Batt. 4th Regiment	669
	1st Batt. 27th Regiment	698
	1st Batt. 40th Regiment	761
4th Hanoverian Brigade Col. Best	Landwehr Batt. Verden	621
	Landwehr Batt. Luneburg	624
	Landwehr Batt. Osterobe	677
	Landwehr Batt. Munden	660
Artillery Lieut.-Col. Bruckmann British Reserve Artillery	Maj. Unett's British Foot Battery Capt. Sinclair's British Foot Battery Lieut.-Col. Sir Hew Ross's Horse Battery Maj. Beane's Horse Battery Maj. Morisson's Foot Battery Capt. Hutchesson's Foot Battery Capt. Tibert's Foot Battery	

CAVALRY

MEN

British and Kings German Legion

1st Brigade Maj.-Gen. Lord E. Somerset	1st Life Guards	228
	2nd Life Guards	231
	Royal Horse Guards	237
	1st Dragoon Guards	530
2nd Brigade Maj.-Gen. Sir V. Ponsonby	2nd Dragoons (Scots Greys)	391
	1st or Royal Dragoons	394
	6th or Inniskilling Dragoons	396
3rd Brigade Ma.-Gen. Sir V. Dornberg	1st Light Dragoons, K.G.L.	462
	2nd Light Dragoons, K.G.L.	419
	23rd Light Dragoons	387
4th Brigade Maj.-Gen. Sir J. Vandeleur	11th Light Dragoons	390
	12th Light Dragoons	388
	16th Light Dragoons	393
5th Brigade Maj.-Gen. Sir Colq. Grant	2nd Hussars, K.G.L.	564
	7th Hussars	380
	15th Hussars	392
6th Brigade Maj.-Gen. Sir H. Vivian	1st Hussars, K.G.L.	493
	10th Hussars	390
	18th Hussars	396
7th Brigade Col. Sir F.V. Arentsschildt	3rd Hussars, K.G.L.	622
	13th Light Dragoons	390

British Horse Batteries attached to the Cavalry

(1) Maj. Bull's Howitzers
(2) Lieut.-Col. Webber Smith's
(3) Lieut.-Col. Sir Robert Gardiner's
(4) Capt. Whinyate's (with rockets)
(5) Capt. Mercer's
(6) Capt. Ramsay's

Hanoverian Cavalry

1st Brigade Col. von Estorff	Prince Regent's Hussars	596
	Bremen and Verden Hussars	589
	Cumberland Hussars	497
	Brunswick Cavalry	

ARTILLERY

British

	GUNS	MEN
7 Foot Batteries of 6 guns each	42	3,630
3 Foot Batteries of 4 guns each (18 pdrs)	12	1,400
8 Horse Batteries of 6 guns each	48	

K.G.L. Artillery

	GUNS	MEN
1 Foot Battery of 6 guns	6	526
2 Horse Batteries of 6 guns	12	

Hanoverian

	GUNS	MEN
2 Foot Batteries of 6 guns	12	465

The Waterloo Medal was awarded to General Colville's division, which was out on the right flank and took no part in the actual fighting. The medals to members of his division are not so highly prized by collectors. His division was composed of the 2/35, 1/54, 2/59, 1/91 Foot.

Regiments present: Two squadrons each of 1, 2 Life Guards; two squadrons Royal Horse Guards; 1 Dragoon Guards; 1 Royal Dragoons; 2nd Royal North British 'Dragoons (Scots Greys); 6 Inniskilling Dragoons; 7, 10, 15, 18 Hussars; 11, 12, 13, 16, 23 Light Dragoons; R.A.; Corps of Artillery Drivers; R.E.; Sappers and Miners; Waggon Train; Staff Corps; Medical Staff; Ordnance Department; Commissariat Department; 2, 3 Grenadier Guards; 2 Coldstream Guards; 2 Scots Guards; 3/1, 1/4, 3/14, 1/23, 27, 28, 2/30, 1/32,* 1/33, 2/35,† 1/40, 1/42, 2/44, 1/51, 1/52, 1/54,† 2/59,† 2/69, 1/71, 2/73, 1/79, 1/91,† 1/92, 1/95, 2/95, 3/95 (two companies) Foot.

The following eight medals were not awarded to British troops. They are included solely on account of their connection with the Battle of Waterloo, the Peninsular War and Napoleon.

HANOVER MEDAL

Granted by the Prince Regent to survivors from his German dominions.

Obverse   Laureated head of the Prince Regent facing right, with date "1815" underneath, and the legend "GEORG PRINZ REGENT."

Reverse   Military Trophy with legend "HANNOVERSCHER TAPFERKEIT" above. Below the trophy, in large lettering is
"WATERLOO
JUN XVIII."

Ribbon   Bright crimson with light blue edges of watered silk, which is attached to the silver piece by a ring similar to the English Waterloo Medal.

BRUNSWICK MEDALS

One medal was awarded by the Prince Regent. It was said to have been made from the metal of captured guns and is, therefore, of bronze.

Obverse   Head of Duke Frederick William of Brunswick (who was killed at Quatre Bras, 17th June, 1815), facing left and wearing cap; with legend "FRIEDRICH WILHELM HERZOG."

Reverse   An oak and laurel wreath surrounding the inscription "BRAUN-SCHWEIG SEINEN KRIEGERN QUATREBRAS UND WATER-LOO."

Size   The piece is 1·35 in. diameter.

Ribbon   1½in. wide, yellow with pale blue stripes near the edges.

Designer   C. Häseler.

In 1824 another medal was issued by the Duke of Brunswick to those who had fought in the Peninsular War. The medal, which was given in silver gilt to officers and bronze to men, bears the word "PENINSULAR" on the obverse, surrounded by a wreath the left half of which is composed of oak leaves and the

* Captain D. Davies, 32nd Foot, received two of these medals. He also gained the M.G.S. Medal with bars for Corunna, Pyrenees, Nivielle and Nive.

† These regiments did not take part in the fighting at Waterloo.

right those of laurel. The reverse shows a collection of military trophies on a stand, consisting of three flags, a drum and a cannon with three cannon balls. In the centre, askew, is a shield. The medal was suspended from a crimson ribbon similar in colour to that of the Victoria Cross. It was not, of course, as the name thereon shows, given for service at Waterloo.

DUTCH STAR

This is a very plain five-pointed silver star with the date "1813" on the obverse and "1815" on the reverse.

SAXE-GOTHA-ALTENBURG MEDAL

This medal was given in bronze to soldiers and bronze, part gilt to officers of the Foreign Legion of Saxe-Gotha-Altenburg. The medals measure 1·6 in. diameter. The design is very simple, suspension being from a bright green ribbon with black edges through which is threaded, horizontally, thin gold silk to form gold stripes. The ribbon is threaded through a 0·7 in. diameter ring which in turn passes through a ball attached to the top of the piece.

Obverse   The crown of Saxe Gotha surrounded by the legend "IM KAMPFE FUER DAS RECHT." The edge of the medal is engraved with the name of the Duchy and the dates "MDCCCXIV" and "MDCCCXV."

Reverse   A five-petalled rose surrounded by an ornate design.

NASSAU MEDAL

This, the first Waterloo medal issued, was distributed by Frederick Duke of Nassau on 23rd December, 1815, to his troops who had been present. The medal, which is of silver, is only 1·1 in. diameter, and is suspended from a dark blue ribbon with narrow yellow edging, which passes through a ring directly connected to the piece.

Obverse   The head of the Duke of Nassau, facing right.

Reverse   A figure of Victory crowning a warrior. The date "DEN 18 JUNI. 1815" is in the exergue. The medals were issued unnamed.

HANOVERIAN JUBILEE MEDAL, 1865

This medal was subscribed for by the people of Hanover for issue to survivors of the Battle of Waterloo. The medal is of bronze and bears on the obverse the Arms of Hanover surrounded by the inscription "STADT HANOVER DEN SIEGEN VON WATERLOO 18 JUN 1815." The reverse shows a laurel wreath surrounding the inscription "ZUR 50 JAHRIGEN JUBELFEIER am 18 JUN 1865."

39 ST. HELENA MEDAL (1857)

This fine medal, though issued in bronze, has something rather pathetic about it as it was not instituted until 12th August, 1857, on the instigation of Emperor Napoleon III, to survivors of Napoleon's Grande Armée. History relates how surprised Napoleon was when he boarded H.M.S. *Bellerophon*, on the first stage of his road to captivity, to notice that the seamen wore no marks of merit.

The medal is oval and bears on the obverse the laureated head of Napoleon, facing to the right, with the inscription "NAPOLEON I EMPEREUR." On the reverse within a laurel wreath is the inscription "A SES COMPAGNONS DE GLOIRE SA DERNIERE PENSEE STE HELENE 5 MAI 1821." Around this again is the further inscription "CAMPAGNES DE 1792 A 1815." Above the oval is the Imperial Crown, surmounted again by a small cross. A ring of suspension passes through the top of the piece, through which passes the 1½ in. wide green ribbon with five thin red stripes and thin red edges.

PISTRUCCI WATERLOO MEDAL

This medal, which was to have been about 5½ in. diameter, was intended by the Prince Regent to be issued to the heads of Allied countries who participated in the downfall of Napoleon. After various squabbles over who should design it, the whole idea of giving a medal was abandoned in 1849, by which time the alliances of 1815 were somewhat moth-eaten, so that the presentation of this or any other medal would not have had the desired effect. However, electrotypes are seen from time to time.

It might interest collectors of the Long Service and Good Conduct and Distinguished Conduct Medals to know that the early issues were designed by Benedetto Pistrucci, an Italian, who was chief medallist at the Royal Mint at the time of their inception by Royal Warrants dated 30th July, 1830, and 4th December, 1854, respectively.

40 NAVAL GENERAL SERVICE MEDAL (1793-1840)

Obverse	The diademed head of Queen Victoria and legend "VICTORIA REGINA" with the date "1848."
Reverse	The figure of Britannia, holding a trident, seated sideways on a seahorse. The exergue is blank.
Size	1·42 in. diameter.
Ribbon	White with dark blue edges, 1·25 in. wide.
Suspension	By a plain straight swivelling suspender.
Designer	W. Wyon, R.A.
Naming	Indented in Roman capitals. The recipient's rank is only given on medals to officers and warrant officers. The name of the ship is never given, but this can be traced by means of the medal rolls.
No. of bars issued	There were 231 bars sanctioned. One hundred and seventy-six of these were for actions fought by His or Her Majesty's warships, which will be dealt with first, and fifty-five for what were termed Boat Actions. These will be explained later when we come to them. For seven of these 231 bars there were no claimants. In addition to the above there was an unpublished bar for Boat Service, dated 6th May, 1814.
Number of medals issued	There were 20,901 medals issued with a single bar. A total of about 24,000 bars were issued altogether. The medal was not issued without a bar.

This medal, which was originally intended to cover the period from 1793 to 1815, was later extended to cover that from 1793 to 1840. It was not issued until 1849. A list was published in 1848 stating for which actions and boat services medals would be given. Those who considered themselves entitled to the medal had to give their names to the Staff Officer of Pensions in the district where they lived by 30th April, 1849. In those days many could not read the papers or notices, which in any case would not have had a very wide circulation outside the towns. The medals previously issued, the medals given by Mr. Davison for Trafalgar were, in many cases, thrown into the sea, so that there must have been a certain apathy towards medals. By 1849* many who would have been entitled must have died. These facts, together with the general illiteracy of the period, probably account for the very few medals issued, and for the fact that there were no claimants at all for some of the awards sanctioned.† It is worth noting that no boat action services were recognized after 1814, thirty-five years before the issue of the medal. It is thought that over 500 medals were issued after the original lists were closed for which there are no medal rolls. This factor should be noted if a medal is reported "not on roll but appears to be perfect."

The maximum number of bars issued with any one medal was seven. There are three such medals, which were awarded to Captain James Alexander Gordon, R.N., Lieutenant John Hindmarsh, R.N. (later Rear Admiral and first Governor of South Australia 1836-38) and Thos. Haines. Five medals were issued with six bars and fourteen with five.

Rear-Admiral Sir George Cockburn received a medal with six bars and in each case was in command at the action. His bars were: 14th March, 1795; Minerve, 19th December, 1796; St. Vincent; Egypt; Martinique; Boat service, 29th April, 1813. This officer escorted Napoleon to St. Helena in H.M.S. *Northumberland* and, it is believed, holds the record for *continuous* naval service — namely, sixty-eight years. He served fifty-six years afloat. His was the only medal indented to a Rear-Admiral.

Another interesting medal is that awarded to Stephen Lawrie, who earned all his six bars whilst serving in H.M.S. *Phoebe*. The dates of his bars show a period of apparently nearly seventeen years' continuous service in one ship — a truly remarkable record. His bars were as follows: *Phoebe*, 21st December, 1797 (as Boy); *Pheobe*, 19th February, 1801 (as Boy); Trafalgar (as Ableseaman). Off Tamatave, 20th May, 1811 (as Ableseaman); Java (as Ableseaman), *Phoebe*, 28th March, 1814 (as Captain of Foretop).

During the battle of the Glorious First of June a son was born to Mrs. McKenzie, who was on board H.M.S. *Tremendous*, and he received the names of Daniel Tremendous and was duly awarded his medal and bar. As applications for the medal were not made until 1848, it must surely be unique for a man to apply fifty-four years later for a medal awarded for a battle fought on the day he was born. In these days, when we hear so much about the youthful age at which men go to war, we would do well to remember Daniel Tremendous McKenzie!

It is thought that the Naval General Service Medal was the first service medal ever awarded to a woman. Jane Townsend, who was aboard H.M.S. *Defiance* during the Battle of Trafalgar, received, according to my roll, her medal and bar. Although someone has written "not admissable" alongside her name on the official roll.

A unique rank is that of "Passenger" which is mentioned for one of the medals awarded to H.M.S. *Venerable* when she captured two French frigates off the Canary Islands on 16th January, 1814.

The first action in British history for which a clergyman received a medal is that of the Glorious First of June, 1794. The recipient was Thomas Morgan, who

---

* The final date for submitting claims for the medal was extended to 1st May, 1851.

† Naval General Service Medals were awarded to the next-of-kin of applicants who died between the time of their application and the distribution. This statement must not be taken as meaning that medals were awarded to the next-of-kin of all the men who would have been entitled to them. They were not.

served on H.M.S. *Alfred*. He also got the bar for Mars, 21st April, 1798.

There were 121 military recipients of this medal — many of them for occasions when regiments served on board as marines. Some were awarded to artillery men and engineers who were co-opted for special services.

Where the bar is particularly rare the names of the recipients are given.

There were a few recipients of two of these medals; for instance, Lieutenant William Parker, R.N., received one with the bars for 14th March, 1795, St. Vincent and Nile, and another with the bar for Egypt. Incidentally, he also received the Sultan's Gold Medal. Ordinary Seaman Samuel Challis received a medal with the bar for 4th November, 1805, and another with that for Basque Roads. Clerk Thomas Bastin received a medal with a bar for Boat Service, 27th June, 1803, and another with those for Boat Service, 4th June, 1805; off Rota, 4th April, 1808; *Grasshopper*, 24th April, 1808.

The approximate number of medals issued to officers and ratings of individual ships for the major actions is indicated thus, 4/21 = 4 officers and 21 ratings.

	No. of H.M. Ships Engaged	No. of Bars Issued	
Nymphe, 18th June, 1793	1	4	For the capture off Start Point by the *Nymphe*, 36 guns (Capt. Ed. Pellew) of the French frigate *La Cléopatra*, 40 guns, which was afterwards added to the Royal Navy as H.M.S. *Oiseau*.
			RECIPIENTS Qr. Mr. J. Gaze; Cpl. J. Kelly, R.M.; Gunner's Crew J. Simpson; Captain's Servant J. Smart.
Crescent 20th Oct., 1793	1	12	For the capture of the French frigate *La Réunion* by the *Crescent* (Capt. J. Saumarex) off Cherbourg.
			RECIPIENTS Lieuts. G. Parker & Peter Rye R.N; Master's Mate J. Tancock; Mids. T. Mansell, J. Marrett; Capt's. Servant John Jones, Qtr. Gnr. William Madge, A.Bs. John de Page, T. Handford, Richard Jeune, J. Kitt & John Soames.
			An engraving was published on 20th January, 1794, the legend stating: "The Submission of the French frigate *La Réunion* to H. Majesty's frigate *Crescent*, Capt. Sir Jas. Saumarez, to whom and his officers, this print and its companion is most respectively inscribed by their obedt. servt. Robt. Dodd." Beneath this is the interesting statement: "It is singularly remarkable that tho' this action lasted two hours and twenty minutes there was not a man on board the *Crescent* either killed, wounded or hurt by the enemy, but the loss on their side was 120 killed and wounded, their vessel a complete wreck in hull, sails and

rigging. Their national colours were shot away early in the action and their temporary one was also shot down three times and in token of submission they brought the remnants to the gangway, held them up and bowed over them to the gallant British Commander."

The size of the forces engaged is quoted as: English force — *Crescent*, 36 guns, 250 men; French foce — *La Réunion*, 36 guns, 320 men, and a cutter of 12 or 14 guns.

	No. of H.M. Ships Engaged	No. of Bars Issued	
Zebra, 17th March, 1794	1	2	For the part played by the *Zebra* (Capt. R. Faulknor) in the capture of Fort Royal, Martinique.

It seems extraordinary that this ship should be singled out for reward for her part in the capture of the island. She accompanied the boats from the other ships, manned by 1,250 men, only twenty-nine of whom received the bar for the Boat Action. However H.M.S. *Zebra* accompanied H.M.S. *Asia* in an attempt to break through the harbour boom. The latter failed to take up her position so that the task was performed by the *Zebra* alone.

The island was restored to the French under the Treaty of Amiens in 1802, and recaptured in 1809.

An interesting naval event is indirectly connected with this island off the southeast of which lies the Diamond Rock. This was taken by the Navy and commissioned and rated as a sloop in 1804. (see "Anholt 27 March 1811") and "BS 21 Jan. 1807". It is now the custom for shore establishments to be rated as men-of war, but one wonders whether this is not one of the earliest instances of "stone frigate".

RECIPIENTS Lieut. Henry Hill, R.N., and Joseph Bass.

	No. of H.M. Ships Engaged	No. of Bars Issued	
Carysfort, 29th May, 1794	1	0	For the recapture of H.M.S. *Castor* off Newfoundland by the *Carysfort* (Capt. Francis Laforey). The *Castor* had been captured from us on 10th May off Newfoundland.

RECIPIENTS No bars were issued.

1st June, 1794 37 583 This was the date of the action known as the Glorious First of June. Readers are referred to Medal No. 22 for particulars of the gold medal issued for this action.

Ships present: Lord Howe's flagship *Queen Charlotte* 4/21,* and *Alfred* 4/22, *Aquilon* 1/5, *Audacious* 1/13, *Bellerophon* 2/17, *Barfleur* 1/15, *Brunswick* 1/18, *Caesar* 2/17, *Culloden* 6/19, *Defence* 4/15, *Gibraltar* 3/11, *Glory* 4/17, *Impregnable* 3/20, *Invincible* 2/14, *Kingfisher* 1/-(?), *Latona* -/9, *Leviathan* 1/16, *Majestic* 1/11, *Marlborough* 1/16, *Montagu* 2/16, *Niger* 1/4, *Orion* 1/12, *Pegasus* -/7, *Phaeton* 1/8, *Queen* 5/14, *Ramillies* 3/11, *Royal George* 4/35, *Royal Soveriegn* 4/22, *Russell* 1/16, *Southampton* 1/3, *Thunderer* 3/7, *Tremendous* -/21, *Valiant* 3/17, *Venus* -/5.

Sloops: *Ranger* 1/-, *Rattler* -/2.

Fireships: *Comet* 1/1, *Incendiary*, *Kingfisher* 1/-.

Hospital ship: *Charon* 1/7.

Special Gold Medal: Admiral Lord Howe received a special gold medal suspended from the same chain as that given with the large gold medal.

RECIPIENTS OF THE LARGE NAVAL GOLD MEDAL AND CHAIN Vice-Admirals Graves and Hood, Rear-Admirals Bowyer, Pasley and Gardner, and Captain of the Fleet Sir Roger Curtis.

Rear-Admiral B. Caldwell, who was on board the *Impregnable*, did not receive a gold medal, and neither did Captain of the fleet Sir Roger B. Westcott.

SMALL GOLD MEDAL RECIPIENTS Capt. Sit Andrew S. Douglas (*Queen Charlotte*), Capt. W. Domett (*Royal George*), Capt. Henry Nichols (*Royal Sovereign*), Capt. Cuthbert Collingwood (*Barfleur*), Capt. John Hutt (*Queen*), Capt. John Elphinstone (*Glory*), Capt. William Hope (*Bellerophon*), Capt.

*See explanation of numbers on page 59.

James Pigott (*Tremendous*), Capt. Thomas Pringle (*Valiant*), Capt. Henry Harvey (*Ramillies*), Capt. William Barker (*Audacious*), Capt. John Bazeley (*Alfred*), Capt. James Gambier (*Defence*), Capt. Lord Hugh Seymour (*Leviathan*), Capt. Hon. Thomas Packenham (*Invincible*), Capt. John T. Duckworth (*Orion*), Capt. John W. Payne (*Russell*), Capt. Hon. C.G. Berkeley (*Marlborough*).

The roll gives the name of Thomas Morgan, Chaplain. This, therefore, is the first action in British history for which a clergyman received a medal. He also received the bar "Mars, 21st April, 1798."

The Queen's and the 1st Bn. The Worcestershire Regiment served with the fleet as Marines and carry a naval crown superscribed "1st JUNE 1794." The King's Own Scottish Borderers were also serving in the fleet as Marines, but carry no distinction to commemorate the fact. The following members of the Army received the N.G.S. Medal with this bar: 2nd Foot (Queen's Regiment): Lieut. A. Pilkington, (H.M.S. *Royal George*), Sergt. D. Wainwright (H.M.S. *Russell*).

25th Foot (K.O.S.B.): Pte. Thomas Burchley, Pte. Luke Thayyers (H.M.S. *Gibraltar*).

29th Foot (The Worcestershire Regiment): Lieut. B. Egerton, Pte. Wm. Robinson (H.M.S. *Thunderer*), Ensign L.A. Northey, Cpl. R. Cook (*Alfred*), Pte. T. Robson (H.M.S. *Brunswick*),* Pte. T. Smith (H.M.S. *Alfred*), Ptes. S.R. Bamford and Jas. Kilgrove (H.M.S. *Glory*).

	No of H.M. Ships Engaged	No of Bars Issued	
Romney, 17th June, 1794	1	2	For the capture of the French frigate *Sibylle*, which was at anchor in Mykonos Harbour (Capt. The Hon. Wm. Paget).

RECIPIENTS Midshipmen Manly Dixon, C. Woodley.

*Thos. Robson also received the M.G.S. Medal with bars for Roleia, Vimiera, Talavera and Albuhera.

	No of H.M. Ships Engaged	No. of Bars Issued	
Blanche, 4th Jan., 1795	1	5	For the extremely fierce fight between the *Blanche* (Capt. R. Faulknor, late of the *Zebra*) and the French frigate *Pique*, which was chased and captured off Grandeterre, Gaudaloupe. Capt. Faulknor was killed in this action, and later a monument was erected to his memory in St. Paul's Cathedral.

RECIPIENTS Lieut. Frederick Watkins, R.N.; Mid. Thos. L. Prescott; AB Henry Greely and Thos. Evans; Boy 3rd Class Joseph Clark.

	No of H.M. Ships Engaged	No. of Bars Issued	
Lively, 13th March, 1795	1	6	For the capture of the French ship *Tourterelle* off Ushant by the *Lively* (Capt. Geo. Burlton).

RECIPIENTS Mid. J. Groves, Vol. 1st Class B. Simpson, Boy 3rd Class, R. Wilcox, also verified aboard ABs I. Buckmaster, T. Holland and Pte RM W. Laverton with St Vincent clasps.

	No of H.M. Ships Engaged	No. of Bars Issued	
14th March, 1795	31	114	Given for the defeat of the French fleet off Genoa by Admiral Hotham.

Ships present: Admiral Hotham's flagship *Britannia* 2/4, and *Agamemnon* 1/-, *Astraea*, *Bedford* 3/8, *Boyne* -/1, *Captain* 1/3, *Courageux* -/2, *Diadem* 2/6, *Egmont* 1/3, *Fortitude* 1/-, *Inconstant* 1/3, *Illustrious* 1/7, *Lowestoffe* 1/4, *Mediator*, *Meleager* 1/1, *Minerva*, *Moselle* 1/1, *Pilade*, *Poulette* -/1, *Princess Royal* 5/3, *Robust* -/2, *Romulus* -/1, *Russel* -/2, *Saint George* 4/8, *Tancredi*, *Terrible* 1/3, *Thunderer* -/1, *Windsor Castle* 3/7. Brig: *Tarlton*. Cutter: *Fox*.

The K.O.S.B., E. Lancs, and 2nd Bn. The Welch Regiment were serving on board the fleet, and the following members of these regiments received the N.G.S. Medal with this bar:

K.O.S.B. (25th Foot): Sergt. J. Ward (H.M.S. *St. George*). E. Lancs (30th Foot): Lieut. D. Maxwell (H.M.S. *Princess Royal*). The Welch Regiment (69th Foot); Capt. Caleb Chute (H.M.S. *Britannia*), who also received the bar for St. Vincent.

The medal awarded to Capt. Chute is probably unique, being the only N.G.S.

No. of H.M. Ships Engaged	No. of Bars Issued	
		medal to the Army carrying two bars. J.G. Bussell, chaplain, received this bar.
Astraea, 10th April, 1795	1	2	For the capture of the French frigate *Gloire* off Brest by the *Astraea* (Capt. Lord Henry Paulet). RECIPIENTS Lieut. John Talbot, R.N.; Ord. Wm. Mainland.
Thetis 17th May, 1795	1	2 ⎫	For the capture by H.M.S. *Thetis* (Capt. Hon. A. Cochrane) and *Hussar* (Capt. J.P. Beresford) of the French ships *Prevoyante* and *La Raison* off Cape Henry in Chesapeake Bay. RECIPIENTS H.M.S. *Thetis* — Surgeon's 1st Mate R. Hume; Mid. William George Maude. H.M.S. *Hussar* — Vol 1st Class James Read.
Hussar, 17th May, 1795	1	1 ⎭	
Mosquito, 9th June, 1795	1	0	For the action which the *Mosquito* (Lieut. Macarthy, R.N.) fought with a French privateer, as a result of which the *Mosquito* was lost with the entire crew. (As this fact must have been known to the committee which approved of the engagements for which bars were to be awarded, it seems particularly futile to have sanctioned a bar for this action.)
17th June, 1795	8	42	This bar was given for Vice Admiral The Hon. William Cornwallis's repulse of about thirty French ships off Ushant. Ships present: Cornwallis's flagship *Royal Sovereign* -/7, and *Bellerophon* 2/3, *Brunswick* -/2, *Kingfisher, Mars* 1/11, *Pallas* -/2, *Phaeton* 1/3 and *Triumph* 4/6. (Master S.P. Pritchard of H.M.S. *Royal Sovereign* later served as Captain of H.M.S. *Blenheim* in China, 1842.) H.M.S. *Kingfisher* left Spithead with Cornwallis's squadron, but must have been detached before the action or, alternatively, there may have been no claimants from her, as he does not appear on the rolls.
23rd June, 1795	32	200	For the defeat of the French fleet by Admiral Bridport off the Isle de Groix. Ships present: Admiral Bridport's flagship *Royal George* 4/15, and *Aquilon*

	No. of H.M. Ships Engaged	No. of Bars Issued	

2/4, *Astraea, Babet* 1/1, *Barfleur* 1/7, *Boyne* -/1, *Colossus* -/7, *Galatea* 1/1, *Irresistible* -/8, *Leviathan, London* 4/4, *Nymphe* -/2, *Orion* 5/9, *Pallas, Prince of Wales* 2/2, *Prince George* 3/8, *Queen* 1/13, *Queen Charlotte* 4/9, *Revolutionnaire* 2/2, *Robust* 2/8, *Russell* 4/7, *Sans Pareil* 4/14, *Standard* 1/3, *Teazer* -/1, *Thalia* 1/4, *Thunderer* -/2, *Valiant* -/5.

Fire Ships: *Incendiary* and *Megaera*.
Cutters: *Argus* and *Dolly*.
Hospital ship: *Charon* -/2.

My roll quotes Andrew McKenzie, private soldier (H.M.S. *Barfleur*), whose regiment is not stated, as having received medals with this bar, also Samuel Cole, Chaplain (H.M.S. *London*). The last is the third medal to a chaplain that is known.

Dido, 24th June, 1795	1	1	
Lowestoffe, 24th June, 1795	1	6	

H.M.S. *Dido* (Capt. G.H. Towry) and *Lowestoffe* (Capt. R.G. Middleton) captured the French frigate *Minerve* and defeated the *Artemise* off Toulon.

RECIPIENTS H.M.S. *Dido* — Ord Charles Ledditt. H.M.S. *Lowestoffe* — Mid. Edward Libby, AB Thos. Kemp, John Smith, George Salvedore and Gilbert White; Boy 2nd Class Wm. Gibson.

Spider, 25th August, 1795	1	1	

The Lugger *Spider*, whilst cruising in the North Sea, encountered two small French brigs and captured the *Victorieuse*.

RECIPIENT John Lean.

Port Spergui, *(17th March, 1796)*	3	4	

The *Diamond* (Capt. Sir Sidney Smith), *Liberty* (Lt. Geo. M'Kinley RN), and the lugger *Aristocrat* (Lieut. Abraham Gossett), went into the harbour of Erqui, on the Brittany coast, and captured and set on fire the French corvette *Etourdie* and also estroyed seven other small French warships.

RECIPIENTS H.M.S. *Diamond* — Surgeon D. McArthur, Mid. J. Boxer and W.F. Carroll. H.M.S. *Liberty* — Lt. Geo. M'Kinley, RN.

	No. of H.M. Ships Engaged	No. of Bars Issued	
			There were no claimants from H.M.S. *Aristocrat*.
Indefatigable, 20th April, 1796	1	8	The *Indefatigable* (Capt. Sir Edward Pellew) captured the French frigate *Virginie* in the English Channel, off Ushant, after a fifteen-hour chase.

Indefatigable, 20th April, 1796 — 1 — 8

The *Indefatigable* (Capt. Sir Edward Pellew) captured the French frigate *Virginie* in the English Channel, off Ushant, after a fifteen-hour chase.

RECIPIENTS Master's Mate T. Groube, Mid N.L. Pateshall, Vols 1st class Hon George Cadogan and John Harry, Qtr Gnr. J. McKerlie, AB John Jones. Vfd. Abd. Mid. John Gaze and AB Joseph Simpson.

Unicorn, 8th June, 1796 — 1 — 4
Santa Margaritta, 8th June, 1796 — 1 — 3

The *Unicorn* (Capt. T. Williams) and *Santa Margaritta* (Capt. T. Byam Martin), when cruising off the Scilly Islands, encountered the French frigates *Tamise* and *Tribune* together with the corvette *Legère*. The two French frigates were captured after the *Unicorn* had chased the *Tribune* for 220 miles. Capt. Williams was knighted for this action.

RECIPIENTS H.M.S. *Unicorn* — Mid. C.J. Austen; Ord. W. Dexter; Pte. John Green, R.M.; Surgeon's Mate J. Mather. H.M.S. *Santa Margaritta* — Capt. T.B. Martin RN,* Q.M's Mate T. Price, and Joseph Bullen (unknown Rate/Rank).

Southampton, 9th June, 1796 — 1 — 8

For the boarding and capturing of the French frigate *Utile*, off Toulon, by the *Southampton* (Capt. Macnamara).

RECIPIENTS Yeoman of B.S. Room J. Strachan, L.M. Joseph Goodall and Privates James Dallimore and S. Spill, R.M Vfd. Abd; A.B. John Wakeham, Ords John Davies and Thomas Haines (7 clasps) and Pte D. Griffiths R.M.

Dryad, 13th June, 1796 — 1 — 6

In this action the *Dryad* (Capt. Lord A. Beauclerk) captured the French frigate *Prosperpine* off Cape Clear.

RECIPIENTS Lieut. E.D. King RN; 2nd-Lieut. Thomas Sharman, R.M.; Master's Mate Ed. D. King; Ordinary Seaman John Allen; L.M. John Pusey; and Edward Verling whose rank is not stated.

*Chairman of the N.G.S. medal committee.

	No. of H.M. Ships Engaged	No. of Bars Issued	
Terpischore, 13th Oct., 1796	1	3	For the action in which the *Terpischore* (Capt. R. Bowen) captured the Spanish frigate *Mahonesa* off Carthagena and then towed her to Lisbon.

RECIPIENTS Pte. T. Ashford, R.M.; Ord. T. Beautyman; Vol. 1st Class W.L. Paterson.

	No. of H.M. Ships Engaged	No. of Bars Issued	
Lapwing, 3rd Dec., 1796	1	2	For the action between the *Lapwing* (Capt. Robert Barton), and the French ships *Vaillante* and *Decius* off St. Kitts, Antigua. The *Decius* was captured.

RECIPIENTS Able seaman T. Morrod and L.M. Wm. Levey.

	No. of H.M. Ships Engaged	No. of Bars Issued	
Minerve, 19th Dec., 1796	1	4 ⎫	Commodore Horatio Nelson in the *Minerve* (Capt. Geo. Cockburn), accom-
Blanche, 19th Dec., 1796	1	4 ⎬	panied by the *Blanche* (Capt. Bruce),

was on his way from Gibraltar to fetch stores left at Porto Ferrajo, on the north coast of the island of Elba, when he fell in with the Spanish frigates *Sabina* and *Ceres*. The *Minerve* (which was pre-viously the French-owned frigate *Minerve* captured by the *Dido* on 24th June, 1795) engaged the *Sabina*, which surrendered. Nelson placed a prize crew on board under Lieuts. John Culverhouse and Thomas Hardy (later to be his Captain on the *Victory* at Trafalgar) and proceeded to tow her. Whilst so engaged the Spanish frigate *Matilda* approached. The *Minerve* cast off her tow and en-gaged the new arri val, but di ring this second action three more Spanish ships appeared and so the Minerve had to seek flight and abandon the *Sabina*.
Much the same happened to the *Blanche*, which had forced the *Ceres* to surrender, and whilst accepting it the arrival of the *Matilda* and *Perla* forced her to relin-quish her capture and seek safety in flight.

RECIPIENTS H.M.S. *Minerve* – Capt. Geo. Cockburn R.N. Lieut. W.H. Gage; Able seamen S. Blackmore and P. Brown. H.M.S. *Blanche* – Mid. R. Pridham; Vol 1st Class J. Clark. and Vfd. Abd. ABs Thomas Evans and H. Greely.

	No. of H.M. Ships Engaged	No. of Bars Issued
Indefatigable, 13th Jan., 1797	1	8 ⎫
Amazon, 13th Jan., 1797	1	6 ⎭

For the action fought by the *Indefatigable* (Capt. Sir Edward Pellew) and *Amazon* (Capt. C. Reynolds), which started off the south of Ireland and ended with the *Amazon* and the enemy ship *Droits de l'Homme* going ashore on the French coast. The crew of the *Amazon* was captured on shore. The *Indefatigable* was almost a wreck, having several feet of water in her, but she managed to get home.

The French ship, when sighted off the mouth of the Shannon, had on board General Humbert and about 1,350 soldiers and crew, so that the loss in the *Droits de l'Homme* during the action, which lasted thirteen hours, and the further loss when she went ashore was appalling — over 900 being either killed or drowned.

General Humbert at the time was in command of a division of 6,000 men, which, together with troops from Spain and Holland, all under General Hoche, hoped to land in Ireland to assist the Irish rebels under Lord Edward Fitzgerald.

It is pleasant to record that the survivors of the *Amazon* and others rescued by the *Droits de l'Homme* were treated with every care. Those who had been in the French ship were nursed back to health and returned by special ship to England in March, the remainder of the crew of the *Amazon* were exchanged in September of the same year.

RECIPIENTS H.M.S. *Indefatigable* — Mid. H. Hart, J. Gaze, and N.L. Pateshall Vols 1st Class Geo. Earl of Cadogan and J. Harry; Master's Mate Thomas Groube, Surgeon's Mate R.P. Williams. Schoolmaster John McKerlie. Vfd. Abd. ABs John Jones and Joseph Simpson. H.M.S. *Amazon* — Mids. B. Reynolds, and A. Dixie; Vol 1st Class Richard Devonshire; ABs John Brown and Alex Dixie; L.M. John Ellender.

St. Vincent *(14th February, 1797)*	24	364

For the battle off Cape St. Vincent fought by Admiral Jervis to prevent the uniting of the Dutch, Spanish and French fleets off the west coast of Spain.

In this action Commodore Nelson captured two of the four ships taken from the enemy — namely, the *San Josef* and *San Nicolas*

It was when the *San Josef* surrendered that Nelson ordered the Spanish Captain to summon his (the Spanish) officers to the quarterdeck. Here Nelson relates that "Extravagant as the story may seem, did I receive the swords of the vanquished Spaniards, which, as I received, I gave toWilliam Fearney, one of my bargemen, who put them with the greatest sangfroid under his arm." Some of the Welch Regiment (then the 69th, South Lincolnshire Regiment) were serving as Marines during this action on Nelson's ship, H.M.S. *Captain*. They had previously served with him on H.M.S. *Agamemnon*, from which fact they earned their soubriquet of "Old Agamemnons" from him.

Ships present: Admiral Jervis's flagship *Victory* 5/18, and *Barfleur* 6/23, *Blenheim* 8/16, *Britannia* 5/16, *Captain* 2/17, *Colossus* 1/12, *Culloden* 4/23, *Diadem* 2/11, *Egmont* -/17, *Emerald* -/1, *Excellent* 3/18, *Goliath* 4/16, *Irresistible* 1/12, *Namur* 3/2, *Orion* 1/21, *Prince George* 3/32; frigates *Dido*, *Lively* 1/6, *Minerve* 2/2, *Niger* -/1, *Southampton* 1/8; sloops *Bon Citoyenne* -/5, *Raven* -/1; cutter *Fox*.

RECIPIENTS OF THE LARGE GOLD MEDAL Admiral Sir John Jervis; Vice-Admiral Charles Thompson; Vice-Admiral Hon. William Waldegrave; Rear-Admiral William Parker; Commodore Horatio Nelson; Capt. of the Fleet Robert Calder.

RECIPIENTS OF THE SMALL GOLD MEDAL Capt. George Gay; Capt. Thos. Foley; Capt. James Richard Dacre; Capt. John Irwin; Capt. Thos. Lenox Frederick; Capt. James Hawkins-Whitshed; Capt. Ralph Willett Miller; Capt. Sir Charles H. Knowles, Bart.; Capt. Cuthbert Collingwood; Capt. Sir James Saumarez; Capt. George Murray; Capt. John Sutton; Capt. Thomas Troubridge; Capt. George Martin; Capt. George

Henry Towry.

MILITARY RECIPIENTS OF THE N.G.S. MEDAL WITH THIS BAR 11th Foot — Ptes. Samuel Huston (H.M.S. *Diadem*) and James Moorfield (H.M.S. *Captain*). 49th Foot — Pte. John Smith* (H.M.S. *Blenheim*) (who also got M.G.S. bar for Corunna when serving with the 51st Foot). 50th Foot — Pte John Milgrove (H.M.S. *Diadem*). 69th Foot† — Capt. Caleb Chute, Pte. Samuel Chadwick (H.M.S. *Britannia*). (Surgeons 3rd Mate (Later Sir) Wm. Burnett [H.M.S. *Goliath*] received the N.G.S. medal with this bar and those for Nile, Egypt and Trafalgar.)

San Fiorenzo, 8th March, 1797	1	8
Nymphe, 8th March, 1797	1	5

The *San Fiorenzo* (Capt. Sir Harry Neale) and *Nymphe* (Capt. John Cooke) intercepted and captured the French frigates *Résistance* and *Constance* which were returning to France after carrying an expeditionary force of scallywags who hoped to destroy the town of Bristol and then that of Liverpool. As a matter of fact 1,400 of them landed at Fishguard, on the Pembrokeshire coast, but surrendered to 600 civilians and the Pembrokeshire Yeomanry. The interest lies in the fact that this regiment received "Fishguard" as a Battle Honour, the only one for home service.

RECIPIENTS H.M.S. *San Fiorenzo* Lieut. T. Renwick R.N.; Mid. R. Mitford; Ords J. Brookman and J. Emmerson; Boys Benjamin Shepherd, W. Dally, Wm. Lewis. H.M.S. *Nymphe* — Surgeon B.F. Outram; Mid. J.H. Godby and R. Bastin; Master's Mate J.D. Markland; Pte John Cook, R.M.

Camperdown (*11th October, 1797*)	25	336

For the defeat of the Dutch fleet off their coast by Admiral Duncan.

* It is probable that this man was serving with the 51st Foot on board H.M.S. *Blenheim*, on which there were twenty-five other members of the Regiment. As the 49th were in the West Indies at the time, either the medal roll is incorrect or there was a mistake when the medal was named. As there is no similarity between these two numbers the first of these two suppositions is more likely to be correct.

† In 1891 Queen Victoria granted this regiment the right to bear "St. Vincent" on its Colours.

The ships present with the approx. number of recipients from each were: Admiral Duncan's flagship H.M.S. *Venerable** 2/17, and *Active* 1/2, *Adamant* 4/4, *Agincourt* 4/9, *Ardent* 3/8, *Beaulieu*, *Bedford* 2/27, *Belliqueux* -/11, *Braakel* -/2, *Director* 2/13, *Isis* -/6, *Lancaster* 1/13, *Martin* 1/-, *Monarch* 5/19, *Montague* 2/20, *Monmouth* 2/13, *Powerful* -/23, *Russel* 7/14, *Triumph* 3/20, *Veteran* 2/19; frigates *Beaulieu* 3/8, *Circe* 3/4, *Martin* -/1; cutters *Active* -/3, *Diligent*, *King George* 1/2, *Rose* -/1; lugger *Speculator*.

RECIPIENTS OF THE LARGE NAVAL GOLD MEDAL Admiral Duncan and Vice-Admiral Richard Onslow.

RECIPIENTS OF THE SMALL NAVAL GOLD MEDAL Capt. Edward O'Brien, Capt. John Knight, Capt. Sir Thomas Byard, Capt. William O'Brien Drury, Capt. William Essington, Capt. John Inglis, Capt. John Williamson, Capt. John Wells, Capt. Richard Rundell Burgess, Capt. George Gregory, Capt. William Bligh, Capt. James Walker, Capt. William Mitchell, Capt. William Hotham, Capt. Francis Fayerman, Capt. Peter Halket, Capt. Hon. Charles Paget.

Phoebe, 21st Dec., 1797 — 1 — 5

For the capture of the French frigate *Néréide* in the Bay of Biscay by the *Phoebe* (Capt. Sir Robert Barlow).

RECIPIENTS Mid. S.J.B. Pechell and Charles Prowett; Yeoman of Sheets Robert Allen; Ordinary Seaman John Reedin. and Boy 3rd Class Stephen Lawrie.
(For further particulars of Boy Lawrie see the introduction to the N.G.S. Medal.)

Mars, 21st April, 1798 — 1 — 26

The *Mars* (Capt. Alex Hood, who was killed in the action), when cruising off

*The Town of Sunderland presented a special silver medal to Jack Crawford for nailing the flag to the mast after it (the flag) had been shot away. The obverse of this medal bears a shield with the arms of Sunderland supported by two sailors. Below, on a scroll, is the motto "ORBIS EST DEI." Under these is the inscription "THE TOWN OF SUNDERLAND TO JOHN CRAWFORD FOR GALLANT SERVICES ON OCT. 11th 1797." On the reverse is a scene of the action with, above, the legend "DUNCAN AND GLORY" and below "BRITISH VALOUR."

	No. of H.M. Ships Engaged	No. of Bars Issued	

Brest in consort with the *Ramillies* and *Jason*, sighted the French ship *L'Hercule*. The *Mars* chased her and, with the help of the *Jason* which came up towards the end of the action, forced her to surrender. The *L'Hercule* was towed to Plymouth and transferred to the Royal Navy under the name of H.M.S. *Hercules.*

Isle St. Marcou (2 bars: 3)
(6th May, 1798)

As a sort of trial run for Napoleon's intended invasion of Britain an expedition consisting of flat-bottomed boats attacked the two small islands of St. Marcouf off Le Havre, which were defended by the crews of the *Badger* and *Sandfly* together with some Marines, all under the command of Lieut. C.P. Price, R.N. It was not a naval action, though fought, on our side, entirely by the crews of the two ships.

RECIPIENTS H.M.S. *Badger* — 2nd Lieut. T.L. Lawrence, R.M., and Pte. John Campbell, R.M.; H.M.S. *Sandfly* — 2nd-Lieut. J. Ensor, R.M.

Lion, (1 bar: 23)
15th July, 1798

For the capture of the Spanish ship *Santa Dorotea* off Carthagena by the *Lion* (Capt. Manly Dixon).

Nile (16 ships: 351 bars)
(1st August, 1798)

For Nelson's victory in Aboukir Bay for which he was created Baron Nelson of the Nile and Burnham Thorpe. The King of Naples conferred on him the title of Duke of Bronte. The Commodore of the French flagship *Orient* was Casa Bianca, whose young son was on board. It was about the fate of this lad that Mrs. Hemans wrote her well-known poem which starts "The boy stood on the burning deck" ("Casabianca"). It was from the timber of the *Orient* that Nelson's coffin was made in which he lay in state in the Royal Naval Hospital, Greenwich.
Ships present: Rear-Admiral Nelson's flagship *Vanguard* 6/21, and *Alexander* 6/29, *Audacious* 1/13, *Bellerophon* 4/19, *Culloden* 5/25, *Defence* 2/24, *Goliath* 6/19, *Leander* -/9, *Majestic* 3/20, *Minotaur* 5/21, *Orion* 4/14,

No. of H.M. Ships Engaged	No. of Bars Issued	

Swiftsure 5/21, *Theseus* 2/13, *Zealous* -/17; lugger *Speculator* o; sloop *Mutine* 1/5.

RECIPIENTS OF LARGE NAVAL GOLD MEDAL Rear-Admiral Sir Horatio Nelson, K.B.

RECIPIENTS OF LARGE NAVAL GOLD MEDAL Captains Edward Berry, Thomas Troubridge, Henry D'Esterre, Darby, Thomas Louis, John Peyton, Alexander John Ball, Samuel Hood, Davidge Gould, Thomas Foley, George Bladgen Westcott, Benjamin Hallowell, Ralph Willett Miller, Thomas Boulden Thompson.

Espoir, 7th Aug., 1798 — 1 — 1

For the capture of the *Liguria*, a large Genoese pirate ship, which closed with the *Espoir* (Comdr. L.O. Bland) and summond her to surrender.

RECIPIENT Ordinary Seaman Henry Chambers.

12th Oct., 1798 — 9 — 79

This bar was awarded for the defeat by Sir John Borlase Warren of the attempted invasion of Ireland, and was fought off Tory Island. The French ship *Hoche* and two frigates were captured.
Ships present: Sir John Borlase Warren's flagship *Canada* 2/16, and *Amelia* -/3, *Anson* -/7, *Arethusa* -/1, *Doris, Ethalion* 1/7, *Foudroyant* 4/15, *Magnamine* 3/3, *Melampus* -/3, *Robust* 3/8.
There is a medal to Ordinary Seaman John Boon of H.M.S. *Canada* with this bar and those for St. Domingo, Java, and Algiers.
Cpl. Wim. Hodgson, R.M., received a medal with this bar for service on H.M.S. *Ethalion*. He received another medal with the bar for Egypt for service as a sergeant on H.M.S. *Sensible*.

Fisgard, 20th Oct., 1798 — 1 — 9

For the defeat of the French frigate *Immortalité*, off Brest, by the *Fisgard* (Capt. Thos. Byam Martin). The *Fisgard* was formerly the French frigate *Résistance* captured by the *San Fiorenzo* on 8th March, 1797, for which a bar was awarded.

RECIPIENTS Capt. T.B. Martin, R.N.; Lieut. J.S. Carden; Mid. Daniel Little Couch; Yeoman of Sheets Thos. Price; Master's Mate John Fleming; L.M. Geo. Bright; Boys Chas. Brady, Richard Maxworthy, and John Tiver.

Sybille, 28th Feb., 1799 — 1 — 12

For the capture of the French frigate *Forte* by the *Sybille* (Capt. Ed. Cooke) off the Hoogly in the Bay of Bengal.

RECIPIENTS Lieut. Nicholas Manger, R.N.; Mid. Arthur Lysaght; Ordinary Seamen James Coombe, Thos. Hurley, and John Triggs; Able seamen W.E. Wright, Samuel Butler and James Long; Vol 1st Class Joseph Wright; Boy 2nd Class Peter Cloosterman and Supernumeraries (Unrated) J. Piercy and R. Ratcliffe.

Telegraph, 18th March, 1799 — 1 — 0

The small brig *Telegraph* (Lieut. J.A. Worth) captured the French privateer *Hirondelle* off the Isle de Bas, near Brest. There were no claimants for this award.

Acre, 30th May, 1799 — 3 — 50

Given for the defence of Acre, but the date is wrong as the siege was terminated on night of 20/21st May. It was the inability of Napoleon to capture Acre and thus open the way to the conquest of the East, and India, that caused him to remark that his destiny was foiled by an English post-captain. He was, of course, referring to Commodore Sir Sidney Smith, who had worked out the plans for the defence of Acre.
Ships present: *Alliance* 3, *Theseus* 16, *Tigre* 31.

Schiermonnikoog, 12 Aug., 1799 — 5 — 9

Given for the attack on the island of Schiermonnikoog, off Holland, during which the Dutch schooner *Vengeance* was captured and the British gunboat *Crash* recaptured.
Ship present: *Courier, Espiegle, Juno, Latona* and *Pylades.*

RECIPIENTS H.M.S. *Courier* Lieut. T. Searle R.N.; Gunner John Besbeech; Able seaman Richard Keys. H.M.S. *Espiegle* Able seamen David Wilson;

	No. of H.M. Ships Engaged	No. of Bars Issued	

H.M.S. *Juno* — Mid. Eaton Travers.
H.M.S. *Pylades* — Pursuer's Steward John Feary; Landsmen, William Briscoe, George Kilner and John Stroud.

Arrow, 13th Sept., 1799	1	2	For the capture of the Dutch brig *Draak*, of Harlingen, by the *Arrow* (Cdr. Portlock). During the same action the *Wolverine* captured the Dutch brig *Gier*, but there appear to have been no claimants for the medal from her crew.
Wolverine, 13th Sept., 1799	1	0	

RECIPIENTS H.M.S. *Arrow* — Clerk J.M. Perkins and Boy 2nd Class George Ricketts.

Surprise with Hermione *(25th October, 1799)*	1	7	Capt. Edward Hamilton of the *Surprise* found the Spanish frigate *Hermione* moored in Puerto Cabello Harbour, Venezuela, and covered by the shore batteries. He decided to capture her by a cutting-out expedition. The boats of the *Surprise*, which were manned and led by Capt. Hamilton, were rowed alongside the *Hermione*. After a desperate struggle the *Hermione* surrendered, and then, partly by sail and partly by being towed by the row boats, she was taken out of the harbour and eventually reached Port Royal, Jamaica, on 1st November.

The previous history of the *Hermione* is probably unique. In 1797, the year in which the Naval Mutinies occurred, she was the 32-gun British frigate *Hermione*, commanded by Capt. Hugh Pigot. His tyrannical manner so annoyed the crew that on 21st September, 1797, whilst the ship was cruising off Porto Rico in the West Indies, they mutinied. They murdered all the officers except two, and sailed the ship to La Guayra and handed her over to the Spaniards, who re-armed her and added her to their fleet.

It is fitting to conclude this short account with a few words about the gallant commander during the action between the *Surprise* and *Hermione*. Capt. Hamilton was wounded no less than six times, so that in the following April he had to return to England for medical treatment. During the voyage he was captured by a French privateer and subsequently taken to Paris. Here his record was personally investigated by Napoleon, who agreed to exchange him for six midshipmen! His return was greeted with tremendous enthusiasm and he was made a Freeman of the City of London. The Jamaicans presented him with a superb gold and enamel sword and he received a small Naval Gold Medal.

RECIPIENTS OF SMALL NAVAL GOLD MEDAL Capt. Edward Hamilton, R.N.

RECIPIENTS OF N.G.S. MEDAL Capt. Ed. Hamilton R.N.; Ship's corporal Ed Bartlett; Pte John Ingram R.M.; Ords John Young and T. Turner; LM Dennis McGivern; Boy 3rd Class C. Robardo.

Ship	No. of H.M. Ships Engaged	No. of Bars Issued
Speedy, 6th Nov., 1799	1	3
Courier, 22nd Nov., 1799	1	3
Viper, 26th Dec., 1799	1	2
Harpy, 5th Feb., 1800	1	4
Fairy, 5th Feb., 1800	1	4

The *Speedy* (Cdr. Jahleel Brenton) defended a convoy which was attacked by fifteen Spansih gunboats off Gibraltar.

RECIPIENTS Master's Mate G. Pedlar; Clerk C.S. Ricketts; A.B., John Luscombe.

The cutter *Courier* (Lieut. Thos. Searle), whilst cruising off Flushing, captured the French privateer *Guerrier*.

RECIPIENTS Lieut. Thos.Searle (see bar for Schiermonnikoog, 12th August, 1799), Gunner AB Henry Keys, J. Besbeech.

The cutter *Viper* (Lieut. John Pengelly) captured the French privateer *Le Furet* in the English Channel.

RECIPIENTS Mid. S.H. Paddon and Able Seaman C. File.

For the capture of the French frigate *Pallas*, off St. Malo, by the *Harpy* (Cdr. Henry Bazeley) and the *Fairy* (Cdr. Sydney Horton), assisted later in the action by the *Loire*, *Danae* and *Rallieur*. The *Pallas* was added to the

Navy under the name of *Pique*, which figures again on 26th March, 1804. It is extraordinary that the *Danae* and *Railleur* should have gone unrewarded, or alternatively that there were no claimants from them.

RECIPIENTS H.M.S. *Harpy* — Able Seaman R.P. Jones; Vol 1st Class R.B. Mathews; Boys 2nd Class, William Talbot and R. Rider. H.M.S. *Fairy* — Purser's Steward J. Benhamen; Clerk J. Hewitt; L.M. Thomas Beddrell; Vol 1st Class A. Clark.

	No. of H.M. Ships Engaged	No. of Bars Issued	
Loire, 5th Feb., 1800	1	1	H.M.S. *Loire* Mid. Sir W. Owen Pell, who lost his left leg in this action, and later became a Rear-Admiral may have received this clasp or *Harpy* or *Fairy* named clasp.
Peterel, 21st March, 1800	1	2	The *Peterel* (Cdr. F.W. Austen) captured the French frigate *La Ligurienne* from almost under the guns of the forts at Marseilles.

RECIPIENTS Cdr. F.W. Austen R.N.; and Ord S. Horn.

	No. of H.M. Ships Engaged	No. of Bars Issued	
Penelope, 30th March, 1800	1	11 ⎫	General Vaubois, who was blockaded in Valetta Harbour, Malta, dispatched the *Guillaume Tell* to obtain help from Napoleon, but she was intercepted by the *Penelope* (Capt. Henry Blackwood) and *Vinciego* (Cdr. G. Long). Later
Vinciego, 30th March, 1800	1	2 ⎬	

H.M.S. *Lion* and *Foudroyant* arrived and, after a terrific but one-sided contest, the Frenchman surrendered. The *Guillaume Tell* was the last survivor in the French Navy of the Battle of the Nile, and, as H.M.S. *Malta*, became the second largest ship in the Royal Navy.

RECIPIENTS H.M.S. *Penelope* — Mid. William Borough, John Carter, Henry Prescott; Vol. 1st Class James Bayley; Master's Mates Charles Elphick, Robert Yule; Ableseaman John Small; Ord Seaman Darby Collins; Carpenter's Mate James Brown;* Marine Charles Ogden; Boy William Manning. H.M.S. *Vinciego*

*James Brown also received the bar for Basque Roads.

Lieut. E.A. Down and Master's Mate John Osborne. H.M.S. *Lion* — Able-seaman Richard Parslon (Or Parslow) and Ordinary Seaman Robert Ripp. Claims from H.M.S. *Foudroyant* and *Lion* were "disallowed".

Capture of the Désirée
(8th July, 1800)

18   24

For the capture of the French frigate *Désirée*, which was lying in Dunkirk Roads. It is the only case in which the bar is named after the enemy's ship. Probably this was done for brevity, as the following ships took part: H.M.S. *Dart, Rosario;* fireships *Comet, Falcon, Wasp;* gunbrigs *Biter* and *Boxer;* cutters *Ann, Camperdown, Kent, Nile, Selbu, Stag, Teazer, Vigilant;* and boats from H.M.S. *Andromeda, Babet* and *Nemesis.*

Seine,
20th August, 1800

1   7

The *Seine* (Capt. David Milne) captured the French frigate *Vengeance* off Porto Rico.

RECIPIENTS Lieut. Ed. Chetham R.N.; (also named Strode) Mids. Wm. C.C. Dalyell and Robert Oliver, ABs Wm. Crotty and James Fitzgerald, Pte Jas. Jarrett.

Phoebe,
19th Feb., 1801

1   6

For the capture of the French frigate *Africaine*, off Gibraltar, by the *Phoebe* (Capt. Sir Robert Barlow). The former was added to the Navy and renamed *Amelia.*

RECIPIENTS Mid. S.J.B. Pechell and C.Prowett; Sergt. Wm. Ward, R.M.; AB J. Reedin; Vol 1st Class R. Meredeth, Boy 2nd Class Stephen Lawrie. (See Introduction to the N.G.S. Medal for full particulars concerning Stephen Lawrie/Laurie).

Egypt
(8th March—
2nd September, 1801)

117   511

Though 117 ships served off Egypt between 28th March and 2nd September, 1801, medals were only awarded to claimants from the following 115. This bar, like that for Egypt to the Military General Service Medal, was not sanctioned until 12th February, 1850. Ships present to which medals were awarded (approx. numbers to each shown in brackets): Admiral Lord

Keith's flagship *Foudroyant* (33), and *Agincourt* (9), *Ajax* (26), *Alexander* (1), *Alligator* (6), *Athenian* (3), *Astraea* (3), *Blonde* (2), *Bonne Citoyenne* (3), *Brakel* (3), *Cameleon* (5), *Ceres* (4), *Charon* (6), *Cyclops* (7), *Cynthia* (4), *Dangereuse* (3), *Delft* (6), *Determinée* (4), *Diadem* (8), *Dido* (2), *Diana* (5), *Dictator* (8), *Dolphin* (1), *Dover* (1), *Dragon* (8), *Druid* (2), *Eurus* (3), *El Carmen* (5), *Europa* (13), *Expedition* (4), *Experiment* (3), *Flora* (5), *Florentina* (5), *Forte* (2), *Fox* (1), *Gibraltar* (4), *Good Design* (1), *Greyhound* (8), *Haerlem* (6), *Hebe* (6), *Hector* (12), *Heroine* (2), *Inçonstant* (3), *Inflexible* (6), *Iphigenia* (1), *Kangaroo* (1), *Kent* (27), *Leda* (8), *Madras* (15), *Minerva* (10), *Minorca* (1), *Minotaur* (17), *Modeste* (8), *Mondovi* (5), *Monmouth* (17), *Niger* (7), *Northumberland* (22), *Pallas* (5), *Pearl* (7), *Pegasus* (6), *Penelope* (1), *Peterel* (3), *Pigmy* (2), *Pique* (9), *Port Mahon* (3), *Regulus* (3), *Renomee* (8), *Renown* (11), *Resource* (3), *Roebuck* (9), *Romney* (7), *Romulus* (5), *Salamine* (1), *Santa Dorothea* (5), *Santa Theresa* (2), *Sensible* (2), *Sheerness* (2), *Spider* (1), *Stately* (10), *Swiftsure* (16), *Termagant* (4), *Thetis* (8), *Thisbe* (4), *Tigre* (30, *Trusty* (5), *Vestal* (10), *Victor* (2), *Virago* (1), *Wilhemina* (2), *Winchelsea* (3), *Ulysses* (2).

Bomb boats: *Fury* (3), *Tartarus* (1). Sgt. Wm. Hodgson, R.M., received one medal with this bar for service on H.M.S. *Sensible*, and another medal with the bar "12th Oct. 1798" for service as a corporal on H.M.S. *Ethdion*.

Copenhagen, 1801 *(2nd April, 1801)*	36	545

Ships present: Lord Nelson's flagship *Elephant* 5/14, and *Agamemnon* 1/14, *Ardent* 4/21, *Bellona* 5/28, *Defence* 3/8, *Defiance* 5/29, *Edgar* 6/33, *Ganges* 6/8, *Glatton* 2/13, *Isis* 2/10, *London* 5/13, *Monarch* 7/29, *Polyphemus* 6/20, *Raisonnable* 1/7, *Ramillies* 1/20, *Russel* 4/25, *Saturn* -/12, *Veteran* 3/14.

Frigates: *Amazon* 4/10, *Alcmene* 3/9, *Blanche* 1/9, *Desiree* 5/4, *Jamaica* 3/5. Sloops: *Arrow* -/3, *Cruiser* -/3, *Dart* -/2,

Harpy 1/5.
Bomb vessels: *Discovery* -/4, *Explosion* -/3, *Hecla* -/1, *Sulphur* -/1, *Terror* 1/4, *Volcano* 1/2, *Zebra* 1/3.
Brigs: *Otter* 2/1, *Tigress* 1/-, *Zephyr* 1/4.
Also: *Asp* -/1, *Caesar* -/1, *Eling* -/4, *Hasty* 1/1, *Hyena* -/1, *Kite* 1/-, *Lecla* 1/-, *Lynx* -/1, *Powerful* -/1, *St. George* 3/24, *Shannon* -/1, *Standard* 1/-, *Teazer* 1/-, *Victorious* -/1, *Warrior* 1/13.

MILITARY RECIPIENTS Royal Artillery — Gunner Andrew Smith (H.M.S. *Zebra*). 49th Foot — Capt. Chas. Plenderleath, Ensign John Armstrong (H.M.S. *Ardent*); Lieut.-Col. Roger H. Sheaffe, Pte. Robert Young, Drummer Anthony Walsh (H.M.S. *Bellona*); Cpl. J. Cronchy, Ptes. Wm. Booth, Wm. Donnelly (H.M.S. *Defiance*); Ptes. Laurence Dooley, Dennis Slaynes, Andrew Jameson (H.M.S. *Edgar*); Capt. Hugh Arbuthnot, Volunteer George Brock, Pte. Edward Liston (H.M.S. *Ganges*); Asst. Surgeon Robert Brown, Volunteer Harry S. Ormond (H.M.S. *Glatton*); Lieut. James Dennis (H.M.S. *Monarch*); Capt. William Bird Bleamire, (H.M.S. *Polyphemus*); Drummer Charles Hawkes (H.M.S. *Ramillies*); Pte. Richard Cornerford (H.M.S. *Russel*); Pte. John Long (H.M.S. *Saturn*). 95th Foot — Rifleman Hugh Pasley (H.M.S. *Isis*) and James Stiff (H.M.S. *St. George*).
Ensign John Armstrong of H.M.S. *Ardent* also received the M.G.S. Medal with bars for Busaco, Fuentes d'Onor, Cieudad Rodrigo, Badjoz and Salamanca when serving with the 88th Foot.

Speedy, 6th May, 1801   1   7

This is probably one of the most extraordinary actions for which this medal was awarded. Capt. Lord Cochrane with the little *Speedy*, which carried only fourteen 4-pounder guns, and a crew of 6 officers and 54 men, chased and boarded the 32-gun Spanish frigate *Gamo*. Laying the *Speedy* alongside, he boarded the Spaniard with the whole of his crew except for the doctor and two seamen! The *Gamo*, which had a crew of over 300, surrendered and was sailed to Port Mahon, on the east coast of Minorca. One of the boarding party was Lord Cochrane's brother, Mid. The Hon. Archibald Cochrane, whose name, however, does not appear on the medal roll.

RECIPIENTS Cdr. Thos. Cochrane R.M.; Mid. C. Ricketts; Coxswain John Thomson; Actg Carpenter David Rust; Able Seamen John Luscombe, David Gray and Wm. Hutchinson (alias John Campbell).

Gut of Gibralter, **11** **144**
12th July, 1801

For the action with the Spanish fleet off Algeciras.
Ships present: Admiral Saumarez's flag-ship *Caesar* 6/7, and *Audacious* 2/10, *Calpe* 1/2, *Carlotta*, *Hannibal* -/1, *Louisa*, *Pompée* 1/18, *Spencer* 4/17, *Superb* 7/20, *Thames* 5/7, *Venerable* 2/21.
(James Bull, 57th Foot, received the Naval General Service Medal with this bar as Boy 2nd Class and the Military General Service Medal with bars for Busaco, Vittoria and Pyrenees.)

Sylph, **1** **2**
28th Sept., 1801

It is presumed that the *Sylph* (Cdr. Charles Dashwood) engaged the French frigate *Artémise* when cruising off the Spanish coast. Whatever the name of the enemy ship was, she mounted 44 guns to the *Sylph's* 28, and after a two hour's battle sought safety in flight. For this engagement Cdr. Dashwood was promoted Captain.

RECIPIENTS Cdr. Charles Dashwood R.N.; and Lieut. S. Burgess, R.N., who received a medal with five bars, 1st June, 1794; *Sylph*, 28th Sept., 1801; Trafalgar; Boat Service, 27th July, 1809; and Algiers.

Pasley, **1** **4**
28th Oct., 1801

For the capture of the Spanish privateer *Virgen del Rosario* by the *Pasley* (Lieut. Wooldridge), who received promotion for this action off Cape de Gata, south-east Spain.

RECIPIENTS Lieut. P.H. Douglas, R.N.; Boatswain W. Bignell; A.Bs R. Glanvill and J. Hill.

	No. of H.M. Ships Engaged	No. of Bars Issued	
Scorpion, 31st March, 1804	1	4	This was really more of a boat action than a naval engagement. Boats from the *Scorpion* (Cdr. G.N. Hardinge) and *Beaver* (Cdr. Pelley) entered the Texel Roads and captured the Dutch brig *Atlante*, which they eventually sailed back to England. Both the Commanders received promotion for this action.
Beaver, 31st March, 1804	1	0	

RECIPIENTS H.M.S. *Scorpion* — AB. George Salvedore (who also got bars for 14th March, 1795; and *Lowestoffe*, 24th June, 1795); LM. T. Hacker (or Hasker); AB W. Thoms and R. Flaxman.

Centurion, 18th Sept., 1804	1	12	Note the similarity in the name of one of the enemy ships with that of one in the last action quoted. This bar was awarded for the action in which the *Centurion* (Capt. J. Lind), whilst waiting in Vizagapatam Roads ready to escort merchant ships to Madras, was attacked by the French Admiral Linois, who appeared in the Roads with the three ships *Atalante, Marengo* and *Sémillante*. After a most half-hearted exhibition, and in spite of having seriously crippled the *Centurion*, he made off. (See bar for *Amazon*, 13th March, 1806.)

RECIPIENTS Lieut. J.R. Philips, R.N. (who also got the bar for *Camperdown*); A./Lieut. Wm. Carroll (who also received the M.G.S. Medal with bar for *Maida*, 4th July, 1806); Lieut. Thos. Colby (who also got the bars for *Camperdown*; 12th October, 1798; *Trafalgar*; and and unlisted Boat Service, 19th April, 1814); Qtr Gunner John Ward; QM's Mate John Symes; Clerk N. Haydon; Able Seamen Thos. Anderton, George Webb; Ord. James Cole. (Vfd. Aboard. Masters Mate George Bowen Carps. crew Jacob Mears and AB John Thompson.)

Arrow, 3rd Feb., 1805	1	8	The sloops *Arrow* (Cdr. R.B. Vincent) and *Acheron* (Cdr. A. Farquhar) were protecting a large convoy which was attacked by the French frigates *Hortense* and *Incorruptible* when off the coast of Algeria. Both the *Arrow* and *Acheron*
Acheron, 3rd Feb., 1805	1	2	

No. of
H.M. Ships
Engaged

No. of
Bars
Issued

were forced to surrender after a twenty-four hours' battle. The *Arrow* eventually sank and the *Acheron* was so badly damaged that the French set her on fire.

RECIPIENTS H.M.S. *Arrow* — Lieut. C.F. Daly, R.N.; AB George Longridge; Ordinary Seamen Richard Dane, Robert Greatrex, John Hurley; Landsmen Benjamin Brown, Thos. Wheeler; Carpenter Archibald Gray, R.M.; H.M.S. *Acheron* — Mid. J. Simpson; Ordinary Seaman J. Wheelan.
C.F. Daly also received the bar for *Comet*, 11th August, 1808 — a unique combination.

San Fiorenzo,
14th Feb., 1805

1   13

For the capture of the French frigate *Psyche* off Ganjam on the Malabar coast of India, by the *San Fiorenzo* (Capt. Henry Lambert).

RECIPIENTS Lieut. Edward Collier; Mid. Samuel Marsingall; Ordinary Seamen George Barney (who also got the bar for *San Fiorenzo*, 8th March, 1808) and George Love; Landsman John Acton; AB. Peter Hughes, Nathaniel Kenny, John Pacey and David Piggott; Ship's Corp. P. Trout, R.M.; Ptes. William Beck and Daniel Hoskins, R.M. (Vfd. Abd LM Samuel Finn.)

Phoenix,
10th Aug., 1805

1   29

For the capture of the French frigate *Didon* off Cape Finisterre by the *Phoenix* (Capt. Thomas Baker). The *Didon* was towed into Plymouth, where she was repaired and recommissioned into the Royal Navy. This is a rare bar.

Trafalgar
(21st October, 1805)

33   1,710

A medal for this action was awarded to Jane Townsend, who was on board H.M.S. *Defiance*. This is the first that can be traced to a woman.
Ships present: Lord Nelson's flagship *Victory* 18/107, and *Achilles* 7/52, *Africa* 6/31, *Agamemnon* 7/39, *Ajax* 6/33, *Belleisle* 14/59, *Bellerophon* 6/50, *Britannia* 11/78, *Colossus* 10/41, *Conqueror* 6/50, *Defence* 8/52, *Defiance* 6/37, *Dreadnought* 10/49, *Leviathan* 5/53, *Mars* 6/47, *Minotaur* 6/28, *Neptune* 10/49, *Orion* 7/45, *Polyphemus*

7/15, *Prince* 16/53, *Revenge* 10/49, *Royal Sovereign* 6/86, *Spartiate* 13/46, *Swiftsure* 8/39, *Temeraire* 7/49, *Thunderer* 7/34, *Tonnant* 7/46.
Frigates: *Euryalus* 5/16, *Naiad* 5/24, *Phoebe* 8/19, *Sirius* 2/17.
Schooner: *Pickle* 3/1, which brought home the news of the victory.
Cutter: *Entreprenante.*

RECIPIENTS OF LARGE NAVAL GOLD MEDALS Vice-Admiral Cuthbert Collingwood, second-in-command, H.M.S. *Royal Sovereign*; Rear-Admiral William — Earl of Northesk, third-in-command, H.M.S. *Britannia.*

RECIPIENTS OF SMALL NAVAL GOLD MEDALS Captains Thos. Hardy, Ed. Rotheram, Chas. Bullen, Eliab Harvey, Richard Grindall, Thos. Francis Fremantle, John Conn, Chas. Tyler, Wm. Hargood, Robert Moorsom, George Duff, Sir Francis Nicoll Morris, Henry Wm. Bayntun, Richard King, John Cooke, Chas. John Mansfield, Ed. Codrington, Wm. George Rutherford, Robert Redmill, Henry Digby, Sir Ed. Berry, Lieut. John Pinfold, who was acting Captain of the *Ajax*, and Lieut. John Stockham, who was performing the same role in the *Thunderer*, were also awarded Gold Medals on reaching the rank of Captain.

4th Nov. 1805   8   297

For the destruction of the remainder of the French Fleet after Trafalgar, off Finisterre, by Capt. Sir Richard Strachan in H.M.S. *Caesar* 4/61, accompanied by the *AEolus* 2/14, *Courageux* 1/29, *Hero* 6/50, *Namur* 1/55, *Phoenix* 3/24, *Revolutionnaire* 1/29 (some books give *Revolution*), and *Santa Margarita* 1/12.

RECIPIENTS OF THE SMALL NAVAL GOLD MEDAL Capt. Sir Richard John Strachan, Bart., H.M.S. *Caesar*; Capt. The Hon. Alan Hyde Gardner, H.M.S. *Hero*; Capt. William Laurence Halsted, H.M.S. *Namur*; Capt. Richard Lee, H.M.S. *Courageux*. Ord. Smn. Samuel Challis (H.M.S. *Namur*) received two Naval General Service Medals, one with this bar and another with the clasp for Basque Roads, 1809 and BS 27 Sept., 1810 as a Steward's mate.

St. Domingo 11 406
(6th February, 1806)

For the destruction of the French Fleet under Admiral Leissegues which had been carrying stores to the island of St. Domingo and was preparing to sail home again.

Ships present: Admiral Sir John Duckworth's flagship *Superb* 16/56, and *Acasta* 4/23, *Agamemnon* 8/32, *Atlas* 4/27, *Canopus* 11/58, *Donegal* 8/37, *Epervier* 1/4, *Kingfisher* 3/7, *Magicienne* 1/12, *Northumberland* 9/41 and *Spencer* 8/32.

RECIPIENTS OF THE LARGE NAVAL GOLD MEDAL Vice-Admiral Sir John Duckworth; Rear-Admiral A. Cochrane; Rear-Admiral Louis.

RECEIPIENTS OF THE SMALL NAVAL GOLD MEDAL Captains Goodwin Keats, Morrison, Hon. Robert Stopford, Pulteney Malcolm, Pym, Sir Edward Berry, F. Austin.

Amazon, 1 30)
13th March, 1806
London, 1 27)
13th March, 1806

The French Admiral Linois, when on his way home from the East Indies, with the *Marengo* and *Belle Poule* (the *Atalante* having been lost), encountered the *Foudroyante, Amazon* and *London* when nearly home. The *Amazon* (Capt. Wm. Parker) chased the *Belle Poule* and the *London* (Capt. Sir Harry Neale) chased the *Marengo*. Both the French ships were brought to action off Brest and surrendered. (See bar for Centurion, 18th September, 1804.)

Pique, 1 8
26th March, 1806

For the capture of the two French brigs *Phaeoton* and *Voligeur* off Porto Rico by the *Pique* (Capt. Charles Ross).

RECIPIENTS Lieut. Christopher Bell R.M.; Lieut. Wm. Ward, R.N.; Mid. Richard Lloyd; Caulker Thos. Moulding; AB. John Williams, LM. John Trusse and Ord. Wm. Hungate.

Sirius, 1 20
17th April, 1806

For the capture by H.M.S. *Sirius* (Capt. Wm. Prowse) of the French corvette

Bergère off Civita Vecchia, on the west coast of Italy. In this action the small *Sirius* of 16 guns attacked a French flotilla, which appears to have made off, leaving the small *Bergère* of only 19 guns to her fate.

RECIPIENTS Surgeon Thos. Robertson; Mid. Morgan G. Crofton and John Turner; 1st Lieut. Wm. Magin, R.M.; Carpenter Robert Beatson; Able Seaman John Cremer, Landsmen Ed. Sheehy, Wm. Thomas and Henry Curley; Sergt. John Ingram, R.M.; Pte. Patrick Connolly, R.M.; Boy 3rd Class John Hennessey (who also got the bar for Trafalgar); and Wm. Norman, whose rank is not stated. (Also Vfd. Aboard and at Trafalgar Gunner Hugh Perry, ABs John Davis and Jonathan Pricely; Ord. Edward Mealy; Landsmen John Brownrigg, John Cremer, William German, Edward Sheehy and Pte. Isaac May R.M.)

Blanche, 19th July, 1806   1   22

For the capture by H.M.S. *Blanche* (Capt. T. Lavie, who was knighted for this action) of the French frigate *Guerriere* off the Faroe Islands.

Arethusa, 23rd August, 1806   1   17 ⎫
Anson, 23rd August, 1806   1   11 ⎭

For the capture of the Spanish frigate *Pomona* off Havana Harbour, Cuba, by H.M.S. *Arethusa* (Capt. Charles Brisbane) and H.M.S. *Anson* (Capt. C. Lydiard).

RECIPIENTS H.M.S. *Arethusa* — Lieut. Henry Higman, R.N.; Mid. J.W. Aldridge, John H. Bellairs and Curtis Reid; Purser John Elliott; Ord. Edward Fielding Jas. Smith; Boy 2nd Class George Greengrass. (Vfd Abd and at Curacoa (on Roll) AB. Charles Fishington; Ords. Peter Concannon, William Griffin, James Smith; LMs John Cowan, James Hagley; Boy 2nd Class George Greengrass. Cpl. John Field R.M. and Pte. Michael Chapple R.M.; AB. James Shepherd.) H.M.S. *Anson* — Lieut Thos. Ball Sullivan; Coxswain Wm. Jeffrey; Qtr. Gnr. Robert Henley; Ord. James Burkley LM. Christopher Coucher; Pte.

Stephen Coward, R.M.; (Vfd. Abd and at Curacoa (on Roll) Yeoman powder room Richard Leverton; Ords. James Duglass, George Simons; Boys 2nd Class Thomas Costello and 3rd Class Charles Salmon).

Curacoa,   4   67
1st Jan., 1807

For the capture of the island of Curacoa in the West Indies. Commodore Charles Brisbane, with the four frigates *Arethusa* (flying his pennant), *Anson*, *Fisguard* and *Latona* is said to have given the town exactly five minutes to surrender. Receiving no reply, he promptly boarded a Dutch frigate lying in the harbour whilst Capt. Lydiard of the *Anson* boarded another. Having captued these two ships, the boarding and landing parties then went ashore and captured the forts of Amsterdam and Republique guarding the harbour. The mere site of these parties seems to have terrified the Dutch garrison, which hastened to surrender the forts and the island. The island was restored to the Dutch in 1814.

The numbers awarded to each ship were: *Arethusa* 24, *Anson* 15, *Fisguard* 9, *Latona* 19.

RECIPIENTS OF THE SMALL NAVAL GOLD MEDAL Commodore Charles Brisbane and Captains Lydiard, Bolton and J.A. Wood.

Pickle,   1   2
3rd Jan., 1807

For the capture of the French privateer *La Favorite* off the Lizard by H.M.S. *Pickle* (Lieut. D. Calloway).

RECIPIENT Actg. Sub-Lieut. Charles Hawkins, and Bosun's Mate James Rowden.

Hydra,   1   12
6th August, 1807

For the capture of the French ships *Caroline*, *L'Eugene* and *Rosario* in Burgur Harbour, in Spain, as the result of a cutting-out expedition by the boats of H.M.S. *Hydra* (Capt. George Mundy) under Lieut. Drury, who was promoted for this action.

RECIPIENTS Capt. Geo Mundy, R.N.; 1st Lieut. Robert Hayes, R.M.; Mid.

No. of H.M. Ships Engaged	No. of Bars Issued	

John Finlaison; Captain of Fore Top James Huntley; Captain Main Top David Smith; Landsmen George King and Thos. Dredge; Clerk R.H. Goddard; Boy 2nd Class B.E. Quadline; Cpl. John Lee, R.M.; Pte. John Bennett, R.M. and Mid P.G. Panton verified aboard (St Domingo on Roll).

Comus, 15th August, 1807 — 1 — 9

For the capture of the Danish frigate *Frederickscoan* off Helsingor by the *Comus* (Capt. Edmund Heywood).

RECIPIENTS Lieut. Geo. E. Watts, R.N.; Mid. W.L. Wraxall and Chas. H. Seale; AB. Wm. Finley; Coxswain John Miller; Purser W.C. Hilier; Able Seaman W. Scammel; Purser's steward James Thain; L.M. Thos. Saunders. (Thos. Saunders also received the bar for *Mars*, 21st April, 1897.)
Sir Wm. Lascelles Wraxall, Bart., whose medal is indented "WRAXALL," received the Military General Service Medal with bars for Vittoria, Pyrenees, Nive, Orthes, and Toulouse when serving as a Lieutenant in the 34th Foot.

Louisa, 28th Oct., 1807 — 1 — 1

For the defeat of a privateer off the Dalmatian cost by H.M.S. *Louisa* (Lieut. Joseph Hoy).

RECIPIENT Supernumary Lieut. H.B. Powell, R.N.

Carrier, 4th Nov., 1807 — 1 — 1

For the capture by H.M.S. *Carrier* (under temporary command William Milne) of the French ship *L'Actif* off the Dalmatian coast. It is rather extraordinary that the sole recipient of the medal should be the commanding officer.

RECIPIENT Actg. Lieut in command Wm. Milne R.N.

Ann, 24th Nov., 1807 — 1 — 0

The *Ann* (Lieut. Mackenzie) was attacked by ten Spanish gunboats off Tarifa, two of which surrendered. There were no claimants for this bar.

Sappho, 2nd March, 1808 — 1 — 4

The *Sappho* (Cdr. Geo Langford) captured the Dutch brig *Admiral Yawl* off

Scarborough.

RECIPIENTS Mid. Daniel McN. Beatty; Carpenter's Mate Thos. Nicholls; Landsman Chas. Parry; Pte. Wm. Howes, R.M.

San Fiorenzo, 8th March, 1808	1	17

For the capture of the French frigate *Piedmontaise* off the coast of Ceylon after a two-day chase. Capt. Geo. F. Hardinge of the *San Fiorenzo* was killed at the start of the action. Lieut. Dawson then assumed command.

RECIPIENTS Captain of Fo'c'le Peter Trout; Gnr. Robert Bird; Purser Nathaniel Haydon; Able Seamen Wm. Cromer, Henry Gauk, Nathaniel Kenny, John Pacey, Matthew Clark, Wm. Dixon; Ordinary Seamen Geo. Barney, John Finch, David Wyse, Geo. Love; Landsmen John Acton, Samuel Finn; Pte. Daniel Hoskins R.N., and Vfd. Abd. Lieut. Edward Collier R.N. (4 clasp see Amanthea 25 July 1810 − Promoted).

Emerald, 13th March, 1808	1	10

H.M.S. *Emerald*, at the time commanded by Lieut. Charles Bertram, destroyed the batteries at Vivero off the northwest coast of Spain, and captured a small French schooner lying in the harbour.

RECIPIENTS Lieut. Chas. Bertram, R.N. Mids. Edward Saurin, Richard Connor; Master's Mate Daniel Baird; Sailmaker Thos. Potts; Carpenter's Crew John Gillman; Able Seaman Wm. Thompson; Vol. per order John McKillop; Pte. John Norman, R.M.; Boy 2nd Class Edward Wylde.

Childers, 14th March, 1808	1	4

The *Childers* (Cdr. W.H. Dillon R.N.) engaged the Danish brig *Lugen* off the Norwegian coast. For this action Cdr. Dillon received promotion. There appears to be a considerable divergence of opinion as to how the name of the Danish brig should be spelt. Various histories mention the following: Lügn, Lougen, Lugn, Lügen and Lougon. Where there is such variation one is unable to say which is correct.

RECIPIENTS Cdr. Wm. Henry Dillon R.N.; Lieut. Thos. Edmonds, R.N.;

Vol. 1st Class Chas. Parker; Acting Master Geo. Wilson.

(Cdr. Dillon, later Rear-Admiral Sir Wm. Hy. Dillon, also received bars for 1st June, 1794; and 23rd June, 1795. He served as a Midshipman in H.M.S. *Defence* on 1st June, 1794, so that his promotion was very rapid. "Dillons Narrative" in two volumes published by Navy Records Society 1953 and 1956 makes excellent reading.

Nassau, 22nd March, 1808	1	31
Stately, 22nd March, 1808	1	31

The *Nassau* (Capt. R. Campbell) and *Stately* (Capt. Geo. Parker) destroyed the Danish battleship *Prince Christian Frederick* off Grenaa, which is in the Kattegat on the north-east coast of Denmark.

Off Rota, 4th April, 1808	3	19

The *Alceste* (Capt. M. Maxwell), *Mercury* (Capt. James Gordon) and the brig *Grasshopper* (Cdr. Thos. Searle) attacked a Spanish convoy off Cadiz and captured seven of the escorted tartans. A tartan is a small sailing vessel with a triangular sail common to the Mediterranean and the Italian lakes.

RECIPIENTS H.M.S. *Alceste* (3) — Landsman Wm. Disney; Pte. James Simpson, Ord. Smith Nash, (awarded but had not yet joined ship). R.M. H.M.S. *Grasshopper* (4) — Cdr. Thos. Searle R.N.; Mid. Stephen Hodge; Clerk John Gain; Purser Thos. Bastin (who also got the bar for *Grasshopper*, 24th April, 1808). H.M.S. *Mercury* (12) — Capt. James A. Gordon; Lieut. W.O. Pell; Mid. Wm. Parker; 1st Lieut. James Whylock, R.M. (and Syria Acre in Gold); Master's Mate Chas. du Cane; LM Jas. French; Carpenter's Crew Joseph Phillips; Able Seaman John Richardson; Ords. Samuel Watson and John Ragan; Vol 1st Class Geo. Broom (later Midshipman, who also got the bar for Guadaloupe); Boy 3rd Class Joseph Crouch.

Grasshopper, 24th April, 1808	1	7

Three weeks after the last action described the *Grasshopper* (Cdr. T. Searle

	No. of H.M. Ships Engaged	No. of Bars Issued	
Rapid, 24th April, 1808	1	1	and the brig *Rapid* (Lieut. H. Baugh) chased a small convoy escored by four Spanish gunboats when off Faro, on the south of Portugal. The Spaniards took refuge in the port, but the forts were silenced and two of the Spanish gunboats were captured.

RECIPIENTS H.M.S. *Grasshopper* — Cdr. T. Searle R.N.; Mid. Stephen Hodge; Purser Thos. Bastin; Clerk John Gain (all of whom also got the bar for Off Rota, 4th April, 1808); Landsmen James Legge and Samuel J. Pottinger; Pte. James Holdeway, R.M. H.M.S. *Rapid* — Lieut Henry Baugh, R.N.

Redwing, 7th May, 1808	1	7	For the destruction of a Spanish gunboat off Cape Trafalgar by H.M.S. *Redwing*, (Cdr. Thos. Ussher — promoted Captain for this action)

RECIPIENTS Cdr. Thos. Ussher, R.N.; Lieut. John McP. Ferguson, R.N.; Mid. Thos. Hallahan; Actg. Master John Davis; Purser R.L. Horniman; Boatswain Wm. Martin; Vol. 1st Class Wm. H. Brand.

Virginie, 19th May, 1808	1	21	For the capture of the Dutch frigate *Guelderland* off Northern Ireland by the *Virginie* (Cdr. E. Brace).

Redwing, 31st May, 1808	1	7	For the destruction of the batteries at Tarifa and capture of two vessels by the *Redwing* (Capt. Thos. Ussher).

RECIPIENTS Capt. Thos. Ussher R.N.; Lieut. John McP. Ferguson, R.N.; Mid. Thos. Hallahan; Vol. 1st Class Wm. H. Brand; Boatswain Wm. Martin (See *Redwing*, 7th May, 1808.) and verified aboard Acting Master John Davis and Purser R.L. Horniman.

Seahorse with Badere Zaffer *(5/6th July,)* 1808	1	32	Capt. John Stewart in the *Seahorse* encountered the Turkish frigate *Badere Zaffer* in company with the *Ali Fezan*. The latter frigate, having received a broadside from the *Seahorse,* decided that she had had enough and cleared off. The *Badere Zaffer*, however, continued fighting all day and all night, but due to her terrible plight was forced to sur-

	No. of H.M. Ships Engaged	No. of Bars Issued	

render in the morning, having had her masts shot away and no less than 170 men killed and 200 wounded. As a result of this action the *Seahorse* had only five killed and ten wounded — a splendid example of fine gunnery, magnificent seamanship and tactics. This is a rare and much-prized bar in spite of the number issued.

Comet, 11th August, 1808 — 1 — 4

For the capture of the French ship *Sylphe*, in the Bay of Biscay, by H.M.S. *Comet* (Cdr. Cuthbert F. Daly).

RECIPIENTS Cdr. C.F. Daly R.N.;* Pte. E. Vanston, R.M.; Vol. 1st Class G. Dew and Vfd. Abd. Boy 2nd Class Daniel Caffrey (on Java Roll).

Centaur, 26th August, 1808 — 1 — 42)
Implacable, 26th August, 1808 — 1 — 44)

These two bars show the variety of opponents which the Royal Navy had during the period covered by the N.G.S. Medal. As a result of the Russians signing the Treaty of Tilsit on 7th July, 1807, they recognized the Confederation of the Rhine and the appointing of Napoleon's brothers Joseph, Louis and Jerome to the thrones of Naples, Holland and Westphalia. In other words, this meant that Russia was now ranged against us, so Admiral Sir James Saumarez was ordered to the Baltic, with his flag in Nelson's old flagship, *Victory*. During his voyage a Russian squadron of seventeen ships was sighted. The *Centaur* (Capt. Webley), flying the flag of Sir Samuel Hood, and the *Implacable*† (Capt. Byam Martin) were

*See bar for *Arrow*, 3rd February, 1805.

†The *Implacable* was originally the French line-of-battle ship *Duguay Trouin*, launched at Rochefort in 1797. She was present at Trafalgar and later captured by Sir Richard Strachan in the action off Finisterre, for which the bar "4th Novr. 1805" was awarded.

She lay in Portsmouth harbour for many years as a hulk, until finally condemned as unseaworthy and not worth the cost of repair.

On 3rd December, 1949, she was towed out to sea and blown up off the Isle of Wight with the White Ensign and the Tricolour flying side by side at her stem.

On her way out of harbour she passed the aircraft carrier H.M.S. *Implacable*, then flagship of the Home Fleet. The final signal for the detonation of the charges was given from the destroyer H.M.S. *Finisterre*.

It is a strange reflection on the life of modern warships to think that the aircraft carrier *Implacable*, 26,000 tons was launched in 1944 and scrapped in 1955 as out-dated.

ordered to give chase. The *Implacable* overtook and captured the Sevolod, but as the Russian fleet returned the *Implacable* had to retire. On the arrival of the *Centaur* the *Sevolod* was again attacked, captured and eventually ran ashore and was set on fire.

Cruizer, 1st Nov., 1808   1   4

The *Cruizer* (Lieut. T. Wells) was attacked by about twenty Danish cutters off Gothenburg. She captured one and drove off the others.

RECIPIENTS Lieut. J. Allen, R.N.; Mid. F.W. Ellis, Ord. W.J. Walker; Vol. 1st Class James R. Forrest.

Amethyst wh. Thetis *(10th November, 1808)*   1   31

Capt. Michael Seymour in the *Amethyst* whilst off Lorient encountered the French frigate *Thetis*, which was on its way to Martinique. The *Thetis* was captured after a terrific fight, having suffered no less than 134 killed and 102 wounded. After the surrender of the *Thetis*, H.M.S. *Triumph* and *Shannon* arrived and took her in tow, but, having taken no part in the actual fight, received no awards. The *Thetis* was added to the Royal Navy under the name of *Brune*.

RECIPIENT OF SMALL NAVAL GOLD MEDAL Capt. Michael Seymour.

Off the Pearl Rock, 13th Dec., 1808   6   16

The *Circe* (Capt. F. Collier), *Amaranthe* (Capt. E. Brenton), *Stork* (Capt. Geo. Le Geyt), *Express* (Lieut. Dowers), *Morne Fortunée* (Lieut. Brown), and *Epervier* (Capt. T. Tucker) destroyed the French frigate *Cyne* off the Pearl Rock, Martinique. No awards were made to H.M.S. *Express*.

RECIPIENTS H.M.S. *Circe* (5) — Cdr. Francis R. Collier, R.N.; Mid. Chas. H. Crooke; Yeoman of Sheets Alexander Roberts; Ab. John Jago; Ord. George Underwood. H.M.S. *Amaranthe* (4) — Mid. James Rigmaiden; Vol. 1st Class Joseph Willans; Ab. Wm. Weatherhead; Ord. James Garrick. H.M.S. *Stork* (3) — Cdr. Geo. Le Geyt; Pte. R.M. Richard Fry; Ab. George Harding (who also received bar for Martinique). H.M.S.

	No. of H.M. Ships Engaged	No. of Bars Issued	
			Morne Fortunée (3) — Lieut. Commanding J.J. Rorie vfd. Abd. (and at Curacoa on Roll); Abs. Alex Clark and Peter Russel. H.M.S. *Epervier* (1) — Lieut. Joseph Harrison, R.N.
Onyx, 1st Jan., 1809	1	5	The brig *Onyx* (Cdr. Chas. Gill) recaptured the brig *Manly* from the Dutch in the North Sea. For this action Cdr. Gill and Lieut. E. Garrett received promotion. RECIPIENTS Lieut. E.W. Garrett R.N.; Master's Mate W. White; Qtr. Gunner H. Edwards; Clerk Hewson Dutchman; Ord. J. Barnes.
Confiance, 14th Jan., 1809	1	8	Capt. Sir L. Yeo in the *Confiance,* with the assistance of 500 Portuguese troops captured Cayenne, the present capital of French Guiana. RECIPIENTS Mid. Wim. Moore; Yeoman of Sheets J. Blackman; Boatswain George Byerle; L.M. Christopher Hosan; Ord. T. Himnick; Vol. 1st Class H.J. O'Callaghan; Cpl. T. Ward, R.M.; Mid. Edward Bryant.
Martinique, *(2nd-10th Fenruary, 1809)*	44	506	For the capture of the island of Martinique in conjunction with the Army. There were no military recipients of the Naval Medal, though there were six naval and marine recipients of the military one, whose names are given when dealing with the bar for Martinique on the Military General Service Medal (*vide* pages 42 and 43). Ships present: Rear-Admiral Cochrane's flagship *Neptune* 17/61, and *Acasta* 5/16, *Aeolus* 5/7, *Amaranthe* 3/9, *Belleisle* 6/32, *Captain* 3/25, *Cherub* 2/3, *Circe* 2/8, *Cleopatra* 3/10, *Eclair* 1/-, *Ethalion* 6/18, *Eurydice* 2/6, *Express* 1/1, *Fawn* 3/6, *Forester* 3/8, *Floric* 2/-, *Gloire* 3/3, *Gorée* 1/4, *Haughty* 1/4, *Hazard* 2/4, *Intrepid* 7/14, *Pelorus* 2/2, *Penelope* 4/17, *Pompée* 11/43, *Recruit* 1/4, *Star* 1/7, *Stork* 1/7, *Swinger, Ulysses* 3/8, *Wolverine* 4/4, *York* 7/23. Schooners: *Bacchus, Bellette* 1/2, *Cuttle* 1/-, *Demerara* -/3, *Dominica* 1/-, *Eliza-*

	No. of H.M. Ships Engaged	No. of Bars Issued	
			beth -/1, *Liberty* -/1, *Mozambique* 1/-, *Port d'Espagne* 4/-, *Poltustle* -/2, *Ringdove* -/5, *Snap* 2/1, *Subtle, Supérieure* 2/1, *Surinam* 3/8.
Horatio, 10th Feb., 1809	1	13 ⎫	The *Horatio* (Capt. George Scott) and the *Supérieure* (Cdr. W. Ferrie) captured the French frigate *Junon* off Saintes in the Virgin Islands.
Supérieure, 10th Feb., 1809	1	1 ⎬	

RECIPIENTS H.M.S. *Horatio* — Drummer Thos. Young R.N.; Purser John Warden; 1st Lieut. Richard Blakeney, R.M.; Able seaman Richard Plumb; Mid. Nicholas Webb; Ord. Joseph Allen; Pte. Joseph Crawford, R.M.; Lieut. Manly Hall Dixon R.N.; L.M. Morris Hurley; Boy 3rd Class Samuel Beswick; Sgt. Geo. Vincent, R.M.; Boy 2nd Class G.R.T. Disney; Capt. of Foretop John Lane; also H.M.S. *Supérieure* Actng. Master B.G.S. Day.

Amethyst, 5th April, 1809	1	27	With Capt. Michael Seymour in command, the *Amethyst* engaged the French frigate *Niemen* in the Bay of Biscay. When the *Niemen* was on the point of capitulating the *Arethusa* came on the scene and, strange to say, the *Niemen* surrendered to her and not to the *Amethyst*. No awards were given to the *Arethusa*. Capt. Seymour was given a baronetcy for this action.
Basque Roads, 1809 *(12th April)*	35	551	For the complete destruction of the French fleet in the Basque Roads, off St. Nazaire, which was due to the enterprize and skill of Lord Cochrane, who organized and led the fleet of warships and fireships into the Roads. Lord Cochrane was given the Order of the Bath and Lord Gambier, who was the senior officer present, received a court martial. The Court not only exonerated him for his pusillanimity but seems to have gone out if its way to express extreme approbation of his conduct! In O'Meara's *Napoleon in Exile*, Napoleon is quoted as having remarked when referring to the French ships in the harbour: "Lord Cochrane could not only have destroyed them, but he might

and would have taken them out had your Admiral supported him as he ought to have done."

Ships present: Admiral Lord Gambier's flagship *Caledonia* 8/22, and *Aetna* 5/11, *Aigle* 5/11, *Armide* -/1, *Arrow* -/1, *Beagle* 2/9, *Bellona* 4/7, *Caesar* 17/22, *Christian VII* -/4, *Conflict* 1/-, *Contest*, *Defiance* -/1, *Doterel* 3/5, *Donegal* 7/13, *Dreadnought* -/1, *Emerald* 3/9, *Encounter* -/2, *Fervant* -/1, *Foxhound* 1/1, *Gibraltar* 10/24, *Goldfinch* 1/-, *Growler, Hero* 3/4, *Illustrious* 3/20, *Impérieuse* 6/18, *Indefatigable* 5/25, *Insolent* 1/4, *Lyra* 2/5, *Martial* 2/2, *Mediator* -/2, *Pallas* 3/8, *Redpole* 2/4, *Resolution* 4/33, *Revenge* 7/24, *Theseus* 6/30, *Thunder* 2/6, *Unicorn* 3/17, *Valiant* 9/20. Schooner *Whiting* -/2, *Zephr* -/1.

Cutters *King George* and *Nimrod* 1/-.

Recruit, 17th June, 1809	1	7
Pompee, 17th June, 1809	1	47
Castor, 17th June, 1809	1	13

The date on this bar is obviously wrong, because the action for which it was awarded took place on 17th April. It is difficult to understand how such an error could pass without coming to the conclusion that there must have been considerable lack of verification or checking of the findings of the Board of Flag Officers which recommended the actions for which awards should be given. The French seventy-four *Hautpoult*, which had escaped from Lorient, was in company with two others of her size and three frigates when they were sighted by the *Pompée* (Capt. W. Fahie) and the brigs *Recruit* (Cdr. Charles Napier) and *Hazard*, all of which gave chase together with other British ships present. The two brigs were eventually outstripped, whereupon the *Latona* and *Castor* (Capt. W. Roberts) took up the action. The latter engaged, giving time for the *Pompée* to arrive. The Frenchman surrendered and was added to the Royal Navy under the name of H.M.S. *Abercromby*. Cdr. Charles Napier, as a reward for the gallant way in which the *Recruit* had behaved during the action, was given command. The action took place off Isle de Saintes, a small island

(Obverse)
No. 22. The Small Naval Gold Medal.

(Obverse)
No. 37. The Small Army Gold Medal.

(Obverse)
No. 37. The Peninsular Gold Cross.

(Obverse)

No. 38. The Hanover Waterloo Medal, 1815.

(Obverse)

No. 38. The Nassau Waterloo Medal 1815.

(Obverse)

No. 38 The Brunswick Waterloo Medal, 1815.

(Obverse)

No. 39. The St. Helena Medal, 1857.

(Obverse)

No. 38. The Saxe-Gotha-Altenburg Waterloo Medal 1815.

To face page 97

off the south coast of Guadaloupe. A company of the 63rd Foot was on board H.M.S. *Pompée* during the action. There was only one medal with this single bar issued, and that was awarded to Lieut. W. Cosby of the 63rd Foot, and he also received the M.G.S. Medal with bars for Martinique and Guadaloupe.

RECIPIENTS H.M.S. *Recruit* — Cdr. Charles Napier, R.N.; Qr. Mr. J. Pearson; Carpenter R. Mustard; L.M. Robert Pattinson; Boy 3rd Class J. Davis. and Capt. Forecastle J. Mott, Carp's. Crew James Stewart. H.M.S. *Castor* — Lieut. M. Raven, R.N.; Lieut. W.B. Sellon, R.N.; Surgeon J. McCarogher; Mid. J.T.T. Dixon; Pte. J. Ross, R.M.; Boy 2nd Class W. Andrews (and Vfd Abd. with Guadaloupe clasp. Cook A. Peveriny; Abs. James McLaughlan, A. Nesbitt; Ptes. Joseph Huson, Samuel Mills and George Packe.)

	No. of H.M. Ships Engaged	No. of Bars Issued	
Cyane, 25th and 27th June, 1809	1	5	
L'Espoir, 25th and 27th June, 1809	1	5	

Capt. T. Staines in the corvette *Cyane* in company with the brig *L'Espoir* (Cdr. T. Mitford) was attacked off Naples by the French frigate *Ceres* and corvette *Fama*. The action was too one-sided and in the end the *Cyane* and *L'Espoir* had to withdraw after being very badly damaged. Capt. T. Staines was knighted for this action.

RECIPIENTS H.M.S. *Cyane* — 1st Lieut. W. Stuart, R.M.; Mids. J. Allnutt and John Taylor; Purser J. Tapson. Boy 3rd Class J. Crogan. H.M.S. *L'Espoir* — Cdr. R. Mitford R.N.; Lieut. W.H. Higgs, R.N.; A./Lieut. R. Oliver R.N.; Ord. E. Boyce and LM. John Taylor.

Bonne Citoyenne with Furieuse *(6th July, 1809)*	1	12	

The French frigate *Furieuse* had escaped from the blockade of Guadaloupe and was on her way back to France when, in mid-Atlantic, she encountered the sloop *Bonne Citoyenne* (Capt. W. Mounsey). After a battle lasting seven hours, the Frenchman had expended all his powder and so was forced to surrender.

No. of H.M. Ships Engaged	No. of Bars Issued	
		RECIPIENT OF SMALL NAVAL GOLD MEDAL Capt. Mounsey.
		RECIPIENTS Lieut. Wm. Sandom, R.N.; Lieut. Joseph Symes, R.N.; Mid. Nathaniel Routh; Capts. of Foretop Richard Roberts, and Eliazer Taysand; Carpenter Thos. Atwaters; Ord. Wm. White and Ed. Buttonshaw; Boy 2nd Class John Crosdale; Ptes. Joseph Smith, James Jolley and Richard Chapman, R.M.
Diana, 11th Sept., 1809	1	8	For the capture of the Dutch brig *Zephr* (or *Zefir*), which was anchored off Amurang, in the north-east of the island of Celebes in the East Indies, by the *Diana* (Lieut. W. Kempthorne).
			RECIPIENTS AB. George Wilson; Ord. R. Rowell; Ptes. A. Brown and N. Brittal, R.M.; Boy 2nd Class James Burke (and Vfd. Abd. with BS clasp 24 December 1810; Mid. John B. Knocker; Ship's Corporal George White; Ord. J.J.F. Newell.)
Anse la Barque, 18th Dec., 1809	9	51	A British squadron consisting of the *Sceptre* (Capt. S. Ballard), *Blonde* (Capt. V.V. Ballard), *Freija* (Capt. J. Hayes), *Thetis* (Capt. G. Miller), *Castor* (Capt. Roberts), *Hazard* (Capt. Cameron), *Ringdove* (Capt. Dowers), *Cygnet* (Capt. Dix) and *Elizabeth* (Lieut. C. Finch) encountered the French frigates *Loire* and *Seine*, which wer escorting troops and stores to Guadaloupe. The latter ships sought protection under the batteries of Anse la Barque, but both they and the batteries were captured. This is a rare bar in spite of the number issued.
Cherokee, 10th Jan., 1810	1	4	For the capute of the French privateer *L'Aimable Nelly* in Dieppe Harbour by the *Cherokee* (Capt. Richard Arthur).
			RECIPIENTS Lieut. J.R.R. Webb, R.N.; Supn. Pilots H. Barber and H. Pilcher; Ord. G. Arguile.
Scorpion, 12th Jan. 1810	1	8	The *Scorpion* (Capt. P. Stanfell) captured the French brig *L'Oreste* off the island of Guadaloupe. The *L'Oreste*

was repaired and added to the Royal Navy as H.M.S. *Wellington.*

RECIPIENTS Lieut. George C. Blake, R.N.; Mid. J.R. Benson; Able seaman Adam Peters; Landman Thos. Hacker Lieuts. Samuel Strong and (?) John Scott. Bosun's Mate Robert Flaxman; Sailmaker William Toms.

Guadaloupe, Jan.-Feb., 1810   45   484

For assisting in the capture of the island of Guadaloupe. From its discovery by Christopher Columbus in 1493 its career, as regards ownership, is a bit difficult to follow, and as its name appears so frequently when dealing with the N.G.S. Medal perhaps collectors will be interested in this very short history.

As a result of its discovery by Columbus, the island was claimed for Spain by Ferdinand and Isabella, who financed his voyage, which incidentally included the discovery of Cuba, the Bahamas, and other West Indian islands. The French took possession in 1635 and spent a considerable sum in colonizing it in time for us to capture it in 1759. In 1763 it was handed back to France, but recaptured again in 1779, 1794 and 1810. After all this trouble it was given to Sweden as an incentive to join the alliance against France. On the ratification of the Treaty of Paris (14th May, 1814) the island was again returned to France, only to be again taken by the British on 10th August, 1815, and yet again restored to France in the following July! Since then it has remained a French possession. It came into the limelight again during 1940 when part of the French fleet took refuge there and had to be demilitarized.

Ships present: Vice-Admiral Sir A. Cochrane's flagship *Pompée* 12/45, and *Abercrombie* 6/18, *Alfred* 6/29, *Alcmène* 5/13, *Asp* 3/7, *Aurora* 1/8, *Amaranthe* 1/5, *Achates* 2/2, *Attentive* -/3, *Bacchus* 1/1, *Ballahou, Bellette* -/1, *Blonde* 4/14, *Castor* 2/9, *Cherub* 3/1, *Cygnet* 1/2, *Eclair* 2/-, *Elizabeth, Fawn* 2/4, *Forester* 1/3, *Freija* 3/15, *Frolic* 1/3, *Gloire* 2/7, *Grenada* 1/-,

	No. of H.M. Ships Engaged	No. of Bars Issued	

Guadeloupe 1/2, *Hazard* 2/5, *Laura* 1/1, *Loire* 5/19, *Melamphus* 4/10, *Morne Fortuné* -/2, *Netley* -/2, *Observateur* 2/4, *Orpheus* 1/15, *Pelorus* 2/5, *Perlen* 4/19, *Plumper* 3/2, *Pultusk* -/1, *Ringdove* 1/3, *Rosamund* 2/7, *St. Christopher* 1/-, *St. Pierre* 1/-, *Savage* 1/-, *Sceptre* 6/34, *Scorpion* 3/5, *Snap* 3/3, *Star* 2/6, *Statira* 5/12, *Subtle*, *Superieure* 2/1, *Surinam* 2/4, *Thetis* 5/6, *Tompee* -/1, *Vimiera* 1/6, *Wanderer* 1/3.

Thistle, 10th Feb., 1810 — 1 — 0

For the capture of the Dutch corvette *Havik* off Bermuda by the *Thistle* (Lieut. Peter Proctor). There were no recipients of this bar.

Surly, 24th April, 1810 — 1 — 1

Firm, 24th April, 1810 — 1 — 1

The correct date for this bar is 20th April, 1810, when the *Surly* (Capt. R. Welch)* and *Firm* Capt. J. Little)* captured the French privateer *Alcide* in Granville Bay, on the east coast of the island of Grenada in the West Indies. H.M.S. *Sharpshooter* was also engaged, but does not appear to have been rewarded, or at any rate there were no claimants for this medal from her.

RECIPIENTS H.M.S. *Surly* — Clerk, Abraham Norster. H.M.S. *Firm* — Pte. Henry Wigley R.M.

Sylvia, 26th April, 1810 — 1 — 1

For the capture of the Dutch ship *Echo* and two transports in the Sunda Sea between Java and Celebes by the *Sylvia* (Lieut. A. Vere Drury).

RECIPIENT Actg. 2nd Master J.C. Chesnaye.

Spartan, 3rd May, 1810 — 1 — 30

Capt. Jahleel Brenton in the *Spartan* was the subject of a special expedition by Murat (one of Napoleon's marshals who had usurped the throne of Naples). Capt. Brenton had been cruising off Naples, causing the Neapolitans a good deal of trouble. Murat sent the frigate *Ceres*, the corvette *Fama*, and several

*The ranks of these officers are various quoted as Lieutenant, Commander and Captain. The name Welch is also found spelt Welsh. The commanding officer's report of this action quoted the date as the 20th Apri, 1810.

	No. of H.M. Ships Engaged	No. of Bars Issued	

small brigs and guboats to destroy the *Spartan*. Events did not materialize as intended by Murat, for the *Ceres*, which had embarked special troops to act as a boarding party, was terribly mauled, the *Fama* sheered off, and one of the brigs, the *Sparviere*, surrendered.

Royalist, 1 3 The correct dates for this clasp should
May and June, 1810   have been Nov. 1809-Feb. 1810. (Capt. G.S. Maxwell) the *Royalist* 1809, was patrolling the Channel on the watch for French privateers. The actions fought by her were with the following five privateers in 1809: *La Princesse* and *Le Grand Napoleon*, 17th November; *L'Heureuse Etoile*, 6th December; *Le Beau Marseille*, 10th December; *Le Francois*, 31st December; and the *Prince Eugène* on the 24th February, 1810. She captured her opponent in each of these actions, but was not engaged during either May or June, 1810.

RECIPIENTS Mid. H.A.D. Thornton, Supn. Pilot Anthony Bowles, and Boy 3rd Class George Selby.

Amanthea, 3 23 The *Thames* (Capt. Hon. G. Waldegrave),
25 July, 1810   *Pilot* (Capt. T. Nicolas) and *Weazel* (Henry Prescott) fought an action with a number of gunboats and destroyed some transports off Amanthea, Calabria, on the "toe" of Italy.

Banda Neira 4 68 Capt. C. Cole in the *Caroline*, together
(9th Aug., 1810)   with the *Piedmontaise* (Capt. Chas. Foote) and the brig *Barracouta* (Cdr. R. Kenah), together with a landing party of 100 of the Madras European Regiment, arrived off the island on the night of 8th-9th August. Early on the 9th the landing parties attacked the batteries and the castle guarding the town, which then surrendered. It seems strange that the forts, mounting a total of nearly 130 guns and over 1,500 defenders, should give in so easily against three ships mounting a total of only 92 guns and a landing party of only 180 seamen, marines and soldiers. Eventually the remaining islands of the Banda

group in the Banda Sea, about 700 miles due north of the Northern Territory in Australia, surrendered, only to be handed back to the Dutch in 1816.

RECIPIENT OF THE SMALL NAVAL GOLD MEDAL Capt. Christopher Cole. The numbers of bars awarded to the three ships were as follows: *Caroline* 35, *Piedmontaise* 20, and *Barracouta* 13.

	No. of H.M. Ships Engaged	No. of Bars Issued	
Staunch, 18th Sept., 1810	1	2	⎫
Otter, 18th Sept., 1810	1	8	⎬
Boadicea, 18th Sept., 1810	1	15	⎭

The *Ceylon* (Capt. Chas. Gordon) sailed from Madras with detachments of the 69th and 89th Foot and Major-General Abercromby on board. When off Réunion she encountered the French frigate *Venus* and corvette *Victor*. The *Ceylon* was forced to surrender. Shortly after, Commodore Rowley in the *Boadicea*, accompanied by the *Otter* (Capt. J. Tomkinson) and *Staunch* (Lieut. B. Street), sighted the *Victor* towing the *Ceylon*, and the *Venus*. released the *Ceylon* and made off, leaving the *Venus* to fight the three ships. Almost as soon as the *Boadicea* engaged her the *Venus* surrendered. She was taken to St. Paul's Bay and renamed *Néréide*.

RECIPIENTS H.M.S. *Staunch* — Actg. Sub-Lieut. R.T. Sainthill, R.N.; Ord. J. Edwards, (also at Malaga 29 April 1812) H.M.S. *Otter* — Actg. Purser F. Taylor; Master's Mate J. McGladery; Ord. J. Sutherland and Ab. John Jeffery; Qtr. Gunner T. Manning; Pte. J. Grassum, R.M.; Boy 2nd Class Owen Hearn and Pte. Benjamin Pratt, 69th Foot. H.M.S. *Boadicea* — Lieuts. Thos. L.P. Laugharne and Edward Lloyd, Actg. Lieut. H.J. Clifford; Mid. Samuel Ramsey, and John Chamberlayne; Ord. Wm. Carey; Able Seaman Wm. Page; L.M. Philip Lamb; Boys 3rd Class Stewart Stocker and James Wilson; Ord. Wm. Taylor; Cpl. Thos. Roberts, R.M.; Ptes. Richard Griffiths, John Borrows and James Swigg, R.M.

	No. of H.M. Ships Engaged	No. of Bars Issued
Briseis, 14th Oct., 1810	1	2

For the capture of the French privateer *Sans Souci* in the North Sea by H.M.S. *Briseis* (Acting Cdr. G. Bentham).

	H.M. Ships Engaged	No. of Bars Issued	
			RECIPIENTS Actg. Cdr. George Bentham, R.N.; and Lieut. George Welsh R.N.
Lissa *(13th March, 1811)*	4	124	The combined French and Venetian fleet, when cruising off Lissa in the Adriatic, was engaged by Capt. W. Hoste in the *Amphion* with the *Active* (Capt. J.A. Gordon), *Cerebus* (Capt. H. Whitby) and *Volage* (Capt. P. Hornby). After a severe fight the three French frigates *Facourite, Danae* and *Flora* and the Venetian ships *Corona, Bellona, Carolina*, and *Mercure* and four small vessels were severely beaten so much so that only the *Danae* and *Carolina* managed to escape capture or destruction. The *Flora* surrendered and then escaped, which in those days was not considered very laudable. The numbers of medals awarded to each ship were Active 44, *Amphion* 34, *Cerebus* 26, *Volage* 20.
			RECIPIENTS OF THE SMALL NAVAL GOLD MEDAL Capts. Sir Wm. Hoste, James Alexander Gordon, H. Whitby, and Phipps Hornby.
Anholt, 27th March, 1811	2	40	Capt. J.W. Maurice, whilst commanding the garrison of 350 Marines and 31 Marine artillerymen on the small island of Anholt in the Cattegat, was attacked by a large flotilla of gunboats and 1,500 Danish troops. No less than 520 Danes surrendered and many were killed. After the attack the *Tartar* (Capt. J. Baker) and *Sheldrake* (Cdr. J. Stewart) chased the fleeing expedition and captured three gunboats and a lugger and a further sixty men. This is a rare bar. (Island commissioned as H.M. Ship. See Master List ADM 37/3513).
Arrow, 6th April, 1811	1	0	For the action fought with French *chasse marées* off the coast of France by the *Arrow* (Lieut. Samuel Knight R.N.). No awards were claimed.
Off Tamatave,	4	87	The *Astaea* 9/15 (Capt. C. Schomberg),

Phoebe 5/17 (Capt. J. Hillier),* *Galatea* 7/15 (Capt. J. Losack), *Racehorse,* 4/9 (Capt. J. de Rippe) and others Vfd. Abd. captured the French frigates *Néréide* and *Renommée*, which were carrying munitions to Mauritius. It is nice to know that the *Renommée* was re-named, this time *Java*, and the *Néréide* was rechristened *Madagascar*.

Hawke, — 1 — 6
18th August, 1811

The *Hawke* (Cdr. Henry Bouchier) captured the French brig *Heron* near Barfleur. This action, according to the commanding officer's report, took place on the 19th August.

RECIPIENTS Cdr. Henry Bouchier R.N.; Lieut. David Price, R.N.; Mid. John Langworthy; Ords. John Keady and Wm. Perkis; Carpenter's Crew John Monteith.

Java — 33 — 695
(4th August - 18th
September, 1811)

For the assistance given by the Navy in capture of the island of Java. This Island, like so many others over which we had spent so much blood and money, was handed back to the Dutch in 1814. The attack on Java provides the only case known of when two ships of the same name were on the same side. In this case there was H.M.S. *Psyche* and the H.E.I. Company's cruiser of the same name.†

For the troops engaged see the Military General Service Medal from page 22 Ships present: Rear-Admiral Hon. R. Stopford's flagship *Scipion* 20/63, and *Akbar* 3/16, *Barracouta* 2/9, *Bucephalus* 2/11, *Caroline* 4/28, *Cornelia* 2/23, *Dasher* 1/2, *Doris* 5/8, *Harpy* 3/11, *Hecate* 2/6, *Hesper* 5/8, *Hussar* 7/33, *Illustrious* 14/52, *Leda* 3/19, *Lion* 10/3, *Minden* 6/37, *Modeste* 3/22, *Nisus* 8/31, *Phaeton* 4/31, *Phoebe* 6/24, *Presidente* 8/41, *Procris* 3/11, *Psyche*, *Samarange* -/8, *Sir Francis Drake* 3/21.

* This officer is quoted as given above and also as Captain T. Hillyar, whilst Captain Losack's initial is found as W. as well as J.

† Captain G. Sayer, of H.M.S. *Leda*, landed in command of a large party of seamen and marines from the *Hesper*, *Illustrious*, *Leda*, *Procris*, and *Scipion*, for which service he received an Army Gold Medal, the only one awarded to a Naval officer. Captain Richard Bunce, R.M., received a similar medal.

No. of H.M. Ships Engaged	No. of Bars Issued	

H.E.I. Company's Cruisers: *Ariel* 1/-, *Aurora* 1/-, *Malabar* 1/-, *Mornington* 1/-, *Nautilus* 1/-, *Psyche*, *Thetis* 1/-, and *Vestal* 1/-.

Skylark, 11th Nov., 1811	1	4 ⎫
Locust, 11th Nov., 1811	1	2 ⎬

For the capture of a French brig off Boulogne, after an action with the Boulogne Flotilla, by the *Skylark* (Cdr. J. Boxer) and *Locust* (Lieut. J. Gedge).

RECIPIENTS H.M.S. *Skylark* — Cdr. James Boxer R.N.; Lieut. W. Walford, R.N.; Boy 2nd Class Wm. Bird, unknown alias aboard or rate Richard Dyer. H.M.S. *Locust* — Lieut. John Gedge, R.N., and Ab. Samuel Bachell.

Pelagosa, 29th Nov., 1811	3	74

For the action off Pelagosa in which the *Active* (Capt. James A. Gordon), *Alceste* (Capt. Murray Maxwell), and *Unité* (Capt. E. Chamberlayne) encountered the French frigates *Pauline* and *Pomone*, which were escorting the store-ship *Persanne*. The *Pomone* surrendered; the *Pauline* escaped to Ancona. The *Persanne* was also trying to escape thither, but was overhauled by the *Unité* and surrendered. In spite of the numerous awards, this is a scarce bar. The distribution of bars is as follows: H.M.S. *Active* 44 *Unité* 19, and *Alceste* 11.

Victorious wh. **Rivoli** (22nd February, 1812)	1	67 ⎫
Weazel, 22nd Feb., 1812	1	6 ⎬

These two bars were given for what was really the same battle, though in a sense each of our two ships fought a separate action. When cruising off Venice, Capt. J. Talbot in the *Victorious*, in consort with the *Weazel* (Cdr. J.W. Andrew), encountered the French 74-gun *Rivoli* and the brig *Mercure*. Whilst the *Victorious* fought the *Rivoli*, the *Weazel* engaged the *Mercure*, which after about an hour, blew up. Having finished off her own adversary so satisfactorily, the *Weazel* then engaged the *Rivoli*, which by then was quite ready to surrender and did so.

RECIPIENTS OF THE SMALL NAVAL GOLD MEDAL Capt. Talbot, of the *Victorious*.

	No. of H.M. Ships Engaged	No. of Bars Issued	
			RECIPIENT OF THE N.G.S. MEDAL H.M.S. *Weazel* — Cdr. J.W. Andrew R.N., Asst. Surg. F. Kiernan; Ord. J. Milly and J. Saxton; Ptes. J. Feather and Wm. Young, R.M.
Rosario, 27th March, 1812	1	7	The *Rosario* (Capt. B. Harvey) and *Griffon* (Cdr. G.B. Trollope) captured two French brigs off Boulogne.
Griffon, 27th March, 1812	1	3	
			RECPIENTS H.M.S. *Rosario* — Surgeon Wm. Watson; Mid. Jas. Rothery; Pilot Jas. Gillman; Purser George Starr; Gnr. John Webber; Actng. Master John Brown; Pte. George Norris, R.M.; H.M.S. *Griffon* — Cdr. G.B. Trollope; Lieut. B. Shepherd, R.N.; Master's Mate C. Price.
Malaga, 29th April, 1812	4	18	The boards from the *Hyacinth* (Capt. T. Ussher), *Goshawk* (Capt. J. Lilburn), *Resolute* (Capt. J. Keenan) and gunboat No. 16 (Lieut. T. Cull), captured the French corsairs *Brave* and *Napoleon* off Malaga, on the south coast of Spain.
			RECPIENTS H.M.S. *Hyacinth* (9) — Capt. Thos. Ussher, R.N.; Clerk J.M. Hoffmeister; Armourer Thos. Wiltshire; Ord. John Andrews; Pte. John Barber, R.M.; Capt. of Foretop Geo. Weeks; Acting Bosun Joseph Bell; Lieut. Thos. Hastings R.N.; Clerk Chas. Blatchley; (Vfd. Abd. Carp's. crew John Edwards with clasp for Staunch 18 Sept., 1810). H.M.S. *Goshawk* (5) — Carpenter Wm. Leaper; Yeoman of Powder Room Chas. File; Master George L. Parrott; Ab. Chas. Shackle; Lieut. Allen Otty R.N.; H.M.S. *Resolute* (3) — Ptes. Richard Bird and John Vassey; and Pte. Marshal Heaviside R.M.
Northumberland, 22nd May, 1812	1	63	The *Northumberland* (Capt. Hon. Henry Hotham) and *Growler* (Lieut. J. Weeks) were detailed to watch for the French frigates *Arienne* and *Andromaque* (*Andromache*?) and the brig *Mamelouc* which had been causing considerable depredations to our merchantmen. They were sighted on their return to port off the Isle de Groix off Lorient. It is rather extraordinary that as a result of the action that followed, all three French
Growler 22nd May, 1812	1	1	

No. of H.M. Ships Engaged	No. of Bars Issued	

ships blew up! In spite of the number issued, the bar to H.M.S. *Northumberland* is rare.

RECIPIENTS H.M.S. *Growler* — Mid. Hy. Edwards. (Mid. Wm. L. Stephens; Ab. Robert Rowe and L.M. Robert Dillon on Growler Roll but all were aboard Northumberland).

Off Mardoe, 6th July, 1812 — 4 — 47

For the destruction of the Danish frigate *Nayaden* and three brigs off Mardoe, on the Norwegian coast, by the *Dictator* (34) (Capt. J.P. Stewart), *Calypso* (7) (Cdr. H. Weir), *Podargus* (5) (Cdr. W. Robilliard) and *Flamer* (1) (Lieut. T. England).

Sealark, 21st July, 1812 — 1 — 4

For the capture of the French privateer *Ville de Caen* off Start Point by the *Sealark* (Lieut. T. Warrand).

RECIPIENTS Lieut. T. Warrand, R.N.; Gnr's. Mate J. Cummings; Ab. Thomas Dunford; Cpl. J. Wakeham, R.M.

Royalist, 29th Dec., 1812 — 1 — 4

For the capture by the *Royalist* (Cdr. G. Downie) of the French privateer *La Ruse* which was then off Hythe.

RECIPIENTS Mid. L. Rees; Coxswain A. Brown. Ab. Henry Hackman; Surgeon W.F. Carter was entitled to this bar, but his name does not appear on the roll.

Weazel, 22nd April, 1813 — 1 — 8

For the destruction of six French gunboats in the Adriatic by the *Weazel* (Cdr. J. Black).

RECIPIENTS Lieut. M. Quinn, R.N.; Asst. Surgeon F. Kiernan; Ords. John Bryan, J. Saxton, and W. Watson. (Also aboard with clasp for Weazel 22 Feb., 1812, Ab. John Milly; Ptes. R.M. James Feather and Wm. Young).

Shannon wh. Chesapeake *(1st June, 1813)* — 1 — 42

Capt. Philip Bowes Vere Broke reconnoitred Boston Harbour, where he found the *Constitution* and *Chesapeake* refitting. He lay off the harbour and sent Capt. Lawrence of the *Chesapeake* a challenge to come out. At noon on 1st June, the *Chesapeake* came out, accompanied by several pleasure boats. The action lasted exactly fifteen minutes. Capt. Broke was severely wounded on board the *Chesapeake* when leading a boarding party. The *Chesapeake* suffered 48 killed and 96 wounded. The *Shannon* was taken out of action by Lieut. Provo Wallis (later Admiral, who died at the age of 101), and Lieut. Falkiner assumed command of the *Chesapeake* and took her to Halifax, where she arrived on 6th June. She was added to the Navy under the same name. This medal is much sought after and commands a high price.

RECIPIENT OF THE SMALL NAVAL GOLD MEDAL Capt. Philip Bowes Vere Broke.

	No. of H.M. Ships Engaged	No. of Bars Issued	
Pelican, 14th August, 1813	1	4	

For the capture of the American brig *Argus*, which had taken the American minister to France and on her way back had caused depradations in the Bristol Channel. The *Pelican* (Cdr. J.F. Maples) sailed from Cork and encountered the *Argus* which had recently captured a Spanish wine ship. It would be unwise to jump to conclusions, but the fact remains that the *Pelican* seemed to have had little trouble in capturing her, during which process she suffered only one killed and five wounded.

RECIPIENTS Mid. Henry Cox (also Gold and Silver Life Saving Medals); Cook F. Fox; Ab. William Baker; Pte. Wm. Maides, R.M.

St. Sebastian (*August-September, 1813*)	18	288	

For assisting in the capture of St. Sebastian. For the troops engaged, see the Military General Service Medal. Some ships' boats were employed in the inner blockade. In many cases the name of their parent ship is not quoted among those of the blockading squadron. Ships present: Captain Sir G. Collier's ship *Surveillante* 4/34, and *Ajax* 13/38, *Andromache* 6/20, *Arrow* 1/1, *Beagle* 1/13, *Challenger* 2/4, *Constant* 2/5, *Dispatch* 2/10, *Epervier* -/1, *Freija* 4/6, *Holly, Juniper* -/5, *Leda* -/1, *Lyra* 4/3,

No. of H.M. Ships Engaged	No. of Bars Issued	

Magicienne 8/14, *Magnificen* -/1, *Nimble, President* 8/21, *Revolutionnaire* 7/24, *Rover* 1/-, *Royalist, Sparrow* 7/5, *Stork* 2/1 and Gunboats Nos. 14 -/2, 16 1/1, 19 1/3, 20 -/1 and 22 -/1; *Racer* 1/-. The following from H.M.S. *Reindeer* which is not given among the list of ships present, received this bar: Lieut. Robert Loney, R.N. (who also received bars for Basque Roads, 1809, and Java). Acting Master Richard Johns; Captain of Forecastle, Joshua Carson; Ordinary Seaman James Wallace. Capt. P. Faddy, R.A., who was on board H.M.S. *Freija*, received the N.G.S. Medal with this bar.

Thunder, 9th Oct., 1813	1	9

For he capture of the French privateer *Le Neptune* off the Owers by the *Thunder* (Cdr. W. Owen Pell).

RECIPIENTS Cdr. W. Owen Pell R.N.; (Had lost his left leg Feb., 1800). Lieut. T.H. McKenzie, R.N.; Mid. Wm. S. Whittmee; Qr. Mr. David Finn; Qr. Mr's Mate Thomas Thompson; Purser C.E. Cotterel; Gunner's Mate James Webb (also aboard with Basque Roads clasp, Ab John Ham, and Ord. John Elmore).

Gluckstadt, 5th Jan., 1814	6	45

For the capture of the Fortress of Gluckstadt, near the mouth of the Elbe, by Capt. A. Farquhar, in the *Desirée*, (24) together with the *Shamrock* (3) (Capt. J. Marshall),* *Hearty* (3) (Capt. J. Rose), *Blazer* (2) (Capt. F. Banks),* *Piercer* (2) (Cdr. J. Kneeshaw), *Redbreast* (2) (Cdr. Sir G.M. Keith), and eight gunboats numbered 1, 2, 3, 4, 5, 8, 10, 12 in *Flotsilla* (9) This is a scarce bar.

Venerable, 16th Jan., 1814	1	42 }
Cyane, 16th Jan., 1814	1	7 }

The *Venerable* (Capt. A.J. Worth) and the *Cyane* (Capt. T. Forrest) captured the French frigates *Alcmene* and *Iphigenia* off the Canary Islands.

RECIPIENTS H.M.S. *Cyane* (7) — Surg. Wm. Aiton; Act. Lieut. Edward Grant R.N.; Mr's. Mate James Thompson;

* The ranks of these officers vary with different histories.

	No. of H.M. Ships Engaged	No. of Bars Issued	

Mid. Daniel Young; Capt. Mast John Truss (who also got the bars for Copenhagen, 1801; *Pique*, 28th March, 1806; Anse la Barque, 18th Dec., 1809; and Guadaloupe). and Supnmy. Boys 2nd Class J. Hurwood, Wm. Scull.

Eurotas,
25th Feb., 1814 — 1 — 32

Captain J. Phillimore in the *Eurotas* captured the French frigate *Clorinde*, off Brest. The *Clorinde* was added to the Navy as H.M.S. *Aurora*. The *Clorinde* actually surrendered to the *Achates*, which, in company with the *Dryad*, arrived on the scene whilst the original contestants had broken apart to repair damage.

Hebrus with L'Etoile
(27th March, 1814) — 1 — 40

On 27th March, 1814, the French frigate *L'Etoile* was returning from the Cape Verde Islands, where she had fought a desperate action with H.M.S. *Creole* and *Astraea*, when she was sighted by the *Hebrus* (Capt. E. Palmer) off the island of Alderney. After suffering over one hundred casualties she surrendered and was added to the Navy as H.M.S. *Topaze*.

RECIPIENT OF A SMALL NAVAL GOLD MEDAL Capt. E. Palmer.

Phoebe,
28th March, 1814 — 1 — 36
Cherub,
28th March, 1814 — 1 — 7

The *Phoebe* (Capt. James Hillyar) and *Cherub* (Capt. T. Tucker) had been cruising up and down the South American coast in search of the American frigate *Essex*, which had destroyed several merchantmen and whaling ships. Early in February, 1814, she was found sheltering in the harbour of Valparaiso with her prizes and a sloop called the *Essex Junior*. Capt. Porter of the *Essex*, having failed in one or two attempts to escape, lay in harbour until 28th March, when a heavy off-shore wind drove him out to sea. The *Essex* surrendered after a short fight. The *Essex Junior* did not take any part in the action, but was captured, together with all the prizes.

RECIPIENTS H.M.S. *Cherub* — Cdr. Thomas T. Tucker, R.N.; Surgeon Peter Ramsay; Supn. L.M. Wm. Crombie; Ord. Wm. Salter; Abe Seaman Thos.

No. of H.M. Ships Engaged	No. of Bars Issued	

Skiddy; Vol. 1st Class John Randall and Boy 2nd Class Jonathan Griffin.

The Potomac,
17th Aug., 1814

8   108

For the destruction of American ships nearly fifty miles up the Potomac river. This is a scarce bar in spite of the number issued.

Ships present: *Aetna* 6, *Devastation* 9, *Euryalus* 30, *Meteor* 4, *Seahorse* 40. Rocket Vessels: *Erebus* 13 and *Fairy* 4. *Regulus* (2) (not present).

Endymion wh.
President
(15th January, 1815)

1   58

The *President* had been blockaded in New York, but, having escaped, was chased by the *Endymion* (Capt. Henry Hope) and brought to action off Sandy Hook. Owing to the *Endymion* having suffered considerable damage to her sails, the *President* managed to get away, but was again brought to action by H.M.S. *Pomone* and *Tenedos*, to whom she eventually surrendered. Whilst taking the prize to Bermuda a terrible gale was encountered and when they eventually arrived the *Endymion* and *President* were practically empty, as everything movable had been jettisoned. The *Endymion* had lost two of her masts and the *President* all three! This is a scarce bar.

The *Pomone* and *Tenedos* were not awarded any bars.

RECIPIENT OF THE SMALL NAVAL GOLD MEDAL Capt. Henry Hope. This was the last Naval Gold Medal issued.

Gaieta,
24th July, 1815

2   89

For the attack on Gaieta, near Naples, by the *Berwick* (Capt. Edward Brace) (49) and *Malta* (Capt. W. Fahie) (37). This, in spite of the numbers issued, is a somewhat scarce medal.

The names of Pte. Ed. Hooper, R.M., and Pte. Wm. Spooner of H.M.S. *Woodlark* appear on my roll, but I cannot trace the presence of this ship. These two names are, however, included in the number 89. Also one award to H.M.S. *Augusta* (Ab. Edward Richmond) which was not present.

	No. of H.M. Ships Engaged	No. of Bars Issued
Algiers *(27th August, 1816)*	26	1,362

For the action off Algiers in which the combined English and Dutch fleets attacked the town. The combined fleets were under the command of Admiral Lord Exmouth, of whom we heard before when he was Capt. Edward Pellew of H.M.S. *Nymphe*, which gained the first bar to the N.G.S. Medal for the action fought on 18th June, 1793, and again as Sir Edward in command of H.M.S. *Indefatigable*, 20th April, 1796, and 13th January, 1797. He commanded H.M.S. *Phaeton* at Java, August and September, 1811. He died on 23rd January, 1833, so consequently did not receive a medal.

There were 19 Military recipients of the N.G.S. Medal with this bar, as follows:

MILITARY RECIPIENTS Rocket Troop, R.H.A. — Lieut. John Thomas Fuller, Sergt. Edward Howe, Ordnance Clerk John Miller (H.M.S. *Minden*); Conductor Edward Sargent, Artificer John Dickenson, Gunner Daniel McLeod (H.M.S. *Queen Charlotte*); Gnr. Joseph Allen (H.M.S. *Granicus*); Sappers and Miners — Lieut. Frederick William Whinyates; Sappers Thomas Jewry and Richard Parry; Drummer Alexander Smith (all H.M.S. *Impregnable*). Capt. William Reid; Lieut. George Hotham; Sergt. Nemen Melville; Sappers James Bond, Thomas Farmer, Alexander McKenzie, Francis Rogers, William Stuart (all H.M.S. *Queen Charlotte*, which had on board 84 men of the 7th Company, 1st Battalion Royal Sappers and Miners).

Ships awarded medals: Lord Exmouth's flagship *Queen Charlotte* 39/193, and *Albion* 18/92, *Beelzebub* 6/12, *Britomart* 4/12, *Cordelia* 4/11, *Dart* 1/-, *Falmouth* 1/3, *Firebrand* -/1, *Fury* 6/8, *Granicus* 10/54, *Glasgow* 22/70, *Hebrus* 8/44, *Hecla* 13/13, *Heron* 5/19, *Impregnable* 21/150, *Infernal* 2/9, *Jasper*, *Leander* 19/85, *Lively* -/1, *Minden* 22/105, *Mutine* 5/19, *Prometheus* 5/16, *Severn* 17/47, *Superb* 26/125.

	No. of H.M. Ships Engaged	No. of Bars Issued	

Navarino
(20th October, 1827)

12   1,137

For the Battle of Navarino, in which the combined fleets of Britain, France, and Russia took part under Vice-Admiral Sir Edward Codrington. Only three or four of the Turkish and Egyptian fleets, numbering over eighty at the start of the battle, were left afloat.

Ships present: Flagship *Asia* 26/202, and *Albion* 21/157, *Cambrian* 11/87, *Dartmouth* 11/90, *Genoa* 24/177, *Glasgow* 15/91, *Talbot* 14/66. Brigs *Brisk* 3/14, *Mosquito* 7/21, *Philomel* 6/23. Corvette *Rose* 5/26. Cutter *Hind* 1/1.

One would particularly value a medal to H.M.S. *Hind* (Lieut. J. Robb), which with ten 6-pdr. guns and a crew of only thirty took on two frigates, a corvette and a brig, and then rammed another frigate for good measure and ended the day with only fifteen of her crew not killed or wounded.

James Hawkins received a medal with this bar and a second medal with a bar for Syria.

The only military recipient of this bar was Lieut.-Colonel John Hobart Cradock for service on board H.M.S. *Asia*. His regiment is not stated.

Syria
(November, 1840)

34   7,057

In 1840, Mehemit Ali, Viceroy of Egypt, broke his agreement to leave Syria alone and invaded it. As Britain, Austria, Russia and Prussia had guaranteed to act in the event of any further trouble, a combined fleet, under Admiral Stopford, was sent to evict him. Acre was bombarded and captured on 3rd November.

Ships present: Admiral Sir Robert Stopford's flagship *Princess Charlotte*, and *Asia, Bellerophon, Benbow, Cambridge, Carysfort, Castor, Daphne, Dido, Edinburgh, Fury, Ganges, Hastings, Hazard, Hecate, Implacable, Lady Franklin, Magicienne, Medea, Pique, Powerful, Revenge, Rodney, Talbot, Thunderer, Vanguard, Wasp, Zebra* and the following steamers, as they were then called: *Cyclps, Gorgon, Hydra, Phoenix, Stromboli*, and *Vesuvius*.

Seventy-two officers and men of the army received the medal with this bar.

ST. JEAN D'ACRE MEDAL, 1840

Obverse	The Turkish flag flying over the Fortress of Acre, six stars and an Arabic inscription. "The country of Syria and the fortress of Acre, 1256."
Reverse	The Sultan's cipher within a laurel wreath.
Size	1·15 in. diameter.
Ribbon	1 1/10 in. wide, pink with white edges.
Naming	The medals were issued unnamed.

For the capture of Acre and services along the Syrian Coast in 1840, the Sultan of Turkey awarded a special medal which was given in gold to Naval Captains and Field Officers and above, in silver to all other officers and warrant officers, and bronze to seamen, marines and soldiers. It was awarded to all who received the N.G.S. bar for Syria except for those who served on board the *Dido, Fury*, and *Lady Franklin* — a distinction for which one is unable to account.

Boat Service Bars

We now come to the bars issued with the Naval General Service Medal for what are termed Boat Actions. The bars are inscribed: "28th AUG. BOAT SERVICE 1809; 28th JUNE BOAT SERVICE 1810"; etc. The words "BOAT SERVICE" separate the month and year. The bars were only sanctioned for occasions on which an officer received promotion, usually the leader of the expedition or action concerned.

As will be seen, more than one boat action took place on some of the dates. In the case of some of the bars no corroborative evidence can be found that any action took place on the dates mentioned.

In the column headed "No. of H.M. Ships engaged" the number of warships is given from which the small boats were supplied.

	No. of H.M. Ships Engaged	No. of Bars Issued	
15th March, 1793	1	1	Boats from H.M.S. *Syren* captured some French guns erected to bombard the fortress of Willemstadt, Holland. RECIPIENT Midshipman The Hon. F.W. Aylmer.
17th March, 1794	28	29	The boats from Admiral Jervis's flagship *Boyne* and the other ships captured the French frigate *Bienvenue* in Fort Royal Bay, Martinique. H.M. Ships engaged: Flagship *Boyne*, and *Alarm, Asia, Assurance, Audacious, Aurora, Avenger, Beaulieu, Blonde, Dromedary, Experiment, Irresistible, Nautilus, Quebec, Rattlesnake, Roebuck, Rose, Santa Margarita, Seaflower, Spiteful, Tormentor, Ulysses, Vengeance, Venom, Vesuvius, Veteran Winchelsea, Woolwich, Zebra.*

No. of H.M. Ships Engaged	No. of Bars Issued	
		The ships to receive awards were: *Veteran* (6), *Boyne* (4), *Irresistible* (4), *Quebec* (3), *Vengeance* (2), *Assurance* (2), and one each to *Alarm*, *Blonde*, *Dromedary*, *Experiment*, *Nautilus*, *Rose*, *Ulysses* and *Vesuvius*.

29th May, 1797 — 2 — 3

The boats of the *Minerve* and *Lively* captured the small French brig *Mutine* at anchor in Santa Cruz Bay.

RECIPIENTS H.M.S. *Minerve* – Lieut. W.H. Gage, R.N.; Actg. Lieut. T.J. Maling R.N., Able Seaman A.B. Blackmore. *Lively* (nil).

9th June, 1799 — 1 — 4

For the action in which boats from the *Success* captured a Spanish polacca* in La Selva Harbour.

RECIPIENTS Lieut. G. Stupart, R.N.; Master's Mate J. Gregory; Ord. Geo. Harding; Pte. Edward Smith, R.M.

20th Dec., 1799 — 2 — 3

The boats of the *Queen Charlotte* and *Emerald* recaptured the British ship *Lady Nelson* off Cabitra. The *Lady Nelson* had been previously captured by 3 French privateers.

RECIPIENTS 2nd-Lieuts. W. Ferguson and T. Peebles, R.M.; A.B., Joseph Perkins.

29th July, 1800 — 2 — 4

The boats from the *Viper*, *Impetueux* and *Amethyst* captured the French brig *Cebère* in Port St. Louis.

RECIPIENTS – *Impetueux* (3) Master's mate Nicholas L. Pateshall, Mid. Henry Hart and L.M. Hugh Dunn. *Viper* (1) Mid. Silas H. Paddon.

29th Aug. 1800 — 9 — 25

Twenty boats from the *Amelia*, *Amethyst*, *Brilliant*, *Courageux*, *Cynthia*, *Impeteux*, *London*, *Renown* and *Stag* attacked and captured the French privateer *Guepe* off Vigo.

27th Oct., 1800 — 1 — 5

Three boats from H.M.S. *Phaeton* captured the Spanish polacca *San Josef* in Fuengirola Harbour, near Malaga.

---

* A polacca is a small three-masted vessel common to the Mediterranean.

	No. of H.M. Ships Engaged	No. of Bars Issued	
			RECIPIENTS Lieut. Francis Beaufort, R.N. (of windscale repute); 2nd-Lieut. D. Campbell, R.M.; Gunner E. Deagon; Master's Mate A.B.P.P. Hamilton; A.B., John Sherrard.
21st July, 1801	5	7	The boats from the *Beaulieu, Doris, Robust, Uraine,* and *Ville de Paris,* captured the French corvette *Chevrette* in Camaret Bay. Of the fifteen boats which left the warships with 280 men, only nine, under Lieut. Maxwell, actually took part in the attack.
			RECIPIENTS H.M.S. *Beaulieu* (1) — Pte. Wm. Beck, R.M.; H.M.S. *Doris* (3) — Capt. Edward Boxer, R.N.; Master's Mate J. Clephan. Sergt. John Inch, R.M. H.M.S. *Uraine* (3) — Yeoman of Sheets J. Morice; Able Seamen J. Barry and R. Biggins.
27th June, 1803	1	5	Two boats from H.M.S. *Loire* captured the French brig *Venteux* off the Isle de Bas.
			RECIPIENTS Lieut. F. Temple, R.N.; Mid. G. Ferguson; Ab. James Cameron and R. Whittaker; Clerk Thomas Bastin (he has the almost unique distinction of receiving two N.G.S. Medals; his other had the following three bars — Boat Service, 4th June, 1805; Off Rota, 4th April, 1808; *Grasshopper,* 24th April, 1808).
4th Nov., 1803	1	1	A boat from the *Blanche* captured a French schooner off St. Domingo.
			RECIPIENTS Mid. Maurice F.F. Berkeley.
4th Feb., 1804	1	10	Four boats from the *Centaur* captured the French brig *Cureux* in Fort Royal Bay, Martinique.
			RECIPIENTS Carpenter's Crew John Messervey; A.B., Joseph Edwards and Henry Manning; Ord. Jeremia Dobson, John James and George Warner; Boy Benjamin Windsor; Ptes. Joseph Back-

No. of H.M. Ships Engaged	No. of Bars Issued	
		house, Richard Church and Robert Cockburn, R.M.
4th June, 1805	1	10	The boats from the *Loire* landed and demolished some forts at Muros, near Cape Finisterre, where the garrison commander and about one hundred men surrendered.

RECIPIENTS Lieut. Charles Bertram, R.N.; Lieut. Joseph Douglas, R.M.; Mid. Richard Connor; Vol. 1st Class John McKillop, Edward Saurin; Ab. James Cameron, Richard Collins and Richard Whitaker; Ord. John Southern; Clerk Thos. Bastin (see bar for Boat Services, 27th June, 1803).

16th July, 1806   9   52

Twelve boats from H.M.S. *Achille,** *Centaur, Conqueror, Indefatigable, Iris, Monarch, Polyphemus, Prince of Wales* and *Revenge* cut out two French corvettes in the River Gironde. The only casualties were suffered by the crew of the *Revenge*.
The number of awards to each ship was as follows: H.M.S. *Achille* 3, *Centaur* 11, *Conqueror* 5, *Indefatigable* 4, *Iris* 3, *Monarch* 12, *Polyphemus* 6, *Prince of Wales* 4, *Revenge* 4.

2nd Jan., 1807   1   3

The boats of H.M.S. *Cerberus* captured two French privateers in St. Peirre Harbour, Martinique.

RECIPIENTS Lieut. W. Coote, R.N.; Mid. G. Sayer and Drummer T. Gilmore, R.M.

21st Jan., 1807   1   8

The boats from the *Galatea* fought the French corvette *Lynx* off Caracas, Venezuela.

RECIPIENTS Ab. Wm. Mills,* Jas. McCarthy,* and John Norris; *L.M. Benjamin Rouse, Wm. Howard and Caulker Thomas Burnett; Ptes. James Williams and M.L. Browning, R.M. (*Had joined from H.M.S. *Diamond Rock* — see Note to *Zebra* 17 March 1794).

*This ship is not mentioned by some historians.

	No. of H.M. Ships Engaged	No. of Bars Issued	
19th April, 1807	1	Nil	The boats of the *Richmond* captured the small Spanish privateer *Galliard* in Paderneira Harbour, Portugal.
13th Feb., 1808	1	2	Two boats from the *Confiance* captured the French gunboat *Canonnier* in the mouth of the River Tagus.

RECIPIENTS Surg. David Lewis; Yeo. of Sheets John Blackman.

10th July, 1808	1	8	The boats of the *Porcupine* captured an armed merchant vessel off Port d'Anzio. This is the same Anzio which became famous for its beach-head in the Second World War. It is about thirty miles south along the coast from the mouth of the Tiber, on which Rome stands. The merchantman was lying under the protection of the batteries of Mount Circio and guarded by two gunboats.

RECIPIENTS Master H. Smartley; Master's Mate H. Parry; Clerk G. Anderson; Vol. 1st Class C.J. Adams; Ab. John Campbell; L.M. G.D. Lane; Pte. Thos. Townsend, R.M.; Boy Francis Johns.

11th Aug. 1808	3	17	The boats of H.M.S. *Brunswick, Edgar* and *Superb* under Capt. J. Macnamara of the *Edgar* entered Nyborg Harbour in the Baltic and captured the small Danish brig *Fama*. Of the seventeen clasps issued, H.M.S. *Brunswick* received two, H.M.S. *Edgar* ten, and H.M.S. *Superb* five.
28th Nov. 1808	1	2	Three boats from H.M.S. *Heureux* captured two French vessels in Mahaut Harbour, Guadaloupe.

RECIPIENTS Lieut. D. Lawrence, R.N., and Carpenter J. Milne.

7th July, 1809	4	35	Seventeen boats containing 270 men from H.M.S. *Bellerophon, Implacable, Melpomene* and *Prometheus* attacked eight Russian gunboats off Percola Point in the Baro Sound, off Finland. The number of bars awarded to each ship were: *Bellerophon* 13, *Implacable* 16, *Melpomene* 5, *Prometheus* 1.

	No. of H.M. Ships Engaged	No. of Bars Issued	
14th July, 1809	1	7	The boats of the *Scout* stormed and captured the batteries commanding the mouth of the River Rhone.
			RECIPIENTS Lieut. John Farrant, R.N.; Mid. John Adams; Capt. of Foretop Thos. Howard; Carpenter Robert Blackmore; Ab. Thomas Atkins, Philip Brown; Pte. James Houlder, R.M.
25th July, 1809	1	Nil	Two separate actions were commemorated by a clasp of this date. No applicants claimed for this affair which involved the cutting out and capture of a French cutter and a schooner in St. Marie Bay, Guadaloupe by boats from H.M.S. *Fawn*.
25th July, 1809	4	36	Seventeen boats from H.M.S. *Cerberus, Minotaur, Princess Caroline* and *Prometheus* attacked four Russian gunboats at Frederikshamm in the Gulf of Finland. The numbers of bars awarded to each ship were: *Cerebus* 4, *Minotaur* 12, *Princess Caroline* 16 and *Prometheus* 4.
27th July, 1809	5	10	This bar was awarded for the attack on French troops and destruction of the forts at Gessendorf, near Cuxhaven, by the boats from H.M.S. *L'Aimable, Briseis, Ephira, Mosquito* and *Pincher*.
			RECIPIENTS H.M.S. *L'Aimable* (3) — Lieuts. John Reeve, R.N.; A.M. Hawkins R.N. and D.J. Thomson, whose rank is not stated. H.M.S. *Briseis* (2) — Lieut. Geo. Welsh, R.N.; Surg. Wm. Hy. Banks. H.M.S. *Ephira* (1) — Cdr. Geo. Ed. Watts. H.M.S. *Mosquito* (2) — Ab. Edward Frost and Pte. Wm. Bird, R.M.; H.M.S. *Pincher* (2) — Lieut. Cdr. Samuel Burgess and Mid. R.E. Cotgrave.
29th July, 1809	3	11	The boats from the *Acorn, Bustard* and *Excellent* entered Duino Harbour, near Trieste, and attacked the batteries covering the harbour. They also captured several fully laden merchant ships which had just arrived in convoy.
			RECIPIENTS H.M.S. *Bustard* (7) — Cdr. J.D. Markland, R.N.; Lieut. John Hilton, R.N.; Purser James Wise; Mr.

Mate Samuel Laston; Ord. Wm. Richards Pte. Thos. Sainsbury, R.M.; and Wm. Wolfe. H.M.S. *Excellent* (4) — Lieut. John Harper, R.N.; Mids. James John Foord and Wm. Prowse; Pte. Thos. How, R.M.

28th Aug. 1809   1   15

The awards were given to the crew of the boats of H.M.S. *Amphion* who stormed a battery at the mouth of the Piave, in the Adriatic and demolished the guns and also captured six Italian gunboats at Cortelazzo.

RECIPIENTS Lieuts. C.G.R. Phillpott, Wm. Slaughter; Surg. John Angas; Mids. Charles Bruce, Chas. H. Kempthorn, Chas. Henry Ross and Joseph Gape. Lieut. Thomas Moore R.M.; Master's Mates John W. Dallings and Thomas Boardman. Capt. of F'c'le Francis Blyth; Yeoman of Sheets David Buchanan; Ord. John Bailey; L.M. Wm. Whisker; Pte. George Weston, R.M.

1st Nov., 1809   8   100

Boats from the *Appollo, Cumberland, Philomel, Scout, Tigre, Topaz, Tuscan* and *Volontaire* attacked a convoy in Rosas Bay, off the extreme north-east coast of Spain. The convoy consisted of five warships and seven merchant vessels all of which were destroyed (Lieut. J. Tailour, R.N.).
This is a rare bar in spite of the number issued.
The number of bars awarded to each ship was: *Apollo* 13, *Cumberland* 18, *Philomel* 5, *Scout* 5, *Tigre* 20, *Topaz* 21, *Tuscan* 4, *Volontaire* 12. In addition to these, Vol. John McDougall and Wm. Waldegrave of H.M.S. *Ville de Paris* were awarded this bar.

13 Dec., 1809   5   9

Boats from the *Achates, Attentive, Bacchus, Pultusk* and *Thetis* captured the French corvette *Nisus* in Hayes Harbour, Guadaloupe.

RECIPIENTS H.M.S. *Achates* (1) — Cdr. Thomas Pinto, R.N.; H.M.S. *Attentive* (2) — Ab. John Ross; Ord. Alexander Underhill. H.M.S. *Bacchus* (1) —

No of H.M. Ships Engaged	No. of bars Issued	
		Mid. William Hole. H.M.S. *Pultusk* (1) — Lieut. John Davis Mercer, R.N. H.M.S. *Thetis* (4) — 2nd Lieut. Jervis Cooke, R.M.; 2nd Lieut. George Ruel, R.M.; Purser Benjamin Soden; Boatswain Daniel Murrey.
13th Feb., 1810	3 20	Three boats from H.M.S. *Christian VII*, three from H.M.S. *Armide* and two from H.M.S. *Seine* destroyed the French ships which were aground off La Rochelle in the Basque Roads. RECIPIENTS H.M.S. *Christian VII* (12) — *Armide* (8), *Seine* (Nil).
1st May, 1810	1 15	A landing party 105 strong from H.M.S. *Néréide* went ashore at Jacotel, in the Bay of Biscay, and destroyed a battery. They then captured a French merchant ship and sailed it out of the harbour.
28th June, 1810	3 27	Boats from the *Active, Amphion*, and *Cerberus* destroyed stores and captured twenty vessels in Grado Harbour, northeast of Venice.
27th Sept., 1810	3 36	Boats from the *Armide, Caledonia* and *Valiant* captured two French brigs off Pointe du Ché, in the Basque Roads. H.M.S. *Armide* received 6 bars, H.M.S. *Caledonia* 19 and H.M.S. *Valiant* 11.
4th Nov., 1810	1 1	Boats from H.M.S. *Blossom* captured the small Spanish privateer *Caesar* off Cape Sicie. RECIPIENT Ord. James Barrington.
23rd Nov., 1810	24† 42	The boats of Rear-Admiral Sir R. Keats's squadron, under command of Capt. R. Hall, attacked the French fleet lying off Point St. Mary during the siege of Cadiz by the French. The siege lasted from 1810 to 1812. It was not until after Wellington's defeat of Marshall Marmont at Salamanca on 22nd July, 1812, and his subsequent entry into Madrid, that Napoleon, already heavily engaged in eastern Europe, decided to withdraw from southern

†Excluding gunboats.

Date	No. of H.M. Ships Engaged	No. of Bars Issued	
			Spain. Historians are inclined to lay emphasis on the parts played by the boats of H.M.S. *Devastation, Aetna* and *Milford*, though it has been impossible to trace any award of medals to the first named. Captain George Landmann, R.E., received the N.G.S. Medal with this bar for his service on H.M.S. *Milford*. *The following* are the names of the ships present, together with the number of bars that can be traced as having been awarded to each: H.M.S. *Achille* 4, *Aetna* 3, *Alfred* 3, *Atlas* 3, *Colossus* 2, Gunboat *Flotilla* 5, *Hardy* 2, *Hound* 2, *Milford* 9, *Norge* 7, *Revenge* 2, *Thunder* 3, and unnamed vessel (1).
24th Dec., 1810	1	6	Boats from H.M.S. *Diana* completed the destruction of the French frigate *Elisa* which was ashore in the La Houge Roads. RECIPIENTS Mid. Julius J.F. Newell; Master's Mate John B. Knocker; Vol. 1st Class Wm. Maxwell; Ship's Corporal George White; Ptes. Noah Brittal and Ambrose Brown, R.M.
4th May, 1811	2	10	Seamen and marines from the *Alceste* and *Belle Poule* destroyed a French brig in Parenzo Harbour, off Istria in the north-east Adriatic. It is interesting to note that although over 300 men took part only 10 bars were claimed. RECIPIENTS H.M.S. *Alceste* (3) — Mid. John King and Chas. Croker; L.M. P. Stanbury. H.M.S. *Belle Poule* (7) — Lieut. Robert B. Boardman, R.N. Mid. Chas. M. Chapman, Abs. Arthur Gros, Geo. Belly; Ord. Geo. Rowcliffe; Ptes. Robert Woodward and James Bowden, R.M.
30th July, 1811	1	4	Capture of Forth Marrack, Java by two boats of *Minden*. RECIPIENTS H.M.S. *Minden* — Lieut. Edmund Lyons, R.N.*; Qr. Gunner Wm. Ellmore; ABs. Stephen Roberts and Wm. Scott.

*Later Naval C-in-C. Crimea

	No of H.M. Ships Engaged	No. of Bars Issued	

2nd Aug., 1811 — 6 — 9

Ten boats containing 117 men from H.M.S. *Alert, Exertion, Princess Augusta, Quebec, Raven* and *Redbreast* entered the River Jade, in north Germany, and captured four French gunboats at Nordeney.

RECIPIENTS H.M.S. *Alert* (1) — Pte. John Smith, R.M.; H.M.S. *Exertion* (1) —Sub. Lieut. Thomas Hare R.N.; H.M.S. *Princess Augusta* (2) — Abs. Edward Wright (or Richmond?), Wm. Russel. H.M.S. *Quebec* (4) — Lieut. Chas. Wolrige R.N.; Master's Mate Robert Cock; L.M. Benjamin Hawkins; Pte. John Tate, R.M.; H.M.S. *Raven* (1) — Carpenter's Crew Wm. Clark.

20th Sept. 1811 — 1 — 6

Boats from H.M.S. *Victory* entered Wingo Sound, in the Baltic, where they captured and brought out two Danish privateers.

RECIPIENTS Lieut. David L. St. Clair; Mid. Edward Purcell; Qtr. Gunner Gabriel Land; AB. Joseph Roston; Ptes. John Bason, Charles Mountford, R.M.

4th Dec., 1811 — 1 — 19

For the capture of the French brig *Languedoc* off Bastia, on the north-east coast of Corsica, by boats from H.M.S. *Sultan*.

4th April, 1812 — 1 — 4

For the capture of a French xebec off Cape de Gatt, south-east Spain, by the boats of H.M.S. *Maidstone*.

RECIPIENTS Master's Mate Wm. Caswell, R.N.; Lieut. A.C. Rea, R.M.; Ord. George Lightbody, Pte. Wm. Smith, R.M.

1 and 18 Sept., 1812 — 1 — 21

A party of sixty-five men from H.M.S. *Bacchante* cut out and captured two French gun-boats, the xebec *Tisiphone* and seven vessels of a convoy.

17th Sept., 1812 — 1 — 11

Boats from H.M.S. *Eagle* attacked coastal trading vessels in the mouth of the River Po in northern Italy, capturing twenty one of them.

RECIPIENTS Lieut. B.M. Festing R.N.; 2nd Lieut. S. Lloyd R.M.; Mate Chas.

No. of H.M. Ships Engaged	No. of Bars Issued	
		Moore; Qr. Mr. Jas. Nicholson; Caulker's Mate Charles Clarke; L.M. Robert Bines; Ord. Chas. Hussey; ABs. Joseph Cemmett, and Samuel Seymour; Ptes. John Good, and Richard Heine.
29th Sept., 1812 2 25		A small party from H.M.S. *Aboukir, Ranger* and gun-boats attacked the booms and batteries guarding Mittau in the Gulf of Riga.
		RECIPIENTS H.M.S. *Aboukir* (24), Gun-boats (1).
6th Jan., 1813 2 25		Boats from the *Bacchante* and *Weazle* attacked French gunboats in Otranto Harbour. H.M.S. *Bacchante* received 23 bars and the *Weazle* only 2.
21st March, 1813 2 3		Boats from the *Blazer* and *Brevdageren* went up the Elbe and captured two Danish gunboats.
		RECIPIENTS H.M.S. *Blazer* — Pte. Charles Whiteman, R.M.; H.M.S. *Brevdageren* — Mid. Frederick Devon; Asst. Surgeon Thos. Davies.
29th April, 1813 1 2		Boats from the *Orpheus* under Lieut. Dance burnt the American ship *Whampoa** off the North American coast.
		RECIPIENTS Lieut. W.F. Dance R.N.; Mid. G.G. MacDonald.

*The *Whampoa* was a "Letter of Marque" and is quoted in some books as Danish, which is probably wrong.

As this is the only occasion on which this term has been listed in actions dealing with the award of medals, perhaps the following account may be interesting.

A "Letter of Marque" is a letter of authority from the owner's government permitting the captain of a private ship to act as a commerce raider against the declared enemy of the government concerned. The crew did not wear uniform and neither was the ship compelled to fly its colours during the engagement, so that it really amounted to a form of licensed piracy. This form of privateering was very prevalent during the early seventeenth century, the Spaniards making particular use of it in their war with Holland.

These "letters" were purchased from the government by the owner for £3,000 when his ship had a crew of over 150 men. Those with smaller crews paid half this sum. The owner reimbursed himself by capturing and bringing into port as many prizes as he could, because he received a percentage of the subsequent sale of his prize and her cargo.

The European powers decided to abolish privateering in 1856, but the Americans refused to agree unless the right of blockade was also abolished. The system was in use during the American Civil War under the authority of the President of the Southern Confederacy, Jefferson Davies. Abraham Lincoln, however, declared it to be piracy and strange to say, on the 19th April, 1861, ordered the blockade of the southern ports.

	No. of H.M. Ships Engaged	No. of Bars Issued	
April and May, 1813 *(29th April and 3rd May, 1813)*	9	56	This bar was given for two separate actions fought on 29th April and 3rd May, both up the Elk river in Chesapeake Bay. The same landing parties under the personal command of Rear-Admiral Sir George Cockburn were engaged in each action. 29th April, 1813: The boats from H.M.S. *Dolphin* (1), *Dragon* (14), *Fantome* (5), *Highflyer* (2), *Maidstone* (3), *Marlborough* (22), *Mohawk* (2), *Racer* (-), and *Statira* (7) went up the river to destroy five American ships and stores. This took until the early hours of the morning of 3rd May. 3rd May, 1813: On the way back to their ships they were fired on by a battery on the banks of the river, so they landed and destroyed it. Two differently dated clasps were issued, early applicants receiving one dated "29 April" later ones were engraved "AP and MAY". The change took place probably to avail confusion with previous Boat Service clasp of similar single dates.
2nd May, 1813	4	48	One hundred marines under Captain M. Ennis, R.M., from H.M.S. *Redwing, Repulse, Volontaire* and *Undaunted* landed in the small harbour of Morgion, near Toulon, and destroyed a battery. In the meantime, another party captured some laden merchant-ships which they sailed out of the harbour (Lieut. Isaac Shaw). The bars were awarded as follows: H.M.S. *Redwing* 4, *Repulse* 16, *Volontaire* 13, *Undaunted* 15.
8th April, 1814	4	24	This bar was given for the destruction of twenty seven vessels and a considerable quantity of stores up the Connecticut river by men from H.M.S. *Boxer, Endymion, Hogue* and *Maidstone*.

One has been unable to trace the earliest use of these letters, but probably some similar system was used as far back as the thirteenth century. There was a very thin line between what we would now call the armed merchantman and the licensed pirate. As long as somebody was having a crack at the actual, or supposed enemy his authority for doing so does not appear to have been very closely investigated!

Privateering and the use of "Letters of Marque" were not universally abolished until 1898.

	No. of H.M. Ships Engaged	No. of Bars Issued	
			RECIPIENTS H.M.S. *Boxer* (2), *Hogue* (15), *Maidstone* (5), *Endymion* (2).
24th May, 1814	1	14	The boats from H.M.S. *Elizabeth* under Lieut. M. Roberts captured the French ship *L'Aigle* off Vide, in Corfu. Some histories quote this action as having been fought on 29th April, 1814.
			RECIPIENTS Lieut. Mitchell Roberts, R.N.; Mid. Edwin Lipscombe; Master's Mate Richard Kearp (Keays?); Carpenter's Crew Daniel McAdam; Ord. John Dearness, John Evans, Henry Taylor; L.M. Wm. Aaron, John Savory, John Stoddard (who also got the bars for Trafalgar and St. Domingo); Henry Towning; Ab. Thos. Robinson; Pte. John Collier, R.M.; and Thos. Gibbons, whose rank is not stated.
3rd and 6th Sept., 1814	1	1	The only bar issued was awarded to Lieut. Andrew Bulger of the Royal Newfoundland Fencible Infantry, which was being blockaded on Lake Huron. The boats from H.M.S. *Nancy* assisted the Regiment to destroy the American schooners *Tigress* and *Scorpion*, and were under the command of Lieut. Miller Worsley. (Lieut. Bulger also received the M.G.S. Medal with bars for Fort Detroit and Chrystler's Farm.)
14th Dec., 1814	22	205	This action, which took place off New Oreleans, was the largest-scale boat action for which awards were given. Prior to capturing the town of New Orleans, the guard-ships had to be destroyed. A fleet of ships' boats, all under the command of Capt. Nicholas Lockyer, carrying about a thousand men altogether, were sent off by Admiral Cochrane to do the job. By capturing one of the enemy's guard ships and using it against the others they eventually destroyed them all.

The boards came from Admiral Cochrane's flagship *Tonnant* 37, and the *Alceste* 8, *Armide* 5. *Asia* 5, *Bedford* 18, *Belle Poule* 2, *Carron* 1, *Cydnus* 9, *Diomede* 5, *Gorgon* 1, *Hydra* 1, *Meteor* 4, *Norge* 17, *Ramillies* 25, *Regulus* 2,

Royal Oak 23, *Seahorse* 21, *Sophie* 11, *Traave* 6, *Weser* 2 and (2) unknown ships.

Lieut. de Lacy Evans of the 3rd (King's Own) Light Dragoons received the N.G.S. Medal with this bar for service on H.M.S. *Meteor* — he was later to command The British Legion in the Cardish War (1835-40).

This concludes a short summary of all the bars awarded with the N.G.S. Medal, and it gives ample proof, though none is needed, of the extraordinary versatility of the Navy. A study of the brief descriptions will show that the destruction of dreams of world conquest or a shore battery were all in a day's work.

When reading the full account of all the actions mentioned, one is amazed at the hardships which the sailors of those days had to endure. One reads not once, but scores of times, of men with the most terrible wounds undergoing amputations without any anæsthetic, of being on deck when their ship has received broadsides at pistol or even half pistol range. They cleared away broken masts and rigging within a few yards of the enemy. No finer example of the range at which these fights took place can be given than the reminder that the greatest Admiral in our history in the most important naval action in which we have ever been involved received his mortal wound from a musket-ball fired from the mizen-top of one of the enemy's ships.

Reading these accounts one realizes that even today we are using, or have used, many ideas which are only elaborations of what these men were using. They had their hand grenades, incendiary shells, landing barges, convoys, rockets and many other ideas which we are inclined to think originated in the 1914-1918 or 1939-1945 wars.

41 THE NEPAUL WAR MEDAL (1814-1816)

Obverse	A scene of hills and stockades; on the left is a field gun.
Reverse	A Persian inscription.
Size	2in. diameter.
Ribbon	The medal was suspended from either a ribbon or cord of no specified colour in a similar manner to the medal for Seringapatam (see No. 25).
Suspension	A loop is riveted to the top of the piece through which the ribbon or cord is threaded.
Designer	The dies were engraved and the medals struck at the Calcutta Mint.
Naming	It was issued unnamed.

The issue of this silver medal (300 thought to have been awarded) was sanctioned by a General Order, signed at Fort William on the 20th March, 1816, for award to native troops who had shown zeal and gallantry. The British troops who took part received the Army of India Medal with the bar Nepaul, as did the native troops who were not awarded the Nepaul War Medal. For the regiments present see the bar for Nepaul awarded with the Army of India Medal 1799-1826 (No. 44).

Nepaul was first conquered by the Gurkhas in 1768 and treaties of friendship were signed between them and the British in 1791 and 1801. In spite of these, however, they made continuous raids over the border until it became necessary to invade their country.

War started on the 1st November, 1814, and ended on the 27th April, 1815, and a new treaty was signed on the 2nd December, 1815, but in January, 1816, trouble broke out again and a further expedition under Major-General Sir David Ochterlony, K.C.B., was sent into the country.

After battles at Mukwampore and Sierapore the Rajah of Nepaul sued for peace and a further treaty was concluded on the 4th March, 1816. After this treaty Prince Jung Bahadoor came to London and opened an embassy.

The Nepaulese remained loyal during the Mutiny and since then the bravery and devotion of the Gurkhas has never failed to earn the admiration of all.

42 THE CEYLON MEDAL (1818)

Obverse	The inscription "CEYLON 1818" surrounded by a wreath.
Reverse	The name of the recipient in the centre surrounded by the inscription "REWARD OF MERIT".
Size	1.5 in. diameter.
Ribbon	1.5 in. wide blue ribbon.
Designer	The medals were issued by the Ceylon Government. It has not been possible to ascertain who actually designed them.
Naming	On the reverse of the medal as described above.

The silver medal was awarded for gallant conduct during the Kandian Rebellion — only forty-five were issued.

Regiments present: 73 Foot and 1 and 2 Ceylon Regiment.

43 THE BURMA MEDAL (April, 1824-February, 1826)

Obverse	The elephant of Ava crouching before the British Lion.
Reverse	A scene of the storming of the Pagoda at Rangoon, the Irrawaddy flotilla and General Campbell directing the attack from under a palm tree.
Size	1.5 in. diameter.
Ribbon	1.5 in. wide, crimson with blue edges.*
Designers	Obverse W. Daniell, R.A. Reverse W. Wyon, R.A.
Suspension	Either by means of a ring attached to a steel clip which passes through the piece or by a suspender similar to the one illustrated.
Naming	The medal was issued unnamed.
No. of bars issued	Nil.

This medal was sanctioned at Fort William on the 22nd April, 1826. It was issued in gold and silver; about 750 of the former were awarded to native officers and officials and about 24,000 silver ones to native troops from Bengal and Madras. Some silver medals were probably also issued to the members of the Royal Indian Marine present.

*This was the first ribbon issued by the Honourable East India Company.

For a complete list of the British troops and units of the Royal Navy and Royal Indian Marine see the bar for Ava awarded with the Army of India Medal, which follows immediately (No. 44).

Native Regiments present: 1 Madras Cavalry; 4, 5, Bengal Artillery; 2 Madras Artillery; 1st Company Bombay Foot Artillery; 1, 3, 7, 8, 9, 10, 16, 2/17, 18, 22, 26, 28, 32 Madras N.I.; 2, 7, 14, 26, 39, 44, 45, 49, 52 Bengal N.I.; 61 Native Pioneers; Native Levies.

The war in Ava, as it is generally called, was caused by the continual depredations of the Burmese into Sylhat and Cachar.

A force was organized under Brigadier-General Sir Archibald Campbell to capture Rangoon and blockade the Irrawaddy river, whilst another one under Brigadier-General Morrison advanced through the Aracan.

The length of the war was mainly caused by the difficult nature of the country, rain, fog, inundations and the difficulty of maintaining supplies, not to mention the stout resistance of the Burmese.

Most of the fighting took place in the neighbourhood of Rangoon. The following nine battles were fought:

1824: Kemmendine, 10th June.

1825: Syriam, 12th January; Bassein, 24th February; Aracan, 1st April; Donabew, 2nd April; Prome, 1st December.

1826: Melloon, 13th January; Moulmein, 28th January; Pagham Mew, 9th February.

44 ARMY OF INDIA MEDAL (1799-1826)

Obverse	The diademed head of Queen Victoria with the legend "VICTORIA REGINA."
Reverse	A seated figure of Victory holding a laurel branch in her right hand and a wreath in her left. In the left background is a palm tree. Around the top is the wording "TO THE ARMY OF INDIA". In the exergue are the dates "1799-1826".*
Size	1.42 in. diameter.
Ribbon	1.25 in. wide of light blue.
Suspension	By an ornate swivelling suspender.
Designer	W. Wyon, R.A.
Naming	In indented capitals similar to the M.G.S. to British troops. In either indented capitals or script to natives.
No. of bars issued	21.

An Order dated the 21st March, 1851, authorized the East India Company to issue a medal to all survivors (and this point must be remembered) who served in India between 1799 and 1826 It should be noted that the first action commemorated was that of Allighur, fought on the 4th September, 1803. A similarity occurs here with the M.G.S. and N.G.S. medals in that Queen Victoria was not born when many of the actions were fought and the date of the first action not agreeing with the first date in the exergue.

The order of the bars is different from most medals in that the last award is placed nearest the piece — *i.e.,* the correct order reads downwards. The medal was not issued without a bar.

*Medals are to be found on which the length of the hyphen between the dates varies. Those with the long hyphen are thought to have been sent out to India unnamed and were then named in Calcutta and issued to those serving or living in India when the claims were made. Those with a short hyphen with the designer's initials "ww" were mostly issued to the Queen's Ships and Regiments.

The greatest number of bars on any one medal was on that awarded to Drummer William Colston, who received the following seven: Allighur, Battle of Delhi, Laswarree, Battle of Deig, Capture of Deig, Nepaul, and Bhurtpoor. He served with the 2/15th Bengal Native Infantry in all the actions. Three were issued with six bars, nine with five bars and twenty-four with four bars.

As is only natural when twenty-one bars were issued, there are a great variety of combinations in existence and medals with three or more bars are extremely rare. The Army of India medal roll compiled by Major G.H. Edwards, M.B.E., gives a full list of European recipients as well as an extensive summary of combinations etc. However this has been partly superceded by a further roll compiled by Mr. R.W. Gould and Captain K.J. Douglas-Morris, R.N.

The Duke of Wellington received bars for Assaye, Argaum and Gawilghur, of which combination only thirteen were issued. Glazed silver gilt specimens of this combination appear on the market.

The records of medals awarded to native troops are very sketchy indeed and therefore all figures quoted should be treated as guides rather than facts.

It is curious to note that whilst the bars for Ava and Bhurtpoor are the commonest, only the following twelve medals were awarded with this dual combination:

Lieut. David Williams	Sub-Assistant Commissariat General.
Assistant Surgeon William Mitchelson	Field Hospital.
Lieut. E.C. Archbold	8th Cavalry.
Lieut. R.G. MacGregor	Artillery.
Brevet Capt. G.T. Finnicane	14th Foot.
Lieut. Francis Hawkins	44th Foot.
Lieut. A.R.J. Swinton	22nd and 3rd N.I.
Capt. R. Seymour	26th N.I.
Capt. George Chapman	36th N.I.
Capt. James Steel	41st N.I.
Lieut. W.C. Ormsby	63rd N.I.
Lieut. E. M. Orr	58th N.I.

Lieutenant J.C.C. Gray, 1st Grenadiers and 21st N.I., was awarded the medal with three bars, Nepaul, Ava and Bhurtpoor.

It seems to have escaped the notice of many collectors that the medal was not issued for one campaign, though a reference to the dates of the actions for which it was awarded cover a period of twenty-three years!

Much fighting had taken place between the times of the battles commemorated by the medal and the date of its issue, to survivors only, so that the number of recipients is very small compared with those involved.

The medals to the 76th Foot are particularly interesting, as they were the only European regiment present under General Lake in the Second Mahratta War, 1803-4. Five men of this regiment received medals with five bars, Allighur, Battle of Delhi, Laswarree, Battle of Deig, Capture of Deig, and four received four bars (Allighur, Battle of Delhi, Laswarree, Battle of Deig). Surgeon C. Corfield of the regiment received the bars for Allighur, Battle of Delhi and Laswarree.

SECOND MAHRATTA WAR, 1803-4*

At this time, native rajahs had their own armies, among the most powerful of which were those of Holkar of Indore, Peshwa of Poona, Scindiah of Gwalior,

---

*The First Mahratta War, for which the Deccan Medal was awarded, took place 1778-84. See No 19.

the Rajah of Berar and the Guicowar of Baroda. These armies were trained by foreigners, mostly Frenchmen. They had their own artillery together with all the, then implements of war. Holkar, the most powerful, had defeated the others and then invaded British territory. Lord Lake, the Commander-in-Chief, crossed the Mahratta border on the 7th August, 1803. The first encounter was at Allighur where Colonel Pedron,* a Frenchman, commanded the garrison. Holkar's forces were then heavily defeated in front of Deig. They took refuge in Deig, where they were assisted by the Rajah of Bhurtpore's forces until an attack seemed imminent, when the whole garrison withdrew. Peace was concluded with Holkar shortly afterwards.

NEPAUL WAR, 1814-16

The bar for Nepaul was given for the campaign already referred to when dealing with the Nepaul War Medal, No. 41, *quod vide*.

PINDAREE, OR THIRD MAHRATTA WAR, 1817-18

In November, 1817, it was found that the Peishwar was inciting trouble among the natives in Poona and was also threatening to attack it. The garrison, under Colonel Burr, was moved out to Kirkee. Then, on the principle that attack is the best defence, the Mahrattas were attacked. They retired on Poona, which was attacked by the combined forces of Colonel Burr and Brigadier-General Lionel Smith, who had arrived with reinforcements. The Peishwar abandoned the city and retired southwards.

Without any warning at all, the Rajah of Berar suddenly attacked the garrison at Seetabuldee. This was a small fortified hill post on the outskirts of Nagpore. At the same time he took up a position in and around Nagapore. The garrison at Seetabuldee, under Colonel Scott, withstood the attack. When Brigadier-General Doveton arrived with reinforcements, the Rajah pretended to surrender, but occupied Nagpore and had to be driven out.

Just prior to the attack on Seetabuldee by the Rajah of Berar, Holkar assembled a large army at Maheidpoor. He was attacked and heavily defeated by General Hislop.

After being driven out of Poona by Colonel Burr, on the 16th November, the Peishwar remained in the district. Colonel Burr, fearing another attack, sent for reinforcements from Seroor, fifty miles away. Captain Staunton, with a small force of natives, was on his way to Poona, when he encountered the Peishwar's army of nearly thirty thousand men. He took up a position in the village of Corygaum where he put up a superb defence.

WAR IN AVA, 1824-6

This bar was awarded for the campaign in Burma which I dealt with under the Burma Medal, No. 43, *quod vide*.

SIEGE OF BHURTPORE, DECEMBER, 1825-JANUARY, 1826

Doojan Sal, the nephew of the late and friendly Rajah Baldeo Singh, usurped the throne which the British had agreed should go to Baldeo Singh's son. Repeated remonstrances having produced no result, the city was attacked by Lord Combermere. After heavy fighting it surrendered.

---

*Readers have written to say that this name should be Perron, but they are probably confused by the similarity of names. Perron was the Frenchman who commanded the Scindian army. At the time of the occupation of Allighur he had withdrawn to Agra, leaving his subordinate, Colonel Pedron, to hold the fortress.

Allighur *(4th September, 1803)*

Regiments present: 27 (20), 29 (14) Light Dragoons; 1, 2, 3, 4 Bengal Cavalry; 76 (20), Foot; 4 (1), 1/15 (3), 17 Bengal N.I. H.E.I.C. Arty.

The assault on this fortress was carried out by four companies of the 76th Foot, 1/4, 2/4, 2/12, 1/15, 2/15, four companies 17 Bengal N.I. and two guns of the Bengal Artillery. The 27th Light Dragoons also received casualties. A total of 66 bars awarded to Europeans (none as singles).

General Mossom Boyd received a medal with bars for Allighur, Battle of Delhi and Laswarree.

The latter medal and that awarded to Sepoy Sunkhar Bhowun, 23 N.I., are the only ones with this single bar that have come to notice.

Battle of Delhi *(11th September, 1803)*

Regiments present: 27 Light Dragoons (20); 2, 3 Bengal Light Cavalry; 76 Foot (18); Pioneers; 1/2, 2/2, 1/4, 2/4, 2/8, 2/9, 1/12, 2/12, 1/14, 1/15, 2/15, 2/16 Bengal N.I. Four companies of the 2/17 Bengal N.I. were acting as baggage guard and took no part in the fighting.

There is an impressed medal to Newal Singh Jagarnath, Pioneer, with this bar and another medal with this bar and Capture of Deig to Sepoy Kedar Nath of the 30th N.I., which was then numbered 1/15 N.I.

Two medals were awarded to Europeans as a single bar. They were awarded to J. Cook, 27 Light Dragoons, and H.S. Montagu, 15 N.I. 58 bars in all awarded to Europeans.

Lieutenant Curzon, 6 Light Cavalry, was awarded bars for Battle of Delhi, Capture of Deig, Nagpore and Bhurtpore, but he must have been serving with some other regiment at the time.

There is a medal named to Sepoy Kedah Nath which has appered with bars for Battle of Delhi, Laswarree and Capture of Deig or, more modestly, with only those for Battle of Delhi and Capture of Deig which has never been verified.

Assaye *(23rd September, 1803)*

This battle, which is spelt Assye on the bar, was the first of Major-General Arthur Wellesley's great victories. With about 4,000 troops he routed the Rajah of Berar's forces of over 50,000.

Regiments present: 19 Light Dragoons (10); 4, 5, 7 Madras Cavalry; 3rd, 5th Companies Bombay Artillery; Madras Pioneers; 74 (15), 78 (34) Foot. The following are the only native infantry that actually took part in the attack: 1/2, 1/4, 1/10, 2/12 Madras N.I.

This bar was awarded singly to ten Europeans. Eighty-eight in all were awarded to Europeans. The sole occasion on which it was awarded in conjunction with other bars to this medal, one of which was not that for Argaum, was in the case of the medal to John McGough, 78 Foot, who received bars for Assye and Gawilghur. This is a unique medal and, incidentally, he also received the Military General Service Medal with the bar for Java.

Medals with single bars to Armourer C. Skeet and P. Dougherty, 78 Foot, are not contained in the roll, whilst one to Sepoy Kabad Rama (or Ramu) with bars for Assye and Nagpore is suspect!

Asseerghur *(21st October, 1803)*

It is difficult to understand why this rare bar, of which only forty-eight were awarded, was sanctioned, as the fort surrendered without being attacked, after an hour's bombardment.

Regiments present: 3, 6 Madras Cavalry; 94 Scotch Brigade (40) (which later became the 2nd Bn. The Connaught Rangers); 2/2, 5, 1/6, 2/7, 2/9, 1/11, 2/11, 19 Madras N.I.; 2 Madras Pioneers.

Major J.L. Basden, 89th Foot, received a medal with this bar and those for Argaum, Gawilghur and Ava; he was serving with the Scotch Brigade as a Lieutenant at the time.

Laswarree *(1st November, 1803)*

8 (28),* 27 (18), 29 (14) Light Dragoons; 1, 2, 3, 4, 6 Bengal Light Cavalry; Bengal Artillery*; 76 Foot (17)*; 1/2, 2/2, 1/4, 2/4, 2/8, 2/9, 1/12, 2/12,* 2/15, 2/16,* 2/17 Bengal N.I. One hundred bars were awarded to Europeans.

There is a medal to Lieutenant-Colonel Parlett Starling, 32nd N.I., then numbered 2/16th Bengal N.I., with this bar and that for Bhurtpoor.

Argaum *(29th November, 1803)*

This is an extremely rare bar, of which only 126 were awarded to Europeans. The Artillery, 74th, 78th Foot and 2nd N.I. received bars for Assye, Argaum, and Gawilghur on one medal.

Regiments present: 19 Light Dragoons (10); 3, 4, 5, 6, 7 Madras Cavalry; 3rd, 5th Companies Bombay Artillery; Madras Artillery. two companies Bombay Pioneers; 74 (15), 78 (33), 94 (40) Foot; 1/2, 2/2, 1/3, 2/3, 1/6, 2/7, 1/8, 1/11, 2/11, 2/12, 2/18 Madras N.I.

Gawilghur *(15th December, 1803)*

This is an extremely rare bar of which only two single ones and one hundred and ten in all were issued to Europeans.

Regiments present: 19th Lt. Dragoons (7); 74 (14), 78 (25), 94 (37) Foot; 1/2, 2/2, 1/3, 2/3, 1/6, 2/7, 1/8, 1/11, 2/11, 2/12, 2/18 Madras N.I.

Defence of Delhi *(8th-14th October, 1804)*

I have only been able to trace five of these bars to Europeans. The first was awarded to Lieutenant-General Sir John Rose, K.C.B., who was serving as Lieutenant and adjutant of the 2/14 N.I. at the time. The second was awarded to General Edmund Frederick Waters, who was serving as a lieutenant in the 2/17 N.I. at the time. He also received the bar for "Battle of Delhi". The third was awarded to Virzhall Tulsidass of the Sappers and Miners. The fourth, together with that for "Capture of Deig", was awarded to Lieutenant Sir A. Galloway, 2/14 N.I. The fifth to C.J. Davis, 4th Bengal Lt. Cav.

No British regiments took part in the defence. The regiments present were the following: 2/4, 2/14, 2/17, 1/21 Bengal Native Infantry. 3rd and 4th Ben. Ltd. Cav.

Battle of Deig *(13th November, 1804)*

Medals with this bar are extremely rare. Only forty-seven were awarded, eight as single bars (to Europeans).

Regiments present: 2, 3 Bengal Light Cavalry; Bengal Horse Artillery; 76 Foot (20) and 1 Bengal European Regiment (10) (later to become the 1st Bn. Royal Munster Fusiliers); 1/2, 1/4, 7, 1/8, 1/12, 2/15, 2/22 Bengal N.I.

*These were the only units to sustain any casualties.

Capture of Deig *(11th-23rd December, 1804)*

Regiments present: 8 (38), 27 (8), 29 (8) Light Dragoons; 2, 3, 6 Bengal Light Cavalry; two companies each of 22 (8) and 76 (16) Foot; 1 Bengal European Regiment (1); 1/2, 1/4, 1/8, 1/12, 2/12, 1/15, 2/15, 2/22 Bengal N.I. One hundred and three bars were awarded to Europeans.

Nepaul *(October, 1814-March, 1816)*

Natives who had received the H.E.I. Co. Medal (see No. 41) did not receive this bar, which was only issued to those who had taken part in actual fighting and not to those who were merely in Nepaul during the campaign.

Regiments present: H.E.I.C. Horse Arty.; 8 Light Dragoons (14); Skinner's Horse; Gardner's Horse; 2 Rohilla Cavalry; 2, 6, 7, 8 Bengal Cavalry; 14 (12), 17 (53) 24 (96), 53 (14), 66 (90), part of 67 (7), 87 (53), Foot; 1/1, 1/2, 2/2, 2/3, 2/4, 1/5, 2/5, 1/6, 2/6, 1/7, 2/7, 1/8, 2/8, 1/9, 2/9, 1/10, 2/10, 1/11, 1/12, 2/12, 1/13, 1/14, 2/14, 1/15, 2/15, 1/16, 1/17, 2/17, 1/18, 2/18, 2/19, 1/21, 2/21, 1/22, 2/22, 2/24, 1/25, 2/25, 1/26, 1/27, 1/30 Bengal N.I. A total of five hundred and five were issued to Europeans.

Kirkee *(5th November, 1817)*

These are extremeley rare bars of which I have only traced five to Europeans (all single bars). They were awarded to Cornet F. Hunter, 1st Cavalry; Joseph Morgan, 65th Foot (the only bar awarded to this regiment); W. McKenzie, Bombay European Regiment; Sepoy Gopal Bhave, 7th Bombay N.I.; Sepoy Nadir Rai, 12th Bombay N.I.

Regiments present: Detachment of 6th Company Bombay Artillery; small detachments of Madras Artillery and Pioneers; detachment of 65 Foot (1); Bombay European Regiment (2); 2/1, 2/6, 1/7 Bombay N.I.; Dapuri Battalion.

Poona *(11th-16th November, 1817)*

Only forty-two bars issued to the 65th Foot and thirty-three to other Europeans.

Regiments present: 14 (2); 65 (42) Foot; Bombay European Regiment (5); 2/1, 1/2, 1/3, 1/4, 2/6, 1/7, 2/9 Bombay N.I.; Madras and Bombay Pioneers; H.E.I.C. Arty.

T. Curtis and J. Strong, 38th Foot, who was serving with the 65th Foot at Poona, received a medal with this bar and that for Ava.

Kirkee and Poona *(5th-16th November, 1817)*

Sixteen of these single bars were awarded to the 65th Foot and seventy-two to other Europeans.

Regiments present: 65 Foot (16); Bombay European Regiment (46); 2/1, 2/6, 1/7 Bombay N.I.; H.E.I.Co. Arty.

Seetabuldee *(26th-27th November, 1817)*

This bar is extremely rare, only one was awarded to Europeans (W. Pegge, Arty.).

Regiments present: Madras Bodyguard; 6 Bengal Cavalry. Detachment of Madras Artillery; 1/20, 1/24 Madras N.I.; 61 Native Pioneers.

Nagpore *(16th December, 1817)*

Only one hundred and fifty-five were awarded to Europeans.

Regiments present: 6 Madras Nat. Cavalry; 6 Bengal Nat. Cavalry (6); Madras

Horse and Foot Artillery; 2/1 Foot (95); 1/2, 1/11, 1/12, 2/13, 2/14, 1/20, 1/22, 2/24, Madras N.I.; 6, 1/22 Bengal N.I.; 61, 81 Native Pioneers.

Seetabuldee and Nagpore (*26th − 27th November and 16th December, 1817*)

A total of twenty-one bars were awarded to Europeans serving in the 3rd 26th Bengal Cavalry, 20, 24 and 28 Madras N.I.; Artillery and Staff.

The 1/24 Madras N.I. were later renumbered 1/1 and medals to them are so numbered.

Maheidpoor (*21st December, 1817*)

Regiments present: 22 Light Dragoons (29); 3, 4, 8 Madras Cavalry; Mysore Horse; Madras Horse Artillery and Rocket Train; 1 Foot (38); Madras European Regiment; 1/3, 2/6, 1/14, 2/14, 1/16 Madras N.I.; Detachment of 22 Bengal N.I.

Corygaum (*1st January, 1818*)

This bar was issued to Europeans once only as a single medal and three times in conjunction with others. The total strength of the garrison, when attacked by three divisions, was only about 600.

Regiments present: Madras Artillery; Poona Auxiliary Horse; 2/1 Bombay N.I. 2nd Native Inf.

The four Europeans who received this bar, were: Pte. G. Bainbridge of the 65th Foot, who also got the bar for Poona. He must have been attached to a staff officer. Asst. Surgn. J. Wylie; J. Nicholas, Bombay Rifle Corp., and C. Swanston, Poona Aux. Horse.

Ava (*1824 − 1826*)

No native troops received this bar, as they were given the H.E.I. Company's medal for Burma, 1824-26 (No. 43). European officers of native regiments did, however, receive it: 2,325 bars were awarded.

Regements present: 1 (117), 13 (109), 38 (115), 41 (150), 44 (96), 45 (120), 47 (173), 54 (76), 87 (189), 89 (203) Foot: 1 Madras European Regiment (104).

Three hundred and thirteen medals were awarded to the R.N., the approximate numbers to each ship were: H.M. ships: *Alligator* (29), *Arachne* (25), *Bodicea* (59), *Champion* (19), *Larne* (30),* *Liffey* (48), *Slaney* (33), *Sophie* (26), *Tamar* (20), *Tees* (14). Fifty three medals to members of Bombay Marine in the following vessels. (The numbers shown are approximate, since many men served in two or more vessels: − *Amhurst* (−), *Arracan Flotilla* (4), *Asseerghur* (2), *Diana* (−)*, *Ellen* (−), *Emma* (1), *Ernaard* (1), *Exeter* (1), *Flora* (1), *Feudall* (−), *Goliath* (−), *Gunga Saugor* (−), *Gun Boats* (3), *Hastings* (3), *Helen* (−), *Henry Meriton* (1), *Investigator* (2), *Margaret* (1), *Matchless* (2), *Mercury* (2), *Narcissa* (1), *Nereide* (1), *Ness* (−), *Planet* (−), *Pluto* (1), *Prince of Wales* (1), *Psyche* (−), *Research* (1), *Sophia* (1), *Surma* (−), *Teignmouth* (6), *Ternate* (1), *Thetis* (5), *Trusty* (−), *Transports* (2), *Tyzer* (−), *and Vestal* (3).

*It is interesting to recall that H.M.S. *Diana* was the first steam warship to go on active service, and the H.M.S. *Larne* was commanded by Commander Marryat, the famous author.

Bhurtpoor (*Siege of, 17th-18th January, 1826*)

Regiments present: 8th Light Dragoons (2), 11 Light Dragoons (190); 16 Lancers (178); 3, 4, 6, 8, 9, 10 Bengal Cavalry; Bengal Horse and Foot Artillery; Bengal S. & M.; 14 (266). 59 (185), Foot; 1 Bengal European Regiment (90); 6, 11, 15, 18, 21, 23, 31, 33, 35, 36, 37, 41, 44 (1), 58, 60, 63 Bengal N.I.; one hundred men from each of the Nusseeree* and Sirmoor Bns. of Goorkhas. 1,059 medals were awarded to Europeans.

45 COORG MEDAL (April-May, 1837)

Obverse	A Coorg holding a knife in his raised right hand and a musket in his left, and a Canarese inscription around the perimeter, "A MARK OF FAVOUR GIVEN FOR LOYALTY TO THE COMPANY'S GOVERNMENT IN SUPPRESSING REBELLION IN THE MONTH OF APRIL AND MAY, 1837."
Reverse	Some war trophies and the inscription "FOR DISTINGUISHED CONDUCT AND LOYALTY TO THE BRITISH GOVERNMENT." At the bottom is "COORG APRIL 1837."
Size	1.97 in. diameter and of various thicknesses.
Suspension	Medals awarded to officers were suspended from chains which passed through a loop in the piece. Medals awarded to other ranks were suspended from a cord of no specified colour.
Designer	The dies were engraved and the medals struck at the Calcutta Mint.
Naming	They were issued unnamed.

Only forty-four gold and three hundred silver medals were issued to natives who remained loyal during the Canara rising. Some of these medals are to be found with a decided flaw in them as if made from a cracked die.

Copper specimens occasionally apeear which, in some cases, give the appearance of having been worn. None were officially awarded and the only inference can be that they are copies.

The order authorizing this medal was dated the 28th August, 1837.

THE FIRST AFGHAN WAR, 1839-42

The following is the historical detail forming the background of medals No. 46, 47, 48, and 49.

The medals awarded for this war consist of the Ghuznee Medal, the Candahar, Ghuznee and Cabul series of Medals, the Jellalabad Medal and one for the Defence of Khelat-i-Ghilzie, all of which follow immediately.

The historical reasons for their award are so correlated that a brief account of the war will show why so many medals were given. We must remember that at this time the principle of awarding bars had not been instituted, though at a later date medals were issued to commemorate actions fought prior to those to which we shall now refer.

Afghanistan was considered a "Buffer State" between India and Persia, so that it was necessary for the tranquillity of the former that whosoever ruled in Afghanistan should be strong and above all friendly.

The ruler at the time was Shah Soojah-ool-Moolk, who was weak and thoroughly unpopular. He was driven out by the Persians under Prince Mahomed

---

*This name is found spelt Nusseeree, Nusuree and Nasiri.

Khan, who then proceeded to divide Afghanistan into several states and to nominate their chiefs.

To drive the Persians out and reinstate Shah Soojah-ool-Moolk, an army, 27,000 strong, subsequently known as "The Army of the Indus," was formed. The command of it was given to Lieutenant-General Sir John Keane. This army was divided into the Bengal and Bombay Columns under Major-Generals W. Cotton and T. Willshire respectively.

The Bombay Column advanced up the Indus and occupied Hyderabad. It then crossed the Bolan Pass and occupied Dadur and then Quetta, where it halted. When the advance was continued, Candahar, the capital of Western Afghanistan, was reached on the 27th April, 1839, after several skirmishes with recalcitrant tribes on the way.

On the 27th June the column moved off again on its way to Ghuznee, which had been heavily fortified by Hyder Khan. When the fort was reached, on the 21st July, it was considered to be too strong to attack until the walls had been breached by explosive. This task was performed under a covering party of the 13th Foot and the fort occupied on the 23rd, and Mahomed Khan fled for safety towards Cabul, the capital of Eastern Afghanistan.

Whilst the fighting for Ghuznee was taking place large numbers of Afghans had remained in the neighbourhood waiting to see which horse to back. Having learnt of the defeat of Mahomed Khan they dispersed, so that Cabul was entered unopposed.

Shah Soojah-ool-Moolk was replaced on the throne and a British envoy appointed in Cabul.

It was to show his appreciation at his reinstatement that Shah Soojah intended to present the medal for Ghuznee to all who had taken part in the siege, and the Order of the Dooranee Empire to field officers and above.

This weakling became so unpopular that in October, 1841, the Afghans rose in revolt and murdered the British envoy in Cabul.

The 44th Foot (1st Bn. Essex Regt.), who formed the garrison, were forced to retreat towards Jellalabad. On their way they were attacked and annihilated. Dr. Brydon was the only officer who survived.

Prior to the attack on Cabul the 13th Foot had formed part of the garrison, but they had been sent out to quell local disturbances. They were on their way back to Cabul when the trouble broke out. Rather than let them fight their way to Cabul it was decided that they should withdraw to Jellalabad and hold it until the garrison in Cabul could get out. As already stated, this garrison was annihilated during its withdrawal.

On arrival at Jellalabad, Major-General Sir Robert Sale placed it in a state of defence and then withstood a siege from the 12th November, 1841, to the 7th April, 1842, when, as a result of an attack in force by the garrison and a threatening one from the relieving column under Major-General Sir George Pollock, Mahomed Khan (who had again come on the scene) cleared off with his Afghan followers.

General Pollock's movements had really been little more than a threat as he met with stiff opposition in the Khyber Pass on the 5th April and did not reach Jellalabad until the 16th, when he found that the garrison had, by their own efforts, relieved themselves.

It will make the account of the war easier to follow if we continue the story of General Pollock's movements until he reached Cabul, though the relief of that city did not take place until after that of Candahar and Ghuznee.

After his arrival at Jellalabad, General Pollock tried to impress on the Government-General the necessity for the reoccupation of Cabul, but for reasons which do not concern us here he was not allowed to move out until the 20th August. During this period the troops suffered severely from the heat and the results of constant raiding of the convoys by the local tribes, the Shinwarees in particular. A brigade, under Brigadier-General Monteath, was sent out to deal with them. They were defeated at Mazenia, which figures on some of the unauthorized bars to be found.

The route to be followed by General Pollock from Jellalabad to Cabul exactly suited the tactics of the Afghans, who took up a strong position in the Tazeane Pass from which they had to be driven out. This action is also commemorated by some unofficial bars.

In this action Mahomed Khan was so completely defeated that there was no further opposition to the advance and Cabul was entered on the 15th September, 1842.

We must now turn to Candahar, where Major-General Sir William Nott, who had refused to surrender, was being besieged by Prince Sufter Jung, the son of Shah Soojah.

The defence was far from a static one, for many foraging and punitive sorties were made by the garrison into the surrounding country. One of these sorties, under the immediate command of Colonel Wymer, relieved the garrison of Khelati-i-Ghilzie, the defenders of which received a special medal.

General Nott's relief was similar to that of General Sale in Jellalabad in that he bided his time until the weather was favourable and the disposition of the Afghans gave him an opportunity to defeat them *en masse*. The similarity is heightened by the fact that Major-General Sir Richard England was on his way to relieve him in the same way that General Pollock was on his way to relieve General Sale.

The situation in Ghuznee was worse than that in Candahar and Cabul because the garrison, through starvation and under orders from Major-General Elphinstone, had been compelled to surrender.

On the 10th August General Nott set out from Candahar to relieve Cabul. On the 30th August he encountered and defeated a strong force of Afghans at Gonine. On the 5th September he reached the outskirts of Ghuznee, which were strongly held by the enemy. Dispositions were made for the attack, but on the morning of the 6th it was found that the enemy had evacuated their positions and Ghuznee, which was immediately entered.

The force remained here until the 10th, when the advance to Cabul continued.

Cabul was reached on the 17th, or two days after its relief by General Pollock.

Collectors will now understand why medals were awarded bearing the single name of Candahar or that of Cabul, also the two names Ghuznee and Cabul and the three names Candahar, Ghuznee and Cabul.

Those who are interested in history will note that in 1842 there was the march, just described, from Candahar to Cabul, and in 1880 there was the more famous one undertaken by General Roberts in the reverse direction.

Those who are interested in small details will note that in 1842 both these places were spelt with a "C," whereas in 1880 they were spelt with a "K."

We shall come across similar alterations of spelling, for which one cannot account when dealing with the Ashantee War, 1873-4, and the Ashanti War, 1900. In the first of these a bar was awarded for Coomassie, whereas on that for the second medal it was spelt Kumassi.

46 GHUZNEE MEDAL (21st-23rd July, 1839).* *(See footnote to page 139)* First Afghan War

Obverse   The fortress of Ghuznee with the word "GHUZNEE" below.

Reverse   The recipient's name above a mural crown. At the top is the date "23RD JULY" and at the bottom is the year "1839." The whole is surrounded by two laurel branches.

138

Size	1.46 in. diameter.
Ribbon	1.5 in. wide. Half crimson and half green in vertical stripes, the green half being to the right when facing the wearer.†
Suspension	The ribbon passes through a plain straight suspender fixed to the top of the piece. It does not swivel.
Designer	The medal was designed by a committee. The dies were engraved and the models struck at the Calcutta Mint.
Naming	The medals were issued unnamed, but they are found named in various ways as follows: (1) Engraved in neat capitals in the field. (2) Engraved in running hand in the field. (3) Engraved in large capital letters on the rim. (4) In some cases there is no naming on the piece. Sometimes attached to the ribbon is a buckle with three flat bars. On the upper one is the word "AFGHANISTAN," on the centre one is the recipient's name, on the lower one are the words "GHUZNEE & KELATT."
No. of bars issued	Nil.‡

There must have been two sets of dies, as medals struck from one depict the fortress as being narrower and taller, whilst the detail on the reverse is much clearer. It may be merely coincidence, but the only specimens seen made from these dies were awarded to the 17 Foot and of course the unnamed numbers awarded: European Commissioned Officers, 239; Native Commissioned Officers. 153; European Warrant Officers, 6; Sergeants and Havildars, 456; Rank and File, 7,467; Misc. 50.

Regiments present: 4 Light Dragoons; 16 Lancers; 1 Bombay Light Cavalry; 2, 3 Bengal Light Cavalry; Skinner's Horse; Poona Irregular Horse; 2/2 Brigade Bengal Horse Artillery; 2/6 Bengal Foot Artillery; 3, 4 Troops Bombay Horse Artillery; 2/2 Battalion Bombay Foot Artillery; 1/Shah Soojah's H.A.; 1 Company Golundaz Native Artillery; 2, 3 Companies Bengal Sappers and Miners; 2, 13, 17 Foot; 1 Bengal European Regiment (later 1 Royal Munster Fusiliers and often named to European Light Infantry); 16, 35, 48 Bengal N.I.; 19 Bombay N.I.

*It was the intention of Shah Soojah to give these medals to all who took part in the capture of Ghuznee. He died before the medals were ready, so the Government of India bore the cost of their manufacture and subsequent issue.

To field officers and above, he presented the Order of the Dooranee Empire, which consists of a combination of a gold Maltese cross and two crossed swords. There were three classes to the Order, the Star of the first and second classes consists of a blue and green circular centre-piece, around the circumference of which are fourteen or more pearls according to the class. These jewels surround a Persian inscription "DURI-DAURAN" (Pearl of the Age). Eight first, eighteen second and forty third class were awarded.

†The original ribbon was half yellow and half green. One has been unable to trace when, or why, it was altered. Medals with both a wide and thin border around the edges on both sides have been seen. One medal had the suspender removed and replaced by a ring similar to those found on the Seringapatam Medal.

‡Unofficial bars are found inscribed Ghuznee, Kelat (or Kelatt), Ponulla (or Punulla) Monsantonsh (or Munsantosh) and Mnaher (or Monohur).

How unofficial and absurd these bars really are may be guaged by the fact that the piece itself bears the name Ghuznee, 1839. The action at Kelat was fought on the 13th November, 1839, that at Ponulla on the 26th November, 1844, and that at Monsantonsh and Mnaher on the 20th January, 1845.

The facts that Ghuznee is in Afghanistan and Mnaber is on the borders of the Portuguese possession of Goa, also that over five years intervene and that the troops were transported by sea (in H.E.I. Company's frigate *Auckland*) are worth noting.

There is a distance of over 1,300 miles, as the crow flies, between the first- and last-mentioned places.

In addition to the above, certain units of Shah Soojah's Force also received the medal.

There is an unpublished issue of this medal in tin. These are fitted with a ring at the top of the piece and thence by a swivel on to a triangular suspender. The edges are inscribed with the Sepoy's name and regiment.

47 CANDAHAR, GHUZNEE AND CABUL MEDALS (October, 1841-October, 1842). First Afghan War

There are four different strikings of this silver medal, authorized by a General Order, issued in Simla, on the 4th October, 1842, not counting the two which appear to have been mistakes. The first of the latter kind have the legend "VICTORIA REGINA" on the obverse instead of "Victoria Vindex"; the second, which refers to the medal for Cabul only, has this place spelt "CABVL". Fifteen of these medals were issued.

As all the types are the same except for the reverses, one general description will suffice and the reverses will be dealt with separately. The order of rarity is as follows: (1) Ghuznee, Cabul; (2) Candahar; (3) Candahar, Ghuznee, Cabul; (4) Cabul.

Obverse	The diademed head of Queen Victoria with the legend "VICTORIA VINDEX".
Size	1.42 in. diameter.
Ribbon	1.75 in, wide. Rainbow pattern watered red, white, yellow, white and blue.
Suspension	By means of a straight steel suspender fastened by a pin to a steel clip affixed to the piece.
Designer	W. Wyon, R.A.
Naming	Some in script, some in indented capitals, whilst a few were issued unnamed. The medals of the 40th Foot and the Artillery are generally found engraved in script, whilst those to the 41st Foot are named in indented Roman capitals.
No. of bars issued	Nil.

Candahar *(May, 1842)*

Reverse	"CANDAHAR" with the date "1842" underneath and surmounted by a crown: the whole surrounded by a laurel wreath.

Europeans received approx. 130 medals and natives 2,485.

Regiments present. Staff and details (5); H.M. 40th Foot (64); H.M. 41st Foot (26); 3/1st Btn. Bombay Artillery (2); 3/2nd Btn. Bengal Artillery (1); 4/2nd Btn. Bengal Artillery (28); 1st Troop, Shah's H. Artillery (127); 2nd Troop, Shah's H. Artillery (1); 1st Bengal Irregular Cavalry (17); 1st Shah's Cavalry (198); 2nd Bengal N.I. (65); 16th Bengal N.I. (31); 38th Bengal N.I. (107); 42nd Bengal N.I. (79); 43rd Bengal N.I. (37); 1st Shah's Infantry (640); 2nd Shah's Infantry (592); 5th Shah's Infantry (595).

Cabul *(15th September, 1842)*

Reverse	"CABUL" with the date "1842" underneath and surmounted by a crown -- the whole surrounded by a laurel wreath. Also the very rare variety with "CABVL".

The bars for "Marzenia 1842"* and "Tazeane 1842"* are found attached to this medal, but they are quite unofficial.

Europeans received approx. 3,500 medals and natives 9,241.

Regiments present: Staff, etc. (38); 3/1st Brigade Bengal H. Artillery (129); 3/2nd Brigade Bengal H. Artillery (139) 2/2nd Btn. Bengal Artillery (97); 2/6th Btn. Bengal Artillery (123); 4/6th Btn. Bengal Artillery (109); Mountain Train (56); E Company Syce Drivers (153); H.M. 3rd Light Dragoons (489); 1st Bengal Light Cavlary (453); 5th Bengal Light Cavalry (142); 10th Bengal Light Cavalry (498); 3rd Tait's Irregular Cavalry (739); H.M. 9th Foot (731); H.M. 13th Foot (745); H.M. 31st Foot (826); 6th Bengal N.I. (3rd Co. only) (112); 26th Bengal N.I. (1,004); 30th Bengal N.I. (920); 33rd Bengal N.I. (947); 35th Bengal N.I. (837); 53rd Bengal N.I. (915); 60th Bengal N.I. (1,012); 64th Bengal N.I. (927); 5th Co. Bengal Sappers & Miners (125); Shah's Sappers (Broadfoot's) (375).

Ptes. M. Doyle of the 50th Foot received this medal, as did Wm. Hewett of the 22nd Foot & I. Simpson. Pte. Ed. Branagan, 40th Foot, received one of the Victoria Regina medals.

Ghuznee and Cabul

Reverse   Two laurel wreaths forming the letter W. The word "GHUZNEE" is written in the first loop and "CABUL" in the second. The whole is surmounted by a crown, and the date "1842" appears at the bottom under the wreaths.

Europeans received approx. 360 medals and natives 1,163.

Regiments present: Staff and details (3); H.M. 40th Foot (3); H.M. 41st Foot (105); 1st Troop, Bombay H. Artillery (138); 3/1st Btn. Bombay Artillery (25); 3/2nd Btn. Bengal Artillery (87); 4/2nd Btn. Bengal Artillery (38); Bengal Sappers and Miners (details 2nd and 3rd Cos.) (24); Madras Sappers and Miners, C Co. (28) 3rd Bombay Light Cavalry (354); 1st Bengal Irregular Cavalry (17); 1st Shah's Cavalry (1); 2nd Bengal N.I. (4); 16th Bengal N.I. (4); 38th Bengal N.I. (1); 43rd Bengal N.I. (169); 3rd Shah's Infantry (521).

Candahar, Ghuznee, Cabul

Reverse   The names of these three places with the date "1842" underneath — on four lines. The whole is surmounted by a crown and surrounded by a laurel wreath.

Europeans received approx. 400 medals and natives 4,811.

Regiments present: Staff and details (23); H.M. 40th Foot (669); H.M. 41st Foot (494); 3/1st Btn. Bombay Artillery (91); 3/2nd Btn. Bengal Artillery (17); 4/2nd Btn. Bengal Artillery (10); 2nd Troop, Shah's H. Artillery (121); Bengall Sappers and Miners (details 2nd and 3rd Cos.) (3); Madras Sappers and Miners, C Co. (1); 1st Bengal Irregular Cavalry (282); 1st Shah's Cavalry (469); 2nd Bengal N.I. (893); 16th Bengal N.I. (795); 38th Bengal N.I. (854); 42nd Bengal N.I. (852); 43rd Bengal N.I. (637).

---

*The battle of Mazenia, or Mazeena, was fought on the 26th July, 1842, by the 31st Foot and the 32nd and 53rd Native Infantry.

The battle of Tazeane, or Tazeen, was fought in, and for, the Tazeen Pass on the 13th September, 1842. The complete defeat of Akkbar Kahn in this action annihilated his forces and opened the way to Cabul, which was reached on the 15th September, 1842.

No regiment is allowed to add bars to medals unless they have been authorized by a General Order and therefore medals fitted with such bars are interesting curios.

48 JELLALABAD MEDALS (12th November, 1841-7th April, 1842). First Afghan War

This medal was issued in two distinct types, generally referred to as (1) Mural Crown and (2) Flying Victory. The first type was considered inartistic, and as regards the obverse quite rightly so. In any case, not enough of the first type were struck to issue to the next of kin, so it was decided to strike a further issue in London — the first issue having been minted in Calcutta. Though a free exchange was offered to those who received the first type it is recorded that only five men of the 13th Foot made the change.*

First Type.

Obverse	A mural crown superscribed "JELLALABAD".
Reverse	The date "VII APRIL, 1842" occupying three lines.
Size	1.52 in. diameter.
Ribbon	Rainbow pattern watered red, white, yellow, white and blue 1¼ in. wide.
Suspension	By means of a plain straight suspender fitted to the rim of the piece, though some are to be found suspended from a ring.
Naming	This seems to vary considerably, so that the medal cannot have been named when issued. Some are found with names on the edge and others with the name of the recipient on the obverse under the crown. The medals issued to the 13th Foot were named round the edge at the Commanding Officer's expense, though some are seen to this regiment with the name above the crown and the regiment underneath, also with the name impressed on the rim as well as on the reverse.
No. of bars issued	Nil.

Second Type

Obverse	The diademed head of Queen Victoria with legend "VICTORIA VINDEX"*, but a few medals were struck with "VICTORIA REGINA".
Reverse	The winged figure of Victory with wreaths in her right hand and holding the staff of a Union Jack in her left hand whilst flying over the fortress of Jellalabad. Around the top is the inscription "JELLALABAD VII APRIL". In the exergue is the date "MDCCCXLII".
Size	1.4 in. diameter.
Ribbon	As above.
Suspension	A straight suspender fastened by means of a pin to a steel clip affixed to the piece.
Designer	W. Wyon, R.A.
Naming	The recipient's name and regiment are indented on the edge in block capitals.
No. of bars issued	Nil.

*Another account states that two hundred of the second issue were struck for exchange, but that only fifty men of the 13th Foot, would agree to do so. In 1860, one hundred and thirty-nine of these medals were sold to a Mr. Nash. If this account is correct it still leaves eleven medals unaccounted for.

A medal issued as late as 1876 which is fitted with the scroll type of suspender is known. Whether the above-mentioned eleven medals were retained in case of any late applications one cannot say. If they were, then perhaps this medal was one of them and was fitted with the type of suspender (*i.e.* scroll type) then in use for the India Service General Medal, 1854.

1 Sqd. 5th Ben. Ltd. Cavy. (Capt. Oldfield).	160
1 Sqd. Shah Soojah's Horse (Lt. Mayne)	100
Political Agent (Capt. MacGregor) and party of Duran's Horse .	25
Abbott's Bty. Bengal H.A.	150
Backhouse's Mtn. Trn., Shah's Arty.	65
Broadfoot's Sappers (3 Cos. — Broadfoot)	375
13th Lt. Inf. (Col. Dennie)	780
35th Bengal N.I. (Col. Monteath)	800
Followers including camel drivers	125
Brigade H.Q.	14
Dr. Brydon — Sole survivor from Kabul	2
	2596

Incidentally, the Mural Crown Medals were awarded by the Governor General, Lord Ellenborough, at Ferozepore to Major General Sale's force in November 1842 and were the first awarded for the war. As the awarding of medals went, and goes now, this is pretty prompt service. Compare this lapse of seven months with the fifty-six years in the case of the first bar to the Naval General Service Medal 1793-1840.

49 DEFENCE OF KELAT-I-GHILZIE (February-May, 1842). First Afghan War

Obverse	A shield, with "KELAT-I-GHILZIE" thereon occupying three lines. The shield is surrounded by a laurel wreath and surmounted by a mural crown.
Reverse	A collection of military trophies surmounting a rectangular plaque with "INVICTA MDCCCXLII" thereon.
Size	1.42 in. diameter.
Ribbon	Rainbow pattern of watered red, white, yellow, white and blue, 1¾ in. wide.
Suspension	The ribbon passes through a straight steel suspender which is affixed to the piece by a somewhat crude metal clip.
Designer	W. Wyon, R.A.
Naming	The recipient's name and regiment are engraved in script on the edge.
No. of bars issued	Nil.

This silver medal, whose issue was sanctioned by a General Order from Simla dated 4th October, 1842, was awarded to the garrison under Captain John Halkett Craigie, which consisted of 55 Europeans and 877 natives as follows: Staff (7); 4th Company 2nd Battalion Bengal Artillery (86); details from the 2nd and 3rd Bengal Sappers and Miners (23); three companies of the 43rd Bengal N.I. under Captain Webster (247); and 569 men of the 3rd Shah Soojah's* Infantry.

Lieutenant G. Piercy, 2nd Foot, received this medal in addition to that for Ghuznee. It was also awarded to Surgeon-General C. Mackinnon, who also received the C.B., Ghuznee 1839 Medal, Ghuznee-Cabul 1842 Medal, Punjab Medal and the Mutiny Medal.

Kelat-i-Ghilzie was a fort between Cabul and Candahar, about eighty miles north-east of the latter, which withstood siege for four months until relieved by Major-General Nott on the 26th May, 1842.

*This name is variously spelt Shoojah, Soojah, Soujah and Sujah.

For its gallant conduct during the siege the Shah's regiment was subsequently added to the establishment of the Bengal Army as the 12th (Kelat-i-Ghilzie Regiment) Bengal N.I. They later became the 2nd Battalion (Kelat-i-Ghilzie) Bombay Pioneers. They were disbanded on the 10th February, 1933.

50 FIRST CHINA WAR (5th July, 1840-29th August, 1842)

Obverse	The diademed head of Queen Victoria with the legend "VICTORIA REGINA".
Reverse	A collection of war trophies with an oval shield with the Royal Arms in the centre, all positioned under a palm tree. Above is the inscription "ARMIS EXPOSCERE PACEM". In the exergue is the word "CHINA" and the date "1842" underneath.
Size	1.42 in. diameter.
Ribbon	1.5 in. wide with a crimson stripe .9 in. wide down the centre and yellow edges.
Suspension	A straight nickel silver suspender with a .2 in. neck in the centre, which is sweated directly on to the piece.
Designer	Wm. Wyon, R.A.
Naming	Impressed in bold well-spaced Roman capitals. The space between the above-mentioned neck either before and/or after the naming is filled in with stars.
No. of bars issued	Nil.

The awarding of this medal was originally suggested by the Governor General of India in October, 1842, for presentation to all ranks of the Honourable East India Company's forces. It was, however, subsequently awarded by the Home Government in 1843 to those who had taken part in the capture of the island of Chusan, in Hangchow Bay, on 5th July, 1840, and the operations in the Canton River, during 1841. The campaign ended with the capture of Nanking.

The original design of the medal was different from that subsequently issued. The reverse depicted a lion with its forepaws on a dragon. This was considered to be offensive to the Chinese and therefore unsuitable. In the exergue was "NANKING, 1842".

Regiments present: 1 Coy. 8 Bn. R.A. C. Tp. Madras H.A., B and C. Co's. 2 Bn. and D. Co. 3 Bn. Madras F.A.,; A, B, F and a few from C, D and E Companies Madras Sappers and Miners; 18, 26, 49, 55, 98 Foot; 2, 6, 14, 36, 37, 39, 41 Madras N.I.; 1, 2 Bengal Volunteers.

H.M. Ships: *Algerine, Alligator, Blenheim, Blonde, Calliope, Cambiran, Childers, Clio, Columbine, Conway, Cornwallis, Cruiser, Dido, Druid, Endymion, Hazard Harlequin, Herald, Hyacinth, Larne, Melville, Modeste, Nimrod, North Star, Pelican, Plover, Pylades, Royalist, Samarang, Starling, Sulphur, Vixen, Volage, Wanderer, Wellesley.* Indian and Bengal Marine ships: *Ariadne, Atlanta, Auckland, Enterprise, Nemesis, Phlegethon, Pluto, Prosperine, Queen, Sesostris, Tenasserim.* Troopships: *Bellisle, Apollo, Jupiter, Rattlesnake, Sapphire.* Hospital ship *Minden.*

The ships present varied considerably in size, consequently, the numbers issued affect the value.

The troubles which led to this war had been brewing for some time. They centred round the importation and sale of opium. The fact was, and it seems almost unbelievable, that the British resident merchants insisted on having the monopoly of the importation of the drug from India, whereas the Chinese Government refused to have any importation at all. They burnt the warehouses containing huge stocks and refused to pay any compensation.

The British Commissioner, Captain Elliot, R.N., and residents were forced to evacuate Canton on the 24th May, 1839, and hostility towards the British was shown in many acts of incendiarism and pillage all over China.

Hong Kong was taken by Captain Elliot on the 23rd August, 1839, and ceded to Britain on the 20th January, 1841.

On the 3rd November, 1839, H.M.S. *Volage* and *Hyacinth* were attacked by a large fleet of junks. On the 6th December, 1839, an edict was published prohibiting all trade with Britain.

Sir Gordon Bremer commenced the blockade of Canton on the 28th June, 1840, and a small force under Brigadier-General George Burrel was dispatched from Madras. This consisted of the 18th, 26th and 49th Foot, together with Bengal Artillery and Sappers, also a composite unit of Bengal Volunteers. It arrived off Ting-lai on the island of Chusan, in Hanchow Bay, on the 2nd July. The island surrendered on the 5th.

A blockade of the whole coast of China was started and treaties and agreeents were signed with a bewildering frequency. The situation gradually became worse until finally the Chinese were offering a reward of 40,000 dollars for a dead or a live Englishman with a special bonus of 10,000 dollars for a chief!

On the 1st March, 1841, the Navy moved up the river to Canton and General Sir Hugh Gough, who had arrived with considerable reinforcements, took over the military command.

It would take up too much space to give a full account of all the engagements which took place during the war. They were, briefly, Canton taken 26th May, 1841, and a ransom paid; hostilities ceased and trade restarted 1st June, 1841; hostilities restarted and Amoy taken on the 16th August, 1841; Chusan recaptured 1st October, 1841; Chinhae, 10th October, 1841; Ningpo, 13th October, 1841. On the 10th March, 1842, the Chinese attacked the garrison at Tingpo, but were repulsed; on the 13th June, 1842, a naval squadron proceeded up the Woosung river and anchored off Shanghai on the 16th.

Nanking was taken on the 4th August and on the 29th a treaty of perpetual friendship was signed on board H.M.S. *Collingwood* by Sir Henry Pottinger, our special envoy, and Keying Elepoo.

As we shall see later this everlasting friendship lasted until 1857 from the point of view of open war, but anyone who cares to read the history of China at that period would doubt whether the Chinese idea of friendship was quite the same as ours.

During this outbreak of peace and fraternity, the pretender Emperor Yeh* is credited with over 100,000 beheadings, but we must also credit him with a certain amount of tact for seeing that the beneficiaries of this great kindness were mostly Chinese!

51 SCINDE CAMPAIGN MEDALS (6th January-24th March, 1843)

There are three different strikings of this silver medal, which differ only as regards their reverses, which will be dealt with separately:

Obverse   Diademed head of Queen Victoria and legend "VICTORIA REGINA".

Reverse   See individual headings.

Size   1.42 in. diameter.

*The career of this usurper is very hard to follow as he continually changed his name. During his early period he styled himself Tien-teh, which means Celestial Virtue. Whether modesty or prudence compelled him to adopt another alias, one cannot say.

Ribbon	1.75 in. wide. Rainbow pattern watered red, white, yellow, white and blue.
Suspension	Either by a straight suspender, or a large ring, passing through a steel clip attached to the piece.
Designer	W. Wyon, R.A.
Naming	In block lettering.
No. of bars issued	Nil.

Lieutenant-Colonel J.L. Pennefather of the 22nd Foot led the attackers, numbering about 2,800, at Meeanee. He was wounded in this action and did not take part in that at Hyderabad, during which the Regiment was commanded by Capt. F.D. George. When the medals were issued, Lieutenant-Colonel Pennefather at his own expense, had all the steel suspenders removed from those awarded to the 22nd Foot and had them replaced by silver ones.

Medals for Meeanee only, are very rare, whilst the other two could be classified as rare.

The medal was authorized on the 22nd September, 1843, to be awarded to those who had accompanied Sir Charles Napier in his campaign to punish the Amirs of Scinde, Rustram, Nasir Khan and Shere Mahomed, for continually raiding our convoys on their way to and from Afghanistan.

The first operation was the destruction of the unoccupied fortress of Emaum Ghur on the 14th-15th January. This defeat cut off their retreat and drove them southwards. Sir Charles followed them up and found that they had taken up a position on the Indus near Meeanee. After considerable slaughter they were defeated on the 17th February, when most of the Amirs surrendered. The chief exception was Meer Shere Mahomed, who refused to parley and so was attacked and defeated at Dubba, on the outskirts of Hyderabad, on the 24th March, 1843.

This campaign is notable for the magnificent march of eighty days across the desert, over which the guns were drawn by hand.

The 22nd Foot particularly distinguished itself and on its return to Bombay the whole garrison paraded and saluted it.

Sir Charles also paid special tribute to the valour and loyalty of his native troops.

Meeanee *(17th February, 1843)*

Reverse   "MEEANEE" above the date "1843" and surmounted by a crown and surrounded by a wreath.

Regiments present: 9 Bengal Cavalry; Scinde (90) and Poona Horse (14); 2/2 Bn. Bombay Artillery (63) and 3 Co. Bombay F.A.; 3 Golandaz (native artillery) Company; C Company Madras Sappers and Miners (14); 22 Foot (65); 1 Bombay Grenadiers (148); 12 (153). 25 (206) Bombay N.I.

European members of the following ships received forty medals and native members seventy.

Indus flotilla ships *Planet* and *Satellite* (40 to European members of the flotilla).

Hyderabad *(24th March, 1843)*

Reverse   "HYDERABAD" within a wreath and surmounted by a crown above the date "1843".

Regiments present: 3 Bombay Cavalry; 9 Bengal Cavalry; Scinde and Poona Horse, 1 Troop Bombay Horse Artillery; 2/1, 2/2 3 and 5 Co's. Bombay Artillery; Madras Sappers and Miners; 22 Foot; 1 Bombay Grenadiers; 6, 8, 12, 21, 24, 25 Bombay N.I.

European members of the following ships received sixty medals and natives fifty-five.

Indus flotilla ships: *Comet, Meteor, Nimrod* (60 to European members of the flotilla and 55 to local seamen).

Two of these medals were awarded to Lieutenant Frederick Foster Taylor, 3rd Bombay Cavalry. He also received the medal for Ghuznee and Cabul.

Meeanee and Hyderabad *(1843)*

Reverse   "MEEANEE, HYDERABAD" on two lines surrounded by a wreath and surmounted by a crown.

Regiments present: 9 Bengal Cavalry; Scinde and Poona Horse; Bombay Artillery; Madras Sappers and Miners; 22 Foot; 12, 25 Bombay N.I.

Two men of the 40th Foot received this medal, one of whom was William Arbott. He also got the medal for Candahar.

Thomas Nugent, 32nd Foot, and Ensign W. Pirie, 1st Grenadier N.I., received this medal, but one cannot trace the presence of either regiment.

One was also awarded to an Assistant Pilot of the Indian Marine.

52 GWALIOR CAMPAIGN STARS (December, 1843)

Obverse   The centre of the main bronze star carries, a small silver one of the same pattern. in the centre of which is the date "29th DEC." in two lines. Around the date is the name of the action for which it was awarded, either "PUNNIAR" or "MAHARAJPOOR", and the year "1843".

Reverse   Plain, except for the naming.

Size   The stars are 1.7 in. wide and 2 in. high.

Ribbon   1.75 in. wide of the then usual Indian pattern of watered red, white yellow, white and blue.*

Suspension   As described below.

Designer   Both the stars were produced and probably designed by the Calcutta Mint.

Naming   In script on the reverse.

No. of bars issued   Nil.

By a General Order dated the 4th January, 1844, sanction was granted for the award of bronze stars, made from captured guns, to all troops who had taken part in the campaign under Sir Hugh Gough or Major-General Grey, which was necessitated by the continual reluctance of the Regent, Dada Khasgee Walla, to refrain from insulting the British authority.

On the 29th December, 1843, it became necessary to cross the border, where Sir Hugh Gough found the Mahrattas in a fortified position at Maharajpoor and defeated them.

On the same day General Grey also crossed it on his way to Punniar, where he found that the Mahrattas had entrenched themselves on the hills around the town. Another sanguinary battle took palce, as a result of which, and that at Maharajpoor, the power of the Mahrattas was broken.

*As the stars were issued with hooks for suspension, it is obvious that there can be no *official* ribbon, so that the wearing of them suspended from the usual Indian pattern one must have crept in as a custom which was winked at by higher authority.

It appears that the stars were originally intended as decorations to be worn on the jacket, for which purpose brass hooks were fitted. This was altered after the issue of the stars and it seems to have been left to the individual to design his own method of suspension. Many different ones were employed though the more usual are by means of a straight suspender or large ring fitted to the back of the piece towards the top of the upmost point.

There are two of these stars, generally referred to as the Punniar and Maharajpoor Stars named after the actions for which they were awarded. As these actions were both fought on the same day, it was naturally impossible for one recipient to receive both. The two places are about twelve miles apart. It is recorded that owing to the expense which would have been involved the original design of the stars was altered slightly, the inner star as issued replacing a small silver elephant.* The inner circle is detachable by unscrewing two small nuts at the back of the piece.

The Earl of Ellenborough, Governor-General of India at the time, presented a star to each of the four ladies present at the battle of Majarajpoor. They were Lady Gough, Lady Smith, Mrs. Curtis and Miss Gough. They were of gold with circular centre pieces. Beyond the fact that they were six-pointed they could hardly be described as similar to those awarded to the soldiers. The obverses bear the Queen's head in the centre of a blue enamelled circle. The reverses have the word "MAHARAJPOOR" around the top half with the date "29 DECEM^R" around the bottom half with the year "1843" on a red enamelled centre.

Maharajpoor Star *(29th December, 1843)*

Regiments present: 16 Lancers; 1, 4, 5, 8, 10 Bengal Light Cavalry; 4 Irregular Cavalry (*N.B.* — The 5th and 8th Bengal Light Cavalry only had detachments present); 2/2, 3/2, 2/3 Bengal H.A.; 1/1, 1/4, 2/4, 3/4 and 4/4 Bengal Foot Arty.; 3, 4, 5, 7 companies Bengal Sappers and Miners; 39, 40, 50 (1)† Foot; 2, 4, 14, 16, 31, 43, 56, 62, 70 Bengal N.I. (The 62nd and 70th were not engaged in the fighting.)

Punniar Star *(29th December, 1843)*

Regiments present: Two squadrons of 9 Lancers; 5, 8, 11 Bengal Light Cavalry; 8 Irregular Cavalry; 3/2, 1/3 and 3/3 Bengal H.A.; 6/6 Bengal F.A.; 1 Company Bengal Sappers and Miners; 3, 50 Foot; 39, 50, 51, 58 Bengal N.I.

53 SUTLEJ CAMPAIGN MEDAL (18th December, 1845-22nd February, 1846)

Obverse The diademed head of Queen Victoria with the legend "VICTORIA REGINA".

Reverse The standing figure of Victory, facing left. In her outstretched right hand she holds a wreath and in her left an olive branch. At her feet is a collection of trophies. The legend "ARMY OF THE SUTLEJ" is written around the circumference. There are four different exergues which contain either of the following: (1) "MOODKEE 1845"; (2) "FEROZESHUHUR 1845"; (3) "ALIWAL 1846"; or (4) "SOBRAON 1846".

Size 1.42 in. diameter.

Ribbon 1.25 in. wide. Dark blue with crimson edges.

---

*The star awarded to Sir Hugh Gough had a silver elephant in the centre.

†This star was awarded to Major Thomas Ryan, Knight of Hanover, of the 50th Foot, who was attached to the 39th Foot.

Suspension	An ornamental swivelling suspender.
Designer	Wm. Wyon, R.A.
Naming	Indented in capital letters or light Roman skeleton lettering.
No. of bars issued	Three.

The medal awarded for this campaign was the first with bars to be given to both officers and men. The Peninsular Gold Medals and Crosses were only awarded to officers. The previously issued China 1842 Medal had no bars. The Army of India Medal, though awarded to commemorate much earlier battles, was not issued until 1851.

The first action in which the recipient took part was given in the exergue on the reverse, so that four distinct types of piece had to be issued. This is the only time this has been done in the case of a battle, though we find the date, or dates, of the campaign either in the exergue or on the reverse as is the case with the medals for Afghanistan 1878-80, Egypt 1882, and the British South Africa Company's medals for Matabeleland, 1893, etc.

The symmetry of the medal is excellent, and it is a great pity it was not adhered to for all future Indian medals, as it is considered that that for Afghanistan 1878-1880 looks very crude by compairson.

Collectors should note that the only regiments present as a whole at all four actions were the 31st and 50th Foot, the 24th and 47th Bengal N.I. and the 5th Bengal Light Cavalry. consequently, the rivets joining the bars should be carefully examined for fakes as three-bar medals are rare. The only Ferozeshuhur Medal that is known of with two bars was awarded to Henry Allward, 62nd Foot. The Moodkee Medals with the Ferozeshuhur — Aliwal combination are rare.

Sanction was given by a General Order dated the 17th April 1846, for the award of a medal to the Army of the Sutlej, as it was called.

The war was caused by the unexpected invasion of the Punjab by the Sikh Army, nearly 100,000 strong, which crossed the Sutlej on the 11th December, 1845, with the object of capturing Ferozepore and Ludhiana.

Taken by surprise, it was necessary for the Commander-in-Chief, Sir Hugh Gough, to march from Umballa to meet them, a distance of about 150 miles. The march started on the 11th December. On the 17th the troops from Ludhiana joined the force which encountered the Sikhs at Moodkee on the 18th.

In quick succession, as will be seen by their dates given below, the Sikhs were defeated in four major battles, until finally compelled to sign a treaty at Lahore on the 22nd February, 1846.

Moodkee *(18th December, 1845)*

Regiments present: 3 Light Dragoons (57 killed, 526 medals claimed); 4, 5 Bengal Light Cavalry; 4, 11 Irregular Horse; 1/1, 2/1, 3/1, 1/3, 2/3 and 4/3 Bengal H.A.; 3/4 and 2/6 Bengal F.A., and Bengal Sappers and Miners; 9 (899), 31 (877), 50 (703), 80 (824) Foot; 2, 9 (899), 16, 24, 26, 42, 47, 48, 73 Bengal N.I.

Ferozeshuhur *(21st December, 1845)*

Regiments present: 3 Light Dragoons (55 killed, 6 medals claimed with Fer. in exergue, total issue of 52); 4, 5, 8 Bengal Light Cavalry; 3, 8, 9 Irregular Horse; 1/1, 2/1, 3/1, 5/1 (including 6 medals with Sobraon bar), 1/3, 2/3, 3/3 and 4/3 Bengal H.A.; 2/4, 3/4, 4/4, 2/6, 4/6 and 2/7 Bengal F.A.; No. 6 Company Bengal Sappers and Miners; 9 (866), 29 (784), 31 (721), 50 (509), 62 (120 killed, 870 claims), 80 (817) Foot; 1 Bengal European Regiment (later 1st Btn. Royal Munster Fusiliers) (696) (131 as Fer. only and 565 with Sobraon bar); 2, 12, 14, 16, 24, 26, 33, 41, 42, 44, 45, 47, 48, 54, 62, 73 Bengal N.I.

Aliwal *(28th January, 1846)*

Regiments present: 3 Light Dgns. (51, 46 having Aliwal in the exergue) 16 Lancers (551); 1, 3, 5 Bengal Light Cavalry; 4 Irregular Cavalry; Bodyguard Cavalry; 1/1 (13 with no bar), 1/2, 3/2 and 2/3 Bengal H.A.; 2/7 Bengal F.A. and Detachment of No. 6 Company Bengal Sappers and Miners; 31 (524), 50 (629), 53 (708), 62 (4 as Aliwal only and 47 with Sobraon), 80 (6 as Aliwal only and 18 with Sobraon) Foot; 13, 24, 30, 36, 47, 48 Bengal N.I.; 1, 2, Goorkhas.

Sobraon *(10th February, 1846)*

Regiments present: 3 Light Dragoons (391, 10 with Sobraon in the exergue), 9 (637), 16 (436) Lancers, 3, 4, 5 Bengal Light Cavalry; 2, 8, 9 Irregular Cavalry; Bodyguard Cavalry; 1/1, 2/1 (3 with no bar), 3/1 (3 with no bar), 5/1, 1/2, 2/2, 3/2, 1/3, 2/3, 3/3, 4/3 Bengal H.A.; 2/2, 3/3, 4/3, 1/4, 2/4, 3/4, 4/4, 1/6, 2/6, 3/6, 4/6, 2/7 Bengal F.A.; 2, 3, 4, 5, 6, 7 Companies Bengal Sappers and Miners; 9 (637), 10 (778), 29 (612), 31 (503), 50 (571), 53 (760), 62 (662), 80 (694) Foot; 1 Bengal European Regiment (565) (later 1st Btn. Royal Munster Fusiliers); 4, 5, 9, 12, 16, 24, 33, 38, 41, 42, 43, 45, 47, 59, 63, 68, 73 Bengal N.I.; 1, 2 Goorkhas.

54 PUNJAB CAMPAIGN MEDAL (7th September, 1848-14th March, 1849)

Obverse	The diademed head of Queen Victoria with the legend "VICTORIA REGINA".
Reverse	Major-General Sir Walter Gilbert, on horseback receiving the surrender of the Sikhs. In the background is a hill with a large palm tree on it. Around the top is the inscription "TO THE ARMY OF THE PUNJAB". In the exergue is the date "MDCCCXLIX".
Size	1.42 in. diameter.
Ribbon	1.25 in. wide. Dark blue with a yellow stripe near each edge.
Suspension	An ornamental swivelling suspender.
Designer	Wm. Wyon, R.A.
Naming	In impressed Roman capitals. The name of the recipient's ship, in the case of medals awarded to the Indus flotilla, is not given.
No. of bars issued	Three — "MOOLTAN", "CHILIANWALA", and "GOOJERAT".

The bars to this medal should read downwards — *i.e.*, the more recent award nearest the piece. As the bars were issued to be affixed locally we find a great number of genuine medals with the bars in the wrong order. It should be noted that medals to the 1/60th with the single bar for Mooltan are rare, and as a general rule the medals to units which were present at Mooltan and Goojerat are more valuable with the single bar than the double. For this reason medals with the single bar for Mooltan should be carefully examined to see whether there are any signs of a second bar having been taken off.

Many medals are found with no bars. The units which received the medal and yet saw no fighting are the following: 2nd Bengal European Regiment (35), 7th Bengal Cavalry, Bengal Horse and Foot Artillery, 53rd (367) Foot, 98th Foot (503), Bengal Pioneers, two regiments of the Sikh Infantry and the 1, 3, 4, 18, 22, 29, 37, 50, 53 (367), 71, 73 Bengal N.I. Fifty-four medals were awarded with bars to members of the Indus flotilla and these command good prices.

At the Battle of Chilianwala the 24th Foot suffered twenty-one officer and 503 other-rank casualties and therefore the medals to them are much prized.

There were no medals issued with three bars, and no unit received a medal with the bars for Mooltan and Chilianwala.

A General Order dated the 2nd April, 1849, granted the award of a medal to all employed in the Punjab between the 7th September, 1848, and the 14th March, 1849.

This campaign was practically a continuation of the Sutlej one which was ended by a treaty signed at Lahore on the 22nd February, 1846.

In spite of, or perhaps because of, their heavy defeats in that campaign the feelings of hatred still persisted among the Sikhs. This hatred culminated in the murder of the British Resident in Mooltan.

This was the signal for Mulraj Singh to start a rebellion. He had little difficulty in collecting serveral thousand followers among the recently disbanded Sikhs, but it is extraordinary where he managed to get the guns and other weapons which were to cause such grievous losses. It seems to have been true throughout the ages that no shortage of money or weapons will stop a people from having a jolly good rebellion or war if they want one.

Lord Gough again commanded in the field. After three more defeats the Sikhs surrendered and the Punjab was annexed.

The famous Kohinor, or Mountain of Light, diamond was handed over by Shuleep Singh and eventually presented to Queen Victoria on the 3rd July, 1850. The gem weighed about 800 carats, but was so badly damaged in the cutting that its weight was reduced to about 280 carats. Later it was again re-cut and reduced to its present weight of about 102 carats.

When one considers that the largest known diamond at that time was the Russian one weighing only (by comparison) 193 carats one realizes what was the real value of the Kohinor. The sum of £104,000 and an annuity of £1,040 for life was refused for the Russian gem, which later became part of the Czar's sceptre. I wonder where it is now.

Numbers claimed shown in brackets.

Mooltan *(Siege of, 7th September-22nd January, 1849)*

Two thousand nine hundred of these bars were issued to Europeans and 16,067 to natives.

Regiments present: Guides Cavalry; 1, 2 Scinde Horse; 1 Bombay Light Cavalry; 11 Bengal Light Cavalry; 7, 11 and 1 Squadron 14 Irregular Cavalry; 4/1, 4/3 Bengal H.A.; 2/2, 3/3, 4/3, 6/7 Bengal F.A.; 3 Bombay H.A.; 2/1, 4/2, 1/4, 2/4 Bombay F.A.; 1, 2, 3 Companies Bengal and 1, 2 Companies Bombay Sappers and Miners; 2, 3 and part of 5 Bengal Pioneers; 10 (843), 24 (2), 32 (1105), 1/60 (998, 100 of which were single bars), 103 (102 as single bars and 789 with Goojerat) Foot; 8, 49, 51, 52, 72 Bengal N.I.; 3, 4, 9, 14th, 19. Bombay N.I.; Scinde and Camel Corps; a hundred men from the Indus flotilla with bar and fifty four without bar. (The name of the recipient's ship is rarely given on the medal.)

Chilianwala *(13th January, 1849)*

Four thousand three hundred bars were awarded to Europeans and 16,153 to natives.

Regiments present: 3 Light Dragoons (586), 9 Lancers (651 but only 1 as a single bar). 14 Light Dragoons (564); 1, 5, 6, 8 Bengal Light Cavalry; 3, 9 Irregular Cavalry; 1/2, 2/2, 3/2, 4/2, 1/3, 2/3 Bengal H.A.; 1/1, 3/1, 1/4, 2/4, 4/4, 2/7, 3/7 Bengal F.A.; 4, 5, 6, 7 Companies Bengal Pioneers; 24 (497 killed and wounded, 1,060 medals), 29 (948), 61 (835) Foot; 2 Bengal European Regiment (36 single bars and 700 with Goojerat); 20, 25, 30, 31, 36, 45, 56, 69, 70 Bengal N.I.

Goojerat *(21st February, 1849)*

Six thousand two hundred bars were issued to Europeans and 26,760 to natives.

Regiments present: 3 Light Dragoons (565); 9 Lancers (666 but 14 only as a single bar); 14 Light Dragoons (549), 1, 8 Bengal Light Cavalry; Guides Cavalry; Scinde Irregular Horse; 3, 9, 11, 14 Irregular Cavalry; 1/2, 2/2, 3/2, 4/2, 1/3, 2/3, 4/3 Bengal H.A.; 1/1, 3/1, 2/2, 3/3, 4/3, 1/4, 2/4, 4/4, 3/7 Bengal F.A.; 3 Bombay H.A.; 2/1 Bombay F.A.; 2, 3 Companies Bengal Sappers; 1 Company Bombay Sappers and Miners; 2, 3, 4, 5, 6, 7 Bengal Pioneers; 10 (790), 24 (694), 29 (824), 32 (975), 53 (611), 1/60 (912), 1/61 (888) Foot; 2 Bengal European Regiment (13 single bars and 700 with Chilianwala); 1 Bombay European Regiment; 8, 15, 20, 21, 25, 30, 31, 36, 45, 46, 51, 52, 56, 69, 70, 72 Bengal N.I.; 3, 19 Bombay N.I.

The following troops were in reserve: 5, 6 Bengal Light Cavalry; 2/1 Btn. Bombay Artillery; 45, 69 Bengal N.I.

55 SOUTH AFRICA CAMPAIGNS (1834-1853)

Obverse	The diademed head of Queen Victoria and the legend "VICTORIA REGINA".
Reverse	A lion, stooping to drink, whilst standing in front of a protea bush; above him is the wording "SOUTH AFRICA". In the exergue is the date "1853".
Size	1.42 in. diameter.
Ribbon	1.25 in. wide. Orange watered with two wide and two narrow dark blue stripes.
Suspension	An ornamental swivelling suspender.
Designer	Obverse — W. Wyon, R.A.; Reverse — L.C. Wyon.
Naming	Indented in Roman capitals.
No. of bars issued	Nil.

On 22nd November, 1854, sanction was given for the awarding of a medal for the three campaigns in South Africa against he Kaffirs between 1834-1835, 1846-1847, and 1850-1853.

Local volunteers and levies did not receive it except in a few instances and then only in exceptional circumstances. The medals were only awarded to survivors and then only to British regulars, all bore the date 1853 in the reverse exergue. The way to tell for which campaign a particular medal was awarded is to check it with the regimental roll, because, as will be shown later, some regiments were present in more than one.

It is difficult to understand why the date 1853 was placed on the medal, as it is quite pointless as regards the first two campaigns and only denotes the final year of the last for which it was awarded.

There is considerable controversy as to whether the ribbon for the 1834-1835 campaign should be paler than that for the other two, but one cannot see how this can be so, as all the medals, and the bits of ribbon to go with them, were issued at the same time. The ribbons for these three earlier campaigns were not paler than those issued withe the 1877-1879 medals.

It should be noted that the 1877-1879 medals issued without bars, did not bear the date 1853 in the exergue. The date is replaced by a Zulu shield and crossed assegais.

A breakdown of the 1853 medals awarded for the different date has been supplied by Capt. W. Morgan:

(Obverse)

No. 40. The St. Jean d'Acre Medal, 1840.

(Obverse)

No. 41. The Nepaul War Medal, 1814-16.

(Obverse)

No. 43. The Burma War Medal, 1824-26.

(Reverse)*

No. 44. The Army of India Medal, 1799-1826.

* Reference should be made to page 425 for medals with identical obverses.

To face page 152

(Obverse)

No. 45. The Coorg Medal, 1837.

(Obverse)

No. 46. The Ghuznee Medal, 1839.

(Reverse)*

(Reverse)*

No. 47. The Candahar, Ghuznee and Cabul Medals, 1842.

* Reference should be made to page 425 for medals with identical obverses.

To face page 153

Unit	Officers				Other Ranks			
	1834-1835	1834-1835 & 1846-1847	1846-1847	1846-1847 & 1850-1853	1834-1835	1834-1835 & 1846-1847	1846-1847	1846-1847 & 1850-1853
Staff	—	—	—	1	—	—	1	—
Commissariat	2	—	9	7	—	—	2	—
7th Dragoon Gds.	—	—	16	—	—	—	152	—
12th Lancers	—	—	—	?	—	—	—	378 (total)
Royal Artillery	—	—	3	—	4	—	19	—
Royal Engineers	—	—	6	3	4	—	21	13
2nd Foot	—	—	—	?	—	—	—	570 (total)
6th Foot	—	—	13	6	—	—	65	88
7th Foot	1	—	—	—	—	—	—	—
12th Foot	—	—	—	?	—	—	—	456 (total)
14th Foot	1	—	—	—	—	—	—	—
17th Foot	—	—	1	—	—	—	—	—
27th Foot	6	2	13	—	43	20	128	1
43rd Foot	—	—	—	?	—	—	—	592 (total)
45th Foot	—	—	9	1	—	1	25	7
60th Foot	—	—	1	—	—	—	—	—
62nd Foot	—	—	—	—	—	—	1	—
72nd Foot	9	—	—	—	126	2	2	—
73rd Foot	—	—	10	1	—	—	57	40
74th Foot	—	—	—	?	—	—	—	530 (total)
75th Foot	11	—	—	—	127	—	—	—
87th Foot	—	1	—	—	—	—	—	—
90th Foot	—	—	14	—	2	—	273	1
91st Foot	—	—	22	3	—	1	209	13
95th Foot	—	1	—	—	—	—	—	—
Rifle Brigade	—	—	8	29	—	—	118	145
Cape Mtd. Rifles	—	1	10	16	3	—	13	28
No. Regt. stated	—	—	11	5	—	—	—	—

Medals were also awarded to Officers and men serving in South African units such as:— European Levies, Native Levies, Colonial Levies, Cape Town Levies Catty's Rifles, Particular Service and also to recipients without names of units included i.e. Storekeeper, Asst. Chaplain, Committee Clerk and Acting A.D.C. etc., most of the above being represented in the Mitchell collection.

H.M. ships: *Castor* (326), *Dee* (46), *Hermes* (92), *Radamanthus* (55), *Styx* (136) and one awarded to a Lieut. of the Norwegian Navy.

(The naval medals bear the name and rating only; the recipient's ship is not stated.)

It was when taking troops to this campaign that the troopship *Birkenhead* struck a rock and sank on 26th February, 1852. The epic bravery of the troops on board so impressed King William of Prussia that he had the full story read out on parade in every barracks in Germany. Medals to survivors who later took part in the campaign are particularly sought after. The number aboard the ship amounted to 15 Officers and 476 other ranks, the numbers lost being 9 officers and 349 other ranks. H.M.S. Radamanthus was the first naval vessel to reach the scene of disaster involving the Birkenhead, and picked up many survivors.

From now onwards we must differentiate between the different races of Africa or else we shall get confused as to why so many medals have been awarded for services in that continent.

Kaffraria, or that part of Africa inhabited by Kaffirs lies to the S.W. of The Transkei or in other words in the extreme East of Cape Colony.

In 1819 the Kaffirs, under Chief Mokannia, attacked Grahamstown, but were heavily defeated. Being nomadic and smarting under any form of restriction, they lived on their wits and the the result of plunder.

A punitive expedition became essential, so that a force was formed of the units enumerated above, under Major-General Sir Benjamin D'Urban K.C.B., with Sir Harry G. Smith as his Second-in-Command. The operations involved great feats of endurance and tact, because only certain tribes were causing trouble. In April, 1835, peace was signed with Chief Hintza, who had led the Tambooki and Amapondi tribes in their forays.

In April, 1846, the depredations of the Gaika Kaffirs under Chief Sandilli necessitated another expedition. This time two small forces were formed from the units mentioned above. The natives had, by now, received firearms, with the result that we suffered several casualties before Sandilli surrendered in October, 1847.

In December, 1850, Chief Sandilli again caused trouble and practically block-aded Sir Harry Smith, who had now become Governor, in Fort Cox. Much severe fighting took place, and not altogether in our favour, so that Sir Harry Smith was replaced by Sir George Cathcart. Further reinforcements were sent out together with a few rifles which were issued at the rate of six per company (this shows a great similarity to the issue to home troops in the dark days of 1940). These rifles were called Minié rifles. They were supposed to be effective up to a range of a thousand yards if "suitably directed". The men issued with them were termed "marksmen"; here the 1852-1940 comparison ends!

The Kaffirs were driven into the mountains, which considerably added to our difficulties, but broke them up into small bands which were eventually forced to surrender. Chief Mocomo, the Hottentots and the Basutos under Chief Moshesh sued for peace on the 20th December, 1852, as did Chief Sandilli.

Peace was proclaimed on the 12th March, 1853.

One must enlarge a bit on the events that took palce in December, 1850, so as to bring into correct perspective the story leading up to the award of what has become known as Sir Harry Smith's Gallantry Medal,* see following Medal.

At the time in question Sandilli's Kaffirs had surrounded the small garrisons in Fort Hare, Fort Cox, and King William's Town. Members of the Kaffir Police, and even a few of the Cape Mounted Rifles, mutinied and deserted, so Sir Harry decided that he had better break out of Fort Cox with his whole force to stren-gthen that at King William's Town about a dozen miles away. Accordingly, therefore, he made the dash with his remaining two hundred and fifty or so Cape Mounted Riflemen.

---

*Recipients of Sir Harry Smith's Medal for Gallantry (see p. 155). 1. J. Hassall; 2. Frs. Meades C.M.R.; 3. David Faroe; 4. John McVarrie; 5. J. Mouatt C.M.R.; 6. Hendrick Ferara; 7. Piet Jan Cornelis; 8. Thos. Duncan; 9. Capt. Skead R.N.; 10. John Keiberg; 11. H. McKain *Sotheby 1878 (Cheylesmore Colln) Glendining 1930 and 1963*; 12. Adrian Strauss *Glendining June 1918*; 13. Fundi (Bantu native policeman); 14. R.S.M. Wm. Richd. Dakins (?Hoskins) *Dr. Payne's Colln. 1911, Glendining 1949*; 15. Paul Arendt *Glendining 1911, Col. Gaskell's Colln.*; 16. Thos. Dicks *Glendining 1925*; 17. Sapper R. Dunning R.E. *Sothebys, 28.11.1907*; 18. Henry Evans *Debenhams 1898, Glendining 1933. Kennard Sale, Sotheby's 1924*; 19. John Main *Fleming Colln. 1871 plus* Unnamed, at least 11 (Eleven).

N.B. Cast copies of numbers 1-10 inclusive are known, in addition unnamed castings have appeared from time to time.

SIR HARRY SMITH MEDAL FOR GALLANTRY

Obverse   Lion standing on a reproduction of the veld and above, a wreath of laurel and below, in the exergue, the date of 1851.

Reverse   "His Excellcy. Sir H.G. Smith Bart. G.C.B. to —" and surrounding "Presented by. For Gallantry in the Field."

Size   1.36 in. in diameter.

Riband   The Sutlej riband was adopted.

Suspension   A steel claw not unlike the Waterloo Medals in design and a curved bar.

Designer   The name Hopkins is usually seen in the "veld" on the obverse although it is thought that the responsibility for the design was Mr. Charles Bell's, Surveyor General at the Cape.

Naming   Engraved on the reverse centre below the word "to" although it is believed that some of these medals were issued unnamed.

No. of bars issued   Nil.

This medal which is purely of local South African interest is very rare and the first medal worn by South African troops. (See latter section of previous medal.)

In spite of the fact that only a few medals appear to have been awarded it is known that they were struck from several different dies. At least 2 different obverse dies are known and 6 reverse dies. The full details of these differences, etc., can be found in an admirable article by Doctor F.K. Mitchell.

30 are thought to have been struck but only 25 are actually known to exist plus a bronze specimen in the Africana Museum.

For reasons which we have been unable to trace, he wished to reward about thirty men for gallantry and wrote to the Colonial Secretary. The following is an extract from his letter, which is quaintly worded and dated 7th March, 1851.

"I wish you would have some thirty or forty medals struck, made in the same way of the make of the Waterloo medal, but about two-thirds the size, with the same device, if we can make it. I wish to give them to some of the Cape Corps and of the levies who distinguished themselves. Inscription: 'Presented by Sir H. Smith for gallantry in the field.'"

Though the medal subsequently awarded by him bore no resemblance to the Waterloo medal, there is nothing whatever in this letter to suggest that he had any other designs in mind.

See end of page 154 for list of recipients.

56 BALTIC MEDAL (March, 1854-August, 1855)

Obverse   The diademed head of Queen Victoria and the legend "VICTORIA REGINA".

Reverse   The seated figure of Britannia holding a trident in her right hand and looking over her left shoulder. Behind her are depicted the fortresses of Bormarsund and Sveaborg. Around the top is the word "BALTIC". In the exergue are dates "1854-1855".

Size   1.42 in. diameter.

Ribbon   1.25 in. wide. Yellow with blue edges.

Suspension   An ornamental swivelling suspender.

Designers   Obverse—W. Wyon, R.A.; Reverse—L. C. Wyon.

Naming   The medals were issued unnamed except for those awarded to the Royal Sappers and Miners mentioned below (one hundred and two in all). Many recipients had their medals named in block capitals of the same type as the Crimean Medals.

No of bars issued   Nil.

These medals are to be found in two thicknesses, which neither adds to nor subtracts from their value.

There are two different types of claws; one is plain like that illustrated, the other is a bit more ornate at the top.

Lieutenants C. B. P. Nugent, R.E., and J. C. Cowell, one sergeant and nineteen Royal Sappers and Miners were on board H.M.S. *Duke of Wellington*. Captain F. W. King, R.E., commanding No. 2 Company, eighty strong sailed ou board the transport *Julia*. The medals to these four officers and their men are named in impressed Roman capitals. Those to the men give their rank, name and corps. Collectors should be on their guard against *inscribed* specimens which are not official issues. They are nothing more than the common Baltic Medal engraved with a probably fictitious number, rank and name.

The following ships were present: Sir C. Napier's flagship, *Duke of Wellington*, and *Aeolus, Ajax, Alban, Algiers, Amphion, Archer, Arrogant, Basilisk, Belleisle,* * *Blenheim, Boscawen, Bulldog, Caesar, Calcutta, Conflict, Cornwallis, Colossus, Cossack, Cressy, Cruiser, Cumberland, Dauntless, Desperate, Dragon, Driver, Edinburgh, Eolus, Esk, Euryalus, Eurydice, Exmouth, Falcon, Geyser, Harrier, Hastings, Hawke, Hecla, Hogue, Impérieuse, James Watt, Leopard, Lightning, Locust, Magicienne, Majestic, Merlin, Miranda, Monarch, Neptune, Nile,*† *Odin, Orion, Pembroke, Pique, Porcupine, President, Prince Regent, Princess Alice, Princess Royal,* ** *Pylades, Retribution, Rosamond, Royal George, Saint George, St. Jean d'Acre, Tartar, Valorous, Virago, Volcano, Vulture.* The following floats, mortar ships and tenders were also present: *Badger, Beacon, Biter, Blazer, Carron, Dapper, Drake, Growler, Gleaner, Havock, Lark, Magpie, Manly, Mastiff, Pelter, Pickle, Pincher, Porpoise, Prompt, Redbreast, Redwing, Sinbad, Skylark, Snap, Snapper, Starling, Stork, Thistle, Weazel.*

This medal was sanctioned on the 23rd April, 1856, as an award for services in the Baltic under Admiral Sir Charles Napier and Rear-Admiral the Hon. R. Dundas.

Admiral Napier entered the Baltic in March, 1854. The forts at Hango Head were attacked and later, when a French Fleet under Admiral Dechasnes arrived, an attack was made on Cronstadt. Russian merchant ships were destroyed in the Gulfs of Bothnia and Riga.

Bomarsund was attacked in August, 1855, and the Sappers and Miners were landed to place demolition charges against the forts, which surrendered on the 16th.

At about this time Captain Lyons (son of Admiral Lyons, later Naval C.-in-C. Crimea), with the *Miranda* and *Brisk*, entered the White Sea and attacked Kola. The port of Petropaulovski, on the Kamtschatka Peninsula in the north-east of Russia in Asia, was attacked by Captain Sir Frederick Nicholson, who had with him the *President, Pique, Virago, Forte* and *Eurydice*. The attack was in charge of a French admiral, who was present with three French ships. Seven hundred

---

* The *Belleisle* was a hospital ship.

** H.M.S. *Princess Royal*: See "A Middy's recollections" R/Admiral The Hon. V. A. Montague, 1898.

† H.M.S. *Nile* was subsequently renamed *Conway* and became the famous training ship. She met a sad end in that she slipped her tow when being moved and ran aground in the Menai Straits and was not considered worth salvaging. She caught fire in October, 1956, when being broken up.

156

seamen and marines were landed under Captain Burridge of the *President*, but the affair was not a success.

In March, 1855, another fleet, this time under Rear-Admiral Dundas, was sent to the Baltic, Sveaborg was attacked from the 9th to 11th August, and Helsingfors (now called Helsinki), farther up the Sound, was practically burnt out. It is interesting to note that specially constructed mortar and rocket boats were used in these attacks.

Nothing further was done after the destruction of Helsingfors and the fleet withdrew from the Baltic in December, 1855.

57 CRIMEA WAR MEDAL (28th March, 1854—30th March, 1856)

Obverse	Diademed head of Queen Victoria with the date "1854" underneath, and the legend "VICTORIA REGINA".
Reverse	A Roman warrior holding a sword in his right hand and a circular shield in front of him with his left whilst being crowned by a small winged figure of Victory. The word "CRIMEA" is written vertically on the left.
Size	1·42 in. diameter.
Ribbon	1·15 in. wide, light blue with yellow edges.
Suspension	By means of a foliated suspender peculiar to this medal.
Designers	Obverse—W. Wyon, R.A.; Reverse—B. Wyon.
Naming	The medals were originally issued unnamed, but could be returned for naming free of charge. Those which were officially named were done in indented square or engraved capitals.
	In the Public Record Office there is a memo from Lord Panmure to a Mr. Elliott "Officers and men who have received medals without names in the Crimea, if they require their names to be engraved on them, and send them in for the purpose, Lord Panmure has no objection to its being done" 5th Dec. 1855. This note *may* indicate that all the medals sent out to the Crimea were unnamed whilst those issued in the U.K. were named.
	Those awarded to members of five selected ships were officially impressed, namely:— H.M. ships *High Flyer* (265), *London* (750), *Niger* (184), *Rodney* (880), *Wasp* (180).
No. of bars issued	Five—Alma, Balaklava, Inkermann, Sebastopol and Azoff. The maximum number of bars awarded to any one man was four.

This medal, of which 275,000 were awarded is often found with the bars arranged in the wrong order, the correct being from the bottom upwards—that is Alma, Balaklava, Inkermann, Sebastopol.

It is interesting to note that the medal and bars were not authorized at the same time.

The deeds of the Army so stirred the Queen that orders were issued on 15th December, 1854, for a medal with bars for Alma and Inkermann to be awarded to all present. The bar for Balaclava was sanctioned on 23rd February, 1855, and that for Sebastopol on 31st October, 1855. Many medals were issued before the last bar was distributed, consequently one finds a variety of fittings and, be it noted, many recipients did not bother to fit it on at all or sewed it on to the ribbon. It must also have happened that many men died from wounds, etc., before the award of the bar for Sebastopol, though they had been present at some time during the siege.

It was intended that all recipients of the bars for Inkermann and Balaklava should receive that for Sebastopol, but for reasons already stated this bar was not added, so that medals with the Inkermann—Balaklava combination only are found.

The fact that the medal was orginally awarded to commemorate the battles of Alma and Balaklava only accounts for it bearing the single date "1854" and not the dual ones as does that for the operations in the Baltic. The colours of the two ribbons were intended to be the same though arranged in the reverse positions.

The British Medal was awarded to some of our French military and naval allies. Some of them do not bear the date "1854" on the obverse. Sometimes found with two bars, Traktir and Mer d'Azoff.* The latter bar is somewhat smaller than the former and has different-sized acorns. The French medals were all awarded unnamed.

The medal for Alma with the single bar is rare. There were, of course, many awarded without bars to those who were present in the Crimea, but had not taken part in any of the actions for which bars, with the leaf and acorn pattern which is unique, were awarded.

In the middle of the nineteenth century, Europe seems to have had a sort of epidemic of "Questions". There were the Eastern Question, the Far Eastern Question, and others. These became, if suitably handled, excuses to go to war with self-bestowed blessings and the avowed belief that mass slaughter was the only way to uphold ideals. The fact that peace itself is the greatest ideal of all has been consistently overlooked throughout history.

Stripped of all excuses, the Crimean War was fought to keep Russia out of the Bosphorus. Those who wish to trace the original source of the trouble will find it in squabbles between the Greek and Latin monks in Palestine as to who should hold the key of the church of Bethlehem. It would be difficult to find a more quixotic reason than this for any war.

The Russians supported the Greeks, the French and the Sultan of Turkey supported the Latins. The Sultan's support could only be described as an invisible asset.

Thinking that Turkey, then described as the "sick man of Europe", was in the throes of disintegration, the Czar ordered Russian troops to invade the Turkish provinces of Moldavia and Wallachia whilst proclaiming his right to protect Christian subjects in the Ottoman Empire.

On the 28th March, 1854, Britain and France declared war on Russia. Later they were joined by the Italian kingdom of Sardinia which, when joined to that of Savoy in 1861, became the kingdom of Italy with King Victor Emmanuel I as its first sovereign. The kingdom, after riding two winning horses in two major wars, suffered a nasty fall whilst changing them in the third, with the result that the monarchy was run over and the last crowned sovereign, Victor Emmanuel III, died in exile in Alexandria on the 28th December, 1947.

Britain—unready as usual—having booked her place in the war, prepared to send an expeditionary force, which, if stories are correct, was well supplied with right-footed boots and summer clothing for the campaign.

The whole story of the campaign reads more like comic opera than war. Lord Cardigan, for instance, commanded the famous Light Brigade from his yacht *Dryad*, lying in Balaklava Bay, on which he dined and slept every night by permission of the Commander-in-Chief. He came ashore on the morning of the 25th October, led the famous charge the length of North Valley up to the Russian guns, left his men there, and walked his horse back, and returned to his yacht! The orders to charge were not his, so, having obeyed them, and having not the slightest use for his divisional Commander, Lord Lucan, or his Commander-in-Chief, he washed his hands of the whole affair! Subsequently, in true British

---

* The French also awarded a bar for Malakof.

fashion, he became a hero, Inspector General of Cavalry, a K.C.B., and Colonel of the 11th Hussars.

The British troops under Lord Raglan and the French under Marshal St. Arnaud gathered at Varna, on the west coast of the Black Sea. Sailing thence on the 3rd, they disembarked at Old Fort, about thirty miles north of Sebastopol, on the 14th, 15th and 16th September, 1854.

On the 20th the Russians, under Menschikoff, were attacked in their strong position on the River Alma. They were defeated and the way lay open to Sebastopol. Lord Raglan favoured an immediate advance, but the French disagreed. The result was that the brilliant Russian engineer Count Franz Todleben was given time to put the place in a state of defence. The combined allied forces were insufficient to surround the town, so a base was made at Balaklava, about ten miles to the south-east of it on the shores of Balaklava Bay.

The Russians, having consolidated Sebastopol, attacked the allied positions in and around Balaklava on the 25th October, 1854, but were driven back, as they were again to be in the epic Battle of Inkermann on the 5th November.

This latter action, which took place at night and in fog, was probably the last to be fought in the history of war as a purely hand-to-hand struggle. Of generalship there was none, of ammunition even less. Bayonets, butts and fists were the weapons, stark courage the deciding factor, victory for the allies the result.

After the Battle of Inkermann the siege proper of Sebastopol began. It was now that the gross inefficiency of the supply and transport services became manifest. There were no proper hospitals. The death-rate among those admitted to the hastily converted buildings exceeded 88 per cent. Four men died from disease to every one killed by enemy action.

On the 8th September, 1855, the key positions in the defence of Sebastopol, the Malakoff and the Redan were stormed. The French captured the first; the British were repulsed at the second. On the next day the Russians set fire to the town, sank their fleet and crossed the small estuary of the River Tchernaya on which Sebastopol stands.

With the fall of the fortress the war virtually came to an end except for an engagement between the Russians and the French at Eupatoria.

Though the fighting ceased, reinforcements continued to arrive, so that by November the allied strengths were approximately 51,000 British, 25,000 French, 20,000 Turks and, as is not generally known, a German Legion 10,000 strong.*

With the Austrians acting as intermediaries, peace terms were sent to St. Petersburg in December, 1855, a treaty of peace being signed in Paris on the 30th March, 1856.

The Crimea was evacuated in the following July.

There was one incident that took place in the campaign which is of interest and very far from generally known. It concerns the inventiveness, experiences and pluck of Boatswain John Shepheard, R.N., for which he was awarded the Victoria Cross.

In the 1914—18 War the Italians sank the Austrian battleship *Viribus Unitis* when in Pola harbour by means of an explosive charge placed against her hull. This charge had been carried in a small two-man torpedo through the boom defences. In the 1939—45 War a similar feat was performed by the Italians on 18th December, 1941, against H.M.S. *Queen Elizabeth* and *Valiant* whilst they were in Alexandria Harbour.

---

* The subsequent history of this Legion is most interesting, though outside the scope of this book. Suffice it to say that at the end of the Crimean War many of them accepted the offer of settlement in South Africa. In 1878 they and/or their descendants were recruited by Commandant Schermbrucker and formed into the Kaffrarian Rifles for service against Chief Sekukuni. (See No. 64.)

Boatswain Shepheard, of H.M.S. *Jean d'Acre*, constructed a sort of punt with a freeboard of only three inches in which he proposed to carry an explosive charge. He was then going to paddle it into the harbour of Sebastopol and attach the charge to the Russian flagship *The Twelve Apostles* and explode it by means of a time fuse.

His scheme met with a certain amount of opposition and ridicule until he showed the feasability of his idea by attaching a large dummy bomb to his own admiral's flagship.

It is a sidelight on how war was carried out in those days to read that both Admiral Lyons and Lord Raglan considered the whole idea very unsporting, and so would not sanction its use against the enemy. The French, however, had no such qualms and borrowed Shepheard and his boat.

On the 15th July, 1855, Shepheard entered Careening Bay, and although he got past the guard ships undetected he could not get through the large number of small boats that were ferrying troops across the bay. He managed to hide his craft and himself all the next day, whilst keeping careful watch of the enemy's movements. He returned to his starting-point the next night with much useful information. He repeated his performance on the 16th August, but once again was unable to dodge the traffic running across the bay.

Though he sank no enemy ships, there can be little doubt that the germ of the idea of limpet bombs and one-man torpedoes originated, or at any rate grew, in Shepheard's mind.

Alma *(20th September, 1854)*

Regiments present: 4, 8, 11, 13 Hussars; 17 Lancers; C and I Tps. H.A.; 1/3, 8/3, 2/8, 1/11, 3/11, 4/11, 5/11, 4/12 R.A.; Sappers; Medical and Transport Corps; 3/1, 1/2, 1/3 Foot Guards; 2/1, 4, 7, 19, 20, 21, 23, 28, 30, 33, 38, 41, 42, 44, 46 (6 officers and 225 men), 47, 49, 50, 55, 63, 68, 77, 79, 88, 93, 2/95 Foot; 1st and 2nd Bns. Rifle Brigade.

(Surgeon J. B. Greene received a medal with this single bar and another medal with bars for Alma, Inkermann and Sebastopol. A naval officer, who was A.D.C. to Lord Raglan, received a medal with bar Alma.)

Balaklava *(25th October, 1854)*

Regiments present: The Light Brigade composed of 4th Lt. Dgns., 8th and 11th Hussars, 13th Lt. Dgns., and the 17th Lancers. The 13th Lt. Dgns. and the 17th Lancers formed the Light Brigade Front line, the 11th Hussars the 2nd line and the 4th Lt. Dgns. and 8th Hussars the 3rd line. On the anniversary of Balaklava, 25th October, 1913, there were fifteen known Light Brigade survivors still alive.

Boxall, John	Pte.	4th Hsrs. age 83 living at Tunbridge Wells
Whitehead, John	Pte/Sgt.	4th Hsrs. age 89 living at Camberley
Wilsden, Henry	Pte.	4th Hsrs. age 92 living at Oxford
Phillips, Edward	Lt./Maj.	8th Hsrs. age — living at Reading
Fulton, Wm.	Pte.	8th Hsrs. age 81 living at Edinburgh
Gibson, Geo.	Pte.	13th Hsrs. age 82 living at Linlithgow
Mustard, Jas.	Pte./Sgt.	17th Hsrs. age 87 living at Twickenham
Watt, Thos.	Pte.	11th Hsrs. age 86 living at Dorchester
Parkinson, John	Pte./Sgt.	11th Hsrs. age 84 living at Birmingham
Smith, Percy	Lt./Capt.	13th Hsrs. age 88 living at Southampton
Olley, Jas.	Pte.	4th Hsrs. age 88 living at Elsing, Norfolk

(Obverse)
Mural Crown

(Reverse)
Flying Victory

No. 48. The Jellalabad Medals, 1842.

(Reverse)

No. 49. The Defence of Kelat-i-Ghilzie Medal,
1842.

(Obverse)

No. 50. The First China War Medal, 1842.

(Reverse)*

No. 51. The Scinde Campaign Medal, 1843.

(Reverse)*

No. 53. The Sutlej Campaign Medal, 1845-6.

No. 52. The Gwalior Campaign Stars, 1843.

* Reference should be made to page 425 for medals with identical obverses.

To face page 161

Kilvert, John   Cpl./T.S.Maj.   11th Hsrs. age 87 living at Wednesbury
Pennington, Wm.   Pte./Cpl.   11th Hsrs. age 80 living at Stoke Newington, died 1923.
Hughes, Edwin   Pte./S.S.Maj.   13th Hsrs. age 96 living at Blackpool
Maclean, Sir Fitzroy (Born 1835 died 1936)—the last survivor of "The Gallant Six Hundred".

The Heavy Brigade was composed of: 4, 5 Dragoon Guards; 1, 2, 6 Dragoons.

The famous Thin Red Line was composed of the 93 Foot (2nd Bn. The Argyll and Sutherland Highlanders), which is the only line regiment to receive Balaklava as a Battle Honour.

In addition to the 93rd Foot and cavalry regiments which received Balaklava as a Battle Honour, medals with this bar are found awarded to almost every unit present in the Crimea, though they, as a whole, took no part in the fighting.

What was known as a "Battalion of Detachments" was formed. These detachments consisted of about one officer, one sergeant and thirty men from several regiments. Medals were issued to the following regiments, but this list must not be considered as in any way complete. 20, 23, 42, 46, 55, 63, 68, 79, 88 (35) Foot; Rifle Brigade, C and I Troops H.A.; 1/3, 2/8, 1/11, 3/11, 5/11, 4/12 R.A. and the Royal Marine Brigade drawn from a number of ships.

Inkermann *(5th November, 1854)*

Regiments present: 5 Dragoon Guards; 6 Dragoons; 4, 8, 11, 13 Hussars; 17 Lancers; C Troop H.A.; 1/3, 8/3, 2/8, 3/11, 4/11, 5/11, 6/11, 7/11, 8/11, 1/12, 2/12, 3/12, 4/12, 6/12, 7/12 R.A.; Sappers; 3/1, 1/2, 1/3 Foot Guards; 1, 4, 7, 19, 20, 21, 23, 28, 30, 33, 38, 41, 44, 46 (6 officers and 201 men), 47, 49, 50, 55, 57, 63, 68, 77, 79, 2/95 Foot; 1st and 2nd Rifle Brigade; Naval Brigade and Royal Marine Brigades drawn from a large number of ships.

Sebastopol *(11th September, 1854—9th September, 1855)**

Regiments present: 1, 4, 5, 6 Dragoon Guards; 1 Royal Dragoons; 2, 6 Dragoons; 4, 8,* 10, 11, 13 Hussars; 12, 17 Lancers; R.H.A.; R.A.; Sappers; Medical and Transport Corps; 3/1, 1/2, 1/3 Foot Guards; 1/1, 2/1, 1/3, 1/4, 7, 9, 13, 14, 17, 18, 19, 20, 21, 23, 28, 30, 31, 33, 34, 38, 39, 41, 42, 44, 46, 47, 48, 49, 50, 55, 56, 57, 62, 63, 68, 71, 72, 77, 79, 82, 88, 89, 90, 93, 95, 97 Foot; 1st and 2nd Rifle Brigade and Royal Marine Brigades drawn from a large number of ships.

H.M. ships: *Agamemnon, Albion, Arethusa, Bellerophon, Britannia, Cyclops, Firebrand, Furious, Highflyer, London, Lynx, Niger, Queen, Resistance, Retribution, Rodney, Samson, Sanspareil, Sphinx, Spitfire, Terrible, Trafalgar, Tribune, Triton, Vesuvius.*

It is interesting to note that in the early days of the siege our men were paid for each Russian shot that they salvaged so that they could be fired back again!

Azoff *(25th May—22nd September, 1855)*†

This bar was only awarded to Naval personnel and Marines who entered the Sea of Azoff.

* The dates for the Royal Navy were 1st October, 1854—9th September, 1855.

† The *London Gazette* of 2nd May, 1856, gives the final date as 22nd November for officers and men who were employed in operations in the Sea of Azoff, but a later *Gazette*, dated 5th August, 1856, quotes the inclusive dates as given above.

H.M. ships: *Agamemnon* (86), *Algiers* (144), *Ardent* (83), *Arrow* (77), *Beagle* (79), *Boxer* (32), *Clinker* (34), *Cracker* (26), *Curlew* (130), *Danube* (37), *Fancy* (32), *Grinder* (32), *Hannibal* (62), *Industry* (48), *Jasper*, *Lynx* (71), *Medina* (105), *Miranda* (236), *Moslem* (25), *Princess Royal* (59), *Recruit* (65), *Royal Albert* (63), *Snake* (80), *Sphinx*, *Stromboli* (151), *St. Jean d'Acre* (62), *Sulina* (33), *Swallow* (130), *Vesuvius* (159), *Viper* (79), *Weser* (72), *Wrangler* (77).

TURKISH CRIMEAN MEDALS*

The Sultan of Turkey issued medals to the English, French and Sardinian troops who had taken part in the war. These medals are of three different types, the differences being in the arrangement of the Allied flags on the obverse. Owing to the loss, by shipwreck, of the ship carrying the medals for issue to the English troops, it would appear that our men were issued quite indiscriminately with either one of the salvaged medals or one of the other two types.

Obverse   British medal—A cannon with "CRIMEA 1855" in the exergue and Union Jack second from the right. French medal—A cannon with "LA CRIMEE 1855" in the exergue and French flag second from the right. Sardinian medal—A cannon with "LA CRIMEA 1855" in the exergue and Sardinian flag second from the right.

Reverse   The Sultan's cipher within a wreath of laurel, also the year of the Hegira, 1271.

Size   1·45 in. diameter.

Ribbon   Watered crimson with green edges. The original ribbon was ½ in. wide, but the medals were often altered so that the normal 1¼-in. ribbon could be worn.

Suspension   Many and varied. The medals were orginally issued with a small ring through which the ribbon was passed. These rings were usually taken off and either a similar suspender as that to the Crimean Medal fitted or one of the type used with the usual Indian medals.

Naming   The medals were issued unnamed, but as many of the recipients had their British medals named privately they must have had these done at the same time, as some are to be found named in similar ways.

No. of bars issued   Nil.

Sardinian medals are seen which, one assumes, were made privately of purer silver content than any of the general issues, with excellent relief work, and the initials "C.B".

With no date to go by, it is probable that these medals, which are of slightly different size from the usual ones, were made at the instigation of certain officers who were disappointed, to say the least, with the workmanship of their originals. As the sizes were not the same, it would be safe to classify them as "unofficial".

One cannot say who "C.B." was, how many medals were struck, or why the Sardinian issue was copied. This may have been because, the instigator of the idea of having the original copied and improved upon, had himself been awarded the more common Sardinian type, so could hardly wear a copy of a medal of which he had not been awarded the original.

* See Varia, p. 383, for further Turkish awards.

INDIAN MUTINY MEDAL (1857–1858)

Obverse	Diademed head of Queen Victoria with the legend "VICTORIA REGINA".
Reverse	A standing helmeted figure of Britannia holding a wreath in her outstretched right hand and over her left arm is the Union Shield. Behind her is the British Lion and above the word "INDIA". In the exergue are the two dates "1857–1858".
Size	1·42 in. diameter.
Ribbon	1·25 in. wide. White with two ¼-in. scarlet stripes.
Suspension	This and the China 1857–1860 medal have most unusual suspenders which are horn-shaped, attached to the piece by a rather high swivelling claw.
Designers	Obverse—W. Wyon, R.A.; Reverse—L. C. Wyon.
Naming	The recipient's name and regiment, or ship, is indented in Roman capitals.
No. of bars issued	Five—Delhi, Defence of Lucknow, Relief of Lucknow, Lucknow and Central India. These bars are fish-tailed and separated from the suspender and each other by rosettes. Bars should read downwards.

This medal was sanctioned by General Order No. 363 dated 18th August, 1858, and No. 733 of 1859, to the troops engaged against the mutineers. General Order No. 771 of 1868 (note the lapse of time) extended the award to all persons who had borne arms or had been under fire.

The latter order may account for the large number of these medals, the last of the Honourable East India Company's to be found without bars from the total of 290,000 awarded.

On January 21st, 1859, the Government of India sanctioned the reissue of medals gratis to all officers and men who had lost their awards during the Mutiny. This is an important point to bear in mind when considering war medals issued prior to the Mutiny, as re-issues are not generally considered as valuable as originals.

Members of the Naval Brigade from H.M.S. *Shannon* could get two bars—namely, Lucknow and Relief of Lucknow. The Brigade from H.M.S. *Pearl* as a complete brigade received no bars, though perhaps some members of it received the one for Lucknow.

The issuing of greased cartridges to the native soldiers was no more the only cause of the Indian Mutiny than the assassination of the Austrian Archduke Ferdinand, at Sarajevo in July, 1914, was the sole reason for the First World War, 1914–18. Both these events were enlarged upon and then used in such a way that only the most gullible person would believe that they, and they only, were the sole causes of the catastrophes that followed.

Trouble in India had been brewing for some time. Serious unrest started after the annexation of the provinces of Oudh and the Punjab in 1856, because the native princes feared that they would lose their territories and their thrones.

In July, 1855, there was a mutiny of the Sonthals, a tribe of Northern India, which was not suppressed until May, 1856.

On the 7th February, 1856, the Province of Oudh (or Oude) was annexed. The King and Queen of Oudh went to London to appeal against this annexation, but to no avail. It is certain that when he returned to India, embittered by what had happened, the King fomented trouble and kindled a hatred against the British presence in the country and the British rule in particular.

Anyone who knows anything about natives of any continent realizes that if the chief, or medicine man, has a really good grouse his main concern for some time is to see that no one is left in ignorance of the fact. When he has got his followers grousing, they are all teed up ready to be driven into war, rebellion or religion, according to which is on the agenda.

The cause of the failure of so many mutinies is that some mutineers drive off before the event is timed to start and thus annoy their fellow members who are unprepared. The Indian Mutiny was no exception. Serious as it was, there was no concerted action on the part of the rebels.

In March, 1857, seven companies of Bengal Native Infantry mutinied at Barrackpore. A rumour got round the sepoys that they were all going to be Christianized and another that a new type of ammunition was going to be introduced which required greasing with cow or pig fat. The seeds for the coming general outbreak were now well sown.

On the 10th May, 1857, the sepoys mutinied in Meerut, the first soldier killed in the Mutiny was Colonel Finnis, Commanding officer of the 11th Bengal Native Infantry at Meerut. They then murdered every white man, woman and child in the cantonment of the city and then fled to Delhi, where they were joined by other mutineers. Here they proclaimed the Great Mogul Emperor of India. They besieged Lucknow, Cawnpore and other cities of lesser note.

The bar for Central India was awarded for services against the mutineers in Rathghur, Saugur, Jubbulpore, Garakota, Serai, Marowra, Jhansi and many other towns in the Central Provinces.

The mutiny was not finally quelled until the 20th December, 1858, when Sir Colin Campbell, later Lord Clyde, announced that the last rebel had been driven out of the country.

On the 2nd August, 1858, the authority of the Honourable East India Company was transferred to the Crown, but it was not until the 1st January, 1877, that Queen Victoria was proclaimed Kaisar-i-Hind, Empress of India, by simultaneous proclamations in Delhi, Calcutta, Madras and Bombay.

Now for a few words concerning the parts played by the Naval Brigades.

In May, 1857, the news reached Calcutta of the disasters at Delhi and Meerut, whereupon the Governor-General, Lord Canning, immediately asked for help.

At this time Lord Elgin was on his way to China with reinforcements for the campaign which had started out there. Whilst waiting at Hong-Kong he heard of Lord Canning's predicament and, in agreement with Admiral Sir Michael Seymour, it was decided that the three ships H.M.S. *Sanspareil* (Captain Key), *H.M.S. Shannon* (Captain Peel) and H.M.S. *Pearl* (Captain Sotheby) should be dispatched to Calcutta at once.

On arrival at Calcutta, Captain Key landed his Marines at Fort William, whilst Captain William Peel, son of Sir Robert Peel, founder of the Police Force, formed a naval brigade of 408 seamen and marines from his crew. He also prepared for use ashore the following artillery pieces which were to prove so useful later on: six 68-pdrs., two 8-in. howitzers, eight 24-pdrs., two small guns and, be it noted, eight rocket tubes.

On the 13th August, 1857, the brigade started on its march to Allahabad, where it was joined on the 20th October by a contingent of 124 volunteers, under Lieutenant Vaughan, from the merchant shipping lying at Calcutta. It remained in Allahabad until the 28th October, when it left for Cawnpore, being joined on the way by Colonel Powell and part of the 53rd Regiment. The brigade reached Futtehpore on the 31st. Here it was joined by a detachment of the 93rd Highlanders.

On the 1st November, the force attacked the mutineers at Kudjna, where Colonel Powell was killed and Captain Peel assumed command. The mutineers were defeated and the advance to Lucknow was continued. It is worth noting that this must be one of the very rare occasions in which a naval officer has commanded a mixed force in action in the field.

Reaching the Alum Bagh on the 15th November, the brigade came under the command of Sir Colin Campbell, who ordered it to start bombarding the defences, part of which consisted of the Shah Nujeef, a mosque surrounded by a garden and a high wall, which had been heavily reinforced and defended. This mosque was to be the particular task of the Naval Brigade, which earned four Victoria Crosses in the process of its capture. The recipients were Lieutenant Thomas Jones, Lieutenant Nowell Salmon, John Harrison and Captain of Foretop William Hall, who was a negro from Nova Scotia.

Lieutenant Salmon earned his V.C. for sniping from a tree which he had climbed to get a view over the wall. Whilst so employed he was kept supplied with loaded rifles by a private of the 93rd.

In these days when the mention of the words Combined Operations conjures up visions of fleets of landing craft, bombarding squadrons, air cover and all the paraphernalia of modern war, one likes to think of this sailor, up a tree, 500 miles from the nearest sea, with his ghillie below, giving a very good example of a Combined Operation on the 16th November, 1857!

After the relief of Lucknow the brigade took part in the relief of Cawnpore.

The *Pearl* Brigade under Captain Sotheby, R.N., 249 strong, operated under Brigadier Rowcroft. It fought in no fewer than ten battles during its existence of fifteen months.

The awards to the *Shannon* and *Pearl* Brigades were as follows:

Ships	Bars	Officers	Other Ranks	Remarks
Shannon	Relief of Lucknow and Lucknow	15	155	2 forfeited, one of which was restored
Shannon	Relief of Lucknow	2	27	17 were awarded to Royal Marines
Shannon	Lucknow	13	256	4 forfeited
Shannon	Nil	3	61	
Pearl	Nil	22	227	
		55	726	

The maximum number of bars carried on one medal was four. Less than 200 of these four-bar medals were awarded to the 3rd Co. Bengal Arty. including 85 to natives serving in the unit.

The 9th Lancers were the only British Regiment to have been awarded as many as three bars.

The following British Units were in India during the period of the Mutiny, 10th May, 1857-30th December, 1858, and many of their members received a medal without a bar:

Cavalry: 1, 2 (69), 3, 6 (495), 7 Dragoon Guards; 6 Dragoons; 7 (103), 8, 14 (689) Hussars; 9 (95), 12 (90), 17 Lancers.

Royal Artillery: Y and J Btys. 3rd Bn.; 4 and 5 Bns.; V Field Bty; 6th Bn.; 8 and 14 Bn. R.H.A.: D and E Troops. **Bengal Artillery:** 1 and 2 Cos. 1st Bn., 1 and 3 Cos. 2nd Bn., 1, 2, 3 and 4 Cos. 3rd Bn., 2, 3 and 4 Cos. 4th Bn., 1, 2 and 4 Cos. 5th Bn., 1, 2 and 4 Cos. 6th Bn. Bengal Horse Artillery: 1 and 2 Troops, 2nd Bde., 1 and 3 Troops, 3rd Bde. **Madras Horse Artillery:** B Troop. **Nagpore Irregular Force Artillery; Hyderabad Contingent** − 2nd Co. Artillery; **Engineers; Medical Services; Commissariat Dept.; Ordnance Dept.**, 2nd Btn. **Military Train; Civil Service; Chaplains.**

Infantry: 1/4 (208), 1/5 (159), 1/6, 8 (310), 1/10 (236), 1/13 (980), 1/20, 1/23, 1/24 (281), 27 (925), 28, 29 (326), 32 (267 with no bar), 33, 34 (196), 35 (471), 37, 38 (501), 42 (54), 43 (755), 51, 52 (44), 53 (337), 54, 56 (22), 1/60 (332), 2/60 (363), 3/60, 61 (79), 64 (600), 66, 69, 70 (634), 71 (716), 72, 73, 74 (444), 75 (101), 78 (121), 79 (135), 80 (811), 81 (960), 82, 83, 84 (167), 86, 87 (1,073), 88 (134), 89 (80), 90 (74), 92 (428), 93, 94, 95, 97 (90), 98, 99 Foot; 2nd and 3rd Bns. Rifle Brigade; 1 Bengal Fusiliers (100); 1 Madras European Regt.; 1 Bombay Fusiliers; 2 Bengal Fusiliers; 2 Madras European Light Infantry; 2 Bombay European Regt. (271); 3 Bengal European Infantry (1,005); 3 Madras European Regt. (150); 3 Bombay European Regt. 4 European Light Cavalry.

Bengal Light Cavalry: 3rd. **Madras Cavalry:** 3, 5 and 7th. **Bombay Light Cavalry:** 2 and 3rd. **Bengal Native Infantry:** 3, 6, 12, 18, 21, 32, 36, 37, 38, 44, .47, 58, 59, 61, 62, 63, 66, 67, 73 and 74th. **Madras Native Infantry:** 17, 24, 26, 28, 33 and 35th. **Bombay Native Infantry:** 4, 24, 26 and 28th. **Hyderabad Contingent:** 4, 5 and 6 Infantry. **Punjab Units:** 4th Punjab Rifles, 16 and 23rd Punjab Infantry, 2nd Sikh Cavalry, 1st Sikh Infantry. Darjeeling Sappers and Miners; Belooch Btn.; Golconda Local Corps; 1st Khandeesh Bheel Corps; 2nd Khandeesh Bheel Corps; Kumaon Levy; Kuppoorthulla Contingent; Musseeree Ghoorka Btn; Sawunt and Warree Local Corps; Sylhet Lt. Infantry; Behar and Shahabad Police; Dumoh Military Police; Jubbulpore Police Btn.; 11th Regt. Oudh Police; Alexanders Horse; Benares Horse; Bengal Yeomanry Cavalry; 2nd Troop Bengal Yeomanry Cavalry; Jat Horse Yeomanry; Maynes Horse; Mooltanee Regt. of Cavalry; Mysore Horse; Nagpore Irregular Cavalry; 1st Nagpore Irregular Cavalry; Pathan Horse; Poona Irregular Horse; Rohilcund Horse; Sind Irregular Horse; 1st Regt. South Mahratta Horse; Volunteer Cavalry.

Naval Brigades: H.M.S. *Shannon* (Captain Peel); H.M.S. *Pearl* (Captain Sotheby).

Indian Naval Brigade, including many small river vessels: *Berhampooter, Calcutta, Coromandel, Dallah, Damoodah, Diana, Enterprise, Fire Queen, Ganges, Hoorungotta, Jumna, Koladyne, Lord Wm. Bentinck, Loorma, Mahanuddy, Megna, Myoo, Nemesis, Nerbuddah, Phlegathon, Pluto, Prosperine, Punjab, Sanspareil, Sesostris, Soornia, Tenasserim, Thames* and *Zenobia*.

Delhi *(30th May-14th September, 1857)*

This bar was awarded to the troops employed in the recapture of the city. The relieving forces, owing to illness and death, had no fewer than four commanders between 14th May and 14th September, 1857. They were General Sir George Anson, General Reed, Major-General Sir Henry Barnard, and finally Brigadier-General Archdale Wilson.

Regiments present: 6 Dragoon Guards (223), 7th Hsrs. (1); 8th Hsrs. (13); 9 Lancers (533); 1, 2, 5 Punjab Cavalry; 4 Irregular Horse; Guides Cavalry; Multan Horse; 1/1, 2/1, 3/1, 5/1, 2/3, 3/3 Bengal H.A.; 3/1, 2/2, 3/3, 1/4, 2/4, 3/4, 4/4, 2/5, 3/6, 4/6, 2/8 Bengal F.A.; Peshawar Mountain Train Battery; Bengal Engineers; Bengal S. and M. (129); 8 (636), 52 (716), 1/60 (680), 61 (871), 75 (798) Foot; 1 (763), 2 (748) Bengal Fusiliers; 1, 2, 4, 24 Punjab N.I.; 4 Sikh Infantry; 20 and 60 Bengal N.I.; 6th Bengal Light Cavalry; Guides Infantry; a battalion of each of the Sirmoor, Kumaon and 1 Balooch N.I.; Towana Horse; Jummoo Contingent.

Defence of Lucknow *(29th June-22nd November, 1857)*

The medals to the original defenders, under Sir Henry Lawrence, and after his death under Major-General Sir John Inglis, are the most prized. The first relief force under Sir Henry Havelock also received this bar. So as to show clearly which these medals are we give the composition of the two forces. A few civilians received medals with this bar.

Original Defenders: These numbered 1,538 soldiers and 160 civilians who were co-opted to serve. 4/1 Bengal F.A.; 32 Foot (19 officers and 517 other ranks); 84 Foot (50); 4/1 Bengal Arty.; 7 Bengal Lt. Cav.; Oudh Irregular units: 1, 2 and 3 Cavalry, 1, 4, 5, 7, 9 and 10 Int., 3rd Horse Bt. Arty.; and 1,099 natives of the 13, 15, 41, 48, 71 N.I.

1st Relief Force under Sir Henry Havelock: 12 Irregular Cavalry (95); Volunteer Cavalry composed of civilians (20); 3/8 R.A.; 2/3 Bengal F.A.; 1/5 (370), 64 (137), 78 (640), 84 (190), 90 (440) Foot; 1 Madras Fusiliers (1 Royal Dublin Fusiliers) (376); 14 Ferozepore Sikhs (448); Military Train; Barrow's Vol. Cavy.

Relief of Lucknow (*November, 1857*)

This bar was awarded to the troops under Sir Colin Campbell engaged in the relief of the city, who were composed as follows:

Cavalry: 8th Hussars (19); 9 Lancers (330); 1, 2, 5 Native Cavalry; Hodson's Horse.

Artillery: 4/5, 11, 5/13, 6/13 R.A.; 1/1, 2/2, 2/3, 3/5, Bengal H.A., 3/1, 1/5, 3/6 Bengal F.A.; E. Tp. Madras H.A. Peshawar Mountain Train Bty.

Engineers: One Company R.E. and two companies of Bengal and Punjab Sappers and Miners.

Infantry: 5 (208, 16 as single bars); 8 (331); 23 (wing); 32nd L.I. (23); 53 (wing 73); 64 (183); 75, 78 (358); 82 (two companies), 84 (5 Officers and 23 Other Ranks); 90 (419, 47 as singles); 93 (963 including 113 as singles) Foot; 1 Madras Fusiliers (1 Royal Dublin Fusiliers), 1 Bengal Europeans (1 Royal-Munster Fusiliers 414); 2, 4 Punjab N.I. Regt. of Ferozepore; 57 Bengal N.I. Naval Brigade from H.M.S. Shannon and H.E.I.C. ship Calcutta.

Seventeen medals with this bar were awarded to the Royal Marine Artillery.

Lucknow (*November, 1857-March, 1858*)

This bar was awarded to the troops under Sir Colin Campbell who took part in the final operations which resulted in the capture of the city.

Cavalry: 2 Dragoon Guards (464); 7 Hussars (435); 8 Hussars (6); 9 Lancers (462, 73 as single bars); 1, 2, 5 Punjab Cavalry; Hodson's Horse; Benares Horse.

Artillery: E and F Tps.; 8/2, 3/8, 6/11, 5/12, 5/13, 6/13, 3/14 R.A.; R.H.A.; 1/1, 2/1, 2/3, 3/3 Bengal H.A.; 4/1, 2/3, 1/5, 3/5, 4/5 Bengal F.A.; A/4 Madras F.A.

Engineers: Royal Engineers; Bengal and Madras Sappers and Miners.

Infantry: 5 (449), 1/8, 10 (719), 20 (714), 23, 32, 34 (586), 38 (993), 42 (893), 53 (386), 75 (12), 78 (550), 79 (846), 82, 84, 90 (683), 93 (850), 97 (657) Foot; 2 and 3 Bns. The Rifle Brigade; 1 Bengal Fusiliers (103 1 Royal Munster Fusiliers); 1 Madras Fusiliers (1 Royal Dublin Fusiliers); 2, 4, 24 Punjab N.I.; 32 Bengal N.I.; six battalions of Goorkhas; Barrow's Vol. Cavy.; 2nd Hodson's Horse; 27 Madras N.I.; 1 and 3 Sikh Cavy.

Military Train.

Naval Brigade from H.M.S. *Shannon.*

Central India (*January-June, 1858*)

This bar was awarded to those who served under Major-General Sir Hugh Rose against Jhansi, Calpee and Gwalior, and those who served with Major-General Roberts in the Rajpatana Field Force, and Major-General Whitlock of the Madras Column, between January and June, 1858.

Cavalry: 8 (511), 14 Hussars; 12 (387), 17 Lancers; 3 Sikh Cavalry; 4, 6 Madras Light Cavalry; 1, 2, 3, 4 Hyderabad Contingent Cavalry; 1, 2, 3 Bombay Light Cavalry; Meades Horse.

Artillery: 5/14, 6/14, 7/14 R.A.; 3/1, 1/4, 2/6 Bengal F.A.; 1, 2, 3 Bombay H.A.; 1/2, 4/2, 2 and 4 Reserve Cos., 3/3 Bombay F.A.; A and E Trps. Madras H.A.; A/4, B/4 Madras F.A.; Peshawar Mountain Train Bty.

Engineers: Royal Engineers; Bombay and Madras Sappers and Miners.

Military Train.

Infantry: 70,* 71 (119), 72 (637), 80 (153), 83, 84, 86, 88 (874), 95 (752) Foot; 3 Rifle Brigade (detachment); 3 Madras European Regiment (806) (2 Royal Inniskilling Fusiliers); 3 Bombay European Regiment (689) (2 The Prince of Wales's Leinster Regiment); 13, 15 Bengal N.I.; 10, 12, 19, 13, 24, 25 Bombay N.I.; Sikh Police, Camel Corps; Rajpootana Field Force; 1, 10, 19, 25, 27 and 50 Madras N.I.; 3rd Hyderabad Infantry; 22 Punjab Infantry.

59 SECOND CHINA WAR MEDAL (1857-1860)

Obverse	The diademed head of Queen Victoria and the legend "VICTORIA REGINA".
Reverse	A collection of war trophies with an oval shield, with the Royal Arms in the centre, all positioned under a palm tree. Above is the legend "ARMIS EXPOSCERE PACEM". In the exergue is the word "CHINA".
Size	1.42 in. diameter.
Ribbon	1.25 in. wide. A variant had five equally spaced stripes, reading from the left, blue, yellow, red, white and green. The adopted ribbon was crimson with yellow edges.
Suspension	Exactly the same as that for the Mutiny Medal, namely by a horn-shaped suspender, which is attached to the piece by a high swivelling claw.
Designer	Wm. Wyon, R.A.
Naming	The medals issued to the Royal Navy were unnamed; a few of those to the Marines and Indian Marine are, however, to be found named as those to the Army, namely in neat indented Roman capitals.
No. of bars issued	Six.

There is one five-bar medal and that was awarded to Thomas Cole, R.M.A., H.M.S. *Cruiser* (although the roll only supports four bars), who received all the bars except that for China, 1842. There is an amazing number of made up five-bar medals on the market and when further particulars are requested the excuse is generally given that they are unnamed and so issued to the Navy, or Mint specimens.

The medal is often found without bars, so we give a complete list of all Naval and Military forces present during the period covered for the award — *i.e.*, 25th May, 1857, to 13th October, 1860 — as approved by Royal Warrant on 6th March, 1861. Fifteen members of the British Embassy Staff were awarded the medal without bar.

Owing to the few men of the regiment engaged, the medals awarded to the 1st Dragoon Guards are sought after most.

Regiments present: two squadrons 1st Dragoon Guards (3 issued without bars); 11, 19 Bengal Cavalry; 4/2, 1/4, 2/4, 6/12 (9), 3/13, 4/13, 7/14, 8/14 Batteries R.A.; A/5 Madras Artillery; 1/5 Supplemental Artillery and a Mountain Traun; R.E.; "A" and "K" Companies Q.O. Madras Sappers and Miners; 2/1

---

*Only a detachment of the 70th Foot received this bar. Most of the regiment received the medal without any bar.

(15 without bar), 1/2 (22 without bar), 1/3, 2/31 (10 without bar), 44 (36), 59, 2/60, 67 (7 without bar), 99 Foot; 15, 23 Sikhs; 19, 20, 22, 27 (37) Punjab N.I.; two officers and forty men of the 38 Madras N.I.; 3, 5 Bombay N.I.; Military Train; Medical Staff Corps.

H.M. ships: *Acorn, Acteon, Adventure, Algerine, Amethyst, Assistance, Bante, Barracouta, Beagle, Belleisle, Bittern, Bouncer, Bustard, Calcutta, Cambrian, Camillia, Centaur, Chesapeake, Clown, Cockchafer, Comus, Cormorant, Cruiser, Drake, Elk, Encounter, Esk, Firm, Flamer, Forester, Furious, Fury, Grasshopper, Hardy, Haughty, Havoc, Hesper, Highflyer, Hong Kong, Hornet, Imperieuse, Inflexible, Insolent, Janus, Kestrel, Lee, Leven, Magicienne, Nankin, Niger, Nimrod, Odin, Opossum, Pearl, Pioneer, Pique, Plover, Prince Arthur, Racehorse, Raleigh, Retribution, Reynard, Ringdove, Roebuck, Sampson, Sanspareil, Scout, Simoon, Sir Charles Forbes, Slaney, Snake, Snap, Sparrowhawk, Spartan, Sphinx, Starling, Staunch, Surprise, Sybille, Tribune, Urgent, Valiant, Volcano, Vulcan, Watchful, Weazel, Winchester, Woodcock.*

Indian Marine ships: *Auckland, Berenice, Coromandel, Ferooz, Prince Arthur, Zenobia.* (Issued with impressed medals with full details.)

There were a few other ships present, such as tugs and gunboats, to which no medals were awarded.

China 1842

The details of the issue of this bar have always been veiled in obscurity, however a letter from the Secretary of State for India to the Governor General dated 28th February, 1861 makes the position clear. "A clasp for China 1842 has been especially granted *in addition* to the clasps already approved for the 1857 medal. The 1842 bar is to be awarded to those of Her Majesty's forces who have *already* received the China 1842 Medal *and* have served in the operations from 1857-60. The Admiralty state that 93 bars were issued for China 1842.

Instructions were given that in the preparation of the rolls for the 1857 medal that those already in possession of the 1842 Medal should receive the clasp only for services 1857-60. In other words it was expected that those who had received the 1842 Medal should not be issued with a second medal but would be awarded bars to be added to their first medal. However it appears to have been overlooked that the suspender of the 1842 Medal was not at all suitable to carry clasps and this aspect seems to have been discovered after the issue of the loose bars had commenced. Consequently it would appear that the 1842 recipients were then sent medals from the 1857-60 die so that the medal could be married up with the loose bar already sent. In the meantime however it is more than likely that some had already fixed their bars to the 1842 Medal by altering the original suspender at their own expense. Unfortunately as the second medal was issued unnamed (unlike the 1842 Medal), it makes it impossible to check these with the rolls.

It is known that General Sir James Hope Grant was issued a medal for the Second China War, this having a China 1842 bar as well as two others for the 1857-60 period, the medal was fully impressed as "Commander of the Army". However a group to an Admiral in the Douglas-Morris collection has the 1842 medal with a suspender from the 1857 medal with a bar affixed for 1842.

Fatshan 1857 *(25th May-1st June, 1857)*

This bar was only awarded to Naval and Marine personnel from H.M. ships *Bustard, Calcutta, Coromandel, Cruiser, Elk, Forester, Fury, Haughty, Highflyer, Hong Kong, Hornet, Nankin, Niger, Plover, Raleigh, Starling, Staunch, Sybille, Tribune.*

Canton 1857 *(28th December 1857-5th January, 1858)*

Regiments present: 4/2, 4/12, 6/12 (105); R.A.; R.E.; R.M.L.I.; Medical Staff Corps; 59 Foot; 38 Madras N.I. (2 officers and 40 men).

Naval Brigade from H.M. ships: *Acorn, Actaeon, Calcutta, Cruiser, Esk, Furious, Fury, Highflyer, Hornet, Inflexible, Nankin, Niger, Racehorse, Samson, Sanspareil, Sybille.*

Taku Forts 1858 *(20th May, 1858)*

This bar was only awarded to Naval and Marine personnel from H.M. ships. *Bustard, Calcutta, Cormorant, Furious, Fury, Magicienne, Nankin, Nimrod, Opossum, Slaney, Staunch.*

(There is a medal to Henry Muggleton, Ordnance Corps, with this bar.)

Taku Forts 1860 *(21st August, 1860)*

Regiments present: 1 Dragoon Guards (two Squadrons, approx. 317 − 15 as single bars); 11 Probyn's and 19 Fane's Horse (11 and 19 Bengal Cavalry); 4/2, 1/4, 2/4, 6/12 (133), 3/13 (231), 4/13, 7/14, 8/14 R.A.; 1 Madras F.A.; R.E., Military Train; R.M.L.I.; 2/1 (51 as singles), 1/2 (613), 1/3, 2/31 (890), 44 (960), 57 (1),* 2/60 (760), 67 (851), 99 (8) Foot; 20, 22, Punjab N.I. (then numbered 8 and 15), 23 Punjab N.I.

H.M.S. *Chespeake, Clown, Drake, Furious, Janus,* and *Woodcock*; Indian Marine ships *Coromandel, Ferooz* and *Prince Arthur.*

Pekin 1860

Regiments present: Two Squadrons of 1 Dragoon Guards (approx. 318 as 2 bar medals, 1 only as a single bar); 11, 19 Bengal Cavalry; 1/4, 2/4, 6/12, (127), 3/13 (25), 4/13, 7/14, 8/14 R.A.; R.E.; 2/1 (17 as single bars); 1/2 (532), 2/31 (51), 44 (28), 2/60, 67 (751), 99 (531) Foot; 20, 22, 23 Punjab N.I. Medals were awarded to members of both the Royal Navy and Royal Indian Marine (Zenobia).

The causes that led up to this war were very similar to those that caused the First China War in 1842 − namely, maltreatment of Europeans.

On the 8th October, 1856, the Chinese in Canton boarded the *Arrow†* and took off twelve of her crew of fourteen. The flag was also hauled down. Admiral Sir Michael Seymour demanded redress, but none was forthcoming. On the 23rd October, 1856, he seized the Barrier Forts and entered the city. The forces at his command were not strong enough for the work in hand, so he appealed to the Governor-General of India for troops and the Home Government for naval reinforcements. They all arrived during March, 1857. In May, 1857, Commodore Elliot destroyed the Chinese fleet in Escape Creek and Admiral Seymour, with Commodore Keppel, those in Fatshan Creek.

The Indian Mutiny had drained our military resources so that, although a few troops had arrived, it was not until December, 1857, that the commanders on the spot felt justified in commencing combined operations on a large scale.

Major-General Sir Charles Van Straubenzee was given command of the British troops. The French also supplied a Naval Brigade.

Canton was captured on the 5th January, 1858; Yeh (see ref. China 1842) was taken prisoner and sent to Calcutta, where he died on the 9th April, 1859.

*This medal was awarded to Lieutenant Edward Brutton, who was serving on the staff. He also obtained the New Zealand medal dated 1861-66.

†The *Arrow* was a lorcha sailing udner British colours. A lorcha is a type of vessel peculiar to the Chinese coast. Their hulls look of European build, whilst their sails are of distinctly Chinese origin and design like those of a junk.

For the scene where the last three bars to this medal were gained we must go some three thousand or more miles northwards to the Gulf of Pechilli.

Lord Elgin had insisted that the Treaty of Peace should be signed in Pekin, but when the envoys arrived off the mouth of the Peiho river they met with a most hostile reception and a blank refusal to be allowed to pass up to Tientsin. It was obvious to Admiral Seymour that the Taku Forts which guard the mouth of the river would have to be attacked. After a heavy bombardment by a combined British and French fleet a landing party went ashore. The forts surrendered on the 20th May. On the same day, Tientsin was reached and a treaty signed by Lord Elgin, Baron Gros (for the French) and Keying Elepoo, who had signed the treaty after the first war.

It was soon made very obvious that the Chinese had not the slightest intention of honouring any treaty and simply looked upon them as a means of lulling suspicion and getting their forts rearmed and collecting fresh supplies of warlike materials.

By the peace signed in May, 1858, it was agreed that Britain and France should be represented by ambassadors at Pekin. Sir Frederick Bruce, whilst on his way to Pekin to take up his appointment, was stopped in the Peiho River by fire from the Taku Forts. Admiral Sir James Hope, who had succeeded Admiral Seymour, was forced to stage a full-scale attack on the 18th and 19th June, 1859. This attack was unsuccessful, so the Mission and the fleet had to withdraw. No bar was awarded for this action, presumably because it was a failure.

Matters could not be left like this, so the British and French Governments decided that a combined expeditionary force should be sent to China. This was composed of about 13,000 European and Indian troops with a French contingent 6,700 strong. In addition there was, of course, a combined fleet. The British troops were commanded by Lieutenant-General Sir Hope Grant, the French by General Montauban.

Operations started in August, 1860, and the Taku Forts* at the mouth of the Peiho river were captured on the 21st. On our arrival at Tientsin, which is about forty miles up the Peiho river, the Chinese again tried to bargain for time, but both the allied commanders agreed that it was essential to get to Pekin. The capital was entered on the 13th October after two severe actions at Chang-kia-wan on the 18th September and Pa-li-chian on the 21st.

A further treaty was signed on the 24th October. Kowloon was exchanged for the island of Chusan and a large indemnity had to be paid. Pekin was evacuated on the 5th November.

Affairs in China after this were far from peaceful as an extraordinarily complicated inter-state struggle then started between the Chinese, Tartars and Taepings on the mainland, whilst at sea piracy, smuggling and banditry of all forms continued on a large scale for many years.

We shall return to the scene again when dealing with the Third China War in 1900.

60 NEW ZEALAND MEDAL (1845-1847 and 1860-1866)

Obverse   Diademed head of Queen Victoria with a veil covering the back of her head. Around the head is the legend "VICTORIA D : G : BRITT : REG : F : D :"

Reverse   In the centre, surrounded by a wreath of laurel, is the date or dates of service. Above are the words "NEW ZEALAND" and below "VIRTUTIS HONOR."

---

*Breech-loading rifled artillery, which had been invented by Sir William Armstrong in 1859, was first used in war against the entrenchments at Sinho on 12th August, 1860 and next against these forts.

Size	1.42 in. diameter.
Ribbon	1.25 in. wide, dark blue with a red stripe $\frac{3}{8}$ in. wide down the centre.
Suspension	By means of a straight ornamental swivelling suspender of a design only used for this medal.
Designers	J.S. Wyon and A.B. Wyon.
Naming	Indented in very neat well-spaced capitals. Some of the medals which bear no date on the reverse are to be found with a date, or dates, engraved on the edge. The rolls indicate many late claims, some after 1900, which probably explains later style naming (often engraved) sometimes found. The New Zealand Ministry of Defence released a number of unclaimed medals to registered N.Z. collectors about 1969. The original names were partly obliterated by an engraved line and "specimen".
No. of bars issued	Nil.

Medals with engraved dates could quite possibly be late issues where the relief dates have been officially removed.

As the medals for these two campaigns are the same, except for the date or dates on the reverses, they have been taken together.

The medal was sanctioned on 1st March, 1869, for issue to survivors only of those who had taken part in suppressing the Maori risings in the North Island between 1845 and 1846, and for those in the South Island during 1847 and further service in New Zealand between 1860 and 1866.

The medal was issued to those officers and men of the Royal Navy who had taken part in the war, but generally only to those members of the crews who had actually landed and been engaged with the enemy.

There were twenty-nine different medals issued. Twenty-eight of these bore a date or dates on the reverse and one was undated. (A friend of mine has a medal with the dates "1846 to 1866" struck in relief. As it is unnamed it was obviously a specimen and so I have not included it although a few were issued unnamed.

Dated medals for the first war were given to the Navy only, those to the Army were undated.

Owing to the lax way in which the records were kept it seems to have been admitted that a man was entitled to a medal though the years during which he served in New Zealand were not recorded.

The undated medals, therefore, may signify service during either of the periods 1845-47 or 1860-66, and have no significance as regards any particular campaign.

This has been an extremely difficult medal to get particulars about, probably due to the fact that it is a dated one and so was not awarded for any particular action, or actions, but for service in an area during a period.

One fact must be borne in mind throughout, which is that because a unit was present for the period of, say, 1863-66 it does not *necessarily* mean that it was awarded medals for *all* the intervening periods for which they were given, *viz.*: 1863, 1863-64, 1863-65, 1864, 1864-65, 1864-66, 1865, 1865-66 and 1866.

We have endeavoured to give against the dates only those units which were awarded medals with that particular date, or dates, so that this is the way the expression "Regiments present" must be read, most units earned a few "odd" dates.

The particulars which have been obtained concerning the naval awards (which represent about 8% of the total) will be found after the medal dated 1866.

The following local forces received medals but no trace has been found of the dates, most were probably issued without dates or 1860-61.

Medals with no dates: These are to be found to the following units: Staff Corps; Artillery; Engineers; Army Hospital Corps; Commissariat Corps (64); 12 (146), 14, 18, 40, 43, 50 (276), 57, 58, 65, 68 (67), 70 and a few to 96 (for 1844-6), (25) and 99 (101) Foot, Military Train, 1, 2, 3, 4 Waikato Militia; Auckland Militia.

The following local forces received medals which were all *undated* and which were engraved by the jeweller in the district to which the medals were sent. Members of local forces and civilians who were employed by the Imperial Commissariat Corps were issued with an impressed medal dated 1861-66 although a few medals of the undated variety were impressed to members of the Waikato Militia.

Alexandra Cavalry Volunteers	1	Napier Cavalry Volunteers	3
Arawa Contingent	2	Napier Military Settlers	18
Armed Constabulary	478	Napier Militia	119
Armed Police	3	Napier Rifle Volunteers	40
Auckland Cavalry Volunteers	3	Native Contingent	94
Auckland Coastguard	1	New Zealand Militia	30
Auckland Defence Force	14	Onehunga Naval Volunteers	2
Auckland Engineer Volunteers	17	Opotiki Rangers	5
Auckland Militia	356	Otahuhu Cavalry Volunteers	6
Auckland Naval Volunteers	12	Patea Rangers	18
Auckland Rifle Volunteers	28	Patea Rifle Volunteers	16
Auckland Volunteers	57	Patea Yeomanry Cavalry	7
Bay of Islands Militia	1	Petone Cavalry	5
Bay of Islands Volunteers	2	Poverty Bay Cavalry	10
Bay of Plenty Coulenter Cavalry	6	Poverty Bay Volunteers	9
Carlyle Volunteers	1	Pukekohe Rifle Volunteers	6
Chatham Islands Guard	1	Taita Militia	2
Civilians in Imperial		Taranaki Bush Rangers	22
Commissariat Corps	239	Taranaki Cavalry Volunteers	20
Clive Milita	1	Taranaki Military Settlers	203
Colonial Defence Force	90	Taranaki Militia	142
Commissariat Transport Corps	9	Taranaki Mounted Volunteers	13
Corps of Guides	3	Taranaki Rifle Volunteers	228
East Cost Expeditionary Force	2	Tauranga Cavalry Volunteers	6
European Contingent	4	Wairea Rifle Volunteers	41
Forest Rangers	86	Waiuku Volunteers	6
Friendly Natives	108	Wanganui Rangers	31
Hawke's Bay Cavalry	3	Wanganui Cavalry	91
Hawke's Bay Military Settlers	29	Wanganui Militia	50
Hawke's Bay Militia	12	Wellington Defence Force	15
Hawke's Bay Volunteers	12	Wellington Militia	12
Howick Royal Cavalry Volunteers	2	Wellington Rangers	22
Hutt Militia	8	Wellington Rifles	33
Interpreters to the Forces	7	1st Waikato Regiment	595
Kai-iwi Volunteer Cavalry	37	2nd Waikato Regiment	483
Mauku Rangers	4	3rd Waikato Regiment	663
Mauku Rifle Volunteers	25	4th Waikato Regiment	17

Undated medals to the 96th Foot are rare.

1845-46 It is not accurate to say that medals with these dates were only issued to the Navy, as fifteen gunners of the Bombay European Artillery who served on board H.E.I.C. ship *Elphinstone* received them. Medals to G. Williams, 99th Foot and Capt. W.M. Biddlecomb, R.E., are also known which must be almost, if not quite, unique. A medal to Commander's Cook J. Crew, H.M.S. *Racehorse* was awarded.

1845-47 A medal to the Army with these dates has never been seen so it is suggested that those who were present from 1845-47 received the undated ones. Gnr. J. Simpson, Bombay Arty. was awarded the medal for service aboard the H.E.I.C. Ship *Elphinstone*. However the Northamptonshire Regt. Museum report that they have a medal dated 1845-47 to Lt. G.H. Page, 58th. Foot.

Medals purporting to have been awarded to J. Richards and J. Shea of H.M.S. *Raceborse* should be examined closely as they may be re-engraved, especially as Commander's Cook J. Crew of *Raceborse* received the 1845-46 medal.

1846-47 Medals with these dates were only issued to the Navy are are consequently rare.

H.M.S. *Calliope, Inflexible.*

SOME RECIPIENTS: H.M.S. *Calliope* — T. Coombs, A.B.; Robert Essary, A.B.; John Blake, Capt. Fore Top; Henry Monks, A.B.; C.J. Polkinghorne, 2nd Master; J. Tickle, Sailmaker's Mate; J. Friend, Boy, 1st Class; Henry Montes; B.B. Graham, Master; Richard Brenchley, Coxswain of Launch; J. Wright, Captain's Coxswain; Pte. C. Easterbrook, R.M.; J. Adkin, Fifer, R.M.; J. Belsey, A.B.; John Phillips; H. West, A.B.; J. Friend, Boy, 1st Class; W. Beard, Caulker; J. Dyer, Sgt. R.M. H.M.S. *Inflexible* — Sergt. W. Hayward, R.M. (an engraved medal).

1846 Ten medals with this date were awarded to H.M.S. *Driver* and one to Captain William Thorp, R.N., of H.M.S. *Calliope* (in lieu of 1846-47).

1846-65 One awarded to Col. R.H. McGregor, C.O. of the 65th Rgt. and now in the Napier Museum.

1847 Medals with this date are very rare and only twenty have been traced, all to H.M.S. *Inflexible* and one to Capt. T.B. Collinson, R.E.

1848 The only known medal bearing this date was awarded to Lieutenant-Colonel Andrew Clarke, R.E.

1860 To Lt. W.H. Blake, R.N. (Niger) and to Commander C.E.H. Vernon, of H.M.S. *Cordelia*. Others were awarded to Daniel Catmore, A.B., and C.M. Cooke, H.M.S. *Iris* (all in lieu of 1860-61), Capt. Chas. Pasley, R.E., Asst. Mil. Sec. to General Pratt, Lt. Col. V.T. Mairis, R.E., and six other ranks of the Sappers.

Australian volunteers were present during this year.

1860-61 Thirty-two Royal Engineers received medals with these dates, though most of the recipients were Naval or Marine personnel. 12th Foot (3), 40th Foot (13) and Lt. E.C. MacNaughton, R.A. received medals with these dates. Some of the naval medals were issued with undated reverse with 1860-61 on the edge.

1860-63 Only three medals with these dates are known namely those awarded to No. 6108 Sapper Thomas Ellis, R.E., Corporal Henry Barnes, R.E., No. 2124 James Phillips, 4th Battalion Military Train.

1860-64 This is a scarce medal.

Regiments present: No. 3 Battery, 12 Brigade R.A. (31); J. Battery, 4th Brigade R.A. (12); R.E.; 12 (4), 40, 65 Foot.

Some recipients: Gnr. George Jaques, Gnr. James Wood, Gnr. J. Pollerton, R.A.; Eighteen to the R.E.; Sgt. J. Sullivan, J. Smith, J. Williams, W. Malone, G. Carnell, J. Eustace, G.H. Boggs, M. Pain,

Adjt. J.T. Whelan, 40th Foot; Capt. Mair, 12th Regt.; Sgt. E, McKenna 65th Foot who also gained V.C. in 1863, his Cross is in the Auckland museum.

1860-65 This is a scarce medal.
Regiments present: 2 Battery Coast Brigade, J Battery, 4th Brigade (3) R.A.; 12 (9), 40, 65, 70 Foot.
Some recipients: 3523 Gnr. Ed. Singer, R.A.; Spr. Wm. Masters; Chas Wallace; Henry Dykes; Ralph Leigh; Wm. Walker; Thos. Ewing; W.M. Burrows; J. Mattock; R. Cole; W. Roberts; Thos. Boyle. 65th Foot: Col. Sgt. Jeremiah Ford, Geo. Jeffries. 70th Foot: J. Halfpin.

1860-66 This is a scarce medal, only thirteen are known.
Some Recipients: 1/12 Foot; 40 Foot, Henry Williams, Wm. Ashworth, Wm. Wall; Spr. Jas Mount; Cpl. J. Broughton, 12th Bde. R.A.

1861 Medals with this single date are extremely rare and the only known ones were awarded to Lieutenant Arthur Stewart Hunter, R.A., and No. 349 Driver William Matthews, "C" Battery, 4th Brigade, R.A. although Gnr. B. Donegan, R.M.A. (Murray Sale 1886) of H.M.S. *Falcon* received one with this date.

1861-63 No trace of any verified medals with these dates can be found, though an unverified medal to 2377 Serg. Chas Moore, 57th Foot and D. Gleed, 57th Foot are known.

1861-64 This is a scarce medal.
Regiments present: 12 (5), 40, 57 Foot, R.A., R.E.
Some Recipients: 40th Foot: E. Caplan, J. Sheenan and J. Bellow. 524 J. Buckley, 57th Foot: Wm. Reeves. 3rd Bty. 12th Brigade R.A. — Sgt. Jas. Arthur.

1861-65 This is an extremely rare medal of which only one is known.
Regiment present: 65 Foot.

1861-66 Regiments present:* C Battery, 4th Brigade R.A. (27); R.E.; 1/12 (85), 2/14, 57 (349), 68, 70 Foot; 1, 2, 3 Waikato Regiments. Auckland Militia.

1862-66 The issue of a medal so dated has always been questioned, however Sotheby's sold, in November 1977, a medal to Capt. Edward Mills, 57th Foot, and Glendinnings sold Ensign C. Picot's (57th) medal in December 1969, both medals bearing the dates 1862-66.

1863 This is an extremely rare medal. Medals are known to No. 3380 Pte. L. Connolly, No. 227 Pte. P. Mahon and No. 494 Pte. T. Hulmes, all of the 40th Foot. In addition two are listed to the R.E.: Lt. C. O'Neil Ferguson and Spr. R. Loader.
Regiments present: 1/12, 2/14, 2/18, 40 (14), 50 (29), 57, 65, 70 (3) Foot; Military Train and a Naval Brigade.

1863-64 Regiments present: R.E. (19), 12 (20), 40, 43 (30), 50 (15), 65, 68, 70 (66) Foot.

1863-65 Regiments present: 12 (27), 14, 2/18 (1), 40, 43 (71), 50 (3), 65 (8), 68 , 70 (3) Foot; H.M.S. *Eclipse.*

*Medals are known to: Drmr. J. Hall, 2/14th; 57th Foot, Lieutenant H.D.C. Barton, Cpl. John Shea, John Fills; 68th Foot, James Hillman, Patrick Murphy; 2nd Waikato Regiment, Sgt. J. Sullivan, Cpl. W. Ellen; 3rd Waikato Regiment, T. King.

1863-66	Regiments present: C (58) and J (8) Batteries 4th Brigade, 17 Brigade, R.A.; R.E. (7); Military Train; 1/12 (243), 2/14, 2/18 (463), 43 (377), 50 (342), 57 (10), 65, 68, 70 Foot.

1864 This is a rare medal.*

Regiments present: J Battery 97) R.A., 11th R.A.; R.E. (2); 40 (33), 43 (5), 50 (1), 68, 70 Foot; 4 Bn. Military Train; (Major von); Commissariat Transport Corps.

1864-65 Regiments present: J Battery (3) 4th Bde., 17 Brigade R.A.; 2/18 (1), 50 (1), 65 (25), 68, 70 (65), Foot and Spr. J. McIntyre.

1864-66 9th Battery 2nd Brigade (25), 10th Battery R.A.; 1 Bn., 11 Brigade, R.A., 2 Bn, R.A., 5, 7, 19 Bn. Costal Bde. R.A.; C (40) and J (36) Batteries 4 Brigade R.A.; R.E. (3); Gunner Riding Establishment; 1/12 (158). 2/18 (68), 40, 43 (109), 50 (102), 57 (61), 65, 69 Foot; Commissariat Staff Corps (13).

1865 Regiments present: 2/18, 43, 50, 65† (38), 68 Foot.

As the Navy is said to have taken no active part after the attack on the Gate Pah on the 22nd and 23rd April, 1864, one is unable to account for the award of medals to it with this date.

Medals with this single date are rare. Namely eight to the 65th Foot, three to H.M.S. *Brisk*† (though thirteen names are given on the Admiralty roll) and five to H.M.S. *Eclipse*. † There is a re-engraved medal to Spr. J. McLaghlan, R.E., and to Spr. J. Trivian.

1865-66 Regiments: present: R.A.; R.E. (14); 2/18 (30), 43, (possibly 3, including Asst. Surgn. O. Owen), 57 (40), 68, 70 Foot; 4th Bn. Military Train (76).

1866 Regiments present: 1/12, 14, 18 (3), 50 (8), 68 Foot; 4 Bn. Military Train.

The following British regiments were engaged in New Zealand between 1845-47 and 1860-66, but not necessarily for the whole of both periods: R.A.; R.E.; Military Train; 1/12, 2/14, 2/18, 40, 43, 50, 57, 58, 65, 68, 70, 96, 99 Foot.

Naval Medals

The awards to the Navy are in the form of a chart, but this cannot be considered to be complete.

*The following military recipients have been traced: 40th Foot: T. Cox, J. Connelly, J. Morrison, E. Drew, T. Heeney, T. McGinty, T. Whiteside, R. Weatherall, R. Jackson; 4th Bn. Military Train: Joseph Clare, Saddler Sergt. Isaac Saunders, Charles Tranter, William Leadon, H. Cranham, Cpl. Joshua Smith, Trumpeter W. Walters, James Butler, Farrier H. Horton, Henry Grundy, Wm. Warby, 2715 Charles Hunter, Thos. Ackers, Sgt. W. Mushet and Thos. W. Bennett

†Nine recipients of the medals to the 65th Foot that have been traced were James Delaney, Wm. Brown, Wm. Blakeley, James Wilson, Thos. Wm. Jones, Thos. Waters, Wm. Moorhouse, P. McLaughlin and Cpl. Michl. McQuire.

The four medals traced to H.M.S. *Brisk* were awarded to Sub. Lt. J.J.F. Bell, A.B., Edward Pomeroy. Lt. C.S. Fitton, R.N. John Davis. The traced medals to H.M.S. *Eclipse* were awarded to Ord. Smn. T. Bath, Pte. H. Rowe, R.M., and F. Browning, John Davis, Boys 1st class. Asst. Paymstr. A. le B. Corrie, Gnr. E.J. Parker, R.N., and Boy M. Swain (all received 1865 in lieu of 1863-65).

(Obverse)

(Reverse)

No. 54. The Punjab Campaign Medal, 1848-9.

(Reverse)*

No. 55. The South Africa Medal, 1834-53.

(Reverse)*

No. 56. The Baltic Medal, 1854-5.

* Reference should be made to page 425 for medals with identical obverses.

To face page 176

(Obverse—British)

(Reverse—French)

No. 57. The English and French Crimean Medals, 1854-6.*

(Obverse—Sardinian)

(Obverse—Sardinian)

No. 57a. The Sultan of Turkey's Crimean Medals, 1854-6.

* The brooches illustrated at the top of these medals are unofficial.

Where a question mark appears we know that medals were awarded, but cannot give the authentic numbers. This often prevents the complete authentic totals awarded to each ship being given in the right-hand column (pages 178 and 9). It should be noted that medals were only issued to the survivors who actually landed and engaged the enemy.

New Zealand was first discovered by Tasman in 1642. It was circum-navigated by Captain Cook, in the *Endeavour*, during the voyage in which he went round the world (30th July, 1768-12th June, 1771).

Captain Hobson, the first Governor, landed on the 29th January, 1840, and signed the Treaty of Waitangi, on the 6th February, as a result of which the native chiefs agreed to the ceding of large tracts of land.

There can be little doubt that the outbreak of war in 1845 was caused by the natives resenting the gradual infiltration of the white man, who obviously began taking a lot more than the Treaty permitted. Whatever the real cause, the natives rose in rebellion, headed by their chiefs Hone-Heke and Kawiti.

The only regiment in the country at the time was the 99th Foot, under Colonel Despard. After considerable bush fighting the troubles ended in the North Island in 1846, and in the South Island in 1847.

During this period about thirty-five officers and 360 men of the Royal Navy and Marines were employed. The discrepancy between these figures and the number of naval medals awarded is probably due to their not having been sanctioned until 1869, and then only to survivors who had landed *and* engaged the enemy.

It was during this campaign that our troops first encountered the native fortifications known as "pahs". These were high wooden stockades, generally of two walls with earth in between and surrounded by a deep ditch. They were, of course, proof against the small firearms of those days.

In March, 1860, the Maoris, under Chief Wiremu Kingi, again rose in revolt due to their belief, not without considerable foundation, that they were being made to part with their lands at prices all too favourable to the Government.

The natives of Tauranga, south of Auckland on the Bay of Plenty, who had remained quiet during the fighting of 1845-47, were incited by the natives of Waikato to revolt. The incitation was acted upon with such enthusiasm that it became necessary to dispatch troops from Burma, India and home to Tauranga and Taranaki, on the West Coast.

General Pratt, who arrived first with troops from Australia, took command. The natives were defeated at Mahoetahi on the 6th November. Peace was again established in March, 1861.

On 4th May, 1863, fighting broke out again and spread rapidly. More troops were sent, some of whom encamped at the end of a narrow peninsula called Te-pap. Incredible as it sounds today, the natives were allowed to build an enormous pah between the camp and the mainland which effectively isolated our troops from the region they had come thousands of miles to enter! This pah, being the gate to the mainland, became known as the Gate Pah.

On the 28th of April, 1864, the attack on the Gate Pah started. Owing to confusion and no little panic among the sailors and soldiers involved we suffered — and no amount of glossing will conceal the fact — a good hiding.

The war continued until the 3rd July, 1866, though it cannot be said that all native disturbances ceased much before 1881. The last British troops were withdrawn from New Zealand in January, 1870.

It is worth noting that although there was no "official" fighting between 6th November, 1861, and 4th May, 1863, medals were issued bearing these dates and many with dates which include them.

H.M.S.	No Date	1845 - '46	1845 - '47	1846	1847	1846 - '47	1860	1860 - '61	1861	1863 - '64	1863 - '65	1863 - '65	1864	1865	Total to Ship
Brisk	?													13[1]	13
Calliope	?	?				63									63?
Castor		69	see note 11												69
Cordelia	?						1[2]	29							30
Curacoa	?									190					190?
Driver	?	1[18]		10[3]											11
Eclipse		6[17]								1[15]	75			6?[4]	80?
H.E.I.C. Ship Elphinstone		6[17]													6
Esk	3									120					123
Falcon													12		12
Harrier	1[9]	35								79					80
Hazard[14]				?								1[13]			36?
Himalaya										1[5]					1
Inflexible					20[6]	?									20?
Iris	?						2[10]	72							74?
Miranda	?									92					92?
North Star[14]	?	41?													41?
Niger	?						3[8]	66							69?

Some undated medals were issued (after 1850) to satisfy late claims whilst others received engraved dates, these engraved dates appear to have been issued between 1875 and 1880. These factors have made it difficult to be absolutely certain regarding numbers issued, especially the undated varieties.

H.M.S.	1845 - '46	1845 - '47	1846	1847	1846 - '47	1860	1860 - '61	1861	1863 - '64	1863 - '65	1863 - '66	1864	1865	Total to Ship
Osprey	11													11
Pelorus	?						116							117?
Racehorse[7]	1[16]	36												37
Colonial Ship *Victoria*							40[12]							40
Auckland Naval Vols														9

1. The recipients from H.M.S. *Brisk* were: Lieut. C.S. Fitton (also received the Baltic); Sub-Lieut. J.F. Bell; Coxn. of Pinnace G. Collings; Captain M. Top; J. Long; Master's Asst. G.H. Stoate; Leading Seamen B. Crow, T. Hunt, S. Stevens; Able Seamen J. Churchill, J. Pook, Edwin Pomeroy; E. Harvey and P. Lyons.
2. This medal was awarded to Commander C.E.H. Vernon.
3. To Lieut. M.C. Connelly, R.N.; Able Seaman J. Darley and Ord. J. Cobden; Gnr. Wm. Barnes, Q.M., J. Harvey, Pte. J. Small, RmM., Lts. Chas. Bromley & Chas. Marcuard, R.N. Ord. G.H. Radmore & M.A.A., Aquila Alpe (see note 18).
4. Medals to Pte. T. Archer, R.M., Pte. H. Rowe, R.M., Pte. T. Bath, R.M. and Boy 1st Class M. Swain. Boy 1st Class Hy. Balcon. Asst. Pay. A. Le B. Corrie.
5. To Capt. E. Lacey who accompanied General Cameron in the action at Rangiiriri on Nov. 20, 1863.
6. We have traced medals to the following: Ropemaker J. Turner, Pte. John Alford, R.M., Gunner Robert Austen, R.M.A., Cooper's Crew J. Lloyd, and Able Seamen R. Roach, T. Stodden and W. Hird, Paymaster J.G. Aldridge, E.M. Johnson, Bosun's Mate & Boy N. Gordon (Gippy).
7. H.M.S. *Racehorse* was wrecked on 4th November, 1864, off Cape Chefoo, on the north-east coast of China, with a loss of ninety-nine lives.
8. Lt. (later Capt.) W.H. Blake, Actg. Mate Wm. W. Smythe and Lt. Wm. Watson-Smyth.
9. T. Rodda, A.B., H.M.S. *Harrier* (Issued 9.5.1911).
10. Danl. Catmore, A.B. and Chas. M. Cooke, A.B.
11. It would appear that the 69 medals were issued with the dates for 1845-6 or 1845-7.
12. It is believed that only 10 medals were distributed.
13. One to Lt. Klintberg, Swedish Navy.
14. Approx. 22 of the Hazard and 31 of the North Star also received China 42.
15. W. Clay, Captain of the Foretop.
16. Commanders Cook, Joseph, Crew.
17. Asst. Surgn. F. Broughton, Mid. H.H. Garrett, Mid. W.M. Pengelly, Paymaster J.A. Keys, A/B R. Collins and Gnr. J. Simpson, Bombay Arty.
18. Master-at-arms, A. Alpe (L.S. & G.C. known separately).
19. Lt. W. Thorpe.

61 ABYSSINIAN WAR MEDAL (4th October, 1867-19th April, 1868)

Obverse	A small veiled and coroneted bust of Queen Victoria surrounded by an ornate nine-pointed star, between each point of which is one of the letters of the word "ABYSSINIA".
Reverse	The name of the recipient with his regiment or ship within a laurel wreath.
Size	1.25 in. diameter.
Ribbon	1½ in. wide. White with a broad red stripe down the centre.
Suspension	Above the circular piece is the imperial crown at the top of which is a ring through which the ribbon is threaded.
Designers	Designed by Owen Jones and engraved by Joseph S. Wyon and Alfred B. Wyon.
Naming	In embossed lettering in the centre of the reverse for British and some native Indian troops, though most of the latter received medals with their names engraved thereon.
No. of bars issued	Nil.

About 14,000 (12,000 to the Army and 2,000 to the Navy) of these medals were issued for the expedition under Lieutenant-General Sir Robert Napier, who afterwards became Lord Napier of Magdala. This campaign was one of the most bloodless in which we have ever been involved, the total casualties amounting to two killed and twenty-seven wounded. It may have been this fact which tempted the Italians to embark on a similar expedition which resulted in almost total annihilation of their forces at Adowa on the 1st March, 1896.

The disembarking and final embarking were in the hands of one who was later to become famous, Major Frederick Roberts, who became Field-Marshall Earl Roberts of Kandahar, V.C.

The medal, which was sanctioned on 1st March, 1869, is said to be the most expensive of all our general-issues, on account of the fact that the recipients' names were embossed, thus necessitating a separate die for each medal. It should be noted, however, that some of those issued to the Indian troops were engraved.

The following troops and H.M. ships took part in the campaign: 3 Dragoon Guards (219); 11 Hussars (9); 3 Scinde Horse; 3 Bombay Light Cavalry; 10 (643), 12 (483) Bengal Cavalry; G/14 (148), 3/21, 5/21 (116), 5/25 (124) Batteries R.A.; No. 1 (Bombay) Mountain Battery; Murray's Armstrong Battery; Munition Battery; 1, 2, 3, 4 Companies Bombay Sappers and Miners; G, H, K Companies Madras Sappers and Miners (368); 10 Company R.E.; Bombay Medical Dept.; Army Hospital Corps; Army Works Corps; Commissariat; Land Transport Corps; Ordnance Corps; 1/4, 26 (800 approx.), 33, 45 (644), 96 (1),* 108 Foot (10); 109 (15) Foot; 1,† 2, 3, 4, 5, 8,* 10, 18, 21 (785), 25, 27 Bombay N.I.; 23 Punjab Pioneers (755), James Pollard, 102 Foot, received this medal.

A Naval Brigade under Captain Fellowes, R.N., drawn from some of the following ships: H.M.S. *Argus* (180), *Daphne* (165), *Dryad* (152), *Nymphe* (169), *Octavia* (642), *Satellite* (292), *Spiteful* (180), *Star* (102), *Vigilant* (101), hospital ships *Golden Fleece, Queen of the South* and *Mauritius*.

This war was caused by the penchant of King Theodore for imprisoning foreigners, among whom were Captain Cameron, the British Consul, as well as missionaries and other British subjects. Most of them were put in chains and sent to Magdala, the capital, in November, 1864. In 1865 the British Political Resident in Aden, Mr. Hormuzd Rassam, together with Lieutenant Prideaux and Doctor

*Lieutenant D. du M. Gunton.
†These regiments did not land in time to take part in any lof the fighting.

Blane, negotiated for nearly a year with the Emperor, with the result that the prisoners were released in March, 1866, and arearrested the next month, together with the negotiators. At about this time, with amazing aplomb on the part of the Emperor and extraordinary imbecility on ours, workmen were asked for and sent from England as a result of a visit by Mr. Flad, the Emperor's representative. On his return, Mr. Flad was thanked and, like the workmen who arrived later, put in prison.

Now came a period occupied in dispatching ultimatums or formal letters. The first, which apparently never arrived, was sent in September, 1867; then came a proclamation by Sir Robert Napier, commanding the Bombay army; then the Queen proclaimed war in a speech on 19th November. This was followed by another ultimatum from Sir Robert, who landed at Annesley Bay, below Massowah, in January, 1868.

As soon as sufficient troops had arrived and the necessary arrangements had been made he started on the 300 or more miles to Magdala. The battle of Arrogie was fought on 10th April, and Magdala entered on the 13th. It was found that Theodore had committed suicide, so that there was nothing more to be done, and the place was razed to the ground on the 17th and the return journey started.

The Royal Navy supplied a Naval Brigade eighty-three strong, which manned twelve 12-pounder rocket tubes. Seldom have sailors served in such mountainous country. The heat by day was terrific, and the cold at night intense. It is recorded that no spirits were available in either bottles or jars, but the excellent quality of the human kind together with hard work brought the force on 8th April to the Talanta plateau, from which rose three mountains, the Fahla, Selasse and the highest of them all on which stood the fortress of Magdala. Prior to the assault the Abyssinians rushed out of their stronghold straight into a volley of rockets, which so unnerved them that they lost heart and bolted down the opposite side of the mountain from the attack. Soon after this the fortress was captured.

On the conclusion of the war Commander Fellowes was promoted, and the brigade received the thanks of Parliament.

Naval awards were made to all the crews of the ships on duty in the Red Sea and to those whose service was in any way connected with the war. They were not confined to those who landed or formed part of the Naval Brigade, so that naval medals are no rarer than any others.

A good sidelight on the expense involved in even these small wars may be judged from the fact that this campaign necessitated the transportation of a total of 43,000 men (of whom only 14,683 were soldiers), 36,000 transport animals, 7,000 camels, and last, but by no means least, 44 elephants.

62 CANADA GENERAL SERVICE MEDAL (1866-1870)

Obverse	A veiled bust of Queen Victoria with the legend "VICTORIA REGINA ET IMPERATRIX".
Reverse	The Canadian flag surrounded by a maple wreath with the word "CANADA" above.
Size	1.42 in. diameter.
Ribbon	1.25 in. Divided equally red, white, red.
Suspension	A plain straight suspender.
Designers	Obverse, T. Brock; Reverse, G.W. de Saulles.
Naming*	These medals are to be found with several different types of naming as follows:

*Medals to English regiments bear the regimental numbers and the territorial title — viz., "2/17, .EIC. R."; 4th, 60th, K.R.R.C."

(a) In large indented block capitals.

(b) In indented lower case letters.

(c) Engraved in large or small capitals. The Naval medals are generally found done in the latter.

(d) The medals to the English regiments were impressed in capitals or engraved.

No. of bars issued — Three — Fenian Raid 1866; Fenian Raid 1870; Red River 1870. The medal was not issued without a bar or bars. 4 different dies were used to strike the 1866 bar, 5 for 1870 and 3 for Red River.

By Army Order No. 7 of January, 1899,† approval was given for the Canadian Government to issue a medal to members of the Imperial and Canadian Forces which had taken part in the suppression of the Fenian Raids and Riel's First Rebellion, the latter generally referred to as the Red River Expedition under Colonel Wolseley. Approximately 17,600 were issued including 15,300 to Canadians.

A friend whose father was awarded this medal has given a most interesting account as to how these medals were dispatched so as to reach the recipients on Christmas Day, 1899. He goes on to relate how many of the veterans of the Crimean War looked down on the medal and declined to apply for it. This fact, together with the period that elapsed between the campaigns and the date of the issue, probably accounts for the differences between the numbers of men engaged and the numbers of medals awarded.

As so little appears in books on medals as to the origin of the troubles which caused the fighting for which this medal was issued, perhaps a brief account may not be out of place.

As early as 1837 a typical tub-thumper called Louis J. Papineau stirred his followers into rebellion with a view to overthrowing the authority of the Crown in Canada, or in other words to persuade Canada to sever her loyalty to Britian. This was no easier to do then than now and had the same result as the strange bleatings we used to hear from Germany on the subject of the breaking away of the Dominions should England be attacked. The Canadians realized that something would have to be done about it and promptly set to work to organize their militia forces on a sound basis.

Fenians is the name of the old Irish National Militia which took the title of "Brotherhood" in the United States and vowed its intention to "liberate Ireland and establish a Republic". The Fenian oath is as follows: "I promise by the divine law of God to do all in my power to obey the laws of the society F.B. and to free and regenerate Ireland from the yoke of England. So help me God."

In the eighteen-sixties it must be admitted that the Fenians in Canada and those in the United States did not have much difficulty in gathering many thousands of adherents; in fact, it is said that there were upwards of 350,000 of them. On 4th March, 1866, they went so far as to hold a mass meeting in New York and threatened to invade Canada. The Fenians appear to have had maritime aspirations as well, because on 1st May, 1866, the Fenian schooner *Friend* captured the British schooner *Wentworth* off Long Island.

On 13th April, 1861, the American Civil War began and the relationship between the Northerners and Canadians became more strained than ever, a fact of which the Fenians took full advantage.

When the Civil War was finished it left in its trail, as wars always do, thousands of free-lance freebooters who accepted ranks far beyond their military capabilities

†Army Order No. 256 of 1906 extended the period for applying for the medal to 1st July 1907, which was later extended to the end of 1928.

in the Fenian organization. After all this talk and with these large numbers of scallywags something had to be done, so on 31st May, 1866, "Colonel" John O'Neil (or was it General O'Neil?) crossed the Niagara River to invade Canada, and made his headquarters at Limeridge. At Ridgeway the force defeated a unit of the Canadian Militia but when they heard that a stronger force was arriving they withdrew to the United States side of the border, where many, to their great surprise, were arrested. President Johnson proclaimed against the Fenians on 7th June, 1866, and this seems to have so upset them that they remained comparatively quiet until 1870.

On 26th May, 1870, O'Neil again crossed the border, but was captured by the United States on his hasty return. On his release he instigated another invasion, this time of Manitoba, but did not attend in person, as he was again arrested by the United States before he crossed the border.

To find the reason for the Red River Expedition we must go back again several years to pick up the thread.

The Hudson Bay was first discovered by Cabot in 1512; then again by Henry Hudson in 1610 when searching for a way into the Pacific from the Atlantic. Hudson remained on the land he discovered. Later the famous Hudson's Bay Company was founded, which obtained a Royal Charter from Charles II in 1670. On 9th April, 1869, the Charter having expired, the whole of what was known as the Hudson Bay Territory was transferred to the Dominion for £300,000 and incorporated into the State of Manitoba. This transference was resented by many people, and Louis Riel, styling himself a General, seized the Company's treasury in January, 1870, seized Fort Garry, imprisoned many British residents, and started a rebellion. One of his prisoners, Thomas Scott, escaped and was recaptured by Riel, and after a sham court-martial was ordered to be shot. The firing party only wounded him twice; he was then shot in the face at point-blank range, but still not killed. He was then placed in a rough wooden box, in which he remained alive for a further ten hours.

The rebellious nature of Riel's activities sounded like a clarion call to the Fenians and they promptly threatened to cause trouble with a further invasion. In the last four years the Canadian Militia had become organized and guarded the United States-Canadian borders, so that the Fenian activities, as already explained, did not get very far.

The fact that British subjects were imprisoned, murdered and maltreated was the concern of the Government, which promptly ordered Colonel Garnet Wolseley to lead an expedition to Fort Garry. The composition of this force will be given under the bar Red River 1870. Colonel Wolseley's expedition left Toronto on 14th May and reached Fort Garry on 24th August, 1870, having covered 1,118 miles almost entirely up the Winnipeg and Red River, on which latter Fort Garry stands.*

Riel escaped before Wolseley's arrival and we shall hear of him again when dealing with the North-West Canada Medal of 1885.

Fenian Raid 1866

British Regiments present: R. Fus. (158); 15 York R. (20); 16 Beford R. (121); 17 Leicester R. (145); 22 Cheshire R. (1); 25 K.O.S.B. (99); 30 E. Lancs. R. (94); 47 Loyal R. (119); 53 Shropshire R. (2); 1/60 K.R.R.C. (6); 4/60 K.R.R.C. (109); 69 S. Lincs. R. (160); 1/Rifle Bde. (92); 4/Rifle Bde. (175); R.A. (280); R.E. (40); A.H.C. (1); A.S.C. (16); Staff (10).

*A few remains of the old Fort Garry may still be seen in Winnipeg, the capital of Manitoba. The fort is commemorated by a Canadian regiment, The Fort Garry Horse. The 6th Battalion Canadian Infantry have a part of the old fort incorporated in their badge.

The medal awarded to No. 1173 Pte. R. Birmingham, 30th Foot, with this bar and that for "Fenian Raid 1870" is the only two-bar one that is known to this regiment.

The Dunville Naval Volunteers (29).

H.M. ships: *Aurora* (121), *Baracouta* (1); *Britomart* (13), *Cherub* (7), *Constance* (2), *Demon* (6), *Duncan* (13), *Fawn* (7), *Heron* (11), *Lily* (1), *Niger* (39), *Pylades* (57), *Rescue* (1), *Rosaria* (14), *Royal* (4), *Simoon* (1), *Wolveron* (7).

On the 19th June, 1866, Pte. Timothy O'Hea, of the 1st Bn. the Rifle Brigade, won the Victoria Cross for putting out a fire in an ammunition wagon. This is the first occasion that I can recall of the Cross having been won for bravery when not in the presence of the enemy.*

The George Cross, instituted by Royal Warrant, dated the 24th September, 1940, is now awarded to men and women, whether in the fighting services or not, for special acts of heroism when not in the presence of the enemy.*

Fenian Raid 1870

British Regiments present: 7. R. Fus. (3); 17 Leicester R. (32); 25 K.O.S.B. (4); 1/60 K.R.R.C. (16); 4/60 K.R.R.C. (7); 69 S. Lincs. R. (1); 1/rifle Bde. (74); 4/Rifle Bde. (69); R.A. (29); R.E. (8); A.S.C. (6); Staff (3).

Red River 1870

British Regiments present: 7 R. Fus. (1); 16 Bedford R. (1); 1/60 K.R.R.C. (123); 4/60 K.R.R.C. (6); 69 S. Lins. R. (1); 4/Rifle Bde. (1); R.A. (6); R.E. (8); A.S.C. (7); Staff (5).

The following figures concerning the number of bars awarded may be of interest:

Total number of medals issued: 16,488. Three bars: Fenian Raid 1866, Fenian Raid 1870, Red River 1870 (11). Two bars: Fenian Raid 1870, Red River 1870 (13). Two bars: Fenian Raid 1866, Red River 1870 (81). Two bars: Fenian Raid 1866, Fenian Raid 1870 (1,325). One bar: Fenian Raid 1866 (10,467). One bar: Fenian Raid 1870 (4,240). One bar: Red River 1870 (351).

For a very comprehensive list of local units, see War Medals and Decorations by Prof. Ross W. Irwin and the C.G.S. roll produced in 1973 by the Military Collectors Club of Canada.

63 ASHANTEE WAR (9th June, 1873-4th February, 1874)

Obverse	The diademed head of Queen Victoria, wearing a veil; also the legend "VICTORIA REGINA".
Reverse	A scene of bush fighting round a tree with a native in a half-lying attitude in front.
Size	1.42 in. diameter.
Ribbon	1.25 in. wide. Yellow with black borders and two thin black stripes down the centre.
Suspension	By a straight suspender.
Designers	Obverse — L.C. Wyon, Reverse — Sir Edward J. Poynter, R.A.

*Assistant Surgeon Campbell Mills Douglas, together with Ptes. T. Murphy, J. Cooper, D. Bell and W. Griffiths of the 2 R. Warwickshire Regiment, all won the Victoria Cross on 7th May, 1867, for taking a boat through dangerous surf to rescue seventeen of their comrades who formed part of an expedition sent to the Andaman Islands in the Bay of Bengal.

(Reverse)*

No. 58. The Indian Mutiny Medal, 1857-8.

(Obverse)

No. 61. The Abyssinian War Medal, 1867-8.

(Reverse)*

No. 59. The Second China War Medal 1857-60.

(Obverse)

(Reverse)

No. 60. The New Zealand Medal, 1845-7 and 1860-6.

* Reference should be made to page 425 for medals with identical obverses.

To face page 184

(Obverse)   (Reverse)

No. 62. The Canada General Service Medal, 1866-70.

(Obverse)

No. 63.* The Ashantee War Medal, 1873-4.

(Reverse)

No. 78.* The East and West Africa Medal,
1887-1900.

* The obverses and reverses of these two medals are the same.

To face page 185

Naming	In engraved Roman capitals with the date 1873-74. The lettering is filled in in black.
No. of bars issued	One. The bar is inscribed "COOMASSIE" and was awarded to all who crossed the River Prah and to those who took part in the actions at Amoaful and Ardahsa* on 31st January and 4th February, 1874, respectively. However those who later qualified for the East & West Africa medal were awarded the bar(s) only for attaching to the previously issued Ashantee medal.**

This medal, sanctioned on 1st June, 1874, was awarded for Major-General Sir Garnet Wolseley's campaign against King Coffee Kalkali, who resented the transfer of the port of Elmina from the Dutch to the British. Although Wolseley landed with his Staff on 2nd October, 1873, the main advance could not start until troops from England had arrived and all the plans for the campaign had been worked out. The troops arrived on 17th December, 1873, and the advance on Coomassie began on 5th January, 1874,† and was completed on 4th February, 1874. During this period four V.C.s were won.

It should be noted that the capital is spelt Coomassie on the bar to this medal and Kumassi on that for the 1900 campaign.

This medal, with bar, in bronze is very rare.

The sickness rate in this campaign was about the worst on record and no less than 98 per cent. of the naval force engaged on land reported sick during the period they were employed ashore.

This campaign, like so many others, was one in which the Navy played a most important part.

Before the arrival of Sir Garnet Wolseley, the only forces in the country were a hundred Marines, under Colonel Festing, who landed on the 9th June, 1873. On 5th July, Commodore Edumnd J. Commerell, V.C., assumed command. With boats from the *Rattlesnake* and *Argus*, he went up the Prah river and shelled the town of Chamah. The Commodore, and Commander Luxmore, of the *Argus*, were wounded and the command was then taken over by Captain Freemantle. Commander J. Glover, R.N., was sent into the interior with a small naval detachment to take the Ashantees in the rear. Sir Garnet, with two hundred seamen and Marines under Captain Freemantle, together with a battalion of the West India Regiment, disembarked at Elmina‡ and defeated the enemy at Essaman on the 14th October. Colonel Festing also defeated them at Escabeo on the 17th October. A small naval force under Lietenant Wells, R.N., was attacked by the enemy at Abrakrampra on 5th November, but they were driven off. On the 27th December a Naval Brigade of 159 officers and men under Captain Blake, R.N. (and later under Captain Luxmore) marched towards Prahsu. After crossing the Prah, they defeated the enemy at Borborassie on the 19th January, 1874. On the 31st January the Brigade, now divided into two units under Captains Luxmore and Hunt-Grubbe, R.N., was in the action at Amoaful.

Peace was signed on 13th February, but King Coffee was reluctant to pay the indemnity demanded until he heard the approach of Captain Glover, who,

*The name of this battle is found spelt in the following ways: Ardahsa, Ordahsa, and Ordahsu.
**Those awarded the Witu 1890 bar for wear with this medal were:— R. Admiral Freemantle, Lt. A.H.D. Ravenhill, Lt. W. Ainger, Staff Paym. F.R.C. Whidden, Cmdr. A.M. Gardner and P.O. 2nd., W.H. Still.
†The difference between this date and the first inclusive one for the award should be noted.
‡This port was originally founded by the Portuguese, from whom it was captured by the Dutch in 1637. King Coffee had received a sort of *ex gratia* payment for its use, but when the British took over the payment was stopped. This fact annoyed the king, who promptly attacked the Fantis who lived around Cape Coast Castle and were quite friendly towards the British.

together with other naval officers present, received the thanks of Parliament. The following troops and naval ships were employed during the campaign: 17 Battery R.A. (20); Raits Artillery. 28th Company R.E. (*93/60), 2/23 (617/302), 1/42 (688/651), 2 Rifle Brigade (700/621); 1, 2 West India Regiments; Glover's Force; Army Hospital Corps (133/22), Army Hospital Services (76/31); Army Service Corps (61/10); Wood's and Russel's Native Regiments; Houssas (210), Kassoos (100), Eliminas (50); Armed Police (10); Control Department.

H.M. Ships: *Active* 564 (113 with bar); *Amethyst* 235 (36 with bar); *Argus* 176 (30 with bar); *Barracuta* 301 (3 with bar); *Beacon* 90, no bars; *Bittern* 106, no bars; *Coquette* 68, no bars; *Decoy* 69, one bar; *Dromedary* 81, no bars; *Druid* 213 (48 with bar); *Encounter* 229 (1 with bar); *Himalaya* 278, one bar; *Merlin* 62, no bars; *Rattlesnake* 295, (31 with bars); *Seagull* 90, no bars; *Simoon* 200, 6 bars; *Tamar* 223, (1 with bar); *Victor Emanuel* 275, no bars.

Also medal without bar to Lt. C.S. Shuckbur R.N., Transport *Manitoban*.

In addition to the above numbers medals with and without bars were issued to native Koomen etc.

Brevet Major J. Lazenby, 1 Leinster Regt., received this medal. Several British regiments contributed between one and three men.

Coomassie

The only one of the units just mentioned which did not gain a number of these bars was the 1st West India Regiment, though Lieutenant Colonel W.W.W. Johnson and Pte. J.F. Holden of this regiment received it.

64 SOUTH AFRICAN WAR MEDAL FOR ZULU AND BASUTO WARS (25th September, 1877-2nd December, 1879)†

DESCRIPTION OF MEDAL: The medal, sanctioned in 1880, is exactly the same as that for the previous campagins between 1834 and 1853 except that the date on the reverse is replaced by a Zulu shield and four crossed assegais. The recipients. names are engraved in capital letters together with their units. Six bars were awarded, but only one to each medal, which bear the date or dates during which the recipient served. Those who were mobilized but remained in Natal between 11th January and 1st September, 1879, received the medal without a bar — such as the Royal Durban Rifles (later the Royal Durban Light Infantry), these medals are rare.

This medal commemorates much severe fighting in operations:

(a) Against the Galekas and Gaikas from 26th September, 1877, to 28th June, 1878.

(b) Against Chief Pokwane from 21st to 28th January, 1878.

(c) Against the Griquas, 24th April to 13th November, 1878.

(d) Against the Zulus, under Cetewayo and his lieutenants, from 11th January to 1st September, 1879.

(e) Against Chief Sekukumi, 11th November to 2nd December, 1879.

(f) Against Chief Moorosi in the Drakensberg mountains, 25th March to 20th November, 1879.

A full history of these operations would necessitate a great deal of space, so that a brief summary of the period must suffice.

In 1877, the Galekas and Gaikas attacked the Fingoes, which was a small friendly tribe under our protection. Lieutenant-General Sir Arthur Cunynghame, K.C.B., who was G.O.C. at the Cape, went to punish them with a small

*When known the 1st figure indicates medals issued without bar, second figure medals with bar Coomassie.

†Mr D. Forsyth of Johannesburg has just completed a concise roll of 269 pages, containing in excess of 39,000 names.

186

force composed of about fifty mounted infantrymen of the 1/24th Foot, the 88th Foot, and a Naval Brigade, 300 strong, under Captain Wright from H.M.S. *Active*. A large number of local units were engaged in the Gaika-Galeka War of 1877-78. These two expeditions ended by the 18th June, 1878.

There was fighting against Pokwane and the Griqua tribes in the Griqualand West area not far from Kimberley between 21st January and 13th November, 1878, in which only Colonial units took part.

In December, 1878, King Cetewayo, who had been crowned King of the Zulus on the 1st September, 1873, caused trouble, so he was sent an ultimatum demanding the release of certain prisoners captured during a raid. As no answer was received, Lord Chelmsford, who assumed command in April, 1878, crossed the Tugela river into Zululand on 11th January, 1879. His force was composed of five columns, one of which remained near the border at Isandhlwana. This was attacked by Dambulamanzi, Cetewayo's half-brother, on the 22nd January. The casualties at Isandhlwana were:

KILLED AT ISANDHLWANA: 22ND JANUARY' 1879

EUROPEANS:

	Officers	N.C.O's & Men
Staff	2	9
R.A. N/5	1	61
R.A. Rocket Battery	1	6
R.E.	1	4
1/24th	16	400
2/24th	5	178
A.S.C.		3
A.H.C.	1	10
Army Medical C.	1	1
Mounted Infantry		13
Natal Mounted Police		26
Natal Carbineers	2	20
Newcastle Mtd. Rifles	2	5
Buffalo Border Guard		3
Sikali's Horse	1	
1st Bn. 1st Regt. N.N.C.	2	10
1st Bn. 3rd Regt. N.N.C.	8	29
2nd Bn. 3rd Regt. N.N.C.	9	28
Total Europeans	52	806

Natives killed — Reported total	471
Total Reported Killed	1329

On the same night, flushed with their success, the Zulus moved about ten miles down the Tugela river to Rorke's Drift. Here the small garrison of 139 men who were guarding the sick and wounded were attacked by about 3,000 Zulus. During this epic defence the garrison, under Lieutenants Bromhead and Chard, won no fewer than eleven Victoria Crosses.

In the meanwhile, Colonel Pearson with the 2/3rd and 99th Foot, together with a Naval Brigade, was surrounded at Eshowe, and Colonel Evelyn Wood, V.C., had to fall back to Kambula. It was not until after the defeat of Ambulamanzi at Ginghilovo, on 2nd April, that Colonel Pearson was relieved. Colonel Wood defeated the Zulus, under Cetewayo's lieutenant Umbelini, in the Zlobani mountains on 28th March, but suffered heavy casualties. On the next day he again defeated them at Kambula.

The unsatisfactory nature of the fighting caused the authorities at home to send out further reinforcements. Sir Garnet Wolseley was sent out and arrived at the Cape on 23rd June, but took no part in any of the fighting.

On 4th July, Cetewayo was defeated at Ulundi by Lord Chelmsford. On 1st September a meeting between Sir Garnet Wolseley and the Zulu Chiefs was held, after which the Zulu War was proclaimed to be at an end.

However, an entirely separate comapign took place in Sekukuniland (N.E. Transvaal near the border with Portuguese East Africa) the Force being under the command of Colonel Russel, the campaign coming to an end on 2nd December, 1879.

Another Basuto Chief, Moirosi, refused to pay taxes and took up a strong position in the Drakensberg mountains, where he defied capture for some time. He was eventually rounded up and killed.

From December, 1877, to December, 1879, the Navy played a part which is worthy of a longer account than space permits. In December, 1877, a brigade of three hundred seamen and Marines from H.M.S. *Active* was landed at East London under Captain Wright, R.N. They fought under Colonel Glynn, against Pokwane in the battle of Quintana early in 1878. In 1878, men of this brigade also fought against the Gaikas in the Peri Bush and then rejoined their ship. On 19th November, 1878, a further brigade, under Captain Campbell, R.N., and Lieutenants Craigie and Hamilton, landed at Durban. It was 172 strong with three guns and two rocket tubes. It formed, together with forty reinforcements from H.M.S. *Tenedos*, part of the garrison at Eshowe for some time. A Naval Brigade, under Captain Brackenbur, R.N., was present at Ginghilovo. When Lord Chelmsford crossed the Tugela river into Zululand he took with him a Naval Brigade consisting of forty-one officers and 812 seamen and Marines. The Admiralty supplied the following figures as regards the naval awards of this medal:

1877-8	. .	76
1878	. .	Nil
1878-9	. .	Nil
1877-8-9	. .	124
1879	. .	848

1,048

There are some inconsistencies in the awards to Colonial units as shown by the medal rolls and other documents. It will be noted that certain units appear to have been awarded the bars for "1877-8" and "1879", but not that for "1877-8-9". Many of the titles that I give were obtained from the medal rolls, so I suggest that medals with the bar "1877-8-9" be verified by reference to the units that obtained those for "1877-8" and "1879".

The Colonial units changed their titles with such bewildering frequency that they may have been mentioned twice against the same bar or given the wrong title at the time. The medals were, of course, issued after the campaigns, and one suspects that those entitled to a medal gave the present title of their unit if still serving or the title at the time of the campaign if they had been demobilized. This would account for two titles to the same unit and, with the constant changes already referred to, probably a good many more. As a result of the general confusion medals with two bars are known. In many cases although the rolls indicate that reasonable numbers were issued, a large proportion were returned to Woolwich; where the number returned is known these are shown thus: (60.W20).

Some Members of the following S.A. units received the 1877-79 medal *without* clasp:—
Buffalo Bdr. Guard; Carbutts Border Rangers; Durban Mtd. Reserve; Durban Vol. Arty.; Maritzburg Rifles; Natal Carbineers; Natal Light Horse; Natal Mtd. Police; Natal Native Contgt.; Natal Native Horse; Natal Nat. Pioneers; Newcastle Mtd. Rif.; Royal Durban Rifles; Sansoms Horse; Southeys Rangers; 1st Stockenstroom Vol. Rifles; Civilian Doctors; H.M. Ships *Active* (200), *Boadirea* (247), *Euphrates* (261), *Himalaya* (229), *Orontes* (226), *Shah* (308), *Taunar* (215), *Tenedes* (141).

1877* The advance against the Galekas did not start until 26th September, 1877, so that this bar is particularly rare.

List of "1877" Bars on South African 1877-79 Medal,
to Colonial Units, after deducting numbers returned to Woolwich

Aliwal North Mounted Vols.	16
Bowkers Rovers	34
Prince Alfred's Volunteer Guard	24
Fort White Mounted Vols.	11
Sidbury Mounted Rangers	5
East London & Chalumna Cavalry	6
Miscellaneous	11
Add medals known but not found on rolls	3
Total:	**110**

The following medals with this bar are known, quoted is the unit as given on the medal. The Cape Mounted Rifles were not formed at the time and only two of these units are mentioned above as having been present. Pte. A. Freeman, P.A.V.G.; Tpr. J. Pentland, Bowker's Horse; No. 422 Pte. J. Hennetz, 88th Foot; Trooper J. Kemp, Bowker's Rovers; Pte. T. Murray, P.A.G. Rifle Volunteers; No. 1806 Pte. J. Wales; Lieut. Vononheim, Cape Mounted Rifles; Pte. H.F. McLachlan, P.A.G. Rifle Vols.; Tpr. J. Kemp, Bowkers Rovers; Tpr. Searle, Bowker's Rovers; Tpr. J.C. McCall, Aliwal N. Mtd. Vols; Pte. C. Hickey, Fort White Mtd. Vols.; Pte. S. Roberts, P.A.G. Rifle Vols. and Civil Practitioner E.S. Stevenson.

*The authority that sanctioned the different dated bars makes no specific mention of a bar for 1877 but as Dr. Mitchell points out, the order mentions that bars were authorised to cover the year(s) of service which explains why a few 1877 bars were awarded. These were probably issued to those who volunteered for three months service in 1877 and who did not renew or extend their agreements. It cannot be argued that the bar for 1877-8 would not have been suitable in these cases. Furthermore the Royal Mint certainly supplied 1877 bars to the War Office.

Imperial Troops present: N/5 (7), 8/7 (23), 11/7 (9) R.A.; R.E. (33); 1/13, 1/24, 2/24 (44), 80, 88 (195), 90 (70) Foot. A.H.C., A.S.C., Army Dept. Commissariat and Transport.

Colonial Troops present: Adelaide Vol. Cav. (74.W*28); Albany Fingoe Levy (53.W49*); Albany Mounted Rangers (or Rifles) (43); Albert Burghers (262.W148); Albert Vols. (37.W23); Alexandra Mounted Rifles (42.W15); Aliwal North Mounted Volunteers; Barber's Horse (75.W58); Beaufort Rangers Cavalry Volunteers (59); Berlin Volunteer Cavalry (122); Berlin Volunteer Mounted Infantry (3); Bolotwa Tembus (136.W32); Bolotwa Volunteers; Bowker's Horse (101.W60); Bowker's Rovers (74.W36); Buckley's Native Levy (51.W45); Buffalo Mounted Vol. Rifles (18.W7); Buffalo Vol. Rifles and Levy (104.W53); Cape Field Arty. (10); Cape Munted Rifles (392.W159); Cape Mounted Rifles Frontier Armed Mounted Police (14.W3); 1 Chalumna Volunteers (Cavalry); Clan-William Vol. Corps (40); Colesburg Light Horse (53); Cradock Vol. Rifles (11); Diamond Fields Horse; District Native Police (8); Duke of Edinburgh's Own Vol. Rifles (55.W16); East London Burghers (20.W10); East London Engineers; East London Volunteer Guard (28); First City Volunteers (53.W20); Fort Beaufort Mounted Volunteers (84); Fort White Mounted Volunteers (12); Frankfort Burghers (41.W27); Frontier Armed Mounted Police (74.W22); Frontier Armed and Mounted Police (146.W30); Frontier Light Horse (98.W1); Frontier Mounted Rifles (210); German Burghers Horse Arty. (73.W16); German Grahamstown Horse Artillery; Grahamstown Rifle Volunteers (11); Hottentot Militia (or Levy) (149); Kaffrarian Volunteer Artillery (12.W3); Kaffrarian Mounted Rifles (36); Kaffrarian Rangers (110); Kaffrarian Volunteers (117); Khama's Levies (113.W40); Keiskama Hoek Burghers (40); Keiskama Hoek Vol. Rifles (20); Keiskama Volunteer Infantry (20); Keiskama Hoek Mounted Volunteers (59); Kimberley Horse (29); Kingwilliamstown Veterans (29); Komgha Fingoe Levy (103); Leach's Fingoes (94.W69); Lonsdale's Horse; Murraysburg Volunteer Cavalry (31); Muray's Orange Revers; Natal Native Contingent (21); Nelson Burghers (18.W5); Northern Border Horse (9); Northern Border Police (56.W26); Officer's Fingoe Levies (10); Port Elizabeth Militia (42.W28); Port Elizabeth Vol. Horse (56); Prince Albert's Guard Rifle Volunteers (130.W28); Prince Albert's Arty. Vol. (27.W2); Prince Alfred's Own Cape Vol. Arty. (44.W6); Pullein's Rangers (37); Pullen's Fingoe Levy (51.W45); Queenstown Burghers Force (115.W84); Queenstown Burghers Force Levies (26.W24); Queenstown Burghers (115.W86); Queenstown Rifle Volunteers (323); Queenstown Volunteer Rifles (21); Queenstown Native Levy (26.W24); Sansom's Horse; Sidbury Rangers (14); Stutterheim Foot Police (32.W27); Stutterheim Mounted Vols. (17.W8); Stutterheim Light Infantry Volunteers (38.W13); Snyman's Burghers (33); Somerset East Volunteers (124); Southeys Rangers (33); Stevenson's Horse (40); Stockenstroom Rangers (28); Streatfields Fingoes (13); Tambookieland Volunteers (5.W1); Transkei Rifles (82); Tshumie Volunteers (153.W141); Upington's Foot (30); Wodehouse Volunteers (6); Yeomanry Regt. (15).

Naval contingents from H.M. ships *Active* (75).

---

*"W" indicates the number of medals which were not claimed and eventually returned to Woolwich.

1877-8-9 Imperial troops present: 1st Royal Dragoons (1); O/2, N/5 (178), 8/7 (11), 11/7 (38) R.A.; 1/13, 1/24 (551), 2/24, 80, 88 (349), 90 (550) Foot.

Colonial troops present: Alexandria Mounted Rangers (8); Baker's Horse (8); Bettington's Horse (7); Cape Field Artillery (41); Cape Mounted Rifles (340.W57); Colesbury Light Horse (4); Fort Beaufort Volunteers (1); Frontier Armed Mounted Police (76.W7); Frontier Mounted Riflemen (200); Grahamstown Volunteer Horse Artillery (6); Keiskama Hook Volunteers; Kimberley Horse; Lonsdale's Horse (4), Natal Horse; Natal Native Contingent (49.W8); Natal Native Infantry (40); Northern Border Horse; Port Elizabeth Volunteers (7); Prince Albert's Guard Volunteer Rifles (5); Queenstown Volunteer Rifles (31); Stevenson's Horse (30); Stockenstroom Rangers (10); Woodhouse Volunteers (9).

124 members of the crews of the ships present in 1877 and 1878 received this bar including H.M.S. *Active* (200), *Boadicea* (4).

1877-9 Mr Forsyth's recent roll includes 11 names of which 4 were returned unclaimed.

1878 Imperial Troops present: 1/13 (25), 1/24, 80 (170), 88, 90 Foot.

Colonial troops present: Baker's Horse (14); Barkly Rangers (63.W38); Bowker's Rovers; Buffalo Volunteer Horse; Cape Town Volunteer Artillery; Colesburg Light Horse (33); Corps of Guides (13.W8); Diamond Fields Horse (2); East London Volunteer Guard (12); Ferrerias Horse (17.W9); First City Volunteers; Fort Whtie Mounted Volunteers (59); Frontier Light Horse; George Town Volunteers (28); Grahamstown Volunteer Horse; Griqualand West Constabulary or Light Infantry (117.W16); Griquatown Burg. Force; Griqualand West Native Contingent (9.W1); Griqualand West Volunteer Arty. (26.W15); Hottentot Militia (or Levy); Humansdorp Volunteer Horse; Jamestown Mounted Volunteer Rifles (40); Komgha Fingoes; Murray's Orange Rovers (68); Northern Border Horse; Northern Border Police; One Star Diamond Contingent (266.W84); Panmure Volunteer Horse; Raaf's Horse; Riversdale Burghers (52); Ronald Maclean's Fingoes; Sidbury Mounted Rifles (10); Siwani's Kaffirs (9.W6); Somerset East Volunteers (78.W51); Tamacha Fingoes; Tarka South Rangers (20); Transvaal Artillery (13.W4); Vincent's Volunteer Horse; Winterberg Grey's Volunteers (29); Woodhouse True Blues (75).

1878-9 Imperial troops present: 11/7 R.A. (6); 3, 1/13, 1/24 (35), 80, 88 Foot.

Colonial Troops present: Baker's Horse; Border Horse (12); Cape Mounted Rifles (37.W12); Cape Town Volunteer Artillery (34); Clarke's Police; Diamond Fields Horse; Farrerias Horse; Frontier Light Horse; Grahamstown Horse Volunteer Artillery; Kimberley Horse (29); Kimberley Rangers; Natal Native Contingent (21); Southey's Rangers; Stockstroom Volunteer Rifles (19); Transvaal Artillery (4).

H.M.S. *Shah.*

1879 Imperial troops present N/5 (146), M/6 (160), N/6 (180), O/6 (160), 8/7 (57), 10/7, 11/7 (97) R.A.; Gatling Train (81); 5 Company R.E.; A.S.C.; Army Hospital R.G.A.; R.E.; A.S.C.; Army Hospital Corps; 1st Life Guards (2); 2nd Dragoon Guards (3); 1 King's Dragoon Guards (600); 16 (6), 17 Lancers; Frontier Light

Horse;* 2/3, 2/4 (1,000), 1/13 (950), 2/21, 1/24), 2/24 (119), 57, 58, 3/60, 80 (820), 88 (336), 90 (380), 91, 94, 99 Foot. Also four to The Scots Greys.

Colonial troops present: Alexandra Mounted Rifles (30); Amangwi Scouts; Amatonga Scouts; Baker's Horse (21); Bolotw Volunteers (18); Border (or Weatherley's Horse) (230); Buffalo Border Guard (196.W91); Cape Field Artillery; Cape Mounted Rifles; Cape Mounted Rifles Artillery; Cape Mounted Yeomanry (250); Duke of Edinburgh's Own Volunteer Artillery; Diamond Fields Horse; Dunn's Scouts; Durban Mounted Rifles (72); Eckersleys Native Contingent; Ferreira's Horse (130); Fort Beaufort Volunteers (33.W26); Frontier Light Horse (5); Grahamstown Horse Artillery Volunteers (7); Griqualand West Border Police; Herschel Mounted Volunteers (59.W3); Herschel Native Contingent (1037.W320); Isipingo Mounted Rifles (101.W46); Mafunzi's Mounted Natives; Murray's Orange Rovers; Natal Carbineers (76); Natal (or Bettington's Horse); Natal Hussars (40); Natal Mounted Police (167); Natal Mounted Volunteers; Natal Native Cavalry (or Horse) (19); Natal Native Contingent (104); Natal Native Pioneers (8); Nettleton Ltd. Horse; Newcastle Mounted Rifles (37); Northern Border Horse; Nourse's Horse; Pietermaritzburg Carbineers; Pietermaritzburg City Guard; Pietermaritzburg Rifles; Piet Uys Horse (or Burgher Force); Pretoria Carbineers (or D'Arcy's Horse); Pretoria Rifles; Pullein's Rangers; Queenstown Volunteer Rifles (35); Rustenburg Contingent; Shepstone's Native Horse (79.W17); Stanger's Rifles (55); Stockstroom Rifle Volunteers (18); Stockstroom Rangers (6); Swazie Contingent; Transvaal Artillery (21); Transvaal Mounted Rifles; Transvaal Rangers (or Raaf's Horse); Transvaal Mounted Volunteer Force (13); Umvoti Mounted Rifles; Victoria Mounted Rifles (49); Weenan Yeomanry (19); Wood's Irregulars; Zoutpansberg Native Contingent.

H.M. Ships: *Active* (56), *Boadicea* (225), *Forester* (111), *Shab* (396), *Tenedos* (59).

It should be added that medals advertised to the 30th and 92nd Foot have been seen but one cannot trace where those units were and if they were there in any large numbers. Pte. J. Connor, 90th Foot, received a medal with the two bars, 1877—8 and 1879, also Lt. Col. E. A. C. Hosmer who also received the Cape of G.H. medal with bar Basutoland. Trooper J. Cooper received a medal with the bar for 1877—8 when serving in the Kaffrarian Rangers and another with the bar for 1879 for service in the Frontier Light Horse.

This is the second medal which can be traced as having been awarded to women. The first was the Naval General Service Medal awarded to Jane Townsend, who was on board H.M.S. *Defiance* at Trafalgar. Excluded, of course, are the four special gold stars awarded to the ladies who were present at the Battle of Maharajpoor in 1843.

65 SECOND AFGHAN WAR (1878—1880)

Obverse The crowned and draped head of Queen Victoria and legend "VICTORIA REGINA ET IMPERATRIX".

*This unit, originally known as Carrington's Horse, was raied by Lieutenant Carrington, 2/24 Regiment. The personnel were paid, equipped and maintained by the Imperial Government and they in no way came under that of the Colony. The title was subsequently changed to the Natal Light Horse.

Reverse	A scene of troops on the march with an elephant carrying a gun in the centre. Around the top is the word "AFGHANISTAN" and in the exergue the dates "1878—79—80".
Size	1·42 in. diameter.
Ribbon	1·25 in. wide. Green with crimson stripe on each edge.
Suspension	By means of a plain, straight swivelling suspender.
Designers	Obverse—J. E. H. Boehm; Reverse—R. Caldecott. The engraving was carried out by L. C. Wyon.
Naming	The medals to the British troops were engraved in upright or sloping capitals and those awarded to natives are found named in capitals or script.
No. of bars issued	Six. The bars are somewhat large, being 1.3/8 in. x 5/16 in. They have no rosettes, as is common with all Indian medals to cover the junctions. The bars were awarded for Ali Musjid, Peiwar Kotal, Charasia, Ahmed Khel, Kabul and Kandahar.

Ali Musjid *(21st November, 1878)*

Regiments present: 10 Hussars; two Squadrons 11 Bengal Lancers; two Squadrons Guides Cavalry; I/C Bty. R.H.A. (56); E/3 Bty. R.F.A. (158); 11/9 Mountain Bty. (104); 13/9 Garrison Bty. (72); No. 4 Hazara Mountain Bty.; Bengal Sappers and Miners; 1/17, 51, 81 Foot and 4 Rifle Brigade; Corps of Guides; 1, 14, 45 Sikhs; 6, 20, 45 Bengal N.I.; 20 and 27 Punjab N.I.; 4 Goorkhas.

(We have never heard of this bar being found on a genuine medal together with that for Ahmed Khel.)

Pelwar Kotal* *(2nd December, 1878)*

Regiments present: One Squadron 10 Hussars (38); 12 Bengal Cavalry; 5 Punjab Cavalry; F/A Bty. R.H.A. (26); G/3 Bty. R.F.A. (74); No. 1 (Kohat) and No. 2 (Derajat) Indian Mountain Batteries; Bengal Sappers and Miners; 2/8, 72 Foot; 2, 5, 29 Punjab N.I.; 23 Pioneers; 5 Goorkhas.

Charasia *(6th October, 1879)*

Regiments present: A Squadron of 9 Lancers (87); 5 Punjab Cavalry; 14 Bengal Lancers; 12 Bengal Cavalry; G/3 Bty. (143); R.F.A. F/A Bty. (58); and No. 2 (Derajat) Mountain Battery; Bengal Sappers and Miners; 67, 72, 92 Foot; 5 and 28 Punjab N.I.; 3 Sikhs; 23 Pioneers; 5 Goorkhas.

Pte. T. Munro, 8th Hussars, received this bar and that for Kabul.

Kabul *(10—23 December, 1879)*

Regiments present: 9 Lancers (253); 10, 14 Bengal Lancers; 5 Punjab Cavalry; Guides Cavalry; F/A Bty. R.H.A. (135); G/3 Bty. R.F.A. (143); No. 1 (Kohat), No. 2 (Derajat) and No. 4 (Hazara) Mountain Batteries; Bengal Sappers and Miners; 2/9, 67, 72, 92 Foot; Corps of Guides; 28 Bengal N.I.; 23 Pioneers; 5 Punjab Inf.; 3 Sikhs; 2, 4, 5 Goorkhas.

Ahmed Khel *(19th April, 1880)*

Regiments present: 19 Bengal Lancers; 1, 2 Punjab Cavalry; A/B Bty. R.H.A. (168); G/4 Bty. R.F.A. (123); 6/11 Heavy Bty. R.A. (96); 11/11 Mountain Bty. R.A.; ten men of P.W.O. Sappers and Miners; 59, 2/60 Foot; 19, 25 Punjab Infantry; 570 men of 2 and 15 Sikhs; 3 Goorkhas.

(This bar on the same medal as that for Ali Musjid is not known.)

* Kotal means pass.

Kandahar *(1st September, 1880)*†

Regiments present: 9 Lancers (244); 3 Bengal Cavalry; 3 Punjab Cavalry; 3 Bombay Cavalry; Central India Horse; Poona Horse; 3 Scinde Horse; E/B R.H.A.; C/2, 6/8, 11/9, 5/11 R.A.; 2 Mtn. Bty.; 2 Bombay Sappers and Miners; 23 Pioneers; 2/7, 22 (6), 50 (13), 2/60, 66 (309), 72, 92 Foot; 2, 3, 15 Sikhs; 24, 25 Punjab N.I.; 1, 3, 4, 9, 28, 29, 30 Bombay N.I.; 2, 4, 5 Goorkhas.

284 of the 66th Berkshire Regiment fell at Maiwand.

The following British regiments served during the war and many members of them received the medal with no bar,‡ in addition to the Artillery, Sappers and Miners and ancillary services: 6 Dragoon Guards; 8, 10, 15 Hussars; 9 Lancers (46); 1/5, 2/5, 2/7, 1/8, 2/8, 2/9, 2/11, 12, 2/14, 2/15, 1/17, 18, 1/25, 31, 34 (31), 51 (454), 59 (13), 2/60, 63 §, 65¶, 66, 67, 70, 72, 78, 81, 85, 92, Foot and Rifle Brigade (83).

The following Artillery units took part in the war and were issued with medals without bars, numbers shown in brackets: A Brigade: D (236), F (177) and I (133) Batteries; B Brigade: A (65), D (136) and E (52) Batteries; C Brigade: H (154) and I (87) Batteries; 1st Brigade: I (144) and H (184) Batteries; 2nd Brigade: C (18), D (188) and F (168) Batteries; 3rd Brigade: C (230), E (38) and G (83) Batteries; 4th Brigade: A (136), C (208), E (175) and C (43) Batteries; 5th Brigade: L (142) Battery;* 8th Brigade: C (29), No. 1 (134), No. 5 (99), No. 13 (102) and No. 16 (10) Batteries; 9th Brigade: 13th (23), 14th (93) and 15th (43) Batteries; 11th Brigade: 5th (29), 6th (19), 8th (11), 9th (4), 10th (90) and 11th (29) Batteries; Siege Train: Kandahar Field Force (26); 1/8, 6/8, 11/9, 12/9, 13/9, 14/9, 5/11, 6/11, 10/11 Batteries R.G.A.; 13/8, 16/8, 8/11 Siege Trains R.A.; 1, 2, 3, 4 Mountain Batteries R.A.; 5 Garrison Battery; 2, 4 Indian Mountain Batteries.

Two officers and 18 men of E. Bty. B. Bde. and the 66th Foot were at Maiwand (27th July 1880), their next of kin were issued the medal without bar.

This medal, sanctioned on 19th March, 1881, was apparently struck both in silver and bronze, although the latter must be very rare indeed.

No explanation whatever can be offered for the existence of the bronze medal. The following extracts from General Order No. 723, dated 16th September, 1887, which sanctioned the award of bronze medals to authorized followers for the campaign in Burma during 1885–7 would infer that it was the first time that such medals had been made the subject of a general issue since the days of the Honourable East India Company.

"*(a)* That the grant of war medals shall extend to all authorized followers accompanying an army in the field, without restriction of their issue to men of the classes heretofore entitled to them;

"*(b)* That all war medals and clasps of such followers shall be made of bronze."

It would take too much space to give a long account of the reasons for this war, so just sufficient detail is given to enable a collector to see why the campaign was necessary.

In 1873 the boundaries between Afghanistan and India were agreed upon by the British and Shere Ali, the Amir, for the peaceful recognition of which he was

---

† General Order No. 30 of 1881 also granted the award of this bar to those who took part in the reconnaissance of the city on 31st August, 1880, but did not participate in the attack on the next day.

‡ Medals to Captain and Paymaster J. L. Hewson, of the 78th Foot, and another to Lieutenant P. E. C. Sheehan, of the 90th Foot are known.

§ A few men of the 1st Bn. The Manchester Regiment received four bars, though the battalion as a whole did not participate in the fighting.

¶ 6 officers and 22 other ranks were employed on lines of communications signals.

to be paid a substantial subsidy. In 1877, Shere Ali refused to have a British Resident at Kabul, raised an army and did all he could to promote bad feeling between the border tribes and the British.

In August, 1878, he signed a treaty with Russia giving her the guardianship of himself and the right to protect Afghanistan. He refused to receive a Mission sent by the Viceroy and threatened the advance party of another led by Sir Nevil Chamberlain which left Peshawur on 21st September, 1877.

Finally an ultimatum was sent to Shere Ali on 28th Octoberm 1878, to which a reply was demanded by 20th November.

In the meanwhile troops had been concentrated at Peshawur, Kohat and Quetta. As no answer was received by 20th November, the Army, which had been organized into three columns, began to cross the frontier on 21st November, 1878. The three columns were as follows: The first, the Peshawur Valley Field Force under Lieutenant-General Sir Samuel Browne, V.C., K.C.S.I., C.B; the second, the Karram Valley Field Force under Major-General Frederick Roberts, V.C., C.B.; the third, the Kandahar Field Force under Lieutenant-General Donald Stewart.

The Peshawur Force crossed the border at Jamrud on 21st November and captured the hill fortress of Ali Musjid on the same day.

The Kurram Force crossed the border and defeated the Afghans in the Peiwar Kotal,* at the entrance to the Kurram Valley route to Kabul, on 2nd December.

After these two actions Shere Ali fled from Kabul and his son Yakoob Khan assumed command. General Roberts annexed the Kurram Valley and after a little more desultory fighting Yakoob Khan, on 30th May, 1879, concluded peace. By this peace he agreed to a British Resident being in Kabul. The Khyber Pass, the Kurram and Pisheen Valleys were to be occupied by the British. The Amir was to be paid an annual subsidy of £60,000 to be on his good behaviour.

Sir Louis Cavagnari, K.C.S.I., was appointed Resident at Kabul, where he arrived on 24th July, 1879. On 3rd September, Sir Louis, and other British residents, together with the bodyguard of the Corps of Guides, was murdered.

General Roberts was ordered to march to Kabul with the Kabul Field Force. He started on 27th September and on the way defeated the Afghans at Charasia on 6th October. He entered Kabul on the 8th, where he was practically surrounded. He concentrated his troops in the cantonments at Sherpur, where they were severely attacked on 23rd December, 1879. Reinforcements under General Gough arrived on the 24th and Kabul was reoccupied. It was for fighting in and around Kabul between the 10th and 23rd December that the bar "Kabul" was awarded.

In April, 1880, General Stewart moved out of Kandahar with a view to clearing the lines of communication to Kabul. When nearing Ghuznee he encountered the Afghans at Ahmed Khel on 19th April and defeated them. He reached Kabul on 2nd May.

On 22nd July, 1880, Abdur Rahman, nephew of Shere Ali, was proclaimed Amir, thus causing Yakoob Khan's brother, Ayoub Khan, a great deal of resentment, which he showed by getting all the tribes in Herat to revolt. General Burrows was sent from Kandahar to oppose him, but was badly defeated at Maiwand, where the 66th Foot lost 62% of their strength, the Sappers and Miners 60% and E. Bty. B. Bde. R.A. 23%, the latter gained two V.C.'s, one C.B., and eight D.C.M's. The remnants of his force retired to Kandahar, closely followed by Ayoub Khan, who promptly surrounded the city and besieged it, together with the forces under General Primrose.

---

* Kotal means pass.

General Roberts, who was then in Kabul, offered to relieve Kandahar, which he did on 1st September.

For this memorable feat the star which follows (No. 66) was awarded.

It is interesting to note that five generals who were holders of the Victoria Cross took part in this campaign. They were Generals Browne, Gough, Macpherson, Tytler and Roberts.

What finer tribute was ever paid to the magnificent Gurkhas than that Lord Roberts should have chosen a member of this regiment and one of the Seaforth Highlanders as the supporters of his armorial bearings? This was done to perpetuate his esteem for the gallantry and comradeship of these two regiments during the attack on the Peiwar Kotal.

The 1st King George V Own Gurka Rifles were originally raised by Lieutenant R. Ross in 1815, and designated the 1st Nasiri Battalion. A very apt title—Nasiri means friendly.

66 KABUL TO KANDAHAR STAR (9th–31st August, 1880)

Obverse	A five pointed star with a ball between all the points except the top two. In the centre is the monogram "V.R.I." around which is a raised circular border. On this border, in raised lettering, is "KABUL TO KANDAHAR", with the date "1880" in the centre at bottom. The star is surmounted by a crown to which is attached the loop for suspension.
Reverse	Plain except for the recipient's name engraved around the hollow centre.
Size	Maximum width 1·9 in. Height 2·5 in. to top of crown, excluding ring for suspension.
Suspension	By means of a ring fixed to the back of the crown near the top.
Designer	Not known, but they were made by Messrs. H. Jenkins & Sons, Birmingham.
Naming	In indented capital letters to British troops. Those issued to natives are found engraved in capitals and in script. A frequent error with specimens that have been named is the use of "Foot" instead of "Regt.".
Ribbon	The rainbow pattern of red, white, yellow, white and blue.
No. of bars issued	Nil.

This bronze star, issued in conjunction with the Queen's medal with the bar Kandhar, was made from captured guns, and awarded to all who had taken part in General Roberts's famous march of about three hundred and ten miles between 9th and 31st August, 1880.* The force consisted of an Infantry Division and a Cavalry and Artillery Brigade as follows:

Cavalry: 9 Lancers (243); 3 Bengal Cavalry; 3 Punjab Cavalry; Central India Horse. Artillery: 6/8, 11/9 British and No. 2 (Hazara) Indian Mountain Batteries. Infantry: 59 (9)†, 2/60, 65 (4), 66 (detachment), 72, 81 (1),‡ 92 Foot; 23 Pioneers; 24, 25 Punjab N.I.; 2, 3, 15 Sikhs; 2, 4, 5 Goorkhas.

* The Garrison of Kelat-i-Ghilzie, which was picked up on the way, was also included in the award. It consisted, among others, of two companies of the 66th Foot under Captain McKinnon.

† 965 R. Hogan; 1420 G. Burbridge; 1081 G. Harrison; 1239 M. Kempson; 1919 J. Curver; 472 G. Tomkinson; Lt. H. A. L. Boulderson; Lt. C. Hodgkinson and 2/Lt. W. G. Small.

‡ L/Cpl. Moon.

Pte. Flynn, West Yorks., and Pte. J. Milne, 1 Manchester Regt. received this star.

67 NORTH WEST CANADA MEDAL (1885)

Obverse	The diademed head of Queen Victoria wearing a veil and surrounded by the legend "VICTORIA REGINA ET IMPERATRIX".
Reverse	The words "NORTH WEST CANADA", surrounded by a maple wreath, and the date "1885" in the centre.
Size	1·4 in. diameter.
Ribbon	1¼ in. wide. Blue-grey with two red stripes almost touching each edge.
Suspension	By a straight suspender.
Designers	Obverse—L. C. Wyon; Reverse—T. Brock.
Naming	The medals were issued unnamed, but a considerable number of them were named locally, whilst some to the steamer *Northcote* were impressed in bold upright letters.
No. of bars issued	One, Saskatchewan (approx. 1,760 issued).

This medal was sanctioned by the Canadian Government for issue on 18th September, 1885, to all who had taken part in the suppressing of Riel's Rebellion. To get a better picture of who Riel was we must go back to the Red River Campaign of 1870 (see Medal 62). We learnt that Riel had escaped when Fort Garry was captured.

The Canadian Government decided to open up the North-West Territory, a fact which was greatly resented by the local Indians. Riel, thinking he saw his chance, styled himself leader of a provisional government and promised a sort of Utopia to all his adherents, Fenians included.

The rising called out practically all of the Canadian forces and the main responsibility for the attack on Riel was given to General Middleton, who with consummate skill organized his forces into three columns. In the operations, which lasted from 24th April to 28th May, 1885, the rebels were completely defeated and Riel captured. After trial he was hanged and thus ended the more serious of the Fenian and other rebellious troubles.

Except for sixteen British officers* who were on the Staff in Canada at the time, no British troops were engaged. To give a complete list† of all the 5,650 medals issued to the Canadian units that took part would be to catalogue the Canadian Militia Force at the time. I will confine myself, therefore, to giving the formation of General Middleton's force and the names of some of the units not included in this force which I know have received medals.

The bar for Saskatchewan was awarded to all who had taken part in any or all three main encounters during the rebellion—namely, those along Saskatchewan and Fish rivers and the battle at Batoche, in which only 850 men took part.

Units present:—

A & B Btys. Can. Art.; Montreal Garrison Arty; Winnipeg Field Bty.

A Troop Cavalry School Corps; Boulton's Mtd. Inf.; French's Scouts; Moose

---

* Major Gen. Melgand; Lt. A. J. Anson, H.L.I.; Lt. L. G. Russell, R.B.; Lt. C. R. Hunter, R.B.; Maj. E. C. Milner; Col. A. Le Coeg, R.A.; Asst. Comm. Gen. F. Shortt; St. Paymstr. F. F. Tereday; Lt. H. Streatfield, Gren. Gds.; Lt. Gen. Lord Russell; Bt. Lt. Col. R. B. Lane, R.B.; Col. W. Black; Capt. R. Nagle; Col. C. S. Akers, R.E.; Asst. Comm. Ordanance W. Booth and Dep. Surgn. Gen. W. Cattell.

† See War Medals and Decorations of Canada by Prof. Ross W. Irwin for a detailed list of Canadian units.

Mountain Scouts; Steele's Scouts; Winnipeg Troop Cavalry; North West Mounted Police; Scouts;

Alberta Mtd. Rifles; Battleford Rifle Co.; Birtle Co. Inf.; C. Co. Inf. Corps School; Halifax Prov. Bn.; Inf. Bn. Winnipeg (95th); Winnipeg Lt. Inf. Bn.; Midland Bn.; Ottawa Sharpshooters; Prince Albert's Vols.; Rocky Mountain Rangers; Yorktown Co. Inf.; York & Simcoe Prov. Bn.; 2nd Bn. Q.O.R.; 7th Bn. Fus.; 9th Bn. Quebec Volt; 10th Bn. Grenadiers; 65th Bn. Mounted Royal Rifles; 90th Bn. Winnipeg Rifles.

Commissariat; D.L.S. Intelligence Corps; Governor General's Bodyguard; Medical Staff; Staff; Transport Officers & Scouts; Red Cross Medical Corps; Saskatchewan Hospital and the steamer *Northcote* (34 medals with bars).

Many of the medals are named in an abbreviated manner; for instance, "9e V.Q.", which stands for Neuvieme Voltigeurs de Quebec; "P.A.V." which stands for Prince Albert Volunteers, etc.

Medals are, from time to time, found with unofficial bars for Batoche, an alternative spelling of Bartouche, and Fish Creek.

68 EGYPTIAN MEDAL (1882—1889)

Obverse	The diademed head of Queen Victoria and legend "VICTORIA REGINA ET IMPERATRIX".
Reverse	The Sphinx on a pedestal with the word "EGYPT" above. In the exergue is the date "1882" for those awarded in the first campaign; those awarded later have a plain exergue.
Size	1·42 in. diameter.
Ribbon	1¼ in. wide with three bright blue and two white stripes of equal width.
Suspension	By a straight swivelling suspender.
Designers	Obverse—L. C. Wyon; Reverse—J. Pinches.
Naming	Dated medals are engraved in sloping capitals.
	Undated medals are impressed in sloping capitals to British troops except those awarded to the Royal Marines, which are named in large upright bold capitals. Medals awarded to Indian troops are named in neat small running script. Those awarded to the Egyptian troops are named in Arabic.
No of bars issued	Thirteen*

It should be noted that there is a great number of medals in existence to units which did not take part in the campaign as a whole. The probable reason for this is that when the war broke out we were, as usual, unprepared, so that troopships on their way to and from India and elsewhere were diverted to Egypt, consequently men of various regiments took part.

Captain J. R. Beech, C.M.G., D.S.O., received a medal with seven bars; there were six issued with six bars, to officers and their gallopers. Medals with five bars are very rare and those with four are not common.

It is worth mentioning that these medals are very difficult to find in really mint conditions, because they were worn next to the pointed Khedive's Star,

* Men who lost their medals and had them *officially* replaced received undated medals irrespective of the type of the original. On some of these one finds bars which would normally be on dated medals. These medals are perfectly genuine, but collectors should be very careful to distinguish between them and made-up fakes.

The manufacturer of some of the bars and clasps was contracted out to Henry Jenkins & Sons of Birmingham.

which pitted them. This remark is especially true as regards medals awarded to mounted men.

Owing to the general poor condition of many of these medals, they had added and subtracted a fascinating assortment of bars. There are a number about that, without a detailed description of it all, one cannot do more than advise special caution before buying medals to mounted units. A great many of those purporting to have been awarded to members of the Camel Corps are renamed and specially made up fakes although it is difficult to accept the logic of this, as in the past the medal was never of sufficient value to warrant any expenditure.

THE EGYPTIAN CAMPAIGNS, 1882–9

EGYPT, 1882

After the opening of the Suez Canal on 16th November, 1869, the affairs of Egypt took on an international aspect, because whoever controlled the country controlled the canal, the use of which was to be free to all nations. At the same time the canal was vital to our trade routes to the East.

After the restoration of peace which followed the action off the Syrian coast for which the last bar to the Naval General Service Medal, 1793–1840, was awarded, Mehemit Ali was proclaimed hereditary Viceroy of Egypt. In 1867 he took the title of Sovereign, and then in 1869 that of Khedive. In 1879 he was deposed and succeeded by his son Tewfik.

Egyptian history is outside the scope of this book, but it would be difficult to nominate a country which at any time had ever been more misgoverned than Egypt between about 1801, when it was handed back to the Turks after we had driven out Napoleon, and 1882. One must realize that, what with the Sultan of Turkey being the real power behind the throne and various Great Powers having considerably more than archaeological interest in the country, it would have been surprising if anything but chaos had resulted.

In 1869 the Sultan of Turkey forbade the Khedive to impose taxes or contract loans, and then in 1872 he followed this up with a firman granting the Khedive a sort of independence except for the right to coin money. In 1875 the Khedive sold his shares in the Suez Canal to the British Government and set up an International Court of Justice. A period of financial chaos followed during which the Khedive gradually lost all authority. In 1881 the Egyptian army mutinied for more pay, but serious trouble was, however, prevented by the joint efforts of the British and French Ministers. In July of the same year Sheik Mahomed Ahmed of Dongola proclaimed himself Mahdi, the Guided by God or Directed One, and in September the Egyptian army, headed by Ahmed Arabi Pasha, again revolted for more pay. The Khedive now favoured the Sultan at the expense of the British and French, who demanded more control of state affairs, which were deteriorating from bad to worse, until eventually rioting and rebellion broke out in Alexandria, where the Arabs attacked all Europeans.

In May, 1882, a British and French squadron arrived off the city to back up the demands for the resignation of Arabi Pasha, who had become Minister for War. He refused to resign, with the result that both the British and French sent ultimatums demanding the restoration of the Khedive's authority. On 11th June, 1882, rebellion and massacre broke out which neither the Egyptian Government nor the suzerain power, the Porte, could or would control. The forts guarding the harbour were fortified in spite of protests by Admiral Sir Beauchamp Seymour and the French Admiral Contad. On the 9th Admiral Seymour threatened to bombard the city if work on the forts was not stopped. On the 10th he demanded the surrender of the batteries on Ras-el-Tin. The French fleet left the harbour on the same day, and thus France surrendered her share of the dual control of

Egypt on which she had previously set such store. At 7 a.m. on 11th July the bombardment started and continued all day until 5.30, when the fleet withdrew out of range and anchored. During the night the town had been set on fire by the Egyptians, who prior to leaving the place had liberated the prisoners from the gaols and given them a free hand to murder and plunder all they could find.

The next morning, the white flag having been hoisted, a force of Marines was landed. Arabi Pasha, together with the Egyptian army, now no longer loyal to the Khedive, had withdrawn, so a very subdued and proably equally frightened Tewfik emerged from Ramleh and took up residence under the protection of British guns. The period 13th—17th was occupied in landing marines and occupying the important places in the city. On the 17th Major-General Sir Archibald Alison arrived with military reinforcements.

The Khedive had now dismissed Arabi Pasha and placed the matter of restoration of law and order in Egypt in our hands. The French declined to assist in any way.

It was obvious that an expeditionary force would be necessary, so troops were dispatched from England and India. The supreme command was given to Sir Garnet Wolseley, who landed at Alexandria on 15th August.

The first task was to seize the Suez Canal and Port Said, as well as to counteract the hostile attitude of M. de Lesseps and the French canal pilots. Captain Fairfax, of H.M.S. *Monarch*, occupied Port Said, while Commander Edwards, of H.M.S. *Ready*, seized all the canal barges and dredgers and occupied the telegraph station at Kantara. In the meanwhile Admiral Hewett had gained command of the canal. With the ports and means of landing a force under our control, the next consideration was to ensure the safety of the water supply, which depended on the fresh water canal between Ismailia and Cairo. It was reported that the rebels were damming this at Magfar (or Mukfar), so they were attacked and driven off on 24th August. They withdrew towards Tel-el-Mahuta and Kassassin, which latter was attacked and captured on the 26th and held against repeated counter-attacks. On 27th August Mustapha Fehmy, Arabi's second-in-command, was captured whilst he was reconnoitring prior, presumably, to the heavy attack launched by the rebels on 9th September at Kassassin. While this fighting and the gradual building up of the British forces was proceeding, Arabi Pasha was strengthening his position at Tel-el-Kebir, which Wolseley reconnoitred in person on the 12th and attacked with two divisions in the early hours of the 13th. The brunt of the fighting was borne by the Highland Brigade under Sir Archibald Alison. The Egyptians were driven out of their positions and pursued so promptly that Cairo was entered on 14th September. Arabi and his army surrendered unconditionally. After his trial he was banished to Ceylon in December, 1882, and pardoned in 1901.

Soon after the entry into Cairo the Khedive dissolved his army and appointed Sir Evelyn Wood, V.C., the commander of a new one. In 1883 (authorized by His Imperial Majesty the Sultan of Turkey) the Khedive signified his desire to express his appreciation of the services rendered by the British Army and Navy by awarding a bronze star.

This is the third award given to British troops for replacing, or maintaining, useless monarchs!

SUDAN, 1884

We must now go south into the Sudan, where, as we have seen, a professed Mahdi had arisen. He quickly obtained thousands of followers who were known as dervishes. The dictionary describes these as mendicant monks of either the howling, whirling or wandering order. These fellows, to save time, combined all three qualifications and added that of fighting. After several clashes between them and the Egyptian troops in 1882 and 1883 they annihilated the Egyptian forces under Hicks Pasha at Kashgil, near El-Obeid, Kordofan, on 3rd—5th November, 1883. On 1st February, 1884, led by Osman Digna, they did the same to another Egyptian army under Valentine Baker Pasha near Tokar.

After this success Osman Digna placed the port of Suakin, on the Red Sea, in a state of siege; but the prompt action of Admiral Sir William Hewett, who landed a Naval Brigade from H.M. ships *Decoy, Euryalus, Ranger* and *Sphinx*, saved it from capture. Reinforcements were sent from Aden and Egypt, which disembarked at Trinkitat on 23rd February, 1884, and defeated Osman Digna at El Teb on 29th February, and again at Tamaai on 13th March. During these two actions a Naval Brigade under Commander E. N. Rolfe, R.N., was present and did splendid work, especially at El Teb.

Following his two defeats, Osman Digna was located at Tamanieb and attacked on 27th March. After this he left the district. The army re-embarked and returned to Egypt, leaving a garrison of Marines at Suakin, which was continually attacked though guarded by a ring of landmines.

After all this bloodshed, trouble and expense the British Government decided to abandon the Sudan, so that the garrison and ships were withdrawn, leaving Osman Digna, the Mahdi and dervishes uncaptured, unrepentant and very much unsubdued.

THE NILE EXPEDITION, 1884—5

This expedition was necessitated by the half-heartedness of the Government, which grossly underestimated the power of the Mahdi and failed to appreciate the complete absence of any authority on the part of the Khedive. With incomprehensible stupidity it was supposed that General Gordon could withdraw the garrison from Khartoum by his will-power or sleight of hand. It should have been obvious that British prestige was inseparably connected with his fate. We had halted in the north and evacuated in the east, so that with nothing to fear the Mahdi, now joined by the greater part of the mutinous Egyptian troops, invested Khartoum. Gordon made repeated and successful sallies, but could never hope to raise the siege without external help.

In August, 1884 (five months after the investment started) preparations were made for his relief. Two expeditions, under the joint command of Sir Garnet Wolseley, were to advance towards Khartoum. One, accompanied by Sir Garnet, advanced up the Nile; the second operated from Suakin. When the Nile column reached Korti on 26th December, 1884, Major-General Sir Herbert Stewart was ordered to take the Camel Corps and a naval brigade under Captain Lord Charles Beresford and cut across the desert to Metemmeh to join up with the Nile steamers sent by Gordon from Khartoum. On the way wells at Gakdul and Abu Klea would have to be captured. The first were found to be unoccupied, so that the force was watered and then continued the advance on 16th January, 1885. Later in the day the scouts of the 19th Hussars reported that the wells at Abu Klea were being held. The action which bears their name was fought on the 17th, after which the enemy withdrew towards the Nile, closely followed by all except the Naval Brigade, who, together with some artillery and engineers, were left behind to guard the wounded. The Nile was reached and a garrison left, while a strong force returned to Abu Klea to assist in the burial of the dead and bring forward the wounded. Subsequently the whole force re-formed and camped at Gubat, from which the four small steamers (*Bordein, Tull-Howeija, Safia* and *Tefikea*) dispatched by Gordon were observed above Metemmeh. An advance towards Metemmeh was made, during which General Stewart was severely wounded and succeeded by General Sir Charles Wilson, who on 21st

January made a useless reconnaissance of Metemmeh which wasted much valuable time. It was found that Gordon's steamers required a certain amount of repairs. These were carried out, and the ships were reported to General Wilson on 22nd January to be ready to make the dash for Khartoum. Instead of sending them off at once, a further useless waste of time was made by ordering Captain Beresford to bombard Shendy. It was not until the morning of the 24th that General Wilson seemed to have remembered the object of the whole expedition. He left for Khartoum with the *Bordein* and *Tull-Howeija*, together with about twenty men of the Sussex Regiment and a few Sudanese from the ships—in all, about 280 men.

The next that was heard of this party was on 1st February, when Lieutenant Stuart-Wortley returned to Gubat with the news that Gordon had been murdered on 26th January, and that the two steamers were wrecked about half a mile or so below Khartoum. Sir Charles Wilson and his men were reported to be on an island about thirty miles upstream and in danger of attack by several thousand Sudanese who were holding an earthwork almost opposite them.

Lord Beresford selected a crew for the *Safia* from his Naval Brigade and a few picked shots from the mounted infantry, together with crews for two Gardner guns, and left on 2nd February. He reached the earthwork the next morning, but when trying to get past it his ship received a shot in the boiler which necessitated running her ashore on the opposite bank. The chief engineer, Mr. Benbow, by a magnificent effort made a plate to cover the hole and got the engine working again in about ten hours. In the meanwhile Sir Charles Wilson had placed his wounded in a nugger to drift down the stream, whilst he and the remainder of his party retired down the right bank of the river.

The expedition had failed in its purpose, and once again the sickening order to retire—with no useful purpose having been served—was issued. Lord Wolseley sent General Redvers Buller, v.c., to Gubat to superintend the withdrawal of the force back to Korti across the same two hundred miles of desert, during which the only bright events must have been to watch the men of Lord Beresford's brigade plugging oakum into any holes shot in the sides of the camels.

Few military forces have deserved more credit than that which left Korti on 26th December, 1884, and returned on 7th March, 1885, after having traversed four hundred miles of desert. No praise could be too high for the members of the Naval Brigade, who acted as gunners, infantry, sailors and vets with conspicuous valour and success.

A study of the course of the Nile between Korti and Metemmeh shows it to be in the shape of an inverted "U" with Khartoum on a continuation of the right-hand arm. The desert column had gone across the opening at the bottom, whilst the other followed the river. The river column was commanded by Major-General W. Earle, who had with him the major part of the relief forces. When the news of Gordon's death was received the column halted for a few days. When the advance continued the Sudanese were found to be holding a position in front of Kirbekan, from which they were driven on 10th February. General Earle was killed, otherwise the casualties were slight. On the 25th orders were received to withdraw to Korti, where on or about 28th March fever broke out before the return of the whole force to Cairo.

We must now turn to the other force at Suakin under the command of Major-General Sir Gerald Graham, v.c.

The plan was that this force should build a railway from Suakin to Berber on the Nile, a distance of about 280 miles, and then methodically reconquer the Sudan. Troops were sent from England, India and Australia. After a reconnaissance it was decided that the main camp should be at Hasheen, some fourteen miles inland. It was known that Osman Digna was in the neighbourhood with considerable forces, so the advance inland was to be made in the usual square formation, leaving Suakin on 20th March. Early on the 22nd General McNeill left Suakin with troops whose intention was to make zarebas, or fortified camps, but he was surprised and attacked at Tofrek whilst the men were having breakfast—not the best time to disturb Englishmen! For a short while all was confusion, but thanks to the steadiness of the Royal Marines and the Berkshire Regiment the fanatics were driven off.

On 2nd April General Graham advanced to Tamaai, but found no one at home, so he burnt the place and then returned to Suakin, and on 17th May the British and Colonial troops left the Sudan, so again another futile expedition was completed.

The Mahdi died of smallpox in June, 1885, and was succeeded by Khalifa Abdullah el Taashi. From 1885 to December, 1888, there was considerable fighting in Egypt and the Sudan for which no bars were awarded, so we can skip that period and return to Suakin in December, 1888, where General Sir Francis Grenfell had arrived with a combined British and Egyptian force, which was as usual surrounded by dervishes. On 20th December he made a sortie and defeated them at Gemaizah, after which the troops at Suakin were again withdrawn except for a small garrison.

The Khalifa, having no opposition in the Sudan, proceeded up the Nile into Egypt, where his forces once again encountered Sir Francis Grenfell, now Sirdar of the Egyptian army, at Toski on 3rd August, 1889, and suffered a heavy defeat.

Medals were awarded without bars to the 1 Cameron Highlanders and some Sudanese troops who served to the south of Wadi Haifa between 30 November, 1885 and 11 January, 1886.

This, then, completes the brief account of all the actions for which the Egypt Medal 1884—9 was awarded, but omits mention of the action of Tokar, south of Suakin, on 19th February, 1891, for which the Khedive awarded an undated bronze star and bar (or bar only to those already in possession of one of the three previous issues of stars) to the crew of H.M. ships *Dolphin* and *Sandfly* and British troops employed with the Egyptian army under Colonel Holland-Smith.

The following medals without bars were awarded: 1st Life Guards (51); 2nd Life Guards (60); Royal Horse Guards (52); 4th Dragoon Guards (208); 7th Dragoon Guards (115); 19th Hussars (202); "N" Bty. "A" Bde. (34); "G" Bty. "B" Bde. R.H.A. (29); A/1 (25), D/1 (19), F/1 (14), H/1 (7), N/2 (19), I/2 (11), C/3 (14), J/3 (10), 1/1 (139). R.A.; 4/1 (106), 5/1 (147) R.A. London Division; No. 7 Mountain Battery (19); 5/1 Scottish Division (144); 6/1 Scottish Division (145); H.Q. R.A. (21); Loyal Malta Artillery (93); Royal Engineers: Staff (26), A Troop (17), C Troop (66), Field Park (32), 8th (28), 17th (12), 18th (103), 21st (56), 24th (187), 26th (144); Grenadier Guards 2nd Bn. (83); Coldstream Guards (49); Scots Guards (58); 18th (63), 35 (927), 38 (1,036), 42 (26), 45/95 (778), 46 (135), 49 (866), 50 (755), 53/85 (785), 63/96 (676), 68, 74 (63), 75 (75), 79 (28), 84 (84), 87 (84) Foot; R.A.M.C., etc; Military Police (15); Army Chaplain's Dept. (18); Interpreters (138); Malta Auxiliaries (214, but many not claimed).

Numerous Naval vessels were present in Egyptian waters including the undermentioned, the crews or part of the complements received the medal without bar with either the dated or undated reverse: *Achilles* (43); *Agincourt* (783); *Albacore* (51); *Arab* (76); *Briton* (200); *Carysfort* (30); *Chester* (21); *Cocatrice* (67); *Condor* (20); *Coquette* (7); *Don* (50); *Dragon* (135); *Dryad* (99); *Eclipse* (224); *Euphrates* (257); *Euralyus* (460); *Falcon* (113); *Hecla* (65); *Helicon* (29); *Humber* (90); *Inconstant* (570); *Iris* (297); *Juma* (180); *Malabar* (269); *Minotaur* (837); *Mosquito* (63); *Myrmidon* (81); *Northumberland* (820); *Orion* (340); *Orontes* (234); *Rambler* (94); *Ranger* (81); *Ready* (81); *Ruby* (234); *Salmis* (88); *Seagull* (108); *Seahorse* (63); *Seraphis* (220); *Sphinx* (68); *Supply*

(24); *Tamar* (214); *Thalia* (460); *Tourmaline* (223); *Turquoise* (190); *Tyne* (65); *Woodlark* (60); *Wye* (76). Indian Government Ship *Amberwitch.*

Alexandria 11th July *(1882)*

Given for the bombardment of Alexandria by the ships under Admiral Seymour.

Flagship *Invincible* (560), *Alexandra* (821), *Beacon* (82), *Hecla* (236), *Inflexible* (481),* *Monarch* (562), *Penelope* (352), *Rambler* (5), *Sultan* (658), *Superb* (623), *Temeraire* (594), *Turquoise* (190). Gunboats *Beacon* (80), *Bittern* (95), *Condor* (104), *Cygnet* (61), *Deacon* (88), *Decoy* (66), *Euphrates.* Despatch Boat Helicon (85).

(Medals to H.M.S. *Coquette* and H.M.S. *Minotaur* are known, which ships, however, did not take part in the bombardment.)

Tel-el-Kebir *(13th September, 1882)*

Regiments present: Three squadrons each of 1 (109) and 2 (103) Life Guards; Royal Horse Guards (108); 4 (335), 7 (450) Dragoon Guards; 1st R. Dragoons (9); 3 (6), 4 (9), 11 (11), 19 (374) Hussars; "N"/"A" (148), "G"/"B" (143) R.H.A.; A/1 (177), D/1 (183), F/1 (186), H/1 (147), N/2 (181), I/2 (187), C/3 (159), J/3 (164) R.A.; No. 7 Mountain Battery (94), H.Q.R.A. (15); R.M.A.; R.E. (570); "A" and "I" Companies Madras Sappers and Miners; 2/1 (660), 2/2 (705), 1/3 (715) Foot Guards; 2/18 (625), 1/42, 46 (645), 50 (One Company) (59), 3/60, 1/63, 1/72 (197), 2/74 (775), 1/75 (766), 78 (564), 1/79 (795), 84 (726), 87 (725), 88 (6), 96 (2) Foot; Mounted Infantry; 2, 6 Bengal Cavalry; 13 Bengal Lancers; 7 Bengal N.I.; 20, 29 Punjab N.I.; Malta Auxiliary Transport; C. and T. Corps; Interpreters (42); Army Veterinary Corps (30); Army Chaplains (10); Army Service Corps; Military Police (59).

A Naval Brigade formed of seamen and marines from the following ships served at the battle of Tel-el-Kebir; H.M.S. *Alexandra* (35); *Carysfort* (28); *Euryalus* (1); *Hecla* (2); *Helicon* (1); *Inflexible; Monarch* (19); *Mosquito; Orion* (41); *Penelope* (22); *Seagull; Superb* (32); *Temeraire* (27).

Medals with bars for "Alexandia 11th July" and Tel-el-Kebir have the date "1882" in the exergue.

Medals are also to be found to the following H.M. ships, but they seldom have any bars. One presumes that they were on duty in the area at the time and that only a few individuals from them took part in the above, and sometimes subsequent, actions: H.M. ships: *Achilles, Agincourt, Amerberwitch, Arab, Calabria, Chester, Cockatrice, Coquette, Dee, Don, Eclipse, Euphrates, Falcon, Hecla, Humber, Inconstant, Inflexible, Iris, Jumna, Malabar, Mariner, Minotaur, Northunberland, Orion, Orontes, Rambler, Ranger, Ready, Ruby, Salamis, Sandfly, Seahorse, Seraphis, Supply, Tamar, Thalia, Tourmaline, Turquoise, Wye.*

The following regiments received the 1882 Medal without bars: 35, 38, 49, 50 (one company received the bar for Tel-el-Kebir), 53, 95, 96 Foot, Royal Marines (840 sent out especially from the U.K.).

El-Teb *(29th February, 1884)*

Four thousand two hundred of these bars were issued. For this and subsequent actions in this campaign the undated medal was awarded to all who had

---

*H.M.S. *Inflexible*, launched at Portsmouth on the 27th April, 1876, was one of the first warships to be fitted with power-operated turrets; in her case they were hydraulic.

not already received the one with the date 1882 in the exergue.

Regiments present: 10 Hussars; 19 Hussars (410); Mounted Infantry (125); 6 Battery R.A. (126); 26 Company R.E. (100); R.M.A.; R.M.L.I.; Carrier and Transport Corps; 1/42, 3/60, 65, 75, 89 Foot; 150 sailors and 400 Marines from H.M. ships: Briton (6), *Carysfort* (38), *Decoy, Dryad* (2), *Euryalus* (20), *Hecla* (7), *Humber, Inconstant, Ranger, Sphinx* (2) and a few from H.M.S. *Ready*.

Medals to the 84, 87 and 92 Foot are known. Captain Wilson, R.N., of H.M.S. *Hecla* gained the V.C. at this action. A medal with this single bar is unusual.

Tamaii *(13th March, 1884)*

It is unusual to find this as a single bar.

Regiments present; One squadron each of 10 (approx. 12) and 19 Hussars; "M" Battery and No. 6 Battery, R.A.; 26 Company R.E.; 42, 3/60, 65, 70, 75, 89 Foot; Native Camel Transport; fourteen officers and 464 seamen and Marines from H.M. ships: *Briton* (36). *Carysfort* (15), *Dryad* (5), *Euryalus* (47), *Hecla* (9), *Humber* (71), *Inconstant, Inflexible, Northumberland, Sphinx, Thalia, Tyne*.

El-Teb — Tamaai

This medal was awared to all those who had taken part in the actions of El-Teb and Tamaii. It is unusual to find a medal with this as a single bar. Pte. J. Stubbs received a medal with this single bar and another medal without a bar and two of the Khedive's Stars. H.M.S. (*Briton* (19), *Dryad* (220), *Euryalus* (28), *Hecla* (23), *Humber* (3), *Sphinx* (12). 7th (17), and 79th Foor (9).

Suakin 1884 *(19th February—26th March, 1884)*

Regiments present: 19 Hussars; 6/1 Scottish Div. R.A.; 24, 26 Co. R.E.; 1/42, 60, 75, 79 (5) Foot.

H.M. ships: *Albacore, Alexandra, Arab* (97), *Briton* (144), *Carysfort* (224), *Coquette, Cygnet; Decoy* (66), *Euryalus* (304), *Falcon, Hecla* (195), *Helicon, Humber* (67), *Inconstant, Inflexible, Iris* (36), *Jumna* (37), *Malabar, Minotaur, Myrmidon, Northumberland, Orion, Orontes* (67), *Ranger* (9), *Ready, Seraphis* (19), *Skylark, Sphinx* (11), *Sultan, Temeraire, Thalia, Tyne, Woodlark*.

The Nile 1884—85

This bar was only awarded to those who served south of Assouan, on or before 7th March, 1885, in the expedition to relieve General Gordon, who was murdered in Khartoum on 26th January, 1885.†

Four camel regiments were formed for this campaign as follows:

Heavy Camel Regiment — Approx. 2 officers and 43 other ranks from each of the following: 1 (39), 2 Life Guards (38); Royal Horse Guards (46); 2, 4 (41), 5 (32) Dragoon Guards; 1, 2 Dragoons; 5, 16 Lancers.

---

†*General Gordon's Star for Khartoum.* During the siege of Khartoum, prior to his death, General Gordon had pewter stars cast, these being in pewter some of which were silver plated or gold plated. These were distributed within the besieged city, the design of the awards being based on the order of Medjidie with a grenade in the centre. In 1957 the Sudanese Embassy stated that the stars were originally issued with a magenta or purple ribbon approx. 1.5 in. wide. Silver stars do exist but it is thought that these were made later on and possibly sold for charity.

Light Camel Regiment — Approx. 2 officers and 43 other ranks from each of the following: 3 (44), 4 (42), 7 (47), 10, 11, 15 (44), 18, 20, 21 Hussars.

Guards Camel Regiment — 2 officers and 43 other ranks from each of the following: 1, 2, 3 Grenadier Guards; 1, 2 Coldstream Guards; 1, 2, 3 Scots Guards; and 4 officers and 102 other ranks Royal Marine Light Infantry.

Mounted Infantry Camel Regiment: 1/13, 19 (10), 1/21, 35, 38, 42, 46, 50, 52 (33), 56, 1, 2 and 3/60, 75, 94, 97 Foot and Rifle Brigade.

Regiments present: 19 Hussars; 1/1 Southern and 5/1 Scottish Divs. R.A.; 18 (647), 35, 38, 42, 46, 50, 56, 75, 79, 88 (27) Foot.

Medals are known with this bar and that for the Abu Klea to the 94th Foot and with this and Suakin 1884 to the Army Pay Department, also to the Comissariat and Transport Corps and R.E., 26th Co.

Naval Brigades from H.M. ships *Albacore, Briton, Carysfort, Condor, Coquette, Cygnet, Dolphin, Falcon, Helicon, Humber, Iris, Monarch, Myrmidon, Rambler, Ranger, Sphinx, Starling, Turquoise, Tyne, Wye* and *Woodlark*.

River gunboats: *Bordein, Sophia, Tewfikea, Tull-Howeija*.

Three hundred and ninety-two Canadian boatmen: Officers 7, Caughnawaga 56, Manitoba 88, Three River's 41, Ottawa 169, Peterborough 15, Sherbrooke 6, Sydney 1, Hospital Staff 1, Wheelmen 8.

Abu Klea *(17th January, 1885)*

This bar, of which 1,581 were issued, is never found singly but always with that for "The Nile 1884—85" and, of course, where applicable with additional ones as well. It is somewhat rare and generally highly prized when on a medal with four bars.

Regiments present: 2 Life Guards (38); R. Horse Guards (46, all with Nile bar); 2nd Dgns. (39); 5th Lancers; 1/1 Division R.A.; 4 Hussars (2); 5th Lcrs. (30); 19 Hussars (135); 2 Coldm. Gds (90); 1 Royal Sussex; 3 K.R.R.C.; Gordon Hldrs. (33); 1st Connaught Rangers (25); Commissariat and Transport Corps and R.M.L.I. (92).

Pte. Russel, 5th Lancers, received this bar.

A Naval Brigade of fifty-five officers and men under Lord Charles Beresford.

Kirbekan *(10th February, 1885)*

This bar, of which 1,200 were issued, is never found singly. but always in conjunction with that for "The Nile 1884—85", and others when applicable. A medal with only these two bars is quite rare. One such medal was awarded to the 2 Essex Regt.

Regiments present: One squadron 19 Hussars (95); two guns 1/1 Southern Division R.A.; 1 South Staffs; 1 Black Watch; D company 1 Gordon Highlanders (82).

A Maxim Gun Detachment from H.M.S. *Wye* was present and 45 Canadian Boatmen who received this bar and "The Nile 1884—1885"—Officers (1), Coughnawaga (3); Manitoba (14); Three Rivers (1); Ottawa (24); Peterborough (1); Sydney (1).

Suakin 1885 *(1st March—14th May, 1885)*

This was the first occasion that Australian units were sent overseas, 720 qualified for the bar.

Regiments present: 5 Lancers (102); 19, 20 (82) Hussars; "G" Battery R.H.A.; 25 and 6 Batteries 1 Scottish Division R.A.; One Field Battery New South Wales

Artillery; 9 Bengal Cavalry; 10, 17, 24, 26 Companies R.E.; 3 Grenadier Guards; 1 Coldstream Guards; 2 Scots Guards; 18, (42), 1/19 (51 plus 10x2 bars), 1/42, 49, 53, 70, 79 (2), 86 (64) Foot; New South Wales Inf.* (500); N.S.W. Arty. (205); N.S.W. Ambulance Corps (22); N.S.W. Band (14); Australian Chaplains (2); Artillery, Ambulance Corps Staff; 3rd Co. C. and T.C. Indian Brigade; 11, 15 Sikhs; 17 Bengal Infantry; 128 Pioneers; 2 Queen's Own Sappers and Miners; Bombay Comm. Dept.

Naval Brigade from H.M. ships: *Alexandra, Carysfort* (32), *Condor* (122), *Coquette* (64), *Cygnet* (84), *Dee* (35), *Dolphin* (115), *Humber* (100), *Northumberland, Sphinx* (185), *Tourmaline, Tyne* (125), and H.M.S. *Starling* (59), Government Launch *Foscolmetto* (1), H.M. Tug *Prompt* (1).

Tofrek *(22nd March, 1885)*

This bar is found only in conjunction with that for "Suakin 1885" and, owing to the small size of the force engaged, it is quite rare to British troops.

Regiments present: One squadron 5 Lancers (102); One Squadron 20 Hussars (82); 6 Battery 1 Scottish Division R.A.; 24 Company R.E.; 1 Royal Berks. Indian Brigade; 11, 15 Sikhs; 17 Bengal Infantry; 128 Pioneers; 2 Queen's Own Sappers and Miners.

Naval Brigade from H.M. ships *Alexandra, Carysfort* (12), *Condor* (7), *Coquette* (2), *Dolphin* (12), *Sphinx* (13), *Starling* (3), and a Royal Marine Br. (542).

For their distinguished conduct at this battle, the Berkshire Regiment gained the prefix "Royal".

General Order No. 68 dated 1st June, 1886, states that all officers and soldiers who served at and to the south of Wadi Halfa between 30th November, 1885, and 11th January, 1886, were to receive a medal with the following two bars providing they had not already received one for any of the previous actions.

Gemaizah *(20th December, 1888)*

Regiments present: 20 Hussars (147); 17 members of the 24 Company R.E.; 2/25, 41, 86 (34) Foot; Egyptian Native Troops.

Naval detachments from H.M.S. *Starling* (Medal & bar 39, bar only 22: total 61), *Racer* (medal & bar 91, bar only 30: total 121), Khedive's *Noor-El-Bahr* (Medal & bar 11, bar only 1: total 12).

Toski 1889 *(3rd August)*

Regiments present: 20 Hussars (93), 83 Foot (29) (the only British troops present); Egyptian troops.

It is most interesting to note how the records vary concerning the number of Hussars present at Gemaizah and Toski. These two bars on one medal are rare even to native recipients. Only Lietenant H. Wiltshire and sixteen men of 20 Hussars received Toski as a single bar.

Four officers and seventy-seven men of the 20th Hussars received both the bars for Gemaizah and Toski. Pte. A. Brooks, 19th Hussars, received these two bars and that for Suakin 1885; this is probably unique. Sergeants H. W. Yates and T. H. Lane and one other N.C.O., R. Irish Rifles, each received a medal with this single bar. They were attached to the Army Medical Corps at the time.

*The citizens of Sydney presented 800 medals, 1·1 in. diameter, to the members of this contingent. They bore the Arms of the Corporation on the obverse; on the reverse was the inscription, "PRESENTED BY THE CITIZENS OF SYDNEY. T. PLAYFAIR, MAYOR, 1885".

This was the first occasion on which Australian units fought with Imperial troops.

69 KHEDIVE'S EGYPTIAN STARS (1882–1891)

Obverse	In the centre is the Sphinx with three pyramids behind. Around this is a raised circle on which is embossed the word "EGYPT", followed by the applicable date or dates. The fourth type has the word "EGYPT" in the centre at the top of this circle.
Reverse	The Kedive's monogram "T.M." within a raised circle.
Size	The maximum width of the star is 1·9 in.
Suspension	A small ring is attached to the piece between two points of the star. To this ring is attached a straight suspender on which is a rectangular bar 1/8 in. x 1.5/8 in., in the centre of which is the Crescent and small five-pointed star.
Ribbon	1½ in. wide. Plain dark blue.
Naming	All the stars were issued unnamed, but most of the 1882 issue awarded to members of the Guards regiments bear the recipient's regimental number and the initials of his regiment, viz. G.G., C.G., or S.G.
No of bars issued	One, for Tokar.

These five-pointed bronze stars, made by Messrs. Henry Jenkins & Sons, Birmingham, to the order of Tewfik Mahommed, were awarded by the Khedive to all who were awarded a medal for the Egyptian Campaigns between 1882 and 1889. There were four issues of these stars, to correspond with the different campaigns. The first three bear the dates on the obverse, the fourth is undated. The relevant dates are as follows:

Star dated 1882, for the Campaign between 16th July and 14th September, 1882.

Star dated 1884, for the Campaign between 19th February and 26th March, 1884.

Star dated 1884–6, for the Campaigns between 26th March, 1884, and 7th October, 1886.

Star undated for the Campaign near Suakin in 1887 and on the Nile in 1889.*

All these stars, no two of which, except by mistake, were given to one man, could be worn in uniform. In 1893 the Khedive made a further issue of the undated stars to commemorate the action at Tokar on 19th February, 1891. Those present who had not already received a star were awarded one bearing the bar with the Arabic inscription "TOKAR 1308H". Previous recipients of the stars received the bar only. By the time the last star was issued, most men had already received one of the earlier ones, so that the undated star with the bar for Tokar is somewhat rare. As there was no British issue to commemorate Tokar, permission was granted for the bronze star and bar to be worn by those entitled to it though they may not have also received the silver medal for services between 1882 and 1889.

70 HONG KONG PLAGUE MEDAL (1894)

Obverse	A Chinaman lying on a trestle table leaning against a man who is fending off the winged figure of death with his left hand. A woman is bending over the sick man. On a scroll in the exergue is the date "1894". To the left of the picture is a Chinese inscription.

*The undated stars are to be found with the word "EGYPT" very crudely embossed.

Reverse	In the centre, in raised lettering, is "FOR SERVICES RENDERED DURING THE PLAGUE OF 1894". Around the outer circumference is "PRESENTED BY THE HONG KONG COMMUNITY".
Size	1.42 in. diameter.
Ribbon	1.25 in. wide. Red with yellow edges and two additional thin yellow stripes down the centre.
Suspension	A loop is soldered on to the top of the piece, through which passes a 0.4 in. diameter ring.
Designer	Designed by Frank Bowcher and struck by A. Wyon, F.S.A.
Naming	In thin well-spaced indented capitals giving the recipient's rank, name and regiment but not number.
No. of bars issued	Nil.

This medal was given by the Hong Kong Community to three hundred men of the Shropshire Light Infantry and fifty members of the Navy and Royal Engineers, also to members of the local police. It is not allowed to be worn in uniform, as it is not a service medal. Approx. 40 medals were given in gold to officers†, a few civilian officials and, possibly, a few nursing sisters, but this has not been verified.

Though the design on the obverse may be considered a bit gruesome, it is beautifully executed and is one of the most symbolical to be found. The colours chosen for the ribbon are particularly apt.

This bubonic plage lasted from 5th May to 3rd September, 1894, when Hong Kong was declared free.

71 INDIAN GENERAL SERVICE MEDAL (1854—1895)

Obverse	The diademed head of Queen Victoria and the legend "VICTORIA REGINA".
Reverse	The winged and standing figure of Victory, who is crowning a seated warrior. In the exergue is a lotus flower and four leaves.
Size	1.42 in. diameter.
Ribbon	1.25 in. wide. Crimson with two dark blue stripes.
Suspension	By means of a floreated swivelling suspender. The rivets at the junction of the suspender and clasp are covered by a rosette, and the junctions of all bars are similarly covered.
Designers	Obverse — W. Wyon, R.A.; Reverse — L. C. Wyon.
Naming	This will be given against each bar as it varies considerably.
No. of bars issued	Twenty-three.

This medal was instituted on 23rd January, 1854, to commemorate the campaign in Burma between 28th March, 1852, and 30th June, 1853. The Governor-General seems to have prophesied considerable further trouble, because his suggestion that for future campaigns on the frontier a bar only should be added to this medal was adopted. It is always referred to as the 1854 Indian General Service Medal, or some combination of these words, so as to distinguish it from the two others we shall come across later.

†Some recipients: Major W. Machaughlin; Major A. F. A. Lyle; Capt. G. H. L. Buchanan; Capt. H. B. Welman; Capt. E. Howell; Capt. J. G. Forbes; Capt. G. C. Vesey; Lieut. R. A. A. Y. Jordan; Lieut. J. A. Strick; Lieut. E. B. Luard; 2nd Lieut. W. J. Robinson; 2nd Lieut. R. T. Carreg and Atr. Mastr. J. C. Wilson.

209

To give a complete account of the campaign for which each bar was awarded is quite beyond the scope of this book, details are very briefly mentioned against each bar as we come to it.

There are a few interesting things about this medal which perhaps collectors may have noticed, but one has been unable to give any explanation for them or to find anyone who can. The oddities, if that is the correct expression, which strike one most forcibly are these.

Firstly, why was the Burma Campaign of 1852—53 commemorated by a bar named "PEGU", when the others in the same country were named "BURMA 1885—7",* "BURMA 1887—89", "BURMA 1889—92"? Here, too, one wonders why the first of these latter bars is identified by the single date at the end instead of the double, *i.e.* 1885—87.

Secondly, why was a separate medal (also a star) awarded for the Afghanistan 1878—80 Campaign if the avowed intention was to avoid a redundancy of medals? It will be noticed that when the 1908 Indian G.S. Medal was current those who served in Afghanistan in 1919 did not receive a separate medal!

Thirdly, it seems extraordinary that the same bar (North-West Frontier) should be awarded for no fewer than sixteen expeditions between 1849 and 1868. To many recipients this bar represented participation in several campaigns spread over five or more years. Brigadier B. B. Chamberlain, for instance, commanded four of them between 4th April, 1855, and 16th April, 1860.

It is believed that a genuine medal exists with the bar for Pegu and Waziristan 1894—95, an interval of forty-one years! Active service on the Frontier meant *active* service, too!

The object of the medal was, as already stated, to avoid the issue of too many medals, but it did not prevent men from receiving two identical ones.

Unfortunately, many medals are found with the bars in the wrong order and this is caused because they were given to the natives to fix themselves. In addition to their being in the wrong order, one might almost describe some of the methods of attachment as weird and wonderful; solder, wire, and bent nails were used. It appears that the local blacksmith turned jeweller and having taken the whole medal to bits forgot the order in which to reassemble it. All this detracts from the value of these medals from the collector's point of view, because it has made it so easy for the faker. In any case, it is extremely difficult to verify native medals, because the natives changed their units so often. Many were combatants in one campaign, followers in another, and combatants in a third. For this reason, I would suggest that collectors should pay more attention to medals of units which they can trace as having been present in the campaigns for which they carry bars.

Whilst the medal itself is very common, there are some bars to it which are very rare indeed; and wheras rarity is rather a matter of opinion, one would say that the order or rareness is as follows: Kachin Hill 1892—93; Hunza 1891; Chin Hill 1892—93; Naga 1879—80; and then North-East Frontier 1891; Lushai 1889—92; Sikim 1888, a good long way behind. I should add that I refer only to the rareness of the bars themselves; if one is particular about the regiments of the recipients then the order of rarity is undoubtedly Kachin Hills 1892—93, to

* The General Order of the Governor-General dated 16th June, 1887, quotes Her Majesty as having approved of a bar inscribed "BURMA 1885—87". The Commander-in-Chief, in his Order dated 1st August, 1887, quotes it as "BURMA 1885—7". The Governor-General, in an Order dated 16th September, 1887, again refers to it as "BURMA 1885—87". On the 11th August, 1887, the Secretary of State refers to it as "BURMA 1885—7".

Nothing can be traced to show how, or why, the bar was not inscribed as originally approved by Her Majesty.

A similar error occurred in the case of the bar for Perak, which was issued without any dates, though Her Majesty sanctioned the award of one inscribed "PERAK 1875—76".

the Yorkshire Regiment, and Chin Hills 1892—93 to the Norfolks. These are considered to be equally, and exceptionally rare.

The naming of the medals varies with the issue of each bar, therefore the type of naming found on the single bar medals is given.

It is well to note that when the medal was originally issued with only a single bar the ears at the top of it were removed so that subsequent bars could not be added above. It is not unusual to find the first awarded bar—for Pegu—at the top and all the other ones in the correct order, that is, reading upwards from the piece.

The maximum number of bars to any medal, which was never awarded without one, that has been heard of is seven. Starting with the issue of the bar for Burma 1885-7, medals were awarded in bronze to authorized followers.

The title Native Infantry was dropped after 1885; the regiments since then have been designated Punjab Infantry, Bengal Infantry, etc. Some time after the Mutiny, the spelling of Goorkhas was altered to Gurkhas, though the old spelling was used on medals for a while after this event.

It will also be realized that the great majority of the Bengal Army disappeared in the Mutiny in 1857 and many of their numbers were allotted to newly raised regiments.

Pegu *(28th March, 1852—30 June, 1853)*

This, the second, campaign in Burma was caused by the refusal of the King of Ava to abide by the Treaty of Yendaboo signed on 24th February, 1826, at the conclusion of the first Burma war, which allowed trading facilities in the port of Rangoon. In addition to the molestation of shipping, the British Resident was insulted and our warships fired upon. After attempts at obtaining satisfaction proved useless, war was declared on 2nd April, 1852. A squadron under Commodore G. Lambert and an expeditionary force under Major-General Godwin were dispatched on 28th March, 1852. Martaban was captured on 5th April; Rangoon on 14th April; Bassein on 19th May; Pegu, which had been captured on 4th April, was recaptured on 21st November; Prome on 10th October. On 20th December the Province of Pegu was annexed. After this a revolution broke out which resulted in considerable banditry, of which Myat-Toon was the chief instigator with his stronghold near Donubyu. It was at the capture of this that Ensign Garnet Wolseley, 80th Foot, distinguished himself.

The war ended on 30th June, 1853.

This bar is slightly narrower than the others.

The naming is in block capitals, those on the Naval medals being slightly smaller than on those awarded to the Army.

Regiments present: Detachment of Irregular Horse; 2, 5 Bn. R.A.; Madras and Bengal Artillery; Madras and Bengal Sappers and Miners; Ordnance Department; Quartermaster General's Department; 18 (1,028), 51 (900), 80 (460) Foot; 1 European Bengal Fusiliers (1 Royal Munster Fusiliers); 1 Madras Fusiliers (1 Royal Dublin Fusiliers); 5, 9, 19, 26, 30, 35, 46, 49, 79 Madras N.I.; 10, 37, 40, 67, 68 Bengal N.I.; 4, 15 Sikhs.

H.M. ships: *Bittern* (139), *Cleopatra* (236), *Contest* (107), *Fox* (447), *Hastings* (576), *Hermes* (160), *Rattler* (169), *Salamander* (142), *Serpent* (123), *Spartan* (245), *Sphinx* (206), *Styx* (153), *Winchester* (518).

Bengal Marine ships: *Bhagurette* (25), *Damoodah* (100), *Enterprise* (93), *Fire Queen* (221), *Indus* (67), *Krishna* (106), *Lord William Bentinck* (116), *Luckia* (24), *Mahanuddy* (120), *Nemesis* (78), *Nerbuddah* (99), *Phlegethon* (131), *Pluto* (173), *Proserpine* (138), *Soane* (26), *Spy* (58), *Sutledge* (30), *Tenasserim* (290).

Indian Marine Ships: *Berenice* (256), *Ferooz* (272), *Hugh Lindsay, Medusa* (85), *Moozuffer* (349), *Sesostris* (182), *Zenobia* (350).

Persia *(5th December, 1856—8th February, 1857)*

The war was caused by the reoccupation of the city of Herat by the Persians. This city, said to be the key to Afghanistan, was formally annexed by them on 25th October, 1856. War was declared on 1st November, and on the 10th an Indian naval squadron commanded by Commodore Young bombarded Bushire, which surrendered. On the arrival of Major-General Sir James Outram with an expeditionary force an advance was made inland from Bushire to Boorzgoon (or Brazjun), where many stores were captured. During the withdrawal the force was attacked at Kooshab on 7th February, 1857. The Persians were heavily defeated. After his return to Bushire, Outram left Major-General Stalker to hold the town, whilst he (Outram) crossed the Persian Gulf to the delta of the Euphrates, up which he advanced to Mohamrah, some sixty miles inland. On 26th March the Navy bombarded the strong Persian positions and forts. After a short while they were either silenced or completely destroyed, so that troops were landed under Brigadier-General Havelock, who promptly entered the city and captured a further large supply of stores. He very generously gave full credit for the ease with which he accomplished his mission to the Navy, who in turn owed its immunity from heavy casualties to the foresight of Commander Rennie, who gave orders for the bombarding ships to be surrounded with trusses of hay!

The Persians withdrew to Akwaz, about a hundred miles up the Karoon river, where they were again attacked by Commander Rennie and a small force composed of about 300 men of the 64th and 78th Foot under Captain Hunt. The town was captured on 1st April, after which the force returned to Mohamrah, where it learnt that peace had been signed in Paris on 4th March under the terms of which Herat was to be evacuated by the Persians.

The North Staffordshire Regiment and the Durham Light Infantry both carry Bushire and Koosh-ab on their colours.

The naming is in block capitals. The Naval medals are named slightly smaller than those to the Army.

Regiments present: 14 Light Dragoons (366); 3 Bombay Cavalry; Scinde Horse; Poona Horse; Aden Irregular Horse; 3, 5 Light Field Batteries, R.A.; D. Battery, 19th Brigade, R.A.; 4th Troop Bombay Horse Artillery; 1st Company 2nd Bn. (Bombay) Foot Artillery; 4th Company 4th Bn. (Native) Artillery; 2, 4 Companies Bombay Sappers and Miners; Ordanance Department; 64 (1,025), 78 Foot; 1, 2 Bombay Fusiliers (1,040) (2 D.L.I.); 2, 3, 4, 5, 6, 8, 9, 11, 15, 19, 20, 21, 22, 23, 25, 26, 28, 29 Bombay N.I.

Indian Marine ships: *Ajdaba* (325), *Assaye* (332), *Assyria* (39), *Berenice*, *Clive*, *Comet*, *Constance*, *Euphrates*, *Falkland*, *Ferooz*, *Hugh Lindsay*, *Moozuffer*, *Napier*, *Nitocris*, *Planet*, *Punjaub*, *Semiramis*, *Victoria* and the steam vessels *Napier*, *Victoria* and *Vincent*.

(Two medals were issued to Comdr. A. B. Kemball of the *Comet*, one of them as an artillery officer!)

North West Frontier *(3rd December, 1849—22nd Octoberm 1868)*

This bar was awarded for expeditions spread over nearly nineteen years. Service in one or more of the expeditions earned the bar. When one considers that the Great War of 1939-45 produced eight stars and some medals for nearly six years' fighting it makes one realize just how much service some of these old bars represented. It is well to remember that no bars or medals were awarded to those who did office work at the bases. Though these bars did not represent service in a blitzkrieg, they certainly did not represent time spent in "sitzkrieg".

As it may be of interest, the composition of each force in the expeditions conerned in the award of the bar is given.

The medals are named in running script to natives and block capitals to British officers. Medals awarded to British officers serving in the Indian Army were generally named in block capitals, but this was not a hard-and-fast rule.

1. *3rd—11th December, 1849.* — Two expeditions under Lieutenant-Colonel J. Bradshaw, C.B., to Yusafzai to collect revenue from the village of Sanghao.

Regiments present: 13 Irregular Cavalry; 2 Troop 2 Brigade R.H.A. (52 Battery R.F.A.); 1 Bombay Sappers and Miners; 60 (77), 61 (74) Foot; 3 Bombay N.I.

2. *9th—15th February, 1850.* — An expedition under Brigadier-General Sir Colin Campbell, K.C.B., to the Kohat Pass to punish troublesome Afridis.

Regiments present: 15th Irregular Cavalry; 1 Punjab Cavalry; two troops of 2nd Brigade R.H.A. (52 Battery R.F.A.). (This battery used elephant transport to carry its 25½ in. mortars.) Two companies each of 60, 61, 98 Foot; 23, 31 Bengal N.I.; 1 Sikhs.

3. *11th March—22nd May, 1852.* — An expedition under Brigadier-General Sir Colin Campbell, K.C.B., against the Ranizais, in Turangai between 11th and 22nd March, 1852, and another in Shakot and Dargai from 15th to 24th May, 1852.

Ranizai Expedition: Regiments present—15 Irregular Cavalry; 1 Troop 1 Brigade R.H.A.; 32 (600) Foot. A wing of the 29 Bengal N.I. and 66 Goorkhas (now the 1 King George's own Gurkha Rifles).

Shakot and Dargai Expedition: Regiments present—Guides Cavalry; 2nd Irregular Cavalry; two squadrons of 1 Punjab Cavalary; one troop 1 Brigade R.H.A.; detachment of 3 Company 4 Bn. R.A.; detachment of 19 Light Field Battery; two companies Sappers and Miners; 32 (350) Foot Guides Infantry; 1, 28 Bengal N.I.; 66 Goorkhas.

4. *15th April—14th May, 1852.* — Two expeditions, under Brigadier-General Sir Colin Campbell, K.C.B., against the Mohmans at Panjpao on 15th April, 1852, and another against the Utman Khel villages of Nawadan and Prangarh between 28th April and 14th May, 1852.

Panjpao Expedition: Regiments present—7 Light Cavalry (87); 15 Irregular Horse (179); 2 Troop 1 Brigade R.H.A.

Nawadan and Prangarh Expeditions: Regiments present—One squadron 2 Irregular Cavalry; one squadron Guides Cavalry; 1 Troop 1 Brigade R.H.A.; detachments of 2 and 3 Companies 4 Bn. R.A.; 19 Light Field Battery; two companies Bengal Sappers and Miners; 32 Foot; Guides Infantry; 1 (300), 28 (300) Punjab N.I; 66 Goorkhas.

5. *19th December, 1852—2nd January, 1853.* — An expedition under Lieutenant-General F. Mackeson, C.B., against the Hassanzais.

Regiments present: 16 Irregular Cavalry; 5 Troop 1 Brigade R.A.; a Mountain Battery; 7 Company Bengal Sappers and Miners; Guides Infantry; 1 Sikh Infantry; two regiments of Dogras; 3, 12* Bengal N.I.; Rawal Pindi Police (176).

6. *30th March—12th April, 1853.* — Two expeditions under Brigadier-General J. S. Hodgson against the Shiranis from 30th March to 2nd April, 1853, and another against the Kasranis from 11th to 12th April, 1853.

Shirani Expedition: Regiments present—4. 5 Punjab Cavalary; Scinde Camel Corps; 2 Punjab Light Field Battery and detachment of Garrison Artillery; detachments from each of 1 and 3 Punjab N.I. and the 1 and 6 Native Police Battalion.

Kasrani Expedition: Regiments present—1, 4 Punjab Cavalry; 6 Police Battalion.

7. *29th November, 1853.* — A punitive expedition under Colonel S. B. Boileau against the Bori Afridis.

Regiments present: One squadron 7 Irregular Cavalry; 23 Peshawur Mountain Battery (108); Bengal Sappers and Miners; 22 Foot (438); 20 Bengal N.I.

(169); 66 Goorkhas (467).

8. *31st August, 1854.* – An expedition under Colonel S. J. Cotton to the villages of Dabb, Sadin and Shah Mansur Khel.

Regiments present: 10 Light Cavalry, 1 Irregular Cavalry (one squadron each); 1 Troop 3 Brigade R.H.A.; 2 Company 2 Bn. R.A.; Mountain Train Battery; 2 Company Bengal Sappers and Miners; 22 Foot (207); 1 Sikh N.I; 1, 9 Bengal N.I.; Rawal Pindi Police.

9. *27th March, 1855.* – An expedition under Lieutenant-Colonel J. H. Craigie, C.B., against the Aka Khels and Bussi Khels.

Regiments present: Two troops of 16 Irregular Cavalry; Peshawur Mountain Battery; detachments of 4 and 9 and 20 Bengal N.I.

10. *4th April, 1855.* – An expedition under Brigadier-General N. B. Chamberlain to the Miranzai Valley.

Regiments present: 1 Punjab Cavalry; Nos. a and 3 Punjab Light Field Batteries; Bengal Sappers and Miners; 66 Goorkhas; 1, 3 Punjab N.I. and the Scinde Rifle Corps (in 1856 this was renamed 6 Punjab Infantry and leter became 59 Royal Scinde Rifles (Frontier Force).

11. *6th–21st March, 1857.* – An expedition under Brigadier-General N. B. Chamberlain against the Bozdars.

Regiments present: 2, 3 Punjab Cavalary; Nos 1, 2 and 3 Punjab Light Field Batteries; Bengal Sappers and Miners; 1, 3 Sikh N.I.; 1, 2 4 Punjab N.I.

12. *22nd April–5th May, 1858.* – For the operations of the Sittana Field Force under Major-General Sir Sydney J. Cotton, K.C.B., in Panjtar and Lower Sittana.

Regiments present: Guides Cavalry; 7, 8 Irregular Horse; Peshawur Light Horse; Peshawur Light Field Battery and Mountain Train (23rd Peshawur Mountain Battery); Hazara Mountain Train Battery; Bengal Sappers and Miners; 81, 98 Foot; Guides Infantry; 8, 9, 12, 18, 21 Bengal N.I.

13. *15th December, 1859* – An expedition under Brigadier-General N. B. Chamberlain, C.B., against the Kabul Khel Waziris.

Regiments present: Nos. 1 and 2 Punjab Light Field Batteries; Peshawur and Hazara Mountain Train Batteries; Bengal Sappers and Miners; Guides Infantry; 4 Sikh Infantry; 1, 3, 4, 6, 24 Bengal N.I.

14. *16th April, 1860* – An expedition under Brigadier-General N. B. Chamberlain, C.B., against the Mahsud Waziris.

Regiments present: Guides Cavalry; 3 Punjab Cavalry; Multani Cavalry; Nos. 2 and 3 Punjab Light Field Batteries; Peshawur and Hazara Mountain Trains; Bengal Sappers and Miners; Guides Infantry; 4 Sikh Infantry; 1, 2, 3, 4, 6, 14, 24 Punjab N.I.; Hazara Goorkhas; 6 Native Police Battalion.

15. *5th December–2nd January, 1864.* – Between these dates Sultan Muhammed Khan attacked the fort of Shabkadar with a body of Mohmands and Bajouris and was defeated by a force under Brevet-Colonel A. F. Macdonell, C.B.

Regiments present: Three troops of 7 Hussars (155); 2, 6 Bengal Cavalry; D Battery 5 Brigade R.H.A. (54); 79 Foot (131); 3 Bn. Rifle Brigade (716); 4 Sikh Infantry; 2 Goorkhas.

16. *3rd–22nd October, 1868.* – An expedition under Major-General A. T. Wilde, C.B., C.S.I., against the Bazotee Black Mountain Tribes.

Regiments present: Guides Cavalry; 9, 16 Bengal Cavalry; D/F Battery R.F.A.; E/19 Battery R.F.A.; 2/24 Battery R.G.A.; Peshawur and Hazara Mountain Trains; 2, 7 Companies Bengal Sappers and Miners; 1/6 (648), 1/19 (720), 38, 77 Foot; 3 Sikhs; 2, 19, 20, 24, 30, 31 Bengal N.I.; 23 (Pioneers) Bengal N.I.; 1, 2, 4, 5 Goorkhas.

---

* The Kelat-i-Ghilzie Regiment.

For those who are not particularly interested in which campaign or campaigns the units served, given below is a combined list of those entitled to the bar for North-West Frontier.

One must again repeat that medals to a few odd men whose units as a whole or in part were not present are to be found.

Regiments present: Cavalry—7 (155) Hussars; 1, 2, 7, 15, 16, 18 Irregular Cavalry; 1, 2, 3, 4, 5 Punjab Cavalry; 2, 6, 9, 16 Bengal Cavalry; Guides Cavalry; Peshawur Light Horse; Multani Cavalry. Camelry—Scinde Camel Corps. Artillery— D/F Battery R.H.A.; 1, 2, 5 Brigade R.H.A.; 2, 4, 19, 2/24 Garrison Batteries, R.A.; 1, 2, 3, 19 Light Field Batteries (Punjab); Peshawur and Nazara Mountain Batteries. Sappers and Miners—Bengal and Bombay (160). Infantry (British)— 1 Warwicks (650), 1 Yorkshire Regiment (720), 1 Cheshires (160), 1 D.C.L.I. (111), K.S.L.I. (100 approx. issued in error), 1 and 2 K.R.R.C. (105), 2 Glosters (50), 2 Middlesex (claims are reported as disallowed), 2 Loyals (205), 79th Cameron Hldrs. (130), 1 Royal Irish Fus. (37), 2 North Staffs (335) and 3 Rifle Brigade (930). Infantry (Native)—Guides Infantry; 1, 4 Sikhs; 1, 2, 3, 4, 6, 8, 9, 12, 18, 19, 20, 23, 24, 28, 29, 30, 31 Bengal Infantry; 3 Bombay N.I.; 1, 2, 4, 5 Goorkhas (I have also seen a medal to the 7th Goorkhas); Dogras; Scinde Rifle Corps; 6 Native Police Battalion and Rawal Pindi Police.

Umbeyla *(20th October—23rd December, 1863)*

This bar was awarded for an expedition against the Hindustani in Sittana and their village of Malka. We are not concerned with the extraordinary vacillation that went on in India concerning the dispatch of the Yusafzai Field Force, under Brigadier-General Sir Neville Chamberlain, into Umbeyla Pass and Chamla Valley, where it met with opposition beyond its powers to subdue. Reinforcements were dribbled out to it until November, during which month the commander was severely wounded when leading a counter-attack against the famous Crag Piquet. Eventually the Commander-in-Chief, Sir Hugh Rose, decided to send further reinforcements and appointed Major-General Garvock to succeed Brigadier-General Chamberlain. The troops were organized into two brigades which drove the Hindustanis out of the valley, and then a small party under Colonel Reynell Taylor with an escort of Guides went forward and burnt Malka. In this expedition we suffered over 900 casualties, and incidentally gained a good deal of knowledge in the carrying out of this sort of campaign against recalcitrant tribesmen. When things were not going well the Commander-in-Chief sent Major Frederick Roberts, R.A., into the district to make an appreciation of the situation, which he did with that accuracy and charm that so signalized his subsequent military career.

The Yusafzai Field Force consisted of two brigades and some unbrigaded troops. The medals are named in block capitals.

Regiments present: 1st Brigade—Half "C" Battery 19th Brigade R.F.A.; Peshawur Mountain Train; 71 Foot (H.L.I.); 1, 3, 5, 20, 32 (Pioneers) Punjab N.I.; 5 Goorkhas. 2nd Brigade—Half No. 3 Punjab Light Field Battery; Peshawur and Hazara Mountain Trains; 101 Bengal Fusiliers (609) (1 Royal Munster Fusiliers); 6, 14, 23 (Pioneers) Punjab N.I.; 3 Sikhs; 4 Goorkhas. Unbrigaded— Guides Cavalry; 11 Bengal (Probyn's Horse) Cavalry; 4, 5 Companies Bengal Sappers and Miners.

The following units joined the Expeditionary Force in the latter part of November: 1/7 (470), 93 Foot; 3rd Sikhs.

Bhootan *(December, 1864—February, 1866)*

This bar was awarded for service in either of the four columns which advanced into Bhootan to obtain redress for the insults offered to the Hon. Ashley Eden, who headed a mission. The first column crossed the border in December, 1864, and met slight resistance at Dhalimcote, Bhumsong and Charmoorchee, at each of which places posts were established. During the withdrawal of the column it was attacked, with serious results. A further expeditions was dispatched under Brigadier-General Sir H. Tombs, V.C., which reached Dewangiri, a post in the Dungarah Pass, on 3rd April, 1865, after which hostilities ceased for the year. Another expedition was dispatched in 1866.

The medals are named in square capitals to Europeans and in script to natives.

Regiments present: 5, 14 Bengal Cavalry; 7/22, 5/25, 6/25, 3/25 Batteries R.A., and the Eurasian (Christian) Battery; 2, 4, 5, 7, 8 Companies Bengal Sappers and Miners; 55, 80 Foot; 11, 12, 17, 18, 43, 44 Bengal N.I.; 19, 29, 30, 31 Punjab N.I.; 2 and 3 Goorkhas.

Medals are also known to the Bengal Staff Corps, and the 9th and 32nd N.I.

(Sgt. C. Byrne, 80th Foot, received a medal with this bar and another with that for Perak. He also received the South Africa Medal with bar for 1878—9)

Looshai *(9th December, 1871—20th February, 1872)*

This expedition was necessitated by the abduction of a planter named Winchester and his daughter. Two columns known as the Cachar Column, under Brigadier-General G. Bourchier, C.B., R.A., and the Chittagong Column under Brigadier-General C. W. Brownlow, C.B., were formed. They joined and stormed the Looshai stronghold of Lungval, which Lord Roberts, in his delightful book *Forty-One Years in India*, states was vacated after two rounds were fired, only one of which landed in the village! The Looshais sued for peace and returned their captives unharmed.

No British units were engaged.

The medals are named in thin running script.

Regiments present: N. 3 (Peshawur) Mountain Battery; Sappers and Miners; Commissariat Tpt. Corps (800); 22, 27 Punjab N.I.; 42 (500), 44 (500) Assam N.I. (2, 4 Goorkhas); Native Police (100).

(Medals to No. 113 Pte. H. Thompson, 55th Foot and one to the 80th Foot with this bar are known.)

Perak *(2nd November, 1875*—20th March, 1876)*

This bar was awarded to members of an expedition to Perak against Ismail, who had murdered the British Resident and then, getting the other Rajahs to join him, was causing considerable trouble. The expedition was commanded by General Colbourne and during it Brigadier-General Ross distinguished himself by capturing Kintra and Kotah Lama.

The first sentence of General Order No. 111, dated 1st September, 1879, reads: "The Queen having been pleased to command that the grant of the India Medal of 1854, with clasp inscribed 'PERAK 1875—76' shall be extended," etc. etc. The date, however, was omitted from the bar. The reason for the omission cannot be traced.

The naming is in large sloping capitals.

Regiments present: 3rd Battery 5th Brigade and 9 Battery, 2nd Brigade, R.A. (120); "C" Company Madras Sappers and Miners (80); 1/3 (600), 10 (460), a few men of 19, 80 (300) Foot; 66 Gurkhas; Army Hospital Corps; Control Dept.

---

* This date signifies the beginning of the qualifying period for the troops that proceeded from Hong Kong and the Straits Settlements. For those that embarked from India it was the 27th November, 1875.

(Obverse)

No. 64. The South Africa Medal, 1877-9.

(Obverse)

No. 66. The Kabul to Kandahar Star,
1880.

(Reverse)

No. 64. The South Africa Medal, 1877-9.

(Obverse)

(Reverse)

No. 65. The Second Afghan War Medal, 1878-80.

(Reverse)*   (Reverse)*

No. 68. The Egyptian Medal, 1882-9.

(Obverse)   (Obverse)

No. 69. The Khedive's Egyptian Stars, 1882-9. (with bar)

* Reference should be made to page 425 for medals with identical obverses.

This was the first occasion on which the Gurkhas served overseas. At the capture of the Bukit Pass they gained a V.C. (Brevet-Major George Nicholas Channer) and two Indian Orders of Merit.

A Naval Brigade from H.M. ships: *Avon, Charybdis* (256), *Egeria* (140), *Fly* (103), *Hart* (74), *Modeste* (256), *Philomel* (101), *Ringdove* (107), *Thistle* (75).

In 1881 medals with this bar were awarded to the crews of H.M.S. *Charybdis* and *Hart* for service up the Lingie and Lukhut rivers between 27th November and 10th December, 1874.

Jowaki 1877—8 *(9th November, 1877—19th January, 1878)*

The Jowaki Afridis occupy the territory between Peshawur and the Kohat Pass. They had, as border tribes go, been quite well behaved until we decided to construct a road through their territory, when they became truculent, so much so that it became necessary to send two expeditions under Brigadiers C. P. Keyes and C. C. G. Ross to deal with them.

This was the first dated bar awarded with an Indian medal.

It was sanctioned on 1st March, 1879. That for South Africa which bears the same dates, 1877—8, was sanctioned on 1st August, 1880.

The medals are named in impressed block capitals.

Brigadier-General Keye's Force (Kohat Column): Regiments present— 13/9 R.A.; 2 Punjab Cavalry; Nos. 1 and 2 Mountain Batteries; 4, 5, 6, 29 Punjab N.I.; 1, 3 Sikh Infantry; 5 Gurkhas.

Brigadier-General Ross's Force (Peshawur Column): Regiments present— 13/9th R.A. (38); 17 Bengal Cavalry; half of 1/C Battery R.H.A. (137); No. 4 Hazara Mountain Battery; 2, 3 and detachment of 4 Bengal Sappers and Miners; 9 (15 Offrs. and 559 other ranks), 51 Foot (536) and 4 Rifle Brigade; 14, 20, 22, 27 Bengal N.I.

Naga 1879—70 *(December, 1879—January, 1880)*

This bar was awarded for a previous expedition in 1875 as well as those under Brigadier-General J. L. Nation to Konoma, and Lieutenant-Colonel Johnson to Kohima to punish the Nagas for the murder of Mr. Damant, the Local Commissioner, on 14th October, 1879. No British troops were engaged.

Included in Lieutenant-Colonel Johnson's force were 300 men under Prince Takendrajit, who murdered Mr. Quinton and the others referred to under the bar for "N.E. Frontier 1891".

The medals which carry this bar are somewhat rare and are named in very thin running script.

Regiments present: Two 7-pdr. guns; Bengal Sappers and Miners; 18 Bengal N.I.; 42, 43, 44 Goorkhas. (A few Frontier Police were also employed.)

The artillery consisted of the two 7-pdrs. and a hundred 9-pdr. rockets. They were manned by Lieutenant A. Mansel and three bombardiers from the 16/9 Battery, R.A. The gunners were drawn from the 44th Gurkhas. Eighteen elephants were used to transport the artillery and its equipment. It is stated that one elephant fell over a cliff, which had the effect of making the subsequent shooting of the rockets very erratic.

Burma 1885—7 *(14th November, 1885—30th April, 1887)*

The troubles which developed into the cause of our many expeditions into Burma between 1885 and 1892 originated with the behaviour of the mad King Thebaw, whose reign of misgovernment and massacre ended with his interfering with the Bombay and Burma Trading Company's timber trade. Arbitration having failed, the Viceroy of India, Lord Dufferin, sent an ultimatum which demanded protection for British subjects and interests. This was rejected, so that war was declared on 8th November, 1885. An expedition under Major-General H. N. D. Prendergast, V.C., composed of three brigades, was dispatched.

The frontier was crossed and the forts of Minhla and Gurgyong captured on 17th November, 1885. On the 26th Thebaw agreed to unconditional surrender; the Ava forts were occupied on the 27th, and General Prendergast entered Mandaly on the 28th.

After Thebaw's surrender his brother issued a proclamation against the British, whereupon banditry, or dacoitry—call it what you will—broke out in earnest. Engagements between the troops and the dacoits took place at Nyadan on 2nd December, 1885; at Bhamo on the 28th; Moutshobo on the 29th; Kadol on 16th January, 1886; Kunnah on the 16th; Yindawango on 18th March; Zemethen on the 26th; Salem on 12th June; Tummoo on the 19th. The amount of dacoitry increased so much in July that more troops were sent from India, and General Macpherson assumed supreme command on 17th September, 1886. He died on 20th October, and was succeeded by General Sir Frederick Roberts, who arrived in Mandalay on 18th November. Now followed a series of actions far too numerous to quote, with a sort of grand finale of an insurrection in Wuntho which started on 19th February, 1891, and ended with a Durbar held by Brigadier-General G. B. Wolseley, C.B., on 3rd March. The real troubles did not end until the capture of Boh Minlaung, the number one dacoit, who was executed. The others then decided that life in China was preferable, so that the troubles so to speak "fizzled out".

The three bars for Burma with the dates 1885—7, 1887—89 and 1889—92 were given for the same series of troubles. They were, for the purpose of awards, subdivided into two periods of about two years each and one of three years.

For the Campaign 1885-87 a bronze medal was issued to non-combatant troops. This custom remained in force for Indian General Service medals up to and including the bar for "Abor 1911—12".

The medals were named in light script except for some of the Naval ones which were impressed.

Regiments present: 7th Dgn. Gds. (1); 12th Lcrs. (5); 1, 2 Madras Cavalry; 1 Bombay Lancers; 7 Bengal Cavalry; 7, 9 Battery 1 Brigade Northern Division R.A.; Q/1 Battery R.F.A.; 4/1 Battery North Irish Division R.G.A.; 3/1 Battery South Irish Division R.G.A.; 2/1, 9/1 Batteries Cinque Ports Division R.G.A.; 3/1 Battery Scottish Division R.G.A.; 5/1, 6/1 Batteries Scottish Division R.G.A.; 7/1, 9/1 Batteries Northern Division R.G.A.; 4/1, 8/1 Battery London Division; 5/1, 6/1 Batteries Southern Division R.G.A.; Military Staff Corps; 1, 2, 4, 7 Native Mountain Batteries; 2, 4, 5 Companies Bengal Sappers and Miners; 2 Company Bombay Sappers and Miners; 2 Queen's, 2 King's (17), 2 Somersets, Cheshire's (4), 2 Hants, 1 Royal Welch Fusiliers, 1 K.O.Y.L.I.; 2 S.W.B., 2 Munster Fusiliers, 2 Royal Scots Fusiliers, 1 and 4 Bns. Rifle Brigade; 1, 2/2, 5, 11, 12, 13, 15, 16, 18, 26, 27, 33, 44 Bengal N.I.; 3, 12, 13, 15, 16, 17, 21, 23, 25, 27 Madras Infantry; 1, 5, 7, 23, 25, 27 Bombay Infantry; 4 Punjabis; 2, 3 Infantry (Hyderabad Contingent); 2 Gurkhas; Madras Transport and Commissariat Department; Levy Militia; Military Police Battalion; Rangoon Vol. Arty.

H. M. ships: *Bacchante* (249), *Briton, Kingfisher, Mariner* (79), *Osprey, Ranger* (42), *Sphinx* (31), *Turquoise* (132), *Woodlark* (53). Indian Marine ship: *Pagan*. I.F. Company's Steamers *Ashley Eden, Ataran, Kah Byoe, Pulu*, S.S. Co. *Formosa* (1).

(Officers' and native medals to the 4th Hyderabad Cavalry and the 3rd, 5th and 22nd Madras N.I. are also known.)

Sikkim 1888 *(15th March—27th September, 1888)*

Sikkim is a small Himalayan state adjoining Tibet. It had been allied to the Indian Government since 1814, and trade and free passage through the state had been agreed upon.

In early 1888 the Tibetans persuaded the Rajah to erect a fort, in strict contravention of the treaty, at Lingtu to obstruct the route through the state. In spite of remonstrances from the Viceroy the work continued so that in March a force under Colonel T. Graham, R.A., was dispatched to capture the fort and drive the Tibetans out of Sikkim.

The fort was captured on 20th March and destroyed the next day, after which the force withdrew to Darjeeling; but it had to return in July owing to further incursions.

On 24th September the Tibetans were found to be fortifying a position in the Jelapla Pass, from which they were driven on the 25th. After this defeat, in which they suffered about four hundred casualties, the Tibetans retired from Sikkim.

The medals are named in very thin running script.

Regiments present: 4 guns 9/1 Northern Division, R.A.; detachment of 5 Company Bengal Sappers and Miners; two companies 2 Derbys (481); 13 Bengal Infantry; 32 Bengal Pioneers; 2/1 Gurkhas.

(One of these bars was awarded to the 55th Foot, the recipient being L./Cpl. G. J. Montague, also John Bolding, 49th Foot and Sergt. F. Willard, 8th Hussars, received this single bar as well as a few others from this regiment.)

Hazara 1888 *(3rd October—9th November, 1888)*

This bar was awarded to the Hazara Field Force, commanded by Major-General J. W. McQueen, C.B., A.D.C. This is generally referred to as the "Black Mountain Expedition", as it was undertaken against the Black Mountain tribes of Hassanzais, Akazais, Chagarzais, etc.

The cause of the trouble was the murder of Major L. Battye and Captain H. B. Urmiston, together with five sepoys, who were surveying in the territory occupied by the Akazais.

The expedition sent to deal with them advanced in four columns and defeated the Chagarzais at Kotgai and Maidan. Many villages were destroyed before the tribes surrendered. During the operations a force under Colonel Channer had to chase the tribesmen up the Gorapher Peak, which is about 9,500 feet high!

The medals are named in very small running script.

Regiments present: 15 Bengal Cavalry; 3/1 South Irish Division, R.G.A.; 2/1 Scottish Division, R.G.A.; No. 2 (Derajat) and No. 4 (Hazara) Mountain Batteries; 3 Company Bengal Sappers and Miners and Telegraph Section; 2 Royal Northumberland Fusiliers; 1 Suffolks; 2 Royal Irish Regiment; 2 Seaforth; 2 Royal Sussex; 3, 14, 25, 45 Sikhs; 4, 24, 29 Punjab Infantry; 40 Bengal Infantry; 34 Sikh Pioneers; Kaiber (Khyber) Rifles; 5 Gurkhas.

Burma 1887—89 *(1st May, 1887—31st March, 1889)*

As already stated when dealing with the bar for Burma 1885—7, fighting was continuous for eight years, so that this bar represents about a two-year period. The Royal Mint issued a bar reading "Burma 1887—9".

The medals are named in thin running script.

Most of the units who were entitled to the bar for 1885—7 were entitled to this one as well. The following are additional troops who would not have received the bar for Burma 1885—7: No. 2 and 6 Mountain Batteries; 7 Dragoon Gds. (2); 1 Norfolks (6 Offrs. and 200 other ranks); 2 Somerset L.I.; 2 Leicesters; 1 and 2 Cheshires; 1 Hants; 2nd Munster Fus. (238 single bars); 4 Gurkhas; Mimbu and Burma Police (many individuals received both bars). Indian Marine ships *Sir Wm. Peel, Irradwaddy* and *Pagan.*

Chin

Chin Lushai 1889—90 *(13th November, 1889—30th April, 1890)*

This bar was awarded for two expeditions. One, under Brigadier-General W. P. Symons, known as the Burma Column, formed a punitive expedition against the Chins. The other, known as the Chittagong Column, commanded by General Tregear, punished the Lushais. This bar was very well earned, as the country that these expeditions had to go through consisted of trackless jungle. About 3,400 men took part.

The medals are named in bold running script.

Regiments present: Burma Column—No. 1 Bengal Mountain Battery; 5, 6 Companies Madras Sappers and Miners; 7th Dgn. Gds. (Pte. J. Foster—with Lushai 1889—92 and Capt. J. W. Peters—with Hazara 1891 and Burma 1889—92); 1 K.O.S.B. (approx. 520) and detachments of 1 Norfolks (29), 1 Cheshires, Border Rgt. (30) and Wiltshire Regt. (4); 2 Madras Infantry; 10, 38 Bengal Infantry. Chittagong Column— 2 Company Bengal Sappers and Miners; 3, 9 Bengal Infantry; 28 Bombay Pioneers; 2/4 (part), 42 Gurkhas; Surma Valley and Chittagong Police. Indian Marine ship *Irrawaddy.*

Samana 1891 *(5th April—25th May, 1891)*

This bar was awarded to members of the Miranzai Expeditionary Force commanded by Brigadier-General Sir W. S. A. Lockhart, K.C.B., C.S.I. which operated in the Miranzai Valley and against the Samana Heights where the fanatical priest Syed Mir Basha was proclaiming a "jihad".*

The medals are named in thin running script.

Regiments present: No. 1 Column—No. 3 Mountain Battery, R.A.; 1 K.R.R.C.; H.L.I. (7); D.L.I. (2); Wiltshire Rgt. (2); 1 Punjab Infantry; 27 Bengal Infantry; 1/5 Gurkhas. No. 2 Column—No. 3 Peshawur Mountain Battery; 3 Sikh Infantry; 2 Punjab Infantry; 15 Bengal Infantry. No. 3 Column—No. 2 Derajat Mountain Battery; 6 Punjab Infantry; 19, 29 Bengal Infantry. Divisional Troops—Punjab Garrison Artillery; two squadrons 5 Punjab Cavalry; 19 Bengal Lancers; 5 Company Bengal Sappers and Miners; two companies 2 Manchester Regiment; 1/4 Gurkhas.

(Some Military Police were also employed.

Hazara 1891 *(12th March—16th May, 1891)*

This bar was awarded for the operations of the Hazara Field Force under Major-General W. K. Elles, C.B., against the Hassanzais and Akazais in the Black Mountain.

The operation was carried out by two columns, commanded by Colonels Williamson and Hammond respectively, which advanced from Derband. There

---

* It is very difficult to describe the meaning of this word in a few lines. Briefly, it is the proclamation of a Holy War against the unbelievers of Mahomet. These jihads have been proclaimed against certain nations. There have been two directed against the British in comparatively recent times, namely that proclaimed by Shere Ali of Afghanistan in 1878 and that by Arabi Pasha in Egypt in 1882.

was little fighting; what there was consisted mostly in repelling raids on the columns when on the march or road-making. During the operations a party of rebels was chased up, and eventually captured on, the Machai Peak, 9,800 feet high.

The medals were named in running script.

Regiments present: King's Dgn. Gds. (5); 2 (6), 3 (10), 7 Dgn. Gds. (5); 11 Bengal Lancers; 1, 9 Mountain Battery, R.A.; 2 Derajat Mountain Battery; 4 Company Bengal Sappers and Miners; Northumberland Fus. (3); R. Irish Rgt. (9); Wiltshire Rgt. (5); 1 R. Welch Fus.; 1 K.R.R.C.; 2 Seaforth; 2 Manchester Rgt. (8); H.L.I. (8); D.L.I. (3); 4 Sikhs; Guides Infantry; Kaiber (Khyber) Rifles; 11, 19, 27, 28, 32, 37 Bengal Infantry; 2/5 Gurkhas; 32 Punjab Pioneers.

Two members of the Queen's received this bar. They were Major (afterwards General Sir) E. O. F. Hamilton and No. 685 Lce.-Cpl. W. Cheriton, 2nd Bn. The Queen's.

(A few medals were issued to the 1/5th Gurkhas and one to Tpr. C. Gellender, 2nd Dragoon Guards; one to Captain J. S. Cayzer, and Pte. E. Heppell, 7th Dragoon Guards; also one to Pte. W. J. L. Burl of the 1st Bn. Royal Fusiliers.

N.E. Frontier 1891 *(28th March—7th May, 1891)*

About 3,000 of these bars were awarded for the Manipur Expedition, which was divided into three columns, commanded by Colonel R. H. F. Rennick, Major-General H. Collett, C.B., and Brigadier-General T. Graham, C.B., respectively.

The small state of Manipur adjoins Assam and Burma. It possessed a small army, but relied on the British for protection against attacks from the Burmese. In 1886 the Rajah, Chandra Kirti Singh, died, leaving eight sons, each of whom headed a rival party for the throne. One brother, Takendrajit Singh, occupied the post of senaputti or commander-in-chief. He deposed the ruler and appointed his brother Kula Chandra Dhuya Singh to the throne.

On 21st February, 1891, Mr. J. W. Quinton, Chief Commissioner for Assam, was instructed to remove the senaputti. He was well received, but failed to get the senaputti to resign. On 24th February Colonel Skene with 250 men surrounded the senaputti's residence, but when it was entered he had escaped. The Manipuris attacked Colonel Skene's force, but after a while a parley was agreed upon, whereupon the Colonel, accompanied by Mr. Quinton and others went forward to meet the Manipuris. None of the party were ever seen alive again. As the fighting had broken out again, it was decided to withdraw towards Lakhipur, which was reached on 20th March.

In the meanwhile the three columns had started their advance and converged on Manipur on 26th April. The palace had been burnt, and the Regent, senaputti and other princes had fled. The heads of the party that went to the parley were found in the palace grounds.

Chandra Dhuya Singh, his brother Prince Angao Sana and the senaputti were captured in May. The senaputti was tried and executed, and the other two were exiled to the Andaman Islands in the Bay of Bengal.

Medals with this bar are somewhat scarce and are named in running script.

Regiments present: 3rd Foot (10); E. Surrey Rgt. (6); Devon Rgt. (4); Cachar Column—Two guns of No. 8 Mountain Battery (62); 1/2 (708), 42 (99), 43 (275), 44 (112) Goorkhas; 18 Bengal N.I. (364); Calcutta Volunteer Pioneers (48). Kohima Column—Three guns of No. 8 Mountain Battery; 42 (200), 43 (300) Gurkhas; 13 Bengal Infantry; Assam Police (200). Tamu Column—Four guns of No. 4 and 8 Mountain Batteries; 4 K.R.R.C. (443); 12, 32 Madras Infantry; 2/4 Gurkhas. Lines of communication troops—5 Madras Infantry.

(A few medals with this as a single bar were issued to the Surma Valley Light Horse and 2nd Gurkhas, but it has been impossible to trace the presence of these units as a whole. A few Military Police were also present, including the Lakhimpur Mty. Police.)

Bugler Guna Ram, 44 Bengal N.I., who was orderly to Colonel Skene, went forward and was murdered with him.

Hunza 1891 *(1st—22nd December, 1891)**

This bar was awarded for an expedition under Lieutenant-Colonel A. G. A. Durand to Gilgit, Hunza and Nagar, where the tribesmen continually attacked the road-making parties. Colonel Durand was wounded during the capture of the fort at Nilt, which was where the only fighting, to differentiate from persistent sniping, took place.

No British troops were engaged.

This is, probably, the second rarest bar to this medal. A silver medal to the Unorganized Transport is known. It is most unusual for the unorganized native transport personnel to receive silver medals, and this is the only bar to such a unit that is known which has been given in silver. Followers received bronze medals.

A medal is known with this bar and those for Samana 1891 and Waziristan 1894—5 on it to the 5th Gurkhas.† Medals with bars in addition to Hunza 1891 are rare and, in addition to the 5th Gurkhas, would probably have been awarded to the Q.O.S.M. or 20th Punjab Infantry.

The medals were named in running script.

Silver

76 men of No. 4 Hazara Mountain Battery.
12 men of No. 4 Company Bengal Sappers and Miners.
1,030 men of the 1st and 404 men of the 2nd Kashmir Infantry.
32 men of the 20th Punjab Infantry.
200 men of the 5th Gurkhas.
159 men of the Peshawur and Unorganized Transport.
12 Native Signallers.

Bronze

Staff (28; 1/5 Gurkha Rifles (23); 4 Mountain Battery (29); Kashmir Troops (81).

Hunza Nagar Badge, 1891

Obverse   A fort-capped hill with three soldiers in the foreground. In the bottom right-hand corner is the inscription "HUNZA NAGAR 1891".

Reverse   This generally has the original brooch fittings, or the remains thereof, or some fitting around which the ribbon can be threaded. The maker's name is impressed in the centre.

---

* The first paragraph of Army Order No. 168, dated 1st September, 1892, which authorized the award of this bar, reads:—

"1. The Queen has been pleased to command that the India Medal of 1854, with a clasp inscribed 'HUNZA 1891', shall be granted to all troops employed in the late Hunza-Nagar Expedition between the 1st and 22nd December, 1891, both dates inclusive."

The fact that the bar did not take the title of "Hunza-Nagar 1891" should be noted, and also that the title of a previous bar awarded for an expedition into the Naga Hills was inscribed "NAGA 1879—80".

† Sepoy Harakbin Gurung, 5th Gurkhas, was awarded the bars for Jowaki 1877—8, Hazara 1888, Samana 1891 and Hunza 1891. He also obtained the Afghanistan Medal, 1878—90, with three bars and the Kandahar Star.

Size	Rectangular 1 in. x 2.1/10 in.
Ribbon	1·8 in. wide. The stripes run diagonally from top right to bottom left and have serrated edges. The centre stripe is white, 1/5 in. wide; this is flanked by two maroon stripes 2/5 in. wide; the top left- and bottom right-hand corners are green.
Suspension	See text below.
Designer	The badges were made by Messrs. Gurney & Son, London, but one cannot say whether they were designed by them as well.
Naming	The badges were issued unnamed.
No. of bars issued	Nil

This bronze, slightly concave badge was given by the Maharajah of Jummoo and Kashmir to his Imperial Service troops who took part in the Hunza-Nagar Expedition. As originally issued it was intended that it should be worn as a brooch at the neck. This accounts for the brooch fittings, or remains thereof, found on the backs of many of the badges. It was decided later that they could be worn as medals, so that some of the badges had the brooch fittings altered to accommodate the ribbon already described.

Army Order No. 168 of 1st September, 1892, authorized the award of the India Medal of 1854, with the bar for Hunza 1891, to all soldiers of the Kashmir Army who served in the expedition, so that these badges, or brooches, were additional awards.

The small semi-independent states of Hunza and Naga face each other across the Hunza river in the extreme north of the State of Kashmir and are approached through a narrow defile in the mighty Karakoram Range.

They were ruled over by Chiefs or Mirs, with hereditary hostility towards each other, though bosom pals if either became involved in a dispute with a third party. The Hunzas are Ismailis who own allegiance to the Aga Khan and must rank among the finest carriers in the world. Barefooted and carrying a 60-lb load they will cross needle-sharp rocks up or down hill and over swinging bridges made of vines with a speed that leaves one with no more breath to lose at the grandeur of the sight of Baltit, the Hunza capital, with its castle (or fort if you prefer) perched on a precipice on the face of a snow-capped mountain. Where else can one see apricots and snow without moving the head? Where else have nature and man staged such a combined balancing feat and maintained the pose for so long?

As both states were under the nominal control of the Maharajah of Kashmir he, naturally, supplied some of the force that went to punish the Hunzas and Nagas. After the expedition he agreed to pay both the Mirs annual payments on condition they behaved themselves, whilst they, by way of acknowledging their loyalty, returned tributes of unusual variety. The Mir of Hunza paid twenty ounces of pure gold which had been panned from the Hunza river together with two dogs and two horses. The Mir of Naga paid ten ounces of gold obtained from the same source and baskets of apricots.

Burma 1889–92 *(16th April, 1889–18th April, 1892)*

This bar was awarded for eleven punitive expeditions, most of which only lasted for two or three weeks. As they were formed in most cases from troops that have already been enumerated as receiving the previous bars for Burma, there is not much point in giving the full composition of each force. The only recipients that received this bar and neither of the previous ones are given below.

The medals are named in running script.

Regiments present: British troops—Devons (137); Cheshire Rgt; 1 D.C.L.I.; 1 Hants; 2 Oxford and Bucks Light Infantry; 4 K.R.R.C.; 4 Rifle Brigade. Indian troops—22 Madras Infantry; 24 Bengal Infantry; 2nd Sappers and Miners.

(A medal to the Leicestershire Regiment with this bar is known, but one is unable to trace any mention of any members of this regiment having taken part in any of the eleven expeditions during 1889—92. However this cannot be considered as a unique case as many regiments had men on detachment.)

Lushai 1889—92 *(11th January, 1889—8th June, 1892)*

This bar, which was awarded for five small expeditions into the Lushai Hills, must not be confused with those awarded for Looshai in 1872 or Chin Lushai 1889—90.

The medals are named in large, bold, block letters to British troops and in script to natives although engraved script to the 4 K.R.R.C. is known.

Regiments present: Bengal Sappers and Miners; 4 K.R.R.C. (1 Coy); 2, 3, 9 Bengal Infantry; 2 Gurkhas; 28 Bombay Pioneers; 4 Madras Pioneers and Military Police.

(Pte. J. Bishop of the 4 K.R.R.C. received two medals, one of which bore the bar for Lushai 1889—92 and the other N.E. Frontier 1891. A small detachment of civilian telegraphists accompanied some of these expeditions and received the medal with this bar.)

Chin Hills 1892—93 *(19th October, 1892—10th March, 1893)*

This bar was awarded for small punitive expeditions, under Brigadier-General Palmer, against the Chins. The bar to the Norfolks is one of the most prized of the whole set.

The medals are named in small running script.

Regiments present: Two guns 4 Mountain Battery R.A.; Queen's Own Madras Sappers and Miners; 19th Hrs. (5); 200 men of 1 Norfolks; 10, 21 Madras Infantry; 31, 33 Burma Light Infantry; 39 Bengal Infantry; Garhwal Rifles; 21 Madras Pioneers; two battalions of Burma Police; Mimbu Native Police; 21 Military Train; Telegraph (Postal) Department; Indian Medical Service.

(Only fifteen of these bars in silver were awarded to the Artillery, one of which was awarded to Bomb. W. Wallace, 1st Bde., N. Division No. 7 Mtn. Bty., R.G.A., and another to Gunner E. Arundel of the same unit.)

A few bronze medals were awarded to natives of the 7th Mountain Battery.

Kachin Hills 1892—93 *(3rd December, 1892—3rd March, 1893)*

This bar was awarded for punitive expeditions into the Kachin Hills. The medals awarded to the Yorkshire Regiment are considered to be the rarest in the whole set. Those awarded to the other units are rare. There is a medal to Engine Driver (an official rate in the R.I.N.), Essack of the tender *Pagan* with bars for Burma 1885—87, Burma 1887—89, Chin Hills 1892—93, Kachin Hills 1892—93 in the R.N. Museum, Portsmouth which is said to have been verified.

The medals are named in bold running script.

Regiments present: 7 Mountain Battery, R.A.; Bengal Artillery; 2 Yorkshire Regiment (112); D.C.L.I. (6); 1 Sikhs; 2, 4, 6 Punjab Infantry; 20, 33, 38 Bengal Infantry; 1/1, 4, 5 Gurkhas; 21 Madras Pioneers; 10, 32 Madras Infantry; Magwe Battalion; Magaung and Chin Levies; Indian Medical Department; The Ava, Sagaing and Chin Hills Military Police.

Wazaristan 1894–5 (*22nd October, 1894–13th March, 1895*)

The operations were necessary owing to the continual attacks by the Waziris on the Afghan Frontier Delimitation Party, which was commanded by Colonel A. H. Turner. Though the tribesmen suffered heavy casualties from the party's escort, it was not possible to deal with them effectively until the arrival of more troops.

The Waziristan Field Force, commanded by Lieutenant-General Sir Wm. Lockhart, K.C.B., C.S.I., was formed on 2nd December, 1894, and disbanded on 30th March, 1895. This bar was, however, also awarded to the Waziristan Delimitation Escort, composed entirely of some of the troops given below, which operated between 22nd October, 1894, and 13th March, 1895. This was the first campaign in which Lee-Metford rifles and cordite cartridges were used.

Regiments present: 1st Brigade—1 Punjab Cavalry; No. 3 Punjab Mountain Battery; No. 2 Company Bengal Sappers and Miners; 2 Border Regiment; 3 Sikhs; 20 (Punjab) Bengal Infantry; 1/1 Gurkhas. 2nd Brigade—1 and 2 Punjab Cavalry; No. 8 Bengal Mountain Battery; No. 5 Company Bengal Sappers and Miners; one Machine-Gun Section of Devons (10); 4, 33 Punjab Infantry; 38 Dogras; 1/5 Gurkhas. 3rd Brigade—3 Punjab Cavalry; No. 1 Kohat Mountain Battery; one Machine-Gun Section 2 South Wales Borderers; 3rd Foot (8); Devon Regiment (8); Derby Regiment (4); Argyle and Sutherland Highlanders (4); Gordon Highlanders (11); 1 Sikhs; 2, 6 Punjab Infantry.

(A few medals are to be found to the 19th Punjab Infantry.)

The beginner must constantly bear in mind the fact that there is no connection between age and value—none whatsoever. A Medal with the single bar "Waziristan 1925"—in other words the most recent—is worth more than all the others with the single bar for operations in that country added together.

2 ASHANTI STAR 1896 (*7th December, 1895–17th January, 1896*)

Obverse	In the centre is the Imperial Crown surrounded by a raised ring on which is the word "ASHANTI" on top and the date "1896" underneath.
Reverse	In raised lettering are the words "FROM THE QUEEN".
Size	1·25 in. diameter.
Ribbon	1·25 in. wide. Yellow with two black stripes.
Suspension	By means of a ring attached to the top of the central point.
Designer	It is said that it was designed by Princess Henry of Battenberg, whose husband died of fever during the campaign.
Naming	All the stars were issued unnamed, but the Colonel of the 2nd Bn. The West Yorkshire Regiment had those awarded to his battalion named at his own expense.
No. of bars issued	Nil.

Some of the stars are in a highly burnished state, but as originally issued they were of the usual dark gun-metal colour.

This gun-metal star was awarded in 1896 to 2,000 troops who had taken part between the dates mentioned in the Ashanti Expedition under Major-General Sir F. C. Scott against King Prempeh, who had been indulging in cannabalism and human sacrifices. The expedition captured Coomassie, though this fact is not recorded by the star, which is a combination of a four-pointed star and the Cross of St. Andrew.

Regiments present: Detachments of R.A.; R.E.; A.S.C.; A.M.C.; Ordnance

Staff Corps; 2 West Yorkshire Regiment was the only complete battalion present (420). A composite battalion was formed of approx. twenty men each from 2/1, 2/2 (16), 1/3 Foot Guards; 1/5, 2/11, 51, 3/60, 85, 89, 100 Foot, 2 Rifle Brigade and three nursing sisters.

73 CAPE OF GOOD HOPE GENERAL SERVICE MEDAL (1880–1897)

Obverse	The bust of Queen Victoria and the legend "VICTORIA REGINA ET IMPERATRIX".
Reverse	The arms of Cape Colony and "CAPE OF GOOD HOPE".
Size	1·42 in. diameter.
Ribbon	1·25 in. wide. Darkish blue with a sandy-coloured yellow stripe down the centre.
Suspension	By means of a straight suspender.
Designer	G. W. de Saulles.
Naming	Engraved in thin, rather faint, block capitals.
No. of bars issued	Three—Transkei, Basutoland, Bechuanaland.

Just over 5000 of this medal were awarded by the Cape Government for services in suppressing small risings in the places mentioned on the bars. No British units were present*, although fifteen were awarded to 'odd' men.

After the defeat of Chief Moirosi (see South Africa Medal 1879) the Basutos were ordered to hand in their arms. Amongst those who refused to do so was Chief Lerothodi, who made war on the colonists. He was defeated by Colonel Clarke at Mafetang on 21st September, 1880, at Kalabani on 19th October, 1880, and Tweefontein on 14th January, 1881. Peace was concluded on 28th April, 1881.

In April, 1896, a very serious cattle disease broke out in Bechuanaland which necessitated the destruction of a large number of cattle, especially at Pokwani. The natives resented this wholesale slaughtering of their cattle and rose in rebellion. There was a good deal of fighting before order was restored.

The undermentioned list has been submitted by Doctor Frank Mitchell:—

An analysis of the Issue Register at Defence Headquarters, Pretoria reveals the following issues:—

One Bar "Transkei"	562
One Bar "Basutoland"	1589
One Bar "Bechuanaland"	2483
Two Bars "Transkei & Basutoland"	490
Two Bars "Transkei & Bechuanaland"	18
Two Bars "Basutoland & Bechuanaland"	77
Three Bars	23†
No Bar	10†
TOTAL	5252

(It is probable that most of the eleven medals shown without clasp, except that to "Nurse Rogers", were in fact issued with a clasp.)

---

* Private P. Pocock, 3rd K.R.R.C., received the medal and bar for Basutoland, the South Africa Medal for 1879, the Egypt Medal for Tel-el-Kebir, Suakin 1884, Tamaai and the Khedive's Egyptian Star.

†Figures kindly supplied by Mr D. Forsyth of Johannesburg.

Transkei† *(13th September, 1880—15th May, 1881)*

This bar was awarded for operations in Tembuland and Griqualand East, in both of which the natives rose in revolt on account of having to hand in their firearms. They showed marked hostility towards the settlers in the districts of Tsolo, Maclear, Matatiele and Qumbu, in all of which it became necessary to employ troops to restore order.

It is difficult to separate the fighting for which this and the next bar were awarded. Many medals were awarded with both bars, though such medals are now rare.

Basutoland† *(13th September, 1880—27th April, 1881)*

After the termination of the fighting in 1879 (see No. 64) the natives were ordered to hand in their firearms. Certain chiefs, such as Jonathon and Letsi, complied with the order, but no sooner had they done so than they were attacked by Chiefs Lerothodi, Masupha and Moletsane, together with others. In September, 1880, they attacked the white officials. The situation soon became so serious that troops and volunteers were mobilized.

The first encounter took place near Mafeteng on 17th September, when a detachment of Cape Mounted Riflemen, under Colonel F. Carrington, was attacked by Chief Lerothodi. When they reached Mafeteng they were again attacked and the place besieged by rebel Basutos. On 10th and 28th October the Basutos attacked Maseru, but were repulsed on both occasions. On 19th October Brigadier-General M. Clarke, now in command of all the forces was attacked at Kalabani. Kerothodi's village was stormed and captured by Colonel F. Carrington on 22nd October, and on the 31st that of Moletsane by Brigadier-General Clarke.

From November, 1880, to February 1881, there were several encounters. In the latter month an armistice was arranged, but sporadic skirmishes continued until peace was concluded in May, 1881, though Chief Masupha did not submit until September. The troubles continued in 1882, 1883, and 1884, in which latter year there were battles between the Chiefs Khetisa and Masupha on one side and Lerothodi on the other.

In response to representations by the Basutos the Home Government agreed that Basutoland should becaome a Crown Colony. The change-over took place in March, 1884.

Bechuanaland *(24th December, 1896—30th July, 1897)*

In April, 1896, a severe cattle disease broke out in Bechuanaland which necessitated the slaughtering of cattle belonging to the natives. They resented this and rose in revolt. The first engagement took place at Pokwani, where the natives under Chief Galishwe attacked a detachment of the Cape Mounted Police on 24th December. In January, 1897, the Batlaros rose in revolt, to be followed shortly by practically all the other native tribes. It became obvious that a considerable force would be necessary, so that units were raised, equipped and placed under the command of Lieutenant-Colonel Dalgety, of the Cape Mounted Rifles. The main actions were the attacks on Gamasep Kloof and Riet Kloof, but in neither of these actions were the rebels completely defeated, so that there had

† Acknowledgments are due to Mr. H. H. Curson and the Editor of *The Nongqai*, Pretoria, for their spontaneous help and interest in enabling one to obtain the names of the Regiments present at these three campaigns and much other information on the campaigns in South Africa between 1854 and 1902. The same remarks apply to Major G. Tylden, who put in a great deal of work on my behalf.

to be a pause in the operations whilst more reinforcements were raised for the Bechuanaland Field Force. In July, when all was ready, a "drive" started which ended with the action at Langberg on 30th July—1st August, 1897, as a result of which the ringleaders were either killed or surrendered.

Medals issued without clasps (the remaining seven names in the roll are suspected of being incorrectly recorded):
Nurse G.A. Rogers
Pte. P.A. Williams, Cape Mounted Rifles
L/Sgt. J. Wilson, Cape Mounted Rifles

Medals issued with all 3 clasps:
Dvr. J. Bobbins, P.A.O.C.V.Arty.
Capt. A.L. Chiapini, C.M.Yeo.
Gnr. E.C.A. Coombs, Cape F.Arty.
Pte. J. Wirran, Nesbitts L.Horse.
Sgt. E.H. Dye, Cape Police Dist. No.1.
Lieut. F.W.H. Gillwald, Cape Police Dist. No.1.
Surg. Maj. E.B. Hartley V.C., C.M. Rifles.
Capt. A.N.M. Hutcheons, Wodehouse B. Rovers.
Pte. J. Lust, Nesbitts L.Horse.
Sapper R. McArthur, C.T.V. Engrs.
Sgt. H. McDonald, Nesbitts L.Horse.
Tpr. E. McGuire, C.M.Yeo.
Capt. R. McLean, Buffalo Vol.
Sgt. Maj. C.S. March, Landreys Horse.
Pte. C. Nielsen, Nesbitts L.Horse.
Sgt. T.C. Peakman, C.F. Arty.
Lieut. R. Pillans, D.E.O.V. Rifles.
Pte. R. Quine, C.T. Rifles.
L/Cpl. T. Rodwell, D.E.O.V. Rifles.
Pte. S. Strutt, Nesbitts L.Horse.
Pte. A. Turner, Ushers Contgt.
Sgt. A.J. White, C.M. Rifles.
Pte. W.D. Willemite, C.T. Rangers.

Imperial Recipients

	BASUTOLAND	TRANSKEI	BECHUANALAND
3rd. K.R.R.C.	3	8	1
3rd. R.Irish Fus.	—	—	1
7th. Hussars.	—	—	2

Local Units

Basutoland	Transkei	Bechuanaland
Abalondolozi Regt. (14)	Abalondolozi Regt. (17)	Albany Rangers (2)
Adelaide Mounted Infantry Infantry (9)	Adelaide Mounted Infantry (10)	Army Ordnance Corps (1)
Albany Rangers (25)	Albany Rangers (2)	Bakers Horse (2)
Albert Burghers (4)	Albert Burghers (1)	Beaufort West Vol. Rifles (1)
Aliwal North Contgt. (1)	Alexandria Burghers (14)	Bechuanaland F.F. (11)
Aliwal North Vols. (3)	Aliwal North Contgt. (1)	Buffalo Mounted Vols. (2)
Amatembu Regt. (1)	Aliwal North Vols. (1)	Cape Field Artillery (6)
Baca Contgt. (2)	Ametembu Regt. (5)	Cape Medical Staff Corps. (24)
Bakers Horse (31)	Baca Contgt. (7)	Cape Mounted Riflemen (133)
Barkley's Native Contgt. (1)	Bakers Horse (53)	Cape Mounted Yeomanry (13)
Basutoland Mounted Police (5)	Barkley Vols. (1)	Cape Police Dist. No.1. (574)
	Basuto Native Contgt. (1)	Cape Police Dist. No.2. (192)
		Cape Police (131)

Basutoland

Basuto Native Contgt. (10)
Beaufort Rangers. (4)
Beaufort West Burghers (1)
Beaufort West Vol. Rifles (2)
Bedford Burghers (1)
Bredasdorp Burghers (1)
Buffalo Mounted Vols. (28)
Buffalo Rangers (4)
Bullers Mounted (1)
Burghersdorp Burgher F. (2)
Caledon Burghers (1)
Cape Field Artillery (32)
Cape Infantry (1)
Cape Medical Staff
  Corps. (1)
Cape Mounted Riflemen
  (355)
Cape Mounted Yeomanry
  (314)
Cape Police Dist. No.1. (9)
Cape Town Rangers (40)
Cape Town Rifles (50)
Cape Town Vol.
  Engineers (3)
Cathcart Burghers (6)
Chalumna Mounted Vols.
  (5)
Colesburg Burghers (9)
Colonial Forces (5)
Commissariat Dept. (18)
Cradock Burghers (21)
Despatch Rider (1)
Diamond Fields Arty. (1)
Diamond Fields Horse (6)
Dicks Kaffrarian Levies (7)
D. of Edinburgh Own Vol.
  Rifles (187)
Dymes Rifles (38)
East Griqualand Forces (1)
East London Arty. (1)
East London Vol. Infantry
  (3)
Ferreiras Horce (4)
Field Force (2)
Fingo Levies (1)
First City Vols. (71)
Fort Beaufort Vols. (1)
Fort White Vols. (1)
Frontier Armed and
  Mounted Police (2)
Frontier Carabineers (1)
General Clarke's Staff (3)
George Burghers (2)
Gonubie Horse (1)
Graff Reinet Burghers (5)
Graff Reinet Rovers (4)
Grahamstown Vol. Horse
  Arty. (13)
Griqualand West Brigade (1)

Transkei

Beaufort Rangers (4)
Beaufort West Burghers (4)
Beaufort West Vol.
  Rifles (10)
Bedford Burghers (12)
Border Police (1)
Bredasdorp Burghers (3)
Buffalo Mounted Vols. (21)
Buffalo Rangers (2)
Bullers Mounted (1)
Caledon Burghers (1)
Cape Field Artillery (12)
Cape Infantry (1)
Cape Mounted Riflemen (32)
Cape Mounted Yeomanry
  (29)
Cape Police Dist. No.1. (4)
Cape Town Rangers (42)
Cape Town Rifles (3)
Cape Town Vol. Arty. (1)
Cape Town Vol. Engineers
  (51)
Cathcart Burghers (4)
Ceres Burghers (6)
Colonial Forces (1)
Commissariat Dept. (10)
Diamond Fields Horse (4)
Dicks Kaffranian Levies (3)
D. of Edinburgh Own Vol.
  Rifles (10)
Dymes Rifles (2)
East London Vol.
  Infantry (4)
Ferreiras Horse (1)
Fingo Scouts (1)
First City Vols. (2)
Frontier Carabineers (10)
Frosts Column (2)
George Burghers (13)
Gonubie Horse (10)
Gordonia Vols. (1)
Graff Reinet Burghers (26)
Graff Reinet Rovers (4)
Grahamstown Vol. Horse
  Arty. (3)
Grays Gonubie Vols. (5)
Griqualand West Native
  Contgt. (2)
Hampshire Arty. (1)
Harveys Horse (10)
Helvens Horse (1)
Herschell Native Contgt. (4)
Humansdorp Burghers (2)
Idutwa Milita (2)
Intelligence (1)
Jamestown Vols. (1)
Kaffranian Rifles (4)
Kaffranian Vol. Arty. (2)
Kamatone Fingos (2)

Bechuanaland

Cape Town Highrs. (110)
Cape Town Rangers (1)
Cape Town Rifles (1)
Cape Town Vol. Engineers (1)
Colesburg Burghers (1)
Commissariat Dept. (9)
Cradock Burghers (1)
Dennisons Horse (7)
Despatch Riders (6)
Diamond Fields Arty. (23)
Diamond Fields Horse (127)
D. of Edinburgh Own Vol.
  Rifles (241)
Dymes Rifles (3)
Fingo Levies (1)
First City Vols. (106)
Frontier Carabineers (1)
Geluk Mounted Vols. (1)
Gordonia Vols. (76)
Grahamstown Mtd. Infy. (1)
Griqualand West Brigade (11)
Hunts Vols. (1)
Intelligence (3)
Kaffrarian Levies (1)
Kaffranian Rifles (87)
Kimberley Light Horse (4)
Kimberley Rifles (176)
Landreys Light Horse (3)
Leaches Rifles (1)
Leribe Native Levy (1)
Mafeking Mounted Rifles (1)
Malmesbury Levies (1)
Mount Temple Horse (4)
Natal Mounted Rifles (1)
Native Basuto Levy (1)
Nesbitts Light Horse (7)
Ordnance Department (2)
Oudtshoorn Vol. Rifles (42)
Papkuil Rifles (13)
Prince Alfred's Own Cape Vol.
  Arty. (40)
Prince Alfred's Vol. Guard
  (138)
Queenstown Rifle Vols (66)
Ross Light Horse (2)
Schermans Burghers (1)
Stellaland Light Horse (18)
Tarkastad Burghers (1)
Taungs Gun Detachment (1)
Telegraphic and Intell.
  Staff (1)
Thompson Relief Column (1)
Transkei Mounted Rifles (1)
Transkei Native Contgt. (7)
Transport Corps (19)
Umtata Volunteers (1)
Upington Special Police (1)
Ushers Contgt. (1)
Victoria Rangers (1)

Basutoland

Griqualand West Native
  Contgt. (4)
Hampshire Arty. (1)
Harveys Horse (2)
Herschell Native Contgt. (14)
Hopetown Burghers (7)
Hunts Vols. (1)
Irregular Horse (Nettleton)
  (1)
Kaffrarian Levies (3)
Kaffrarian Rifles (1)
Kaffrarian Vol. Arty. (16)
Kamatone Fingos (2)
Keiskama Hoek Vols. (9)
Kimberley Light Horse (63)
Kimberley Rifles (1)
Knysna Vols. (1)
Kokstad Mounted Rifles (10)
Landreys Light Horse (70)
Leaches Rifles (3)
Leribe Native Levy (3)
Lonsdale Rifles (3)
Maclear Constab. (1)
Mafeteng Contgt. (6)
Malmesbury Burghers (2)
Malmesbury Levies (1)
Maseru Native Levies (1)
Maseru Vols. (1)
Middleburg Burghers (3)
Mohali Hoek Contgt. (1)
Muters Rangers (10)
Natal Mounted Police (28)
Natal Mounted Rifles (1)
Native Contgt. (3)
Native Levies (1)
Nesbitts Light Horse (105)
Ordnance Department (2)
Oudtshoorn Burghers (2)
Paarl Burghers (18)
Paarl Western Levies (1)
Port Elizabeth Rifles (2)
Prince Alfred's Own Cape
  Vol. Arty. (1)
Prince Alfred's Vol. Guard
  (135)
Pullens Rangers (1)
Queenstown Burghers (17)
Queenstown Rifle Vols. (1)
Qutheng and Masitisi Native
  Contgt. (1)
Richmond Burghers (9)
Ross and Hicksons Horse (1)
Ross Light Horse (1)
Salem Rangers (1)
Somerset East Burghers (18)
Special Border Police (2)
Stanfords Police (1)
Stantons Light Horse (9)
Stellenbosch Burghers (4)
Sterkstroom Rifles (1)

Transkei

Kimberley Light Horse (2)
King Williams Town Vol.
  Arty. (11)
Kokstad Mounted Rifles (22)
Komgha Mounted Vols. (2)
Lady Frere Native Levy (1)
Landreys Light Horse (34)
Leaches Rifles (2)
Learys Native Levies (1)
Maclear Constab. (4)
Malmesbury Burghers (15)
McNicholas Horse (1)
Mount Ayliff Vol. (2)
Murraysburgh
Muters Rangers (10)
Natal Constabulary (1)
Natal Mounted Police (1)
Native Contgt. (1)
Native Contgt. Tembuland
  (1)
Native Levies (1)
Nesbitts Light Horse (102)
Ordnance Department (5)
Oudtshoorn Burghers (19)
Paarl Burghers (18)
Paarl Western Levies
Prince Albert Burghers (2)
Prince Alfred's Own Cape Vol.
  Arty. (40
Prince Alfred's Vol. Guard (5)
Pullens Horse (1)
Queenstown Burghers (9)
Queenstown Division (1)
Queenstown Flying Col. (1)
Queenstown Rifle Vols. (2)
Qumbu Contgt. (1)
Ross and Hicksons Horse (1)
Ross Light Horse (12)
Scouts (1)
Southeyville Levies (1)
Special Border Police (2)
Stanfords Police (2)
Stellenbosch Burghers (12)
Stockenstroom Hott. Cont. (3)
Stockenstroom Rangers (3)
Strachans Native Contgt. (2)
Swellendam Burghers (13)
Tarka Vol. Rifles (2)
Tarkastad Burghers (8)
Tembu Levies (4)
Thompson Relief Column (1)
Transkei Native Contgt. (7)
Transport Corpos (3)
Transuaal Horse (5)
True Blues (1)
Tsolo Native Militia (3)
Uitenhage Burghers (13)
Umtala Volunteers (17)
Ushers Contgt. (1)
Ushers Rangers (2)

Bechuanaland

Victoria Rifles (1)
Vol. Medical Staff Corps (11)
Vryburg Vols. (39)
Websters Rovers (1)
Western Rifles (1)
Willowvale Native Contgt. (3)
Wodehouse Border Rangers (4)

Basutoland	Transkei	Bechuanaland
Stockenstroom Burghers (3)	Victoria Rangers (17)	
Stockenstroom Hott. Contgt. (1)	Vol. Medical Staff Corps. (1)	
Stockenstroom Rangers (3)	Walkers Rifles (20)	
Strachans Native Contgt. (1)	Warells Column (2)	
Stutterheim L.I. Vols. (7)	Websters Rovers (9)	
Swellendam Burghers (1)	Western Levies (4)	
Tambookie Ward Burghers (1)	Willoughby's Horse (31)	
Tarkastad Burghers (4)	Willowmore Burghers (1)	
Tembu Levies (1)	Winterburg Greys (3)	
Transport Corps. (3)	Wodehouse Border Rangers (18)	
Transvaal Horse (43)	Worcester Burghers (14)	
Uitenhage Burghers (4)		
Umtata Volunteers (2)		
Ushers Contgt. (1)		
Ushers Rangers (1)		
Victoria Rangers (1)		
Walkers Rifles (20)		
Warells Column (2)		
Websters Rovers (1)		
Western Levies (4)		
Willoughby's Horse (39)		
Willowmore Burghers (1)		
Winterberg Greys (16)		
Wodehouse Border Rangers (3)		

The preceeding list of units and their medals have been extracted from the Cape of Good Hope General Service Medal Roll prepared by Mr. D.R. Forsyth of Blackheath, Johannesburg. The roll referred to was prepared by Mr. Forsyth with great care from microfilm housed in the Africana Museum, Johannesburg, however Mr. Forsyth wishes to make it perfectly clear that the extracts above are not an indication that this number only took part in the three campaigns.

74 ROYAL NIGER COMPANY'S MEDAL (1886—1897)

Obverse	The crowned and veiled head of Queen Victoria and legend "VICTORIA · REGINA · IMPERATRIX". *
Reverse	A shield with the words "PAX, JUS, ARS", arranged in the form of a Y with two flags above. The whole is surrounded by a wreath of laurel.
Size	1·51 in. diameter.
Ribbon	1·25 in. wide with three equal-width stripes of yellow, black and white.
Suspension	By a straight suspender.
Designer	The medals were designed and made by Messrs. Spink & Son, London.
Naming	The silver medals given to Europeans are impressed in bold capitals. The bronze medals awarded to natives are unnamed but bear the recipient's number. Medals numbered between 15 and 2,236 are known, but we would not say that these are the highest and lowest numbers issued. They have also been seen unnumbered.

* Originals had "Spink & Son Lond." below the bust. Obv. die renewed 1933 with Spink & Son Ltd." below bust.

One bar reading "NIGERIA 1886—97" to the silver medals, and one reading "NIGERIA" to the bronze.

Specimens of this medal are either struck with heavy gauge blanks or "S" of "Son" obliterated and "Copy" on the rims.

This silver medal was awarded by the Company in 1899 to its white officers (36), officers and N.C.Os of H.M.'s Forces (49) and R. Niger Constabulary (12) for services in several small punitive expeditions in the Company's territory between 1886 and 1897. Expeditions in which no casualties occurred did not count for the award. They bore a bar inscribed "NIGERIA 1886—97" irrespective of the date of the actual service rendered. Two hundred and thirty-eight bronze medals were awarded to members of the native constabulary who were still serving at the time of the award in 1899. These bronze medals bore a bar with the single word "NIGERIA".

It seems strange that the award was not given to natives who may have taken part in several expeditions but who did not happen to be still in the Company's service at the time of issue.

The National African Company was incorporated in 1882. In 1886 it was chartered as the Royal Niger Company, with Lord Aberdare as Chairman. On 9th August, 1899, the charter was revoked and the territory was taken over by the Imperial Government.

There were numerous expeditions in the Company's territory between 1886 and 1897, but there were also some which involved considerable fighting in 1898 and 1899, such as the expedition which operated in June, 1898, against the Lapai and Argeyes tribes.

It would be interesting to know why the dates 1898 and 1899 were not included on the bar.

75 BRITISH SOUTH AFRICA COMPANY'S MEDAL (1890—97)

Obverse   The crowned and veiled head of Queen Victoria with the legend "VICTORIA REGINA".

Reverse   A charging lion with a spear sticking in its chest. In the background is a mimosa bush, and in the foreground are a native shield and spears. Above are the name and date of the campaign for which the award was originally made, and below is the wording "BRITISH SOUTH AFRICA COMPANY".

Size   1·45 in. diameter.

Ribbon   1·4 in. wide with four yellow and three dark blue stripes. The ribbon is narrower than the suspender bar.

Suspension   By a wide flat suspender which is composed of representations of roses, shamrocks and thistles.

Designer   R. Caton Woodville. The medals were made in Birmingham.

Naming   Usually in engraved upright but sometimes sloping capitals. The medals for Matabeleland 1893 and Rhodesia 1896 are also found named in indented capitals.

No. of bars
issued   Four. Mashonaland 1890, Matabeleland 1893, Rhodesia 1896, Mashonaland 1897.

In 1896 the Queen sanctioned the issue by the British South Africa Company of a medal to the troops engaged in the Matabeleland Rising in 1893, and in 1897 another for those engaged in Rhodesia in 1896. In 1897 the Queen sanctioned a further issue of a medal to those who operated in Mashonaland in 1897. The three medals are the same except for name and date above the lion on the reverse. The three wordings above the lion denote the campaign for which the medal was issued, viz., Matabeleland 1893, Rhodesia 1896, and Mashonaland 1897.

In 1927, a similar medal was issued to recognize services in Mashonaland in 1890. It bore no place or date on the reverse.

As this medal is extremely rare and its existence not generally known, the Government Notice No. 267 dated 30th April, 1926, as published in the *Southern Rhodesia Government Gazette* is quoted.

"It is hereby notified that His Majesty the King has been graciously pleased to approve of a medal with clasp inscribed 'MASHONALAND 1890' being awarded to the Colonial Forces who were engaged in the expedition which marched into and occupied Mashonaland in September, 1890, on the following conditions:

"(1) The medal, which will be designated the 'Mashonaland 1890, Medal', will be in silver, and similar to that sanctioned by Her Late Majesty Queen Victoria, to be granted by the British South Africa Company for military operations in Matabeleland, 1893, but with the superscription 'Matabeleland, 1893' omitted from the reverse.*

"(2) The riband will be identical with that of the Matabeleland War Medal, 1893.

"(3) Members of the Pioneer Corps and escort of British South Africa Company's Police who have already been awarded the medal granted for operations in Matabeleland 1893, or Rhodesia 1896, will surrender that medal and receive in lieu thereof the "Mashonaland 1890, Medal' with clasp 'Mashonaland 1890' and 'Matabeleland 1893' or 'Rhodesia 1896' respectively. Those members who were not entitled to the medal granted for operations in Matabeleland 1803, or Rhodesia 1896, will receive the 'Mashonaland, 1890, Medal' with clasp 'Mashonaland 1890'.

"(4) Provided claims are approved by the competent authorities, the medal with clasp will be granted to all officers, warrant officers, non-commissioned officers and other ranks who actually served on the establishment of the Pioneer Corps or British South Africa Company's Police and who entered Mashonaland between the 1st June and the 12th September, 1890."

It is rather extraordinary that no mention was made about the "Mashonaland 1897, Medal" which was awarded under the authority of Government Notice No. 168, dated the 23rd August, 1898.

Four ment were entitled to the medal with four bars, but the only one known to have been issued is the one illustrated.

The medal, illustrated by kind permission of the recipient and the Government archivist, Salisbury, Southern Rhodesia (whose help in supplying some of the data is much appreciated), was awarded to M. E. Weale of the B.S.A. Company's Police. A medal is known to Corporal J. W. Corderoy of the Pioneers with bars for Mashonaland 1890 and Rhodesia 1896, and one other medal with the single bar for Mashonaland 1890.

Those who had received one of the three earlier issues and in 1927 claimed the bar for Mashonaland 1890, were expected to hand their original medal in for exchange, but a number did not do so.

---

* Both the obverse and reverse of this medal have milled edges.

† Marmaduke Howell Gwynne Mundell, Walter Frederick George Moberley, George Frank Vizard, and Mansell Edye Weale.

Mashonaland 1890 *(1st June—12th September, 1890)*

On 29th October, 1889, a charter was granted to the British South Africa Company to develop the district between the Lower and Central Zambesi on the north and the Transvaal border on the south. The Portuguese sent an exploring expedition, as they called it, under Lieutenant Cordon, into the same territory and claimed the province of Zumbo on 7th November, 1889. Protests were made to the Portuguese Government by the Marquis of Salisbury, who referred them to the agreements made with King Lobengula of Mashona and Makalakaland in 1888 and to those made with other tribes. The Portuguese Foreign Minister, Senor Barros Gomez, replied that Portugal maintained her claims as a result of exploration and prior occupation of the territory. This attitude was followed up by the sending of a force of about 4,000 men, under Major Serpo Pinto, to form a camp in the Makolo country. He displeased the natives and demanded that British settlers should submit to Portuguese authority. Lord Salisbury insisted that British subjects should not be attacked, but he received a reply to the effect that the Portuguese action was justified owing to the disturbed state of the country. Lord Salisbury then suggested that the matter be referred to a conference of the Powers in accordance with the Treaty of Berlin (1878), and in the meanwhile demanded the immediate withdrawal of the Portuguese troops. Senor Gomez reported that this had been done, but on 9th January, 1890, Lord Salisbury learnt that not only had the force not been withdrawn but, what is more, they were treating Nyasaland as a Portuguese colony. He then demanded the withdrawal to take place by 10 p.m., 11th January, 1890. He further informed the Portuguese Government that if this was not done, H.M.S. *Enchantress* would enter the Tagus and embark the personnel of the British Legation and all British subjects in Lisbon. This had the desired effect and the demands were complied with, though the complete evacuation did not take place until March, prior to which a survey party under Mr. Selous had entered the territory and had not been molested.

In July it was considered advisable to send a column into Mashonaland—not with any hostile intentions, yet prepared to use force if necessary.

This column, under the command of Lieutenant-Colonel E. G. Pennefather, was composed of the company's policemen and enlisted pioneers—real pioneers —totalling about 700 men.

On the 11th September as a result of a report received from a scouting party that Mount Hampden had been sighted, Colonel Pennefather with his second-in-command and the Chief Scout rode forward to reconnoitre. The three of them followed the southbank of the strongly flowing Makabusi River until they reached a kopje (then known as Harare Kopje after a local native chief and shortly to be renamed Salisbury Kopje). In the vicinity of the Kopje they crossed the river and headed northwards in the direction of Mount Hampden.

A survey of Mount Hampden area revealed there was insufficient water for a settlement of any size. Col. Pennefather then decided on the site in the vicinity of Harare Kopje and the Makabusi River. The Chief Scout was sent back to the Column with instructions to take them to this area. The Column reached the area where the Anglican Cathedral now stands about midday on the 12th September. This site is about 12 miles south-east of Mount Hampden. A parade was held at 10.00 a.m. the following morning and the Union Flag hoisted.

Major Johnson, in his Orders of the Day, announced that the place where the Column had halted should be called Fort Salisbury after Lord Salisbury, the Prime Minister of Great Britain. The Pioneer Corps did not dismiss until the 30th September, when they held their last parade. Mount Hampden had been named by F. C. Selous on one of his earlier hunting expeditions "after that good Englishman who gave his life in the defence of the liberties of his country".

As it turned out, this bar, or medal, was not awarded for combatant service. In view of what had been going on in the territory, nobody knew what might have happened.

The Medal Roll contains 687 names, 207 medals were issued:117 to members of the company's police; eighty-five to pioneers; four to men who were transferred from one force to another; and one to a prospector who, though not formally attested, did duties with the rest.

Matabeleland 1893 (16th October—24th December, 1893)

In July, 1893, the Matabeles raided the Mashonas, who had been quite well behaved, and then they invaded the British settlement at Fort Victoria; but it is doubtful whether it was at the instigation of King Lobengula, who, I think, was peacefully inclined but lacked control over his subordinates. Be that as it may, it was necessary to defend the settlers and punish the Matabeles, so three mounted columns were organised; one at Tuli, one at Salisbury, and the third at Fort Victoria.

When all was ready the Salisbury and Fort Victoria columns moved off and joined at Intaba Zimbi (Iron Mine Hill) on 16th October. They were attacked on the Shangi river on 24th October and on the Mbembesi (M'Bembezu) on 1st November. It transpired later that Lobengula had sent envoys for peace but that they had been shot at Tati by mistake on or about 23rd October, so the advance to Buawayo was undertaken with the object of capturing Lobengula, who, however, had fled by the time his kraal was entered on 4th November. Messages were sent to him offering him a safe conduct, but as no answer was received a force under Major Forbes was sent off on the 14th to capture him. The Shangani river was reached on 3rd December, hot on Lobengula's trail, and a small party of about thirty men under Major Allan Wilson was sent across the river to arrest him. Whilst these men were on the other bank the river rose rapidly in flood, so that they were cut off. They were attacked by an overwhelming force of Matabeles. The epic stand they made forms one of the bright pages of history.

The Matabele chiefs surrendered on 14th January. Lobengula died of fever on the 23rd.

Army Order 202 of December, 1896, authorized the award of a medal to all officers, non-commissioned officers and men of the Regular Forces, Bechuanaland Police, and British South Africa Company's Forces who were employed in connection with the operations in Matabeleland within the country west of Iron Mine Hill, north of Palla Camp and east of the boundary of the German possessions in South-West Africa, between the 16th October and 24th December, 1893. The grant of the medal to officers of the Regular Forces was limited to those who had official sanction to be present.

The name and date of this campaign are on the medal, so that only those who received one of the undated medals previously referred to were awarded a bar.

A total of 1,574 of these medals was awarded, though the rolls give the names of 927 men of the Company's Forces and 694 men of the Imperial Forces as being entitled to an award for the campaign.

There are no records to show how the 47 men who did not receive their award were divided between the two forces.

Regiments present: Imperial troops—3 Dragoon Guards (three); 7 Hussars (11); two guns of 10 Mountain Battery, R.A.; section of R.E.; Medical Corps; eighteen men of 42 Foot (Black Watch); one company of 76 Foot (53) (2 Duke of Wellington Regiment); three men of 84 Foot (2 York and Lancs). There were a few officers from British regiments present, and also a total of about fifty other ranks who volunteered for service as mounted infantrymen. We have not seen one of the latter medals, but the unit they formed was styled "Special Service Mounted Infantry".

Colonial troops—Bulawayo Field Force; Matabeleland Relief Force. In some cases included and in others additional to the above were: Raaffs' Column (249) (named after Commander Pieter Johannes Raaff, C.M.G.,); Cape Mounted Rifles (one officer and thirty-five men); Salisbury Horse (265); B.S.A. Police; Bechuanaland Border Police (558); Victoria Column (399); Rhodesia Volunteers; Matabeleland Mounted Rifles; Grey's Volunteeers.

Rhodesia 1896 *(24th March—31st December, 1896)*

In 1895 the territories subject to the British South Africa Company were named Rhodesia after Cecil Rhodes. Rhodesia was divided into Northern Rhodesia (which in turn was subdivided into North Eastern and North Western Rhodesia, or Barotseland) and Southern Rhodesia. North Eastern Rhodesia was administered from Fort Jameson; North Western Rhodesia from Kalomo; and Southern Rhodesia from Salisbury, in Mashonaland.

In March, 1896, the Matabeles, under Chief Olimo, revolted and were joined by a few of the native police in the Insega and Filibusi districts. They massacred some settlers, Constable Bentley and Assist. Native Commissioners Graham and Handley. Relief forces were formed which took the names of the Bulawayo Field Force, the Matabeleland Relief Force, and others as mentioned later on.

Several small and not-so-small encounters took place, among which may be mentioned those in the Shiloh district between 4th and 8th April; the attack on Captain Brand's patrol on the Tuli Road, 10th April; the action on the Umgusa River on 22nd April; the two actions at Gwelo on 1st May and 6th June.

In June the Mashonas also rose in revolt, so that martial law was proclaimed in Salisbury. Commissioner Graham was murdered at Inyati; the mission station at Ingwengwesi River was destroyed, and severe fighting took place at Umfuli on 22nd June. Chief Olimo was killed during the fighting in the Matoppo Hills and a heavy defeat inflicted on the rebels at Thbas-I-M'hamba on 5th July. Chief Secombo's stronghold in the Matoppos was stormed by Colonel Plumer's force; Colonel Alderson captured Chief Makoni's kraal in August, and the chief himself was captured in September near Umtali and shot, as was Chief Aweenya. Chief Mtigeza surrendered together with other chiefs in September. Finally an indaba was held between Mr. Rhodes and the native chiefs, during which peace terms were agreed upon on 20th September, though peace was not declared until 13th October.

Army Order 96 of July, 1897, authorized the award of a medal to all those who were employed in connection with the operations in the provinces of Matabeleland and Mashonaland, known as Southern Rhodesia, between the 24th March and the 31st December, 1896, both dates inclusive.

The medal was of exactly the same design as that previously issued for Matabeleland 1893, except that it bore the inscription "Rhodesia 1896" instead of "Matbeleland 1893" on the reverse.

Those who had been awarded the medal for Matabeleland, or subsequently received the undated medal previously referred to, received a bar inscribed "Thodesia 1896" for addition to their medal.

Regiments present and number of Rhodesia 1896 medals issued:

7th Hussars	251	"M" Troop, B.F.F. Corps	14
10 Mtn. By. R.A.	20	Grey's Scout Corps	62
25 and 26 West Dn. – R.A.	6	Swanson's Volunteers B.F.F. Corps	35
Leic. Regt.	3	Africander Corps	8
2/K.R.R. Corps	2	"A" Troop, Africander Corps	120
A.O. Corps	5	"B" Troop, Africander Corps	106
Med. Staff	35	Engineer Corps	58
Vet. Dept.	1	Artillery B.F.F. Corps	141
Mtd. Infantry Staff	1	Gwelo Burghers Corps	63
2nd Battalion Wiltshire Regt.	1	Mangwe Field Force Corps	118
3 Drag. Gds.	2	Staff, Belingwe Column Corps	11
6th Dragoons	1	Maxim Troop Belingwe Column	
2 Norfolk Regt.	31	Corps	30
2/R Welch Fus.	2	"A" Troop, Belingwe Column Corps	23
2/Hamp. Regt.	25	"B" Troop, Belingwe Column Corps	23
1/Derby Regt.	8	"C" Troop, Belingwe Column Corps	22
2/R.W. Kent Regt.	2	"D" Troop, Belingwe Column Corps	54
3/K.R.R. Corps	28	"E" Troop, Belingwe Column Corps	36
4/K.R.R. Corps	33	Scouts Belingwe Column Corps	7
I/R. Ir. Rif.	29	Gwelo Volunteers Corps	329
2/R. Ir. Fus.	28	M.M.P. Corps	93
I/R Dub. Fus.	33	Matabeleland Relief Force Corps	1033
4/Rif.: Bde.	31	M.M. Police Corps	246
I/Y Lancs. Regt.	1	B.S.A. Police Corps	1436
1st Royal Dragoons	1	H.Q. Staff, Mashonaland Field Force	
R.E.	3	Corps	4
Med. Staff Corps.	51	Mounted Troop, Rhodesia Horse	
South Wales Bordrs.	1	Volunteer Corps	136
1/S. Wales Bord.	2	Umtali Volunteer Corps	386
E/Yorks L.I.	1	Umtali Artillery Corps	21
A.S.C.	5	Chisawasha Garrison, Salisbury Rifle	
A.O.C.	1	Corps.	17
1/W Yorks Regt.	1	Salisbury Volunteer Corps	14
24/West Dn. R.A.	8	Honey's Scout Corps	15
2/W. Rid. Regt.	312	Natal Troop, Volunteer Corps	65
43 Co.: R.E.	59	Artillery Troop Corps	77
Royal Highlanders	1	B.S.A. Police Corps (See above)	
Royal Artillery	1	43rd Company, Royal Engineers Corps	42
1/R Irish Regt.	30	2nd Batt., York and Lancaster Regt	
A.S.	4	Corps	51
2/Rif. Bde.	31	Salisbury Field Force Corps	427
W. Rid. Regt.	1	1896 Addenda–B.S.A.P. Corps Mat-	
Staff, Infantry Brig. Gibraltar	1	abeleland	8
S. Wales Bord.	1	H.Q. Staff Corps.	1
East Kent Regt.	1	Volunteer Defence Corps	28
2/Y & Lanc. Regt.	154	Native Commissioners Dept. Corps	6
Commandant–Gen. Staff Corps	4	Rand Bulawaya Field Force Corps	18
H.Q. Staff Corps	18	Bulawayo Field Force Corps	117
Staff Bulawayo Field Force Corps	33	Addenda–Swanson's Volunteer Corps	9
Post and Telegraph Staff Corps	12	Belingwe Field Force	3
Ambulance Corps B.F.F. and Med.		Gwelo District Volunteers	4
Staff Corps	57	Africander Corps	12
Commissariat Dept. B.F.F. Corps	24	Matabeleland Relief Force Corps	36
Transport Dept. B.F.F. Corps	29	M.M.P. Corps.	22
Remount Dept. B.F.F. Corps	29	Municipal Police Corps	51
Gifford's Horse Corps	173	Umtali Burghers Corps	142
"C" Troop, B.F.F. Corps	88	Charter Garrison Corps	28
"D" Troop, B.F.F. Corps	85	Enkeldoorn Garrison Corps	56
"E" Troop, B.F.F. Corps	142	Victoria Rifle Corps.	153
"F" Troop, B.F.F. Corps	102	Victoria Transport Convoy Corps	2
"G" Troop, B.F.F. Corps	180	Salisbury Field Force Corps	296
"H" Troop, B.F.F. Corps	109	No. 10 Mountain Battery, R.A.	50
"K" Troop, B.F.F. Corps	71	Colenbranders Cape Boy Corps	413
"L" Troop, B.F.F. Corps	112	Robertson's Cape Boy Corps	190

Mashonaland 1897 *(24th March, 1896-31st October, 1897)*

Though peace had been declared in October, 1896, the smouldering embers of revolt had not been stamped out, so that troubles started almost at once — in fact, it is difficult to see how they could ever have been considered to have finished.

On 19th October, 1896, Gatze's kraal was taken by Major F.S. Evans; Lieutenant-Colonel Baden-Powerll captured eight more kraals between the 16th and 28th and burnt that of Chief Dango on the 30th; Colonel Paget dispersed the rebels in the Thaba Insimba Hills on 20th November; Major Gosling captured Seka's kraal on 15th January, 1897. Many more kraals were captured in February, which prompted the company to report that the troubles were over. The prospectors, however, had other views on the subject and appealed for Imperial aid. How right they were was very soon shown by the seriousness of the continued troubles. Marandella's kraal was stormed and captured on 26th May; heavy fighting broke out in July on the Umyami and near Fort Charter; more kraals, including that of Chief Matshayongombi, were taken on the same day.

The troubles may be considered to have stopped in September, though the final surrender of all the Mashona chiefs did not take place until 29th October.

Government Notice No. 168, from the Secretary's Office, Salisbury, notified the grant of the medal for operations in Rhodesia between the 27th March and 31st December, 1896, being extended to those employed in the subsequent operations in Mashonaland up to the 31st October, 1897, inclusive. The medals awarded to those who only served in Mashonaland in 1897 were to have the inscription "Mashonaland 1897" on the reverse. Those who had received either of the previous medals were to be awarded a bar inscribed "Mashonaland 1897" to be affixed to their medals. Two types of bar exist, one with Mashonaland 1897 in 2 lines and the other with the name, place and date in 1 line only, the 2 line version is more frequently seen.

This medal is the rarest of the three which bear the place and date on the reverse.

Regiments present: Imperial troops — 3rd Dragoon Guards (2); 7 Hussars (15 medals and 187 bars). Mounted sections, consisting of one officer and thirty other ranks, were formed from each of the following regiments: 2 Norfolks; 1 Royal Irish Regiment; 1 South Lancs; 1 Derbys; 3 and 4 K.R.R.C.; 2 Hants; 1 Royal Irish Fusiliers; 2 Royal Irish Fusiliers; 1 Royal Dublin Fusiliers; 3 and 4 Rifle Brigade. Commandant General's Staff (5).

Colonial units — B.S.A.P., Umtali Volunteers, Mount Darwin Volunteers, Garrison Volunteers and the Native Commissioner's Department.

The following information, which is taken from the official records, concerning these four medals should be noted.

Only four Matebeleland medals were awarded with the single bar for "Mashonaland 1897". The recipients were Captain C.D.L. Monro, Maj. Sadler*, Cpl. T. Gardner and 1972. Tpr. A. Knight, B.B. Police.

76 CENTRAL AFRICA MEDAL (1891-1898)

Obverse and Identical with the East and West Africa Medal (No. 78).
Reverse

Ribbon The ribbon, 1.25 in. wide, is of three colours of equal width symnolical of the troops taking part. Reading from left to right

---

*Major R.H. Sadler, K.O.Y.L. was serving as a Special Service Officer with the 7 Hussars during the operations in Mashonaland.

racing the wearer they are black for the Zanzibar, white for the British and terracotta for the Indian troops.

Suspension By means of a small swivelling ring through which the ribbon passes, those issued with a bar had a plain straight suspender.

Designers Obverse — L.C. Wyon; Reverse — Sir Edward J. Poynter.

Naming Many medals are found unnamed and others named in script or in impressed capitals.†

No. of bars issued One.

Care must be taken to distinguish this medal from the East and Central Africa and East and West Africa Medals, which follow immediately, owing to the similarity of names and the periods for which they were issued.

The medal was issued on two occasions, firstly in 1895 to commemorte ten small campaigns in Central Africa between 1891 and 1894, and again in 1899, for several more in the same area.

On the first occasion, the piece was suspended by a swivel ring and no bar was awarded.

On the second occasion a bar inscribed "Central Africa 1894-98" was given, and the piece was fitted with a plain straight suspender. A few were issued in bronze.

The medal with the bar is very rare, and that with the swivel suspender is far from common.

The expeditions for which the medal without the bar was awarded were undertaken against native chiefs who were imprisoning and maltreating slaves. The expeditions were as follows:

July-August, 1891: Expedition agasint Mlanje.

October-November, 1891: Expedition against Makanjira under Commissioner H.H. Johnston and Captain Maguire.

November, 1891: Expedition against Kawinga under Captain Maguire, who withe thirty Sepoys went to release slaves. Captain Maguire was killed on this expedition.

January-February, 1892: Expedition against Zarifa.

January-February, 1893: An expedition into the Upper Shire.

August-October, 1893: A further expedition against Mlanje.

November, 1893-January, 1894: Commissioner Johnston, assisted by two lake gunboats, captured Makinjira's position and released many slaves.

December, 1893: An expedition against Chirodzulu.

December, 1893-February, 1894: An expedition against Unyoro.

April-June, 1894: An expedition against Mruli.

Recipients: 15, 23, 24, 25, 31, 32, 36 Bengal Infantry; 22 Punjabis (6); 23 Pioneers (26); 24 (14), 26 (5), 28 (19), 30 (13), 31 (14), 32 (20), 35 (16), 36 (27), 45 (17) Punjabis; 1 Sikh Lancers (23); 1 Sikh Infantry (15); 15 Sikhs (14); British Central African Rifles; 1st, 3rd Lancers K.C. (Hyderabad Contingent). Also to Lt. Chaworth-Masters, 3rd Hrs.

A hundred Sikhs who accompanied the crews of the *Adventure* and *Pioneer* to Lake Nyassa in 1893 received this medal. (See bar for Lake Nyassa 1893, to the East and West Africa Medal.)

---

†The author possessed one with the bar "CENTRAL AFRICA 1894-98" awarded to a native of the 2nd British Central African Rifles, which was named in script followed by the words "PRESENTED BY THE KING".

Central Africa 1894-98

For fixing this bar the ring was removed so that the medal and suspender are the same as that for East and West Africa (No. 78).

This bar was awarded for several small expeditions as follows:

January, 1894: Operations around Fort Johnson.

March, 1895: Expedition against Kawinga.

September-November, 1895: Expeditions against Zarafi, Mponda, Matipwiri, Makanjira.

December, 1895: Expeditions agains Mlozi and Mwani.

January, 1896: Expeditions against Tambola.

October, 1896: Expeditions against Odeti, Chikusi, and Mkoma.

August, 1897: Expedition against Chilwa.

January-February, 1898: Expedition against Mpezeni. (Mpseni?)

April, 1898: Expedition to Southern Agoniland.

Regiments present: 15, 31, 35 Bengal Infantry; British Central African Rifles; Civilian Volunteers.

Twenty-one medals were issued to the Navy and a few to the Royal Marines.

Silver medals were also awarded to Major F. Trollope, Grenadier Guards, Capt. L.P. de V. Stokes, 4th King's Own, Lieutenant J.S. Brogden, R.M.L.I. and Sgt. Maj. P. Devoy, R.A., and in bronze to Bhisti Nihal Singh, 31st Bengal Infantry and to a Dooley Bearer, 36th Bengal Inf.

77 EAST AND CENTRAL AFRICA MEDAL (1897-1899)

Obverse	The half-length figure of Queen Victoria wearing a small crown and veil and holding a sceptre in her right hand, and legend "VICTORIA REGINA ET IMPERATRIX".
Reverse	The standing figure of Britannia holding a trident in her right hand. In her left hand, which is extended, she is holding an olive branch and a scroll. Behind her is a fine figure of the British Lion. In the right background is the rising sun, and in the exergue "EAST & CENTRAL AFRICA".
Size	1.42 in. diameter.
Ribbon	1.25 in. wide, half yellow (to the left facing wearer) and half red.
Suspension	By a straight, plain suspender.
Designer	G.W. de Saulles.
Naming	The recipient's rank and name are in rather thin sloping or upright capitals.
No. of bars issued	Four: Lubwa's, Uganda 1897-98, 1898, and Uganda 1899. A few were awarded medals without a bar including Armr. Sgt. A.W. Strong, Ord. Corps. & Sgt. T. Scott, R. Scots. Fus.

Lubwa's *(23rd September, 1897-24th February, 1898)*

This bar, which is usually found in conjunction with that for Uganda 1897-98, was awarded for service against 510 mutinous Sudanese troops who refused to go on to exploratory mission. They held Fort Lubwas, where they were attacked by Major Macdonald on 12th October, 1897.

After very heavy fighting the mutineers escaped and crossed the Nile, but were overtaken by forces under Major Macdonald and Captain Moloney at Kabagambi, on Lake Kioga.

In the period covered by the award about thirty Europeans were killed

Regiments present: Uganda Rifles (55); 27 (1 Baluch Battalion) Bombay

240

(Obverse)

67. The North West Canada Medal,
1885.

(Obverse)

No. 70. The Hong Kong Plague Medal,
1894.

(Reverse)

No. 67. The North West Canada Med
1885.

(Obverse)

(Obverse)

No. 71. The Hunza Nagar Badge, 1891.
(Pages 222/3).

(Reverse)

No. 71. The India General Service Medal, 1854-95.

To face page 240

(Obverse)

No. 73. The Cape General Service Medal, 1880-97.

(Reverse)

No. 73. The Cape General Service Medal, 1880-97.

(Obverse)

No. 72. The Ashanti Star, 1896.

(Obverse)

(Reverse)

No. 74. The Royal Niger Company's Medal, 1886-97.

To face page 241

Light Infantry; 14, 15 Sikhs. Also a few women who nursed the sick.

Capt. C.E. Bagnall, 41 Yorks Rgt. received the medal with bars for Lubwas and Uganda 1897-98.

Uganda 1897-98 *(20th July, 1897-19th March, 1898)*

This bar was awarded for an expedition under Lieutenant-Colonel W.A. Broome into the Teita country.

Sergt. R. Thompson of the Seaforth Highlanders received this bar, as did Mr. S.D. Shaw, J.D. Wilson, S. Ormsby and W. Grant.

Regiments present: Indian Contingent — 27 (1 Baluch Battalion) Bombay Light Infantry; 14, 15 Sikhs; 1 Uganda Rifles (259). Also eight women who nursed the sick.

1898 *(12th April-3rd October, 1898)*

This bar was awarded for service in the Ogaden against rebellious Somalis. The force was commanded by Major W. Quentin.

Regiments present: 4 Bombay Rifles; 27 (1 Baluch Battalion) Bombay Light Infantry; 1 Uganda Rifles; East African Rifles; 46th Native Field Hospital (18).

Uganda 1899 *(21st March-2nd May, 1899)*

This bar was awarded to members of the forces under Major Martyr and Colonel Evatt which advanced down the Nile and then defeated and captured both Kabarega dn M'Wanga in the Uganda Protectorate and continued on to Nandi.

Regiments present: 27 (1 Baluch Battalion) Bombay Light Infantry (344); 1 Uganda Rifles.

Medals were also awarded to Lieutenant C. de Vere Beauclerk, K.R.R.C., and Sergt. S.W. Bone, South Lancs Regiment, and a bronze medal to Bhisti Len Singh, 4th Bombay Rifles.

A total of eighty-one medals were issued to civilians.

78 EAST AND WEST AFRICA MEDAL (1887-1900)

This medal is slightly thinner than that awarded for the Ashantee Campaign of 1873-74. In all other respects, including the ribbon, it is the same (see page 184).

Those who had received the medal for the Ashantee War, either with or without the bar for Coomassie, were only awarded the appropriate bar, or bars, for further service in East and West Africa between 1887 and 1900. Those who had not received the Ashantee Medal received the East and West Africa Medal.

The only way, therefore, to ascertain whether the recipient had taken part in the Ashantee War but had not received the bar for Coomassie is to compare the thicknesses of the two pieces.

The first issue was authorized on 1st November, 1892, and altogether over twenty bars were awarded. For the M'wele Campaign in 1895-96 no bar was issued, but the name and date were engraved round the rim. This seems an extraordinary idea, because without examining the rim of the medal there is no way of distinguishing it from one issued, without the bar for Coomassie, for the Ashantee, 1873-74, Campaign. The latter is the thicker.

The greatest number of bars seen on this medal is seven, but this may not be the maximum, because all those seen were dated between 1890 and 1894.

Some of the bars are extremely rare. Some are seen bearing the dates 1896-97 and 1896-99, but there appears to be no mention in official records.

White officers and N.C.O.s who were serving with the West India Regiment, and other native forces, had their medals named with their parent regiment, so it must not be thought that the whole of their unit was present. For instance, Lieutenant A.C.A. Jerrard, 4th Dragoon Guards, received the bar for Sierra Leone 1898-99, but it is obvious that this complete cavalry regiment was not out there.

The medals, which were issued in silver and a few in bronze, are named in thin capitals; those to natives for M'wele are named in sloping script, with the word M'wele in indented capitals on one side of the claw and the date on the other.

It should be noted that number shown after H.M. ships represent the number of *single* bars issued.

1887-8 *(13th November, 1887-2nd January, 1888)*

This bar was awarded for operations against the Yonnie Tribe.

Regiments present: 1 West India Regiment; Political Officers; Sierra Leone Frontier Police (47).

Sizty two medals were awarded to the crews of H.M.S. *Acorn* (17),* *Icarus* (22), *Rifleman* (23).

Witu 1890 *(17th-27th October, 1890)*

This bar was awarded to members of the undermentioned ships who composed the expedition to punish the Sultan of Witu, who had murdered several German Europeans. The following is the composition of the force: 750 seamen and marines; 150 Indian police; 200 Sultan of Zanzibar's troops.

H.M. ships: *Boadicea* (327), *Brisk* (90), *Conquest* (190), *Cossack* (79), *Humber* (20), *Kingfisher* (96), *Pigeon* (10), *Redbreast* (47), *Turquoise* (131). Dispatch Boat *Somali* and Imp. E. Africa Cos. S.S. *Juba*.

In addition the rolls list medals to 218 Seedies attached to the ships.

A/B., W. Whitehead also received Benin 1897 on a separate medal.

1891-2 *(29th December, 1891-2nd February, 1892)*

This bar was awarded to three hundred members of the Gambia Expedition against Chief Cabba.

Regiments present: 2 West India Regiment (six officers and one hundred and seventy-six other ranks) Gambia Police and a Naval Brigade from:— H.M.S. *Alecto*, (6 — all R. Marines) *Racer* (80), *Sparrow* (46), *Swallow* (43), *Thrush* (46), *Widgeon* (55) and the colonial steamer *Lily*.

Duplicates were issued to A/B., J. Connell and E. Holland, Ord. Smn. E.P. Hawton and H. Lee and also T. Bestman all of H.M.S. *Racer*. Also S.B.A., I. Davies, H.J. Triff and J. Newman of H.M.S. *Thrush* and A/B., H. Rogers and Dom. 3rd cl., T. Peter of H.M.S. *Sparrow*.

1892 *(8th Darch-25th May, 1892)*

This bar was awarded for expeditions against Tambi, Toniataba and the Jebus.

Regiments present: Tambi Expedition (8th March-11th April, 1892) — 1 West India Regiment; 2 West India Regiment (60); Bathurst Police (20); Gold Coast Constabulary (125); Sierra Leone Frontier Police (213); Lagos Houssa Force.

---

*Represents throughout the number of *single* bars issued to R.N. ships.

Toniataba and Jebus operations (12th March-11th April and 12th-25th May, 1893): 1 West India Regiment; Naval Brigade from H.M.S. *Alecto, Racer* (5), and men from the Colonial steamer *Counterss of Derby* (23).

Witu August 1893 *(7th-13th August, 1893)*

This bar was awarded for an expedition under Captain G.R. Lindley, R.N., which landed at Lamu to punish the Sultan of Witu. Bars were awarded as follows: seventy natives of the West India Regiment and Niger Constabulary; ten officers, two hundred and twenty seamen and thirty-six Marines from H.M. ships *Blanche* (70 single bars), *Sparrow* (4 single bars) and *Swallow* (69 single bars).

Liwondi 1893 *(February-March, 1893)*

This rare bar was awarded to Lieutenant-Commander G.S.Q. Carr, R.N., two officers and thirty men of H.M. ships *Herald* (16) and *Mosquito* (16) for an expedition up the Shire river against Chief Liwondi, who had arrested H.M. Commissioner Mr. H.H. Johnston. It should be noted that C. Banks was issued with three medals over a period. Ten Volunteers also accompanied this expedition but it is not known that they were awarded medals.

Juba River 1893 *(23rd-25th August, 1893)*

Lieutenant P. Vaughan Lewes, R.N., with forty naval volunteers from H.M.S. *Blanche* and Count Lovatelli successfully carried out a small expedition to Gobwen to rescue Captain Tritton and Mr. McDougall from the Somalis and some rebellious natives of the Hyderabad Contingent.

Twenty-one of these bars in conjunction with that for Witu August 1893 were awarded to Europeans and three to natives.

Lake Nyassa 1893 *(November, 1893)*

Only twenty-six single bars were awarded and those to European officers and men who manned two small boats called the *Adventure* (9) and *Pioneer* (17). These were built at Jarrow-on-Tyne and sent out to Africa in sections. They were hauled over two hundred miles of virgin country to the edge of the lake, where they were assembled.* The object of all this trouble was to punish Chief Makaujira, who lived in this then almost unknown and inaccessible region.

One hundrded and one Sikhs accompanied the expedition, and for some reason they did not receive the same medal as the sailors, but were awarded the Central Africa Medal with the swivel ring suspender already described (See No. 76.)

(J. Symes, A.B., and Carpenter's Mate W. Maber, of H.M.S. *Pioneer*, received the bar for Lake Nyassa 1893, as did Ldg. Stoker J. Bramble, who also had the Egyptian Medal, Khedive's Star, Queen's Sudan Medal, Khedive's Sudan Medal, and the L.S.G.C. Medal. Carpenter's Mate W. Mater received triplicate medals and A/B. G. Powell duplicate medals, both served aboard H.M.S. *Pioneer*.)

*The most extraordinary case of ship transportation that is known is that of the steamship *Inca* on Lake Titicaca in Peru. Built at Hull in 1905, 200 feet long, of 1,000 tons, she sailed out to Mollendo. Here she was taken to bits and transported by rail to the shores of the lake, where she was reassembled. She does, or did, a regular run of 123 miles at over $2\frac{1}{3}$ miles above sea-level!

Later a similar ship was sent out from Hull in segments and reassembled in the same manner.

The journey from Puno in Peru to Guaqui in Bolivia is the highest steamship journey in the world, and on it medal collectors and others may obtain the rare combination of mountain and lake sickness!

1893-94 *(16th November, 1893-11th March, 1894)*

This bar was awarded for services against the Sofas between 26th November, 1893, and 20th January, 1894, and also for operations up the Gambia river between 22nd February and 11th March, 1894. As the Navy only took part from 22nd February, 1894, onwards, they were not eligible for this bar so, consequently, received that awarded for Gambia 1894, which follows.

Regiment present: Fifty men of the 1 West India Regiment. (C.S.M. Gifford, R. Sussex Regt., received this bar.)

The Sierra Leone Frontier Police and the Colonial steamer *Countess of Derby* (25) received a medal with this bar.

Gambia 1894 *(23rd February-13th March, 1894)*

This bar was awarded for considerable fighting during the short period that it covers.

In February a Naval Brigade, commanded by Captain Gamble, R.N., (H.M.S. *Raleigh*), went inland to attack Chief Fodi Silah. On its way back it was ambushed. Lieutenants W.H. Arnold, F.W. Hervey, and Sub-Lieutenant F.W. Meister and fifteen men were killed. A further attack was made on a force commanded by Lieutenant-Colonel Corbet. Reinfrocements were sent under Major S.G. Fairclough and Major G.C. Madden. Gonjur was bombarded by Rear-Admiral Bedford's squadron. Chief Silah surrendered to the French in Senegal.

About fifty men of the 1st West India Regiment and six hundred and seventy-two members of the crews of H.M. ships *Alecto* (47), *Magpie* (41), *Raleigh* (349), *Satellite* (164), and *Widgeon* (8) received this *single* bar.

Duplicates have been issued to: *Alecto*, J. Allen. *Magpie*, G. Huse, R.W. Jane and Tom Walker (Native). *Raleigh*, W. Aldred, R. Browning, T. Davis, G. Harrold, G. Heathfield, E.R. Lakey, H.L. Road, E. Tablock, W.F. White, H. Worth and Tom Lee (Native). *Satellite*, H. Bummage, W. Gatrell, C.H. Green, H.J. Pope, F.J. White, J. Wingard and G.W. Woodruff.

Benin River 1894 *(August-September, 1894)*

This bar was awarded to members of an expedition that went up the Benin river to punish Chief Nana.

Some officers of the Niger Coast Protectorate and a few Houssas received this bar but the chief recipients were members of the Navy under the command of Rear-Admiral Bedford.

H.M. ships: *Alecto* (43), *Philomel* (165), *Phoebe* (190), *Widgeon* (4) as *single* bars.

Brass River 1895 *(17th-26th February, 1895)*

This bar was awarded for operations against King Koko and was issued to H.M. ships: *Barrosa* (19), *St. George* (23), *Thrush* (22), *Widgeon* (5) as single bars.

(Major A.G. Leonard, Commissariat and Transport Corps, received this bar, also the Afghanistan medal, 1878, the Egypt medal (5 bars) and the Khedive's Star.)

M'wele 1895-1896

There was no bar issued for the operations against Chief Rashid of M'wele (region of Mombasa). The word "MWELE" was impressed on the rim of the medal to the left of the claw and the date "1895" or "1895-6", to the right. As previously mentioned, it is impossible to distinguish this medal from that for the Ashantee War, which does not carry the bar for Coomassie, except by comparing the thicknesses of the two pieces, the latter being the thicker.

Bronze medals were issued for these operations as well as silver ones.

Regiments present: 24, 26 Bombay Infantry; 1 Punjabis.

H.M. ships: *Barrosa* (5), *Phoebe* (4), *Racoon* (70), *St. George* (22), *Thrush* (4), *Widgeon* (1) as *single* bars.

1896-97

As previously stated this bar has been quoted, but there is no trace of any official record of it.

1896-98 *(27th November, 1896-27th June, 1898)*

This bar was awarded for several expeditions into the Northern Territory of the Gold Coast between 27th November, 1896, and 27th June, 1898. Not many men appear to have seen service in each of these three years so that the bar is rare.

Regiments present: 1 and 2 West India Regiment (two companies).

Niger 1897 *(6th January-26th February, 1897)*

This rare bar was awarded for the expedition to Egbon, Bida and Ilorin and for garrison duty at Lokoja and Fort Goldie between 6th January and 26th February, 1897. The recipients were twenty British and five hundred natives of the Niger Company's force of constabulary. Included in the twenty British were a few instructors, one of whom was Bombardier A.E. Bosher, R.A. and Lt. A.S. Arnold, 3rd Hrs.

The medal with this bar was awarded to fourteen civilian employees of the Niger Company including Mr. H.J. Drew who was in charge of the transport.

Benin 1897 *(6th February-7th August, 1897)*

This bar was awarded to members of a punitive expedition in the Benin Territory under Lieutenant-Colonel Bruce Hamilton and to the personnel of a flotilla under Rear-Admiral Rawson which captured Gwato and Sapobo. A total of 1,400 bars were issued.

H.M. ships: *Alecto* (76), *Barrosa* (31), *Forte* (320), *Magpie* (86), *Philomel* (337), *Phoebe* (258), *St. George* (456), *Theseus* (551), *Widgeon* (79).

(A medal was also issued to two R.N. officers who served on S.S. *Malacca* and three to nursing sisters.)

Dawkita 1897 *(28th March, 1897)*

This bar was awarded to forty-two men of the Gold Coast Constabulary for the defence of Dawkita under Lieutenant F.B. Henderson, R.N., when it was attacked by Sofas.

1897-98 *(September, 1897-August, 1898)*

This bar was awarded to those who took part in the expeditions to the hinterland of Lagos between September, 1897, and 14th June, 1898, or in Borgu. It was also awarded for the following expeditions which took place in 1898: Lapai, Ibonza, Anai, Barua, Bessama, Siama, Angaima, Illah, Dama and the Central Division Expediton, providing, of course, that the recipient had seen service during 1897 as well.

Regiments present: 1 West India Regiment; 2 West India Regiment; Gold Coast Constabulary; 2nd Gold Coast Constabulary (48); Lagos Houssa Force

(290); Artillery (30); N. Nigeria Regiment (63); 2nd Nigeria Regiment.

A medal was also issued to a man in the Hampshire Regiment who was probably an instructor to one of the native regiments and Capt. W.G. Murray, 3rd Hrs.

1898

This bar, somewhat rare to the native troops, and very rare to the Navy, was awarded to those who took part in any of the expeditions during 1898 which were mentioned under the last bar.

Regiments present: 1 West India Regiment; 2 West India Regiment; Lagos Houssa Force (150); Gold Coast Constabulary; 1st W.A.F.F. (413); 2nd W.A.F.F. (35); W.A.F.F. Artillery (13); Rifle Bde. (13); N. Nigeria Regiment. Capt. C.F. Goldie-Taubman, Lanc. Rgt., and Cpl. A. Wilkinson, 1st H.L.I.

Ten of these bars were awarded to the Navy, all to H.M.S. *Heron*.

Four of them were awarded for the Borgu Expedition and six for the Illah Expedition.

Sierra Leone 1898-99 *(18th February, 1898-9th March, 1899)*

This bar is deeper than any of the others awarded with this medal, as the inscription occupies two lines. It was awarded for services in the Sherboro District and on the Brempe river. It may be considered as rather rare to the Navy, but not to native troops. In this case, a very clear distinction was made between awards to the Naval personnel and those to the natives. It was only awarded to Naval personnel who had been under fire, whereas every native participant in the above and Lokko and Kittam river expeditions received it. Only medals issued with this bar were named in square block capitals.

Regiments present: R.A.M.C. (26); A.S.C. (27); A.O.C. (9); 1, 2, 3 West India Regiment; Waterloo Vol. Corps (61); Sierra Leone Volunteers (127); Sierra Leone Police and R.G.A. (70).

Naval Brigade from H.M. ships *Alecto* (35), *Blonde* (111), *Fox* (87) and Colonial Steamer *Countess of Derby* (19).

1896-99

These dates have been quoted, but there does not seem to be any official record of such a bar.

1899 *(February-May, 1899)*

This rather rare bar was awarded for the expedition under Major Carter and Captain R. Gabbett to Bula, and the Central Division Expedition in February and March; also for the Benin Territory Expedition in April and May under the same officers.

A naval rocket detachment (5 awarded) under Lieutenant V. Buckland, R.N.R.

Regiments present: 3rd Nigeria Regiment; Niger Coast Protectorate Police Force; W.A.F.F.

1900 *(4th January-8th May, 1900)*

This rare bar was awarded for the Kaduna Expedition between 20th February and 8th May, 1900, and also for the Munshi Expedition from 4th January-19th March, 1900, under Lieutenant-Colonel Lowry-Cole.

Regiments present: 24, 26 Bombay Infantry; 2 Northern Nigeria Regiment; and a few members of the Royal Niger Company's Police.

Colour-Sgt. W. Flicker, the Queen's, Cpl. A. Watt, The King's Regiment and Lt. G. Lewis-Lloyd, 57th, received this bar.

79 THIRD CHINA WAR MEDAL 1900 (10th June-31st December, 1900)

Obverse   The crowned and veiled head of Queen Victoria and legend "VICTORIA REGINA ET IMPERATRIX".

Reverse   The same as that for the China 1860 Medal (No. 59), with the addition of the date "1900" under the word "CHINA".

Size   1.42 in. diameter.

Ribbon   1.25 in. wide. Crimson with yellow edges.

Suspension   By a plain, straight suspender.

Designer   Obverse — G.W. de Saulles. Reverse — W. Wyon.

Naming   Indented in thin block capitals similar to the Q.S.A. Impressed in skeleton Roman caps or engraved in script similar to the I.G.S. 1895.

No. of bars issued   Three: Taku Forts, Defence of Legations, Relief of Pekin; but two are the maximum number issued with any one medal.

The troubles in China during this period are better known as the Boxer Rebellion. The Boxers formed a Chinese secret society known as the I-ho-chuan (league of United Patriots), but as the first part of the title can also be pronounced to mean "fists", the title "Boxers" (or Red Fists) soon followed. No useful purpose would be served by trying to arrive at the very origin of the troubles, so let me start the story by saying that in March, 1899, Yu Hsien, one of the founders of the anti-foreign and anti-Christian Boxer Movement, was made governor of the Province of Shahtung. On 11th January, 1900, the Rev. Brooks was murdered in that province, after which edicts were issued. It is difficult to understand whether these were exhortations to the Boxers to continue or threats of suppression. In addition to the Boxers, there were other secret societies which had the avowed intention of evicting all foreigners. Things became so bad that the Great Powers demanded the suppression of all these societies, but no notice was taken of this demand. On 2nd June, 1900, two more missionaries were murdered, and the flame of rebellion spread rapidly to all, or most of, the provinces.

On 9th June, 1900, a Royal Edict was issued which not only made the murder of foreigners a free sport but actually decreed that they should be murdered.

The Powers had been sending troops and warships to the Chinese ports to protect their nationals and interests, so that when this latest edict was issued Admiral Sir Edward Seymour took action. He defeated the Boxers at Langfang on 11th June; captured the Taku forts on the 17th (these same forts were captured by us on 21st August, 1860), and an arsenal near Tientsin on the 22nd. Tientsin was occupied on 14th July. Of the total allied casualties incurred in the capture the British Naval contingent suffered 26 killed and 149 wounded.

From June to the end the actions of the Boxers are too numerous and revolting to follow in detail. They include the massacre of all Christians and foreigners in Pekin and the burning of their buildings 12th-24th June, the murder of the German Minister in Pekin on 19th June, the issue of special anti-foreign edicts on 22nd June, actual war declared against all foreigners on 26th June, and an attack on all the foreign settlements in Tientsin on 3rd-4th July. In July anarchy broke out in Manchuria, and the Roman Catholic Bishop Guillon was burnt alive in Mukden. On 9th July fifty-four missionaries were murdered in the province of Shansi. On 9th August British troops arrived at Shanghai, and then the fighting between the Chinese and Europeans started in earnest, as trouble had become general throughout the country. The allied forces numbering some 20,000 were composed mainly of British, American, French, Italian, Japanese, Russian and German troops under the supreme command of the German Field-Marshal Count von Waldersee.

The most spectacular — or shall we say the best known? — event during the whole rebellion concerned the defence and relief of the legations in Pekin. Defending and relieving places was rather a popular pastime in 1900, as will be seen by referring to the Boer War, which was a counter-attraction going on at the same time. In 1900 there were also the defence and relief of Kumassi.

On 14th January, 1901, a peace protocol was signed in Pekin and ratified by the Emperor on the 17th. The troubles in China were not really over. When will they ever be?

A few civilian doctors received the silver medal and native servants, etc., the bronze without bar. 15 Lady nurses were awarded the silver medal without bar.

Sergt. E. Beedle, R.E., received two of these medals and also the Khedive's and Queen's Sudan Medals. A medal is known to J. Sheppard of the Hampshire Regiment, with the bar for the Relief of Pekin.

The bar for the Defence of the Legations was awarded to three British officers seventy-nine other ranks and two interpreters of the Legation (one to J. Peachey), and is very rare indeed. The total allied strength of the Legation guard was eighteen officers and 389 other ranks.

The following are the particulars concerning the dates covered by each of the three bars:

Taku Forts, 17th June, 1900; Defence of Legations, 29th June-14th August, 1900; Relief of Pekin, 10th June-14th August, 1900.

The following troops and H.M. ships took part in the war.

Cavalry: 1, 16 Bengal Lancers; 3 Bombay Cavalry; 1 Jodhpur Lancers. R.H.A.; R/2 Ammunition Col. (5); B Battery (153); 1, 2, 3 (43), 4 (45) and 5 (45) Vickers Maxim Gun Sections; Vickers Maxim Gun Battery (131); R. Garrison Arty; 15th Siege Train (97), 62nd Co. (194); 91st Co. (218); Hong Kong and Singapore Battery. British Infantry: Norfolk Rgt. (24); Beds & Herts (11 - no bar); Cheshire Regiment (12); 2 R. Welch Fusiliers (530); Rifle Bde. (7); Native Infantry; 4, 20, 24 Sikhs; 3, 28, 31 Madras Infantry; 2, 6, 7, 9, 26 Bengal Infantry; 4, 20, 24 Punjab Infantry; 22, 26, 30 Bombay Infantry; Alwar and Bikanir Infantry; 1/4 Gurkhas. Sappers and Miners; 4 Bengal; 2 Bombay; 3 Madras; companies Sappers and Miners. Native Pioneers: 1, 34 Madras Pioneers; 8 Mule Corps; Shanghai Volunteers; Wei Hai Wei Volunteers (31); 26th Baluchistan Infantry; Teintsin Volunteers (65); Newchang Volunteers (34); 1st Chinese Regt.; Hong Kong Vol. Corps (37).

In addition to the 300 men of the Royal Welch Fusiliers, generally regarded as being the only British infantry present at the Relief of Pekin, small detachments of six or seven men were sent from several regiments in India for duty as telegraphists and hospital orderlies. Four men of the Royal Irish Rifles were also present.

Victorian Naval Brigade; New South Wales Naval Brigade (562 medals to Australians).

The medal without bar was also awarded to fourteen members of the St. John Ambulance Brigade serving aboard the American hospital ship *Maine*.

To given an example of the fascination of collecting a campaign medal to all the units present we give right a chart showing the numbers issued to the various vessels, etc., engaged.

Name of Ship, etc.	Medals without bar	Medals with bar Relief of Pekin	Medals issued with Taku Forts	Medals with both bars	Total Medals issued
Terrible	1000	252			1252
Barfleur	782	279	19	64	1144
Centurion	737	402	25	20	1163
Endymion	632	286	8	25	951
Goliath	580	1			581
Aurora	553	256	11	46	863
Undaunted	534				534
Orlando	532	191	37	80	835
Dido	479				479
Isis	446				446
Hermione	340				340
Bonaventure	331				331
Arethusa	312				312
Pique	293				293
New South Wales Contingent	256				256
Marathon	234				234
Wallaroo	230				230
Victoria Contingent	197				197
N.W. Fort Taku	197				197
R.I.M.S. Clive	177				177
Wei-Hei-Wei Naval Depot	156	12			156
Daphne	139				139
R.I.M.S. Canning	138 + 10 bronze				138
Alacrity	138	1	8	42	187
Algerine	9	5	98	9	118
R.I.M.S. Dalhousie	115				115
R.I.M.S. Clive	177 + 9 bronze				177
Rosario	110				110
Phoenix	109	13	12		134
Humber	104				104
South Australian Gunboat Protector	102				102
Esk	100				100
Linnet	97				97
Plover	88				88
Waterwitch	86				86
Peacock	83				83
Pigmy	79				79
Redpole	78				78
Whiting	65		57		122
Fame	3	2	58	3	66
Hart	57				57
Woodcock	45				45
Woodlark	36				36
Snipe	27				27
Fleet Transport S.S. Penarth	?				?
Fleet Transport S.S. Salamis	?				?
Civilians	21				21
Lady Nurses at Wei-Hei-Wei	13				13
Pilots employed in H.M. Ships	19				19
S.S. El Dorado*	1				1?
Hospital Ship Gwalior					
Hospital Ship Carthage					

*Capt. L.H. Tamplin

80 INDIA MEDAL (1895-1902)

Obverse	The crowned and veiled head of Queen Victoria and legend "VICTORIA REGINA ET IMPERATRIX".
Reverse	A British and a native soldier both supporting the same standard. On the left is the word "INDIA" and on the right the date "1895".
Size	1.42 in. diameter and slightly thicker than the I.G.S. 1854 Medal.
Ribbon	1.25 in. wide. Crimson with two dark green stripes down the centre.
Suspension	By an ornamental pattern suspender of the same type as the I.G.S. 1854 Medal.
Designer	Obverse — T. Brock; Reverse — G.W. de Saulles.
Naming	The medals were named in script, except those awarded to the Highlands Light Infnatry for Punjab Frontier 1897-98 and Tirah 1897-98, which were done in block capitals.
No. of bars issued	Six to the medal with the Queen's head and one to that with the head of Edward VII.

Twenty-three bars having been issued with the India General Service Medal of 1854, it was considered that it was time to institute a new one. Consequently, this medal, generally referred to as the "India 1895 Medal", was introduced in 1896. As Queen Victoria died before the last bar was issued, we find that the last issue bears the head of Edward VII, and with this issue the date 1895 was removed from the reverse. Since the bar for Punjab Frontier 1897-98 was not awarded till 3rd June, 1898, it cannot be understood why the date was not removed then, as it is almost as incongruous to award bars for operations 1897-98 as for 1901-2 to a medal which bears the date 1895. The point also arises as to why, when the Edward VII issue was made, the opportunity was not taken to strike a new medal, as the obverse had to be completely different and the reverse altered. Apparently in December, 1908, when the first bar for the next India Medal was sanctioned, the illogicality became sufficiently apparent!

The medal was issued in silver and bronze.

The bar for the Defence of Chitral is very rare and that for Malakand is not common.

The three bars for Punjab Frontier 1897-98, Samana 1897 and Tirah 1897-98 are generally found in that order, which is contrary to the sequence of the final inclusive dates of their award.

NORTH WEST FRONTIER OPERATIONS 1895-1902

Chitral is a small state on the North West Frontier of India. On 30th August, 1892, the Mehtar of Chitral was assasinated. His son Afzul-ul-Mulk, who seized the throne, was promptly murdered by his uncle, who, however, after his defeat by the Nizam-ul-Mulk, found the seat a bit too warm, so cleared off into Afghanistan. This round of unmusical bumping-off concluded with the recognition of Nizam-ul-Mulk by the British, who sent Surgeon-Major Robertson as Political Agent into the district in January, 1893. The Nizam was murdered by his brother Amir-ul-Mulk on 10th January, 1893, and at about the same time the state was invaded by an adventurous thug called Umra Khan. Dr. Robertson returned to Chitral and formally but temporarily recognized Amir-ul-Mulk as Mehtar in January, 1895. In March he did the same to Shujah-ul-Mulk and put Amir-ul-Mulk under surveillance. In the same month Umra Khan was joined by Sher Afzul from Cabul. The British then proclaimed against Umra Khan, who started operations without delay, with the result that there were many engagements with the tribesmen. Lieutenants Edwardes and Fowler were besieged in Reshun and their relief force attacked in the defile at Karagh on 8th March. The small

British force accompanying the Agent, Dr. Robertson, was besieged in Chitral until relieved by Lieutenant-Colonel J.G. Kelly.

The trouble had now got serious, so that an expeditionary force under Major-General Sir Robert Low crossed the Malakand Pass to the Jandol Valley, and eventually Umra Khan was driven out of Chitral.

On 26th July, 1897, a fanatical rising broke out in the Swat Valley, where the Mullah's followers attacked the garrisons in the Malakand Pass and Chakdara; then the Shabkadr Fort on 7th August. By now almost the whole of the North West Frontier was in revolt. The Swatis, the Mohmands and Afridis were united against us.

The bar for Malakand was awarded for service against the Swatis, that for Tirah for service against the Afridis, and that for Punjab Frontier for all service along that frontier, which accounts for its being the commonest of the three.

Returning to our story, we find Brigadier-General W. Meiklejohn attacked in the Malakand Pass by the Swatis, Lieutenant Rattray besieged in the fort at Chakdara, and thousands of Afghans and Mohmands attacking Shabkadr.

An expeditionary force of one division known as the Malakand Field Force was mobilized under Major-General Sir Bindon Blood, whilst another was prepared under Major-General E.R. Elles.

The punishing of the Swatis did not take long, so that General Blood then attacked the Mohmands in conjunction with General Elles's division. These two divisions then jointly formed the Mohmand Field Force.

Whilst these operations were going on trouble broke out on the Samana Ridge, where a force under Major-General Yeatman-Biggs was occupied with the joint predatory efforts of the Afridis and Orakzais, who attacked the forts with great vigour.

The tribes along the northern frontier of India were mainly ruled on the principle of *divide et impera*, but in 1897 the dividing part of the business broke down, with the result that all the border tribes united against the British. The Afridis, Waziris, Swatis, Tochis, Afghans, Mohmands, Orakzais, Miranzais, Zakkakhels, Akakhels and Bunerwals were in the first eleven with some other lesser-known tribes to complete the first fifteen. They made a strong combination which required the mobilization of the Tirah Field Force to keep them out of our posts and to maintain our position.

This force, as will be seen by a reference to the bar for Tirah 1897-98, was composed of many columns all under the supreme command of General Sir William Lockhart. There were too many encounters between October, 1897, and April, 1898, to mention.

The story ends with Sir William Lockhart's friendly farewell of the Afridis in April, 1898 — so one account states. Whether that was true or not, there is no doubt that there were to be many more contests on the same ground.

In 1901 the Mahsuds and Waziris again caused trouble by ambushing a column in the Gomal Pass. Though the operations were more prolonged than the usual tribal ones, there was no serious fighting.

Defence of Chitral 1895 (*3rd March — 19th April, 1895*)

This very rare bar was awarded to the garrison under Brevet-Major C. V. F. Townshend, C.B. The following troops composed the garrison: 88 men of the 14th Sikhs; 100 Punyalis (local levies);* 300 men of the 4th Kashmir Rifles; 40 camp followers, who received bronze medals.

In addition to the above, each of the four syces present received a bronze medal.†

*The medals are named "Gilgit Levy."
†They were Sepoy Sujen Singh, Bhisti Ami Chand, Bhisti Khim Singh and Bhisti Ala Vaux.

Jummoo and Kashmir Medal 1895

This medal, made by Messrs. Gurney in London, was given, in bronze only, by the Maharajah of Jummoo and Kashmir to his native troops who had taken part in the Defence of Chitral.

Obverse	Two natives supporting a coat of arms.
Reverse	A large fortress with troops in the foreground.
Size	The medal is kidney-shaped, being recessed at the centre of the top and bottom. It is 1½in. wide from side to side, and $1\frac{5}{6}$in. from top to bottom at its narrowest part.
Ribbon	1¼in. wide. Red with a central green stripe, bordered by two white ones.
Suspension	The same type of suspender as the I.G.S. Medals.
Naming	These are either found very crudely impressed in block letters or unnamed.
No of bars issued	One, Chitral 1895, the bar being of exactly the same pattern as that of the I.G.S. Medals. The medal was not given without this bar — the reverse of the bar reads "Gurney, London".

Relief of Chitral 1895 (*7th March — 15th August, 1895*)

This bar was awarded for service under:

1. Lieutenant-General Sir R.C. Low, G.C.B., between 2nd April and 15th August, 1895.
2. Brevet-Colonel J. G. Kelly, C.B., A.D.C., between 26th March and 20th April, 1895.
3. Captain F. J. Moberley, D.S.O., 37th Bengal Infantry, at Mastuj.
4. Lieutenant S. M. Edwardes, D.S.O., 2nd Bombay Infantry, at Reshan.
5. Captain C. R. Ross, 14th Bengal Infantury, who left Mastuj on the 7th March to succour Lieutenant Edwardes at Reshan.

Regiments present: **Colonel Kelly's Force:** Two guns of 1st Kashmir Mountain Battery; 32 Pioneers (400); Kashmir Infantry (100); Kashmir Sappers and Miners (34); Hunza and Punnial Levies (100). **Lieutenant-General Sir Robert Low's Force:** 1st Brigade — Guides Cavalry; 3 Mountain Battery R.A.; 4th D. Gds. (7); 5th Lancers (3); 11 (12), 18 (16), 19 (6) Hussars; 1 Royal Scots (13); Buffs (3rd Foot); Devons (15); East Surrey's (21); 1 Beds. and Herts.; 1 Northampton Rgt.; 1 King's Royal Rifle Corps; 15 Sikhs; 37 Dogras. 2nd Brigade — Guides Cavalry; 2 K.O.S.B.; 1 Gordons; Machine Gun Section of 1 Devons; Guides Infantry; 4 Sikhs; 11, 15 Bengal Infantry. 3rd Brigade — 8 Mountain Battery R.A.; No. 2 Derajat Mountain Battery; 1, 4, 6 Companies Bengal Sappers and Miners; 1 Buffs; 2 Seaforth; 25 Punjabis; 2/4 Gurkhas. Lines of Communication troops; 11 Bengal Lancers; Guides Cavalry; 1 East Lancs; 23 Pioneers; 13 Rajputs; 30 Punjab Infantry. Also present: 9 Bengal Lancers; 15 Field Battery R.A.; 3, 8 Mountain Batteries R.A.; 1 Kashmir, and 1 and 4 Derajat Mountain Batteries; No. 4 (Hazara) Mountain Battery; No. 7 (Bengal) Mountain Battery; 6 Company Bengal Sappers and Miners; 1 P.W.O. Sappers and Miners; R.E. and Indian Medical Service; 4 Sikhs; 26, 29, 30 Punjab Infantry; 34 Pioneers; 2/1, 2/3, 2/5 Gurkhas; Gwalior and Jodhpore Carrier Corps; Kurram and Border Military Police.

Captain G. Marshall received this bar and, incidentally, the Ashanti Medal with bar for Kumassi.

Punjab Frontier 1897-98 (*10th June, 1897 — 6th April, 1898*)

To give the full details regarding the award of this bar would necessitate enumerating a bewildering number of places and dates, so that it will serve our purpose if we abbreviate all the details and merely add that it is very common to find medals with the single bar for Punjab Frontier 1897-98.

Medals with this bar to the Highland Light Infantry are named in block capitals.

This bar was awarded to the defenders of Shabkadr Fort on 7th August, 1897, and to the members of the Mohmand Field Force under Major-General E. R. Elles, C.B., which operated from 15th September to 4th October, 1897. It was also given to the Tirah Expeditionary Force under Lieutenant-General Sir W.S.A. Lockhart, K.C.B., K.C.S.I., which operated between 2nd October, 1897, and 6th April, 1898.

Mohmand Field Force (Major-General E. R. Elles, C.B.). 1st Brigade — Somerset L.I.; 2/1 Goorkhas; 20 Bengal Infantry. 2nd Brigade — 11, 13 Bengal Lancers; 5 Bombay Mountain Battery; No. 8 Bengal Mountain Battery; No. 3 Mountain Battery R.A.; 4 and 5 Companies Bengal Sappers and Miners; North Fus.; 1 D.C.L.I.; 2. K.O.S.B.; Devon Rgt; Norfolk Rgt; Argyll and Sutherland Hldrs; 2 Ox. and Bucks L.I.; Q.O. Corps of Guides; 27 Bengal Infantry; 9 Gurkhas. 3rd Brigade — two squadrons 4 Dragoon Guards; 5th Lancers (14); 11 Hussars; two squadrons (15) 11 Bengal Lancers; "K" Battery R.H.A.; 1 Mountain Battery R.A.; 3 Company Bengal Sappers and Miners; 2 Queen's; 2 H.L.I.; 88th Foot (15); Argyll and Sutherland Hldrs; 22, 39 Bengal Infantry.

Unbrigaded troops: Corps of Guides; 24 Bengal Infantry.

C.T. Dept.

Lieutenant R. Gordon, Queensland Mounted Infantry, received a medal with this bar and that for Tirah 1897-98 and so did six members of the 19th Hussars and the 16th Lcrs. (48).

Malakand 1897 (*26th July — 2nd August, 1897*)

This bar was awarded to all who took part in the Defence and Relief of Chakdara and Malakand. The garrisons were commanded by Colonel W. H. Meikeljohn, C.B., C.M.G., and were drawn from: 11 Bengal Lancers; No. 8 Mountain Battery; No. 5 Company Madras Sappers and Miners: 45 Sikhs; 24, 31 Punjab N.I.

The relief force, known as the Malakand Field Force, was commanded by Major-General Sir Bindon Blood, K.C.B., and was composed as follows:
1st Brigade — 1 R.W. Kent; 45 Sikhs; 24, 31 Punjab Infantry. 2nd Brigade — 11 Bengal Lancers; No. 5 Company Bengal Sappers and Miners; 1 Buffs; Guides Infantry; 35 Sikhs; 38 Dogras. 3rd Brigade — 1 Queen's; 38 Bengal Infantry; 39 Garhwals; 22 Punjab Infantry. Divisional troops; One squadron each of 10, 11 Bengal Lancers; Guides Cavalry; 10 Field Battery R.F.A.; Nos. 1 and 7 Mountain Batteries R.A.; No. 8 Bengal Mountain Battery; No. 3 (Bombay), 4 (Bengal), 5 (Madras) Sappers and Miners; 21 Punjab Infantry. Lines of communication troops; 2 Highland Light Infantry.

Samana 1897 (*2nd August — 2nd October, 1897*)

This bar, which is never found singly, was awarded to the garrisons beyond Kohat. The medals to the 36th Sikhs who defended Fort Gulistan, the gateway to the Afridi Hills, deserve special notice. The rare tribute of a special memorial at Amritsar was paid to the gallant defenders of Saragarhi, which consisted of a native officer and twenty Sikhs, who were all killed. The troops under Major-General Yeatman-Biggs, R.A., which formed the garrisons, as under, joined the Tirah Field Force on 2nd October, 1897.

12, 18 Bengal Lancers; two squadrons 3 Punjab Cavalry; 3, 9, 11 Field Batteries R.A.; No. 2 Mountain Battery R.A.; No. 2 Derajat Mountain Battery; No. 4 Company Bombay Sappers and Miners; 2 R.I. Regiment; 2 R. Scots Fusiliers; 5th North Fus; 1/ Northampton Rgt., 9th Norfolk Regt; 1 D.C.L.I.; 2, 5 Punjab Infantry; 3, 15, 36 Sikhs; 21 Madras Pioneers; 1/2, 1/3, 5 Gurkhas; Kurram Militia.

A medal is know to Pte. W. Reidy, I.R.I. Regiment, with this bar.

Tirah 1897-98 (*2nd October, 1897 — 6th April, 1898*)

This bar, never awarded singly, was awarded to the Tirah Expeditionary Force, which included the Kurram Column, Peshawur Column, and the Rawal Pindi Brigade. The troops on the lines of communication and those in the Swat Valley also received the award.

Tirah Field Force (Lieutenant-General Sir W. S. A. Lockhart, K.C.B., K.C.S.I.). 1st Division: 1st Brigade — 1 Devon; 2 Notts and Derbys; 1 Queen's; 2 Green Howards; 20 Bengal (Punjab) Infantry; 2/1 Gurkhas; No. 6 Brigade and 34 Native Field Hospital. 2nd Brigade — 1 Queen's; 2 Green Howards; 3 Sikhs; 2/4 Gurkhas; 28 Bombay Pioneers; Kapurthala Imperial Service Infantry; Nos. 8 and 14 British and 51 Native Field Hospitals. 1st Divisional troops: Two squadrons 18 Bengal Cavalry; No. 1 Mountain Battery R.A.; No. 1 (Kohat) Mountain Battery; No. 2 (Derajat) Mountain Battery; 3, 4 Companies Bombay Sappers and Miners; Maler Sappers and Miners; 28 Bombay Infantry (Pioneers); Nabha Imperial Service Infantry; No. 13 British and 63 Native Field Hospitals.

2nd Division: 3rd Brigade — 1 Dorsets; 1 Gordons; 1/Connaught Rgnrs (11); 15 Bengal (Sikh) Infantry; 1/2 Gurkhas; 24 British and 44 Native Field Hospitals. 4th Brigade — 2 K.O.S.B.; 1 Northants; 36 Bengal (Sikh) Infantry; 1/3 Gurkhas; sections of No. 9 and 23 British and No. 48 Native Field Hospitals.

2nd Divisional troops: Machine Gun Detachment of 16 Lancers; two squadrons 18 Bengal Lancers; 8, 9 Mountain Batteries R.A.; 5 Bombay Mountain Battery; Rocket Battery; 4 Company Madras Sappers and Miners; Sirmoor Sappers and Miners; 21 Madras Pioneers; Jhind Imperial Service Infantry; 13 British and 42 Native Field Hospitals.

Kurram Column (Colonel W. Hill): 6 Bengal Cavalry; 38, 39 Central India Horse; one troop of 3 Field Battery R.A.; 12 (Khelat) Bengal Infantry; 1/5 Gurkhas; Karpurthala Infantry; Nabha Infantry; "D" section of No. 46 British and all No. 62 Native Field Hospital.

Peshawur Column (Brigadier-General A. G. Hammond, V.C., C.B., D.S.O., A.D.C.): 9 Bengal Cavalry; 57 Field Battery R.A.; No. 3 Mountain Battery R.A.; No. 5 Company Bengal Sappers and Miners; 2 Ox. and Bucks.; 2 R. Inniskilling Fusiliers; 45 Sikhs; 9 Gurkhas; No. 5 British and No. 45 Native Field Hospitals.

Rawal Pindi Brigade (in reverse) (Brigadier-General C. R. Macgregor, D.S.O.); Jodhpur Imperial Service Lancers; 1 D.C.L.I.; 2 K.O.Y.L.I.; 27 Bombay Infantry; 2 Hyderabad Infantry; No. 12 British and No. 53 Native Field Hospitals.

Lines of communication troops (Lieutenant-General Sir A. P. Palmer, K.C.B.); 3, 18 Bengal Cavalry; 9 Field Battery R.A.; No. 1 Kashmir Mountain Battery; No. 1 Company Bengal Sappers and Miners; 39 Bengal Infantry; 2, 22 Punjab Infantry; 2/2 Gurkhas; Jodhpore and Gwalior Transport Corps; Ordnance, Engineer and Veterinary Services; Nos. 11, 25 British and 42, 47, 53, 64 Native Field Hospitals.

Swat Valley: 2 R. Sussex.

(The 1 R. Scots Fusiliers also received this bar, as did four officers and ten other ranks of the 2 Durham Light Infantry, six members of the 19th Hussars and 1 member of 2/Suffolk.)

Waziristan 1901-2 (*23rd November, 1901 — 10th March, 1902*)

This bar was authorized in 1903 to those engaged in the Mahsud and Waziri districts. As Queen Victoria died in 1901, the original medal had to be considerably altered. The obverse bears the head and shoulders of King Edward VII in field-marshal's uniform, wearing a coat, and the reverse has had the date "1895" removed. The medal is much thinner than the original issue, whilst the bronze medal is even thinner still.

Both the silver and bronze medals are named in thin running script.

This medal is rather scarce, and to find this bar on a Queen Victoria Medal is rare and would require careful verification. It should be noticed that only three Europeans, except, of course, British officers of Indian units, took part.

There was no expedition in the usually accepted term, but mobile columns were formed, as sort of counter-raids, against the Mahsuds in the Kabul Khel country. Major-General C. C. Egerton, C.B., formed four columns of all arms drawn from the following troops:

1, 2, 5 Punjab Cavalry; No. 2 (Gujerat) (Bengal) Mountain Batteries; 1, 2, 9, 27, 28, 29 Punjab Infantry; 3, 4, 35, 45 Sikhs; 17 Bengal Infantry; 9, 23, 24 Bombay Infantry; 38 Dogras; 23, 32 Pioneers; 13 Rajputs; 3 Gurkhas; North and South Waziri Militia, 43 Native Field Hospital. Three men of 1 Bn. Cheshire Regiment who were on H.Q. Staff also received this medal and a small number of R.E. officers.

(Medals are known to the 8th Mule Corps, 5th Punjab Infantry, and the Supply and Transport Corps.)

81 QUEEN'S SUDAN MEDAL, 1896-97

Obverse	The crowned half-length figure of Queen Victoria and the legend "VICTORIA REGINA ET IMPERATRIX."
Reverse	A very fine figure of Victory, who is seated, holding a palm branch in her right hand and laurel wreath in her left. At her feet is the word "SUDAN" on a plaque supported by three lilies. Behind her and on either side are the British and Egyptian flags. This is one of the most pleasing of all the reverses which include the figure of Victory.
Size	1.42in. diameter.
Ribbon	1.25in. wide. Left half yellow, right half black with a thin dividing stripe of red, $\frac{1}{16}$ in. wide.
Suspension	By a plain, straight suspender.
Designer	G. W. de Saulles.
Naming	This varies, as some are engraved in very neat sloping capitals, others in upright capitals, and many were issued unnamed. A few were impressed in thin Roman capitals and some in Arabic.
No. of bars issued	Nil.

It was awarded in 1899 to all the forces engaged in the reconquest of the Sudan; that means to those who took part in any of the first six actions for which the Khedive's Sudan Medal, which follows immediately, was given. The 21st Lancers who took part in the charge at Omdurman suffered 21 killed, their medals are, of course, more sought after.

It was awarded in silver and bronze.

82 KHEDIVE'S SUDAN MEDAL, 1896-1908

Obverse	An Arabic inscription which reads "ABBAS HILMI THE SECOND" with the Mohammedan year 1314. which is 1897 by our calendar.
Reverse	An oval shield bearing three stars and crescents in the centre and surrounded by lances and flags. The whole is superimposed on two crossed rifles and a cannon with a pyramid of six cannon balls. Beneath the whole is the Arabic inscription "THE RE-CONQUEST OF THE SUDAN, 1314."
Size	1.54in. diameter.
Ribbon	1.5in. wide. Yellow with a broad blue stripe down the centre symbolic of the Nile flowing through the desert.
Suspension	By a plain, straight suspender.
Designer	G. W. de Saulles.
Naming	Those issued to British troops are named in sloping capitals, those to Indian troops mostly in script, whilst those to native troops are named in Arabic. Most of the later issues were unnamed.
No. of bars issued	Fifteen. They were named in English and Arabic.

The London Office of the Sudan Government and the Public Relations Office, Khartoum, are to be thanked for the information they have given concerning the dates of the actions for which this medal was awarded and for much of the other information.

The medal, which is rare to British troops with more than two bars (*i.e.*, those for Atbara and Khartoum), was sanctioned by a special Egyptian Army Order on the 12th February, 1897, to commemorate the reconquest of the Dongola Province. It was to be worn on the *right* of the Khedive's Bronze Star. It was issued in both silver and bronze. Those who served at and south of Sarras between 30th March and 23rd September, 1896, or in Brigadier-General Egerton's Force at Suakin, between the same dates, received the silver medal without a bar, as did the crews of H.M.S. *Melita* (139) and *Scout* (149), a few Nile steamers and 'G' Co. R. Dublin Fus.

It has been awarded with as many as ten bars being 7in.long without riband (Firket, Hafir, Sudan 1897, Abu Hamed. The Atbara, Khartoum, Gedaref, Sudan 1899, Bahr-el-Ghazal 1900-02 and Nyam-Nyam), this is the greatest number of bars to any one campaign medal since the Military General Service Medal.

Firket (*7th June, 1896*)*

The first phase of the reconquest of the Sudan was the occupation of Dongola. On 2nd June, 1896, headquarters were established at Akasha, from which the advance was continued on 5th June towards Firket, where, on 7th June, 1896, the Emir Osman Azraq was defeated.On 2nd June, 1896, headquarter

Regiments present: Egyptian Cavalry; Camel Corps; 16 Eastern Division R.G.A.; 2 Company R.E.; 1 N. Staffs (18);† Connaught Rangers (7);† 2, 3, 4, 7, 8 Egyptian Infantry; 9, 10, 11, 12, 13 Sudanese Infantry.

---

*The Special Army Order of 12th February, 1897, and an Army Order of April, 1897, use the spelling "Ferket" throughout.

†Only the machine-gun sections of these two regiments were present.

Hafir (*19th – 26th September, 1896*)

After the Battle of Firket the advance continued and reached Kerma on 19th September, Merowe on 26th September, and Dongola on 15th October, 1896. Hafir is on the west bank of the Nile opposite Kerma, and it was here that the battle was fought. The bar was awarded to those who had taken part in the operations south of Fareig on 19th September, 1896.

Regiments present: 16 Eastern Division R.G.A.; Egyptian Artillery; Egyptian Cavalry; R.E.; R.A.M.C. (20); 1 N. Staffs (588); 1/Connaught Rangers (6); 1, 2, 3, 4, 5, 7, 8, 15 Egyptian Infantry; 9, 10, 11, 12, 13 Sudanese Infantry, also Capt. B. Y. McMahon, 1st R. Dgns.

H.M. gunboats: *Abu Klea, El Teb, Metemma, Tamai, Zafir.* Approx. 17 bars to the R.N.

Abu Hamed (*7th July, 1897*)

This bar was awarded to members of Major-General A. Hunter's Force which set out from Kassingar to capture Abu Hamed, which it did on 7th July, 1897.

Regiments present: 1 Troop Egyptian Cavalry; No. 2 Field Battery Egyptian Artillery 3, Egyptian Infantry; 9, 10, 11 Sudanese Infantry; Madras Sappers and Miners.

Sudan 1897 (*15th July – 6th November, 1897*)

This bar was not awarded for any particular action, but was given to those who had already received the medal and were south of Kerma and south of No. 6 Station between the 15th July and 6th November, 1897.

Regiments present: R. E.; Camel Corps; No. 2 Field Battery Egyptian Artillery; 3, 8 Egyptian Infantry; 9, 10, 11, 13 Sudanese Infantry; Royal Navy (14).

The Atbara (*8th April, 1898*)*

This bar, which it is rare to find singly, was awarded for the Battle of The Atbara fought against the Dervish army commanded by Emir Mahmoud.

Regiments present: Egyptian Cavalry and Camel Corps; 1 R. Warwicks; 1 Lincolnshire Regiment; 1 Seaforth; 1 Cameron Highlanders; 16 Battery, Eastern Division R.G.A.; 1, 2, 4, 5 Batteries Egyptian Artillery; 2, 3, 4, 7, 8 Egyptian Infantry; 9, 10, 11, 12, 13, 14 Sudanese Infantry; also H.S.H., Prince Francis of Teck, 1st R. Dgns. who received the medal with bars Hafir and Khartoum and 6 bars to the R.N.

Khartoum (*2nd September, 1898*)*

This bar was awarded for the Battle of Omdurman. Though the entry into Khartoum followed immediately, it is unusual to find a bar inscribed differently from the battle for which it was awarded. A similar case occurred after the Ashantee campaign of 1873, when a bar inscribed "COOMASSIE" was awarded for the action at Amoaful.

Regiments present: Four squadrons 21 Lancers (21 killed in the charge); Egyptian Cavalry and Camel Corps; 32 (159); 37 (71) Field Batteries R.F.A., detachment from 16 Eastern Division R.A.; 1, 2, 3, 4, 5 Field Batteries Egyptian Artillery; No. 2 Company R.A.; 2 R.E. (14); 1 Grenadier Guards; 1 R. Northumberland Fusiliers (approx. 60 without bars); 1 R. Warwicks; 1 Lincolnshire

---

*Medals are to be found to individuals with bars for either Atbara or Khartoum, and sometimes both. For instance, Bandsman J. Marriott, 1 Leicestershire Regiment, received a medal with both bars.

Regiment; 2 Lancashire Fusiliers; 1 Seaforth Highlanders; 1 Cameron Highlanders; 2 Rifle Brigade; and a machine-gun detachment of the Royal Irish Fusiliers (102); 1, 3, 4, part of 5, 7, 8, 15, 17, 18 Egyptian Infantry; 9, 10, 11, 12, 13, 14 Sudanese Infantry.

H.M. Gunboats: *Abu, Klea, El Teb, Fateh, Hafir, Melik, Metemmeh, Nazir, Saffiyeh, Sheikh, Sultan, Tamai, Zafir, Zapi.* Thirty-five bars to the R.N.

Gedaref (*7th September – 26th December, 1898*)

This bar was awarded to those who took part in the fighting in the Eastern Sudan against Ahmed Fedil, who had established himself at Gedaref. The operations lasted from 7th September, 1898, when Colonel Parsons left Kassala to occupy Gedaref, until 26th December, 1898, when Ahmed Fedil escaped by crossing the White Nile near Kosti.

Regiments present: Camel Corps; 16 Egyptian Infantry; 9, 10, 12, 14 Sudanese Infantry; twenty men of the Royal Irish Fusiliers with two machine-guns, R.A. (3); Medical Corps (2) and 495 Irregulars under 3 Sheikhs.

H.M. gunboats: *Dal, Hafir, Melik, Sheikh.* 9 bars to the R.M.A.

Gedid (*22nd November, 1899*)

Ahmed Fedil, after his escape from Gedaref, rejoined the Khalifa, who had been routed after the Battle of Omdurman. Though attempts had been made to bring these two to action they proved too elusive and it was not until 12th November, 1899, that they were again encountered. On this day the Khalifa attacked the gunboat *Sultan* opposite Aba Island. Sir Reginald Wingate, with 2,300 men, was sent out to catch him. On 22nd November, 1899, the enemy was defeated at Gedid. The Khalifa and Ahmed Fedil were both killed and the reconquest of the Sudan completed.

Regiments present: One troop Egyptian Cavalry; Camel Corps; 2 Field Battery Egyptian Artillery; 9, 13 Sudanese Infantry; one company of 2 Bn. Egyptian Infantry. 1 bar issued to the R.N.

Sudan 1899

This bar was awarded to all who served on the Blue and White Niles south of Khartoum during 1899, including six to the R.N. one being to Cmdr. H. Escombe.

Bahr-el-Ghazal 1900-02 (*13th December, 1900 – 28th April, 1902*)

This bar was awarded to five British and eleven native officers together with three hundred and fifty native troops for policing operations under Sparkes Bey. The bar was also awarded to Lieutenant Fell, R.N., and a few Naval ratings for services during November and December, 1900. All these operations took place in the Bahr-el-Ghazal Province.

Lieutenant-Colonel H. Gordon, C.B. C.M.G., received this bar and that for Nyam-Nyam. One bar was also awarded to the R.N.

Jerok (*January – March, 1904*)

This bar was awarded to the force under command of Miralai Gorringe Bey, C.M.G., D.S.O., which attacked the slave raider Ibrahim Wad Mahmud at Gebel Jerok on 11th February, 1904, and finally captured him on 3rd March, 1904. The force consisted of about eight hundred Sudanese Infantry, together with a machine-gun section. These operations took place on the Blue Nile near the Abyssinian border.

Nyam-Nyman (*January – May, 1905*)

This bar was awarded for the suppression of further trouble in the Bahr-el-Ghazal province, on the Belgian Congo border. On this occasion it was caused by the Nyam-Nyam tribe. A force under Boulnois Bey, composed of eighteen British and thirty native officers and about seven hundred men with five machine-guns, was sent to restore order. It was organized in January and withdrawn in May.

Talodi (*2nd – 15th June, 1905*)

This bar was awarded for the suppression of the Abu Rufas Rising in the Nuba Mountains. El Miralai O'Connell Bey, together with three hundred and eighty camelry and one hundred and fifty men of the 12th Sudanese Infantry, left el Obeid on 2nd June and reached Talodi on the 12th and finally stamped out the rising at Eliri on the 15th.

Katfia (*April, 1908*)

This bar was awarded for the suppression of the rebellion led by Mohammed Wad Habuba, who had styled himself Prophet Isa and avowed his intention of opposing British authority, After treacherously murdering officials who went to interview him, a small force was sent to round him up. He was captured and hanged.

Nyima (*1st – 21st November, 1908*)

This bar was awarded to members of the force under el Kaimakam Lempriere Bey which undertook a punitive expedition in the Nyima Hills. The force was drawn from the Camel Corps and the 10th and 15th Sudanese Infantry.

83 ASHANTI MEDAL (31st March – 25th December, 1900)

Obverse	The bust of King Edward VII with the legend "EDWARDUS VII, REX IMPERATOR."
Reverse	The British Lion facing left and standing on a rock, below which are a native shield and two assegais. Below this again a scroll with the word "ASHANTI" thereon. To the left is the rising sun.
Size	1.42 in. diameter.
Ribbon	3/5 in. wide. Black with two dark green stripes Tin. wide.
Suspension	By a straight suspender.
Designer	G. W. de Saulles.
Naming	Impressed in rather small square capitals.
No. of bars issued	One – for Kumassi.

This medal, the first awarded in the reign of Edward VII, was sanctioned in October, 1901, to be awarded to all who had taken part in the suppression of the Ashanti Rising between 31st March and 25th December, 1900.

The medals are to be found in both high and low relief. They were awarded in silver and bronze.

After the rising in 1895 (for which the Ashantee Star was awarded) there had been comparative peace but no lack of ill-feeling.

One of the native chiefs possessed the "Golden Stool", which was regarded by the natives an a sign of authority. It was decided, therefore, that this stool should be captured. Captain Armitage set off with a small force to find it, and was attacked. Wind of the intention of this force soon got round among the natives, who rose in rebellion. They invested the Governor and his wife, Sir Frederick and Lady Hodgson, in Kumassi. Captain Middlemist, with a force of about fifty men, broke through on 15th April, and Captain Aplix with another on the 17th. Major Morris, with two hundred and thirty reinforcements, got through on 15th May, by which time the situation in Kumassi had become very serious through starvation, disease and casualties.

On 23rd June Sir Frederick and Lady Hodgson, with a force of six hundred under Major Morris and over a thousand non-combatants, left Kumassi. Captains Bishop and Ralph were left behind with a garrison of about a hundred men.

A relief force, under Brigadier-General Sir W. J. Willcocks, K.C.M.G., relieved the town on 28th July. Leaving a small garrison, he took the worst of the sick and wounded back to Bekwai. A further relief force, under Colonel A. P. Burroughs, relieved Kumassi on 7th August.

There was much more fighting until the chiefs surrendered in December.

The Boer War was at its height at this time, so that no European troops could be spared. There were, of course, European officers and a few European N.C.Os. The medals to the latter are found named with their parent units. The actual number of soldiers employed in the campaign was about 3,400. The rest of the force was made up of carriers and local levies. One doctor, and there were probably more, received the medal, though not a member of the forces at the time.

The nature of the fighting and the general conditions involved in this little-known campaign are well illustrated by the casualty returns. These show a total of no fewer than sixty-two white officers and eight hundred natives during the nine months.

Kumassi (31st March – 15th July, 1900)

This bar was awarded to all who had garrisoned Kumassi at any time between 31st March and 15th July, and to those who were members of either of the relieving columns under Brigadier-General Willcocks or Colonel Burroughs.

The troops engaged in the operations, not all of whom received the bar, were:

The H.Q. staff consisted of British officers, civilian doctors and political officers. The fighting troops were as follows: Four 75 mm guns W.A.F.F.; Four 7 pdr. guns W.I.R.; 4 Companies each of 1 and 2 W.A.F.F.; 2 Coys. Southern Nigeria Regt.; 6 Coys. W. Africa Regt.; ½ Bn. each of 1 and 2 Central African Regt.;* Gold Coast Constabulary (700); Lagos Constabulary (300); Sierra Leone Frontier Police (50); Lagos Hausa Force, Lt. H. B. Cooke, The Lincolnshire Regt.; Capt. R. M. Stallard, Bedfordshire Regt., Lieut. T. D. Pottinger, Royal Irish Fusiliers received medals without bars and the Munster Fus. (8 no bar and 1 with bar).

About 900 carriers were employed, all of whom received a bronze medal. There were also numerous levies who may have got them too.

A total of 135 white officers and 35 N.C.Os. received the silver medal, as did three native officers.

A medal with this bar was awarded to the 45th Sikhs. The recipient was serving with the Central African Rifles at the time. Sixty Sikhs took part in the campaign, but we do not know how all their medals were named.

*On 1st January, 1902, the title was altered to the King's African Rifles.

260

Obverse	The crowned and veiled head of Queen Victoria and legend "VICTORIA REGINA ET IMPERATRIX."
Reverse	Britannia with a flag in her left hand and holding out a laurel wreath towards an advancing party of soldiers. In the background are two men-of-war. Around the top are the words "SOUTH AFRICA."
Size	1.42 in. diameter.
Ribbon	1.25 in. wide. Red with two blue stripes and a broad orange one down the centre.
Suspension	By a straight suspender.
Designer	G. W. de Saulles.
Naming	Generally in indented block or sloping capitals. Some including those to officers and certain units were engraved in different styles.
No. of bars issued	Twenty-six.

There were two different strikings of this medal, which was awarded for services during the Boer War.

The first striking can be easily distinguished, because in it the wreath of Britannia points to the "R" in Africa, whereas in the second it points to the "F".

The campaign has been so written about that we will refrain from any historical notes.

Its probable duration was grossly underestimated, because the first issues bore the dates 1899-1900 on the reverse in *raised* figures. Lord Strathcona's Horse was the only unit to receive a limited number of the dated medals as orignally struck. They went home to Canada via London as a complete unit before the war ended and fifty medals with raised dates were awarded by Edward VII at Buckingham Palace. However these 50 medals were issued without bars, the bars were sent out to Canada at a later date and affixed privately. Approx. 3,750 of the normal type with erased dates were issued later to Canadian units.

After the mistake had been realized the dates were removed from the medals before any further issues were made, but on many medals ghost dates can still be seen. Approx. 177,000 of these are thought to have been struck.

The maximum number of bars to any one medal is nine to the Army; and eight to the Navy (see table of R.N. medals). Naval medals with more than four bars are scarce.

Five of what were termed "State" bars were awarded, namely: Cape Colony, Natal, Rhodesia, Orange Free State, and Transvaal. These were given for service in the various states in which so many small actions were fought that it would have been impossible to have recognized each with a bar. The bars for Cape Colony and Natal could not both be gained by one recipient.

The names of every colonial and local unit will be omitted from each bar except on occasions when they formed the major portion of the force engaged, and these remarks also apply to artillery, engineers and other anciliary units.

The rarest bar is that for the Defence of Mafeking, and then come those for Wepener, Defence of Kimberley, and Rhodesia. All the other bars are very common.

This medal is found unnamed, renamed, with added or subtracted bars, spurious bars, bars in wrong order, complete set of incorrect bars for regiment, wrong combination of bars, and, of course, with more than one of these defects. However as most of the medals in the past attracted very little above their silver value it is unlikely that any alteration of bars or renaming was done with the purpose of deceiving collectors. Dated bars were often issued after the original medal had been awarded which could explain why these bars are often found on the Q.S.A. medals with unoffical or crude rivets or even sown on.

The medal was awarded without bars to troops who guarded Boer prisoners on the island of St. Helena, nurses, members of St. John Ambulance Brigade, some naval personnel, and civilians whose work furthered the war efforts, though they took no part in the fighting.

Bronze medals* without bars were given to local natives, Indian troops, and members of the West India Regiments. (I know of a medal to the 3 W.I.R.) No bars were given with them. Medals have been heard of which were issued to white men, many of whom saw considerable service, who did not attest and yet drew the pay of their ranks. These men, probably freelance soldiers or soldiers of fortune, who did not mind fighting but resented any form of contract and wished to be able to get away as soon as the fighting died not come up to their standard, or ceased altogether, or they got bored.

From the point of view of modern war there were a few interesting events which may be worth noting.

Balloons were used for observation purposes both in the defence and relief of Ladysmith.

It would have been interesting to have seen the march, or ride, past of the Photographic Section, which consisted of one officer and one N.C.O. mounted on bicycles. They were most valuably employed with the 1st Cavalry Division on panoramic photography, which was then in its infancy.

Wireless telegraphy was attempted but abandoned as a failure. It is strange to note that the only experiments made seem to have been with equipment captured when on its way to Kruger.

Many will remember the admirable hospital trains in the 1914-18 war. A train, subscribed for by the residents of Windsor, was sent out to South Africa. It was named "The Princess Christian."

The United States fitted out, and supplied free, the hospital ship *Maine.* This was, therefore, the first war in which donations from civilians supplied medical and other comforts to the troops on anything like a large scale. One does not, of course, forget the many individual efforts in the Crimea, Mutiny and Zulu Wars. Whilst on the subject of "Private Enterprise" we might mention that Lord Strathcona raised and equipped the Strathcona Horse entirely at his own expense.

To Colonel Morgan, well known as a medal roll researcher who has supplied much useful information, must go the credit for starting what became known as the Field Force Canteen, in the 1914-18 War the Expeditionary Force Canteen and now, of course, the N.A.A.F.I.

The following units and ships were present:*

Royal Horse Artillery Batteries: "A," "G," "I." "J," "M." "O." "P." "Q." "R." "T." "U."

Royal Field Artillery Batteries: 2, 4, 5, 7, 8, 9, 13, 14, 17, 18, 19, 20, 21, 28, 37, 38, 39, 42, 43, 44, 53, 61, 62, 63, 64, 65, 66, 67, 68, 69, 73, 74, 75, 76, 77, 78, 79, 81, 82, 83, 84, 85, 86, 87, 88.

Royal Garrison Artillery Companies: Eastern Division — 5, 6, 10 Companies;

*A bronze medal is known to Pte. G. Harvey of the 20th Hussars, but we are unable to say why such a medal should have been awarded to him unless he had left the service after the Egyptian Campagin for which he received the silver medal and bronze Khedive's Star. These bronze medals were struck from the dies used for the second striking, i.e. the wreath points to the "F" in Africa. The recipient's name and regiment is indented in capitals on the edge when awarded to non Indian troops and in running script to Indians.

*For Canadian units see War Medals and Decorations of Canada by Prof. Ross W. Irwin.

Western Division — 2, 6, 10, 14, 15, 17, 23 Companies; Southern Division — 14, 15, 16, 36 Companies.

Pom-pom Sections: A, B, C, D, E, F, G, H, J, K, L, M, N, O, P, Q, R, S, V, X, Z, A/A, B/B, C/C, D/D, E/E, F/F, G/G, H/H, J/J, K/K, L/L,.

Mountain Batteries: 4, 10.

Additional Artillery: Cape Garrison; Cape Mounted Rifles; Diamond Fields Horse; Duke of Edinburgh's Own Volunteer; Elswick Volunteer Battery; Honourable Artillery Company (1 Battery); Natal Naval, Natal Volunteer; New South Wales; New Zealand; Prince Alfred's Own Cape Arty; Queensland; Rhodesian; Royal Canadian; South Australian; Tasmanian; Victoria; Western Australia.

Royal Engineers; Army Service Corps; Royal Army Medical Corps; Ordanance Corps; Veterinary and Pay Corps.

Mounted units: Almost every county in the British Isles supplied yeomanry units, and many of them cyclist battalions as well.

In addition to the above, there were the City Imperial Volunteers, 5,363 strong, which included two companies of cyclists.

It must be remembered that small numbers of volunteers were called for from the infantry regiments of the Regular Army to form mounted units, which accounts for the appearance of such titles as the Loyal North Lancs Mounted Infantry, to give only one example; medals to these units are scarce.

90 silver medals to officers of the Indian Army, some with bars; 817 bronze medals to O.Rs. Indian Army, all with no bars; 215 silver medals to S & T Corps; 3,500 bronze medals to S and T Corps.

At the request of many collectors, a list of the units is given, other than those from the British Isles, that served in the South African War, however this list is by no means complete (see later list of Town Guards).

Ashburner's Light Horse; Bayly's Horse; Bechuanaland Rifles; Beddy's Scouts; Bethune's Mounted Infantry; Border Horse; Border Mounted Police; Border Mounted Rifles; Border Scouts; Brabant's Horse (1st and 2nd); British South Africa Police; Burma Mounted Infantry; Bushmen Borderers; Bushveld Rifles; Cameron's Scouts; Canadian Contingent; Cape Cavalry Brigade; Cape Colony Cyclist Corps; Cape Medical Staff Corps; Cape Mounted Police; Cape Mounted Rifles; Cape Police; Cape Railway Sharpshooters; Cape Special Police; Cape Town Highlanders; Cape Volunteer Bearer Company; Ceylon Contingent; Ceylon Mounted Infantry; Clifford's Scouts; Colesburg Mounted Rifle Club; Colonial Defence Force; Colonial Light Horse; Colonial Scouts; Colonical Volunteer Corps; Composite Regiment Mounted Infantry (mostly men from home mounted infantry units); Commander-in-Chief's Bodyguard; Cullinan's Horse; Damant's Horse (formerly Rimington's Guides); Dennison's Scouts; Diamond Fields Horse; District Military Police (these took the name of their districts); District Mounted Troops (these took the name of their districts, such as Modder River District Mounted Rifles, Vryburg Mounted Rifles, etc.); Divisional Scouting Corps; Driscoll's Scouts; Duke of Edinburgh's Own Volunteer Rifles; Durban Light Infantry; East Griqualand Mounted Rifle Volunteers; Eastern Province Horse; Eastern Transvaal Scouts (these were native scouts in Colonel Benson's Column); Engcobo Mounted Rifle Club; French's Scouts; Frontier Light Horse; Frontier Mounted Rifles; Gatacre's Scouts; Gorringe's Fighting Scouts; Gough's Mounted Infantry; Grahamstown (1st City) Volunteers; Griqualand Mounted Rifle Volunteers; Harrismith Light Horse; Heidelburg Volunteers; Heidelburg Scouts; Herschel Mounted Volunteers; Herschel Native Police; Imperial Bushmen; Imperial Light Horse (1st and 2nd); Imperial Light Infantry; Imperial Railway Volunteer Corps; Imperial Yeomanry Scouts; Johannesburg Mounted Rifles; Kaffrarian Rifles; Kenny's Scouts; Kimberley Regiment; Kimberley Light Horse; Kimberley Mounted Corps; Kimberley Mounted Rifles; Kimberley Volunteers (or Kimberely Volunteer Regiment); Kitchener's Fighting Scouts (1st and 2nd); Kitchener's Horse; Komgha Mounted Volunteers; Knysna Rangers; Le Gros Scouts; Loch's Horse; Loxton's Horse; Loyal Farmers' Light Horse; Lumsden's Horse (250); Maclean's Scouts; Malta Mounted Infantry; Maritzani Mounted Irregulars; Marshall's Horse; Matatiele District Defence Force; Menné's Scouts; Midland Mounted Rifles; Montmorency's Scouts; Morley's Scouts; Mounted Pioneers; Murray's Horse; Namaqualand Border Scouts (natives); Natal Bridge Guards; Natal Carbineers; Natal Guides; Natal Hotchkiss Detachment; Natal Police (mounted and dismounted); Natal Mounted Rifles; Natal Royal Rifles; Natal Naval Volunteers; Natal Composite Regiment; National Scouts; Nesbitt's Horse; New England Mounted Rifles; New Zealand Contingent; Orange River Colony Volunteers; Orpen's Horse; Pietersburg Light Horse (formerly Bushveld Rifles) Prince Alfred's Own Volunteer Guards; Prince of Wales's Light Horse; Protectorate Regiment; Queensland Contingent; Queentown Rifle Volunteers; Railway Pioneers Regiment; Rand Rifles; Rhodesian Field Force; Rhodesian Regiment; Rimington's Guides (subsequently Damant's Horse) Roberts's Horse (originally Warren's, then 2nd South Africa Light Horse); Royal Canadian Regiment; Royal Horse Artillery Mounted Rifles (in the latter stages of the war the artillery was reduced, and the men thus released were formed into mounted riflemen. A few colonials were included); Rundle's Scouts; Scottish Horse; Scott's Railway Guards; South African Constabulary; South African Mounted Irregular Forces; South African Light Horse; South African Mounted Infantry; South Rhodesian Volunteers; Steinaecker's Horse; Stellenbosch Mounted Infantry (a unit of the South African Light Horse); Strathcona's Horse*: Struben's Scouts; Swaziland Police; Swellendam Mounted Infantry; Tembuland Mounted Rifle Club; Tempest's Scouts; Thorneycroft's Mounted Infantry; Transkei Mounted Rifles; Transvaal Mounted Infantry; Tucker's Scouts; Uitenhage Mounted Infantry; Uitenhage Volunteer Rifles; Umvoti Mounted Rifles; Utrecht Mounted Rifles; Utrecht-Vryheid Mounted Police; Victorian Contingent (which included Mounted Infantury and Bushmen); Vryburg Mounted Rifles; Warren's Light Horse, which later became 2nd South Africa Light Horse, which became Robert's Horse); Warren's Mounted Infantury; Warren's Scouts; Warwick's Scouts; Western Light Horse; Western Province Mounted Rifles; Wodehouse Yeomanry; Xalanga Mounted Rifles; Younghusband's Horse.

Approx. strength of the 57 Australian Units in South Africa which comprised 15,500 O.Rs. and 840 officers:

New South Wales

N.S.W. Lancers	170
1st Australian Horse (1st Contingent)	34
1st Australian Horse (2nd Contingent)	107
"A" Battery R.A.A.	177
1st N.S.W. M.R.	405
N.S.W. Citizen Bushmen	525
Imperial Bushmen	762
2nd N.S.W. M.R.	995
3rd N.S.W. M.R.	997
3rd N.S.W. Imp. Bushmen (this unit was formed in South Africa, 230 men plus 200 Riverina Bushmen)	
1st Australian Comm. Horse	375
3rd Australian Comm. Horse No active service	371
5th Australian Comm. Horse	

*16 medals known with raised reverse dates.

(Obverse)
All issues

(Reverse)
(Matabeleland 1893 Medal)

(Reverse)
Undated Medal

No. 75. The British South Africa Company's Medals, 1890-7.

(Obverse)
(First issue)

(Reverse)
(Second issue)

(Reverse)

No. 76. The Central Africa Medal, 1891-8.

No. 77. The East and Central Africa Medal, 1897-99.

(Reverse)*

No. 79. The Third China War Medal,
1900.

(Reverse)
First issue

(Obverse)

No. 80. The Maharajah of Jummoo and
Kashmir's Medal, 1895.
(Page 252)

(Obverse)
First issue

(Obverse)
Second issue

No. 80. The India Medal, 1895-1902.

* Reference should be made to page 425 for medals with identical obverses.

South Australia

1st M.R. Contingent	126
2nd M.R. Contingent	119
3rd Bushmens Contingent	99
4th Imperial Bushmen Contingent	234
5th Imperial Contingent	316
6th Imperial Contingent	316
2nd Battalion Australian Comm. Horse	171
4th Battalion Australian Comm. Horse (No active service)	120
8th Battalion Australian Comm. Horse	245

West Australia

1st Mounted Infantry Contingent	130
2nd Mounted Infantry Contingent	103
3rd Bushmen Contingent	116
4th Mounted Infantry Contingent	127
5th Mounted Infantry Contingent	221
6th Mounted Infantry Contingent	228
2nd Battalion Australian Comm. Horse	60
4th Battalion Australian Comm. Horse	120
8th Battalion Australian Comm. Horse	120

Tasmania

1st Tasmanian Contingent	80
1st Tasmanian Contingent (Draft)	47
2nd Tasmanian Bushmen	54
3rd (First Tasmanian Imp. Contingent)	122
4th (2nd Imp. Bushmen)	253
1st Battalion Australian Comm. Horse (Tasmanian ½ Unit)	62
3rd Battalion Australian Comm. Horse (Tasmanian Unit)	121
8th Battalion Australian Comm. Horse (Tasmanian Unit)	120

Queensland

1st Queensland Mounted Infantry	262
2nd Queensland Mounted Infantry	154
3rd Queensland Mounted Infantry	316
4th Queensland Imp. Bushmen	384
5th Queensland Imp. Bushmen	529
6th Queensland Imp. Bushmen	401
Draft	78
Draft	21
1st Australian Comm. Horse (Queensland Unit)	123
3rd Australian Comm. Horse	122
7th Australian Comm. Horse.	490

Victoria

1st Victoria Mounted Infantry Co.	252
2nd Victoria Mounted Rifles	265
3rd Bushmens Contingent	276
4th Imperial Contingent	629
5th Mounted Rifles Contingent	1,037
2nd Battalion Australian Comm. Horse	372
6th Battalion Australian Comm. Horse	489

New Zealand

1st Contingent.	215
2nd Contingent	258
3rd Contingent	264
4th Contingent	466
5th Contingent	595
6th Contingent	578
7th Contingent	600
8th Contingent	1196
9th Contingent	1076
10th Contingent	1168

List of 110 South African Town Guard units awarded medals. (Some of these units whave already been mentioned in the previous list.)

The numbers claimed are shown in brackets but it would appear likely that a fairly large percentage was later returned to the issuing authorities.

Aberdeen (50); Adelaide (70); Albany (50); Alexandria (25); Alice (60); Alicedale (170); Aliwal North (70); Barberton (140); Barkly East (50); Barkly West (85); Beaconsfield; Beaufort West; Bedford (1350: Bethulie (43); Bluecliff and Glenconnor (12); Boshof (18); Brandfort (22) Britstown (35); Burgersdorp (205); Cala (120); Campbell (30); Carnarvon (29); Cathcart (80); Ceres (80); Clanwilliam (35); Colesberg (130); Cookhouse (100); Cradock (440); Cyphergat (75); Danielskuil (26); Darling (11); De-Aar (5); Dordrecht (85); Douglas (50); Dundee (195); Durban Road (23); East London; Edenberg (55); Farmer; Fauresmith (10); Fort Beaufort (59); Fraserberg (26); Fraserberg Road; George (110); Graaf Reinet (266); 1st Grahamstown (41); 2nd Grahamstown (127); Griquatown (37); Hanover (54); Hopetown (29); Hoppesia; Humansdorp (68); Indve (137); Jagersfontein (77); Jamestown (40); Jansenville; Kimberley (2,594); Keindes (4); Kenhardt (50); King Williams Town (329); Klerksdorp (118); Klipdam (11); Kynsna (154); Kokstad (145); Komgha (32); Kuruman (21); Ladybrand (8); Ladygrey (108); Ladysmith; Laingsberg; Mafeking (513); Malmesbury; Maraisberg (17); Middleburg (100); Middleton (36); Molteno (74); Montagu (32); Mossel Bay (118); Naauwpoopt (129); Namaqualand (240); Newcastle (243); Niger River (75); Oudtshoorn (233); Oumbu; Paarl (27); Pearston (14); Petrusville (52); Pietersburg (12); Piquetberg (23); Port Elizabeth (562); Port Nolloth (22); Potchef Stroon (63); Prieska (56); Prince Albert (45); Prince Albert Road; Queenstown (331); Richmond (70); Riversdale (68); Robertson; Rosmead (38); Salt River Works; Sandflats; Somerset East (186); Springbokfontein (12); Starkstroom; Steynsburg (68); Steytlerville (100); Stormburg; Sutherland (26); Swallendam (55); Swallendam Railway (35); Tarkastad (134); Touws River; Tsome (15); Towfre (137); Uuitenhage (893); Upington (4); Victoria West (42); Vryburg (212); Warrenton (55); Wellington (106); Willowmore (109); Windsorton and Wedburg (74); Worcester (153); Zeerust (46).

List of 68 South African District Mounted Troops (D.M.T.) awarded medals.

Aberdeen (100); Adelaide (90); Albany (480, including a few Cape C. bars); Alexandria; Aliwal North (5); Baca (42); Beaufort West; Bedford (135); Burgersdorp (90); Cala (30); Caledon (62); Carnarvon (60); Cathcart (190); Christiana (30); Colesberg (75); East London (300); Elsies River Troop (14); Fort Beaufort (106); Fraserberg (26); Fraserberg Road (20); Graaf Reinet (145); Green River (29); Harrismith (99); Hawick (30); Hay (11); Hex River (23); Highland (15); Hopefield (46); Houw Hoek (26); Humansdorp (107); Indve (19); Jansenville (200); Karkloop (15); Kei Road (36); King William Town (135); Koffy (30);

Komgha; Krom River (18); Kruisfontein (1); Kynsna (36); Ladysmith (47); Laingsberg; Lidgetton (25); Mafeking (66); Malmesbury (89); Malmesbury Police (12); Malbon (22); Matjesfontein (46); Melmoth (17); Middleburg (18); Modder River (3); Montagu (27); Mosita Squadron (59); Mossel Bay (40); Mtshate (14); Naauwpoopt (128); New Hudson (20); Nottingham Road (41); Oudtshoorn (140); Paarl (278); Peddie (251); Piquetsberg (22); Port Elizabeth (80); Prince Albert (60); Prince Albert Road; Queenstown (230); Riversdale (46); Robertson (67); Sandflats (66); Sir Lowry's Pass (15); Somerset East (197); Stellenbosch (84); Steytlerville (117); Storkensheim (76); Stutterheim; Sutherland (38); Swallendam (42); Uitenhage (264); Uniondale (37); Victoria East (139); Warhburg (72); Warrenton (50); Wellington (91); Willowmore (64); Windsorton and Wedburg (105); Worcester (99).

It should be noted that the following units were raised at home: Duke of Cambridge's Own Yeomanry (raised by Lord Donoughmore); Lovat's Scouts (raised by Lord Lovat); Paget's Horse (raised by Mr. George Paget); The Roughriders (raised by Lord Latham).

Cape Colony (*11th October, 1899 — 31st May, 1902*)

Issued to all troops in Cape Colony at any time between 11th October, 1899 and 31st May, who recieve no clasp for an action already specified in the Cape Colony, nor the "Natal" clasp.

Regiments present: 1, 2 Life Guards; Royal Horse Guards; 1, 2, 3, 6, 7 Dragoon Guards; 1 Royal Dragoons; 2, 6 Dragoons; 4. 7, 8, 10, 14, 19 Hussars; 5, 9, 16, 17 Lancers; 1, 2, 3 Foot Guards; 1, 2, 3, 4, 5, 6, 7, 8, 9, 10, 12, 13, 14, 15, 16, 17, 18, 19, 20, 22, 23, 24, 25, 26, 27, 28, 29, 30, 31, 32, 33, 34, 35, 37, 38, 39, 40, 41, 43, 44, 45, 47, 50, 57, 58, 60, 62, 63, 64, 65, 66, 68, 71, 73, 75, 78, 79, 83, 85, 87, 88, 91, 100, 101, (1991), 102 (2,476) Foot; Rifle Brigade. Approx. 2,670 to Canadian units. *New South Wales Units:* "A" Bty. R. Australian Arty.; Imperial Bushmen; 3rd Imperial Bushmen. *S. Australian Units:* 1st and 2nd M.R. Contg; 3rd Bushmen Contg.; 4th Imp. Bushmen; 5th and 6th Imp. Bushmen; 2nd Bn. Aust. Comm. Horse. *Western Australian Units:* 1st and 2nd Mounted Inf. Contgs.; 3rd Bushmen Contg. *Tasmanian Units;* 2nd Tasmanian Contg.; 2nd Tasmanian Bushmen; 1st Tasmanian Imp. Contg.; 2nd Imp. Bushmen. *Queensland Units;* 1st, 2nd and 3rd Queensland Mtd. Infy.; 4th and 5th Queensland Imp. Bushmen. *Victoria Units:* 2nd Victoria Mtd. Rifles; 3rd Bushmen Contg.; 4th Imp. Contg.; 5th Victorian Mtd. Rifles. *New Zealand:* 1, 2, 3, 4, 5, 6, 7 and 8th Contingents.
H.M. ships: See analysis pages 273-5.

Natal (*11th October, 1899-17th May, 1900*)

Granted to all troops in Natal at any time between 11th October, 1899 and 11th June, 1900, both dates inclusive, who receive no clasp for an action in Natal nor the Cape Colony clasp as already specified.

Regiments present: 5 Dragoon Guards; 5, 9 Lancers; 14 Hussars (H.Q., B and C Squadrons); 2, 11, 17, 20 (50); 27, 28, 31, 63, 88, 102 (25); 103 (111) Foot. Strathcona's Horse; 5th and 6th W. Australian Mtd. Inf.
H.M. ships: See analysis pages 273-5.

Rhodesia (*11th October, 1899 — 17th May, 1900*)

Authorised for all troops under the command of Lt. Gen. Sir F. Carrington and Col. Plumer in Rhodesia, between 11th October, 1899 and 17th May, 1900, both dates inclusive, who receive no clasp for the relief of Mafeking.
Regiments present: 10 Mtn. Bty. R.G.A.; "C" Battery Royal Canadian

Artillery; Rhodesia Regiment; Southern Rhodesian Volunteers; 65th (Leicestershire) Company 17th Battalion Imperial Yeomanry; British South African Police; New Zealand Mounted Rifles, 1, 3, 4, 5 and 7th New Zealand Contingents; 18 Imperial Yeomanry; Umvoti Volunteers; Menne's Scouts and Canadian Units. N.S.W. Citizen Bushmen; N.S.W. Imp. Bushmen; 3rd S. Australian Bushmen; 4th S. Australian Imp. Bushmen; 3rd W. Australian Bushmen; 2nd Tasmanian Bushmen; 3rd Queensland Mtd. Inf.; 4th Queensland Imp. Bushmen; 3rd Victoria Bushmen Contg.; 4th Victorian Imp. Contg.

H.M. ships: See analysis pages 273-5.

Relief of Mafeking (*17th May, 1900*)

Issued to all troops under the command of Colonel Mahon, who marched from Barkly West on 4th May, 1900, and to all troops who were under Colonel Plumber's command between 11th October, 1899 and 17th May, 1900, both dates inclusive, and who were south of an east and west line drawn through Palachwe.

Regiments present: Kimberley Light Horse; Imperial Light Horse; Damant's Horse; 2 sections of "M" Battery R.H.A.; "F" section of pom-poms and "C" section R. Can. Arty.; Rhodesia Regiment; Kimberley Mounted Corps; South Rhodesian Volunteers; 100 men from Barton's Fusilier Brigade (composed of men from the 2 Royal Fusiliers, 2 R. Scots Fusiliers, 1 R. Welch Fusiliers and 2 R. Irish Fusiliers); N. S. W. Citizen Bushmen; 3rd Queensland Mtd. Infantry.

Defence of Kimberley (*15th October, 1899-15th February, 1900*)

Issued to all troops in the garrison of Kimberley between 14th October, 1899 and 15th February, 1900, both dates inclusive.

Regiments present: Cape Mounted Police (488); Kimberley Light Horse (427); Loyal North Lancs Mounted Infantry (22); 23rd Company Western Division R.A. (94); R.E. (51); A.S.C. (9); Loyal North Lancs Regiment (422); Kimberley Town Guard (1,439); Diamond Field Volunteers (84); Kimberely Regiment and about 1,000 members of neighbouring Town Guards — 88 Officers (13 British and 75 Colonial) were awarded the bar. No women received the bar. The rarest combination of bars is probably Defence of Kimberley and Paardeberg (110).

H.M.S. See analysis pages 273-5.

Talana (*30th October, 1899*)

Granted to all troops under Lt. Gen. Sir W. Penn Symon's command on 20th October, 1899, who were north of an east and west line drawn through Waschbank Station. These bars are very rare to S. African units.

Regiments present: 18 Hussars; 13, 67, 69 R.F.A.; 1/17, 1/60, 87, 103 (855) Foot, Dundee Town Gd., Dundee Rifle Assoc. Natal Police.

Enlandslaagte (*21st October, 1899*)

Issued to all troops at Elandslaagte on 21st October, 1899, who were on the right bank of the Sunday river and north of an east and west line through Buys Farm.

Regiments present: 5 Dragoon Guards; 5 Lancers; 21, 42 R.F.A.; 1/11, 63, 92 Foot, I.L.H.

This bar was not awarded as well as that for Natal to the same recipient.

Defence of Ladysmith (*3rd November, 1899-28th February, 1900*)

Authorized for all troops in Ladysmith between 3rd November, 1899 and 28th February, 1900, both dates inclusive.

Regiments present: 5 Dragoons; 5 Lancers; 11 (Pte. W. S. Wolfe); 18, 19, Hussars; Natal Carbineers; Natal Mounted Police; Natal Mounted Rifles; Border Mounted Rifles; Imperial Light Horse; 13, 21, 42, 53, 67, 69 Bsyyrtird R.F.A.; No. 10 Mountain Battery; 2 guns Natal Hotchkiss Detachment; 8, 11, 16 (24). 17, 28 (½ Bn.) 1/60, 2/60, 63, 87 (½ Bn.), 92, 2nd Bn. The Rifle Brigade; R. Dublin Fus. (45); 23rd Field Company R.E.; A Balloon and Telegraph Section R.E.; Army Service Corps and Army Ordanance Department; about 250 members of the Ladysmith Town Guard.

H.M. ships see analysis pages 273-5.

Belmont (*23rd November, 1899*)

Awarded to all troops under Lt. Gen. Lord Methuen's command who were north of Witteputs (exclusive), on 23rd November, 1899, however the bar is rare to S. African units.

Regiments present: 9 Lancers; 18, 75 R.F.A.; New South Wales Lancers; 2nd S. Australian Mtd. R; 2nd W. Australian Mtd. Infantry; 1st Tasmanian Contg.; 1st Queensland Mtd. Infantury; 1, 2, 3 Foot Guards; 1/5, 47, 58, 85, 101 (239), 105 Foot; Rimington's Guides, Kitcheners F.S., Cape Medical Staff Corps., Imperial Light Horse, D.E.O.V.R.

H.M. ships: See analysis pages 273-5.

Modder River (*28th November, 1899*)

Granded to all troops under Lt. Gen. Lord Methuen's command who were north of Honey Nest Kloof (exclusive), and south of the Magersfontein ridge (exclusive) on 28th November, 1899.

Regiments present: 9 Lancers: 18, 62, R.F.A.; 1, 2, 3 Foot Guards; 5, 47, 58, 71, 85, 91 101 (75), 105 Foot; N.S.W. Lancers; 1st Australian Horse, Damant's Horse, Rimington's Guides, Kitcheners F.S., Cape Medical Staff Corps., Imperial Light Horse, D.E.O.U.R.

H.M. ships: See analysis pages 273-5.

Tugela Heights (*14th − 27th February, 1900*)

Granted to all troops of the Natal Field Force, exclusive of the Ladysmith garrison, employed in the operations north of an east and west line through Chieveley Station between 14th and 27th February, 1900, both dates inclusive.

Regiments present: 1 The Royal Dragoons; 13, 14, Hussars; 2, 4, 7, 11, 14, 18, 20, 21, 23, 26, 27, 31, 34, 39, 40, 57, 60, 65, 68, 87, 88, 89, 101, 103 Foot (1, 262); The Rifle Brigade; "D" Coy. 6th Mounted Infantury.

H.M. ships: See analysis pages 273-5.

Relief of Kimberley (*15th February, 1900*)

Issued to all troops in the relief column under Lt. Gen. French who marched from Klip Drift on 15th February, 1900, and all the 6th Division under Lt. Gen. Kelly-Kenny who were within 7,000 yds. of Klip Drift on 15th February. Rare as a single bar to S. African units.

Regiments present: 1, 2 Life Guards; Royal Horse Guards; 3, 6 Dragoon Guards; 2 Dragoons; 9, 12, 16 Lancers; 10 Hussars; B Squadron 14 Hussars; 3, 9, 18 (139), 19, 22, 28, 33, 41, 43, 44, 58, 64, 102 (32) Foot; "D" Coy. 6th Mounted Infantry; N.S.W. Lancers; 1st Australian Horse; 1st Queensland Mtd. Infy.; New Zealand Mounted Rifles, Cape Medical S.C., C.G.A., Damant's Horse, D.E.O.V.R., Field Int. Dept., French's Scouts. Kimberley R., Kimberley Lt. Horse, Kitcheners Horse, Rand Rifles, Roberts Horse, Scott's R.G., S.A.C.

H.M. ships: See analysis pages 273-5.

Paardeberg (*17th – 26th February, 1900*)

Awarded to all troops within 7,000 yds. of General Cronje's final laager between midnight of 17th February and midnight of 26th Febuary, 1900, and to all troops within 7,000 yds. of Koodoe's Rand Drift between those dates.

Regiments present: 1, 2 Life Guards; Royal Horse Guards; 3, 6 Dragoon Guards; 2 Dragoons; 9, 12, 16 Lancers; 10 Hussars; 1, 2, 3 Foot Guards; 3, 9, (4 offrs. & 164 O.Rs.), 10, 18 (138), 19, 22, 25, 28, 30, 33, 41, 43, 44, 46, 47, 68, 71, 73, 75, 78, 85, 91, 102 (35) Foot; 1st Australian Horse; 1st N.S.W. Mounted Rifles; 1st Queensland Mounted Infantary; No. 1 Contingent, New Zealand; 2nd (Special Service) Bn., R. Canadian R.; C.M.S.C., Commander-in-Chief's Bodyguard, Dammants H., D.E.O.U.R., F.I.D., French's Scouts, Imp. Lt. H., Kimberley Lt. H., Kimberley Vol. R., Kitchener's H., Nesbitt's H., Rand Rifles, Robert's H., Scott's R.G., S.A.C., Tucker's Scouts.

H.M. ships: See analysis pages 273-5.

Orange Free State (*28th February, 1900 – 31st May, 1902*)

Issued to all troops in Orange River Colony at any time between 28th February, 1900 and 21st May, 1902, who receive no claps which has been already specified for an action in the Orange River Colony. Scarce as a single bar.

Regiments present: 1, 2, 3, 5, 6, 7 Dragoon Guards; 1 Royal Dragoons; 2, 6 Dragoons; 3, 4, 7, 8, 13, 14, 18, 19, 20 Hussars; 5, 9, 12, 16, 17 Lancers; 1, 2, 3 Foot Guards; 1, 2, 3, 4, 5, 6, 7, 8, 9, 10, 11, 12, 13, 14, 15, 16, 18, 19, 20, 21, 22, 23, 24, 25, 26, 27, 28, 29, 30, 31, 32, 33, 34, 35, 37, 38, 40, 41, 43, 44, 45, 46, 47, 50, 54, 57, 58, 60, 62, 63, 65, 66, 68, 71, 73, 75, 78, 79, 83, 85, 87, 88, 91, 96, 98, 101 (3,131), 104, 105 Foot; The Rifle Brigade; *N.S.W. Units:* "A" Bty. R.A.A.; Imperial Bushmen; 3rd Mtd. Rifles; 3rd Imp. Bushmen; 1st Australian Comm. Horse. *S. Australian Units:* 1st and 2nd Mounted Rifles Contg., 3rd Bushmen Contg.; 4th Imp. Bushmen; 5th and 6th Imp. Contg.; 2nd Bn. Australian Comm. Horse. *Western Australian Units:* 1st and 2nd Mtd. Inf. Contg.; 3rd Bushmen Contg.; 4th, 5th and 6th Mtd. Inf. Contg. *Tasmanian Units:* 2nd Tasmanian Bushmen; 3rd Tasmanian Contg; 4th Imperial Bushmen. *Queensland Units:* 1st, 2nd and 3rd Mtd. Inf.; 4th and 5th Imp. Bushmen. *Victoria Units:* 2nd Mtd. Rifles; 3rd Bushmen; 4th Imp. Contg.; 5th Mtd. Rifles; 2, 3, 4, 6, 7 and 9th New Zealand Contingents.

H.M. ships: See analysis pages 273-5.

Relief of Ladysmith (*15th December, 1899 – 28th February, 1900*)

Granted to all troops in Natal north of and including Estcourt between 15th December, 1899 and 28th February, 1900, both dates inclusive.

Regiments present: The Royal Dragoons; 13, 14 Hussars; 2, 4, 7, 8, 2/11, 13, 14, 18, 20, 21, 23, 26, 27, 31, 33, 34, 40, 54, 60, 65, 68, 77, 87, 89, 101, 103 Foot (1,882); The Rifle Brigade.

H.M. ships: See analysis pages 273-5.

Driefontein (*10th March, 1900*)

Awarded to all troops with Army Headquarters and Lt. Gen. French's column – *i.e.,* the left and centre columns, which advanced from Popular Grove on 10th March, 1900.

Regiments present: 1, 2 Life Guards; Royal Horse Guards; 6 Dragoon Guards; 2 Dragoons; 10 Hussars; 12 Lancers; 1, 2, 3 Foot Guards; 3, 18 (33), 19, 22, 24, 28, 32, 33 (500), 41, 43, 44, 73, 75, 78, 85, 91, 102 (36) Foot; N.S.W. Lancers; 1st and 2nd Queensland Mounted Infantry; New Zealand Contingent.

H.M. ships: See analysis pages 273-5.

Wepener (*9th — 25th April*)

Awarded to all troops engaged in the defence of that place between 9th April, 1900 and 25th April, 1900, both days inclusive.

Regiments present. **Kaffrarian Rifles; 1st Imperial Lt. Horse (1); 2nd Imperial Lt. Horse (2); Cape Medical Staff Corps (1); Johannesburg Mounted Rifles (2); 1st. R. Scots (83); R. Engineers (11); S. African Constabulary; Driscoll's Scouts; Cape Mounted Rifles; 2nd Kitchener's Fighting Scouts (8); Prince of Wales Lt. Horse (9); 1st. Scottish Horse (7); 2nd Scottish Horse (2); 1st Brabant's Horse; 2nd Brabant's Horse.

Although 18 were originally issued to H.M.S. *Doris* they were all recalled with one exception.

Defence of Mafeking (*13th October, 1899 — 17th May, 1900*)

Issued to all troops in the garrison of Mafeking between 13th October, 1899 and 17th May, 1900, both dates inclusive. Approx. 1,300 present although some were unclaimed making a nett figure of approx. 1,150 issued.

Regiments present: S. African Constabulary (14); Mafeking Town Guard (513); Mafeking Railway Vols. (26); Mafeking Cadet Corps (38); Protectorate Regiment Frontier Force (424); Bechuanaland Rifles (125); Cape Police District No. 1 (43); Cape Polie District No. 2 (54); Special Police Contingent, Mafeking (5); B.S.A. Police B.P. Division (92); 1st Life Guards (1); Barkly West Town Guard (2); Border Horse (1); Border Scouts (1); 1 Brabant's Horse (1); 2 Btabant's Horse (2); Bushveld Carbineers (1); Cape Medical Staff Corps (4); Colonial Defence Force (1); Commander-in-Chief's Bodyguard (9); Diamond Fields Artillery (2); Driscoll's Scouts (4); 2nd Duke of Edinburgh's Own Rifles (1); French's Scouts (1); Gorringe's Flying Column (2); 1st Imperial Light Horse (1); Imperial Military Railway (2); Johannesburg Mounted Rifles (1); Kaffrarian Rifles (2); Kimberley Volunteer Regiment (7); 1st Kitchener's Fighting Scouts (3); Marshall's Horse (1); Nesbitt's Horse (3); Prince Alfred's Own Cape Artillery (1); Queenstown Rifle Volunteers (1); Railway Pioneer Regiment (2); Robert's Horse (2); Scoutt's Railway Guards (1); Steinaccker's Horse (6); Transkei Mounted Rifles (1); Vryburg Town Guard (5); Western Province Mounted Rifles (2).

Queen Victoria personally presented Mother Mary Joseph with the Royal Red Cross for her devoted work during the siege.)

Transvaal (*24th May, 1900 — 31st May, 1902*)

Issued to all troops in the Transvaal at any time between 24th May, 1900 and 31st May, 1902, who received no clasp for an action in the Transvaal which has already been specified.

Regiments present: 1, 2, 3, 5, 6, 7 Dragoon Guards; 1 Royal Dragoons; 2, 6 Dragoons; 5, 12 Lancers; 3, 4, 8, 10, 13, 14, 19, 20 Hussars; 1, 2, 3 Foot Guards; 1, 2, 3, 4, 5, 6, 7, 8, 9, 10, 12, 13, 14, 15, 16, 17, 19, 20, 21, 22, 23, 24, 25, 26, 27, 28, 29, 30, 31, 33, 34, 37, 38, 40, 41, 43, 44, 45, 46, 47, 49, 50, 51, 54, 57, 58, 60, 62, 63, 65, 68, 71, 73, 78, 79, 83, 85, 87, 88, 91, 98, 100, 101, 102, (2,789, 105 Foot; The Rifle Brigade. *N.S.W. Units:* "A" Bty. R.A.A.; N.S.W. Citizen Bushmen; 2nd and 3rd N.S.W. Mtd. Rifles; 3rd N.S.W. Imp. Bushmen; 1st Australian Comm. Horse. *S. Australian Units:* 1st and 2nd Mtd. Rifle Contgs.; 3rd Bushmen Contg.; 4th Imp. Bushmen; 2nd Australian Comm. Horse. *W. Australian Units:* 1st and 2nd Mtd. Infantry; 3rd Bushmen; 4th, 5th and 6th Mtd. Infantry. *Tasmanian Units:* 2nd Bushmen; 3rd Contg.; 1st

**See the very comprehensive medal roll by S. M. Kaplan

Australian Comm. Horse. *Queensland Units:* 2nd Mtd. Infantry; 4th and 5th Imp. Bushmen; 1st and 3rd Australian Comm. Horse. *Victoria Units:* 2nd Mtd. Rifles; 3rd Bushmen Contg.; 4th Imp. Contg.; 5th Mtd. Rifles; 1, 4, 5, 6, 7, 8 and 9th New Zealand Contingents.

H.M. ships: See analysis pages 273-5.

Johannesburg (*31st May, 1900*)

Awarded to all troops who, on 29th May, 1900, were north of an east and west line through Klip River Station (exclusive) and east of a north and south line through Krugersdorp Station (inclusive).

Regiments present: 1, 2 Life Guards; Royal Horse Guards; 6, 7 Dragoon Guards; 2, 6 Dragoons; 8, 10, 14 Hussars; 9, 12, 16, 17 Lancers; 1, 2, 3 Foot Guards; 6, 9, 10, 18 (104), 19, 22, 24, 25, 30, 35, 37, 44, 45. 46, 64, 68, 75, 79, 85, 98, 102 (30) Foot: "D" Co. 6th M.I.; 1st N.S.W. Australian Horse; 1st N.S.W. Mounted Rifles; 1st and 2nd S. Australian Mounted Rifles; 1st and 2nd W. Australian Mounted Infy. Contg.; 1st Tasmanian Contg.; 2nd Queensland Mounted Infantry; 1, 2 & 3rd New Zealand Contingents.

H.M. ships: See analysis pages 273-5.

Laing's Nek (*12th June, 1900*)

Issued to all troops of the Natal Field Force employed in the operations, and north of an east and west line through Newcastle between 2nd and 9th June, 1900, both dates inclusive.

Regiments present: The Royal Dragoons; 3 Dragoon Guards; 13, 18 Hussars; 2, 4, 8, 11, 13, 14, 17, 18, 20, 26, 31, 40, 41, 60, 63, 65, 68, 77, 89, 92, 102 (735) Foot: The Rifle Brigade.

H.M. ships: See analysis pages 273-5.

Diamond Hill (*11th — 12th June, 1900*)

Awarded to all troops who, on 11th or 12th June, 1900, were east of a north and south line drawn through Silverton Siding and north of an east and west line through Vlakfontein.

Regiments present: 1, 2 Life Guards; 6, 7 Dragoon Guards; 2, 6 Dragoons; 8, 10, 14 Hussars; 9, 12, 16, 17 Lancers; 1, 2, 3 Foot Guards; 1, 2, 3, 6, 16, 18 (74), 19, 35, 41, 44, 45, 79, 102 (29) Foot. *N.S.W. Units:* N.S.W. Lancers; 1st Australian Horse; 1st Mounted Rifles. *S. Australian Units:* 1st and 2nd Mounted Rifles. *W. Australian Units:* 1st and 2nd Mounted Infantry. *Tasmanian Units:* 1st Tasmanian Contg. *Queensland Units:* 1st and 2nd Mounted Infantry. *Victoria Units:* 2nd Victoria Mounted Rifles; 1 and 3rd New Zealand Contingents.

H.M. ships: See analysis pages 273-5.

Wittebergen (*1st — 29th July, 1900*)

Granted to all troops who were inside a line drawn from Harrismith to Bethlehem, thence to Senekal and Clocolan, along the Basuto border, and back to Harrismith, between 1st and 29th July, 1900, both dates inclusive.

Regiments present: 1, 2 Life Guards; Royal Horse Guards; 9, 12, 16, 17 Lancers; 10 Hussars; 1, 3 Foot Guards; 13, 15, 16, 18, 26, 29, 35, 38, 47, 50, 62. 63, 71, 73, 78, 79, 96, 99, 100, 101 (762), 102 (24), 105 Foot; 1st N.S.W. Mounted Rifles; Imperial Bushmen; 1st and 2nd and 4th W. Australian Mounted Infantry; 3rd Tasmanian Contg.; 1st New Zealand Contingent.

Six to Royal Marines serving with the Army.

(Obverse)

(Reverse)

No. 81. The Queen's Sudan Medal, 1896-7.

(Reverse)

No. 82. The Khedive's Sudan Medal, 1896-1908.

(Reverse)

No. 83. The Ashanti Medal, 1900.

(Reverse)
First issue

(Obverse)
Both issues

(Reverse)
Second issue

No. 84. The Queen's South Africa Medal, 1899-1902.

(Reverse)

No. 85.   The Queen's Mediterranean
Medal, 1899-1902.

(Obverse)

No. 87. The Kimberley Star,
1899-1900.

(Obverse)

No. 86. The King's South Africa Medal,
1901-2.

To face page 273

Queen's South Africa Medal to the Royal Navy

Analysis and summaries of medals and bars kindly produced by Mr. W.H. Fevyer

Note: the Roll for H.M.S. Monarch has partially disintegrated and although it has been repaired there has been an 8% loss. Detail has been extropaleted from the roll and the use of Capt. Morgan's notes.

SUMMARY OF MEDALS ISSUED TO NAVAL UNITS

NUMBER OF BARS

H.M.S.	TOTAL	RETURNED	ENTITLED	0	1	2	3	4	5	6	7	8
Barracouta	341	21	320	264	1	36	19					
Barrosa	193	35	158	101	32	1	7	17				
Beagle	139	12	127	110		17						
Blanche	217	44	173	156	4	13						
Doris	803	78	725	351	185	28	32	67	15	9	34	4
Dwarf	289	110	179	179								
Fearless	151	6	145	145								
Forte	688	112	576	421	119	8	1	4	23			
Gibraltar	673	51	622	618	4							
Magiciene	256	20	236	230	6							
Magpie	95	6	89	75	13	1						
Monarch	1262	162	1100	834	54	37	32	21	16	52	37	17
Naiad	274	23	251	134		117						
Niobe	757	117	640	514	125	1						
Partridge	171	13	158	147	8	3						
Pearl	230	26	204	190		14						
Pelorus	249	20	229	216	12	1						
Philomel	269	41	228	152	32	15	3	4	21	1		
Powerful	898	89	809	421	303	13	4	29	18	3	17	1
Racoon	207	29	178	176	2							
Rambler	145	36	109	109								
Rattler	86	10	76	76								
Redbreast	87	4	83	83								
Sappho	274	18	256	255		1						
Sybille	313	42	271	186	80	5						
Tarter	239	45	194	104	57	9	4	1	18	1		
Terpsichore	312	39	273	137		136						
Terrible	1147	59	1088	540	273	261	13		1			
Thetis	297	12	285	183	101	1						
Thrush	117	37	80	67		13						
Widgeon	112	24	88	20	68							
Cape & Transport Staff	46	—	46	35	11							
Marines (not on Ship's)	31	—	31	9	8	3	9	2				
Natal Naval Volunteers	132	9	123	1	72	23	2	2	22		1	
Royal Indian Marine	34	—	34	34								
Grand Total	11534	1350	10184	7273	1570	757	126	147	134	66	89	22

H.M.S.	BELMONT	MODDER RIVER	PAAREBERG	DRIEFONTEIN	WEPENER	JOHANNESBURG	DIAMOND HILL	BELFAST	WITTENBERGEN	DEFENCE OF KIMBERLEY	RELIEF OF KIMBERLEY	DEFENCE OF MAFEKING	RELIEF OF MAFEKING	CAPE COLONY
Barracouta														55
Barrosa			25	24										57
Beagle														17
Blanche														17
Doris	129	108	152	149		43	54	51			13			224
Dwarf														
Fearless														
Forte														1
Gibraltar														4
Magiciene														3
Magpie														14
Monarch	115	99	171	168	—	122	120	107			28			143
Naiad														117
Niobe														125
Partridge														6
Pearl														14
Pelorus														1
Philomel			2	1		2	2	2						2
Powerful	105	79	71	69		22	21	19			19			5
Racoon														
Rambler														
Rattler														
Redbreast														
Sappho														1
Sybille														85
Tartar							4	5						46
Terpsichore														136
Terrible														45
Thetis														1
Thrush														13
Widgeon														
Cape & Transport Staff														11
Marines (not on Ship's)									7					17
Natal Naval Volunteers			1											
Royal Indian Marine														
Grand Total	349	286	422	411	—	189	201	184	7	—	60	—	—	1160

ORANGE FREE STATE	TRANSVAAL	RHODESIA	TALANA	ELANDSLAAGTE	TUGELA HEIGHTS	DEFENCE OF LADYSMITH	RELIEF OF LADYSMITH	LAINGS NEK	NATAL	SOUTH AFRICA 1901	SOUTH AFRICA 1902	TOTAL	
										25	50	130	Barracouta
	17											123	Barrosa
										17		34	Beagle
										13		30	Blanche
13	45				1		1	1	14	55	1	1004	Doris
												—	Dwarf
												—	Fearless
25	28				32		37	28	117	1		269	Forte
												4	Gibraltar
									3			6	Magiciene
											1	15	Magpie
7	1				3		5	1	1	1	1	1095	Monarch
										117		234	Naiad
		1									1	127	Niobe
		5								3		14	Partridge
										14		28	Pearl
									12	1		14	Pelorus
24	28				37		37	28	32	1		198	Philomel
1					3	275	3					692	Powerful
									2			2	Racoon
												—	Rambler
												—	Rattler
												—	Redbreast
										1		2	Sappho
										4	1	90	Sybille
20	19				26		29	20	17		1	187	Tartar
										136		272	Terpsichore
2	1				274	1	292	1	223			839	Terrible
									101	1		103	Thetis
										13		26	Thrush
									68			68	Widgeon
												11	Cape & Transport Staff
9	10	1							5			49	Marines (not on Ship's)
26	26				47	65	49	27	8			249	Natal Naval Volunteers
												—	Royal Indian Marine
127	175	7	—	—	425	341	453	106	603	353	56	5915	Grand Total

TABLE SHOWING THE RELATIVE RARITY OF THE SINGLE BAR QUEEN'S SOUTH AFRICA MEDAL

(Please note that this table has no bearing whatsoever on multiple bar medals)

Bar	Imperial Units (Including Dominions other than South African)					South African Units				
	Common	Scarce	Rare	Extremely Rare	Unknown	Common	Scarce	Rare	Extremely Rare	Unknown
Cape Colony	+					+				
Natal		+							+	
Rhodesia				+				+		
Relief of Mafeking					+				+	
Defence of Kimberley				+			+			
Talana		+							+	
Elandslaagte				+						+
Defence of Ladysmith		+						+		
Belmont		+								+
Modder River			+							+
Tugela Heights	IMPOSSIBLE AS A SINGLE BAR									
Relief of Kimberley				+					+	
Paardeberg				+					+	
Orange Free State		+						+		
Relief of ladysmith		+						+		
Driefontein				+						+
Wepener				+					+	
Defence of Mafeking				+				+		
Transvaal	+						+			
Johannesburg				+					+	
Laing's Nek			+							+
Diamond Hill			+						+	
Wittebergen		+							+	
Belfast			+							+
South Africa 1901		+						+		
South Africa 1902		+						+		

List extracted from a paper presented to the second South African Numismatic Convention by M.G. Hibbard at Cape Town, 7th January 1964.

Belfast (*26th-27th August, 1900*)

Granted to all troops who, on 26th or 27th August, 1900, were east of a north and south line drawn through Wonderfonein (the garrison and troops quartered at Wonderfonein on those dates did not receive this clasp), and west of a north and south line through Dalmanutha Station, and north of an east and west line through Carolina.

Regiments present: 3, 6, 7 Dragoon Guards; 2, 6 Dragoons; 5, 9, 12, 17 Lancers; 8, 10, 14, 18 Hussars; 1, 2, 3 Foot Guards; 1, 6, 8, 11, 17, 18, 19, 27, 41, 44, 60, 63, 75, 92 Foot; The Rifle Brigade; 1st N.S.W. Australian Horse and probably a few New Zealand troops.

H.M. ships: See analysis pages 273-5.

South Africa 1901

This bar was awarded to those who were not eligible for the King's Medal, though they had served at the front between 1st January and 31st December, 1901.

H.M. ships: See analysis pages 273-5.

South Africa 1902

This bar was awarded to those who were not eligible for the King's Medal, though they had served at the front between 1st January and 31st May, 1902, although the Irish Guards only received 30 medals.

H.M. ships: See analysis pages 273-5.

THE IMPERIAL YEOMANRY IN SOUTH AFRICA

Probably more medals were named to the Imperial Yeomanry than to any other unit after the war in South Africa of 1899-1902, and to collectors the medals to this unit have been considered "common".

Be this as it may, let us consider how the medals were named. The medals to those on the Staff of the battalions formed were named with the battalion number and the word STAFF. Some other units may be found named to Base Coy., etc. The bulk of the medals were however named with the man's company number after his name and a considerable number had also the battalion number too. There are to be found a good many medals with just "Imperial Yeomanry" after the man's name — these are medals of late issue and most probably against individual claims of which there are several volumes at the Record Office.

The clasps won by the Imperial Yeomanry are for the most part the Colony clasps: CAPE COLONY, ORANGE FREE STATE, TRANSVAAL, and the two dated clasps, SOUTH AFRICA 1901 and SOUTH AFRICA 1902. The clasps for RHODESIA will be found on the medals on a few Companies and also the clasp for WITTERBERGEN.

When one inspects the rolls it is noticed that some Officers and Non-Commissioned Officers are credited with some of the battle clasps. It is obvious that as the Imperial Yeomanry were not present at these battles the clasps were won with another unit.

The list of Imperial Yeomanry Companies that follows shows in the first column the company number, in the second the County, the third the battalion, the fourth the strength of the original contingent, the fifth the strength of the reinforcements and the last the clasps awarded other than that for CAPE COLONY, ORANGE FREE STATE and TRANSVAAL.

Coy. No.	County of the Yeomanry Cavalry Regiment	Btn. No.	Orig. Congt.	Second Congt.	Clasps awarded other than CAPE COLONY, ORANGE FREE STATE and TRANSVAAL
1	Wiltshire	1	105	140	WITTENBERGEN for O.F.S. S.A. 1901 (61) S.A. 1901 (112); S.A. 1902 (110)
2	Wiltshire	1	120	150	WITTENBERGEN for O.F.S. S.A. 1901 (80) S.A. 1901 (140); S.A. 1902 (140)
3	Gloucestershire	1	120	140	WITTENBERGEN for O.F.S. S.A. 1901 (80) S.A. 1901 (140); S.A. 1902 (130)
4	Glamorganshire	1	118	160	WITTENBERGEN for O.F.S. Combined with 2nd draft Roll for S.A. 1901 (150); S.A. 1902 (150)
63	Wiltshire	1		135	Not TRANSVAAL. S.A. 1901 (115); S.A. 1902 (115)
5	Warwickshire	2	137	146	S.A. 1901 (82) S.A. 1901 (130); S.A. 1902 (120)
21	Cheshire	2	135	154	Not TRANSVAAL. S.A. 1901 (65) S.A. 1901 (150); S.A. 1902 (115)
22	Cheshire	2	125	155	Not TRANSVAAL. S.A. 1901 (70) Few had TRANSVAAL. S.A. 1901 (125); S.A. 1092 (100)
32	Lancashire	2	144	130	CAFE COLONY (a few had O.F.S.). S.A. 1901 (90) S.A. 1901 (115); S.A. 1902 (98)
103	Warwickshire	2	158		S.A. 1901 (130); S.A. 1902 (100)
110	No County given	2	130		S.A. 1901 (130); S.A. 1902 (75)
Gun See.	No County given	3	13		S.A. 1901 (10); S.A. 1902 (1)
9	Yorkshire (Doncaster)	3	165	180	6 men had WITTENBERGEN. S.A. 1901 (85); S.A. 1902 (9) S.A. 1901 (175); S.A. 1902 (150)
10	Sherwood Rangers	3	135	135	S.A. 1901 (60) Only half had O.F.S. S.A. 1901 (120); S.A. 1902 (97)
11	Yorkshire	3	131	175	S.A. 1901 (75); S.A. 1902 (72) S.A. 1901 (150); S.A. 1092 (140)
12	South Nottingham	3	120	160	S.A. 1901 (60) Half had only C.C., a quarter had C.C. and O.F.S. The rest had 3 clasps and S.A. 1901 (150); S.A. 1902 (125)
109	Yorkshire Hussars	3	175		S.A. 1901 (175); S.A. 1902 (140)

Coy. No.	County of the Yeomanry Cavalry Regiment	Btn. No.	Orig. Congt.	Second Congt.	Clasps awarded other than CAPE COLONY, ORANGE FREE STATE and TRANSVAAL
66	Yorkshire	3	150		S.A. 1901 (150); S.A. 1902 (150)
111	Yorkshire Dragoons	3	120		S.A. 1901 (120); S.A. 1902 (95)
6	Staffordshire e	4	120	170	WITTENBERGEN for O.F.S. S.A. 1901 (90); S.A. 1902 (1) S.A. 1901 (140); S.A. 1902 (?)
7	Leicestershire	4	135	140	WITTENBERGEN for O.F.S. S.A. 1901 (100) Few had WITTENBERGEN. S.A. 1901 (135); S.A. 1902 (105)
8	Derbyshire	4	120	170	About two-thirds had WITTENBERGEN for O.F.S. S.A. 1901 (65) S.A. 1901 (170); S.A. 1902 (155)
28	Bedfordshire	4	130	160	JOHANNESBURG for TRANSVAAL. S.A. 1901 (1) S.A. 1901 (155); S.A. 1902 (100)
41	Hampshire	4	140		S.A. 1901 (135); S.A. 1902 (130)
104	Derbyshire	4	114		Most did not have O.F.S. and TRANSVAAL. S.A. 1901 (100); S.A. 1902 (80)
15	Northumberland	5	170		S.A. 1901 (155); S.A. 1902 (140)
16	Worcestershire	5	135	175	S.A. 1901 (75) S.A. 1901 (140); S.A. 1902 (110)
55	Northumberland	5	110		30 of this Coy. had C.C. only. S.A. 1901 (70); S.A. 1092 (60)
100	No County given	5	125		S.A. 11901 (90); S.A. 1902 (80)
101	No County given	5	150		S.A. 1901 (150); S.A. 1902 (150)
102	No County given	5	115		S.A. 1901 (100); S.A. 1902 (100)
17	Ayrshire	6	115		WITTENBERGEN for O.F.S. S.A. 1901 (95); S.A. 1902 (1)
18	Queen's Own Royal Glasgow & Lower Ward of Lanark	6	120		WITTENBERGEN for O.F.S. S.A. 1901 (80); S.A. 1902 (1)
19	Lothian and Berwickshire	6	120		Three only had WITTENBERGEN S.A. 1901 ( ); S.A. 1902 ( )
	Colt Gun 17/18/19		17	450	17. S.A. 1901 (120); S.A. 1902 (100) 18 S.A. 1001 (140); S.A. 1902 (110) 19 S.A. 1901 (110); S.A. 1902 (24)
19	Lothian			70	S.A. included in above
20	Fife and Forfar	6	135	200	40 had C.C. and TRANSVAAL only. S.A. 1901 (80) S.A. 1902 (150)

Coy. No.	County of the Yeomanry Cavalry Regiment	Btn. No.	Orig. Cont.	Second Congt.	Clasps awarded other than CAPE COLONY, ORANGE FREE STATE and TRANSVAAL
107	No County given	6	170		C.C. and WITTENBERGEN. S.A. 1901 (170); S.A. 1902 (!30)
108	Royal Glasgow	6	270		S.A. 1901 (190); S.A. 1902 (135)
25	West Somerset	7	92	173	JOHANNESBURG, DIAMOND HILL, C.C., O.F.S.A. S.A. 1901 (62) 102 had single TRANSVAAL. S.A. 1901 (162); S.A. 1902 (150)
26	Dorsetshire	7	175	160	JOH., D. HILL, C.C., O.F.S. S.A. 1901 (135); S.A. 1902 (2) 150 had TRANSVALL only, others as Orig. Coy, S.A. 1901 (160) S.A. 1902 (130)
27	Devonshire	7	200	145	105 had D. HILL, C.C., O.F.S. The rest had usual three. S.A. 1901 (65) 32 had three clasps. The rest single TRANSVAAL. S.A. 1901 (145); S.A. 1902 (95)
48	North Somerset	7	120	170	JOH., D. HILL, C.C., O.F.S. S.A. 1901 (68); S.A. 1902 (2) Single TRANSVAAL. 5 or 6 with C.C., and O.F.S. S.A. 1901 (155); S.A. 1902 (110)
69	Sussex	7	140		C.C., TRANSVAAL, few with O.F.S. S.A. 1901 (140); S.A. 1902 (95) An Officer of this Company had DEFENCE OF MAFEKING.
23	Lancashire	8	150	180	Only about a quarter had three clasps. Usual C.C. and O.F.S. S.A. 1901 (120); S.A. 1902 (2) Mostly three clasps. S.A. 1901 (170); S.A. 1902 (130)
24	Westmorland and Cumberland	8	140		S.A. 1901 (95); S.A. 1902 (10)
74	Irish (Dublin)	8	165	255	S.A. 1901 (145); S.A. 1902 (110) S.A. 1901 (230); S.A. 1902 (190)
77	Manchester	8	120	140	S.A. 1901 (80) S.A. 1901 (140); S.A. 1902 (90)
99	No County given	8	120		Single clasp C.C. Only 12 had three clasps. S.A. 1901 (17); S.A. 1902 (6)
105	No County given	8	170		S.A. 1901 (160)
29	Denbighshire	9	125 20	140	Clasps C.C. and O.F.S. S.A. 1901 (100); S.A. 1902 (3) C.C., O.F.S. and TRANSVAAL. S.A. 1901 (19); S.A. 1902 (6) S.A. 1901 (140); S.A. 1902 (120)

Coy. No.	County of the Yeomanry Cavalry Regiment	Btn. No.	Orig. Congt.	Second Congt.	Clasps awarded other than CAPE COLONY, ORANGE FREE STATE and TRANSVAAL
30	Pembrokeshire	9	112 17	140	C.C. and O.F.S. C.C., O.F.S. and TRANSVAAL. S.A. 1901 (90); S.A. 1902 (3) Half had C.C. and O.F.S. only S.A. 1901 (125)
31	Montgomeryshire	9	120 50		C.C. and O.F.S. only. S.S. 1901 (130) C.C., O.F.S. and TRANSVAAL. S.A. 1902 (10)
31	Montgomeryshire	9		120 100 71 5	O.F.S. only C.C. only ⎱ S.A. 1901 (120); C.C. and TRANS ⎰ S.A. 1902 (100) C.C., O.F.S. and TRANSVAAL
49	Montgomeryshire	9	130	167	Usual three clasps. S.A. 1901 (80); S.A. 1902 (2) Usual three clasps (C.C. & O.F.S. 2). S.A. 1901 (153); S.A. 1902 (126)
88	Welsh Yeomanry	9	1 130		BRONZE to Indian Servant C.C. only. S.A. 1901 (130); S.A. 1902 (110)
89	No County given	9	18 120		Usual three clasps. Joined at Mafeking. S.A. 1901 Date clasps only shown. S.A. 1901 (120); S.A. 1902 (90)
37	Buckinghamshire	10	125	100	No note of date clasps. S.A. 1901 (110); S.A. 1902 (100)
38	Buckingham	10	120	120	S.A. 1901 (75) S.A. 1901 (120); S.A. 1902 (100)
39	Berkshire	10	93 37	140	Usual three clasps. S.A. 1901 (87); S.A. 1902 (3) WITTENBERGEN for O.F.S. S.A. 1901 (140); S.A. 1902 (110)
40	Oxfordshire	10	11 120	165	WITTENBERGEN for O.F.S. with Knox's Column Usual three. S.A. 1901 (80) S.A. 1901 (149); S.A. 1902 (111)
33	Royal East Kent	11	131	225	6 C.C., WITT. and TRANS.; 25 C.C., O.F.S. and TRANS.; rest C.C. and WITTENBERGEN. S.A. 1901 (85); S.A. 1902 (2) S.A. 1901 (155); S.A. 1902 (105)
34	Middlesex	11	120	160	WITTENBERGEN for O.F.S. S.A. 1901 (65) S.A. 1901 (140); S.A. 1902 (110)
35	Middlesex	11	120	150	WITTENBERGEN for O.F.S. S.A. 1901 (67) S.A. 1901 shows (305) and S.A. 1902 (255). This hardly seems possible!

Coy. No.	County of the Yeomanry Cavalry Regiment	Btn. No.	Orig. Congt.	Second Congt.	Clasps awarded other than CAPE COLONY, ORANGE FREE STATE and TRANSVAAL
36	West Kent	11	120		WITTENBERGEN for O.F.S. S.A. 1910 (81)
				170	S.A. 1901 (150); S.A. (1902. 135)
55	Royal East Kent	11	140		WITTENBERGEN for O.F.S. No note of dates
62	Middlesex	11	150		WITTENBERGEN for O.F.S. S.A. 1901 (120)
112	No County given	11		170	S.A. 1901 (150); S.A. 1902 (80)
41	Hampshire	12	140		WITTENBERGEN for O.F.S. S.A. 1901 (80); S.A. 1902 (1)
42	Hertfordshire	12	120		WITTENBERGEN for O.F.S. S.A. 1901 (55); S.A. 1902 (3)
				170	S.A. 1901 (140); S.A. 1902 (120)
43	Suffolk	12	120		S.A. 1901 (70); S.A. 1902 (3)
44	Suffolk	12	150		WITTENBERGEN for O.F.S. S.A. 1901 (70)
				160	S.A. 1901 (160); S.A. 1902 (122)
46	Irish (Belfast)	12	155 54		C.C. and O.F.S. only Usual three clasps. S.A. 1901 (170); S.A. 1902 (135)
51	Paget's Horse	12	145 85		Usual three clasps. C.C. and TRANSVAAL
53	Royal East Kent	12	15		S.A. 1901 (160); S.A. 1902 (160)
45	Irish (Dublin)	13	100		S.A. 1901 (40); S.A. 1902 (2)
46	Irish (Belfast)	13	130		C.C. and O.F.S. only. S.A. 1901 (65); S.A. 1902 (1)
47	Duke of Cambridge's Own or Lord Donoughmore's	13	140		S.A. 1901 (7)
54	Irish (Belfast)	13	130		C.C. and O.F.S., a few TRANSVAAL. S.A. 1901 (48); S.A. 1902 (1)
53	Royal East Kent	14	120		WITTENBERGEN for O.F.S. S.A. 1901 (75); See 12th Bin.
55	Northumberland	14	120		S.A. 1901 (80); S.A. 1902 (4)
62	Middlesex	14	130		WITTENBERGEN for O.F.S. S.A. 1901 (20); S.A. 1902 (1)
69	Sussex	14	125		JOH., D. HILL, C.C. and O.F.S. S.A. 1901 (75)
56	Buckinghamshire	15	160		S.A. 1901 (85)
				160	S.A. 1901 (140)
57	Buckinghamshire	15	65 75		WITTENBERGEN for O.F.S. Usual three
				130	S.A. 1901 (130); S.A. 1902 (125)

Coy. No.	County of the Yeomanry Cavalry Regiment	Btn. No.	Orig. Congt.	Second Congt.	Clasps awarded other than CAPE COLONY, ORANGE FREE STATE and TRANSVAAL
58	Berkshire	15	140	120	A few had WITT. for O.F.S. S.A. 1901 (85) S.A. 1901 (115); S.A. 1902 (110)
59	Oxfordshire	15	130	185	S.A. 1901 (65) S.A. 1901 (185); S.A. 1902 (170)
63	Wiltshire	16	90		WITTENBERGEN for O.F.S. S.A. 1901 (75)
66	Yorkshire	16	160		WITTENBERGEN for O.F.S. S.A. 1901 (80)
74	Irish (Dublin)	16	100		S.A. (1901) 75. Some C.C. only
50	Hampshire	17	120	140	Usual three plus RHODESIA. S.A. 1901 (85) Usual three only. S.A. 1901 (140); S.A. 1902 (120)
60	North Irish (Belfast)	17	70	60 150	Usualy C.C., O.F.S. and RHODESIA. A few TRANSVAAL C.C., O.F.S. adn RHODESIA. S.A. 1901 (combined 95) Usual three clasps. S.A. 1901 (150); S.A. 1902 (120)
61	South Irish (Dublin)	17	150 15	160	C.C., O.F.S. TRANS. and RHODESIA Single TRANSVAAL S.A. 1901 (90); S.A. 1902 (3) C.C. and O.F.S. only. S.A. 1901 (145); S.A. 1902 (120)
65	Leicestershire	17	120	145	S.A. 1901 (100); S.A. 1902 (2) S.A. 1901 (145); S.A. 1902 (80)
67	Sharpshooters	18	120	160	Four clasp RHODESIA added. S.A. 1901 (80) C.C. and O.F.S. usual, a few TRANS. S.A. 1901 (155); S.A. 1902 (110)
70	Sharpshooters	18	115	150	C.C., O.F.S. and RHODESIA. S.A. 1901 (110) C.C. and O.F.S.; a few TRANS. S.A. 1901 (150)
70/71	Sharpshooters	18	20		C.C. and O.F.S. S.A. 1901 (?)
71	Sharpshooters	18	130	155	Usual three, plus RHODESIA. A few single RHODESIA. S.A. 1901 (90) C.C. and O.F.S. and few RHODESIA. S.A. 1901 (155); S.A. 1902 (120)
75	Sharpshooters	18	120	155	Usual three, plus RHODESIA. S.A. 1901 (100) C.C. and O.F.S. only. S.A. 1901 (155); S.A. 1902 (135)
57	Buckinghamshire	19	4		C.C. and O.F.S. only
68	Paget's Horse	19	2		C.C. and O.F.S. only.

Coy. No.	County of the Yeomanry Cavalry Regiment	Btn. No.	Orig. Congt.	Second Congt.	Clasps awarded other than CAPE COLONY, ORANGE FREE STATE and TRANSVAAL
73	Paget's Horse	19	1		C.C., O.F.S. and TRANSVAAL
–		19	54		C.C. and TRANSVAAL
51	Paget's Horse	19	105		C.C. and TRANS., and a few O.F.S. S.A. 1901 (70)
52	Paget's Horse	19	100		C.C. and TRANSVAAL
68	Paget's Horse	19	115		C.C. and TRANSVAAL S.A. 1901 (80); S.A. 1902 (1)
73	Paget's Horse	19	85 91 5		Usual three clasps C.C. and TRANS. S.A. 1901 (85) Gun Section
72 76 78 79	Rough Riders Ditto Ditto Ditto	20	529		All Companies are mixed together, usual three bars S.A. 1901 (340). Rough extract of numbered entries: 72 (79); 76 (98); (98); 78 (96); 79 (83); no Company numbers (156)
80	No County shown	21	125		S.A. 1901 (125); S.A. 1902 (100)
81	No County shown	21	125		S.A. 1901 (130). this includes a few of other Companies) S.A. 1902 (115)
82	No County shown	21	135		S.A. 1901 (130); S.A. 1902 (100)
83	No County shown	21	110		S.A. 1901 (110); S.A. 1902 (80)
78	Rough Riders	22	60		S.A. 1901 (120), this must take in Company 76); S.A. 1902 (30)
76	Rough Riders	22	135		S.A. 1901 (2); S.A. 1902 (1)
84 85	No County shown No County shown	22 22	150 115		C.C. and O.F.S. only. S.A. 1901 (110) S.A. 1901 (115); S.A. 1902 (95)
86	No County shown	22	120		S.A. 1901 (120); S.A. 1902 (90, C.C. and O.F.S. only)
87	No County shown	22	120		S.A. 1901 (120); S.A. 1902 (100, C.C. and O.F.S. only, too had TRANS-VAAL added later)
90	No County whown	23	140		40 had C.C. and O.F.S. only. S.A. 1901 (135); S.A. 1902 (120)
91	No County shown	23	110		C.C. and O.F.S. only S.A. 1901 (105); S.A. 1902 (85)
92	No County shown	23	120		C.C. and O.F.S. only S.A. 1901 (110); S.A. 1902 (100)
93	No County shown	23	120		Usual three clasps. S.A. 1901 (120); S.A. 1902 (100)

Coy. No.	County of the Yeomanry Cavalry Regiment	Btn. No.	Orig. Congt.	Second Congt.	Clasps awarded other than CAPE COLONY, ORANGE FREE STATE and TRANSVAAL
94	Metropolitan Mounted Rifles	24	150		Usual three clasps. S.A. 1901 (130); S.A. 1902 (75)
95	Ditto	24	140		S.A. 1901 (140); S.A. 1902 (100)
96	Ditto	24	120		S.A. 1901 (115); S.A. 1902 (90)
97	Ditto	24	115		S.A. 1901 (115); S.A. 1902 (90)
115	No County shown	25	1		Usual three clasps
117	Ditto	25	1		Usual three clasps
118	Ditto	25	3		Usual three clasps
120	Younghusband's Horse	26	25		C.C. and S.A. 1901. S.A. 1901 (140); S.A. 1902 (140). Claims for medal on other lists.
—		27	417		C.C., S.A. 1901 and S.A. 1902. Regt. Nos. up to 44575
127	No County shown	28	100		C.C. and S.A. 1902
128	Ditto	28	90		Ditto
129	Ditto	28	130		Ditto
130	Ditto	28	100		Ditto
131	Ditto	29	120		Ditto
132	Ditto	29	100		Ditto
133	Ditto	29	130		Ditto
134 Gun Sect.	Ditto	29	120		Ditto
	Ditto	29	16		Ditto
175	Ditto	29	120		Ditto
176	Ditto	29	105		Ditto
—		30	70		Ditto
			38		Clasp only, S.A. 1902
135	Ditto	30	105		C.C. and S.A. 1902
137	Ditto	30	95		Ditto
138	Ditto	30	95		Ditto
139	No County shown	31	100		C.C. and S.A. 1902
140	Ditto	31	102		Ditto
141	Ditto	31	105		Ditto
147	Ditto	31	100		Ditto
143	Ditto	32	95		Ditto
145	Ditto	32	90		Ditto
146	Ditto	32	100		Ditto

85 QUEEN'S MEDITERRANEAN MEDAL (1899-1902)

This medal, for which no bars were awarded, is exactly the same as the Queen's South Africa Medal except that the word "MEDITERRANEAN" is on the reverse and the words "SOUTH AFRICA" deleted. It was awarded to garrisons in the Mediterranean. The Third Battalions of the following regiments received it:

Royal Northumberland Fusiliers (574); Royal Fusiliers; West Yorks (721); Loyal North Lancs (202); Royal West Kent; King's Own Yorkshire Light Infantry (775); Seaforth Highlanders (784); Royal Munster Fusiliers (498).

86 KING'S SOUTH AFRICA MEDAL (1901-1902)

Obverse   The bust of King Edward VII and legend "EDWARDVS VII REX IMPERATOR."

285

Reverse	As for the second issue of the Queen's Medal.
Size	1.42 in. diameter.
Ribbon	1.25 in. wide. Green, white and yellow in equal widths.
Suspension	By a plain, straight suspender.
Designer	G.W. de Saulles.
Naming	As for the Queen's South Africa Medal (No. 84).
No. of bars issued	Two — "South Africa 1901" and "SOUTH AFRICA 1902".

Queen Victoria having died during the South African War, King Edward VII authorized this medal to be given to all who were serving in South Africa on or after 1st January, 1902, and who would complete eighteen months' service before 1st June, 1902.

Only thirty-one of these medals were awarded to the Navy, as the Naval Brigades returned to their ships in 1901, and men who did not see service ashore were not awarded it (1 to H.M.S. *Doris*, 11 to R.M., and 19 to miscellaneous R.N.). 30 were awarded to Canadians (S.A.C.).

This medal was never issued alone, but always in conjunction with the Queen's Medal, and neither was it issued without a bar, except to nursing sisters, to whom 587 were awarded. This medal was occasionally given with the single bar "South Africa 1902". A man who missed qualifying for the 1901 bar because of wounds etc., but who returned after Jan. 1902 and completed a total of 18 months before 31st May, 1902, could qualify for just the 1902 bar.

87 DEFENCE OF KIMBERLEY STAR AND MEDAL

Neither the Star nor Medal may be worn in uniform, so that they cannot be described as campaign awards. The Stars measure $1\frac{7}{8}$ in. x $1\frac{5}{8}$ in. and have six points, each of which has a small ball on the end. They are made of silver. The obverse bears the Town Shield and name "KIMBERLEY" above, with the dates "1899-1900" below. The usual suspension is by a narrow suspender, but sometimes this is dispensed with and the 1 in. wide ribbon is threaded through a small ring attached to the topmost point of the Star. It would seem that some 5,000 were prepared. Two are known in gold, but these were replicas being made by a jeweller in Kimberley. One striking feature of the replicas is the absence of "Mayor's Siege Medal" on the reverse. The 2 gold medals were presented to the Mayor Mr. H.A. Oliver, J.P., and Mr. R. Archibald of the De Beers Co.

The ribbon was red, white and blue stripes down the centre, with one yellow and one black edge. In relief on the reverse is the wording "MAYOR'S SIEGE MEDAL, 1900".

The medal bears on the obverse the figure of Victory above the Town Hall, and on the reverse are two shields. On one is the wording: "INVESTED 15 OCT. 1899" and on the other "RELIEVED 15 FEB. 1900". There is also the legend "TO THE GALLANT DEFENDERS OF KIMBERLEY", the monogram "V.R.I." and the Imperial Crown. The issue of this medal was suppressed and is therefore rare.

The Stars are quite common adn I am told that there are several fakes to every genuine one. The Medal is now rare. Mr. Augustus Steward, in his book *The A.B.C. of War Medals and Decorations*, states that only the Stars bearing the Birmingham date-mark "a" are genuine for 1900/1. Many with the letter "b" or "c" are to be found which were struck one or two years later.

88 TRANSPORT MEDAL (1899-1902)

Obverse	Bust of King Edward VII in Naval uniform and legend: "EDWARDVS VII REX ET IMPERATOR".

			South Africa 1899-1902	China 1900	Both Bars	Total

Reverse   H.M.T. *Ophir*, above which is part of the map of the world* and the Latin inscription "OB PATRIAM MILITIBUS PER MARE TRANSVECTIS ADJUTAM". (For services rendered in trans-porting troops by sea.)

Size   1.42 in. diameter.

Ribbon   1. 25 in. wide. Red with two blue stripes. On the ribbon the stripes are nearer the edges than on the I.G.S. 1854 Medal, otherwise the colours are the same.

Suspension   By a plain, straight, swivelling suspender.

Designer   Obverse — G.W. de Saulles; Reverse — The design was supplied by the Admiralty.

Naming   Impressed in block letters. Only the recipient's name is given; neither his rank nor the ship on which he served is mentioned. There are, however, official rolls in existence for the purposes of verification.

No. of bars issued   Two — S. Africa 1899-1902 and China 1900.

This medal was sanctioned on 8th November, 1903, for award to the Master, 1st, 2nd and 3rd Officers, 1st, 2nd and 3rd Engineers, Pursers and Surgeons of merchant vessels employed in the Transport Service which took troops to the South African War and to the Boxer Rebellion in China. It seems to have been awarded to the captains and chief officers and also in a few cases to the chief engineers. One hundred and seventeen transports and eleven hospital ships were used in the above two campaigns.

				South Africa 1899-1902	China 1900	Both Bars	Total
Masters	.	.	.	122	37	34	191
Other officers	.	.	.	1,150	286	154	1,590
Totals	.	.	.	1,272	323	188	1,781

It should be noted that the above table does not include those of the 95 eligible recipients who did not claim their medals, but it does include a few which, for unspecified reasons, were returned to the Royal Mint. This number is thought to be nine, but we cannot guarantee this and neither do we know how they were distributed in the above table which is, therefore, only strictly accurate as regards the actual number of medals that were originally awarded.

The interesting fact about this medal is that it was to have been issued in future wars to the officers of the Mercantile Marine who serve in transports.

The following are the names of the eleven hospital ships and a few of the transports:

Hospital ships: *Avoca, Dunera, Lismore Castle, Maine* (which served on the China station after July, 1900), *Nubia, Orcana, Princess of Wales, Simla, Spartan, Trojan, Yorkshire.*

Transports: *Aurania, Australia, Bavarian, Canada, Carinthia* (wrecked), *Cedric, Cephalonia, Colombia, Cymric, Denton Grange* (wrecked), *Fiume, Fort Salisbury, Galeka, Gallea, Gascon, Ismore* (wrecked), *Johannesburg, Kildonan Castle, Kumara, Landaura, Majestic, Malacca, Montrose, Navassa, Ophir, Orcana, Orissa, Waiwera.*

*Note that the greater part of the continent of North America is excluded.

The *Waiwera* sailed from New Zealand for Cape Twon on 1st October, 1899, with the first New Zealand troops to fight overseas.

89 TIBET MEDAL (13th December, 1903-23rd September, 1904)

Obverse	The bust of King Edward VII and legend: "EDWARDVS VII KAISAR-I-HIND".
Reverse	A fine picture, in rather shallow relief, of the fortress of Potala Lhassa with the words "TIBET 1903-4".
Size	1.42 in. diameter.
Ribbon	1.25 in. wide. Green with two white stripes and a thick one of maroon in the centre.
Suspension	By an ornamental scroll swivelling suspender as used for the I.G.S. Medal.
Designers	Obverse — G.W. de Saulles; Reverse — E.G. Gillick.
Naming	In neat, rather thick, running script.
No. of bars issued	One — for Gyantse.

This medal was authorized on 1st February, 1905, to be awarded to all who took part in the Tibet Mission and to the troops accompanying it who served at or beyond Silgari between 13th December 1903, and 23rd September, 1904.

As will be seen, very few British troops were present; consequently, medals to Europeans are rather scarce.

The medal was also issued in bronze, including the bar for Gyantse, when applicable, to the Peshawur Camel Corps and native camp followers, etc.

In July, 1903, a trade Mission, under Colonel Younghusband, was sent by the Indian Government to meet the Tibet and Chinese officials in Gyantse. This Mission met with a hostile reception on the way and when it arrived at Tanu it was advised by the Tibetan general to return to Quatong to avoid bloodshed. This Colonel Younghusband refused to do, but ordered the disarmament of the Tibetan troops.

On 31st March, 1904, the Tibetans fired on the column and suffered heavily for doing so. On the 8th April, the 32nd Sikh Pioneers stormed the Red Idol Gorge. A force under General Macdonald arrived at Gyantse after having had to fight its way there. The Dalai Lama refused to negotiate, so that it became obvious that the way would have to be cleared right through to Lhassa. Colonel Brander was sent from Gyantse with a force to clear the Karo Pass, which he did on 6th May.

The Tibetans surrounded Gyantse and repeatedly attacked it. Colonel Younghusband demanded that the Amban should go to Gyantse with a view to putting an end to the trouble, but this he refused to do. In the end, an expeditionary force 4,600 strong, was employed. The Tibetans were heavily defeated outside Gyantse and a Lama was sent from Lhassa to sue for peace.

In July, Colonel Younghusband stated that the Mission would proceed to Lhassa to demand an apology. Preceded by General Macdonald's force, the Mission arrived on the 3rd August, and a treaty was signed in the Portala Lhassa (which is depicted on the reverse of the medal).

The Mission, after blessings and presents all round, including a golden image of Buddha to Colonel Younghusband, left Lhassa on 23rd September, 1904.

The following troops took part: No. 7 British Mountain Battery; one section from each of the 27th and 30th Mountain Batteries; 3 Bengal and 12 Madras Sappers and Miners; four companies of 1st Bn. Royal Fusiliers; a machine-gun section from the 1st Bn. Norfolk Regiment (18); King's Own R. Lancs. (8) and

(Obverse)

No. 88. The Transport Medal, 1899-1902.

(Reverse)*

No. 89. The Tibet Medal, 1903-4.

(Reverse)

No. 88. The Transport Medal, 1899-1902.

(Obverse)

(Reverse)

No. 90. The Natal Rebellion Medal, 1906.

* Reference should be made to page 425 for medals with identical obverses.

To face page 288

(Obverse)   (Reverse)   (Obverse)

(Reverse)   (Obverse)   (Reverse)

No. 91. The British North Borneo Company's Medals, 1897-1937.

one from the Royal Irish Regiment and 3rd Rifle Bde.; 23, 32 Sikh Pioneers; 19 Punjab Infantry; 8th and machine-gun section of 9 Gurkhas; 55th Cokes Rifles; 40 Pathans; 5, 6, 9, 11, 12, 19, 24 and part of 26 Mule Corps; Peshawur Cooly Corps; Sikkim Cooly Corps; Supply and Transport Corps; Army Veterinary Department; Survey Department; a few volunteer officers; British Officers (160); N.C.O.s and men (600); Indian Officers (60); N.C.O.s and men (2,500).

Gyantse *(3rd May-6th July, 1904)*

This bar was awarded to members of the abovementioned units who took part in the operations around Gyantse between 3rd May and 6th July, 1904.

90 NATAL REBELLION (8th February-3rd August, 1906)

Obverse	The coinage head of King Edward VII facing right, with the legend: "EDWARDVS VII REX IMPERATOR".
Reverse	In the centre are the figures of Britannia and Natalia. The former is holding an orb, surmounted by the figure of Peace in her left hand, and Natalia is holding a large sword in her right hand. In the background are some natives and a kraal. In the exergue is the word "NATAL".
Size	1.42 in. diameter.
Ribbon	1.25 in. wide. Crimson with black edges.
Suspension	By a plain, straight suspender.
Designer	The medal was designed and manufactured by the Goldsmiths and Silversmiths Co., London.
Naming	Impressed in thin block capitals, a few are found unnamed.
No. of bars issued	One — 1906.

On the 9th May, 1907, the Natal Government was authorized to issue a medal to thoe who had taken part in the suppression of the Zulu Rising in 1906. Approx. 10,000 medals issued, about 20% being without bar.

It is thought that the reverse to this medal is the finest issued during the past hundred years. There is nothing depicting triumph, and it is a pleasant change not to have a lion on a medal. The attitude of the natives in the right background is so beautifully in keeping with the solicitous attitude of Britannia, who seems to be sympathizing with the figure of Natalia. It is such a breakaway from the usual not to see Britannia with her usual wreath of laurels. The design of the bar with its mottled background and the stop before and after the date is much more pleasing than any of the others which carry a single date, such as those on the medals for South Africa between 1877 and 1879, and the East and West Africa Medals.

The medal, which was only awarded in silver, was the first campaign one to bear the Sovereign's head facing to the right.

It has been said that the Cameron Highlanders were awarded medals for service in the rebellion, but it is understood that they never left Pietermaritzburg. Furthermore, the Natal Government refused the help of Imperial troops.

It is also to be found stated that the medal was never issued without the bar. This statement is entirely wrong, though the number so issued was small. The medal without the bar was awarded to those who served for a continuous period of from twenty to forty-nine days, whilst those who served for fifty or more continuous days received the bar.

The cause of the rebellion was the native refusal to pay hut taxes, followed by the murder of two Natal policemen on 8th February.

On the 10th Colonel Duncan Mackenzie, C.B., C.M.G., raised a force with a view to a "drive" in the Southern Natal with a further force under Colonel G. Leuchars, C.M.G. These two forces rounded up Chiefs Ngobizembe, Mskofeli and Gobizembe. At a parade at Mapumulo on the 10th March, Colonel Leuchars announced the fines of cattle to be imposed. This brought the first part of the rebellion to a close.

On the 3rd April, Chief Bambata incited the rebels in the Greytwon District to revolt. They ambushed a police column and practically besieged Greytown, Melmoth and Eshowe. A large sum was offered for the caputre of Bambata, who crossed the Tugela River into Zululand, where he was joined by Chiefs Sigananda and N'Dubi in the Nkandhla Forests. It was now decided to raise more forces and drive the forests. The Transvaal raised a force under Lieutenant-Colonel W.F. Barker and the Cape another, under Lieutenant-Colonel J. Dick. In addition to these State forces Colonel J.R. Royston raised a unit known as Royston's Horse. The Naval Corps, under Commander F. Hoare, was mobilized. Sir Abe Bailey raised a small unit from the Lancaster and York Association (which I have seen quoted as the York and Lancaster Regiment!). The Natal Indian Congress raised a stretcher-bearer unit, the Sergeant-Major of which was M.K. Ghandi, who became so well known.*

As soon as these forces were ready the "drive" started and the rebels were driven out of the forests into the mountains. On 16th June Chief Sigananda surrendered. On the 19th, a further outbreak was started by Chiefs Ndhlova and Messini. On the 8th July, the rebels were totally defeated at Izinsimba and both Chiefs surrendered.

This revised fifth edition is greatly indebted to D.R. Forsyth for very kindly allowing the publisher to use the following summary extracted from his Natal Native Rebellion 1906 Medal Roll which he has compiled with meticulous care.

SUMMARY OF:— UNITS, MEDALS AND CLASPS AWARDED

Unit	Clasps	No Clasps	Total
Amabomvu Levy	—	32	32
Amafunze Tribe	—	20	20
Border Mounted Rifles	213	38	251
Cape Mounted Riflemen	70	—	70
Chaplains	4	2	6
Civilian Employees	—	135	135
Doctors	—	4	4
Dundee Borough Reserves	—	35	35
Dundee District Reserves	—	62	62
Dunns Scouts	20	—	20
Durban Light Infantry	539	93	632
Durban Militia Reserves	—	194	194
Escourt Militia Reserves	105	13	118

*He was assasinated on 31st January, 1948.

Unit	Clasps	No Clasps	Total
Greytown Reserves (1st)	—	42	42
Greytown Reserves (2nd)	1	—	1
H.E. The Governor — Staff	2	1	3
Imperial Officers	—	4	4
Indian Stretcher Bearer Corps	—	20	20
Intelligence Service	17	34	51
Klipriver Reserves	—	62	62
Krantzkop Reserves	71	4	75
Lancashire & Yorkshire Contg.	150	—	150
Lower Tugela Reserves	—	35	35
Melmouth Reserves	25	32	57
Militia Reserves Lower Tugela Div.	—	52	52
Militia Transport Service Corp.	45	28	73
Natal Carbineers	878	132	1010
Natal Field Arty. 1st Bdge. Staff	3	2	5
Natal Field Arty. "A" Battery	94	21	115
Natal Field Arty. "B" Battery	101	5	106
Natal Field Arty. "C" Battery	91	10	101
Natal Field Arty. Pom Pom Section	24	—	24
Natal Guides	4	—	4
Natal Medical Corps	104	19	123
Natal Militia Staff	30	1	31
Natal Mounted Rifles	424	38	462
Natal Police Gaolers	50	—	50
Natal Rangers	839	68	907
Natal Royal Regiment	225	33	258
Natal Service Corps	111	8	119
Natal Telegraph Corps	38	6	44
Natal Veterinary Corps	11	2	13
Newcastle Division Reserves	—	88	88
New Hanover Reserves	—	75	75
Nkandhla Town Guard	—	17	17
Northern Districts Mounted Rifles	233	6	239
Nurses	—	7	7
Roystons Horse	714	31	745
Roystons Horse 2nd	93	—	93
Searchlight Section	3	—	3
Sibindies Levies	1	—	1
Sundry Recipients	16	4	20
Transvaal Medical Staff Corps	9	—	9
Transvaal Mounted Rifles	489	46	535
Transvaal Volunteer Staff	3	—	3
Transvaal Volunteer Transport Corps	1	—	1
Umsinga Militia Reserves	6	40	46
Umvoti Division Reserves	61	27	88
Umvoti Mounted Rifles	327	98	425
Zuzuland Chiefs	—	15	15
Zuzuland Field Force	1	—	1
Zuzuland Mounted Rifles	124	31	155
Zuzuland Natives	—	33	33
Zuzuland Police	122	25	147
TOTAL	8045	1934	9979

The main thing to note is that the medal for Tambunan is neither the same nor even remotely similar to the others.

There are several interesting facts about these medals which will be dealt with in turn: Firstly, two distinct types of medals were issued, and three different ribbons; secondly, the first two medals could be worn at the same time, though the pieces are identical; thirdly, that the first three medals were issued in silver and bronze, and that although a free exchange of bronze for silver ones was offered there is nothing that shows whether any were so exchanged; fourthly, that the medals are larger than normal and that for Tambunan thinner than the others — the bronze medal for Tambunan is thinner than the silver one: fifthly, that all the medals were issued unnamed, though a few were privately named afterwards; sixthly, it is difficult to understand why the second medal was issued with a bar which reads "PUNITIVE EXPEDITIONS", when there was only one additional expedition after that covered by the first medal.

In addition to four campaign medals the Company issued a General Service Medal, the full particulars concerning the issue of which are given on page 293. An illustration will be found facing the same page.

The historical particulars are taken from the most interesting book *British North Borneo*, by Owen Rutter, published by Messrs. Constable & Co.

As the medals vary with each issue they are described in their order of issue.

All the medals were manufactured by Messrs. Spink & Son. Specimens issued have either been made in a heavy gauge or with "S" of "Son" stamped out in the reverse exergue and "Copy" on the rim.

(a) Punitive Expedition (1897)

Numbers issued	Twelve silver and seventy-four bronze.
Obverse	The shield of the Company supported on either side by a native. Above the shield are two arms, one clothed, the other nude, supporting the Company's flag. Below the shield is the motto "PERGO ET PERAGO".
Reverse	The British Lion, facing left, standing in front of a bush. Between them is a flagstaff from which flies the Company's flag. Around the top is the inscription "BRITISH NORTH BORNEO". There is an unusually large exergue in the centre of which is a wreath. At the top left of the exergue is "SPINK AND SON", and top right "LONDON".
Size	1.5 in. diameter and 0.2 in. thick.
Ribbon	The original issue was of a watered golden colour 1.25 in. wide, but in 1917 this was altered to one of the same width with 0.3 in. wide marroon edges, then two yellow stripes 0.2 in. wide with a dark blue stripe down the centre. The ribbon is of a heavier material than usual.
Suspension	By a floreated clasp of the I.G.S. Medal pattern.
Naming	The medals were issued unnamed.
No. of bars issued	One. The bar bears the word "PUNITIVE EXPEDITION" in two lines. The bar is 1.45 in. long and 0.3 in. wide and of the I.G.S. Medal pattern.

The medal was given for a small expedition against Mat Saleh conducted by Mr. Hewett, the Resident for Labuan, together with a few police officers, 38 Sikhs, some Sugat policemen, and a 7-pdr. gun. The main action took place in December, 1897, though there had been two smaller ones in July and August.

(b) Punitive Expeditions (1898)

Numbers
issued   Five silver and forty-seven bronze bamed and numbered.

Particulars   Identical with the above.

In January, 1898, Mat Saleh caused more trouble which necessiated another expedition, this time under Captain C.H. Harrington. H.M.S. *Swift* was present at the time, though no members of her crew took part.

(c) Tambunan (1899-1900)

Numbers
issued   Eight silver and one hundred and six bronze.

Obverse   The Company's shield, above which are the words "BRITISH NORTH BORNEO", and, below, the date "1900".

Reverse   One clothed and one naked arm supporting the Company's flag surrounded by a wreath. Around the whole is the motto "PERGO ET PERAGO". At the bottom in very small lettering is "SPINK & SON, LONDON".

Size   1.5 in. diameter. The silver medal is 0.19 in. thick, and the bronze one 0.15 in.

Ribbon   1.25 in. wide. Yellow with a green stripe 0.4 in. wide down the centre.

Suspension By a plain straight suspender, as used with the Queen's South Africa Medal.

No. of bars One − for Tambunan. The bar is of the pattern used for the I.G.S.
issued·   Medals.

This medal was awarded for another expedition, led by Captain C.H. Harrington, against Mat Saleh, who was killed.

(d) Rundum (1915-16)

Number   One hundred and thirteen, all of silver (no bronze medals were
issued   issued with this bar).

Particulars   Identical with those for (a) the Punitive Expedition Medal.

This medal was awarded to a small force under Mr. Bunbury, consisting of three white men, fifteen Sikhs, ten native policemen and eighty-five Dyaks, which relieved the village of Rundum which was besieged by natives.

Those who had already received either of the previous medals would receive the bar only.

(e) General Service Medal.

Obverse   Exactly the same as that of the Punitive Expedition Medal (a).

Reverse   The seated figure of Britannia holding a trident in her left hand. Her right hand is resting on a shield which bears the Union Flag. Around the circumference, above the exergue, is the inscription "NORTH BORNEO GENERAL SERVICE MEDAL". In the exergue is a branch with eleven leaves − tip of end leaf is stamped out in the specimens and in addition "Copy" is stamped on the rimsof those made since 1955.

Size   1.5 in. diameter, 0.1 in. thick.

Ribbon   1 in. wide. Half dark green and half yellow.

| Suspension | By means of a ring which is attached to the piece by an ornate claw. |
| No. of bars issued | Nil. |

This medal was sanctioned by the Company's Official Gazette (Extraordinary) No. 9, dated 6th April, 1937, the first five paragraphs of which read:

1. The Court of Directors have been pleased to approve the creation of a medal to be designated "The North Borneo General Service Medal".
2. This medal will be granted for
   (a) Specially valuable services to North Borneo.
   (b) Long and meritorious service of not less than eighteen years in any capacity in North Borneo, irrespective of whether such service has been rendered in the service of the Chartered Company or not.
   (c) Acts of exceptional courage in North Borneo.
3. After publication of the first list, recommendations for the award of the medal under Regulation 2 (a) and (b) above shall be submitted by the Governor to the Court of Directors annually on the 1st of July; and awards will be published annually in the *North Borneo Gazette* on the 1st of November (Charter Day). Recommendations for the award of the medal under Regulation 2 (c) may be made by the Governor at any time.
4. The medal shall consist of a circular medal in silver, having on the obverse a representation of Britannia within the circle and the words "NORTH BORNEO GENERAL SERVICE MEDAL", and on the reverse the arms of the Chartered Company, and shall be worn on the left side suspended by a ring to a riband of dark green and yellow in equal proportions of one inch and three-eights of an inch in width, with the addition in the case of recipients under Regulation 2 (c) above of a central red stripe of about one-sixteenth of an inch.
5. Recipients who are British subjects are not permitted to wear this medal except in North Borneo.

Forty-two of these mdals were awarded. The medal is now obsolete.

It is NOT a campaign medal pure and simple. The word "General" in its title must be translated as meaning exactly what it says, as recipients were members of the Legislative Council, railway executives, clergy, district officers, rubber planters, members of the local constabulary and native chiefs, etc.

A full list of recipients was contained in th Winter 1973 bulletin of The Orders and Medals Research Society.

92 SUDAN MEDAL (1910)

| Obverse | An Arabic inscription which reads "ABBAS HILMI THE SECOND", with the Mohammedan year 1328* for the issues from 1910 to 1917, those from 1918-1922 contained a new cypher. |
| Reverse | A lion standing on a plinth, which is inscribed with the word "SUDAN" in English. Behind the lion is the River Nile, on the farther bank of which are two clumps of palm trees. In the background is the rising sun with spreading rays. |

*The Mohammedan calendar starts from the hejira, or Hegira, which means departure or flight. The departure referred to is, of course, that of Mohammed (which is spelt in different ways) from Mecca to Medina. The calendar starts from 15th July, 622, though authorities vary as to actual date of the flight. Thirty-three Mohammedan years are equal to thirty-two of those of the normal calendar.

Both Mecca and Medina are in what is now known as the Hedjaz (Saudi Arabia), which borders part of the eastern shore of the Red Sea.

Size	1.42 in. diameter.
Ribbon	1.3 in. wide with a black watered centre with a thin green and red stripe on either side. These colours are said to symbolize the Sudan, guarded by Egypt (the green) and Britain (the red).
Suspension	By a straight, swivelling suspender with the first issue, but non-swivelling with the second.
Designer	Richard Garbe.
Naming	Most of the medals were issued unnamed.
No. of bars issued	Sixteen, each of which is inscribed in English and Arabic.

On 12th June, 1911, His Highness the Khedive authorized the issue of a new medal to replace that which was first issued in 1897.

In 1918 there was a further issue of this medal, which bore the cipher of the new Khedive and, of course, the new date. Both issues are rare.

Collectors should examine the medals very carefully to see that they have the designer's initials immediately to the right of the right-hand spear. The initials are "R.G." done in such a way as to appear like a small R. inside a circular G.

It was awarded in silver and bronze, but no bars were given with the bronze medals, so that there is nothing to show in how many expeditions the recipients of the bronze ones had served. Silver medals are known without a bar, one was awarded to 2nd. Ltd. D.G.A. Allen, R.F.C., and there may well be others. As, too, all the medals were issued unnamed, it is not possible to say whether any man received a silver and a bronze medal, which, without definite authority to the contrary, would be possible if he had taken part in one or more of the earlier expeditions in a combatant role and later as a syce.

The greatest number of bars heard of on one of these medals is five. They were those for S. Kordofan 1910, Mandal, Miri, Darfu 1916, and Fasher.

Atwot *(February-April, 1910)*

This bar was awarded for an expedition against the Atwot Dinkas between 9th February and 17th March, 1910, and another in the Aliab District of the Mongalla Province between 29th March and 4th April, 1910. The troops taking part were drawn from the 13th Sudanese Infantry and were commanded by el Kaimakam Harvey Bey. The crews of the Nile steamers which took part received silver medals. Camp followers and syces received bronze medals.

S. Kordofan 1910 *(10th November-19th December, 1910)*

This bar was awarded for two expeditions to the Kordofan District, which is about two hundred miles to the South-West of Khartoum. The first lasted from 10th to 19th November, and the second from 27th November to 19th December, 1910. The first expedition, commanded by el Lewa Asser Pasha, was composed of cavalry, camelry, artillery and the 10th and 12th Sudanese Infantry. It operated in the Eastern Gebels district. The second expedition consisted of a patrol under el Kaimakam Conry Bey, D.S.O., which operated in the Dilling district.

Sudan 1912 *(March, 1912)*

This bar was awarded to thirteen British officers seconded to the Egyptian Army and twenty-one native officers and four hundred and seven men of the 13th Sudanese Infantry, under Major Leveson, D.S.O. for operations against the Adonga Anuak. Two British and three native officers, toegether with forty-two other ranks, were killed in these operations, which ended on the Abyssinian border.

Zeraf 1913-14 *(December, 1913-June, 1914)*

This bar was awarded to members of a patrol under Captain D.A. Fairbairn, West Ridign Regiment, and detachments from the 9th and 12th Sudanese Infantry, and a few mounted infantry, which operated in the Zeraf District. Owing to the swampy nature of the country it was very difficult to gain and maintain contact with the elusive Gaweir Nuer, so that the operations, which started in December, 1913, were continued for several months.

Mandal *(March, 1914)*

In March, 1914, a patrol of camelry under Captain Romilly, D.S.O., Scots Guards, was dispatched to punish the Nubas for cattle-thieving. As punishment for their depredations the unusual idea of a fine of rifles was imposed.

Miri *(April, 1915)*

In March, 1915, it was learned that Fiki Ali, with his followers in the Miri Hills, intended to attack the District Headquarters at Kadugli. Reinforcements consisting of cavalry, camelry, and four companies of infantry were sent to reinforce the garrison and then Fiki Ali was attacked. The active operations lasted from 15th to 21st April.

Mongalla 1915-16 *(December, 1915-14th March, 1916)*

In December, 1915, it became necessary to undertake active operations in the Imatong and Lafite Mountains. A patrol, consisting of three companies of the Equatorial Battalion under Major D.C. Percy Smith, D.S.O., operated in the Imatongs, where they were joined by another patrol under Captain Hobbs composed of men of the 9th Sudanese Infantry and later by some artillery. The combined force then operated in the Lafite Mountains until the 14th March, 1916.

Darfur 1916 *(March-23rd May, 1916)*

This bar was awarded for operations in Darfur against Sultan Ali Dinar, who, encouraged by Enver Pasha and the Senussi, appeared likely to join the Turks in operations against the British. A force, commanded by Lieutenant-Colonel P.V. Kelly, 3rd Hussars, and composed of sixty mounted infantrymen, four companies of camelry, and eight companies of infantry, together with eight guns and two machine-guns, was assembled at Nahud; moving westwards, Meleit was occupied on 18th May, and the Sultan's army, about three thousand five hundred strong, was found to be holding a strong position north of Fasher. Fasher was occupied on 23rd May, but Dinar had escaped. Some Royal Flying Corps and Army Service Corps personnel also received the medals with this bar. Some recipients:— Capt. E. Bannatyne, Lt. J.C. Slessor, Lt. J.K. Maurice, M.C., R.A.S.C., and Pte. J.E. Clark, R. Warwick Rgt., received this bar, also Captain F. Bellamy, M.C., R.F.C., who received this bar and that for Fasher.

Fasher *(1st September-23rd November, 1916)*

On 1st September, 1916, a force commanded by Major W.H. McCowan, Cameron Highlanders, and composed of four British and fourteen native officers and four hundred and sixty-eight other ranks, left Fasher on patrol to find Sultan Ali Dinar. On 1st November, Major H.J. Huddleston, Dorset Regiment, wth three British officers and about three hundred other ranks, left Dibbis on the same errand. On the 6th November, Ali Dinar was surprised in his camp at Guiba. After a short fight, his troops stampeded and his body was found near the camp. His son, Zakaria, escaped, but surrendered to Major Huddleston on

23rd November, 1916. Three members of the R.F.C., as the R.A.F. was then called, and A.S.C. personnel received the medal with this bar. Medals purporting to be to the Royal Flying Corps should be verified.

Lau Nuer (March-May, 1917)

As a result of consistent raids by the Lau Nuer against the Dinkas in the Bor district of Mongalla and other depredations, it was decided to send out a punitive patrol under Major E.A.T. Byaly, D.S.O., Royal Welch Fusiliers. The patrol, which was composed of Sudanese Infantry, combed the Lau country during March, April and May, and after establishing a post at Nyerol under Captain C.C. Goodwin, The Yorkshire Regiment, was withdrawn.

Nyima 1917-18 (2nd November, 1917-February, 1918)

On 16th January, 1917, Chief Agabna, of the Nubas, who lived in the Nyima Hills, raided Kasha and caused other disturbances which necessitated the sending out of a strong force as soon as the rainy season ended. In November, 1917, a force consisting of thirty-one British officers, one hundred and five native officers and 2,875 other ranks was placed under the command of Lieutenant-Colonel L.K. Smith, D.S.O., Royal Scots, with orders to clear the area. At the end of February, Agabna was captured together with over 2,000 troublesome natives.

Atwot 1918 (1st January-26th May, 1918)

Once again the Atwot dinkas caused trouble, this time under the leadership of Malwal Matiang. A patrol consisting of four companies of infantry and one company of mounted infantry with two machine guns was sent out in January, 1918, and operated until the 26th May, when Matiang surrendered. So as not to confuse this bar with that awarded for similar operations in February-April, 1910, the year 1918 was added to the title.

Garjak Nuer (December, 1919-April, 1920)

The Garjak Nuer are a tribe which live in the Eastern Nuer District of the Upper Nile. In December, 1919, they raided their neighbours, the Burun, who were quite peacefully inclined. To prevent the troubles from spreading to the Lau Nuer two strong columns were sent out, the Northern commanded by Major G.C. Cobden, 9th Lancers, and the Southern commanded by Major C.R.K. Bacon, O.B.E., The Queen's Royal Regiment. Operations continued until the end of April, 1920.

R.A.F. (approx. 30).

Aliab Dinka (8th November, 1919-May, 1920)

This bar was awarded for service against the Aliab Dinka, Bor Dinka, and Mandari tribes, who rose unexpectedly and attacked the post at Menkamon. Two columns commanded by Major R.F. White, Essex Regiment, and Major F.C. Roberts, V.C., D.S.O., M.C., Worcestershire Regiment, were dispatched. The latter column was surprised by the Dinka and, owing to the stampeding of its carriers, was forced to return to Tombe, which it reached on 13th December, 1919. In March, 1920, a further force under Lieutenant-Colonel R.H. Darwall, D.S.O., Royal Marines, composed of mounted infantry, camelry, and Sudanese infantry, established itself at Pap and gradually cleared the country.

Nyala (26th September, 1921-20th January, 1922)

It should be noted that this bar comes before that for Darfur, 1921, though the period of service for which it was awarded continued on much later. In

September, 1921, Fiki Abdullahi el Suheina proclaimed himself to be the Prophet Isa and obtained a considerable following in Southern Darfur. On 26th Setpember he attacked the District Headquarters at Nyala, but was driven off and killed; but this did not put an end to the troubles, which lasted for a further four months. This bar was awarded to forty mounted infantrymen, forty police and a few friendlies for the defence of Nyala, and also to members of the column under Major S.T. Grigg, D.S.O., M.C., West Yorkshire Regiment, which operated south of Nyala until 20th January, 1922.

Darfur 1921 *(26th September-22nd November, 1921)*

It should be noted that this bar follows that for Nyala in spite of the fact that the period for which it was awarded was completed first.

This bar was awarded to those who served at, or west of, Kereinik between 26th September and 22nd November, 1921. It was also awarded for services against Fiki Abdullahi and his followers (see Nyala above).

93 AFRICA GENERAL SERVICE MEDAL (1902-1956)

Obverse	*1st issue:* King Edward VII in uniform, facing left, and legend: "EDWARDVS VII REX IMPERATOR".
	2nd issue: King George V in military uniform, facing left, and legend: "GEORGIVS V BRITT: OMN: REG ET IND: IMP:"
	3rd issue: Queen Elizabeth II, facing right, and legend: "ELIZA-BETH · II · DEI · GRATIA · REGINA · F: D: +."
Reverse	Except for the wording in the exergue, it is the same as that for the East and Central Africa Medal. A standing figure of Britannia holding a palm branch and scroll in her extended left hand and a trident in her right. In the exergue is the word "AFRICA".
Size	1.42 in. diameter.
Ribbon	1.25 in. wide. Yellow edged with black and with two green stripes towards the centre.
Suspension	By means of a plain, straight suspender.
Designers	1st issue: G.W. de Saulles.
	2nd issue: The obverse was designed by Mrs. Mary Gillick, C.B.E.
Naming	In thin impressed block capitals.
No. of bars issued	Thirty-four with the King Edward Medal; ten with the King George V, and one with that of Queen Elizabeth II — a total of forty-five with as many as seven or more bars to a medal.

This silver medal (occasionally issued in bronze) was sanctioned in 1902, to replace the East and West Africa Medal, to which twenty-two bars had been awarded. It was struck in both high and low relief.

There are genuine medals in existence to Indian units that cannot be traced as having been present. It is suggested therefore, that there must have been occasions when the medal was impressed with the name of the unit that the man was serving with before he left India, or after his return.

Indians selected from several units of the Indian Army were employed with the African regiments.

It is suspected that the titles of the units of the King's African Rifles were not strictly adhered to immediately after the change of nomenclature in 1902, so it is recommended that the table which follows be studied, and that a medal not be condemned simply because it is named with, say, the 1st Uganda Rifles instead of 4th King's African Rifles.

King Edward VII died between the issue of the bar for Nandi 1905-06 and that for Shimber Berris 1914-15, so, naturally, we find the later issue bears the head of King George V. This new design was instituted under Army Order No. 89 of 1916.

It is safe to say that all the medals bearing the head of King George V are very rare, as are many of the bars awarded during the reign of King Edward VII.

The pieces of the second issue are thinner than those of the first.

The medal was never issued without one or more bars.

For the sake of easy reference we have grouped together all the bars awarded for Nigeria during King Edward's reign, and also those for Somaliland. The bar for Jidballi is inserted after the campaign in which the battle occurred, i.e. Somaliland 1902-04.

On 1st January, 1902, the various local East African forces were amalgamated into the King's African Rifles. A study of the following table will show which were the former titles of the battalions:

1st Bn. K.A.R., formerly the 1st Bn. Central Africa Rifles.
2nd Bn. K.A.R., formerly the 2nd Bn. Central Africa Rifles.
3rd Bn. K.A.R., formerly the East Africa Rifles.
4th Bn. K.A.R., formerly the 1st B. Uganda Rifles.
5th Bn. K.A.R., formerly the 2nd Bn. Uganda Rifles.
6th Bn. K.A.R., formerly the various local forces in the Somaliland Protec-
torate. In 1909 this battalion was disbanded and was replaced by the Somaliland Camel Constabulary, which was later renamed the Somaliland Camel Corps.

N. Nigeria *(July, 1900-September, 1901)*

A total of 365* of these bars, which bear no date, were awarded to members of the Northern Nigeria Regiment for service in any of the following operations:

(a)   Operations against the forces of Bida and Kontagora under Major W.H. O'Neill, R.A., from July to December, 1900; or under Major G.V. Kemball, R.A., from 19th January, 1900, to 17th February, 1901.
(b)   The expedition against the Chief of Tawari under Major A.W. Cole, Royal Welch Fusiliers, from 6th to 8th December, 1900.
(c)   Operations against the Emir of Yola under Lieutenant-Colonel T.L.N. Morland, K.R.R.C., in August and September, 1901.

N. Nigeria 1902 *(1st February-16th May and 15th June-30th November, 1902)*

Five hundred and thirty-five of these bars were awarded to members of a further expedition under Lieutenant-Colonel T.L.N. Morland, K.R.R.C., to Bornu which lasted from 1st February to 16th May, 1902, and also to members of the Kontagora Force, which operated between 12th and 20th February, 1902.

Army Order No. 4 of 1905 sanctioned the award of this bar to those under the command of Captain G.C. Merrick, R.A., at Argungu and on French convoy duty between 15th June and 30th November, 1902.

The 2nd Northern Nigeria Regiment composed most of the forces.

N. Nigeria 1903 *(29th January-27th July, 1903)*

In October, 1903, sanction was granted for the award of 734 bars to members of an expedition to Kano and Sokoto, under General Kemball, between 29th January and 15th March, 1903. In April, 1905, it was decided that all who had

*Throughout this series one must bear in mind that although relatively large numbers were issued, very few indeed have survived.

operated between Sokoto and Birni between 15th April and 27th July, 1903, should also be awarded this bar.

The recipients were as follows: twenty-four British officers; twelve British N.C.O.s; and natives of the 1st and 2nd Northern Nigeria Regiment, S. Nigeria Regiment and 4th (Lagos) Bn. West African Frontier Force.

N. Nigeria 1903-04 *(23rd December, 1903-12th March, 1904)*

Three hundred silver and four hundred bronze medals were awarded to members of the Bassa Expedition under Captain G.C. Merrick, R.A., between 23rd December, 1903, and 12th March, 1904. Members of the 2nd Northern Nigeria Regiment received three hundred silver medals, and four hundred bronze medals were awarded to native carriers. The N.N. Constabulary received the silver medals.

N. Nigeria 1904 *(March-October, 1904)*

This bar was awarded for services during March, April, July and October, 1904, against small tribes at the head of the Benue river around Yola.

The recipients consisted of a few British officers and N.C.O.s and members of the 2nd Northern Nigeria Regiment.

N. Nigeria 1906 *(14th February-24th April, 1906)*

This bar was given for service under Lieutenant F.E. Blackwood, East Surrey Regiment, and Captain R.H. Goodwin, R.G.A., in the suppression of the Satiru Rising, during which sixty-nine members of the Mounted Infantry Company of the Northern Nigeria Regiment, together with six British officers and sixty-five natives of the 2nd Northern Nigeria Regiment, were present.

It was also awarded for service under Colonel A.W.G. Lowry Cole in the suppression of the Hadeija Rising to 280 Mounted Infantry and 293 members of the 2nd Northern Nigeria Regiment.

The dates of these two risings were 14th February-11th March and 16th-24th April, 1906, respectively.

Colour-Sergt. C.H. Gosling, D.C.L.I., received this bar (and also the L.S.G.C. Medal).

S. Nigeria *(March-May, 1901)*

This bar was awarded to members of the Southern Nigeria Regiment who took part in the Ishan and Ulia Expeditions under Captain W.C.G. Heneker, Connaught Rangers, between March and May, 1901. Note that it bears no date.

Members of the Southern Nigeria Regiment were the only recipients.

S. Nigeria 1902 *(15th June-30th December, 1902)*

This bar was awarded to members of the Southern Nigeria Regiment who took part in one or more of seven patrols, which lasted only a few days each, between 15th June and 30th December, 1902.

S. Nigeria 1902-03 *(7th July, 1902-8th June, 1903)*

This bar was awarded to members of the Southern Nigeria Regiment for service under Colonel A.F. Montanaro, C.B., R.A., against the Uris and the people of Omonoha and Ebima between 7th July, 1902, and 8th June, 1903. It was also awarded for operations under Lieutenant-Colonel W.C.G. Heneker, D.S.O., Connaught Rangers, against Chief Adukukaiku of Igarra and further operations in the Afikpo District in December, 1902, and January, 1903.

S. Nigeria 1903 *(4th February-5th December, 1903)*

This bar was awarded to members of the Southern Nigeria Regiment for the following expeditions:

- *(a)* Under Brevet-Colonel A.F. Montanaro, D.S.O., R.A., on the Nun river in September and October.
- *(b)* Under Brevet-Major A.M.N. Mackenzie, R.A., in the Eket District between 16th and 25th September.
- *(c)* Under Brevet-Major A.M.N. Mackenzie, R.A., in the Mkpani country from the 1st to the 5th December.

Army Order No. 40 of 1906 extended the award of this bar to include the following operations:

- *(d)* Under Captain H.H. Sproule, 4th Cavalry, in the Ebegga country in February.
- *(e)* Under Captain E.L. Roddy, Cheshire Regiment, in the country west of Anan in March.

S. Nigeria 1903-04 *(24th December, 1903-15th January, 1904)*

This bar was awarded to members of the Southern Nigeria Regiment for the expedition, under Brevet-Major I.G. Hogg, D.S.O., 4th Hussars, to the towns of Osea, Oriri and N'doto.

S. Nigeria 1904 *(12th January-3rd June, 1904)*

This bar was awarded for five small expeditions between 12th January and 3rd June, 1904. All the recipients were from the Southern Nigeria Regiment, except for a few British officers who were seconded.
Lieut. Buckland, R.N.R., received this bar.

S. Nigeria 1904-05 *(15th November, 1904-27th February, 1905)*

This bar was awarded to the Southern Regiment for operations under Brevet-Major H.M.T. Trenchard, Royal Scots Fusiliers, through the Ibibio and Kwa Country.

S. Nigeria 1905 *(10th-18th October, 1905)*

This bar was awarded to members of the Southern Nigeria Regiment for operations in the K'wale District.

S. Nigeria 1905-06

Army Order No. 277 of 1906, which authorized the issue of this bar, does not state the inclusive dates of the operations for which it was awarded. The award was for officers and men of the columns which concentrated at Bende and Oka under Brevet-Major H.M. Trenchard, Royal Scots Fusiliers, and Captain G.T. Mair, R.F.A., and took part in the Bende-Onitsha Hinterland Expedition.

East Africa 1902 *(4th September-25th October, 1902)*

This rare bar was awarded to members of the 3rd Bn. King's African Rifles and Police who formed the Maruka Patrol under Lieutenant F.W.O. Maycock, Suffolk Regiment. The Patrol operated between 4th September and 25th October, 1902.

East Africa 1904 *(13th February-17th March, 1904)*

This scarce bar was awarded to members of the Iraini Patrol under Captain F.A. Dickinson, D.C.L.I., which operated between 13th February and 17th

March, 1904. It was composed of members of the East African Police Force and 3rd Bn. King's African Rifles.

East Africa 1905 *(31st May-9th October, 1905)*

This bar was awarded to members of two expeditions; the first, under Major L.R.H. Pope-Hennessy, D.S.O., Oxford and Bucks Light Infantry, to Sotik between 31st May and 12th July, 1905; the second under Captain E.V. Jenkins, D.S.O., The Duke of Wellington's Regiment, to Kisii between 1st September and 9th October, 1905.

These expeditions were composed of members of the East African Police Force, the Uganda Rifles and a unit whose initials are P.C.E., but one cannot say what those initials stand for.

East Africa 1906 *(18th June-19th July, 1906)*

This bar was awarded to members of the 3rd King's African Rifles and East African Police who accompanied Lieutenant F.W.O. Maycock, D.S.O., to the Embu Territory between 18th June and 19th July, 1906.

West Africa 1906 *(9th June, 1906-17th February, 1907)*

This bar was awarded to members of the punitive expedition, under Captain W.C.E. Rudkin, D.S.O., R.F.A., which operated in the Owa Territory between 9th June and 3rd August, 1906.

It was also awarded for two other small expeditions under Lieutenants P. Chapman and E.J. Worsley, which operated between 12th November, 1906, and 17th February, 1907.

The recipients were members of the Southern Nigeria Regiment and 2nd Northern Nigeria Regiment.

West Africa 1908 *(11th-31st December, 1908)*

This bar was awarded to members of the Southern Nigeria Regiment who operated in the Sonkwala district between 11th and 31st December, 1908, under Lieutenant-Colonel G.F.A. Whitlock, R.E.

West Africa 1909-10 *(2nd December, 1909-27th May, 1910)*

This bar was awarded to members of the Southern Nigeria Regiment for operations in the Ogwashi-Oku country under Major G.N. Sheffield, 3rd Bn. Essex Regiment, between 2nd November and 18th December, 1909, and for a further expedition under Major G.L. Bruce between 4th and 27th May, 1910.

Captain H.G. Chapman, Southern Nigeria Regiment, received this bar.

Somaliland 1901 *(22nd May-30th July, 1901)*

This bar was awarded for the first expedition against the Mad Mullah, which lasted from 22nd May to 30th July, 1901. It was commanded by Colonel Sir E.J.E. Swayne, who had under his command twenty-one British officers, fifty Punjabis and about 1,500 Somali levies who were mostly raised locally.

This is a very rare bar, which the Somali levies received in silver or bronze according to whether they fulfilled a combatant or non-combatant role.

Armourer-Sergt. H.H. Goodwin, R. Ordnance Corps, received this bar and also the Queen's South Africa Medal with, among others, the bar for "SOUTH AFRICA 1901". It is rare for a man to get different medals with bars bearing the same date.

Somaliland 1902-04 *(18th January, 1902-11th May, 1904)*

Between 18th January, 1902 and 11th May, 1904, there were three more expeditions against the Mad Mullah, making four against him in all to date, for which both silver and bronze medals were awarded.

This bar was also awarded to the officers who accompanied Colonel A.N. Rochfort, C.B., C.M.G., and the Abyssinian forces which cooperated with the British and 14 of the Liverpool Regiment.

Those who took part in the Battle of Jidballi, or who acted as baggage party during the action on 10th January, 1904, received an additional bar named Jidballi *(quod vide)*. Those who received the bar for Jidballi also received this one, but not necessarily *vice versa*. The bar for Jidballi should be consulted, as some units will be found there and not below.

Second Expedition (8th February to 17th October, 1902, under Colonel Sir E.J.E. Swayne): twelve British Staff Officers; sixty men of the 1 King's African Rifles (Sikhs); three hundred of 2 King's African Rifles (Yaos); five hundred of 6 King's African Rifles (Somalis); 450 Mounted Infantry and Camelry; 1 and 2 Bombay Grenadiers.

Third Expedition (4th November, 1902, to 3rd July, 1903): 4 King's Royal Rifle Corps (147); Mounted Infantry; Somaliland Burgher Corps; Punjab Mounted Infantry; 8 or 28 (Lahore) Mountain Battery (65); King's African Rifles Camel Battery (45); Telegraph Section R.E. (58); Bikanir Camel Corps; 107 Bombay Pioneers (737); 1 (Sikhs), 2 (Yaos), 3 (Sudanese), (5 Sikhs), 6 (Somalis), King's African Rifles; 23 Bombay Rifles (400); 2 (later renumbered 52) Sikhs; 15 British and 58, 65, 69 Native Field Hospitals; 15 Company, A.S.C.

Fourth Expedition (26th October, 1903, to 25th April, 1904): All the above troops were present and the following additional ones. 1 Bn. Hampshire Regiment (326); R. Warwicks (Lieutenant G.D. Martin, 1 Sgt., 1 Cpl., and 25 Ptes.); Essex Regiment (45); 17 and 19 Companies Bombay Sappers and Miners; 27 Punjabis.

This bar is also found to the Yorkshire Regiment and a few others including 2nd R. Dgns. (2), King's Liverpool Regiment (14) and Norfolk Regiment (28 — 1 to an Offr. & 27 to other ranks).

Naval medals were awarded to those engaged in Somaliland between 18th January, 1902, and 11th May, 1904, and to those who accompanied Colonel A.N. Rochfort, C.B., C.M.G., with the Abyssinian forces. The award to the Navy included all those serving on H.M. ships employed in connection with the operations within the limits of a sphere comprising the Somaliland coast from Berbera to Mogdishu* and including Aden, but excluded those serving in torpedo boats.

H.M.S. *Coassack* (197), *Dryad* (154), *Fox* (405), *Harrier* (150), *Highflyer* (533), *Hussar* (125), *Hyacinth* (553), *Merlin* (142), *Mohawk* (205), *Naiad* (283), *Perseus* (329), *Pomone* (311), *Porpoise* (167), *Redbreast* (82).

Royal Indian Marine ships: *Canning, Dalhousie, Mayo.* Hospital ship *Hardinge.* Royal Italian Navy (2).

87 medals were authorised with bars Somaliland 1902-04 *and* Somaliland 1908-10. Foreign representatives appear to have been given this medal, as there is one to Captain Eugenio Finzi, of the Italian Navy.

Jidballi *(10th January, 1904)*

This bar was awarded to those who took part in the engagement and to those who formed part of the guard left behind during it in charge of the baggage

---

*This is the spelling used in the Admiralty Order, but it is also found spelt Mogadishu, Magadoxo and Mukdeesha.

under the command of Major W.B. Mullins, 27th Punjabis.

Those who received it also received the bar "Somaliland, 1902-04", so that this bar is not found singly. The units that follow would be entitled to both bars.

Regiments present: Poona, Umballa and 5 Indian Mounted Infantry; Gadabursi Horse; Bikanir Camel Corps; 8 or 28 (Lahore) Mountain Battery (65); King's African Rifles Camel Battery (45); 19 Company Bombay Sappers and Miners; 1 Hants (259); sections of twenty-five men each of the Royal Warwickshire Regiment (12); Liverpool Regiment (14); Norfolk Regiment, Essex Regiment, York and Lancs Regiment, Yorkshire Regiment, 2 Middlesex Regiment, 4 K.R.R.C. (105), and the Rifle Brigade; 1, 2, 3 King's African Rifles; 27 Punjabis; 2 Sikhs (later renumbered 52); Arab Police Corps.

Medals bearing this bar are to be found to N.C.O.s of regiments not given above. They were instructors to the King's African Rifles or in charge of some of the native labour and carrier units. I know of a medal with this bar to a man in the Leicestershire Regiment who may have been an officer's servant.

The only Naval recipient of this bar was Commander E.S. Carey, of H.M.S. *Naiad*.

Somaliland 1908-10 *(19th August, 1908-31st January, 1910)*

This bar was awarded for further services, under Colonel J.E. Gough, V.C., C.M.G., against the rebellious Somalis.

Regiments present: 1, 3, 4, 6 King's African Rifles; 66 Punjab Infantry; 127 Baluch Light Infantry and 129 Baluchis;† Wilde's Rifles; Sikh F.F.

Ships of the Mediterranean Fleet and East Indies Squadron were employed in the blockade of the Somali coast in connection with the operations. The bar was granted to all who took part in the patrolling, or at Aden between 19th August, 1908, and 31st January, 1910. Occasional visits did not, however, count for the award.

H.M.S. *Barham* (208), *Diana* (397), *Fox* (335), *Hyacinth* (498), *Philomel* (467), *Prosperine* (447). Royal Indian Marine ship *Hardinge*.

89 medals were authorised with both Somaliland bars.

Uganda 1900 *(3rd July-October, 1900)*

This bar was awarded for operations in the Nandi Country, under Lieutenant-Colonel J.T. Evatt, D.S.O., Indian Staff Corps. The recipients were five British officers,* three Indian officers, Quartermaster-Sergt. W. Ramsay, R.E., two hundred and twenty-five members of the 1st Uganda Rifles, and a few members of the Kisumu Police.

B.C.A. 1899-1900 *(August, 1899-December, 1900)*

This bar, for British Central Africa, was awarded for services in any of the following operations:

(a) Operations against Nkwamba from August to October, 1899, under Captain F.B. Pearce, West Yorks.

(b) Operations in North Eastern Rhodesia against Kazembe from September to November, 1899.

(c) Operations in central Agoniland, against Kalulu in December, 1900, under Captain R. Bright, The Buffs.

---

†The medals so named were awarded to men who served with the 127th Regiment during the campaign.

*Including Capt. E. Bagnall, 4/Yorks. Rgt.

Regiments present: 24 Punjab Infantry; 34, 45 Sikhs; 1 King's African Rifles; Central African Rifles.

Jubaland (16th November, 1900-30th April, 1901)

This scarce bar was awarded for service under Colonel T. Ternan, against the Ogaden Somalis, including military forces at Kismayu and to officers and men of the Royal Navy and Marines who landed to supplement the garrison at Kismayu between 16th November, 1900, and 30th April, 1901. The number of medals awarded to Indian troops were about four hundred and sixty-five silver and twenty-six bronze. The medals to African troops were usually marked with the recipient's number and name only.

Regiments present: One section of No. 9 (Murree) Mountain Battery (93); 16 Bombay Infantry; East African Rifles; Aden Camel Corps; Supply and Transport Corps (the only medals that are known have been of bronze).

H.M.S. *Magicienne* (172), *Scout* (16), and *Terpsichore* (39).

Gambia (January-March, 1901)

This bar was awarded to those who took part in the operations under Lieut-enant-Colonel H.E.J. Brake, C.B., D.S.O., R.A. The Naval awards were limited to a few officers, petty officers, and seamen who were under fire in the action at Dumbutu on 11th January, 1901. Those engaged in patrolling rivers, or transporting troops, were not eligible, so that the crews of H.M.S. *Magicienne, Scout* and *Terpsichore*, though present, were not rewarded.

Regiments present: 2 King's African Rifles; 3 West Indian Regiment and District Commissioners who served with the Gambia Expeditionary Force received this bar. There were thirty-seven Naval awards as follows:

H.M.S. *Forte* (29); *Thrush* (3); *Dwarf* (2); *Transport Service* (2).

(A medal to Commander P. Wainewright, Gambia Expeditionary Force is known. Whether he was a Commissioner at the time, or serving with the Navy, one cannot say.)

Aro 1901-1902 (15th November, 1901-23rd March, 1902)

The rather unusual dating of this bar should be noted, the second date being repeated in full. This bar was issued to fourteen British Military Officers and 1,830 native soldiers in addition to the Naval personnel mentioned below. Eleven District Commissioners and officers of the Niger Police were also present, with the Aro Expeditionary Force under Lieutenant-Colonel A.F. Montanaro, R.A.

Regiments present: 4 (Lagos) and 5 Southern Nigeria Regiment; 1, 2 Northern Nigeria Regiment.

Three officers and twenty-seven ratings from H.M.S. *Jackdaw* and fifty-three members of the crew of H.M.S. *Thrush*.

Lango 1901 (24th April-24th August, 1901)

This bar was awarded to members of a punitive expedition under Major C. Delme-Radcliffe, Connaught Rangers, against Sudanese mutineers between 24th April and 24th August, 1901. The only regiment to participate was the 4th Bn. King's African Rifles, to which about sixty bars were awarded.

Kissi 1905 (27th March-28th June, 1905)

This rare bar was awarded to members of the Sierra Leone Bn. of the West African Frontier Force who operated in the Kissi Country under Captain C.E. Palmer, R.A., between 27th March and 28th June, 1905.

Nandi 1905-06 *(18th October, 1905-6th July, 1906)*

This very rare bar was awarded for service in Nandi Country under Lieutenant-Colonel E.G. Harrison, D.S.O., Reserve of Officers, Major Walker, Royal Fusiliers, and Capt. Mackay, Seaforth Highlanders.

Regiments present: 1, 3, 4 King's African Rifles; East African Police Force. Medals are known to an officer whose unit is given as the Mombasa Defence Force, and another to Captain B.R. Graham, Q.O. Corps of Guides.

The subsequent issues of the African General Service Medal, until the award of the bar for service against the Mau Mau tribes in Kenya, bore the head of King George V, but were otherwise, in all respects, the same. This medal was not issued in addition to the King Edward's Medal, those in possession of this received bars in addition to it. Participants in these campaigns *only* were not eligible for any of the medals given for the Great War, 1914-18.

Shimber Berris 1914-15 *(19th November, 1914-9th February, 1915)*

This bar was awarded for two small campaigns against the Dervishes from 19th to 25th November, 1914, and again from 2nd to 9th February, 1915, under Lieutenant-Colonel T.A. Cubitt, D.S.O., R.A. It should be noted that those who took part in these operations only during the period of the First Great War (4th August, 1914, to 11th November, 1918) were not entitled to *any* of the medals awarded for the Great War.

This is a very rare bar, though the total number of officers and men who must have been entitled to silver medals was about eight hundred and seventy-five.

Regiments present: King's African Rifles (250); 23 Sikh Pioneers (detachment); Somaliland Camel Corps (600).

Nyasaland 1915 *(24th January-17th February, 1915)*

This bar was awarded to a few members of the 1st King's African Rifles, a few of the Nyasaland Volunteer Reserve, and native policemen from Blantyre and Nchew, who quelled a small rising in the Shire Highlands between 24th January and 17th February, 1915.

East Africa 1913 *(17th June-7th August, 1913)*

This bar was awarded for operations under Captain Brooks, D.C.L.I., against the Dodingas between June and August, 1913. The recipients were members of the East African Police.

East Africa 1914 *(2nd April-7th July, 1914)*

This bar was awarded for a punitive expedition under Captain R.H. Leeke, The Rifle Brigade; Lieutenant S.W.H. Silver, the Suffolk Regiment, and Lieutenant H.A. Lilley, the Yorkshire Regiment, against the Turkhana Tribe in the North Frontier District of British East Africa and the Uganda Borders West of Lake Rudolf. The recipients were mostly of the East Africa Police.

East Africa 1913-14 *(15th December, 1913-31st May, 1914)*

This bar was awarded for operations under Lieutenant-Colonel B.R. Graham, 3 King's African Rifles, against the Merehan Tribe. The recipients were members of the 3 King's African Rifles, the S. & T.I.A. and C. Coy. 1 King's African Rifles.

East Africa 1915 *(4th February-28th May, 1915)*

This bar was awarded for an expedition under Leituenant-Colonel W.F.S. Edwards, D.S.O., against the Turkhanas between 4th February and 28th May,

1915. Most of the recipients were members of the Uganda Police and East African Police.

Jubaland 1917-18 (23rd July, 1917-24th March, 1918)

This bar was awarded to the 5th Bn; 1/6 Bn. King's African Rifles and one section of No. ((Murree) Mountain Battery for service under Lieutenant-Colonel W.E.H. Barratt, King's African Rifles, Major E.G.M. Porcelli, D.C.L.I., Captain J.F. Wolseley-Bourne, and Captain O. Martin, King's African Rifles, in the military operations against the Northern Aulihan tribe west of the Juba river, or north or east of a line Waregta — Lake Abeleni — Lorian Swamp — El Wak — Dolo.

Twenty-six bronze medals were issued bearing this bar, in addition, of course, to the silver awards.

East Africa 1918 (20th April-19th June, 1918)

This bar, sanctioned by Army Order No. 51 of 1920, was awarded for services under Major R.F. White, The Essex Regiment; Major H. Rayne, M.C., King's African Rifles; and Captain J.H.R. Yardley, D.S.O., Royal Inniskilling Fusiliers, in military operations against Northern Turkhana, Marille, Donyiro and kindred tribes in the vicinity of the southern Sudan boundary and west of Lake Rudolf.

The 5th Bn. King's African Rifles supplied the troops.

Nigeria 1918 (11th June-31st July, 1918)

This bar was awarded under Army Order No. 460 of 1924, for services against the Egba tribe in the vicinity of the Nigerian Government Railway (main line) from Abeokuta in the north to Lagos in the south within the area bounded on the east by a line from Abeokuta through Ijebu — Ode to Lagos, and on the west by a line from Abeokuta to the Ilaro, thence through Igbessa to Lagos.

Captain S.G. Clifton, the West Riding Regiment, Captain F.W. Whetton, the Essex Regiment, Lieutenant A.L. Burt and Sgt. E. Oldfield, R. Lancs received this bar.

Somaliland 1920 (21st January-12th February, 1920)

This bar was awarded for the fifth, and final, expedition against the Mad Mullah. The bar "Somaliland, 1901", was awarded for the first expedition, that worded "Somaliland, 1902-04" for the second, third and fourth expeditions.

The expedition was commanded by Major (temporary Colonel) G.H. Summers, C.M.G., K.G.O. Light Cavalry, Indian Army, under the general direction of the Governor, Sir G.F. Archer, K.C.M.G.

The medal with this bar only does not swivel.

Regiments present: Part of the 2 King's African Rifles; 6 King's African Rifles; Somaliland Camel Corps (700); half of the 1/101 Bombay Grenadiers (400); Somaliland Police; Somaliland Levies; one flight of R.A.F.; R. Sussex Rgt. (1);

The members of the following H.M. ships also received the award for services between 21st January and 12th February; H.M.S. *Ark Royal* (149); *Clio* (147); *Odin* (156).

Kenya (21st October, 1952-17th November, 1956) √

Approval for the award of this bar was given by Her Majesty in 1955.

It is nice to note that the period for eligibility has been extended to ninety-one days on land for all the services which puts it in a class above the tip and run ones that have been made since 1945.

The area of operations is defined as the Central or Southern Province of

Kenya, in the Naivasha, Nakuru or Laikipia Districts of the Rift Valley Province or the Nairobi extra-provincial District.

Apart from the members of the three regular Fighting Serivces, including the W.R.A.C. and Nos. 30, 152 and 208 Sqdns., R.A.F., who took part in operations against the Mau Mau, the personnel of many other units are included in the list of those entitled to the new medal. They are for instance, The King's African Rifles, Kenya Regiment, E. African Rifles Camel Bty., East Africa Pioneer Corps, Civil Police Forces, the Civil Prison Service, and a bewildering list of civil officials ranging from Provincial Commissioners to Headmen. In addition to all these there are the members of the various civilian organizations.

The re-issuing of this medal raises two very interesting points, for it is now that with the longest span of life in our history, and the period that has elapsed between the award of this bar and its predecessor is also the greatest — thirty-five years.

94 1914 STAR (5th August-22nd November, 1914)

General description	This bronze star measures approximately 1¾ in. wide and 2½ in. from top to bottom. The ring for suspension is stamped out solid with the piece. The star has three points; the topmost is replaced by a crown at the top of which is a half-inch diameter ring for suspension. Across the face are two crossed swords, the points and handles of which protrude and thus form what might be considered four additional points.
Obverse	In the centre, on a scroll, is the date "1914"; on two further scrolls, one above and the other immediately underneath the date, are the months "AUG" and "NOV." The "AUG" is on the top scroll. These three scrolls are surrounded by a laurel wreath ¾ in. diameter, on the bottom of which is superscribed G.
Reverse	Perfectly flat and plain, except for the stamping of the recipient's number, rank, name, and regiment.
Size	Maximum width, 1.75 in.; height 2.4 in.. including ring for suspension.
Ribbon	1.25 in. wide. Reading from left to right as seen on the wearer, the colours are red, white and blue shaded and watered.
Suspension	Through a loop, as described in the general description.
Designer	Unknown.
Naming	The recipient's number, rank, initials, name, and regiment are stamped in block capitals on the reverse in three lines for officers and other ranks.
No. of bars issued	One.

This Bronze Star was authorized in April, 1917, to be awarded to those who served in France or Belgium on the strength of a unit, or service in either of those two countries between 5th August and midnight on 22nd/23rd November, 1914. 378,000 issued but it is not known how many of these were awarded the "Mons" bar. 160 medals only without bar to Canadians.

In October, 1919, the King sanctioned the award of a bar to this star to all who had been *under fire* in France or Belgium during, or between the above dates.

It should be noted that there are two categories of recipients, (1) those who served the requisite period under fire, and (2) those who served the same period not under fire.

The bar is of bronze, $1\frac{5}{16}$ in. x $\frac{3}{16}$ in. and bears on it "5TH AUG-22nd NOV. 1914". There are small hoes at each corner enabling it to be sewn on to the ribbon. Those entitled to the bar wear a small silver rose in the centre of the ribbon when the medal is not worn.

Groups are to be found, which include this star, and also the Mercantile Marine Medal. The recipients probably transferred to the Merchant Service subesequent to serving ashore during the qualifying period.

A few women received this Star, sometimes referred to as the Mons Star. One was Miss Ellanore Parker, who died on 15th October, 1965, aged 86, in Victoria, B.C.

Personnel of the Royal Navy were awarded the 1914-15 Star, except for the few who served at Antwerp prior to midnight, 22nd/23rd November, 1914.

95 1914-1915 STAR (5th August, 1914-31st December, 1915)

This star is identical with the 1914 Star in every respect except that the centre scroll bears the dates "1914-15" and the two small scrolls bearing "AUG" and "NOV" are omitted.

The particulars concerning the award of this star are, briefly, as follows:

It was given to all who saw service in any theatre of war against the Central Powers between 5th August, 1914, and 31st December, 1915, except those eligible for the 1914 Star. This statement must be qualified by the remark that it was *not* awarded to those who passed through a theatre of war, or only visited one. For instance, those who passed through any of the theatres as passengers, or visited them in inspections, did not qualify. Neither was it awarded to those who, between these dates, *only* saw service for which the Africa General Service Medal or the Sudan 1910 Medal was granted.

It is interesting to note that those who saw service on the Indian Frontier between 28th November, 1914, and 27th October, 1915, did, however, qualify. This must have been because no bar was awarded to the India General Service 1908 Medal for these operations, but as the star was not awarded without the War and Victory Medals, it is difficult to understand why participants in these operations should have received three medals. Why, one wonders, one medal for the Nyima Expedition, in the Sudan, from October, 1917, to February, 1918, and three medals for operations on the Landakai Ridge in August, 1915? Approx. 2,366,000 issued (283,500 to the Royal Navy and 71,500 to Canadian units).

96 BRITISH WAR MEDAL (1914-20)

Obverse	The coinage head of King George V with legend "GEORGIVS V BRITT: OMN: REX ET IND: IMP:"
Reverse	St. George on horseback facing right. The horse is trampling on the shield of the Central Powers. At the foot is a skull and crossbones, at the top there is the rising sun. Around the edge are the dates "1914" and "1918".
Size	1.42 in. diameter.
Ribbon	1.25 in. wide. A broad orange watered stripe down the centre bordered with white, black and blue ones.
Suspension	By a plain, straight suspender, which does not swivel.
Designer	W. McMillan.
Naming	In rather faint indented block capitals. Medals awarded to officers do not give the name of their regiments, except those of the Royal Artillery.

This medal, which carries no bar, commemorates some of the most terrible battles the world has ever known. The casualties in the Ypres Salient and on the Somme from 1915 to 1918 were more than our total for the Second World War.

The design of the reverse shows a welcome change from the usual, to make them swivel would have added considerably to the cost.

The question of giving bars for certain battles and theatres of operation was raised, about sixty-eight were suggested for Naval recipients and seventy-nine for the Army. The idea was, however, dropped in 1923 on account of the expense involved. The naval bars however were authorised but not issued which explains why miniatures to naval recipients are often seen with bars.

This medal was issued singly without the Allied Victory Medal to certain regular and mobolized personnel who did not see any fighting.

Recipients of a Mention in Despatches who did not qualify for the Allied Victory Medal wore a bronze oak leaf on the ribbon on this medal.

It was issued in bronze (110,000) to Chinese, Maltese and other native Labour Corps and other native personnel who were mobilized for war service and receive pay at military rates.

As foreigners are often seen wearing the ribbon of this medal it would be as well to say that it was the British War Medal and was awarded to all who served in our forces, and many foreigners did so. Those who served with their own forces all the time did not receive it, but they did receive the Allied Victory Medal — that is those whose Governments agreed to issue it, which was not always the case.

The medal was awarded for services after 1918. It was awarded to Naval members of a Mission to Russia in 1919-20, anf for mine clearance in the North Sea between 11th November, 1918, and 30th November, 1919.

Some groups are known which contain two of these medals or two Victory Medals. In one case the two issues were inscribed to entirely different regiments. There are various possible reasons why this happened, not forgetting that the issue of two identical medals to the same man is a mistake. The most probable was that the man may have re-enlisted for service in Russia. It is, of course, quite possible that his name was on the roll of one regiment which made out their nominal roll fairly early, and then he was transferred to another regiment and put his name down again, not mentioning that it was already down elsewhere. Approx. 6,500,000 issued.

97 MERCANTILE MARINE WAR MEDAL (1914-18)

Obverse	The coinage head of King George V with legend "GEORGIVS V BRITT. OMN: REX ET IND: IMP:"
Reverse	The bows of a steamship with a sailing ship in the right background. In the right foreground there is a sinking submarine, which is very hard to distinguish as such. It is between the right-hand wave and the sailing ship. In the exergue is the wording "FOR WAR SERVICE MERCANTILE MARINE 1914-1918" in three lines.
Size	1.42 in. diameter.
Ribbon	1.25 in. wide. Watered green and red divided by a thin white stripe. The green should be to the left facing the wearer.
Suspension	By a straight, non-swivelling suspender.
Designer	Harold Stabler.

This bronze medal, issued by the Board of Trade, was awarded to members of the Mercantile Marine, as the Merchant Navy was then called, who served one or more voyages through a danger zone. It was given in bronze only to officers and men alike, one has never seeen any explanation as to why the Transport Medal, as awarded for the Boer War of 1899-1902 and the Boxer Rising of 1900, was not issued to ships' officers. (See No. 88.)

A few members of the Royal Navy were seconded for service with the Mercantile Marine to man the defensive weapons between 4th August, 1914, and 31st December, 1915. These men received the appropriate Star, the British War Medal and the Victory Medal, as well as the Mercantile Marine Medal.

Certain members of the Mercantile Marine joined the Royal Navy between the above dates. They also received the four medals.

Those who completed the whole of their service at sea with the Mercantile Marine, no matter for how long or between which dates, were only awarded the Mercantile Marine Medal and the British War Medal.

It was, of course, possible for a man who did not qualify for one of the stars to get only three medals — namely, the British War Medal, Mercantile Marine Medal, and the Victory Medal — providing he had not less than six months' service at sea. Those who served this period at sea in pilot and/or lighthouse vessels, Government cable ships or as fishermen also qualified. 133,135 issued.

98 ALLIED VICTORY MEDAL, 1914-18

Obverse	The winged, full-length figure of Victory, with her left arm extended and holding a plam branch in her right hand. The remaining space is left bare.
Reverse	The inscription "THE GREAT WAR FOR CIVILIZATION, 1914-1919" surrounded by a wreath.
Size	1.42 in. diameter.
Ribbon	1.55 in. wide. Watered, reading from the centre outwards, the colours are red, green, blue and violet merged into a rainbow pattern.
Suspension	The ribbon is threaded through a half-inch diameter ring, which passes through a loop fixed to the top of the pice. The ring will move forwards and backwards but not sideways.
Designer	W. McMillan.
Naming	In faint impressed block capitals, giving recipient's number, rank, name, and unit. In the case of medals awarded to officers the name of the regiment was omitted, except in the case of those in the Royal Artillery.
No. of bars issued	Nil.

This bronze medal was awarded to all who received the 1914 or 1914-15 Star and, with certain exceptions, to those who received the British War Medal. It was never awarded alone.

Eligibility for this award consisted of having been mobilized in any of the fighting services and of having served in any of the theatres of operations, or at sea, between midnight, 4th/5th August, 1914, and midnight, 11th/12th November, 1918. Women who served in any of the various organizations in a theatre of operations were eligibile, such as nurses, members of the Women's Royal Naval Service, Women's Army Auxiliary Corps, Women's Royal Air Force, canteen staffs and members of the many charitable organizations of all kinds.

Those who were mentioned in dispatches between 4th August, 1914, and 10th August, 1920, were allowed to wear an oak leaf on the ribbon. The leaf worn on the ribbon with the medal is slightly larger than that worn on the ribbon of the jacket when the medal is not worn. In the rare cases when the recipient on a Mention in Dispatches did not receive a Victory Medal, or the British War Medal, the emblem is worn on the jacket.

Not all the Allies awarded the medal to their nationals. Each government was responsible for the cost of the issue of its medals, and whether they awarded it or not was optional.* There was no central fund for bearing the cost of the issue to all Allied combatants. Approx. 5,725,000 issued.

The South Afircan Government issued this medal with the inscription on the reverse in both English and Afrikaans.

9 TERRITORIAL FORCE WAR MEDAL (1914-19)

Obverse	The coinage head of King George V with legend "GEORGIVS V BRITT. OMN: REX ET IND: IMP:"
Reverse	The legend "TERRITORIAL WAR MEDAL" around the top. Inside a wreath is the inscription "FOR VOLUNTARY SERVICE OVERSEAS, 1914-19".
Size	1.42 in. diameter.
Ribbon	1.25 in. wide. Watered, yellow with two green stripes.
Suspension	By a plain, non-swivelling suspender.
Designer	As the reverse only bears an inscription, no designer was employed
Naming	The medals were named in impressed block capitals.
No. of bars issued	Nil.

This bronze medal was awarded to all members of the Territorial Force including Nursing Sisters, who were members of the service on 4th August 1914, and to those who had completed four years' service before 4th August 1914, providing that they had rejoined on, or prior to, 30th September, 1914. In addition to the above, to be eligible for the award members must have: (a) Undertaken on, or before, 30th September, 1914, to serve outside the United Kingdom; (b) served outside the United Kingdom between 4th August, 1914 and midnight, 11th/12th November, 1918; (c) been ineligible for either the 1914 or 1914-15 Star.

The medal is worn immediately after the Allied Victory Medal and before all subsequently awarded war medals, and, of course, before Long Service and Meritorious Service Medals.

The dates on the reverse should be noted. As eligibility terminated on 11th November, 1918, it is difficult to see whey the date 1919 was put on the medal 33,944 medals issued.

The following countries issued medals: Great Britian, Belgium, Brazil, Cuba, Czechoslovakia, France, Greece, Italy, Japan, Portugal, Roumania, Siam, Union of South Africa and the United States. I believe that one or two of the following countries struck medals for distribution to local museums, but I have not been able to trace any general issue of them to their nationals — Arabia, China, Costa Rica, Honduras, Montenegro, Russia and Serbia.

It was agreed that all the different reverse designs should incorporate the winged figure of Victory on the obverse although the Japanese issue depicts a warrior holding a spear.

100 INDIAN GENERAL SERVICE MEDAL (1908-1935)

Obverse	*1st issue* — Bust of King Edward VII in uniform and legend "EDWARDVS VII KAISAR-I-HIND".
	2nd issue — Crowned bust of King George V in robes, and legend "GEORGIVS V KAISAR-I-HIND". (This issue started with the medal given with the bar for Abor, 1911-12.)
	3rd issue — Crowned bust of King George V in robes and legend "GEORGIVS · V · D · G · BRITT · OMN · REX · ET. INDIÆ · IMP ·" (This issue started with the medal given with the bar for North West Frontier, 1930-31.)
Reverse	A picture of the fort at Jamrud, which commands the Khyber Pass eleven miles from Peshawur. Between a "V" formed by a branch of oak and another of laurel is a tablet on which is the word "INDIA".
Size	1.42 in. diameter.
Ribbon	1.25 in. wide. Green with a 0.6 in. wide drk blue stripe down the centre.
Suspension	By a floral suspender, as used on all previous Indian General Service Medals.
Designer	Richard Garbe.
Naming	The method of naming varies, and so will be given for each bar. (Only one five bar medal and seven with four bars were issued to the R.A.F.)
No. of bars issued	Twelve.

This medal, which was issued both in silver and bronze*, was the last medal awarded in the reign of King Edward VII. Only one bar was awarded during his reign. There were two designs of obverse with the head of King George V; the second one was first used with the issue for the bar for North West Frontier, 1930-31.

The claws of the medals struck by the Calcutta Mint differ from those struck by the Royal Mint, as a study of the illustrations facing page 321 will show.

The bar for Waziristan 1925 is excessively rare, in fact the rarest to Indian Medals since some of those of the very first issue.

Permission was given to some recipients of a Mention in Dispatches during any of the campaigns for which this medal was awarded after 11th August, 1920, to wear a bronze oak leaf emblem on the ribbon.

North West Frontier 1908 *(14th February-31st May, 1908)*

This bar was awarded for service in the Mohmand Field Force, Bazaar Valley Field Force, and for service at Landi Kital and North of Adinazai.

The naming is in running script.

Regiments present: 10 Hussars; 19, 21, 37 Indian Cavalry; Guides Cavalry; 18, 62, 75, 80 Batteries R.F.A.; 71 Company R.G.a.; 2, 3, 8, 21, 22, 23, 28 Mountain Batteries; 1, 6 Companies Bengal and 9 Company Madras Sappers and Miners; 1 Northumberland Fusiliers; 1 Royal Warwicks; 1 West Yorks; 1 Seaforth; 2nd Gordons; 1 Royal Munster Fusiliers; 19, 20, 21, 22, 25, 28, 29, 30, 33 Punjab Infantry; 15, 23, 34, 45, 53, 54, 55 Sikhs; 57, 59 Rifles; Khyber

---

*The issue of Indian General Service bronze medals was discontinued after those awarded with the bar for "NORTH WEST FRONTIER 1908" and "ABOR 1911-12". At least three of the latter are known, namely: Servant Ramtai Thape, 1/8 Gurkha Rifles, Sardar Pasangtamba, No. 1 Gurkha Carrier Corps, Sardar Lalbir Lama, No. 1 Gurkha Carrier Corps.

Rifles; Guides Infantry; 40 Pathans; 1, 4, 5, 6, 8 Gurkhas; 7, 16 Mule Corps. Medals with this bar were awarded in bronze.

Abor 1911-12 *(6th October, 1911-20th April, 1912)*

This was the first bar awarded with the second issue of this medal (see description against obverse).

Except for their British officers, this bar was only awarded to Indian Troops for service under Major-General Sir H. Bower, K.C.B., against the Abors.

The naming is in bold sloping script.

Regiments present: Assam Valley Light Horse; 1 Company King George's Own Sappers and Miners; 1, 2, 1/8 Gurkhas; 32 Sikh Pioneers; 26 Mule Corps; 5 Naga Carrier Corps; Lakimpur Police; No. 1 Gurkhali Carrier Corps; Lushai Hills Bn., Assam Mily. Police.

(I also know of medals to the 30 Lancers, 1/61 Pioneers, 114 Mahrattas and 1/3 Gurkhas, Survey of India, Supply and Transport Corps.)

Medals with this bar were also awarded in bronze.

Afghanistan N.W.F. 1919 *(6th May — 8th August, 1919)*. Third Afghan War

This bar was awarded for service in the Third Afghan War, under General Sir A. A. Barratt, G.C.B., K.C.S.I., K.C.V.O., A.D.C. Note that the year 1919 occupies a second line on the bar, of which 12,500 were struck for distribution.

This is the first occasion on which the Royal Air Force took part in Indian campaigns. The previous service of the Royal Flying Corps which was in action during the Mohmand Blockade in 1916 has been excluded.

The naming is in thin impressed block capitals.

British Army

Cavalry	1 King's Dragoon Guards.
Artillery	One Battery R.H.A.; 4, 28, 74, 77, 79, 89, 90, 101, 102, 1091, 1093, 1096, 1104, 1107 Batteries R.F.A.; 1, 3, 4, 6, 8, 9 Mountain Batteries R.G.A.; 60, 68 Heavy Batteries R.G.A.
Armoured Cars and M.G. Coys.	1, 2, 3, 4, 5, 6, 7, 8, 11 Armoured Motor Batteries; 15, 22, 24 M.G. Squadrons; 3, 15, 19, 22, 222, 260, 263, 270, 281, 285, 286, Machine-Gun Companies.
Infantry	1/4 Royal West Surrey Regiment; 3rd Buffs (115); 1/25 Royal Fusiliers; 2 Kings; 2 Somerset Light Infantry; 1 Yorkshire Regiment; 1 Duke of Wellington's Regiment; 2/4 Border Regiment; 1, 2/6 Royal Sussex; 1/15 Hants; 1 South Lancs; 1/1 Kent Regiment; 1/4 Royal West Kent Regiment; 2 North Staffs; 1 Durham Light Infantry; No. 17 Special Service Bn.; 25 Bn. The London Regiment; 1 Kent Cyclist Bn.

(Medals are known to men of the East Yorks, D.C.L.I., Seaforth Highlanders, H.L.I. and Gordon Highlanders, though no battalions of these regiments were present.)

Indian Army

Cavalry	1, 13, 30, 31, 37 Lancers; 3 Horse; 4, 12, 17, 23, 25, 27, 40, 41, 42 Cavalry; 28, 33 Light Cavalry; Patiala, Alwar, Navanagar and Bhopal Lancers; 40th Mule Corps.
Artillery	22, 23, 24, 27, 28, 30, 33, 35, 37, 38 Mountain Batteries; Frontier Garrison Artillery; 1, 2 Kashmir Mountain Batteries.

Signals	6, 12 Cavalry Brigade Signals; 43, 44, 45, 46, 67, 68 Brigade Signals.
Sappers and Miners	1, 7, 53, 55, 56, 57, 58, 1st Sappers and Miners; 8, 11, 14, 15, 63, 64, 66, 67, 68, 69, 76, 2nd Sappers and Miners; 17, 24, 71, 73, 74, 3rd Sappers and Miners.
Infantry	2/2, 1/11, 2/11, 16 Rajputs; 3 Guides Infantry; 2/3 Gaur Brahmins, 1/5 Light Infantry; 1/6, 2/10 Jats; 14/ 1/15, 2/15, 1/35, 2/35, 2/54 Sikhs; 1/19, 1/22, 2/26, 2/27, 1/30, 2/30, 1/33, 2/33, 1/66, 2/67, 1/69, 2/69, 2/72, 1/76, 82, 2/89, 1/90, 2/90, 1/152, 1/153, 2/153 Punjabis; 37, 1/41, 2/41 Dogras; 3/39. 4/39 Garhwal Rifles; 40 Pathans; 1/55, 2/56, 1/57 Frontier Force; 1/97, 1/98, 1/109, 2/112, 2/113, 2/119, 120, 1/150, 3/150, 1/151, 2/151, 1/154 Infantry; 1/102, 2/102 Grenadiers; 1/103, 110 Mahratta Light Infantry; 1/124, 3/124, 126, 1/129, 2/129 Baluchis; Jind, Gwalior, Patiala, Karpurthala, Nabha, 1st and 2nd Kashmir Rifles of Imperial Service Infantry, and the 2nd Rifle Regiment (Nepalese); Chitral Scouts.
Pioneers	1/12, 2/12, 2/23, 2/34, 3/34, 1/61, 2/61, 1/81, 2/81, 1/107.
Gurkhas	2/1, 3/1, 2/2, 3/2, 4/3, 1/4, 3/5, 3/6, 2/7, 3/7, 2/8, 1/9, 2/9, 3/9, 2/10, 1/11, 2/11, 3/11.
R.A.F.	
	52nd Wing; composed of 20, 31, 48, 114 Squadrons. (Approx. 850 bars.)

Mahsud 1919-20 (*27th November, 1919-7th May, 1920*)

Army Order No. 361 of 1921 sanctioned the award of this bar to all who served under Major-General A. Skeen, west of and including Jandola between 18th December, 1919, and 8th April, 1920. Army Order No. 347 of 1922 also granted the award of this bar to all who served under the G.O.C. Wariziristan Force on the Takki Zam Line north of and including Jandola between 18th December, 1919, and 8th April, 1920. The bar for Waziristan 1919-21 next mentioned should be consulted for units present. This bar is nearly always found on the same medal as that for Warizistan 1919-21; in fact, it is difficult to see how it could have been gained singly, as the Mahsud territory is enclosed by Northern and Southern Waziristan, though medals with this single bar are known to the Royal West Kent Regiment and to the 2nd Queen Victoria's Own Sappers and Miners.

The naming is in thin block capitals. Approx. 175 to the R.A.F.

Waziristan 1919-21 (*6th May, 1919 — January, 1921*)

This bar was awarded for punitive operations against the Tochi and Wana Wazirs and Mahsuds, who had caused considerable depredations since the end of the Third Afghan War. The operations were under Major-General A. Skeen, C.M.G.

The naming is in thin impressed block capitals.

Distribution of troops in Waziristan 6th May, 1919:—

BANNU AREA

Bannu	31 D.C.O. Lancers (less one squadron); one section 33 Indian Mountain Battery; 1/103 Mahratta Light Infantry; 3/6 Gurkha Rifles.

Dardoni	One Squadron 31 D.C.O. Lancers; one section 33 Indian Mountain Battery; 55 Field Company Sappers and Miners; 1/41 Dogras; 2/112 Infantry. Also Northern Waziri Militia and Frontier Constabulary.

DERAJAT AREA

Dera Ismail Khan	27 Cavalry (less one Squadron); 27 Indian Mountain Battery; 1/76 Punjabis; 2/2 Gurkha Rifles; No. 7 Armoured Motor Battery.
Monzai	76 Field Company Sappers and Miners; 1/66 Punjabis. Also Southern Waziri Militia and Frontier Constabulary.

COMPSOITION OF THE THREE ECHELONS OF THE TOCHI COLUMN ON 13TH NOVEMBER, 1919

No. 1 Echelon	One and a half Squadrons D.C.O. Lancers; 35 Indian Mountain Battery; 55 Field Company Sappers and Miners; 2/61 Pioneers; Northern Waziri Militia; 1/55 Coke's Rifles; 1/103 Mahratta Light Infantry; 104 Wellesley's Rifles; 2/112 Infantry; 2/21 Punjabis; 2/76 Punjabis (later transferred).
No. 2. Echelon	74 Field Company Sappers and Miners; 3/34 Pioneers; 2/152 Punjabis; No. 6 Armoured Motor Battery.
No. 3. Echelon	One Squadron D.C.O. Lancers; 33 Indian Mountain Battery, 4/39 Garhwal Rifles; 57 Wilde's Rifles; 82 Punjabis.

STRIKING FORCE – TOCHI AND DERAJAT COLUMNS

Cavalry	Two Squadrons D.C.O. Lancers; one Squadron 21 P.A.V.O. Cavalry.
Artillery	One section 4.5 Howitzers R.F.A.; No. 6 Mountain Battery R.G.A.; Nos. 27, 33, 35 Indian Mounted Batteries.
Sappers and Miners	55, 74 Field Companies.
Infantry	43rd Brigade – 4/39 Garhwal Rifles; 57 Wilde's Rifles; 82 Punjabis. 67th Brigade – 1/55 Coke's Rifles; 1/103 Mahrattas, 104 Wellesley's Rifles; 2/112 Infantry.
Pioneers	3/34 Sikh; 2/61 Pioneers.

Note: The 2/19, 82 Punjabis, 1/103 Mahratta Light Infantry and 2/112 Infantry were transferred to the L. of C. and replaced by the 4/3, 2/5, 2/9, 3/11 Gurkha Rifles.

LINES OF COMMUNICATION – FIGHTING TROOPS
TOCHI

No. 1 Section Bannu L. of C.

Cavalry	31st D.C.O. Lancers (less two Squadrons).
Artillery	One section 33 Indian Mountain Battery; 15-pdr. and 6.3 in. Frontier G.A.
Machine-Gun Corps	No. 5 Armoured Motor Battery.
Infantry	45th Brigade – 2/4 Rajputs; 2/25 Punjabis; 1/150, 2/154 Infantry.

316

No. 2 Section Bannu L. of C.

Cavalry	Two Squadrons D.C.O. Lancers.
Artillery	No. 33 Indian Mountain Battery; one section R.G.A.
Sappers and Miners	No. 74 Field Company.
Infantry	47th Brigade — 2/21, 2/69, 3/151, 3/152 Punjabis.

DERAJAT

No. 1 Section Tank L. of C.

Cavalry	16th Cavalry; 21 P.A.V.O. Cavalry; 27 Light Cavalry.
Artillery	One section 35 Indian Mountain Battery; one section F.G.A.
Machine-Gun Corps	No. 6, 7 Armoured Motor Batteries.
Infantry	62nd Brigade — 2/90 Punjabis; 2/102 Grenaiders; 2/94, 2/113, 2/150 Infantry, 2/127 Baluchis. Southern Waziri Militia.

No. 2 Section Tank L. of C.

Cavalry	One troop 21 P.A.V.O. Cavalry.
Artillery	No. 35 Indian Mountain Battery.
Sappers and Miners	75 Field Company.
Infantry	68th Brigade — 3rd Guides; 2/19, 2/76 Punjabis; 109 Infantry.
R.A.F.	5, 20, 27, 28, 31, 60 and one flight each of 97 and 99 Squadrons (approx. 600 bars).

The following regiments which took part in the later stages of the campaign also received the award: The Queen's, 2 Norfolks, R.W. Fusiliers, Border Regiment, W. Yorks.

Malabar 1921-22 (*20th August, 1921 — 25th February, 1922*)

Malabar lies between the Nilgiri Hills and the Arabian Sea. It is inhabited by Hindus and Mohammedans, most of whom are Moplahs or Mapillas, who specialized in rebellions of various degrees of importance.

On this occasion they attacked the police and communications and defied British rule generally.

Reinforcements were sent to the district, and then a drive was started like that referred to during the Natal Rebellion in 1906 (No. 90). The rebels were chased into the hills, where they were split up into small bodies and then effectively dealt with.

Army Order 50 of 1924 sanctioned the award of this bar to all who took part in the suppression of the Moplah Rebellion in Malabar within the area bounded as follows: On the west by the sea, on the south by the Ponnani river, on the east by a north-and-south line from Gudalur to the Ponnani river, on the north by an east-and-west line from Gudalur to the sea.

The naming is in thin impressed block capitals.

Regiments present: One squadron of Queen's Bays; one section 67 Battery

R.F.A.; 1 Suffolk Regiment (less "C" Company); 2 Dorsetshire Regiment; 1 Leinster Regiment (332); Royal Tank Corps; Madras Sappers and Miners (1 platoon); 64 Pioneers (detachment); 83 Wallajabad Light Infantry; 1/39 Royal Garhwal Rifles; 3/70 Burma Rifles; Malabar Territorial Infantry; 2/8, 2/9 Gurkhas and Special Police.

There were no awards of this bar to the R.A.F.

Waziristan 1921-24 (*21st December, 1921 — 31st March, 1924*)

Army Order 177 of 1926 authorized the issue of this bar to all who served in North and South Waziristan, Bannu, the Dera Ismail Khan Civil Districts and that part of the Mianwali District which lies west of the River Indus, also the military posts of Mari Indus and Darya Khan east of the River Indus between 21st December, 1921, and 31st March, 1924.

The naming is in thin impressed block capitals.

A large number of troops were employed in small garrisons over a wide area. We have, for the sake of easy reference, grouped all the battalions together under their regimental titles. It would be almost impossible to give the names of every unit from which one or more men served in the campaign. We have included in the following list the names of those regiments present as a whole and those to whom I have often seen medals. There were, in addition to those given, Indian Army Service Corps and Medical Service units and a host of small formations such as Soda Water Sections whose titles illustrate the complexity of modern war.

Regiments present:

Cavalry	7, 16, 17, 21, 27, 28 Regiments.
Artillery	128 Howitzer Battery R.F.A.
	15 Pdrs. R.G.A.
	6.3 in. R.M.L. Howitzers.
	10, 13, 47, 128 Medium Howitzer Batteries, R.G.A.
	6, 11, 12, 21, 27, 33, 35, 101, 103, 106, 108, 112, 114, 119, 121 Batteries Pack
	5, 16 Armoured Motor Batteries.
Armoured Car Coys.	7, 9, 10.
Sappers and Miners	5, 12, 13, 14, 19, 20, 21, 94, 96, 113 Companies.
Pioneers	1/1, 2/1 Madras; 1/3, 2/3, 3/3, 21, 32, 34 Sikh; 1/4 Hazara; 48, 2/61, 1/12 Pioneers.
Infantry (European)	2 Queen's; 1 Royal Welch Fusiliers; 1 Border Regiment; 1 Welch Regiment; Sherwood Foresters; Royal Berks.
(Indian)	2/1, 4/1, 2/2, 1/19, 2/21, 2/25, 1/26, 1/28, 1/30, 1/69, 2/69, 82 Punjabis.
	1/3 Brahmans.
	1/4, 2/4, 1/7, 16 Rajputs.
	3/5 Mahratta Light Infantry.
	1/6, 2/6, 4/6, 5/6 Rajputana Rifles.
	1/9, 2/9, 3/9 Jat Regiment.
	4/10, 5/10 Baluch Regiment.
	1/12, 2/12, 3/12 Frontier Force Regiment.
	2/13, 4/13, 5/13 Frontier Force Rifles.

1/17, 37, 2/41 Dogras.
2/18, 1/109, 2/113, 1/119 Infantry.
36 Sikhs.
4/39 Garhwal Rifles.
2/50 Kumaon Rifles
1/73 Carnatic Infantry
2/101, 2/102 Grenaiders
104 Wellesley's Rifles.
2/1, 2/2, 1/3, 2/3, 4/3, 1/4, 1/5, 2/6, 2/8, 1/9, 3/11 Gurkhas.
North West Militia.
South Waziri Militia.
Tochi Scouts.
112 Labour Corps.
3, 9 Mule Corps.
43 Camel Corps.

R.A.F.   5, 27, 28, 31, 60 Squadrons (approx. 600 bars).

Waziristan 1925 (*9th March — 1st May, 1925*)

This bar was awarded for service under Wing Commander R. C. M. Pink, C.B., against the Waziris. It was the first occasion in which the R.A.F. was used independently of the Army and is the only bar awarded to the R.A.F. only for service in India. The full number of recipients shows that it is by far the rarest bar ever given with an Indian General Service Medal.

The medals are named in thin impressed block capitals with the recipient's number, rank and name followed by the letters "R.A.F."

Those who had already qualified for the bar "WAZIRISTAN 1921-24" and who also took part in these operations were given the option of receiving the above bar or that for "WAZIRISTAN 1925," *but not both.*

Recipients

At Tank: Headquarters, Five officers and twenty airmen.

No. 5 (A.C.) Squadron Bristol Fighters — ten places: Fourteen officers, sixty-nine airmen.

At Miramshah: No. 27 (B.) Squadron D.H.9A — eight planes: Fifteen officers, fifty-eight airmen.

No. 60 Squadron D.H.9A — eight planes: Thirteen officers, sixty-seven airmen.

Total: Seventy-seven officers and 198 airmen including one to an army officer and one to a civilian.

North West Frontier 1930-31 (*23rd April, 1930-22nd March, 1931*).

The rebel organization known as Redshirts, under Abdul Ghaffar, had been causing trouble along the Mohmand Frontier and in the border villages, so that it became necessary to establish a blockade line and an improved system of roads. A few minor actions were fought, but most of the period was spent in making roads and building posts, except for a small expedition into Tirah.

This bar was awarded for services in Kohat, Waziristan and the Peshawur District between 23rd April and 30th September, 1930, and also for services between 1st October, 1930, and 22nd March, 1931, in the area bounded as follows: North: Bazar river, Khyber river to the bridge on the Peshawur Jamrud road seven and a half miles from Peshawur. East: From the road from the above bridge to Narai Khwan Post, thence to Frontier Road to Bara Fort-Malaimi.

South and West: From a line from Aimal Chabutra to Point 2498, thence to the Afghan Frontier.

This was the first medal of the third issue (see description against obverse) and was awarded for the suppression of what were officially described as the Afridi and Red Shirt Rebellions.

The naming is in thin impressed block capitals.

15/19 Hussars; Poona Horse; 20th Lancers; Guides Cabalry; 31, 58 Field Batteries R.F.A.; 17 Light Battery R.A.; 8, 16 Mountain Batteries R.A.; 3, 4, 5 Companies Bengal Sappers and Miners; 2 Bombay Pioneers, 1 Light Tank Company R.T.C.; 2 Border Regiment; Royal Sussex; South Lancs; 2 Essex; 2 K.O.Y.L.I., 1 K.S.L.I., 2 D.L.I.; 2 Seaforth, 1/1, 5/2, 1/8 Punjab Regiment, 2/7 Rajput Regiment; 3/10, 5/10 Baluch Regiment; 1/11, 2/11 Sikh Regiment; 2/13 Frontier Force Rifles; 2/17, 3/17 Dogras; 1/1, 1/3, 2/4, 2/5 Gurkhas; 21 D.T.T.; Animal Transport Companies; Police Department.

R.A.F.: 5, 11, 20, 27, 28, 39, 60 Squadrons. (Approx. 1,350 bars.)

Burma 1930-32 (*22nd December, 1930 — 25th March, 1932*)

This bar was sanctioned by Army Order 94 of 1933 for award to all who were dispatched from India and actually served in Burma between 22nd December, 1930, and 25th March, 1932. It was also awarded for service in Shwebo, Bassein, Toungo, Meiktila, Sahaingu, Myaungmya, Tharrawaddy, Pegu, Pakokku, Lower Chindwin, Prome, Insein, Mimbu, Kyaukse, Pyapon, Hanthawaddy, Thayetmyo, Myingyan, Mandalay, Maubin, Henzada, Magwe and Yamethin.

The naming is in very small block capitals.

On 17th October, 1947, Burma received her independence and left the British Commonwealth of Nations.

Regiments present: R.A.; R.E.; one company of Madras Sappers and Miners; 1 Buffs; 2 Ox. and Bucks L.I.; 2 Manchesters; 2/5 Mahratta L.I.; 3/6 Rajputana Rifles; 3/10 Baluch Regt.; 2/15, 3/16 Punjab Regt.; 1/17 Dogra Regt., 2/20, 3/20 Burma Rifles; Burma Military Police; 18 Mule Transport Company.

R.A.F: 36 (Torpedo Bomber) and 205 (Flying Boat) Squadrons. Total of 14 bars to the R.A.F.

Mohmand 1933 (*28th July — 3rd October, 1933*)

The Mohmand Column, which contained no British troops, operated against the Upper Mohmands and was commanded by Brigadier C. J. E. Auchinleck, D.S.O., O.B.E.

The naming is in small thin impressed block capitals.

Mohmand Column
> 18 (K.E.O.) Cavalry; 22 Mountain Battery R.A.; 4 Hazara Mountain Battery; 10 Abbottabad Mountain Battery; 22 Mountain Brigade Signals; 1/7 Rajputs; 5/10 Baluch Regiment; 3/14 Punjab Regiment; 5/12 Frontier Force (Q.V.O.); Nos. 2, 3 (K.G.O.) Bengal Sappers and Miners; Corps of Guides; 2 Field Ambulance; 30, 34, 37, 39 Animal Transport Companies.

L. of C. Troops
> 1/11 Sikhs; 3/2 Punjab Regiment; 5/12 Frontier Force; 1, 32 Animal Transport Companies.

Mohmand Blockhouse Line Force
> 58 Field Battery R.A.; 6 Armoured Car Company.

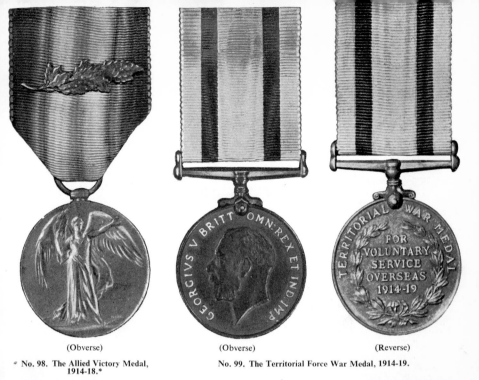

(Obverse)

No. 98. The Allied Victory Medal, 1914-18.*

(Obverse)

(Reverse)

No. 99. The Territorial Force War Medal, 1914-19.

(Obverse)
First issue

(Reverse)
All issues

(Obverse)
Third issue

No. 100. The Indian General Service Medal, 1908-35.

* The oak leaf on the ribbon signifies that the recipient received a "Mentioned in Despatches". Only one
leaf can be worn irrespective of how many times the recipient was "mentioned".

To face page 320

(Obverse)
First issue

(Reverse)
All issues

(Obverse)
Second issue

(Obverse)
Third issue

No. 101. The Naval General Service Medal, 1915-64.

Reserve Force
> 2 Derajat Mountain Battery Frontier Force; 3/11 Sikh Regiment.

Medals to the 3/10 Baluch Regiment; 1/1 Hyderbad Regiment; 21 D.T.T. Company are also known.

R.A.F.
> No. 20 Squadron only (180).

North West Frontier 1935 (12th *January — 3rd November, 1935*)

The naming is in thin impressed block capitals.

Mohmand Force
> 18 (K.E.O.) Cavalry; 4 Field Brigade R.A.; 13, 22 Mountain Batteries R.A.; 15 Medium Battery, R.A.; detachment of 8 A.A. Battery, R.A.; 3, 5 Field Companies K.G.O. Bengal Sappers and Miners; 2 Light Tank Company and one section 8 Armoured Car Company R.T.C.; 4/15 Punjab Regiment; 2/1 Gurkhas.
> 2 officers, 1 sergeant and 8 men of 2 Welch Regiment were attached to Force Headquarters.

Peshawur Brigade
> 2 H.L.I.; 5/1 Punjab Regiment; 1/4 Bombay Grenaiders; 5/10 Baluch Regiment.

Nowshera Brigade
> 2 Duke of Wellington's Regiment; 3/2, 2/15 Punjab Regiment; 5/12 Frontier Force (Q.V.O. Guides).

Rawalpindi Brigade
> 1 Hampshire Regiment; 2/2, 1/15 Punjab Regiment; 3/11 Sikhs (Rattray's).

Thelum Brigade
> 2 Argyll and Sutherland Highlanders; 1/14, 4/16 Punjab Regiment.

R.A.F.
> No. 20 Squadron only.

(Medals are also known to the Royal Northumberland Fusiliers and 21 D.T.T. Company.)

01 NAVAL GENERAL SERVICE MEDAL (1915-1962)

Obverse
> *The first issue* bears the head of King George V in Naval uniform with the legend "GEORGIVS V BRITT: OMN: REX ET IND: IMP:" *The second issue* (1936-1949) has the crowned coinage head of King George VI and bears the legend "GEORGIVS VI G: BR: OMN: REX ET INDIAE IMP:" *The third issue* (1949-1952) has the crowned head of George VI and the legend "GEORGVIS VI DEI: GRA: BRITT: OMN: REX F.D.DEF +." *The fourth issue* has the crowned bust of Queen Elizabeth II facing right and legend "ELIZABETH II D: G: BR: OMN: REGINA F:D." *The fifth issue* (1953-1962) has the crowned bust of Elizabeth II and the legend "ELIZABETH II DEI. GRATIA REGINA F.D. +."

Reverse
> Britannia on two sea horses, with her left hand resting on the Union Shield.

Size
> 1.42 in. diameter.

Ribbon	1.24 in. wide. Crimson with three white strips.
Suspension	By a plain straight suspender, which does not swivel on the George VI and Elizabeth II issues.
Designer	Miss Margaret Winser.
Naming	The first issue is named in rather large impressed block capitals which give the recipient's number, name, rank, and ship. The seccond issue is named in very small impressed block capitals, and the name of the recipient's ship is not given, only the initials "R.N." or "R.M." after the name. The same applies to the third issue.
No, of bars issued	Sixteen.

This medal was instituted to avoid having to issue a separate medal for every small operation in which the Royal Navy might be involved. As we shall see, a similar idea was started in 1918 with the General Service Medal for the Army and R.A.F.

Permission was granted to recipients of a Mention in Dispatches during any of the operations for which this medal was awarded after 11th August, 1920, to wear a bronze oak leaf emblem on the ribbon.

Persian Gulf 1909-1914 (*19th October, 1909 – 1st August, 1914*)

This bar was awarded for services against gun-runners, pirates, etc., in the Persian Gulf, Straits of Ormuz and the Sea of Oman between 19th October, 1909, and 1st August, 1914.

H.M.S. *Alert, Dartmouth, Fox, Harold, Highflyer, Hyaciath, Karanja, Lapwing, Mashona, Minor, Muzbee, Odin, Panter, Pelorus, Perseus, Philomel Proserpine, Sheik Berthua, Shaiklo, Swiftsure, Tamil.*

Ships of the Royal Indian Marine also present: *Lawrence* (336), *Minto* (4,400), *Palihurus* (178).

Basian Coal Depot Staff, Heniam Coal Depot Staff.

The following thirteen Army officers and one of the Indian Police received a medal with this bar:

Major H. H. Austin, R.E., Naval Intelligence Staff.
Major C. C. R. Murphy, I.A., Naval Intelligence Staff.
Captain G. S. G. Crauford, Naval Intelligence Staff.
Captain J. I. Eadie, I.A., attached Naval Staff.
Captain R. F. Woodward, attached Naval Staff.
E. G. Gregson, Indian Police, attached Naval Staff.
Lieutenant-Colonel F. A. Smith, 2 Rajputs, H.M.S. *Pelorus.*
Captain R. T. Arundell, 2 Rajputs, H.M.S. *Pelorus.*
Captain L. Birdwood, I.A., 2 Rajputs, H.M.S. *Pelorus.*
Captain W. R. C. Griffiths, 2 Rajputs, H.M.S. *Pelorus.*
Lieutenant C. D. Noyes, 2 Rajputes, H.M.S. *Pelorus.*
Major J. Stewart, I.A., H.M.S. *Perseus.*
Captain W. L. Watson, Indian Medical Service, H.M.S. *Philomel.*
Lieutenant C. M. Maltby, 95th Russell's Infantry, H.M.S. *Fox.*

Iraq 1919-1920 (*1st July – 17th November, 1920*)

This award was only granted to officers and men who served in River Gun-Boats within the boundaries of Iraq between 1st July and 17th November, 1920, so that it is difficult to see why the bar is dated as it is. A total of nine officers and 119 ratings from the following three ships received the award: This issue has a fixed suspender, the Palestine 1936-39 type naming being used. All are believed to have been awarded after 1935.

H.M.S. *Clio, Espiegel, Triad.*

W.A. Rapley, R.N., H.M.S. *Clio*, received this bar and the Africa General Service Medal with the bar for "Somaliland 1920."

N.W. Persia 1920* (*10th August − 31st December, 1920*)

This bar was awarded to only four officers and four ratings who served in the Naval Mission under Commodore D. T. Norris, C.B., C.M.G., R.N., in North West Persia.

Recipients: Commodore D. T. Norris, C.B., C.M.G., R.N.; Paymaster Lieutenants H. G. Pertwee, D.S.O., R.N., Cavendish and Onslow; Chief Petty Officer H. Dickason; Ableseamen C. B. Haig, Egglestone and Hickman.

Palestine 1936-1939 (*19th April, 1936 − 3rd September, 1939*)

This bar was awarded for service in connection with the Military Forces in Palestine between 19th April, 1936, and 3rd September, 1939. In the case of many of the ships, the period of service was very short. For instance, H.M.S. *Emerald* served from 7th to 8th July, 1938 − one day! The *Imogen* served from 2nd to 8th September, 1937, and the service of some of the other ships did not exceed a fortnight. This bar was awarded with the second issue of the medal unless the recipient was already in possession of the first, in which case he received the bar only. Approx. 13,000 medals and/or clasps issued.

H.M.S.: *Aberdeen, Active, Adventure, Agate, Ajax, Amethyst, Antelope, Arethusa, Beagle, Blanche, Boadicea, Boreas, Brazen, Brigand, Brilliant, Bulldog, Cedar, Clyde, Cornelian, Cyclops, Delhi, Despatch, Douglas, Durban, Emerald, Galatea, Gallant, Garland, Gipsy, Glowworm, Grafton, Grenade, Greyhound, Griffin, Hardy, Hasty, Havock, Hawthorn, Hereward, Hero, Holly, Hotspur, Icarus, Ilex, Imogen, Imperial, Impulsive, Inglefield, Intrepid, Isis, Ivanhoe, Jasper, Keith, Laurel, Lilac, Maine, Magnolia, Malaya, Narwhal, Pangbourne, Pearl, Porpoise, Protector, Reliant, Repulse, Ross, Ruby, Sapphire, Severn, Sussex, Sutton, Syringe, Thames, Topaze, Tourmaline, Turquoise, Valiant, Weston, Willow.*

S.E. Asia 1945-48

To qualify for this award a member of the Naval Forces must have served a total of twenty-eight days afloat within five miles of the operationsl areas given below and within the specified periods. These areas and dates are the same as those which enabled the Army and the Royal Air Force to qualify for the General Service Medal (see page 334).

Naval personnel who served on operational duty ashore qualified under Army rules.

The qualifying period for official vists and inspections was one week.

Naval air crews qualified if they had performed one operational sortie over any of the land operational areas.

Recipients of a King's Commendation, Mention in Dispatches or any British honour for service rendered in any of the specified areas and within the specified

---

*As originally issued the title of this bar was "N.W. PERSIA 1919-20," but those who had received it were expected to hand it back for exchange.

dates were eligible for the award, though they may not have completed the full twenty-eight days' service. Approx. 2,000 awarded.

Curtailment of the specified period through death or by evacuation on account of wounds or disability caused by service did not debar eligibility. The qualifying areas and dates are:

(1)   Java and Sumatra from 3rd September, 1945, to 30th November, 1946, both dates inclusive.

(2)   French Indo-China from 3rd September, 1945, to 28th January, 1946, both dates inclusive.

Minesweeping 1945-51 *(3rd September, 1945-30th September, 1951)*

With the third issue obverse.

The qualifying period for this award was six months' Naval minesweeping service afloat after 3rd September, 1945.

The grant of a King's Commendation, Mention in Dispatches or other British honour for minesweeping service within the qualifying zones and dates qualified the recipient for the award, though he may not have completed the full six months' service.

If the qualifying service was ended by death or curtailed by reason of wounds or any disability due to service, the reduced period of service was considered sufficient to gain the award. Approx. 4,500 issued.

The minesweeping zones and terminal dates of the operations were:

Zone	*Terminal date*
East Indies, South West Pacific and China Coast	30th December, 1946.
Mediterranean (except Greek waters) and approaches to Gibraltar	15th August, 1947.
North West Europe and British Isles, including the North Sea	30th October, 1947 (except for the Thames Estuary).
Red Sea	15th Apri, 1948.
Greek Waters	30th September, 1951.

Palestine 1945-48 *(27th September, 1945-30th June, 1948)*

The Committee on the grants of Honours, Decorations and Awards recommended, and the King approved, the award of a medal, or bar, for service in Palestine subsequent to 27th September, 1945.

The qualifying period was given as (1) twenty-eight days afloat in ships employed on the Palestine Patrol against illegal immigration, or (2) in close support of the defined Army Forces, which means service within three miles of any qualifying land area. Approx. 7,500 awarded.

Naval personnel who served ashore and Naval air crews came under the same qualifications as those for the Army.

Service which was curtailed through death, or other causes due to service, would qualify for the award.

The British mandate in Palestine ended at midnight, 14th/15th May, 1948.

H.M.S. *Ajax, Aurora, Bigbury Bay, Brissenden, Chequers, Charity, Cheviot, Childers, Chieftain, Chevron, Chaplet, Chivalrous, Cardigan Bay, Espiegle, Enard Bay, Fierce, Haydon, Hascosay, Liverpool, Lookout Mauritius, Milne, Matchless, Moon, Magpie, Mermaid, Orion, Octavia, Phoebe, Providence, Peacock, Pelican, Rowena, Sirius, Superb, Saumarez, Stevenstone, Skipjack, Seabear, Stormcloud,*

St. Austell Bay, St. Brides Bay, Troubridge, Talybont, Truelove, Venus, Virago,
Volage, Verulam, Veryan Bay, Welfare, Whitesand Bay, Widemouth Bay, M.F.V.
55, M.F.V. 101.

Malaya *(16th June, 1948-31st July, 1960)*

With either the fourth or fifth issue obverse.

The qualifications for the award of this bar, the first with the third issue of
the medal, consist either of one day's service ashore attached to any of the
Military or Police Forces eligible for the General Service Medal (Army and
Royal Air Force), or, in the case of service afloat, a period of twenty-eight
days patrolling off the coast of Malaya in support of operations ashore.

Naval inspecting officers and visitors had to extend their welcome to a period
of thirty days to qualify. Approx. 7,500 awarded.

Yangtze 1949 *(20th April-31st July, 1949)*

With the third issue obverse.

This bar was awarded to members of all three Services for operations in the
Yangtze river against all Chinese Communist Forces.

It should be especially noted that personnel of the Army and the Royal Air
Force were awarded a Naval medal.

The qualifications for the award were as follows:

ROYAL NAVY

It was awarded to members of His Majesty's ships for service on, or between,
the dates mentioned:

H.M.S. *Amethyst*, 20th April-31st July, 1949.
H.M.S. *Black Swan*, 21st April, 1949.
H.M.S. *Consort*, 20th April, 1949.
H.M.S. *London*, 21st April, 1949.

It was also awarded to the officers who joined H.M.S. *Amethyst* on 21st or
22nd April, 1949, after being flown alongside in a Sunderland aircraft of the
Royal Air Force.

ARMY

It was awarded to personnel who flew to H.M.S. *Amethyst* on 21st or 22nd
Apri, 1949, in the Sunderland aircraft of the Royal Air Force.

ROYAL AIR FORCE

It was awarded to the crew of the Sunderland aircraft which flew to H.M.S.
Amethyst on 21st or 22nd April, and to Flight Lieutenant M.E. Fearnley, who
remained on board the warship as medical officer.

Approx. 1,400 awarded for the incident which originated about 140 miles up
the Yangtze river during the fighting between the Chinese Communists and Nati-
onalist forces, the former of whom held the north bank and the latter the south.

H.M.S. *Amethyst* was ordered up to Nanking to relieve H.M.S. *Consort* and
to take up supplies to the British community. On 20th April, whilst on her way
up, she was heavily shelled by the Communist forces and driven ashore, suffering
seventeen killed and ten wounded casualties, among the latter being the commanding officer, Lieutenant-Commander B.M. Skinner, R.N. H.M.S. *Consort*
hurried down to her relief, but could not stop and reached Kiangyin with
twleve casualties.

When the perilous plight of the *Amethyst* became apparent, the cruiser

H.M.S. *London* (Captain P.G.L. Cazalet, R.N.) and the frigate *Black Swan* (Captain A.D.H. Jay, D.S.O., D.S.C., R.N.) were ordered to proceed up the river to assist her. The attempt was made on 21st April, but the fire from the Communist-held shore was so severe that the two ships had to return. H.M.S. *London* received thirty-two casulaties (fifteen killed, seventeen wounded), and the *Black Swan* had five men wounded.

Whilst these rescue attempts were being made the Royal Air Force flew a British and an American doctor to the *Amethyst*, which had succeeded in moving to a more sheltered position upstream and Lieutenant-Commander J.S. Kerans assumed command.

Negotiations concerning the release of the ship became protracted and the supplies of food and fuel were running short, so Lieutenant-Commander Kerans decided that the ship should escape, and the necessary preparations were made.

By an extraordinarly blend of good preparation, good discipline, good seamanship and the good fortune which invariably favours the brave, the ship rejoined the fleet on 30th July.

She eventually reached England on 1st November, 1949, where the Commander-in-Chief, Plymouth, notified the ship's company that their conduct was "up to standard", which, when compared with the many other Naval occasions mentioned in this book, is a particularly apt description.

Bomb and Mine Clearance 1945-53

With either the fourth or fifth issue obverse.

This bar was awarded for six months' consecutive work (including Australian units) in the disposal of bombs and mines in different parts of the world too numerous to mention. The terminal dates varied from 16th December, 1946, around Hong Kong to 28th April, 1953, for clearances off the Solomon Islands, New Guinea and Papua. Approx. 140 medals and/or bars issued.

Bomb & Mine Clearance, Mediterranean *(1st January, 1953-31st December, 1960)*

This bar was authorized on the 27th July, 1956, for service with the Mediterranean Fleet Clearance Diving Team between the dates given above. A new bar was made by the Mint in 1959 reading "B. & M. Clearance Mediterranean".

Cyprus *(1st April, 1955-18th April, 1959)*

The qualifications for this award are:

ROYAL NAVY AND ROYAL MARINES

A total period of four months (or 120 days), which need not be continuous, ashore or in ships based on Cyprus on patrol within twenty miles of the island.

MERCHANT NAVY

Members of the Royal Fleet Auxiliary qualified as for the Royal Navy. Crews of ships chartered to the Ministry of Transport and Civil Aviation and of Tank Landing Ships based on Cyprus that served with the Army also qualified.

Near East *(31st October-22nd December, 1956)*

The qualifications for this award are:

ROYAL NAVY AND ROYAL MARINES

One or more days ashore in Egypt or on duty off the Egyptian coasts. The qualification for the aircrews was one operational sortie over Egypt or over the

Egyptian warships off Alexandria. The medals do not contain the names of the ships or units.

MERCHANT NAVY

One or more days' service in support of either of the Armed Forces afloat in ships of the Royal Fleet Auxiliary or Landing Ships Tanks. R.N. ships present included the aircraft carriers *Bulwark*, *Eagle* and *Albion* from which many excellent air strikes were mounted which almost destroyed the whole of the Egyptian Air Force.

The Carriers *Theseus* and *Ocean* operated as helicopter assault ships landing 45 Royal Marien Commando. H.M.S. *Newfoundland* (Light Cruiser) was the only ship engaged in a traditional role when she sank in a few minutes the frigate *Domiat* in the Red Sea.

Arabian Peninsular *(1st January, 1957-30th June, 1960)*

Issued for service in or off the Aden Colony or Protectorate, Muscat and Oman and other neighbouring Gulf States.

Brunei *(December, 1962)*

This bar was awarded to the Navy and the Royal Marine landing parties (see G.S. Medal 1918/62 bar Brunei for Army and R.A.F. awards) for their services during a revolt which broke out in the British Protectorate State early in December, 1962. A total of approximately 850 medals with the single bar were awarded and approximately 450 bars for attachment to medals already issued. The only naval unit actually engaged was the 42 Commando. R . M .

02 THE GENERAL SERVICE MEDAL (ARMY AND ROYAL AIR FORCE) (1918-1962)

Obverse	*1st issue (1918-1934)* — The coinage head of King George V facing left and legend "GEORGIVS V BRITT : OMN : REX ET IND : IMP".
	2nd issue (1934-1936) — The crowned head of King George V in robes and the legend "GEORGIVS V . D . G . BRITT . OMN . REX . ET . INDAE . IMP ."
	3rd issue (1936-1949) — The crowned head of King Geoge VI and the legend "GEORGIVS VI D : G : BR : OMN : REX ET INDIAE IMP :"
	4th issue (1949-1952) — The crowned head of King George VI and the legend "GEORGIVS VI DEI GRA : BRITT : OMN : REX FID : DEF +"
	5th issue (1952-1953) — The crowned bust of Elizabeth II and the legend "ELIZABETH II D . G : BR : OMN : REGINA F. D. +."
	6th issue (1953-1964) — The crowned bust of Elizabeth II and the legend "ELIZABETH II DEI GRATIA REGINA F . D. + ."
Reverse	The standing winged figure of Victory, who is placing a wreath on the emblems of the two Services. In her left hand she is holding a trident.
Size	1.42 in. diameter.
Ribbon	1.25 in. wide. Purple with a 0.35 in. green stripe down the centre.
Suspension	By a unique design of ornamental suspender, which does not swivel in the case of the first two issues.

Designer	E. Carter Preston.
Naming	In thin impressed block capitals.
No. of bars issued	Sixteen.

This medal was instituted by Army Order No. 4 dated 19th January, 1923, to be a contemporary to the Naval General Service Medal instituted in 1915. It is to be awarded for services other than on the adjacent frontiers of India, and East, West and Central Africa.

The medal has been issued with three different obverse effigies and several different legends. The first contained the head of George V and has no raised rim. The second effigy was that of George VI with a slightly raised rim not sufficiently high enough to protect the relief.

Permission was granted to recipients of a Mention in Dispatches during any of the campaigns or expeditions for which this medal was awarded after 11th August, 1920, to wear a bronze oak leaf emblem on the ribbon.

S. Persia *(12th November, 1918-22nd June, 1919)*

This bar was awarded for services under (1) Major-General J.A. Douglas, C.M.G., C.I.E., or Brigadier-General A.M.S. Elsmie, C.M.G., at or near Bushire between 12th November, 1918, and 22nd June, 1919, or (2) under Major-General Sir P. Sykes, K.C.I.E., C.M.G., or Lieutenant-Colonel E.F. Orton at or near Bandar Abbas between 12th November, 1918, and 3rd June, 1919. Only Indian units were employed, the complete names of which are not available. There were, of course, a few European recipients apart from the officers, such as Sergt. A. Prangle (1st Bn. the Royal Hampshire Regiment).

Regiments present: 81 Pioneers; 1/55 Coke's Rifles Frontier Force; 1/127 Baluchis.

R.A.F.: 30 Squadron only.

Medals are known to the South Persia Rifles and to a member of the 1 Kent Cyclist Bn.

Kurdistan *(23rd May, 1919-6th December, 1919)* and *(19th March-18th June, 1923)*

This bar was originally awarded for service as follows: *(a)* At Kirkuk or north of a line east and west through Kirkuk between 23rd May and 31st July, 1919; *(b)* at Dohok or north of a line east and west through Dohok between 14th July and 7th October, 1919; *(c)* north of the advanced bases near Akra and Amadia between 7th November and 6th December, 1919.

Army Order 387 of 1924 and Army Instruction (India) No. 132 of 1925 extended the award to cover operations in Kurdistan in 1923 as follows: *(a)* Operations under Air Marshal Sir J.M. Salmond, K.C.B., C.M.G., D.S.O., or Colonel Commandant B. Vincent, C.B., C.M.G., from 19th March to 18th June, 1923; *(b)* operations under Commandant H.T. Dobbin, D.S.O., from 27th March to 28th April, 1923.

During these operations troops were moved by air. This is the first occasion on which aeroplanes were used as troop carriers in military operations, so that the date 21st February, 1923, is worth noting. The troops moved consisted of two companies of the 1/11th Sikhs.

A full list of the military units present in 1919 is not available but medals with this bar were awarded to units such as the South Wales Borderers, North Lancs, Guides Cavalry, 51st and 52nd Sikhs, who do not appear among the units engaged in 1923 as given below.

The operations in 1923 were against the Kurdish, chief Sheik Mahmoud, who, assisted by a small Turkish force at Rowanduz, had installed himself at Salaimani-yah, in the north-east corner of Iraq. Two columns were formed as under:

Koicol (Colonel Vincent):

120th Pack Battery R.A.
2nd Bn. The West Yorkshire Regiment.
2nd Bn. The Cameronians.
63rd Company Madras Sappers and Miners.
1/11, 2/11 and 14 Sikhs.
1/13 Frontier Force Rifles.
3/16 Punjab Regiment.
Iraq Troops.
Signal Section.
Field Ambulance.
Mobile Veterinary Section.
Pack Train.

Frontier Col. (Commandant Dobbin):

Assyrian Levies only.

R.A.F.:

6, 30, 63 Squadrons.

A column operated from Mosul against the Kurds and consisted of the 34th Mountain Bty. R.A.; 52nd Sikhs; 39th Garhwal Rifles; 7th Gurkhas and 8th Co. Sappers and Miners.

(Two Indian battalions, whose titles I cannot trace, but one was probably the 55th. Burma Rifles, joined the force on or about 5th May at Alton Kupri and completed the march to Saliamaniyah.)

Iraq *(10th December, 1919-17th November, 1920)*

This bar was awarded to: *(a)* Those who served at Ramadi or north of a line east and west through Ramadi between 10th December, 1919, and 13th June, 1920, and *(b)* Those who were present on the strength of an establishment within the boundaries of Iraq between 1st July and 17th November, 1920.

6th DIVISION

74th Brigade:
2/7 Rajputs; 1/15 Sikhs; 3/123 Outram's Rifles.

75th Brigade:
2/96 Infantry; 2/116 Mahrattas; 3/70 Burma Rifles.

76th Brigade:
2/23 Sikh Pioneers; 2/89 Punjabis; 2/117 Mahrattas.

Divisional Troops:
F Battery R.H.A.; 17th Brigade R.F.A.; 10, 26, 92 (Howitzer) Batteries; 11, 63, 69 Companies 2nd Sappers and Miners; 1/12 Pioneers; 8th Machine-Gun Battalion.

Additional Troops:
2 East Yorks; 2 D.C.L.I.; 1 K.O.Y.L.I., 3/153 Rifles; 2/5, 2/11 Gurkhas, Kapurthala Light Infantry.

17th DIVISION

34th Brigade:
2 Royal Irish Rifles; 1/99 Deccan Infantry; 108 Infantry; 114 Mahrattas.

51st Brigade:
2 York and Lancs; 2/6 Jat. Light Infantry; 1/80 Carnatic Infantry; 1/10 Gurkhas.

52nd Brigade:
4 Royal Fusiliers; 45 Sikhs; 1/94 Russell's Regiment; 1/113 Infantry.

Divisional Troops:
19th Brigade R.F.A.; 39, 96, 97, 131 (Howitzer) Batteries; 13 Pack Artillery Brigade; 13 (British), 31, 45, 49 Indian Batteries; 17th Divisional Signal Company; 9, 61, 64, 57 Field Companies; 2nd Sappers and Miners; 1/31 Sikh Pioneers; 17th Machine-Gun Battalion; 5th Cavalry and 32, 37 Lancers.

18th DIVISION

53rd Brigade:
2 Manchester Regiment; 8 Rajputs; 86 Carnatic Infantry; 1/87 Punjabis.

54th Brigade:
2 Royal Northumberland Fusiliers; 1/39 Garhwal Rifles; 52 Sikhs; 1/7 Goorkhas.

55th Brigade:
1 Rifle Brigade; 3/9 Bhopal Infantry; 13 Rajputs; 1/116 Mahrattas; 1/3 Gurkhas.

Divisional Troops
13 Brigade R.F.A.; 2, 8, 44, 160 (Howitzer) Batteries; 2 Pack Artillery Brigade; 14 (British), 25, 34, 40, 50 Indian Batteries; 18 Division Signals Company; 2, 6, 8 Field Companies; 1st Sappers and Miners; 106 Hazara Pioneers; 17 Machine-Gun Battalion; 11 Lancers; 35 Scinde Horse; 8, 14 Light Armoured Motor Batteries.

Cavalry Brigade:
1, 7, Dragoon Guards; 16 Machine Gun Squadron; 8 Field Troop 2nd Sappers and Miners.

Army Troops
5th Battery R.G.A.; 9th Company 2nd Sappers and Miners; 132, 133, 138 Railway Construction Companies; 7th Light Armoured Motor Battery; 1 Railway Armoured Battery.

Baghdad Garrison
2/9 Delhi Regiment; 2/119 Infantry.

Lines of Communication Troops
Sam Browne's Cavalry (two squadron); 37 Lancers; 35 Scinde Horse; Royal Irish Fusiliers; 83 Wallajabad Light Infantry; 2/125 Napier Rifles; 2/129 Baluchis; 124, 134, 140 Railway Construction Companies.

R.A.F.
6, 30, 55, 63, 84 Squadrons.
Medals are also found to the 8th Hussars, Leicestershire Regiment and R. Berkshire Rgt. (153 and also 73 with N.W. Persia.)

N.W. Persia *(10th August–31st December, 1920)*

This bar was awarded to members of Noperforce (North Persia Force) and those on the lines of communication, under Brigadier-General H.F. Bateman-Champain, C.M.G., which consisted of the 36th (Indian) Mixed Brigade:

"A" Battery R.H.A.; 19 Company 3 Sappers and Miners; Royal Northumberland Fusiliers; 1 Royal Berks (624 and 73 with Iraq); 2 York and Lancs; 1 Royal Irish Fusiliers; 1/42 Deoli Regiment; 1/67 Punjabis; 122 Rajputana Infantry; 1/2 Gurkhas; 48th Division Signals. Lines of communication troops: Guides Cavalry, 2/26 Punjabis; 64 Pioneers; 79 Carnatic Infantry; 7, 52, 65 Companies Sappers and Miners.

R.A.F.: 6, 30, 63 Squadrons.

Southern Desert: Iraq *(8th January–3rd June, 1928)*

This bar was awarded for services against the Akhwan in the Southern Desert, under Air-Commodore T.C.R. Higgins, C.B., C.M.G., between 8th and 22nd January, 1928, or under Wing-Commander E.R.C. Nanson, C.B.E., D.S.C., A.F.C., between 22nd January and 3rd June, 1928.

It was mainly awarded to the R.A.F.

R.A.F.: 30, 55, 70, 84 Squadrons; 1 British officer; 4 British officers including Capt. C.L.M. Voutes, 10/5 Maharatta L.I. with the Indian and Iraqi armies, 25 to Indians and over 550 to native personnel with the Iraq Army.

Northern Kurdistan *(15th Marcy–21st June, 1932)*

Issued with the crowned Geo. V. obverse.

No British troops were engaged in these operations against Shaik Admed of Barzan in the area Diana – Erbil – Aqra – Suri due north to the Turkish Frontier.

Iraq Levies.

R.A.F.: 30, 55, 70 Squadrons.

Palestine *(19th April, 1936–3rd September, 1939)*

The medals with this and the next five bars bear the crowned coinage head of King George VI and has a small raised rim.

Regiments present: The Royals; Scots Greys; 8, 11 Hussars; R.A.; R.E.; R.C.S.; R.A.S.C.; R.A.M.C.; R.A.O.C.; Coldstream Guards; Scots Guards; Irish Guards; Royal Scots; 2 Queen's; 2 Buffs; King's Own; 2 R. Northumberland Fusiliers; 2 R. Lincolnshire Regiment; 2 West Yorkshire Regiment; 2 East Yorkshire Regiment; 1 Bedfordshire and Hertfordshire Regiment; 1 R. Leicestershire Regiment; Green Howards; 1 R. Scots Fusiliers; 2 Cheshire Regiment; 2 South Wales Borderers; 1 King's Own Scottish Borderers; 1 Worcestershire Regiment; Border Regiment; South Staffordshire Regiment; Black Watch; 1 Essex Regiment; Foresters; 1 Loyal Regiment; 2 Dorsetshire Regiment; 1 Wiltshire Regiment; Manchester Regiment; 1 York and Lancaster Regiment; 2 R. Hampshire Regiment; 2 Highland Light Infantry; 1 Seaforth Highlanders; 2 Cameron Highlanders; R. Ulster Rifles; 1 R. Irish Fusiliers; Rifle Brigade; The Palestine Police.

R.A.F.: 6, 14, 33, 80, 208, 211, 216 Squadrons.

S.E. Asia 1945-46

ARMY

The qualifications for the Army is quoted as entry into one of the areas mentioned below.

For official visits and inspections the time qualification was one week. (The meaning of the wording is not clear, as it would appear that a member of a unit had only to enter one of the areas, even for a day, to qualify, whereas an inspecting officer had to remain the minimum period of a week.)

The areas referred to are:

1. Java and Sumatra from 3rd September, 1945, to 30th November, 1946, both dates inclusive.
2. French Indo-China from 3rd September, 1945, to 28th January, 1946, both dates inclusive.

ROYAL AIR FORCE

The qualifications may be summarized as follows:

1. One operational sortie over the areas mentioned for the Army.
2. One sortie in connection with the removal of prisoners of war and internees in South-East Asia between 3rd September, 1945, and 4th October, 1945, whether the squadron was based within the area mentioned for the Army or not. This service included Java, Sumatra, Malaya, Siam, French Indo-China and the Andaman Islands.
3. Non-aircrew personnel who served in the areas and between the dates given for the Army qualified for the award, as well as those who were members of any squadron which carried out operational sorties as mentioned in the last paragraph, providing that they served for a minimum period of one month with such squadron.
4. For official visits and inspections the qualifying period was one week.
5. The recipient of a King's Commendation, whether non-aircrew or non-operational, was eligible, even though he may not have completed the necessary qualifying period.
6. A reduced period of service caused by death or evacuation due to disability caused by service was considered as sufficient qualification in the case of non-operational personnel.

The following units were concerned in the operations referred to above. It should be noted that some of them are mentioned more than once. This is accounted for by the fact that they operated over more than one area and were also engaged in the removal of internees and prisoners of war.

1. Units operating over Java and Sumatra between 3rd September, 1945, and November, 1946, both dates inclusive: 27, 47, 62, 89, 96, 117, 136, 194, 215/48; also A.C.S.E.A. and Malaya Communication Squadrons and 224 Group.
2. Units operating over French Indo-China between 3rd September, 1945, and 28th January, 1946, both dates inclusive: 62, 96, 117, 159, 194, 215/48, 233, 357, 358 Squadrons.
3. Units engaged in removal by air of internees and prisoners of war in South-East Asia to Singapore or other ports for onward shipment between 3rd September and 4th October, 1945, both dates inclusive: 8, 27, 31, 47, 48, 62, 89, 96, 99, 117, 136, 159, 160, 194, 203, 215. 233, 321, 355, 356, 357, 358; also A.C.S.E.A. and Malaya Communication Squadrons and 224 Group.

No 1341 Special Flight was also employed, as were the following units of the Royal Australian Air Force: 12, 23, 25, Squadrons and No. 200 Flight.

No. 321 Squadron was a Dutch squadron, and only British personnel employed with it, if any, were eligible for the award.

Bomb and Mine Clearance 1945-49
Bomb and Mine Clearance 1945-56

With the third or fourth obverse issues.

The qualification for this award was originally an aggregate of 180 days' active engagement in the clearance of bombs and mines in the United Kingdom and Northern Ireland between 9th May, 1945, and 31st December, 1949. In May, 1956, the Queen approved the extension of the period of eligibility to 1st January, 1955, for service in the Mediterranean.

Any member of the Royal Navy and Royal Air Force employed on this work on land qualified under the same conditions as those for the Army.

The term "active engagement" must be translated as meaning the process of digging down to a bomb or its removal and final disposal. In the case of mines it means the entering of the perimeter of live minefields, disarming the mines or acting as water jet operator.

It should be noted that being a member of a unit so employed did not, in itself, count as a qualification. To be eligible the recipient must have been personally engaged in one or all of the processes from the reaching to the final disposal of the bombs or mines.

Death or the curtailment of the qualifying period through wounds or disability due to service did not debar eligibility, and those who received a King's Commendation or a Mention in Dispatches also qualified, even though they may not have completed the necessary 180 days' aggregate service.

Palestine 1945-48 *(27th September, 1945—30th June, 1948)*
With the third or fourth obverse issues.

This bar was awarded to officers and other ranks (including women) of the British Commonwealth and Colonial Forces, also British personnel of the Palestine Police and Palestine Civil Service on the strength of a unit in Palestine for one or more days between the above dates. Service in Trans-jordan did not qualify.

Once again the incomprehensible clause that official visits and inspections would only be considered as eligibility providing that they lasted more than a certain number of days, in this case thirty, was included.

The subtlety which decides between a period of service of one day and a visit of twenty-nine is delightful!

R.A.F.: The following operational squadrons were based in Palestine for various periods between the qualifying dates: 6, 13, 27 (detachment), 32, 37, 38, 70, 113, 178, 208, 213, 214, 256, 620, 621, 644, 651 (detachment), 680 (detachment) Squadrons.

It should be noted that, in addition to these, a few aircraft of certain squadrons based outside the area visited Palestine from time to time on official duty, and there were also numerous ground units of the Royal Air Force in Palestine during the qualifying period, all of whom qualified for the medal and bar.

Malaya *16th June 1948—31st July, 1960* (Colony of Singapore *16th June, 1948—31st January, 1959)*
With the third or fourth obverse issues.

The qualifications for the award of this bar, the first with the third issue of the medal, are as follows:

ARMY
One or more days' service on the strength of a unit in the Federation of Malaya or the Colony of Singapore since the first qualifying date inclusive.

ROYAL AIR FORCE E
The qualifications are the same as for the Army. Service with detached squadrons normally based elsewhere, or with detachments of squadrons based elsewhere (such as that of No. 45 Squadron) will qualify.

LOCAL FORCES
Members of all the Local Forces, providing they have completed their training, qualify in exactly the same way as the corresponding Regular Force to which they were attached individually or as a complete unit.

CIVIL POLICE FORCES

The period of qualification in their case is three months' full-time service.

CIVILIANS

All the various members of the organizations that supply everything from beer to beauty qualify in the same way as Army personnel, except members of Ferret Force, the Civil Liaison Corps, and Dyaks recruited in Sarawak, whose qualifying period is twenty-eight days.

One cannot help but wonder why the Regular Malayan Police, the Special Constables, and the detachment of the North Borneo Constabulary had to serve ninety-one times as long as Regular personnel to get a medal, and why certain civilian categories had to do twenty-eight times as long as others. It would seem that those who had to do least to get a campaign medal were the members of the Regular Forces!

Judging by the casualty lists, there is little doubt that the local police ran much more risk of being ambushed, sniped, and brutally murdered than the Naval men in their warships off the coast. As the dacoits have neither navy nor air force, the danger of mines and bombing is eliminated, and it would seem that the dangers which they ran were the same as for the land forces.

Regiments present: 1 King's Dragoon Guards; 4 Queen's Own Hussars; 11 Hussars; 12 Royal Lancers; 13/18 Royal Hussars; 15/19 The King's R. Hussars; 2, 25, 26, 48 Field Regt. R.A.; 1 Singapore Rgt. R.A.; 100, 101, 105 Field Batt., R.A.A.; 11 Indep. Field Sq. R.E.; 50 Gurkha Field Engineer Rgt. R.E.; 51 Field Engineer Regt. R.E.; 74 Field Park R.E.; 410 Indep. Plant Troop R.E.; 3 Grenadier Gds.; 2 Coldstream Gd.; 2 Scots Gds.; 40, 42, 45 Commando Royal Marines; 1 Bn. Queen's Royal Rgt.; 1 Bn. Royal Lincolnshire; 1 Bn. Devonshire Rgt.; 1 Bn. The Suffolk Rgt.; 1 Bn. The Somerset Lt. Inf.; 1 Bn. The West Yorkshire Rgt.; 1 Bn. The East Yorkshire Rgt.; 1 Bn. The Green Howards; 1 Bn. The Royal Scots Fusiliers; 1 Bn. The Cheshire Rgt.; 1 Bn. The Royal Welch Fusiliers; 1 Bn. The South Wales Borderers; 1 Bn. The Cameronians; 1 Bn. The Royal Inniskilling Fusl.; 1st Bn. The Worcestershire Rgt.; 1 Bn. The Royal Hampshire Rgt.; 1 Bn. The Sherwood Foresters; 1 Bn. The Loyal Rgt.; 1 Bn. 3rd East Anglian Rgt. (16/44 Foot); 1 Bn. Q.O.R. West Kent 1 Bn. K.O. Yorkshire Lt. Inf.; 1 Bn. The Wiltshire Rgt.; 1 Bn. The Manchester Rgt.; 1 Bn. Seaforth Highlanders; 1 Bn. Gordon Highlanders; 1 Bn. The Rifle Brigade; 22 Special Air Service Rgt.; The Indep. Para. Squadron; 17th (Gurkha) Signal Rgt.; 208 (Commonwealth) Signal Squadron; Malaya Command Signal Squadron; 1/2, 2/2 King Edward VII's Own Gurkha Rifles; 1/6 Queen Elizabeth's Own Gurkha Rifles; 1/7 Duke of Edinburgh's Own Gurkha Rifles; 1/10, 2/10 Princess Mary's Own Gurkha Rifles; 1, 3 Bn. The King's African Rifles; 1 Bn. The Northern Rhodesia Rgt.; 1 Bn. The Fiji Infantry Rgt.; 1 Singapore Rgt.; 1, 2, 3 Bn. The Australian Rgt.; 1, 2 Bn. The New Zealand Rgt.; The New Zealand Squadron (Special Air Service); The Rhodesia Squadron (Special Air Service who were awarded 120 medals of the 3rd issue) 2/6 Queen Elizabeth's Own Gurkha Rifles; 2/7 Duke of Edinburgh's Own Gurkha Rifles and 1st Bn. Rhodesian African Rifles the latter being awarded 894 of the 4th Q.IIR. issue.

Cyprus (1st April, 1955–19th April, 1959)

The qualifications for this award are:

ARMY

Four months' (or 120 days') service with a unit stationed in Cyprus. The service need not be continuous.

ROYAL AIR FORCE

As for the Army, with the addition of the air-crews of Nos. 37 and 38 Mari-

334

time Reconnaissance Squadrons based on Malta who have flown ten or more sorties over Cyprus waters.

POLICE AND FIRE BRIGADE

A total of 120 days' service in the case of regular members of the above, and a total of 822 hours of duty in the case of Special Constables.

CIVILIAN CATEGORIES

All members of the Church and welfare organizations.

GENERAL

Those recommended for a decoration of any kind, a Mention in Dispatches, or a Queen's Commendation qualify irrespective of their length of service.

Near East *(31st October—22nd December, 1956)*

ARMY

One day's service, or part thereof, ashore in Egypt or off the Egyptian coast.

Units present: 1, 2 and 3* Bn. 16th Parachute Regt. (supported by 33rd Parachute Lt. Rgt. R.A.); 6th Royal Tank Regt.; 1st Royal West Kent; 1st Royal Fusiliers; 1st York and Lancs Regt.; W. Yorks. Regt.; Royal Scots; Argyll and Sutherland Highlanders; Detachments of R.E.; Royal Signals, etc.

ROYAL AIR FORCE

As for the Army or the participation in one or more operational sorties over the area of operations from their bases in Cyprus.

CIVILIAN CATEGORIES

Accredited War Correspondents and certain officially appointed advisers.

This is the first award for which part of a day's service is mentioned in the official qualifications.

In these days of prompt evacuation of the wounded it should be remembered that a man could land on a hostile shore, be wounded, and evacuated to many miles away all in the space of a few hours.

Arabian Peninsular *(1st January, 1957—30th June, 1960)*

This bar was authorized by Army Order 9 dated 22nd February, 1961, for award to those who had served 30 days in the Aden Colony or Protectorate and the Sultanates of Muscat and Oman, or any of the Gulf States.

In addition to members of the Army and Royal Air Force it was also awarded to those who served with the N.A.A.F.I., W.V.S., British Red Cross and the Soldiers' and Airmen's Scripture Readers' Association.

A truly bewildering number of Tribal Guards, Police Foces and The T.O.S. (Trucial Oman Scouts) now the Union Defence Force of the United Arab Emirates were also eligible under the same conditions as the Army and Royal Air Force, though the period mentioned does not apply to them in all cases.

Those who were withdrawn from Cyprus for service in any of the above-mentioned territories before completion of the necessary service to qualify for the "Cyprus" bar were granted it and should wear that for the "Arabian Peninsular" immediately after (i.e. above) that for "Cyprus."

The award of a Mention-in-Despatches or a Queen's Commendation are entitled to wear an Oak Leaf emblem on the ribbon. Recipients of either of these, whose service was curtailed through no fault of their own, are entitled to the award irrespective of their length of service.

---

*This unit made the initial air-borne landing and were heavily engaged.

Brunei *(8th—23rd December, 1962)*

This bar was authorised by A.O. 44/1963 for award to members of all the Services of the British, Australian and New Zealand forces who served for a period of one day in the operational areas in the State of Brunei and/or North Borneo and Sarawak between the dates, both inclusive, mentioned.

The Army Order states that the bar will be awarded for any future operations that may become necessary and that, should such be the case, special orders will be issued on the subject. The only units that took part in the fighting were the Queen's Own Highlanders and the 1/2 Gurkha Regiment.

Members of the North Borneo and Sarawak Police Forces were also eligible for the medal if they took an active part in any operation.

The period of service necessary was one day.

The usual rules concerning the wearing of an Oak Leaf and matters concerning awards for bravery apply as do those concerning the curtailment of service for any of the usually recognized causes.

Now-a-days civilians of many recognized organizations are eligible for service medals, these are listed to save constant repetition in the case of future bars unless, of course, any extra service not now included will be included. These civilian services are:

1. Soldiers, Sailors and Airmen's Families Association Nursing Service.
2. British Red Cross Society Welfare Service.
3. Women's Voluntary Service.
4. Mission of Mediterranean Garrisons.
5. Soldiers' and Airmen's Scripture Readers Association.
6. Ministry of Defence (Army Department) Fire Service.
7. Ministry of Defence (Air Force Department) Fire Service.

103 INDIA GENERAL SERVICE MEDAL (1936-39)

Obverse	The Crowned coinage head of King George VI and legend "GEORGIVS VI D:G:BR:OMN:REX ET INDIAE IMP:"
Reverse	A tiger, with raised right front paws. His head is turned right back and almost meets his very long tail, which is curled back. He is standing on a rocky bit of ground. The word "INDIA" is written above, and the remainder of the background has an unfinished look.
Size	1·42 in. diameter.
Ribbon	1·25 in wide. Green with a ·65-in. grey, sandy-coloured centre separated from the green by two thin red stripes.
Suspension	By an ornamental suspender of the usual India Medal pattern.
Designer	H. Wilson Parker.
Naming	In thin impressed block capitals.
No. of bars issued	Two — North West Frontier, 1936-37, and North West Frontier, 1937-39.

This medal, instituted on 3rd August, 1938, replaced the Indian General Service medal, 1908, which, as already described, was used during the reigns of King Edward VII and King George V and had three different designs of obverse.

There are two different strikings of the medal. That done in England has artistic shoulders to the claw, whereas that done in Calcutta is quite plain. The relief work on the reverse of the Indian striking is distinctly crude, there being practically none on the neck and fore-paws of the tiger. The Calcutta Medals are slightly thicker than those struck by the Royal Mint. The bar 1937-39 and the

(Obverse)
First issue

(Obverse)
Second issue

(Obverse)
Fifth issue

No. 102. The General Service Medal (Army and Royal Air Force) 1918-1964.

(Reverse)*
All issues

(Obverse)
Calcutta Mint issue

(Reverse)
Royal Mint issue

No. 102.   The General Service Medal
(Army and Royal Air Force), 1918-1964.

No. 103. The India General Service Medal, 1936-39.
(The difference in the claws of these medals should be noted.)

* As this medal does not swivel, the pin was withdrawn and the piece reversed for photographic purposes.

To face page 336

(Obverse)

No. 104. The 1939-45 Star.

(Obverse)

No. 105. The Atlantic Star, 1939-45.

(Obverse)

No. 106. The Air Crew Europe Star, 1939-44.

(Obverse)

No. 107. The Africa Star, 1940-43.

To face page 337

medal governing this period was not issued in England until after the war, this type does not swivel.

Permission was granted to recipients of a Mention in Dispatches during any of the campaigns for which this medal was awarded to wear a bronze oak leaf. emblem on the ribbon.

North West Frontier 1936-37 *(24th November, 1936—16th/17th January 1937, and 16th/17th January 1937—15th/16th December, 1937)*

Regiments present: R.I.A.S.C.; I.M.S.; 7 (Bengal), 13 (Dardoni), 19 (Maymyo) Mountain Batteries R.A.; 15 Jhelum Mountain Battery; Norfolk Regiment; Leicestershire Regiment; 1 East Yorkshire Regiment (about twenty men); 2 Green Howards; 1 South Wales Borderers; Duke of Wellington's Regiment; Hampshire Regiment; 1 Northamptonshire Regiment; Highland Light Infantry; 2 Argyll and Sutherlands; 2 Sikhs; 3/7 Rajputs; 1/17 Dogras; 2/1, 1/3, 2/4, 1/5, 1/6, 2/6, 1/9 Goorkhas; 12 Company (Madras) Sappers and Miners; South Waziri and Tochi Scouts; 2 Native Road Construction Battalion; Animal Transport Corps.

The following units, and others that one cannot trace, also received the award: 2 (Derajat) Mountain Battery Frontier Force; 2 Fd. Company Q.O. Madras Sappers and Miners; 3/12 Frontier Force Regiment; 3/6 Rajputana Rifles; 4/8 Punjab Regiment; 5/12 Frontier Force Regiment; 6/13 Frontier Force Rifles; 3/16 Punjab Regiment.

R.A.F. 5, 11, 20, 27, 28, 31, 39, 60, 70 (B.T.) Squadrons.

North West Frontier 1937-39 *(15th/16th December 1937—31st December/1st January, 1939), (15th/16th June, 1938—1st/2nd November, 1938), (31st December, 1938—31st January, 1939), (31st December, 1939—1st January, 1940)*

This bar was sanctioned by Army Order 217 of 1940 to be awarded for operations in Waziristan between midnight 15th/16th December, 1937, and midnight, 31st December, 1939/1st January, 1940. The operations were conducted by General Sir John F.S.D. Coleridge, K.C.B., C.M.G., D.S.O., A.D.C., who was the G.O.C. in C. of the Northern Command (India). The two divisions employed were commanded by Major-General E. de Burgh, C.B., D.S.O., O.B.E., and Major-General A.F. Hartley, C.B., D.S.O.

Below, is the list of complete units present but, as for all Indian campaigns, medals are to be found to individuals from several regiments which were not present as a whole.

Regiments present:

Cavalry	Skinner's Horse (1 Duke of York's Own); Probyn's Horse (5th King Edward's Own); 8 (King George's Own); a detachment of the Scinde Horse (14 Prince of Wales's Own).
Artillery	4, 7, 63, 66, 80, 81 Field Batteries. 2, 3, 9 Light Batteries. Section each of 20/21 and 26 Medium Batteries. 2, 3, 4, 5, 7, 8, 12, 13, 15, 17, 18, 19 Batteries and one section of 20 Mountain Battery.
Sappers and Miners	2, 3, 4, 5, 6, 9, 12, 14, 15, 19, 20, 22 Companies.
Royal Tank Corps	1, 6, 7, 8, 9, 11 Tank Companies.

Infantry: European	1 R. Warwicks; 1 Norfolks; 2 Suffolks; 1 Leicesters;* 2 Green Howards; 1 South Wales Borderers; 1 Hants;* R. Ulster Rifles. 1 Northampton's.
Indian†	2/1 Punjab Regiment; 3/1 Punjab Regiment; 1/2, 2/2 Punjab Regiment; 2/4 Bombay Grenadiers; 1/5 Mahratta Light Infantry; 2/6, 3/6, 4/6 Rajputana Rifles; 2/7, 3/7 Rajput Regiment; 2/8, 3/8, 4/8 5/8 Punjab Regiment; 3/9 Jat Regiment; 1/10, 3/10 Baluch Regiment; 1/11, 2/11 Sikhs; 1/12, 3/12, 5/12 Frontier Force Regiment; 1/13, 4/13, 6/13 Frontier Force Rigles; 1/14, 2/14, 3/14 Punjab Regiment; 3/15 Punjab Regiment; 1/16, 3/16, 4/16 Punjab Regiment; 1/17, 2/17, 3/17 Dogras; 1/18 Royal Carhwal Rifles; 1/1, 2/1, 1/2, 1/3, 2/3, 1/4, 2/4, 1/5, 2/5, 1/6, 2/6, 2/8, 1/9 Gurkhas. Road Construction Battalions: 1, 2, 4, 5.
R.A.F.:	5 (A.C.), 11 (B), 20 (A.C.), 27 (B), 28 (A.C.), 31 (A.C.), 39 (B.), 60 (B.), one flight of 70 (B.T.) Squadrons.

World War, 1939-45, Stars and Medals

Those who wish to obtain the full particulars of the awards made for the World War, 1939-45, should consult the pamphlet issued by the Committee on the grant of Honours, Decorations and Medals, and published by H.M. Stationery Office in June, 1946, and subsequent publications.

The 1939-45 Star could be considered as the qualifying one, because those who were entitled to it became entitled to the others on entering the applicable theatre of operations, except in the case of the Atlantic and Air Crew Europe and Africa Stars.

It was decided by the Honours Committee, after due deliberation, that the campaign stars and medals awarded to Imperial troops for service during the 1939-45 War would not be stamped with particulars of the name and unit of the recipients at Government expense, but that they could be added under private arrangement.

Not only will this lower the intrinsic value of all these stars and medals, but it will necessitate a careful scrutiny of the recipient's Record of Service to verify the authenticity of any group.

No one person could receive more than five campaign stars and the two medals, as the following will show:

1939-45 Star.
Atlantic (or France and Germany, or Air Crew Europe Star).
Africa Star.
Pacific Star (or Burma Star).
Italy Star.
Defence Medal.
War Medal.

No individual was awarded more than one bar or emblem to any one campaign star, nor was he entitled to wear more than one emblem on any one of the star ribbons when the ribbon only was worn.

---

* The title "Royal" was granted in November, 1946.
† The regiments are given in their numerical order, which was not that of their seniority in the Indian Army.

All the eight stars are of the same design and differ only in the wording of their title on the central circlet. Their particulars are as follows:

Obverse	The shape of the stars is similar to those awarded for the Gwalior Campaign of 1843. In the centre is the Royal Cipher surmounted by a crown superimposed on a circlet which bears the title of the star.
Reverse	Plain.
Size	1·75 in. across.
Ribbons	These were designed by His Majesty King George VI, and vary with each star. The colours are given in the text of the star concerned. They are all 1·25 in. wide.
Suspension	The ribbon passes through a ring attached to the uppermost point of the star.
Designers	The stars were designed by the Mint engravers.
Naming	All issued unnamed by the British Government.
No. of bars issued	A total of nine which are sewn on the appropriate ribbons.
Composition	Bronze.

104 THE 1939-45 STAR (3rd September, 1939—2nd September, 1945)

This star was awarded for service in the Second World War between 3rd September, 1939, and 2nd September, 1945. (First announced as the 1939-44 Star).

The qualifications were, as regards the United Kingdom Forces, briefly as follows:

NAVY
(1) Six months'* service afloat in areas of active operations.
(2) Naval personnel who did not complete their six months' service afloat but took part in a commando raid, etc., for which the Army were eligible for the star, also received it.
(3) Members of the Fleet Air Arm could qualify for the star, either by six months' service afloat or under any of the qualifications applicable to the Royal Air Force.

ARMY
(1) Six months' service in an operational command, except for service in Dunkirk, Norway and in some specified commando raids and other services for which the qualifying period was one day. Airborne troops qualified if they had participated in any airborne operations and had completed two months' service in an operational unit.

R.A.F.
(1) Operations against the enemy, providing that two months' service had been completed in an operational unit.
(2) Non-aircrew personnel had to complete six months' service in the area of an operational army command, except that service at Dunkirk and in Norway, etc., also counted.

* As the period of a month will often be mentioned in connection with the 1939-45 awards it is as well to call attention to the official duration of such a period. A month is 30 days; two months are 60 days; four months are 120 days; six months are 180 days. The difference between these periods and the corresponding calendar ones should be noted.

MERCHANT NAVY

(1) Personnel who completed six months' service afloat qualified, providing that at least one voyage was made through an operational area. Service performed during the evacuation of Dunkirk also qualified. Service in fishing vessels and in coastal craft was also included.

Service which was curtailed by death, or disability due to service, would qualify for the award.

A recipient of a Decoration, Mention in Dispatches or a King's Commendation qualified for the award, irrespective of the length of service.

Recipients of the star for less than the full qualifying periods of six months', or two months', service must have completed the remainder of their qualifying period in any theatre of operations before being allowed to count service for the Atlantic or Air Crew Europe Star.

In the case of the Royal Navy and the Merchant Navy, a full period of six months' operational service must have been rendered before eligibility for the Pacific, Burma or Italy Stars began.

Members of the crews of fighter aircraft who took part in the Battle of Britain between 10th July and 31st October, 1940, were awarded a silver-gilt rose emblem to be worn when the ribbon alone was being worn, and a bar inscribed "Battle of Britain" to be affixed on the ribbon when the medal is worn.

It should be clearly understood that combat in the air during the qualifying period did not in itself constitute a qualification no matter in what type of aircraft the combat took place. The squadrons that qualified were: Nos. 1, 17, 19, 23, 25, 29, 32, 41, 43, 46, 54, 56, 64, 65, 66, 72, 73, 74, 79, 85, 89, 92, 111, 141, 145, 151, 152, 213, 219, 222, 229, 234, 235, 236, 238, 242, 248, 249, 253, 257, 264, 266, 302, 303, 310, 312, 401 (No. 1 R.C.A.F. Squadron), 501, 504, 600, 601, 602, 603, 604, 605, 607, 609, 610, 611, 615, 616 and the Fighter Interception Unit.

Members of the women's Naval, Military and Air Force organizations were eligible for the star on the same basis as the male members of the services to which they belonged.

The colours of the ribbon are, reading from the left when facing the wearer, dark blue, red and light blue in equal proportions. They symbolize the Royal and Merchant Navies, the Army and the Royal Air Force.

105 THE ATLANTIC STAR (3rd September, 1939—8th May, 1945)

This star, awarded to commemorate the Battle of the Atlantic, was granted for six months' service afloat. The location of the qualifying areas differs in the case of the Royal Navy and the Merchant Navy. The 1939-45 Star must have been earned by six or, in the case of the air crews, two months' service in operations before the qualifying period for the Atlantic Star began.

The qualifying period was from 3rd September, 1939, to 8th May, 1945.

NAVY

(1) Service in the Russian convoys or west of longitude 20° E. was included.
(2) The period of qualification for the France and Germany Star could not run concurrently with that for the Atlantic Star.
(3) Prisoners of war were entitled to the star, providing that they had already completed the qualifying period for the 1939-45 Star and had begun to earn the Atlantic Star at the time of capture.

MERCHANT NAVY

(1) The 1939-45 Star must have been earned by six months' service at sea, and there must have been a further six months' service anywhere at sea rendered

between 3rd September, 1939, and 8th May, 1945, with one or more voyages in the Atlantic and/or Home Waters, including service in convoys to North Russia and service in the South Atlantic west of longitude 20°E. during the second period of six months. Seamen who had not earned the 1939-45 Star but who served in the Merchant Navy at sea in the area specified above during the last six months of operational service up to 8th May, 1945, qualified for the Atlantic Star, provided that service was not subsequently rendered in another operational area. The 1939-45 Star was not awarded in such cases.

(2) Service afloat in fishing vessels and certain coastal craft was excluded from the award of this star, though recognized for the 1939-45 Star, which included at least one voyage through the specified area.

R.A.F.

(1) Members of air crews who had taken part in active operations within the specified area, providing that they completed two months' service in an operational unit after earning the 1939-45 Star.

(2) Four months' service as a member of an air crew in an operational unit was also considered as a qualification for the star, providing that any two of them qualified for this star.

(3) Time spent as a prisoner of war was not counted, unless the period necessary to earn the 1939-45 Star had been completed at the time of capture.

ARMY AND R.A.F.

Army and Air Force personnel who served with the Navy or Merchant Navy qualified in the same way as members of the service with which they served.

Those who were not able to complete the qualifying period for this star, and had not been eligible for the 1939-45 Star, would be awarded the Atlantic Star. The Atlantic Star could, therefore, be gained without the 1939-45 Star.

If a recipient of this star also qualified for the France and Germany Star, he could wear a silver rose emblem on the ribbon of the star first earned. When th the ribbons only are worn, there is no way of showing whether the recipient qualified for the Air Crew Europe Star or the France and Germany Star, as he was only allowed to wear one emblem. The emblem does not signify which of the other stars the recipient had earned, as it was of the same pattern for both. When the star is worn, then the appropriate bar with the title "Air Crew Europe" or "France and Germany" is worn attached to the ribbon.

Service which was terminated by death, or disability due to service, would qualify, as would that of any period in the case of an award of a Mention in Dispatches or a King's Commendation.

The ribbon is of the shaded and watered type of dark blue, white and sea green symbolical of the Atlantic. The dark blue is worn to the left when facing the wearer.

06 THE AIR CREW EUROPE STAR (3rd September, 1939—5th June, 1944)

This star was awarded for operational flying from United Kingdom bases over Europe between the dates mentioned.

(1) The qualifying period was four months' service as a member of an air crew in an operational unit, any two months of which qualified for the Air Crew Europe Star.

(2) Time spent as a prisoner of war was not counted, unless the qualifying period for the 1939-45 Star had been completed before capture.

(3) Service curtailed by death, or disability due to service, would qualify, as

would any service during which an award or a Mention in Dispatches was gained.

(4) Army personnel qualified for this star if they had served on aircrew duties for four months with the R.A.F. operational unit providing that two months of this period was employed on operational flying over Europe and at least one operational sortie was made.

The star could not be earned unless the qualification to earn the 1939-45 Star had been fulfilled.

GENERAL

Those who qualified for this star, the Atlantic Star and the France and Germany Star, or two of these, were awarded the star first earned. To signify that a recipient was also eligible for either or both of the other stars a silver rose emblem is worn on the ribbon of the star first earned. Only one emblem may be worn, whether to denote the eligibility for a further one or two stars. When the star is worn, then the appropriate bar with the title "Atlantic" or "France and Germany" is worn attached to the ribbon.

The ribbon is light blue with black edges and two yellow stripes, representing continuous service by day and by night.

107 THE AFRICA STAR (10th June, 1940–12th May, 1943)

This star was awarded for one or more days' service in North Africa between 10th June, 1940, and 12th May, 1943, both dates inclusive.

The qualifications were:

NAVY AND MERCHANT NAVY

Any service at sea in the Mediterranean between 10th June, 1940, and 12th May, 1943, and/or service in support of the campaigns in Abyssinia, Somaliland and Eritrea.

Naval service ashore in the same areas as the Army would also qualify. Members of the Merchant Navy who took part in the operations off the coast of Morocco between 8th November, 1942, and 12th May, 1943, would also qualify.

The conditions governing the award of this star are in no way connected with those for the 1939-45 Star.

ARMY

The qualifications is the entry into North Africa on the establishment of an operational unit.

Service in Abyssinia, The Somalilands, Eritrea, Sudan and, be it noted, Malta was included, but not that in West Africa.

R.A.F.

The qualifications was to have landed in, or flown over, any of the areas previously mentioned (except West Africa), or territory occupied by the enemy.

Bars and Emblems to the Africa Star

NAVY

Personnel who served inshore or on escort duty off the North African coast between 23rd October, 1942, and 12th May, 1943, were entitled to wear a silver rose emblem on the ribbon to denote entitlement to the bar 'North Africa 1942-43." Those who served with either the Eighth or First Armies were granted a silver emblem of the Arabic figure "8" or "I" according to the army with which they served.

ARMY

Three emblems were awarded to the Army, which consisted of (1) a numeral "8", (2) a numeral "1", or (3) a silver rose emblem to denote the award of the bar "North Africa 1942-43". Only one could be worn. The qualifications were:

(1) The numeral "8" representing the 'Eighth Army' bar was awarded for service in the Eighth Army between 23rd October, 1942, the date of the Battle of El Alamein, and 12th May, 1943.

(2) The numeral "1" ('1st Army') was awarded for service in the First Army in a unit or formation in Tunis or Algeria between 8th November and 31st December, 1942, or thereafter between 1st January and 12th May, 1943, in any unit under the command of the First Army.

(3) The silver rose emblem was awarded to personnel of the Headquarters of the 18th Army Group who did not qualify for either of the numerals. Members of the Union Defence Force attached to the South African Air Force Squadrons, which qualified for the rose emblem, also qualified for it.

R.A.F.

A silver rose emblem denoting award of the bar "North Africa 1942-43" was awarded to those who served under the command of the A.O.C. Western Desert, A.C.N.W. African Forces, A.O.C. Malta, or any others who operated against the Germans or Italians between 23rd October, 1942, and 12th May, 1943.

MERCHANT NAVY

Inshore service on the North African coast between 23rd October, 1942, and 12th May, 1943, and participation in the landings on the Moroccan coast between 8th November, 1942, and 12th May, 1943, qualified for the award of a silver rose emblem (see R.A.F. above).

Service in any vessel in support of the operations in North Africa, during the period 23rd October, 1942, to 12th May, 1943, qualified for the bar "North Africa 1942-43."

GENERAL

Only one bar, or emblem, was awarded to any one individual in conjunction with this star. If, however, an individual qualified for all three bars, then the one to which he first became entitled was awarded.

When the star is worn, then the appropriate bar inscribed with the title "Eighth Army", "First Army" or "North Africa 1942-43" is worn attached to the ribbon.

The colours of the ribbon are pale buff with a central red stripe and two narrow stripes, one of dark blue and the other of light blue. The dark blue stripe is worn innermost, *i.e.* to the left when facing the wearer.

These colours are symbolical of the desert, the Royal Navy, the Army and the Royal Air Force.

08 THE PACIFIC STAR (8th December, 1941—2nd September, 1945)

This star was awarded for service in the Pacific theatre of operations between 8th December, 1941, and 2nd September, 1945, both dates inclusive.

In the case of the Army there is no prior time qualification. Naval and Royal Air Force crews must have completed at least one operational sortie over the appropriate land or sea area. The qualifications for the award were:

ROYAL NAVY AND MERCHANT NAVY

Service in the Pacific Ocean, South China Sea and the Indian Ocean east of a line running approximately south of Singapore.

The 1939-45 Star must have been earned by six months' service before qualification for the Pacific Star could commence, except in the case of those who served in the Pacific zone for less than six months after 2nd March, 1945. There was a special rule in relation to the last six months of operational service up to 2nd September, 1945. Persons who entered operational service during the last six months qualified for the star if they did not serve subsequently in another operational area. In this case the prior time qualification of six months did not apply. The 1939-45 Star was not awarded in such cases where the total operational service amounted to less than six months.

Naval personnel who served ashore qualified under the same rules as those pertaining to the Army.

ARMY

Qualifying service for the Army was restricted to that in territory which had been subjected to enemy or allied invasions. Service in Burma was, however, excluded. Service in China and Malaya between 8th December, 1941, and 15th February, 1942, was included.

R.A.F.

One operational sortie qualified for the star. Ground service qualified under the same rules as for the Army.

GENERAL

Official visits under the authority of the Commanders of the Military or Air Forces engaged did not qualify unless they exceeded thirty days in duration.

Those who qualified for both the Pacific and Burma Stars were awarded a silver rose emblem to be worn on the ribbon of the star that was earned first. The recipient of a Pacific Star who also qualified for the Burma Star was awarded a bar with the title "Burma" to be affixed to the ribbon when the Pacific Star itself was being worn.

The ribbon is dark green with red edges with a central yellow stripe, also a thin one of dark blue and another of light blue. The dark blue stripe should be worn farthese from a left shoulder, i.e. to the left when facing the wearer. The green and yellow symbolize the forests and beaches; the dark blue represents the Navy, the red the Army, and the light blue the Royal Air Force.

109 THE BURMA STAR (11th December, 1941—2nd September, 1945)

This star was awarded for service in the Burma Campaign between 11th December, 1941, and 2nd September, 1945, both dates inclusive.

The qualifications for the different Services are as follows:

ROYAL NAVY AND MERCHANT NAVY

(1) The 1939-45 Star must have been earned by six months' service in operations before eligibility for the Burma Star could begin. In the case of the Merchant Navy there is an extra proviso, which is not mentioned in the case of the Royal Navy, that the previous six months' service must have been followed by further service on or after 11th December, 1941, irrespective of the length of that service, in the area enumerated in the next paragraph.

(2) The area is restricted to the Bay of Bengal, enclosed by a line running from the southernmost point of Ceylon for a distance of 300 miles south, thence to a point 300 miles west of the southernmost point of Sumatra, and continuing east to the western side of Sunda Strait. The Malacca Strait is included.

(3) Those who entered the area after 2nd March qualified for the Burma Star but not for the 1939-45 Star.

(Obverse)

No. 108. The Pacific Star, 1941-45.

(Obverse)

No. 109. The Burma Star, 1941-45.

(Obverse)

No. 110. The Italy Star, 1943-45.

(Obverse)

**No. 111. The France and Germany
Star, 1944-45.**

To face page 344

(Obverse)

No. 112.   The Defence Medal, 1939-45.

(Reverse)*

**No. 114.   The India Service Medal,
1939-45.**

(Reverse)

No. 112.   The Defence Medal, 1939-45

Obverse)

(Reverse)

No. 113.   The War Medal, 1939-45.

* The obverse is identical with that of the War Medal illustrated above.

To face page 345

(4) Naval personnel who served ashore qualified under the same rules as the Army.

ARMY

Service in any part of Burma between 11th December, 1941, and 2nd September, 1945, qualified for the award, as did that in the provinces of Bengal and Assam between 1st May, 1942, and 31st December, 1943, and in the same provinces between 1st January, 1944, and 2nd September, 1945. Service in China and Malaya between 16th February, 1942, and 2nd September, 1945, was also included.

R.A.F.

One operational sortie qualified. Non-aircrew qualified under the same rules as for the Army.

GENERAL

Visits and inspections which were approved by any of the Commanders-in-Chief would qualify, providing that they were of over thirty days' duration.

Those who qualified for both the Burma and Pacific Stars were awarded a silver rose emblem to be worn on the ribbon of the star first earned when the ribbons alone are worn. When the Burma Star itself is being worn the recipient is entitled to wear a bar with the title "Pacific" attached to the ribbon.

The ribbon is dark blue with a wide red stripe down the centre. The blue edges thus formed have a central orange stripe. The red symbolizes the British Commonwealth Forces and the orange the sun.

110 THE ITALY STAR (11th June, 1943–8th May, 1945)

This star was awarded for operational service in Sicily or Italy from the date of the capture of the island of Pantellaria on 11th June, 1943, to 8th May, 1945. The qualifications were:

THE ROYAL NAVY AND MERCHANT NAVY

(1) The 1939-45 Star must have been earned by six months' service in operations before the qualifying period for the Italy Star could commence.
(2) Service in the Mediterranean and the Aegean Seas and operations in and around the Dodecanese, Corsica, Greece, Sardinia and Yugoslavia after 11th June, 1943, would qualify. Those who entered these last five areas after 8th November, 1944, if they did not serve subsequently in another operational area, would qualify for the Italy Star but would not be awarded the 1939-45 Star.
(3) Those who served ashore qualified under the same rules as the Army.

ARMY

(1) There was no prior time qualification.
(2) Operational service in the Aegean, Dodecanese, Corsica, Greece, Sardinia, Yugoslavia and Elba between 11th June, 1943, and 8th May, 1945, qualified.
(3) Service in Sicily after 17th August, 1943, in Sardinia after 19th September, 1943, and in Corsica after 4th October, 1943, did not qualify.

R.A.F.

Qualification consisted of participation in aircrew service within the Mediterranean theatre, including sorties over Europe therefrom.

GENERAL

Entry into Austrian Territory during the last few days of the war qualified for this star, not for the France and Germany Star.

Visits of over thirty days' duration qualified for the award, providing that they were undertaken under the authority of one of the Commanders-in-Chief.

The star was awarded in addition to the other stars, so that no clasps were awarded to it.

The Italian colours are represented on the ribbon, which is red, white, green, white, red in equal width stripes.

111 THE FRANCE AND GERMANY STAR (6th June, 1944—8th May, 1945)

This star was awarded for service in France, Belgium, Holland or Germany between D Day and the German surrender — that is for the period 6th June, 1944, to 8th May, 1945.

The qualifications were:

(1) All service directly concerned with the operations in the invasion of the above countries.

(2) Service off the South of France did not qualify for this star but for the Italy Star.

(3) Service ashore in any of the areas of land operations was a qualification.

ARMY

The only qualification necessary was the participation in any operation on land in any of the above countries.

R.A.F.

Any service over Europe between the above dates constituted a qualification, except those which started from the Mediterranean area, which would qualify for the Italy Star.

Non-aircrew personnel qualified under the same conditions as the Army.

GENERAL

Visits of an official nature which lasted over thirty days would qualify.

The star was not awarded in addition to the Atlantic Star and the Air Crew Europe Star, so that a rose emblem was awarded to be worn on the ribbon of the star first earned when the ribbon alone was worn.

Those who qualified for the Atlantic, Air Crew Europe or France and Germany Star, or two of them, were awarded only the star for which they qualified. The bar with the title "Atlantic" was awarded to be worn on the ribbon to show that service was rendered which would have qualified for the second star. A second bar was not awarded to those who qualified for all three stars. A bar for "Air Crew Europe" was not awarded with this star.

The colours of the ribbon are blue, white, red, white, blue in equal width stripes which are symbolical of the Union flag and those of France and the Netherlands. It will be noted that Belgium is not represented in these colours.

GENERAL REMARKS CONCERNING THE 1939-45 CAMPAIGN STARS

(1) Service in ships making occasional visits to the scenes of operations for refuelling would not necessarily be a qualification.

(2) The expression "entry into operational service" in the case of the Atlantic and Air Crew Europe Stars was subject to the qualification that six or two months' operational service must already have been rendered. For awards to the Royal Navy and the Merchant Navy of the Pacific, Burma and Italy Stars a similar prior time qualification of six months also applied. There were, however, certain exceptions to these rules which have been enumerated in the applicable texts.

(3) A recipient of the 1939-45 Star who qualified for it by less than the six or two months' service respectively had to complete the requisite period before he could begin to qualify for the Atlantic or Air Crew Europe Stars respectively.

In the case of the Royal Navy and Merchant Navy, the applicable qualifying period had to be completed before they could begin to qualify for the Pacific, Burma and Italy Stars.

(4) For the Atlantic or Air Crew Europe Stars in the Armed Forces or Merchant Navy, or for the Pacific, Burma or Italy Stars in the Royal Navy or Merchant Navy, operational service for a lesser period than six or two months as the case may be, which was brought to an end by death, wounds or other disability due to service; or, alternatively, the grant for service in operations of an Honour, Decoration, Mention in Dispatches, King's Commendation for brave conduct or King's Commendation for valuable service in the air, was a qualification for award, without regard to the prior service requirement. The restrictions concerning the alternative awards of the stars still applied.

(5) Time spent as a prisoner of war would count towards the 1939-45 Star, but it would not be counted towards earning any of the other stars unless the full qualifying periods for the 1939-45 Star had been completed before capture. If, however, the candidate had completed his requisite period for the 1939-45 Star and was captured during the period he was qualifying for one of the other stars, then the period spent in captivity would count. In the case of the Merchant Navy, at least one voyage must have been completed in the necessary qualifying area since the completion of the service necessary to qualify for the 1939-45 Star.

(6) Service spent in qualifying for one star could not run concurrently with service qualifying for another, except that an individual who had completed the six or two months' operational service required for the award of the 1939-45 Star was not required to complete this period of qualifying service a second time in order to begin to qualify for the other. A similar arrangement applied to the prior service qualification for awards in the Royal Navy and the Merchant Navy of the Pacific, Burma and Italy Stars. An exception was made to this rule in the case of the Merchant Navy as regards the Atlantic Star which was mentioned in the text referring to it.

(7) No individual was awarded more than one bar to any one star.

(8) The 1939-45 and Africa Stars were awarded to crews of transport aircraft that flew over certain specified routes. The same remarks apply to crews of the Royal Air Force Transport Command that did similar duties.

(9) Personnel of the Royal Navy and Merchant Navy who were on operational service on 8th May, 1945, or during the six months immediately preceding it were granted the Italy Star by virtue of entry into a theatre of operations, and the prior six months' service requirement did not apply. A similar waiving of the prior service requirement extended to the Atlantic Star. The actual requirement for the Atlantic Star was thus reduced in that period until it consisted merely of entry into operational service.

(10) Personnel of the Royal Navy and the Merchant Navy who were in operational service on 2nd September, 1945, received the Pacific or Burma Star, as the case might be, by virtue of entry into a theatre of operations, and the prior six months' service requirement did not apply. In such cases only one star was awarded for service at sea during the last six months in the Atlantic, Italy, Pacific and Burma areas. The star awarded was the one appropriate to the last area in which service was rendered. The 1939-45 Star was not awarded in cases where the operational service amounted to less than the necessary six or two months respectively.

(11) Civilians who performed not less than twenty-eight days' operational service (a) under the Council of Voluntary War Work, (b as recognized Press Correspondents in an operational command, (c) as a member of a civil air transport crew which flew over certain specified areas, or (d) officers who performed meteorological work, R.A.F. education, works service, in uniform, in the area

of Army operational commands were eligible for the Campaign Stars and the War Medal.

112 THE DEFENCE MEDAL (3rd September, 1939—2nd September, 1945)

Obverse	The uncrowned effigy of King George VI and legend "GEORGIVS VI D: BR: OMN: REX F: D: IND: IMP:"
Reverse	The Royal Crown resting on the stump of an oak tree and flanked by two lions. On the top left is the date 1939, and on the top right the date 1945. In the exergue, though not ruled off as such, is the wording "THE DEFENCE MEDAL".
Size	1·42 in. diameter.
Ribbon	Flame coloured with green edges, symbolical of the enemy attacks on our green land. The black-out is commemorated by two thin black stripes down the centre of the green ones.
Suspension	By a plain, straight, non-swivelling suspender.
Designers	Obverse — T.H. Paget; Reverse — H. Wilson Parker.
Naming	Issued unnamed.
No. of bars issued	Nil.

Composition Cupro-nickel although the Canadian version was in ·800 fine silver.

The qualifications for the award were:

(1) Service in the Forces in non-operational areas subjected to air attack or closely threatened, providing such service lasted for three or more years.

(2) Non-operational service in the Forces overseas or outside the country of residence, providing that such service lasted for one year, except in territories threatened by the enemy or subject to bomb attacks, in which case it was six months.

(3) Civil Defence or other similar service in military operational areas providing the civil category was not eligible for campaign stars.

(4) The qualifying period of service in Mine and Bomb Disposal Units was three months.

(5) Those were were awarded Campaign Stars could also, providing they fulfilled the necessary conditions, be awarded this medal.

(6) Service in the United Kingdom Forces in West Africa, Palestine and India would count for the award of this medal, as well as by Dominion Forces, other than operational air crews, in non-operational areas outside their own countries.

(7) Part-time service in the Malta Home Guard also counted.

(8) The closing date for those in the Forces was extended to 2nd September, 1945, for those serving overseas.

(9) Members of any of the civilian services that were entitled to wear chevrons for their war service were eligible for this medal.

(10) Members of the Home Guard resident in the United Kingdom qualified for the medal by rendering three years' service (or three months in the case of those who served in a bomb and mine disposal unit). British citizens from overseas qualified with six months' service or three months in the bomb and mine disposal units.

(11) Service curtailed by death due to enemy action or service wounds was considered eligible. Those who received a personal award conferred by the King were also eligible irrespective of their length of service providing they were serving in a category that qualified for the medal.

(12) Recipients of the George Cross, or George Medal, were eligible for the

Defence Medal whether they were serving in a category eligible for the medal or not, providing that the decorations were gained for service in Civil Defence.

GENERAL

The plastic oval badge granted to civilians who were awarded a King's Commendation for brave conduct was replaced, except in the Merchant Navy, by an emblem of silver laurel leaves to be worn on the ribbon of the Defence Medal. When the Defence Medal was not granted, or the award was for services after the war, the emblem was to be worn directly on the coat, after any ribbons or alone. Approval was given for a small oval badge to be awarded to those civilians who were granted a King's Commendation for valuable service in the air. This badge was to be worn on the coat immediately under any medal ribbons, or in civil air-line uniform on the panel of the left breast pocket.

113 THE WAR MEDAL (3rd September, 1939—2nd September, 1945)

Obverse	The crowned head of King George VI surrounded by the legend "GEORGIBS VI D: G: BR: OMB: REX ET INDIAE IMP:"
Reverse	A lion standing on a dragon which is lying on its back. The lion's right forepaw is resting on the dragon's head which he appears to have raised for the purpose.
Size	1·42 in. diameter.
Ribbon	This embodies the red, white and blue of the Union Flag. It has a narrow red stripe down the centre with a narrow white stripe on both sides of it. The remainder of the sides of the ribbon are equally divided into blue and red stripes with the blue ones next to the white.
Suspension	By a plain, straight, non-swivelling suspender.
·Designer	E. Carter Preston.
Naming	Issued unnamed.
No. of bars issued	Nil.
Composition	Cupro-nickel although the Canadian issue was ·800 fine silver, those issued to the Canadian Merchant Marine were named (700,000 issued, including 4,450 to the Canadian Merchant Marine).

This medal was awarded to all full-time personnel of the Armed Forces wherever their service during the war was rendered. Operational and non-operational service counted, providing that it was of twenty-eight days' or more duration. In the Merchant Navy there was the requirement that the twenty-eight days should have been served at sea.

Operational service that was terminated by death, wounds or a disability due to service, capture or the cessation of hostilities which qualified for one of the Campaign Stars also qualified the recipient for the War Medal even though the total service did not amount to twenty-eight days. This proviso did not, however, apply to those who were not awarded one of the Campaign Stars. If one of the Campaign Stars were awarded for service of less than twenty-eight days, the War Medal was granted in addition. When issued by Canada to a next-of-kin a silver memorial bar engraved with the name and date of death is attached to the ribbon (40,000 issued).

114 THE INDIA SERVICE MEDAL (3rd September, 1939—2nd September, 1945)

On 6th June, 1946, it was announced in Parliament that the King had sanctioned the award of this medal to Indian Forces for three years' non-operational service in India or elsewhere between 3rd September, 1939, and 2nd September, 1945. It was not to be awarded to those who qualified for the Defence Medal. The award was additional to the War Medal and the Campaign Stars and takes precedence immediately after the War Medal.

The obverse is the same as that of the War Medal. The reverse is illustrated facing page 345. The ribbon is dark blue with a central and two other light blue stripes. The light blue is that of the ribbon of the Order of the Star of India, whilst the dark blue is that of the Order of the Indian Empire.

The following were eligible for this medal:

(1) British officers resident in India, Viceroy Commissioned officers, British other ranks and Indian personnel of the Indian Army.
(2) Members of the Indian Territorial and Auxiliary Forces who were called up for service, Indian State Forces which were embodied and the Indian Women's Services.
(3) Non-combatants in military employ who performed duties with a military formation.
(4) British personnel who served with the British or Indian Armies providing that they resided in India prior to 3rd September, 1939.
(5) Indians and Europeans who resided in India prior to 3rd September, 1939, who served with the British Forces in India, or elsewhere, who were not eligible for the Defence Medal.

Those who were serving with the United Kingdom Forces in India during the war, whether stationed there prior to 3rd September, 1939, or not, and those who were recruited from outside India but served with the Indian Army, were *not* eligible. Approximately 222,000 issued.

115 CANADIAN VOLUNTEER SERVICE MEDAL (2nd September, 1939—1st March, 1947)

Obverse	Seven marching figures representing the three fighting services, male and female, together with the Nursing Service. Around the circumference is the inscription "1939 CANADA 1945" at the top and "VOLUNTARY SERVICE VOLONTAIRE" around the bottom. The last three words are separated by maple leaves.
Reverse	The Canadian Coat of Arms.
Size	1·42 in. diameter.
Ribbon	1·25 in. wide, reading from the edge, green, scarlet, royal blue, scarlet and green. Each of the green stripes is 3/10 in. wide. The scarlet stripes are 1/8 in. wide.
Suspension	There is a small ring fitted to the top of the piece through which passes a loose ring, which also passes through a hole in the centre of a straight, non-swivelling suspender of a unique design.
Designer	The obverse was designed by the Canadian Army war artist, Major C.F. Comfort.
Naming	It was decided that the medals should not be named.
No. of bars issued	There are no bars to commemorate any particular action of theatre of service, but there is a straight bar with a maple leaf in the centre to denote service outside the Dominion. Approximately 1,000,000 issued.

The awarding of this silver medal was sanctioned by an order of the King's Privy Council for Canada No. P.C. 8160 of 1943, to which amendments were made in the three following years.

Members of the fighting services and the Nursing Service were eligible for the award, providing that they had completed eighteen months' voluntary service or had been honourably discharged before the full period was completed. Those whose total overseas service amounted to not less than six days, not necessarily continuous ones, were awarded the bar already described. The bar is worn on the ribbon. When the medal is not worn the recipients wear a small maple leaf in the centre of the ribbon. Those who volunteered and were serving on 2nd September, 1939, though under eighteen years of age, were also eligible. Prior service in any of His Majesty's Forces, or those of the United States, also counted towards the award. Posthumous awards were made.

The qualifying period was from 2nd September, 1939, to 1st March, 1947. Those who were serving on voluntary active service on 1st September, 1945, would qualify upon completion of eighteen months' continuous active service, but the service of those appointed, or enlisted, after 1st September, 1945, would not constitute qualifying service.

The medal follows after all the Campaign Stars and the Defence Medal, but precedes the 1939-45 War Medal.

116 THE AFRICA SERVICE MEDAL

Obverse   The map of Africa, with the inscription "AFRICA SERVICE MEDAL" around the left half of the circumference and "AFRIKADIENS-MEDALJE" around the right half.

Reverse   A leaping springbok facing right.

Size   1 7/16 in. (1·4375 in.) diameter.

Ribbon   1·25 in. wide. Tricoloured with a central vertical stripe of orange ¾ in. wide flanked by 1/8 in. wide vertical stripes of the springbok colours of gold and green, the green stripes being at edges.

Suspension   By a straight suspender.

Designers   The designs of the obverse and reverse were suggested by the Prime Minister and Minister of Defence of the Union of South Africa and sketched by a member of the South African Mint.

Naming   In indented block capitals. The prefix "N" indicates a Native whilst "C" indicates a Coloured recipient.

No. of bars issued   Nil.

The award of this silver medal was approved by His Majesty the King on 16th November, 1943, and gazetted in the *Union Government's Gazette* No. 3407, dated 27th October, 1944.

The qualifications for the award were:

(1) The signing of the Africa Oath acknowledging liability for service with the Union Defence Forces anywhere in Africa, and/or
(2) The signing of the General Service Oath acknowledging liability for service with the Union Defence Forces in any theatre of war.

The following also qualified:

(1) Personnel of the Union Defence Forces who served in a full- or part-time capacity.
(2) Personnel of other uniformed services, male or female, who performed full-time service with their respective units. These services include membership of the South African Police, Essential Services Protection Corps, South African Military Nursing Services, V.A.D. officers and members, and women's services.

In the case of full-time service the qualifying period was thirty days. The part-time qualifying period was eighteen hours' non-continuous training. Approximately 192,000 struck.

Issued with a Protea leaf in bronze which is attached to the riband to denote a mention in despatches or a King's commendation.

117 THE AUSTRALIA SERVICE MEDAL (3rd September, 1939—2nd September, 1945)

Obverse:	The crowned effigy of King George VI.
Reverse	The Coat of Arms of the Commonwealth of Australia.
Size	1·4 diameter.
Ribbon	Dark blue, khaki and light blue with intervening stripes of red. The first three colours represent the Navy, the Army and the Air Force respectively. The red stripes represent the Australian Mercantile Marine.
Suspension	By a straight suspender.
Naming	With the regimental or service number (when applicable), initials and surname in impressed capitals.
No. of bars issued	Nil.
Composition	Nickel-silver.

The King's approval of the award of this medal to all members of the Australian armed forces and the Australian Mercantile Marine who served overseas for at least eighteen months between the dates mentioned was announced by the Prime Minister of Australia on 1st December, 1949.

The qualifications are as follows:

(1) Honourable discharge and the completion of a period of continuous training on full-time service of not less than eighteen months or part-time service of three years. Eligibility will include those who served both full- and part-time service. In this case full-time service will count double towards the qualifying period of three years with the proviso that defence duty was performed on not less than sixty days during the service.

(2) Members of the Australian Mercantile Marine must have served eighteen months at sea.

(3) In addition to the Australian armed forces and the Australian Mercantile Marine, the following are also eligible: Civilian members of the R.A.A.F. Reserve who flew over operational zones, official Press representatives, official photographers and all who served in uniform on full-time duty attached to the armed forces.

(4) Civil aircrew personnel must have made three or more flights over, or three landings in, zones of military operations unless para. 5 is applicable to their case.

(5) Service, whether full- or part-time, which was terminated by death, wounds or any disability due to service will qualify.

Approximately 177,000 issued.

118 THE NEW ZEALAND WAR SERVICE MEDAL (3rd September, 1939—2nd September, 1945)

Obverse	The uncrowned effigy of King George VI.
Reverse	The inscription "FOR SERVICE TO NEW ZEALAND 1939/45" above a frond of fern.

Size	1·4 in. diameter.
Ribbon	Black, watered and edged with white stripes 3/16 in. wide.
Suspension	The suspender is composed of two fern leaves joined at the stalk end to form a "U". The tips of the leaves are joined by a thin bar to take the ribbon.
Naming	Issued unnamed.
No. of bars issued	Nil.

The qualifications are as follows:

(1) Personnel of the R.N.Z. Navy, the N.Z. Army (including the National Military Reserve) and the R.N.Z. Air Force (including commissioned ranks of the Air Training Corps) who completed an aggregate of at least 28 days' full-time service or six months' part-time service either at home or abroad between 3rd September, 1939, and 2nd September, 1945, will qualify for the award, provided that the recipient, if not still serving, has been honourably discharged.

(2) Similar periods of service in the Home Guard between 16th August, 1940, and 1st January, 1944, and in the Naval Auxiliary Patrol Service between 31st December, 1941, and 31st July, 1944, will qualify.

(3) Members of the N.Z. Merchant Navy and of the Civil Air Lines registered in New Zealand who rendered service beyond New Zealand will qualify for the award under certain conditions.

(4) Full-time uniformed civilians who served as members of the N.Z. Armed Forces will qualify in the same way as full-time members of such Forces.

(5) "Part-time service" is defined as service rendered by a member of the Armed Forces who was not fully mobilized but was liable to render service by the performance from time to time of short periods of training or other duties and did in fact cary out such training or duties.

(6) The qualifying service, whether part-time or full-time, need not necessarily have been performed in the one service. Short periods of service may be aggregated. In such cases seven days' part-time service is to be taken as equivalent to one of full-time service, and vice versa.

(7) If the service was terminated by capture by the enemy, the recipient must have been free from blame.

(8) Service brought to an end by death on duty, or due to wounds or injuries sustained on duty, or honourable discharge as a direct result of injuries sustained whilst on duty will qualify for the medal, even though the service may not have amounted to 28 days or six months as the case may be.

Approximately 238,000 struck.

119 THE SOUTH AFRICAN MEDAL FOR WAR SERVICES (6th September, 1939-15th February, 1946)

Obverse	The Union Coat of Arms.
Reverse	A wreath of Protea enclosing the figures "1939-1945", the design being circumscribed by the words "SOUTH AFRICA—SUID—AFRICA—FOR WAR SERVICES—VIR OORLOGSDIENSTE."
Size	1 7/16 in. (1·4375 in.) diameter.
Ribbon	1·25 in. wide. Equally divided into three vertical stripes of orange, white and blue reading from the left when facing the wearer.
Suspension	By a straight suspender.
Naming	Unnamed.

No. of bars
issued   Nil., but can be issued with a Protea left in bronze which is atta-
                ched to the riband to denote a mention in despatches or a King's
                commendation.
Composition Silver.

This medal was instituted by a Royal Warrant dated 29th December, 1946,
countersigned and sealed at Cape Town on 6th February, 1946, for award to
both sexes, whether British subjects or not.

The qualifications were:

(1) A minimum of two years' service, one at least of which was continuous,
    rendered voluntarily and without pay, within or without the Union, in one
    or more of the officially recognized voluntary organizations, providing that
    give or more hours were worked every week.
(2) Service counting towards the African Service Medal could not be included.

Approximately 17,000 issued.

119A THE SOUTHERN RHODESIA WAR SERVICE MEDAL (1939-45)

Obverse   Crowned head of George VI and "GEORGIUS VI D: G: BR: OMN:
                REX ET INDIAE IMP:"

Reverse   Arms of S. Rhodesia and "FOR SERVICE IN SOUTHERN
                RHODESIA 1939—1945" surrounding.

Size   1·4 in.

Ribbon   Dark green with narrow black and red stripes at each edge.

Suspension   Straight bar.

No. of bars
issued   Nil.

Composition Cupro-nickel.

Approximately 1,700 issued.

Qualifications: Awarded to those who served at home. Not issued to anyone
qualifying for the campaign stars and medals which, in view of the large proportion who served overseas, explains the rarity of the medal.

120 THE KOREA MEDAL (2nd July, 1950—10th June, 1953)

Obverse   The laureated bust of Queen Elizabeth II facing right surrounded
                by a legend the first issue contained "ELIZABETH II DEI GRA:
                BRITT: OMN: REGINA F: D" and the second scarcer issue,
                "ELIZABETH II: DEI: GRATIA: REGINA F: D:+". Medals to the
                Canadian Forces have the word "CANADA" under the bust.
                (27,500 issued to Canadians.)

Reverse   Hercules, armed with a dagger, with his left arm out horizontally
                holding Hydra, which he is also holding off with his left leg. The
                word "KOREA" is in the exergue.

Size   1·42 in. diameter.

Ribbon   1·25 in. wide. Yellow with two ·25 in. blue stripes.

Suspension   By a plain, straight, non-swivelling suspender.

Designers   Obverse — Mrs. Mary Gillick, C.B.E.; Reverse — E. Carter Preston

Naming   Impressed in thin capitals.

No. of bars
issued   Nil.

Composition Cupro-nickel. The Canadian issue was in ·800 fine silver.

At the end of the 1939-45 War the peninsula of Korea was divided into two countries. The northern part was ruled by a puppet government under Russian control. The southern part had a similar one under United States supervision. When the Russians and Americans had withdrawn their occupying forces the North attacked the South, which, by some means or other, had been recognized by the United Nations.

On 25th June, 1950, the North Koreans attacked the South Koreans, who appealed to the United Nations for military support. This necessitated the dispatch of a liquorice-sorts type of force which the United Nations seem to be able to produce.

The Commonwealth supplied ships and troops, as did the United States and other countries.

When all were partially ready the usual tactical advances and strategic retreats were indulged in, until both side were on the right side of the net – as represented by the 38th Parallel. Then, after a lot of parleying, ending in some sort of agreement, everyone went home.

This medal, whose award was sanctioned by King George VI in 1951, was not issued till the following year, and is, therefore, unusual in this respect.

The qualifications were as follows:

NAVY
Twenty-eight days afloat in the operational areas of the Yellow Sea and Sea of Japan, or one or more days of shore duty.

ARMY
Service of at least one day on the strength of a unit serving in Korea.

R.A.F.
(1) One operational sortie over Korea or Korean waters
(2) Service of one or more days on land.
(3) Service of twenty-eight days afloat in the areas mentioned for the Navy.

Visitors to Korea had to spin out their welcome to thirty days, as time spent in Japan could not be counted.

Many members of civilian organizations were eligible for the medal, which, incidentally, was awarded to those whose service was curtailed by wounds, sickness, etc. Authority was given to the wearing of a bronze oak leaf emblem by those who were Mentioned in Dispatches.

Medals are to be found to practically every regiment in the Army. It is out of place to give the full details as to how reinforcements and replacements were supplied, but suffice it to say that regiments were grouped according to their geographical location at home. This meant that a battalion was made up to strength with men from any regiment in its particular group. The medals were named to the recipient's parent unit, which accounts for the large number to be found to regiments that were not present in Korea as a whole.

However, the Gloucester Rgt's outstanding action at Hill 235 should be mentioned, of 750 men in the 1st Bn. only 40 fought their way back to their own lines whilst 150 held on to the hill until relieved. The remaining 560 were either killed or captured by the Chinese.

The following regiments were recognized by the Battles and Nomenclature Committee as being eligible to claim battle honours for the "Korean Campaign 1950-53":

5th Royal Inniskilling Dragoon Guards, 8th King's Royal Irish Hussars, Royal Tank Regiment, Royal Scots, Royal Northumberland Fusiliers, Royal

Fusiliers, King's Regiment, Royal Norfolk Regiment, Royal Leicestershire Regiment, King's Own Scottish Borderers, Glostershire Regiment, Duke of Wellington's Regiment, Welch Regiment, Black Watch, King's Shropshire Light Infantry, Middlesex Regiment, Durham Light Infantry, Royal Ulster Rifles, Argyll and Sutherland Highlanders.

The following Commonwealth warships were present, but the list is not complete, as we have omitted, with the greatest respect, ancillary craft such as tankers and supply ships and others of the fleet train.

ROYAL NAVY

Aircraft-carriers	*Glory, Ocean, Theseus, Triumph.*
Aircraft Maintenance Carrier	*Unicorn.*
Cruisers	*Belfast, Birmingham, Ceylon, Jamaica, Kenya, Newcastle.*
Destroyers	*Cockade, Comus, Consort, Cossack.*
Frigates	*Alacrity, Amethyst, Black Swan, Cardigan Bay, Hart.*
Headquarter Ship	*Ladybirtd*
Depot ship	*Tyne.*
Hospital ship	*Maine.*

ROYAL CANADIAN NAVY	*Athabaskan. Cayuga, Hyron, Sioux.*
ROYAL AUSTRALIAN NAVY	*Anzac, Bataan, Condamine, Culgoa, Murchison, Shoalhaven, Sydney, Tobruk, Warramunge* and *805, 808, 817 Squadrons Fleet Air Arm.*
ROYAL NEW ZEALAND NAVY	*Hawera, Kanierg, Pukaki, Roboit, Taupo* and *Tutira.*

Nos. 88, 205 and 207 Flying Boat Squadrons, which, based at Seletar, formed the Far East Flying Boat Wing, flew Sunderlands from Iwakuni (Japan) on operational sorties over Korean waters. Also 30, 152, 208, 801 and 810 Squadrons.

R.A.F. fighter pilots flew in Sabre aircraft of the United States Air Force and some photographic interpreters also served with the Reconnaissance Wing of the same forces.

No. 77 Royal Australian (Meteor) Squadron and a South African (Sabre) Squadron also took part in the operations.

20A SOUTH AFRICAN KOREA MEDAL (1950-53)

Obverse	Maps of the Union of S.A. and Korea in relief joined by an arrow with the sea as a background. The whole design partly surrounded by laurel and "KOREA" "VRYWILLIGERS-VOLUNTEERS" "U VAN SA-U OF S.A."
Reverse	Union coat of arms and the Royal Cypher.
Size	1½ in. diameter.
Ribbon	1·25 in. wide. Sky blue, dark blue and orange stripes.
Suspension	Ring and clasp.
Naming	Impressed block capitals.
Composition	Silver.

Instituted by Royal Warrant and signed by Queen Elizabeth 1953.
Qualifications:

(1) Service of at least one day on the strength of an active unit.
(2) Thirty days service for those engaged in inspections, official tours, etc.

Recipients: No. 2 Squadron S.A. Air Force. Ten officers of the S.A. Army who served with the Commonwealth Division. Approximately 800 awarded in all.

20B THE GENERAL SERVICE MEDAL (1962—)

Obverse	The crowned effigy of Queen Elizabeth II with the legend "ELIZABETH II DEI GRATIA REGINA F: D:+"
Reverse	A wreath and crown surrounding the words "FOR CAMPAIGN SERVICE."
Size	1.42in. diameter.
Ribbon	1.25in. wide. Purple with green edges.
Suspension	By a swivelling suspender similar to the third issue of No. 102 illustrated opposite page 361.
Designer	T.H. Paget, O.B.E.
Naming	Impressed in small thin block letters.
No. of bars issued	Five (to date).

This medal, instituted under Ministry of Defence Order No. 61 dated 6th October, 1964, supersedes both the Naval General Service Medal (Army and Royal Air Force 1918-64) which are now, of course, obsolete.

The order of wearing the clasps is that of the date of the periods of service for which the clasps are awarded, not the dates of the relevant Army Orders (i.e. if an earlier period of service qualified for "Radfan" followed by a period which qualified for "Borneo", the "Radfan" clasp would normally have been issued with the medal and the "Borneo" clasp, issued would then be placed above the "Radfan". 68 are thought to have been awarded.

If, as occasionally happens, a General Service Medal with clasp "Borneo" had been issued and it was later confirmed that an earlier period of service had qualified for the "Radfan" clasp, it would be necessary to remove "Borneo" clasp and re-assemble both clasps in the correct order.

From time immemorial until circa 1965 Naval vessels were manned by crews who stayed with the ship throughout her commission. On paying off, the crew were drafted to other ships in the process of being commissioned. This made it very easy to compile medal rolls from the ship's musters.

During the early part of the last decade successive Defence expenditure cuts placed constraints on manpower and it was realised that the traditional methods of collecting crews in barracks ashore until the complement was complete, tied up considerable resources needlessly. As a result 'trickle drafting' was introduced in which every 3 months or so $\frac{1}{8}$ of the crew changed — a completely new crew in a 2 year period. This has resulted in the demise of the composite medal roll. Applications for medals and/or clasps are now made by individuals and as mentioned above the only entry is on the person's service record papers.

Rough assessments of the numbers awarded have been made but it must be emphasised that in the absence of fuller information they must be regarded as tentative only.

Borneo (*24th December, 1962-11th August, 1966*)

This bar was authorized by Ministry of Defence A.O. 2/64 dated 6th October, 1967, and 8/67, for service against the rebels in what was previously known as North Borneo (now Sabah), Sarawak or Brunei between 24th December, 1962 and 11th August, 1966.

The qualifications are:

NAVY AND ROYAL MARINES

(1) Service afloat for an aggregate of 30 days in ships or craft operating on the waters of Sabah, Sarawak, or Brunei, or off the coasts in support of shore operations.

(2) One sortie, or more, as a member of an aircraft crew in support of operations ashore.

(3) Service of 30 days, or more, ashore when posted to units operating in the above areas.

ARMY

Thirty days, or more, service, not necessarily continuous, in the above areas.

ROYAL AIR FORCE

(1) Thirty days or more, not necessarily continuous in the areas mentioned whether serving with the R.A.F. or any unit of H.M. Forces.

(2) One sortie, or more, over the areas mentioned when in direct support of operations. (Approximately 11,000 were awarded to the R.A.F.)

AUSTRALIAN NAVY AND AIR FORCE
ROYAL NEW ZEALAND AIR FORCE

Only members of No. 41 Squadron, based in Singapore, have qualified by one, or more, sorties under the same conditions as the R.A.F.

In addition to the above Services, members of the Royal Fleet Auxiliary Service, Army Fire Service, Womens' Voluntary Service, members of the Meteorological Office serving with the R.A.F., Class "C.C." Commissions, etc., will also qualify.

Those who are awarded anything from a Queen's Commendation to a Victoria Cross and those whose service was curtailed by no fault of their own will be eligible for the award. This is the only post-war second world war campaign where British troops have been engaged, except Korea, in which a V.C. has been awarded (to L/Cpl. Rambahadur Lumbu, 2/10th P.M.O. Gurkha Rifles).

The recipient of a Mention-in-Despatches may wear a bronze emblem on the ribbon, but a rosette may never be worn.

Radfan (*25th April-31st July, 1964*)

This bar was authorised by A.O. 36/65 for award to all members of the United Kingdom Forces and those of the Federal Forces of Arabia who served for a continuous period of 14 days in the South Arabian Federation. The R.A.F. were awarded approximately 5,000 bars. The single bar is more often seen than the combination Radfan and South Arabia.

The usual rules concerning the granting of awards and curtailment of service apply as do those concerning the granting of medals to civilians who wore their prescribed uniform and who were attached to the Federal and/or National Guard of South Arabia for a qualifying period of 30, or more, days from 1st August.

Civilians who wore the approved uniform of their respective organizations also qualify, such as those of the following:

Soldiers' and Airmen's Scripture Readers Association.
Nursing Service.
British Red Cross Society Welfare Service.
Women's Voluntary Service.

Mission of Mediterranean Garrisons.

Soldiers', Sailors and Airmen's Families Association.

Ministry of Defence (Air Force Department) Fire Service.

What one may now almost call the usual rules concerning the wearing of an Oak Leaf, etc., and curtailment of service all apply to this bar.

South Arabia (*1st August, 1964-30th November, 1967*)

Announced in the Army Order 40/66 for continuous service of 30 days or more between the 1st August, 1964 and 30th November, 1967, on the strength of a unit serving in the Federation of South Arabia. The R.A.F. were issued with with approximately 15,000 bars. This bar, in view of the large number issued, should be easily available.

Malay Peninsular (*17th August, 1964-11th August, 1966*)

This bar was authorized in October 1967 for efforts in the Malay Peninsular/ Singapore area during the Indonesian confrontation. The Royal Navy's primary task was patrolling the Malacca and Singapore Straits (approximately 22,000 awarded for service afloat including 1,200 to the Australian and 300 to the New Zealand Navies) while the R.A.F. provided air cover and reconnaissances (approximately 6,500 were issued to the R.A.F.)

The qualifications are:

a. Ashore — Service of 30 days or more, not necessarily continuous, on land in the Malay Peninsular/Singapore between 17th August, 1964 and 12th June, 1965 (both dates inclusive) whilst on the posted or attached strength of any unit or formation in these areas.

b. Afloat — Service of 30 days or more afloat, while in any Royal Navy, Royal Australian Navy, Royal New Zealand Navy or Army Department vessel on duty in the waters surrounding the Malay Peninsular/Singapore between 17th August, 1964 and 12th June, 1965 (both dates inclusive). Service in any Royal Navy, Royal Australian Navy, Royal New Zealand Navy vessel on sea patrol duties between 13th June, 1965 and 11th August, 1966 (both dates inclusive) may also reckon as qualifying service. This service may be aggregated with qualifying service on land as in *a.* above to complete the required period of 30 days.

c. Flying — Completion of 30 or more sorties by aircraft crews of H.M. Forces engaged on operational patrols over the waters surrounding the Malay Peninsular/ Singapore between 13th June, 1965 and 11th August, 1966 (both dates inclusive) may also reckon as qualifying service; each patrol may count as one day's qualifying service and may be aggregated with qualifying service on land and sea as in *a.* and *b.* above to complete the required period of 30 days.

Short Service

In qualifying service was brought to an end before the completion of 30 days on account of death, or evacuation owing to wounds or other disability due to service the reduced period of service will be sufficient qualification for the award.

The grant to individuals for gallantry in the operations on a specific occasion during the uncompleted qualifying period, not amounting to 30 days, or a British Honour, Decoration or Medal of the status of a British Empire Medal or above or a Queen's Commendation or a Mention-in-Despatches will qualify the recipient for the above mentioned Medal and/or Clasp.

Shore Establishments

RN and RM personnel who served for 30 days or more in H.M.S. Terror or other shore establishment in the area between 17th August, 1964 and 12th June, 1965 are eligible.

Personnel on loan to RMN

RN and RM personnel who served on loan with the Royal Malaysian Navy are eligible for the award under the terms of sub-paragraph *a.* above. Consideration will also be given to applications from those who cannot qualify under *a.* but who would quality under *b.* if this applied to RMN as well.

RFA Personnel

Provided they wore uniform of their organisation, RFA personnel will qualify for the award on the same terms as RN and RM personnel as in paragraphs *a. b.* and *c.* above.

The major Army units on emergency duty were: No. 40 Light Regt. R.A.; 1st Bn. Royal Warwickshire Regiment and the 1st Bn. Royal Hampshire Regiment in Borneo and the Green Howards in Singapore. Also New Zealand Forces, and 1/10 P.M.O. Gurkha Rifles.

Casualities were 295 Commonwealth military (114 killed and 181 wounded) and 93 Commonwealth civilian (36 killed, 4 captured and 53 wounded).

The following H.M. Ships completed the qualifying period of 30 days or more in the Malay Peninsular/Singapore area:—

RN Ships	RN Submarines	Royal Australian Navy Ships
Agincourt	Alliance	Curlew
Aisne	Ambush	Derwent
Albion	Amphion	Duchess
Ajax	Anchorite	Gull
Barbain	Andrew	Hawk
Barfoil	Oberon	Ibis
Barrosa		Melbourne
Berwick		Parramatta
Brighton		Snipe
Bulwark		Supply
Caesar		Teal
Camberford		Vampire
Cambrian		Vendetta
Carysfort		Yarra
Cassandra		
Centaur		
Chawton		
Chichester		*Royal New Zealand Navy Ships*
Corunna		Hickleton
Dampier		Otago
Dartington		Santon
Dido		
Eagle		
Eurayalus		
Falmouth		
Fiskerton		
Greatford		
Hampshire		
Hartland Point		
Houghton		
Hubberston		
Ickford		
Invermoriston		
Kent		

(Obverse)

No. 121. Naval Engineers Medal,
1842-6.

(Obverse)
1952 issue

No. 124. The 1904 Polar Medal.

(Reverse)

No. 121. Naval Engineers Meda[l]
1842-6.

(Obverse)

(Obverse)

Varia 12. The Indian Overseas
Badge.

(Reverse)

Varia 4. The Cape Copper Company's Medal for the Defence of Ookiep, 1902.

(Obverse)   (Obverse)   (Obverse)

(Reverse)   (Reverse)   (Reverse)

The 1818-55 Medal.   The 1875-6 Medal.   The 1904- Medal.

No. 124. The Arctic and Polar Medals, 1818-1942.

(Obverse)

(Obverse)

(Obverse)

(Reverse)

120B. The General Service Medal, 1962-.

(Reverse)

120C. Vietnam Medal, 1964.

(Reverse)

South Vietnam Campaign Medal.

RN Ships	RN Submarines	Royal Australian Navy Ships

Kildarton
Lincoln
Loch Fada
Loch Killisport
Loch Lomond
London
Lullington
Manxman
Maryton
Mull of Kintyre
Picton
Plymouth
Puncheston
Salisbury
Sheraton
Thankerton
Tilford
Triumph
Victorious
Whitby
Wilkieston
Woolaston
West

The following H.M. Ships served in the Malay Peninsular/Singapore area but not for a sufficient period to qualify for the award. Personnel who served in these ships would need to aggregate their service with that in other ships or ashore to qualify for the award unless the short service provisions apply:-

RN Ships

Blackpool
Bossington
Cavendish
Londonderry
Lowestoft
Nubian
Penston
Rhyl

Royal New Zealand Navy Ships

Royalist
Taranaki

South Vietnam *(24th December, 1962-29th May, 1964)*

Authorized by Royal Warrant 8th June, 1968 for award to Australian troops only. Qualifications are: 30 days service in ships employed in operations on inland waters and/or off the coast of Vietnam, one day or more on the posted strength of a unit on land, one operational sortie, or 30 days for official visits etc. The usual concession is made regarding termination of service by death, wounds or an award of a gallantry decoration. (The Australian Vietnam Medal with the Queen's effigy was awarded to Australian and New Zealand forces for services after the 29th May, 1964.) 68 clasps awarded, all to members of the Australian Army Training Team. Permission has also been granted to wear the South Vietnamese Government Medal with the General Service Medal.

Northern Ireland (*14th August, 1969 —*)

Awarded in recognition of service in Northern Ireland from 14th August, 1969 inclusive to a future date to be decided in due course, with special regard to the hardships and dangers which have accompanied duty there. Personnel who have already received the General Service Medal (1962) will receive the clasp only.

The qualifications are:

a. Service of 30 days or more, not necessarily continuous, in Northern Ireland between 14th August, 1969 and a date to be decided in the future, while on the posted or attached strength of any Regular Naval, Military or Air Force unit or formation in that area, excluding recruits and junior soldiers under training.

b. Service of 30 days or more, not necessarily continuous, in Northern Ireland between 14th August, 1969 and a date to be decided in the future, as a member of the Ulster Defence Regiment or Services Reserve Forces, on call out for permanent or emergency service in that area.

c. Service of 30 days or more afloat, not necessarily continuous, whilst in a Royal Navy or Army Department vessel on duty in the waters adjacent to Northern Ireland in support of the Land Forces between 14th August, 1969 and a date to be decided in the future. Such service may, if necessary, be aggregated with service on land to complete the required period of 30 days.

Short Service

If the qualifying service is brought to an end before the completion of 30 days on account of death, or evacuation, owing to wounds or other disability due to service, the reduced period of service will be sufficient qualification for the award.

The grant to individuals for gallantry in the operations on a specific occasion during the qualifying period, not amounting to 30 days, of a British Honour, Decoration or Medal of the status of the British Empire Medal, or above, or a Queen's Commendation, or a Mention-in-Despatches will qualify the recipient for the above mentioned medal and/or clasp.

Consideration may be given to the award of the Medal and/or clasp to personnel who have been engaged in special hazardous operations of comparatively short duration.

Civilian Categories

a. Members of the Royal Fleet Auxiliary will be eligible under the same terms as Royal Navy personnel provided that they wore the approved uniform of their organisation.

b. Members of the following organisations and any other organisations as may hereafter be determined who served with Forces in Northern Ireland will be eligible under the 30 day rules provided that they wore the approved uniform of their organisation:

 H.M. Forces Fire Services.
 Ministry of Defence Police.

The following H.M. Ships completed the qualifying period of 30 days or more in the Northern Ireland area between 14th August, 1969 and 31st July, 1977;—

Abdiel	Mersey
Alert	Montrose
Ashton	Northumbria
Belton	Nurton
Bildeston	Opossum
Bossington	Overton
Brereton	Peterel

Brinton	Repton
Bronington	St. David
Chawton	Sealion
Clyde	Sheraton
Crichton	Shoulton
Crofton	Soberton
Curzon	Solent
Cygnet	Tenacity
Fittleton	Thames
Gavington	Upton
Glasserton	Venturer
Highburton	Vigilant
Hodgeston	Wakeful
Hubberston	Wasperton
Iveston	Wilton
Kedleston	Wiston
Kellington	Wotton
Killiekrankie	
Kirkliston	HMAFV Seal
Laleston	Sea Otter
Laymoor	
Lewiston	HMFT A382
Maxton	A510

Dhofar (*1st October, 1969-30th September, 1976*)

Awarded in recognition of service in the Dhofar Province of Oman from 1st October, 1969 to 30th September, 1976 (both dates inclusive) with speical regard to the hardships and dangers which have accompanied duty there. Personnel who have already been awarded the General Service Medal (1962) will receive the clasp only.

The qualifications are:

a. Service of 30 days or more, not necessarily continuous, in the Dhofar Province of Oman between 1st October, 1969 and 30th September, 1976 while on the posted or attached strength of a unit or a formation of H.M. Forces in that area.

b. Thirty or more flights into Salalah airfield in support of operations at a rate of not more than one landing per day during the qualifying period as members of British Service transports or detachments.

c. Service of 30 days or more afloat, not necessarily continuous, while posted to a British Service vessel operating in Oman territorial waters, adjacent to the province of Dhofar in direct support of operations in the Dhofar campaign between 1st October, 1969 and 30th September, 1976. Such service may, if necessary, be aggregated with service on land to complete the required period of 30 days.

Short Service

If the qualifying service is brought to an end before the completion of 30 days on account of death, or evacuation, owing to wounds or other disability due to service, the reduced period of service will be sufficient qualification for the award.

The grant to individuals for gallantry in the operations on a specific occasion during the qualifying period, not amounting to 30 days, of a British Honour, Decoration or Medal of the status of the Queen's Gallantry Medal, or above, or a Mention-in-Despatches will qualify the recipient for the above mentioned Medal and/or clasp.

Personnel on loan

Personnel on loan or under contract to the Sultan's Armed Forces (SAF) will not qualify for the award of the General Service Medal under these conditions while so serving.

Civilian Categories

Members of the Royal Fleet Auxiliary Service will be eligible under the same terms as Royal Navy personnel provided that they wore the approved uniform of their organisation and served directly with units or formations of H.M. Forces in the qualifying area.

Details of ships qualifying for the award of this clasp have not yet been announced.

120C VIETNAM MEDAL 1964

Obverse	The crowned bust of Queen Elizabeth II and the legend "ELIZABETH II DEI GRATIA REGINA F · D."
Reverse	Nude figure of a man pushing one spherical shapre from another representing the keeping apart of two representations of ideological war.
Size	1·42 in. diameter.
Ribbon	1·25 in. wide, on the left edge a dark blue stripe, ¼ in. (Navy) and on the right a light blue stripe (Air Force). Inside of these two stripes are 1/8 in. wide red stripes (Army). The central band is yellow having three very narrow stripes of red in the centre, these being the colours of the national flag of S. Vietnam.
Suspension	By an ornate non-swivelling bar.
Designer	Andor Meszaros being the first operational medal to be designed and produced in Australia.
Naming	Australian Forces: Large impressed Roman capital,; New Zealand Forces; Small fine impressed Roman capitals. Approx. 18,000 have been issued to Australian Forces and 4,000 to New Zealand.

This medal is an Australian and New Zealand issue being awarded to the Australian and New Zealand Armed Forces serving in Vietnam after 28th May, 1964 for a minimum of twenty-eight days service in ships or one day ashore with an operational unit. Official visits must last thirty days to qualify although service may be aggregated. Also awarded to accredited relief societies.

Unrestricted permission has been given for the wearing of the **SOUTH VIETNAM CAMPAIGN MEDAL.** (Chien-dich bôi tinh). This is a six-pointed white enamel star with gold rays between each point. The centre contains a map of Vietnam with red enamel flames. The reverse contains an indented die struck inscription with the recipients number above and name below. To qualify one must spend six months in Vietnam.

Originally recipients were expected to purchase the awards from the government of Vietnam but as those were of very inferior quality the Australian and U.S. Governments produced their own awards. The original awards were unnamed but the later issues by both Australia and New Zealand were impressed.

121 NAVAL ENGINEERS MEDAL (1842-46)

Obverse	A two-masted paddle steamer; a trident in the exergue.
Reverse	An inner circle in which is an anchor surmounted by a crown, surrounded by the words "FOR ABILITY & GOOD CONDUCT." In the space between this inner circle and the edge the name of

the recipient is engraved at the top; his rank, ship and year at the bottom.

Size   1·38 in. diameter.

Size   1·38 in. diameter.

Ribbon No official statement was issued concerning this, so it was the custom to wear the medal from the Naval Long Service and Good Conduct ribbon, which in those days was 1·5 in. wide, dark blue with white edges.

Suspension By a small ring.

Designer W. Wyon, R.A.

Naming See against reverse, above.

This medal, instituted in 1842 and abolished in 1846, was intended to reward "Engineers of the First Class service in Her Majesty's Navy, who by their good conduct and ability deserve some special mark of notice."

Recommendations were made by the captain of the ship through the usual channels to the Comptroller of Steam Machinery to the Board of Admiralty. The final approval was given by the Lords Commissioners of the Admiralty.

It appears to be consistently stated that only six of these medals were awarded, but there follows eight recipients, with the dates of award:

1842, Wm. Shaw, W. Dunkin; 1843, W. Johnstone; 1843, Langley; 1845, G. Roberts, J.P. Rundle, James Urquhart; 1846, S.B. Meredith.

Mr. Shaw obtained testimony of their Lordships' approbation when serving under Commander George W. Smith, on H.M.S. *Tartarus*, steam vessel, on the West Indian and North American stations.

Mr. James Urquhart, when serving on H.M.S.V. *Columbia*, invented a tide motor. The idea was that the incoming tide exerted pressure on a large sort of keel board suspended under the pier, and so revolved a series of gear-wheels linked to an electric generator. On the turn of the tide a link came into operation so that the same direction of revolution of the generator was maintained.

Mr. Meredith was awarded his medal for cutting chains at Obligado when serving as third engineer of H.M.S. *Firebrand*. This rather refutes the original idea of the award being for first-class engineers only.

During a visit to the vicinity of Obligado inquiries were made as to what our ships were doing there in 1845 and I found the following facts.

It appears that in those days the Argentine Confederation had a selection of dictators, one of whom, Rosas, dictator of Buenos Aires, closed the Parana river to all trade and erected strong batteries at and opposite Obligado, which is about 100 miles up the river.

In November 1845, a combined English and French fleet under Captain Hotham left Montevideo to silence the batteries and reopen the river to trade.

The English squadron consisted of the steam warships *Firebrand*, *Fulton* and *Gorgon*, with the sailing vessels *Comus*, *Dolphin* and *Philomel*, also the tender *Fairy*.

When the fleet approached Punta de Obligado, to give it its full name, it was found that both banks of the river were heavily fortified and that heavy chains supported on boats were stretched across the whole half-mile width of the river. The sailing vessels were detailed to engage the batteries, and then Captain Hope in the *Firebrand* went forward and severed the chains and broke a way through the barrier. After a while the batteries were silenced, and a party of about 300 men was landed to complete the work of destruction. The fleet then continued up the river to Corrientes, some 800 miles from the mouth.

In June, 1846, on the return journey the fleet encountered strong opposition at San Lorenzo, where newly erected batteries had to be silenced before it and the merchant vessels that it was escorting could pass.

The whole episode bears a striking resemblance to that in the Yangtze in 1949, but, though our casualties were some forty-odd, no campaign awards were made.

122 NAVAL GOOD SHOOTING MEDAL (1903-14)

Obverse	The bust of King Edward VII in Naval uniform and legend "EDWARDVS VII REX IMPERATOR", or the bust of King George V in Naval uniform and the legend "GEORGIVS V BRITT: OMN: REX ET IND: IMP:"
Reverse	The nude figure of Neptune facing right, grasping five thunder-bolts in each hand. Also shown are the bows of a trireme and three horses' heads. Around the reverse is the legend "AMAT VICTORIA CVRAM", (Victory delights in care).
Size	1·42 in. diameter.
Ribbon	1·25 in. wide. Dark blue with a red centre, with white stripes in between.
Suspension	By a straight, swivelling or non-swivelling suspender.
Designers	Obverse — G.W. de Saulles; Reverse — Miss Margaret Winser.
Naming	The recipient's number, name and rank, also the name of the ship; the year and calibre of gun are impressed in block letters on the rim.
No. of bars issued	None with the medal, but a subsequent winning was rewarded by a bar on which was the name of the ship, year and calibre of gun used.

This medal was instituted in August, 1903, with the object of encouraging good performances in gunnery at the Annual Fleet Competitions. Awards were made to seamen and Marines who scored a very high percentage of hits with their particular weapon. This accounts for the fact that medals were awarded for every type of gun used in the Royal Navy during the period 1903-14.

It is as well to remember that in those days the predominant factor in good shooting was the human element. It was before the introduction of scientific instruments to co-ordinate allowances for speed, course, temperature, etc., now in use. In fact, the skill required by the gun's crew was similar to that required to hit a rabbit with a shotgun.

The medal, which is somewhat rare, is now obsolete.

The following are the numbers of medals and bars awarded for each of the years that competitions were held:

Year	Medals	Bars
1903	81	Nil
1904	86	3
1905	74	3
1906	76	3
1907	79	3
1908	80	7
1909	78	6
1910	81	7
1911	83	5
1912	85	5
1913	80	11
1914	91	9
Totals awarded	974	62

No. 4638 Sergeant G. Boyce, R.M.A., was the only recipient of a medal with three bars. His medal was indented with the above particulars, followed by "H.M.S. ILLUSTRIOUS. 1904. 6 IN. Q.F." His three bars read: "H.M.S. ILLUS-TRIOUS. 1905. 6 in Q.F."; "H.M.S. NATAL. 1908. 9·2 IN. B.L."; and "H.M.S. INFLEXIBLE. 1913. 12 IN. B.L."

Three men received two bars, and there were fifty-three recipients of one bar. A few unnamed examples of these medals are in circulation.

123 THE QUEEN'S MEDAL FOR CHAMPION SHOTS OF THE NEW ZEALAND NAVAL FORCES (1955—)

Obverse	The crowned effigy of the Sovereign facing right.
Reverse	The nude figure of Neptune facing right, grasping five thunder-bolts in each hand. Also shown are the bows of a trireme and three sea horses' heads. Around the whole is the legend "AMAT VIC-TORIA CVRAM."
Size	1·42 in. Diameter.
Ribbon	1·25 in. wide. Dark blue with a red centre, with white stipes in between.
Suspension	By a straight, swivelling suspender.
Designers	Obverse — G.W. de Saulles; Reverse — Miss Margaret Winser.
Naming	The recipient's name will be either stamped or engraved on the rim.
No. of bars issued	Every medal awarded is accompanied by a bar fixed to the ribbon and bearing the year of award thereon. Subsequent awards earn an additional bar and a silver rosette for the ribbon when the medal is not being worn.

This medal was authorized by a Royal Warrant dated 9th July, 1958, with a retrospective effect to 1st January, 1955.

The piece, which is of silver, has the same reverse as the obsolete Naval Good Shooting Medal. The claw and suspender are like those of the Queen's Army Best Shot Medal.

The object of the award is to encourage skill in small arms shooting in the New Zealand Naval Forces. The competition for it is held during February each year at the Trentham Military Camp, which is near Wellington, North Island, New Zealand.

The awarding and, if necessary, forfeiture of the medal comes under the jurisdiction of the Minister of Defence of New Zealand, who is responsible for keeping records of awards made and all to do with it.

The order of precedence is immediately before the Queen's Medal for Champion Shots in the Military Forces.

1955 Chief Ordnance Artificer K.W.M. Southwell.
1956 Lieutenant J.G. Naylor, R.N.Z.N.V.R.
1957 Lieutenant J.G. Naylor, R.N.Z.N.V.R.
1958 Sick Berth Petty Officer N.C.G. Peach.
1959 Sick Berth Petty Officer N.C.G. Peach.
1960 Sick Berth Petty Officer N.C.G. Peach.
1961 Acting Wardmaster Sub-Lieutenant N.C.G. Peach.

124 ARCTIC AND POLAR MEDALS (1818—)

The first issue of medals for Polar expeditions was sanctioned on 30th January, 1857. There are some facts about the sanctioning of these medals which are interesting and unusual, so I will enumerate them briefly.

367

Firstly: The issue of the medal was not confined to personnel of Her Majesty's Forces, but was awarded to members of the French Navy which had also undertaken voyages of exploration in the Arctic Regions. Civilian volunteers, scientists, doctors, etc., were eligible if they had taken part in any expedition.

Secondly: Members of expeditions recognized by the Government of the United States were also eligible, whether they were members of that Government's military forces or not.

Thirdly: The members of all expeditions to the Arctic regions whether financed by the State, the Hudson's Bay Company, or by private enterprise were eligible for the award.

Fourthly: There is no record of any other foreigners except those mentioned above being rewarded.

Fifthly: The first two medals are styled Arctic medals, as they were awarded for service in the Arctic regions only. The later octagonal medals are styled Polar medals, as they were awarded for services in both the Polar regions.

The medals of the first issue are fairly common, those of the second are very rare, whilst all the remainder may safely be said to be extremely rare.

The first two were issued in silver only, but the others were awarded in silver and bronze according to the type of service on which the recipient was employed up to and including the bar Antarctic 1936-39.

Finally, be it noted that the first issue is octagonal, the second circular, the third and subsequent ones are all octagonal.

Arctic Medal 1818-55

Obverse	A very charming head of Queen Victoria wearing a small tiara instead of the usual coronet. The hair at the back comes down lower than on the Indian General Service Medals. The rim is lined with a beaded edge. The word "VICTORIA" appears on the left of the head and "REGINA" on the right.
Reverse	A three-masted sailing ship, with icebergs in the background and a sledging party in the foreground; in the exergue are dates "1818-1855." Around the top is written "FOR ARCTIC DISCOVERIES".
Size	The medal is octagonal, 1·3 in. diameter.
Ribbon	1½ in. wide of watered white.
Suspension	Affixed to the top of the octagonal piece is a small claw above which is a star (symbolical of the Pole Star) which has five large points with five smaller ones between them. On the topmost large point is a swivel through which is a half-inch diameter ring and through this the ribbon is threaded.
Designer	L.C. Wyon.
Naming	The medals were issued unnamed, though many are found named.
No. of bars issued	Nil.

The following ships took part in voyages to the Arctic regions and their crews were eligible for the medal, of which a total of 1,486 were issued: 1,106 were awarded to the Royal Navy, the remainder were issued to crews of private vessels. Sgt. John Ross, R.A. took part in the third expedition 1833-35 under Sir Geo. Black.

Arctic, Advance, Alexander, Assistance, Blossom, Breadalbane, Dorothea, Enterprise, Erebus, Felix, Fox, Fury, Griper, Hecla, Herald, Investigator, Isabella, Lady Franklin, Nancy Dawson, North Star, Phoenix, Pioneer, Plover, Prince Albert, Rattlesnake, Rescue, Resolute, Sophia, Terror, Trent, Victory.

Details and dates of the various expeditions are as follows:

Expedition	No Medals Issued
Officers and men of the Royal Navy 1818-55	1,106
First expedition to the shores of the Polar Seas under the command of Sir George Black. 1819—22	—
Second expedition under the command of Sir George Black. 1825-27 .	—
Third expedition under the command of Sir George Black. 1833-35 .	5
Expedition for survey of the shores of the Arctic Seas under the command of Lieut. afterwards R. Admiral Sir John Franklin. 1821 .	2
Expedition under the command of Captain John Franklin. 1826. .	—
Detachment from Sir J. Franklin's expedition in 1826 commanded by Dr. John Richardson, M.D., Surgeon R.M. Chatham Division . .	1
Private ship *Victory*, 1829-33	6
Searching expedition under command of Sir John Richardson, M.D., C.B., Inspector of Haslar Hospital. 1848	9
Detachment from Sir John Richardson's expeiditon under the command of John Rae Esq., to search Wollaston Sound in 1849 . .	—
Nancy Dawson, 1849	1
Private ship *Lady Franklin*, 1850-51	19
Private ship *Sophia*, 1850-51	10
Felix, 18th May, 1850-11th October, 1851	11
Prince Albert, first voyage 1850 — fitted out by Lady Franklin . .	7
Prince Albert, second voyage 1851-52 — fitted out by Lady Franklin .	5
Expedition to the Arctic Seas in search of Sir John Franklin under the command of Lieut. De Haven, United States Navy. 1850-51 . .	33
Brig Advance (16 medals) and Brig *Rescue* (17 medals) . . .	33
Isabel, 1852	5
Breadalbane, 8th May, 1853-21st August, 1853	5
Expedition to the Arctic Seas in search of Asst. Surgeon E.K. Kane under the command of Lieut. Hy. I. Hartstein, United States Navy. 1855. Bark *Rescue* (26 medals) and Propeller *Arctic* (21 medals). Asst. Surgeon E.K. Kane and Party (16 medals)	63
Fox, commanded by Captain F.L.M. McClintock, R.N. Final expedition fitted out by Lady Franklin, 1857-59	11
Hudson's Bay Company	187
Total	1,486

Arctic Medal 1875-76

Obverse	The crowned and veiled bust of Queen Victoria, and legend "VICTORIA REGINA 1876."
Reverse	An ice-bound ship, somewhat low on the piece. The sky is filled with very heavy clouds.
Size	1·3 in. diameter. Circular.
Ribbon	1¼ in. wide. White.
Suspension	By a plain, straight suspender as used on the King's South Africa Medal.
Designers	Obverse — G.G. Adams; Reverse — L.C. Wyon.
Engraver	J. Pinches.

Naming	In small block lettering giving rank of recipient. It is interesting to note that the rank of dog driver is given on one of the medals. This is a very rare rank in the Navy!
No. of bars issued	Nil.

This silver medal was sanctioned on the 28th Novemberm 1876, to be awarded to the crews of the *Alert* (Captain Sir George Nares, K.C.B.) and *Discovery** (Captain H.F. Stevenson) for Arctic exploration between 17th July, 1875, and 2nd November, 1876. At the same time authority was given for it to be awarded to the crew of the private yacht *Pandora*, which voyaged in the Arctic regions, under the command of Captain Allen Young, between 25th June and 19th October, 1875, and 3rd June and 2nd November, 1876.

The medal, which has a raised milled edge, was awarded to fifty-seven members of the crew of the *Discovery*, sixty-three of the *Alert*, and fifty of the *Pandora*.

Some recipients: *Discovery* — Engineer M.R. Miller; P.O. 1st Class T. Simmonds; P.O. F. Chatel, W. Dougall; Cooper J. Sheperd; Able-Seamen H.W. Edwards, James Hand, J.S. Saggers, J. Hodges, J.E. Smith, D. Girard; J. Thornback; Stoker S. Bulley; Acting Ship's Cook George Leggett; Bombardier J. Cropp, R.M.A.; Gunner E. Rayner, R.M.A.; Ptes. Henry Petty, R.M., and T. Darke, R.M.

Alert — Carpenter's Crew A.J.W. Norris; Dog Driver J.C. Peterson; Qr. Master J. Thores; Cooper J. Hawkins; Ableseaman G. Winstone; Pte. Thos. Smith, R.M.; W.F. Hunt; Robert Joiner.

Pandora — Boatswain W.R. Taylor; Caps's Coxsn. G. Smithers; Able-seamen Alan Gillies, F. Pressley; Stokers H. Denness, E. Griffey; Ship's Steward Wm. H. Edwards, H.C. Vine; Secretary W.J.A. Grant.

Polar Medal 1904-

Obverse†	The effigy of the reigning sovereign in admiral's uniform. The legend in the case of the Edward VII issues is "EDWARDVS VII REX IMPERATOR" and on the George V medals it is "GEORGIVS V BRITT: OMN: REX ET IND: IMP:"
Reverse	The *Discovery* with a sledging party of six in the foreground, and a heavily laden sledge with a square sail.
Size	The medal is octagonal, 1·315 in. diameter.
Ribbon	1·25 in. wide, plain white.
Suspension	By an ornamental swivelling suspender.
Designers	E.G. Gillick and Mrs. Mary Gillick.
Naming	Edward VII, George V and George VI issues in engraved capitals. E II R in small impressed lettering.

* The name *Discovery* was not new to the Arctic regions even in 1875, for a ship of this name which, under the command of Captain George Waymouth, was sent out to "find the passage best to lye towards the parts or kingdom of Cataya or China or the backe side (*sic*) of America" as early as the 2nd May, 1602, It was in this same ship, in 1610, that Henry Hudson sailed into the straits and bay which bear his name. It was used again by William Baffin, who gave his name to Baffin Bay.

† All Polar Medals awarded during the reign of Edward VII and the first issues of those bearing the effigy of George V depict the sovereign in admiral's uniform. There were two subsequent issues of the George V medal depicting him first with crowned head and robed bust, and then with coinage head. All George VI and Elizabeth II issues bear the coinage head.

Ninety-one, the later issues have engraved bars.

This is the current medal for Arctic and Antarctic exploration. It was instituted in 1904 by King Edward VII, and since then has been issued with the heads
of King George V, King George VI and Elizabeth II. It has been awarded in silver
and bronze, and those recipients who made further voyages were awarded bars
to their medals. If, however, the original award was not of the same metal as that
subsequently gained, then another medal was given.

The silver and bronze medals constitute two separate awards and may be
worn at the same time.

Alfred Cheetham was awarded two bars to each of his silver and bronze
medals. There were three other recipients of the two medals. Frank Wild was
awarded four bars to his silver medal.

The only other occasions when it has been permissible for a man to wear two
identical medals were in the cases of the first two issued by the British North
Borneo Company, the Khedive's Sudan and the Sudan 1910 Medals without
bars, and in the case of Pte. G. Bryant of the Wiltshire Regiment, who won the
Queen's Medal at Bisley in 1870 and again in 1871. The Polar, Khedive's and
Sudan Medals were of different metal, the Borneo Medals had different bars.

Those who have been awarded either a silver or bronze Polar Medal may wear
a rose emblem, of the same metal as the medal, on the ribbon to denote participation in subsequent expeditions for which an award was sanctioned. The
wearing of one emblem denotes participation in two expeditions, the wearing of
two emblems the participation in three expeditions, and so on.

We are greatly indebted to the Chief Clerk of the Royal Mint, the Royal
Geographical Society and the Scott Polar Research Institute for much of the
information that follows. We particularly appreciate the kindness of the Royal
Geographical Society and the Scott Polar Research Institute for allowing particulars to be taken from their publications.

The numbers of medals and bars awarded for each expedition do not always
agree with the totals of the names of the members of the expeditions as given in
the records.

When the number of bars awarded for any particular expedition exceeds the
number of medals, the difference signifies the number of members who were
already in possession of the medal. Those already in possession of the medal
received, of course, only the appropriate bar.

Lt. Col. N.W. Poulson in his book ".The White Ribbon" comments:—

"The conditions for the award of the Polar Medal 1904 have significantly
changed since it was first instituted. Currently it is not awarded automatically
to all who go to the Antarctic. Only individuals who explore or acquire notable
knowledge are eligible, provided that in doing so they have undergone the
hazards of the Polar environment. The award may only be made to all members
of a party if the achievement of that party has been exceptional, and it follows
that when a well established site is manned for routine observations the award
is only confered on those whose contribution is outstanding. The same princi-
ples apply to crews and others aboard ships and aircraft."

Antarctic 1902-04

This bar was awarded for Captain Robert Falcon Scott's first expedition in
the *Discovery I.*

The members who formed the landing party received silver awards. The crews
of the supply ships *Terra Nova* (Capt. Harry Mackay) and *Morning* (Capt.
William Colbeck) received bronze medals.

Thirty-eight silver medals and bars were awarded and sixty bronze.

Antarctic 1907-09

This bar was awarded for Sir Ernest Shackleton's "Nimrod Furthese South Expedition" in the *Nimrod*. The expedition reached to within one hundred miles of the South Pole.

Antarctic 1910-13

This bar commemorates Captain Scott's famous, and last, expedition in which that very gallant gentleman, Captain Oates, who was a sick man, walked out into a blizzard to perish so as to ease the strain on the others during their terrible journey back from the Pole.

The expedition, which used the Ship *Terra Nova*, reached the South Pole on 18th January, 1912, only to find that the Norwegian Captain Amundsen had reached it on 14th December, 1911.

Those who had already received a Polar Medal were awarded this bar for attachment thereto. Those who had not already received a medal were awarded one bearing the effigy of King George V with this bar.

Antarctic 1912-14

This award was made for Sir Douglas Mawson's (Australian) Expedition in the *Aurora*.

It was during this expedition that he made his epic journey across King George V Land with two companions, Ninnis and Mertz, which started on 6th November, 1912. On 14th December Ninnis was killed by falling down a crevasse. On 11th January, 1913, Mertz died of starvation and dysentry. From that date until reaching his comrades on 8th February Mawson travelled on alone. His story is grandly, and very modestly, told in his book, *Home of the Blizzard*.

Antarctic 1914-16

This award was made for the Trans-Atlantic Expedition under Sir Ernest Shackleton. The ships used were the *Aurora* and *Endurance*.

Antarctic 1917

This award, which for some inexplicable reason was not gazetted, was given for the Aurora Relief Expedition which left New Zealand in December, 1916, and returned on 9th February, 1917.

Bronze medals without bars were awarded to those who had not previously received a medal. Bars were awarded to those who had already received a medal.

Antarctic 1929-30

This award was made for the first part of the British-Australia-New Zealand Antarctic Research Expedition, known for short as the Banzare Expedition, conducted by Sir Douglas Mawson. The ship used was the *Discovery*.

Antarctic 1929-31

This award was made to those who were present throughout the Banzare Expedition just mentioned.

Antarctic 1930-31

This award was made to those who only participated in the last two years of the Banzare Expedition.

Arctic 1930-31

This award was made for the British Arctic Air Route Expedition under H.G. Watkins.

The ship used was the *Penola*.

Arctic 1935-36

This award was made for the Oxford University Expedition to North East Land, which lies to the north-east of Spitzbergen.

Antarctic 1935-37

This award was made for the British Graham Land Expedition, under J.R. Rymil, which left London on 10th September, 1934. It arrived in the Antarctic on 21st January, 1935, and left on 12th March, 1937, arriving back at Portsmouth on 10th August, 1937.

The ship used was the *Penola*, a 240-ton Brittany fishing vessel, whose engine came loose during the voyage out and thus delayed the landing on Graham Land until early in 1936.

Antarctic 1925-39

Awarded for services in Antarctic research work between the above dates. The bars were dated according to the period during which the recipient served.

The ships employed on this work were the *Discovery II* and the *William Scoresby*. A small motor boat called the *Rapid* was borrowed from the Norwegian whaling station for survey work on King George Island.

This boat got into difficulties through engine trouble, and was rescued by the *Penola* (the ship used by J.R. Rymill during his expedition to British Graham Land between 1935 and 1937), the *Discovery II* and the cruiser H.M.S. *Ajax*, which was to win such fame, together with H.M.S. *Achilles* and H.M.S. *Exeter* at the Battle of the River Plate against the German pocket battleship *Graf Spee* on 13th December, 1939.

Arctic 1940-42

This award was made to the crew of the Royal Canadian Mounted Police ship *St. Roch*, which patrolled extensively in the western Arctic under Sergt. H.A. Larsen, who was promoted to sub-inspector and later received the Patron's Medal of the Royal Geographical Society.

During the course of this patrol work the ship made a complete east to west passage. The *St. Roch* returned later with a different crew, but still under the command of Sub-Inspector Larsen and all received the next bar Arctic 1944.

Arctic 1944

This award was made for the return journey of the *St. Roch*. Three bars were awarded to those who had taken part in the eastward journey and a further eight medals and bars to the new members of the crew.

As all later expeditions received a wide variety of dated bars due to various periods of service it is not practical to list the particular services for every bar but readers are recommended to consult "The White Ribbon" by Lt. Col. Neville Poulson.

SILVER AND BRONZE POLAR MEDALS/BARS AWARDED FOR THE ANTARCTIC

	Silver	Bronze		Silver	Bronze
No Bar (for 1902-04)	——	58	Antarctic 1945-46	1	——
Antarctic 1902-04	37	——	Antarctic 1946	9	——
Antarctic 1907-09	16	14	Antarctic 1946-47	9	——
Antarctic 1910-13	59	6	Antarctic 1947	6	——
Antarctic 1912-14	18	8	Antarctic 1947-48	2	——
Antarctic 1914-16	37	14	Antarctic 1947-49	5	——
Antarctic 1917	10	22	Antarctic 1948	4	——
Antarctic 1925-31	——	2	Antarctic 1948-49	7	——
Antarctic 1925-32	——	2	Antarctic 1949-50	1	——
Antarctic 1925-35	——	3	Antarctic 1950-51	1	——
Antarctic 1925-37	——	1	Antarctic 1950-52	4	——
Antarctic 1925-39	——	6	Antarctic 1950-61	1	——
Antarctic 1926-30	——	4	Antarctic 1951	2	——
Antarctic 1926-33	——	1	Antarctic 1952	5	——
Antarctic 1927-30	——	4	Antarctic 1952-53	7	——
Antarctic 1927-32	——	1	Antarctic 1953-54	3	——
Antarctic 1927-35	——	1	Antarctic 1954-55	12	——
Antarctic 1927-37	——	1	Antarctic 1955	7	——
Antarctic 1927-38	——	1	Antarctic 1955-56	15	——
Antarctic 1928-37	——	1	Antarctic 1955-58	1	——
Antarctic 1929-30	——	16	Antarctic 1956	29	——
Antarctic 1929-30	——	1	Antarctic 1956-57	3	——
Antarctic 1929-31	——	22	Antarctic 1956-58	9	——
Antarctic 1929-32	——	5	Antarctic 1956-59	2	——
Antarctic 1929-33	——	5	Antarctic 1957	40	——
Antarctic 1929-34	——	1	Antarctic 1957-58	54	——
Antarctic 1929-35	——	6	Antarctic 1957-59	5	——
Antarctic 1929-37	——	2	Antarctic 1957-60	3	——
Antarctic 1929-38	——	1	Antarctic 1958	33	——
Antarctic 1929-39	——	7	Antarctic 1958-59	4	——
Antarctic 1930-31	——	18	Antarctic 1958-60	1	——
Antarctic 1930-33	——	1	Antarctic 1958-61	6	——
Antarctic 1930-35	——	3	Antarctic 1959	1	——
Antarctic 1930-36	——	2	Antarctic 1959-60	5	——
Antarctic 1930-39	——	1	Antarctic 1959-61	2	——
Antarctic 1931-35	——	3	Antarctic 1960	3	——
Antarctic 1931-37	——	4	Antarctic 1960-61	9	——
Antarctic 1931-39	——	3	Antarctic 1960-62	3	——
Antarctic 1933-37	——	4	Antarctic 1961	7	——
Antarctic 1933-38	——	2	Antarctic 1961-62	7	——
Antarctic 1933-39	——	2	Antarctic 1961-63	2	——
Antarctic 1934-37	——	1	Antarctic 1962	9	——
Antarctic 1934-38	——	3	Antarctic 1962-63	6	——
Antarctic 1934-39	——	2	Antarctic 1962-64	4	——
Antarctic 1935-37	16	——	Antarctic 1963	14	——
Antarctic 1935-38	——	2	Antarctic 1963-64	7	——
Antarctic 1935-39	——	6	Antarctic 1963-65	2	——
Antarctic 1936-39	——	2	Antarctic 1964	9	——
Antarctic 1944	1	——	Antarctic 1964-65	5	——
Antarctic 1944-45	9	——	Antarctic 1964-66	3	——
Antarctic 1945	3	——	Antarctic 1965	13	——

	Silver		Silver
Antarctic 1966	3	Antarctic 1969	4
Antarctic 1966-67	1	Antarctic 1970	5
Antarctic 1967	8	Antarctic 1971	7
Antarctic 1968	5		

SILVER POLAR MEDALS AWARDED FOR THE ARCTIC

With Bar	No.
Arctic 1930-31	14
Arctic 1935-36	9
Arctic 1940-42	8
Arctic 1944	11
Arctic 1952-53	8
Arctic 1952-54	16
Arctic 1953-54	5

"The White Ribbon" by Lt. Col. N. Poulson is earnestly suggested for a full study of the medals awarded with details of the numerous expeditions.

Before leaving Polar Medals the following notes may be of interest:

1. There is considerable delay in gazetting Polar Medals. For instance, the award "Antarctic 1945" was not gazetted till 14th July, 1953. This was the year that Elizabeth II ascended the Throne. Naturally, therefore, the medal bearing this bar has her effigy though the dates were during the reign of George VI. As a matter of fact, all the bars awarded to members of the Falkland Islands Dependencies Surveys in the Antarctic bearing dates from 1944-45 to 1948-49 were gazetted on the same date originally with a subsequent amendment dated 26th November, 1954.

2. King George V, by a decree dated 16th October, 1933, ordered that in future all Polar Medals were to be struck in silver only. This caused another anomaly, because bronze medals were awarded bearing bars with dates up to 1939. One can only assume that, as some bronze awards had already been made for service in the Antarctic, it was not considered fair to make distinctions for the same service in the same area.

3. There are two different types of wording on the bars. What one might call the normal issue bear the lettering in relief because they were struck from dies which had been engraved. However, sometimes, owing to the pressure of work at the Royal Mint, the plain dies were engraved and that is how the recipients received them. To make this point clear, below is a list of bars which were embossed; all those not mentioned were awarded with engraved dates.

   Arctic 1930-31, 1935-36, and 1944.

   Antarctic 1902-04, 1907-09, 1910-13, 1912-14, 1914-16, 1917, 1929-30, 1929-31, 1935-37, 1957-58, and 1958.

4. Mrs. Mary Gillick's design for the effigy of Queen Elizabeth II is now used for this medal, as it is for all that are required to show the uncrowned one of the Queen. It is unique for a medal to have one side designed by the wife and the other by the husband.

5. Numbers of awards made in silver and bronze since 1902:

Obverse	The diademed and veiled bust of Queen Victoria with the legend "VICTORIA REGINA." The diadem is quite different from that shown on any other medal, so is the arrangement of the veil, and the effigy includes the shoulders.
Reverse	The figure of Fame standing on a dais, facing left; with her outstretched right hand she is placing a laurel wreath on a warrior, who is standing on his right foot with his left raised and resting on the dais. He is supporting on his left knee a target through the centre of which are three arrows. In his right hand he holds a bow and a quiver full of arrows. The exergue is plain.
Size	1·42 in. diameter.
Ribbon	1·25 in. wide. Watered with a ·6 in. wide crimson centre and, reading towards the edges, a black, white and black stripe.
Suspension	By a straight, swivelling suspender.
Designers	Obverse — L.C. Wyon; Reverse — Sir E.J. Poynter, R.A.
Naming	In block letters giving the recipient's rank, name and regiment, followed by the wording "BEST SHOT MEDAL" and the year of the award given thus, "1873-74."
No. of bars issued	Nil.

Instituted by Royal Warrant dated 30th April 1869. The Editor of the *National Rifle Association Journal* has kindly supplied much of the information which follows, also the entire list of all recipient's of the Queen's and King's Medals.

The author having at one time possessed both a Queen's and King's Medals must claim leave to differ from some of the descriptions seen of them.

The medal was first instituted by Royal Warrant dated 30th April, 1869 to be awarded annually to the best shot in the British Army, and was to be styled The Queen's Medal.

Pte. Bryant won the medal in 1870 and again in 1871, and thus had the unique distinction in the records of the British Army of being allowed to wear two medals which were identical. One has alluded to cases where men have received the same medal twice (such as the India General Service Medal, 1854), but in their case the bar, or bars, would have been different. In Pte. Bryant's case there were no bars, so that his medals were identical. The issue in error, as has happened, of two identical medals for the same campaign would not entitle the recipient to wear them both simultaneously.

Two medals were awarded for each of the competitions held in 1875-76 and 1876-77. One was given to the best shot with the Snider rifle, and the other to the best shot with the then newly introduced Martini-Henry rifle.

These silver medals were allowed to be worn in uniform, and the recipient was referred to as a Queen's Medallist.

Type of Medal	Year	No.	Rank	Name	Regiment	General Order
Silver	1869-70	969	Sgt.	T.B. Ryle	2 Bn. Suffolk R.	101 of 1870
"	1870-71	666	Pte.	G. Bryant	1 Bn. Wilts. R.	103 of 1872
"	1871-72	666	Pte.	G. Bryant	1 Bn. Wilts. R.	103 of 1872
"	1872-73	353	Pte.	S. Whitby	2 Bn. K.O.Y.L.I	82 of 1873
"	1873-74	1159	Col. Sgt.	C. Hedges	3 Bn. Gren. Gds.	76 of 1874

Type of Medal Silver	Year	No.	Rank	Name	Regiment	General Order
„	1874-75	1282	Pte.	J. Gardiner	1 Bn. West Yorks	63 of 1875
„	1875-76	3326	Col. Sgt.	T. Wallace	1 Bn. Hants. R.	95 of 1876 Using Martini- Henry Rifle.
„	1875-76	1601	Sgt.	A. Woods	2 Bn. Loyals	95 of 1876 Using Snider Rifle.
"	1876-77	1475	Col. Sgt.	J. Hogan	2 Bn. Lancs. Fus.	90 of 1877 Using Martini- Henry Rifle.
„	1876-77	1551	Pte.	J. Murphy	1 Bn. Devonshire R.	90 of 1877 Using Snider Rifle.
„	1877-78	1497	Sgt.	A. Salmond, D.C.M.	1. Bn. Seaforth Highlanders	135 of 1879
1878-79	1878-79	1261	Sgt.	T. Armstrong	2 Bn. Rifle Bde.	32 of 1880
„	1879-80	1965	Pte.	H. Morgan	2 Bn. Middlesex R.	154 of 1880
„	1880-81	1346	Col. Sgt.	W. Mitcell	2 Bn. R.W. Kent R.	128 of 1882
„	1881-82	1276	Dmr.	J. Savage	2 Bn. N. Staffs.	309 of 1882
„	1882-83	741	Sgt.	E. Andrews	2 Bn. D.C.L.I	163 of 1883

The King's Medal (1923-61)

In 1923, the competition was revived. The same reverse was used as with the Queen's Medal with the head and shoulders of the reigning Sovereign on the obverse. The medal is fitted with a straight non-swivelling suspender and carries a straight bar with the year of the award thereon. Subsequent success is rewarded by the addition of a further bar bearing the year. The ribbon is the same as that for the Queen's Medal. From its inception in 1923 to 1934 inclusive, the medal was competed for by fifty representatives of the Regular Army and fifty from the Territorial Army, and only one medal was awarded. Medals were granted to the Commonwealth Forces, as will be seen from the following Roll of Winners, from 1923 to 1961. Lieutenant (later Major), D.T. Burke of Canada has won the medal on six occasions, 1925, 1927, 1929, 1930, 1931, 1947 this being the record. It has been won three times by the same man on three consecutive occasions, by Lieutenant Burke of Canada in 1929, 1930 and 1931; C.Q.M.S. F.H. Morgan of Southern Rhodesia in 1927, 1928, and 1929; and Sgt. G. Lamont also of Southern Rhodesia.

All the medals are of silver and may be worn in uniform. The recipient is referred to as a King's or Queen's Medallist.

When in undress or service uniform, a recipient may wear a silver rose emblem on the ribbon for every subsequent gaining of the award.

The Queen's Medal (1952-61)

All the medals from 1952 inclusive, bear the head of Elizabeth II.

There appear to be certain gaps in the continuity of the awards. The full list of those supplied from official sources follows.

Queen's Medal (1962-) (for Champion Shots in the Military Forces)

Revised Rules

The medal will be awarded annually to the undermentioned Forces:

(a) The Military Forces at Home except those at (b) hereunder.

(b) The Army Emergency Reserve. Categories 1 and 1 (a) and Territorial Army.

(c) The Military Forces of Canada.

(d) The Military Forces of Australia.

(e) The Military Forces of New Zealand.

(f) The Military Forces of Ceylon.

(g) The Military Forces of Federation of Rhodesia and Nyasaland and the British S. Africa Police.

(h) The Military Forces of The Ghana Armed Forces.

The following do not include new forces such as The Military Forces of Jamaica, Military Forces of the Federation of Rhodesia and Nyasaland, British South Africa Police, Canadian Army (Militia), Royal Canadian Mounted Police.

The Military Forces at Home (Except Categories I(A) and II(A))

The Army Emergency Reserve

1923 Sergt. C. Mapp, Royal Engineers
1924 C.S.M.I.C. W. Churcher, Small Arms School.
1925 R.S.M. W. Jagger, K.R.R.C.
1926 R.S.M. W. Apsey, D.C.M., The Rifle Brigade.
1927 R.S.M. W. Jagger, K.R.R.C.
1928 C.S.M. J. Williams, 4th Bn. R.W. Kent Regiment.
1929 Lieut. G.F. Johnson, 1st Bn. Scots Guards.
1930 Lieut. J.A. Barlow, West Yorkshire Regiment.
1931 Lieut. E.J.C. King-Salter, The Rifle Brigade.
1932 Lieut. N. Boyer, Royal Warwickshire Regiment.
1933 C.S.M.I. A.G. Ellis, Small Arms School.
1934 Sergt. Instructor T. Moore, Small Arms School.
1962 Q.M.S.I. J.D. Gillam, Small Arms School.
1963 Cpl. A. Notley, 3rd Green Jackets, The Rifle Brigade.
1964 Sgt. R. Smith, 2nd Green Jackets.
1965 Sgt. J.H. Wheeler, M.M., The R. Hants. Regiment.

The Military Forces at Home

1935 C.S.M.I. T. Moore, Small Arms School.
1936 C.S.M. W. Edwards, D.C.L.I.
1937 Cpl. White, 1st Bn. Rifle Brigade.
1938 C.S.M.I. P. Walbridge, Small Arms School.
1947 E.Q.M.S. H.E. Malpas, Small Arms School Corps.
1948 Capt. F. Anderson, R.E.M.E.
1949 Major R.M. Parsons, Royal Ulster Rifles.
1950 Major R.M. Parsons, Royal Ulster Rifles.
1951 R.Q.M.S. G. Armstrong, D.C.M., Grenadier Guards.
1952 Q.M.S.I. T. Seaman, Small Arms School Corps.
1953 Capt. B.P. Walker, R.E.M.E.
1954 Major W.H. Baudains, M.M., Royal Ulster Rifles.
1955 R.Q.M.S. G. Armstrong, D.C.M., Grenadier Guards.
1956 Sgt. D.W. Kingdon, R.E.M.E.

1957 Senior Under Officer A.D. Abbot-Anderson, Royal Military Academy, Sandhurst
1958 Q.M.S.K. Argent, Small Arms School Corps.
1959 W.O. Cl. I E. Mitchell, R.E.M.E.
1960 W.O. Cl. I E. Mitchell, R.E.M.E.
1961 Capt. D.O. Carpenter, Royal Army Ordnance Corps

The Army Emergency Reserve Categories I and II(A) and the Territorial Army

1961 W.O. Cl. II J.E. Swann, D.C.M., London Rifle Brigade Rangers.
1963 Sgt. J.A. Mitchison, 7th R.N.T.
1964 Sgt. J.W. Meynell, 6th Bn. Durham Light Infantry.
1965 Cpl. R.I. Russell, London Rifle Brigade Rangers.

Territorial Army

1935 Rfm. W.D. Hodder, Queen's Westminster and Civil Service Rifles.
1936 Major D.M. Lindsay, M.C., 7th Bn. Sherwood Foresters.
1937 Sergt. J. Hamill, 38th A.A. Bn. R.E. (Liverpool).
1938 C.S.M. F.J. Coles, 2nd Bn. The Monmouthshire Regiment.
1939 Lieut. G.W. Nicholson, 6th (Bermondsey) Bn. The Queen's Royal Regiment.
1948 Capt. J. Hamill, 470 H.A.A. Regiment, R.A.
1949 Sgt. J.E. White, 535 Company, R.A.S.C.
1950 Lieut.-Col. B.D. Shaw, M.M., T.D., Nottingham University Officers Training Corps.
1951 Capt. J. Hamill, 470 H.A.A. Regiment, R.A.
1952 Lieut. J.P. Goodacre, 305 Medium Regiment, R.A.
1953 Sgt. J.E. White, 535 Company, R.A.S.C.
1954 R.Q.M.S. F.J. Broughton, 14th Bn. The Parachute Regiment.
1955 Cpl. A.J. Tetlow, Cambridge University Officers Training Corps.
1956 Sapper J. Northcliffe, 106 Field Engineer Regiment, R.E.
1957 L./Cpl. J.W. Meynell, 6th Bn. The Durham Light Infantry.
1958 Sgt. S.J. Graham, North Somerset Yeomanry, 44 Bn. The Royal Tank Regiment.
1959 Sgt. S.J. Graham, North Somerset Yeomanry, 44 Bn. The Royal Tank Regiment.
1960 Capt. J. Hamill, 470 Light Anti-Aircraft Regiment, R.A.
1961 Lieut. J.R. Sadler, 5th Bn. The South Staffordshire Regiment.
1963 Sgt. J.A. Mitchison, 7th Bn. The Royal Northumberland Fusiliers.

India

1923-24* Risaldar Abdul Rauf Khan, 2nd Lancers (G.H.)
1924-25 Naik Suba Sing Lama, 2/2nd King Edward's Own Gurkha Rifles.
1925-26 Jemadar Kalbi Raza, The Hazara Pioneers.
1926-27 Sergt. B. Cartwright, 1st South Staffs.
1927-28 Rfm. A. Lewis, 1st K.R.R.C.
1928-29 Naik Barna Sing Thapa, 2/2nd King Edward's Own Gurkha Rifles.
1929-30 Naik Barna Sing Thapa, 2/2nd King Edward's Own Gurkha Rifles.
1930-31 Jemadar Yakoob Ali, Hazara Pioneers.
1931-32 Naik Barna Sing Thapa, 2/2nd King Edward's Own Gurkha Rifles.
1932-33 Sergt. C.S. Cole, Simla Rifles.
1933-34 Sergt. W.H. Bayes, 13th/18th Hussars.

* The competition was fired during parts of both years, but the bar only bore the first date in every case.

1934-35 L./Cpl. A. Thurbow, 1 Bn. Royal Norfolk Regiment.
1935-36 B.H.M. Nandbahadur Thapa, 1st/5th The Royal Gurkha Rifles Frontier Force.
1936-37 Capt. E.E.E. Cass, D.S.O. M.C., K.O.Y.L.I.
1937-38 Havildar Harkarbir Gurung, 1st/15th The Royal Gurkha Rifles (Frontier Force).

Dominion of Canada

1923 R.S.M.F. J. Goodhouse, C.A.S.C.
1924 Cpl. W.J. Livingstone, The G.G.F.G.
1925 Lieut. D.T. Burke, G.M., The G.G.F.G.
1926 Cpl. W.J. Livingstone, The G.G.F.G.
1927 Lieut. D.T. Burke, G.M., The G.G.F.G.
1928 Major J. Jeffrey, R.C.R.
1929 Lieut. D.T. Burke, G.M., The G.G.F.G.
1930 Lieut. D.T. Burke, G.M., The G.G.F.G.
1931 Lieut. D.T. Burke, G.M., The G.G.F.G.
1932 Capt. J.W. Houlden, The Sherbrooke Regiment.
1933 Lieut. A.B. Coulter, The G.G.F.G.
1934 Capt. J.W. Houlden, The Sherbrooke Regiment.
1935 Sergt. T.W. Gregory, 7th Bn. C.M.G. Corps.
1936 L./Cpl. C. Robins, P.P.C.L.I.
1937 Lieut. G.A. Molecey, Canadian Irish Fusiliers.
1938 Aircraftman T.W. Gregory, R.C.A.F.
1947 Major T.D. Burke, R.C.A.M.A.
1948 Lieut. R.F. Fendick, R.C.E.M.E
1949 Offr. Cadet G.S. Boa, Central Command Contingent (48th Highlanders of Canada)
1950 Lieut. G.S. Boa, 48th Highlanders of Canada.
1951 Lieut. G.S. Boa, 48th Highlanders of Canada.
1952 Lieut.-Col. S. Johnson, O.B.E., E.D., 14th Armoured Regiment (King's Own Calgary Regiment).
1953 Lieut. A.H. McKeage, Canadian Grenadier Guards.
1954 Capt. D.C. Lawford, 1st Canadian Inf. Div. Signals Regiment.
1955 2nd Lieut. E.L. Warner, Sherbrooke Regiment (12th Armoured Regiment).
1956 Sgt. J.R. Hardy, R.C.E.M.E.
1957 Lieut. A.S. Derrick, R.C.E.
1958 Staff-Sgt. L.A. White, Princess Patricia's Canadian Light Infantry.
1959 Capt. J.J. Barrett, The Royal Canadian Regiment.
1960 W.O. Cl. II, C.F. Rowell, C.D., Regiment of Canadian Guards.
1961 Pte. J.W. Matthews, Princess Patricia's Canadian Light Infantry.
1962 Lieut. K.D. Lidgren, Princess Patricia's Canadian Light Infantry.

Canadian Army (Militia) and the Royal Canadian Mounted Police

1963 Lance Sgt. T.A. Richardson, Victoria Rifles of Canada.
1964 Staff Sgt. C. Tremblay, C.D., Les Voltigueeurs de Quebec.
1965 Sgt. G.C. Campbell, New Westminster Regiment.

Military Forces of Canada (Regular)

1963 Sgt. J. Eloi Daigle, Royal 22e Regiment.
1964 Lieut. W.J. Molnar, The Black Watch (Royal Highland Regiment of Canada)
1965 Sgt. R.E. Lawrence, Royal Canadian Engineers.

Commonwealth of Australia

1924 T./Q.M. and Hon. Capt. W.C.G. Ruddock, A.I.C.
1925 S.S.M. 3 Cl. (W.O.II), B. Taylor, A.I.C.
1926 S.S.M. 2 Cl. (W.O.I), Hon. Lieut. E.F. Davies, A.I.C.
1927 S.S.M. 2 Cl. (W.O.I), J.D. Shearim, A.I.C.
1928 S.S.M. 2 Cl. (W.O.I.) Hon. Lieut. J. Hutchinson, A.I.C.
1929 S.S.M. 2 Cl. (W.O.I), J.D. Shearim, A.I.C.
1930 S.S.M. 2 Cl. (W.O.I.), W.H. Hackfath, D.C.M., A.I.C.
1931 S.S.M. 2 Cl. (W.O.I.), J.D. Shearim, A.I.C.
1932 Lieut. C.W. Potter, 3rd L.H. Regiment.
1933 S.S.M. 2 Cl. (W.O.I.), J.D. Shearim, A.I.C.
1934 Bdr. J.C. King, 2nd Survey Co. A.G.A.
1935 Cpl. A.F. Carson, 32nd Battalion.
1936 Pte. E.W. Potter, 43rd/48th Battalion.
1937 Pte. E.W. Potter, 43rd/48th Battalion.
1938 Pte. N.W. Savage, Sydney University Regiment.
1947 Lieut. A Preston, Northern Command Australian Military Forces.
1948 Capt. A.E. Green, Eastern Command Australian Military Forces.
1949 Capt. L.A.J. Eagleson, Royal Australian Armoured Corps. 1 Royal News South Wales Lancers.
1950 W.O. Cl. II, R.D. Archer, 5th Infantry Bn.
1951 Major G.C. Magenis, Royal Australian Armoured Corps.
1952 Major G.C. Magenis, Royal Australian Armoured Corps.
1953 Sgt. G.L. Loveband, Royal Australian Infantry.
1954 Sgt. P.F. Jeffrey, Western Command Australian Regular Army.
1955 Sgt. R.K. Beardman, R.A.A.S.C., Citizen Military Forces.
1956 Major A.E. Green, R.A.E.M.E.
1957 W.O. Cl. II, R.D. Archer, Royal Australian Infantry.
1958 W.O. Cl. I, J.A. Guymer, Royal Australian Infantry.
1959 W.O. Cl. I, R.D. Archer, Royal Australian Infantry.
1960 L./Cpl. C.A. Dennis, Royal Australian Engineers.
1961 W.O. Cl. II, P.J. Pini, R.A.E. and M.E.
1962 W.O. Cl. II, G.L. Loveband, 4th Cadet Battalion.
1963 Capt. G.S. Pratt, 2nd Australian Regiment.
1964 Pte. E.R. French, Royal Australian Infantry Corps.
1965 Capt. M.D. Hanber, Royal Australian Infantry.

Union of South Africa

1924 G.W. Church, Kimberley Rifle Club.
1925 Major R. Bodley, Imperial Light Horse.
1926 No Competition.
1927 L.D. Busschau, Johannesburg, 8th Infantry Bn. (Transvaal Scottish).
1928 Col. Busschau, Johannesburg, 8th Infantry Bn. (Transvaal Scottish).
1929 R.E. Neville, Durban and Coast R.D.A.
1930 Capt. H.A. Viljoen, Phillippolis Commando.
1931 G.W. Church, Kimberley Rifle Club.
1932 Col. F.L.A. Buchanan, M.C., V.D., Commanding 1st Infantry Brigade.
1933 Lieut. M.G. Bodley, East Rand United Rifle Association.
1934 L. Towne, Albany Commando, Grahamstown.
1935 Lieut. J. Liebman, Witwatersrand Rifles.
1936 O.M. Peckham, Maritzburg Defence R.A.
1937 Lieut. J. Liebman, Witwatersrand Rifles.
1938 Capt. J. Liebman, Witwatersrand Rifles.
1948 Lieut. D.C. Welsh, Rand Light Infantry.

1949 Staff-Sgt. J.J. Bezuidenhout, Technical Service Corps.
1950 Pte. J.M. Potgeiter, Kirkwood Rifle Commando.
1951 Sgt. R.V.E Smith, Pietermaritzberg Rifle Commando.
1952 W.O. Cl. II, P. Waterfall, S.A. Instructional Corps.
1953 W.O. Cl. II, J.J. Bezuidenhout, Technical Service Corps.
1954 W.O. Cl. II, P. Waterfall, South African Infantry Corps.
1955 W.O. Cl. II, P. Waterfall, South African Infantry Corps.
1956 Staff-Sgt. W.H. Page, Technical Service Corps.
1957 Lieut. A.J. Maartens, Central South West African Commando.
1958 W.O. Cl. II, P. Waterfall, South Africa Infantry Corps.
1959 W.O. Cl. II, J.J. Bezuidenhout, Technical Service Corps.
1960 Cpl. W.J. Scholtz, Thabazimbi Commands.
1961 W.O. Cl. I, P. Waterfall, South African Infantry Corps.

New Zealand

1923 S.S.M. A.J. Moore, New Zealand Permanent Staff.
1924 S.S.M. H.L.S. Frank, New Zealand Permanent Staff.
1925 No Competition.
1926 Staff-Sgt. J.S. Thomson, New Zealand Permanent Staff.
1927 Lieut. T.J. Denton, New Zealand Permanent Air Force.
1928 L./Cpl. S.W. Barnet, 1st Bn. Wellington Regiment.
1929 S.S.M. (W.O.I.), J.H. Kearney, New Zealand Permanent Staff.
1930 Staff-Sgt. J.S. Thomson, New Zealand Permanent Staff.
1955 Pte. I.R. Larsen, Royal New Zealand Army Ordnance Corps.
1956 L./Cpl. I.R. Larsen, R.N.Z.A.O.C.
1957 Staff-Sgt. I.G. Campbell R.N.Z.A.O.C.
1958 Lieut. J.S. Wooster, Royal New Zealand Electrical and Mechanical Engineers.
1959 L./Cpl. I.R. Larsen, R.N.Z.A.O.C.
1960 Lieut. J.S. Wooster, R.N.Z.E.M.E.
1961 Lieut. J.S. Wooster, R.N.Z.E.M.E.
1962 Lieut. J.S. Wooster, R.N.Z.E.M.E.
1963 W.O. Cl. II, G. Collins, R.N.Z.E.M.E.
1964 W.O. Cl. II, G. Collins, R.N.Z.E.M.E.
1965 W.O. Cl. II, G. Collins, R.N.Z.E.M.E.

Southern Rhodesia

1926 Sergt. F.G. Elliott, British South Africa Police.
1927 C.Q.M.S. F.H. Morgan, Territorial Force.
1928 C.Q.M.S. F.H. Morgan, Territorial Force.
1929 C.Q.M.S. F.H. Morgan, Territorial Force.
1930 Sergt. N.A. Fereday, Territorial Force.
1931 Sergt. N.A. Fereday, Territorial Forces.
1932 Lieut. F.H. Morgan, Territorial Force.
1933 C.Q.M.S. N.A. Fereday, 1st Bn. Sailsbury Regiment.
1934 C.Q.M.S. N.A. Fereday, 1st Bn. Sailsbury Regiment.
1935 Rfm. D.F. Butcher, 2nd Bn. Rhodesia Regiment.
1936 Pipe Major A. MacBean, 1st Bn. Rhodesia Regiment.
1937 Rfm. P.J. Cumming, 1st Bn. Rhodesia Regiment.
1938 Lieut. F.H. Morgan, 2nd Bn. Rhodesia Regiment.
1939 Sergt. A.M. Butcher, The Rhodesia Regiment.
1948 Sgt.-Maj. W.D. Cook, 1st Bn. Royal Rhodesia Regiment.
1949 Sgt. G. Lamont, 2nd Bn. Royal Rhodesia Regiment.
1950 Sgt. G. Lamont, 2nd Bn. Royal Rhodesia Regiment.
1951 Sgt. G. Lamont, 2nd Bn. Royal Rhodesia Regiment.

1952 Inspector H.R. Cooke, British South Africa Police.
1953 Capt. R.V. Allan, D.F.C., 1st Bn. Royal Rhodesia Regiment.
1954 Rifleman A.D. Scates, 1st Bn. Royal Rhodesia Regiment.

Military Forces of Rhodesia and the British South African Police

1960 No competition held.
1961 No competition held.
1962 Inspector D. Hollingsworth, British South Africa Police.
1963 Inspector D. Hollingsworth, British South Africa Police.
1964 Inspector B.W. Pratt, British South Africa Police.
1965 No medal awarded.

Pakistan

1950 Jemadar Sher Akbar, South Waziristan Scouts.
1951 Major Malik Mohammed Amin, 14th Punjab Regiment.
1952 Naik Amir Khan, 14th Punjab Regiment.
1953 Havildar Amir Khan, 14th Punjab Regiment.
1954 No name recorded.
1955 Havildar Zabardast, South Waziristan Scouts.
1956 Jemadar Badshah Khan, South Waziristan Scouts.

Ceylon

1954 Capt. C.L.A. Dirckze, The Ceylon Light Infantry
1955 No name recorded.
1956 No name recorded.
1957 L./Cpl. K.R. Perara, 1st Bn. Ceylon Light Infantry.
1958 Cpl. K.R. Perara, 1st Bn. Ceylon Light Infantry.
1959 No competition held.
1960 No competition held.
1961 No medal awarded.
1962 No medal awarded.
1963 No competititon held.
1964 No medal awarded.
1965 No medal awarded.

Ghana

1959 Sgt. Mawa Konkomba, 2nd Bn. Ghana Regiment of Infantry.

Federation of Rhodesia and Nyasaland and the British S.A. Police

1956 Staff-Sgt. D. Hollingworth, British South Africa Police.
1957 Staff-Sgt. D. Hollingworth, British South Africa Police.
1958 Lieut. M.C. Godfrey, Central Africa Command Training School.
1959 Capt. M.C. Godfrey, 1st King's African Rifles.

The Military Forces of Jamaica

1963 Pte. J.E. Daley, 1st Bn. The Jamaica Regiment.
1964 Sgt. D. de Q.Snall, 1st Bn. The Jamaica Regiment.
1965 L./Cpl. C. Barker, 1st Bn. The Jamaica Regiment.

Queen's Medal (for Champion Shots in the Military Forces)

Revised Rules 1962.
    The medal will be awarded annually to the undermentioned Forces:

    (*a*) The Military Forces at Home except those at (*g*) hereunder.

(b) The Army Emergency Reserve, Categories I and I (a) and Territorial Army.
(c) The Military Forces of Canada.
(d) The Military Forces of Australia.
(e) The Military Forces of New Zealand.
(f) The Military Forces of Ceylon.
(g) The Military Forces of Federation of Rhodesia and Nyasaland and the British South Africa Police.
(h) The Military Forces of The Ghana Armed Forces.

126 THE QUEEN'S MEDAL FOR CHAMPION SHOTS OF THE AIR FORCES (1953-)

Obverse	The crowned effigy of the Sovereign facing right. *1st issue* "ELIZABETH II D: G: BR: REGINA: F:D." *2nd issue* "ELIZABETH II DEI GRATIA REGINA F:D."
Reverse	A representation of the kneeling figure of Hermes throwing a javelin whilst mounted on a hawk in flight.
Size	1·42 in. diameter.
Ribbon	1·25 in. wide Dark crimson with dark blue, light blue and dark blue narrow stripes at the edges.
Suspension	*1st issue* A straight fixed suspender. *2nd issue* A straight swivelling suspender.
Designers	Obverse — Mrs. M.E. Gillick; Reverse — B.R. Sindall.
Naming	The recipient's name is engraved on the rim.
No. of bars issued	Each award carries a bar with the year in relief which is affixed to the ribbon. Subsequent awards earn an additional bar and a silver rosette for the ribbon when the medal is not being worn.

This silver medal, whose title is self-explanatory, was instituted on the 12th June, 1953. It is competed for annually at the Royal Air Force Small Arms Meeting held at Bisley, Surrey.

1953 Senior Technician J.E.P. Witts.
1954 Sgt. C.H. Greenlee.
1955 Cpl. Technician B.R. Cressey.
1956 Sqdn. Leader C.C. Willett, O.B.E.
1957 Flt. Lieut. M. Gill.
1958 Wing Commander P.E.H. Thomas, A.F.C.
1959 Wing Commander P.E.H. Thomas, A.F.C.
1960 Sqdn. Leader D. Young.
1961 Warrant Officer F. Flanagan.
1962 Ch. Tech. B.R. Greasey.
1963 Snr. Tech. D.J. Limby
1964 Flt. Lt. R.S. Hassell.
1965 Cpl. R.N. Van-Gelderen.
1966 Cpl. R.N. Van-Gelderen.
1967 Ch. Tech. H.J. Dillon-Lee
1968 Sgt. R.N. Van-Gelderen.
1969 Sgt. R.N. Van-Gelderen.
1970 Sgt. R.N. Van-Gelderen.
1971 Sgt. R.N. Van-Gelderen.

1 TURKISH MEDALS FOR THE DEFENCE OF SILISTRIA (1854) AND KARS (1855)

In addition to what are generally referred to as the Turkish Crimean Medals, the Sultan awarded the Turkish General Service Medal, the medal for the Defence of Silistria and that for the Defence of Kars to a few British personnel.

The General Service Medal was awarded in gold to Colonel J. L. A. Simmons, R.E., and in silver to sixteen members of No. 10 Company, R.E. It was also awarded in gold to Commander H. Carr-Glyn and in silver to thirty members of the crew of a gun-boat which operated up one of the navigable mouths of the Danube known as the Sulina River, or Suline Bagasi, between 7th July and 19th August, 1854.

The medal is circular, 1·3 in. diameter. The obverse bears the Sultan's Cipher within a beaded circle above which is a star and crescent. The remaining space is occupied by flags and silver olive branches. On the reverse is one large star and three smaller ones. On a curved panel is a Turkish inscription meaning "Medal of Distinction". The ribbon is ·5 in. wide, crimson with narrow green edges.

In May and June, 1854, the Turkish garrison in Silistria, under Mussa Pasha, was surrounded by 30,000 Russians, under Prince Paskievitch. There were seven British officers present with the garrison. They were the previously mentioned Colonel (afterwards Field-Marshal Sir) J. L. A. Simmons, Captain Butler, Lieutenants Ballard, Hinde, Nasmyth and Ogilvy. Colonel Simmons received the medal in gold; the other officers in silver, as well as, I presume, a General Cannon who made his way into the city during the siege and left, under special orders, prior to the conclusion.

The medals are circular, 1·4 in. diameter. They bear the Sultan's Cipher on the obverse and a wreath of oak and laurel leaves. The reverse shows a view of the city together with the year of the Hegira, 1271, which corresponds to our 1854. Suspension is by means of a ring passing through a leafed claw. The ribbon is ·5 in. wide, crimson with narrow green stripes at the edges.

The Sultan awarded silver medals to General W. F. Williams, Colonel Lake, Lieutenant C. C. Teesdale and an artillery soldier-servant for their services during the defence of Kars.

It was here that General Williams organized the Turkish garrison, 15,000 strong, to withstand a siege by 50,000 Russians, under General Mouravieff. After repeated assaults, all of which were repulsed, the garrison was compelled to surrender owing to an outbreak of cholera and famine. On accepting General Williams's surrender, Mouravieff paid, in my opinion, one of the nicest compliments ever paid to a vanquished foe. He said: "General Williams, you have made a name in history; and posterity will stand amazed at the endurance, the courage, and the discipline which the siege has called forth in the remains of an army. Let us arrange a capitulation that will satisfy the demands of war without disgracing humanity."

General Williams was subsequently created a baronet with the title of Sir William Fenwick Williams of Kars. His A.D.C., Lieutenant C. C. Teesdale, R.A., was awarded the Victoria Cross for conspicuous gallantry in rallying the Turks at a critical moment. He was also personally thanked by General Mouravieff for preventing the Turks from butchering wounded Russians.

The medals are circular, 1·4 in. diameter. The obverse bears the Sultan's Cipher surrounded by a wreath of oak and laurel leaves. The reverse depicts a view of Kars with the year of the Hegira, 1272, below. Suspension is by means of two rings. The smaller passes through the piece, the larger takes the ribbon, which is maroon with narrow green stripes at the edges.

1A LIST OF THE RECIPIENTS OF THE FRENCH MILITARY MEDAL FOR THE CRIMEA

4TH DRAGOON GUARDS — Regimental Sergeant-Major William Joyce; Sergeant-Major Joseph Drake; Sergeant Richard Cooke; Private Patrick Hogan.

5TH DRAGOON GUARDS — Regimental Sergeant-Major J. Russell; Troop Sergeant-Majors S. Griffith, William Stewart; Sergeant M. Davidson.

6TH DRAGOON GUARDS — Regimental Sergeant-Major William Lyons; Private Thomas Edwards.

1ST DRAGOONS — Troop Sergeant-Majors John Norris, Matthew Bailey; Private John Savage.

2ND DRAGOONS — Regimental Sergeant-Major John Geene; Troop Sergeant-Major George Tilsley; Lance-Sergeant James Borthwick; Private Andrew Wilson.

4TH LIGHT DRAGOONS — Regimental Sergeant-Major James Kelly; Sergeant John Andrews; Privates Thomas Guthre, George McGregor.

6TH DRAGOONS — Troop Sergeant-Majors T. Wakefield, Andrew Morton; Trumpeter Thomas Monkes; Private Humphrey Polkinghorn.

8TH HUSSARS — Troop Sergeant-Major John Pickworth; Sergeant Charles Macauley; Corporal James Donaghur; Private John Martin.

10TH HUSSARS —Troop Sergeant-Major William Finch.

11TH HUSSARS — Regimental Sergeant-Major G. L. Smith; Troop Sergeant-Major Rourke Trevan; Sergeant Seth Bond; Lance-Corporal Thos. Harrison; Private Cornelius Teehan.

12TH LANCERS — Corporal J. Cannings; Trumpeter John Earson.

13TH LIGHT DRAGOONS — Regimental Sergeant-Major T. G. Johnson; Sergeant Richard Davis; Privates George Dearlove, John Fenton.

17TH LANCERS — Regimental Sergeant-Major Chas. Wooden; Sergeants J. Shearingham, J. Nunnely; Private Chas. Watson.

ROYAL ARTILLERY — Sergeant-Conductors J. Buchanan, J. Boggie, Job Smith; Sergeant-Major W. Flockhart; Sergeants William Kempton, William Scott, F. Iles, Rd. Perkins, Chst. Fitzsimons, John Adams, John Acland, John Fairfax, J. McGarrity, Joseph Smith, J. McPherson, H. Bacchus, T. Walsh, S. Ewing, J. McKown; Corporals Thomas Betts, Patrick Conway, James Browne, M. Fenton, James Hamilton, Joseph Milligan; Bombardiers Willm. Hewitt, John Bower, A. Sutherland, J. Trotter, W. Ramsey; Acting-Bombardiers John Hagan, C. Henderson, D. Jenkins, G. Gibson, W. Burrows; Gunners and Drivers H. Wood, R. Botfield, J. Douglas, J. Cannell, J. M'Ardle, J. Hay, G. Davis, J. Powell, M. O'Donohue, M. Malowney, J. Magee, G. Bines, J. McGrath, J. Norton, J. Vance, P. Knight, R. Woodbridge, T. Margree, E. O'Brien, H. Davis, W. Hovenden, T. Reynolds; Driver Rbt. Smeaton; Trumpeter J. McLaren.

ROYAL ENGINEERS — Colour-Sergeant K. Knight; Corporals W. Lendrim, J. McMurphy, J. Ross, R. Hanson; Second Corporal W. Conning.

GRENADIER GUARDS — Pay-Sergeant R. Powley; Colour-Sergeant C. Sargent; Privates J. Archer, T. Elger, A. Hale, J. King, W. Myers, W. Williams, W. Nurton.

COLDSTREAM GUARDS — Sergeant-Major S. Carter; Drill-Sergeant J. Burnett, Sergeants W. Reed, G. Walden; Corporal F. Vile; Privates J. Winter, P. Balls, C. Tutt, J. Bott.

SCOTS GUARDS — Pay and Colour-Sergeants W. M. M'Gregor, J. Badenoch, G. Attrill; Drill-Sergeants J. Lennox, G. Sharp; Sergeant D. Manson; Corporal J. Judd; Acting Corporal J. Coulter; Private J. Drummond.

1ST REGIMENT — Sergeant-Major S. Hunter; Colour-Sergeant A. Stewart; Sergeants W. Sparks, J. Mulvany; Corporals J. Horsfall, W. Sullivan; Privates D. Moran, J. Colver, A. Campbell, C. Pulfer, F. Lock; Drummer H. Clarke.

3RD REGIMENT — Sergeant W. Heyes; Privates W. Brown, J. Connor, J. Eagan, J. Hall, J. Walsh.

386

4TH REGIMENT — Colour-Sergeants W. O'Grady, A. Flemming, R. Marshall; Sergeant J. Newth; Corporal J. Clarkson; Lance-Corporal J. Fitzgerald; Privates T. Murray, J. Murphy, J. Fitzpatrick.

7TH REGIMENT — Sergeant-Majors J. Bell, W. Bacon; Colour-Sergeant J. Watts; Sergeants J. Laws, T. Poulton, W. White; Corporals P. Hanlon, W. Marshall; Private M. Edwards.

9TH REGIMENT — Sergeants G. Ripton, E. Firmin, A. Rielly; Corporal M. Monaghan; Privates D. M'Mahaon, C. Farrell, J. Redmond.

13TH REGIMENT — Sergeants J. Godwin, T. Coopen; Corporal E. Tallman; Privates V. Corry, F. Stokes.

14TH REGIMENT — Sergeants T. Cooper, J. MacDonald, T. Brown; Privates R. Harrison, T. Caby, P. Canty.

17TH REGIMENT — Sergeant C. Collins; Corporal P. Smith; Privates J. Davis, R. Hogan, T. Lawless, B. Vaughan.

18TH REGIMENT — Colour-Sergeant E. Dunne; Sergeants J. Harvey, J. Gleeson; Corporal N. O'Donnell; Privates J. Cox, E. Langton, J. Byrne.

19TH REGIMENT — Colour-Sergeant W. Britts; Sergeants W. Murphy, W. Smith, H. Strick, T. Murphy, G. Rolins; Privates H. Higgins, J. Duffy, S. Evans.

20TH REGIMENT — Sergeants J. Moss, G. Boxall, J. Brown; Privates J. Brown, G. Kirkham, W. Hennessy, H. Gray, P. Callaghan, J. Lowe.

21ST REGIMENT — Colour Sergeants J. Higdon, R. Ellis; Sergeants J. Sim, P. Kelly, J. Russell, E. Marshman; Privates T. Driscoll, M. M'Phely, P. Crowley.

23RD REGIMENT — Sergeant-Major W. Handley; Colour-Sergeants J. O'Neill, C. Coviton, J. Boyse; Sergeants J. Collins, C. Godden, W. Andrews, W. Parkinson; Privates T. Gerraghty, J. Brown.

28TH REGIMENT — Sergeants W. Cook, G. Dunnery; Privates J. Carson, M. Connell, W. Dunn, J. Blake, J. Tobin, J. Hill, P. Tulley.

30TH REGIMENT — Colour-Sergeants H. McAllister, T. M'Donogh, J. Richardson; Sergeant O. Curran; Lance-Corporal M. Byrne; Privates J. Smith, W. Nicholl, C. Quigley, T. McDonald.

31ST REGIMENT - Colour-Sergeant J. Foley; Privates R. Stapleton, J. Ruth, L. Ryan, J. Spelman.

33RD REGIMENT — Sergeant-Major W. Barwell; Colour-Sergeants W. Meanaing, P. Read, J. Bacon; Sergeants P. Whelan, W. Crane; Privates F. Crotty, W. Douglas, P. M'Guire.

34TH REGIMENT — Colour-Sergeant W. Smith; Sergeants W. Quirk, J. Haydon, W. Carney; Corporal W. Coffer; Privates C. Brophy, W. Gill, T. Loft.

38TH REGIMENT — Sergeant-Major P. M'Fadden; Sergeant A. Clarke; Corporal T. Brennan; Privates J. Walsh, R. Longheed, M. Murphy, B. Newhall, W. Moore, J. Blackmore.

39TH REGIMENT — Colour-Sergeant J. Garrett; Sergeant G. Pegram; Corporal T. Omealy; Privates M. Boyle, L. Lind, M. Ryan.

41ST REGIMENT — Colour-Sergeants J. Smith, A. Madden, W. Davis, J. Kelly; Corporal C. Nelson; Privates P. Garvey, J. Kennelly, T. M'Quade, M. Rogerson.

42ND REGIMENT — Colour-Sergeant T. Ridley; Sergeants W. Strathern, G. Fox; Lance-Corporals R. M'Nair, W. Bennett; Privates D. M'Kenzie, N. Carmichael, A. Cromtie.

44TH REGIMENT — Quartermaster-Sergeant D. Reddin; Colour-Sergeant J. Donelan; Sergeant T. Brown; Corporals R. Murray, J. Drenon, D. Canty; Privates J. Edlow, J. Burnside, T. McCarthy.

46TH REGIMENT — Colour-Sergeant S. Harbour; Sergeants G. Blagdon, W. Brommell, L. Gooding; Corporal W. Watt; Privates J. Hunt, J. Condon.

47TH REGIMENT — Colour-Sergeants G. M'Donald, Gill; Sergeants W. Bowler, R. Court; Corporal C. O'Loghlin; Privates J. McDermond, J. Dinneen, J. Dillon, D. Flanagan.

48TH REGIMENT — Sergeant-Major S. Francis; Corporals T. Kelly, T. Goorly; Private J. Downey.

49TH REGIMENT — Colour-Sergeants G. Vayng, J. M'Coy, J. Thompson, C. Barnes; Sergeant M. Rooney; Corporal W. Reilly; Lance-Corporal A. Pendridge; Private R. McKenna.

50TH REGIMENT — Sergeant-Major R. Foley; Colour-Sergeant W. Turner; Sergeant R. Newcombe; Privates M. Hannan, J. Brennan, W. Cooney, L. Ward.

55TH REGIMENT — Colour-Sergeants H. Hendrick, P. Pope; Sergeants W. Spencer, W. Campion; Lance-Corporal W. M'Lachlan; Privates J. Dunn, J. Wilson, J. Whelan, T. Johnstone.

56TH REGIMENT — Colour-Sergeants W. Dibbs, J. Whittaker, J. Lord, L. Hogan; Private J. Butler.

57TH REGIMENT — Colour-Sergeants J. McCardle, J. Coughlan, J. Jones; Sergeant J. Andrews; Corporal T. Connell, Lance-Corporals W. Kinnarney, T. Anderson; Private J. Murray.

62ND REGIMENT — Sergeants W. Reilly, J. Warren; Privates M. Brophy, J. McKie, T. Carney, J. McCarthy, J. McSharry; Drummer T. Finnigan.

63RD REGIMENT — Sergeant-Major R. Hughes; Colour-Sergeants J. Ward, W. Morris, J. Brophy; Sergeants A. Roberts, W. Ahern; Privates J. McGowan, D. Sullivan.

68TH REGIMENT — Sergeant-Major J. Gibbons; Sergeants P. Delany, T. Watson; Corporals Donohue, P. Finns; Privates J. Sims, W. Ferris, C. Ross, J. Mitchell.

71ST REGIMENT — Colour-Sergeant J. Hughes; Privates W. Don, R. Martin, A. Rattray, J. Cousins, J. Laughlan.

72ND REGIMENT — Corporal A. Duncan; Privates T. Alison, J. Harper, S. McNeish.

77TH REGIMENT — Colour-Sergeant J. Toohey; Lance-Corporal W. Wilson; Privates A. Wright, M. Charleston, W. M'Guire, J. Quinlan, Drummer T. McGill.

79TH REGIMENT — Colour-Sergeants J. Spence, A. Goodbrand; Sergeants C. Campbell, W. Davie, W. Gunn, Privates R. Bruce, J. Wilkie, J. Sloan.

88TH REGIMENT — Sergeant-Major S. Conyngham; Colour-Sergeants H. Kelly, M. Canty; Sergeant J. Myers; Corporal H. McKeon; Privates H. Spellacy, T. Handley, B. M'Namara, M. Ryan; Drummer R. Grannon.

89TH REGIMENT — Sergeant J. Grant; Corporal J. Tremwith; Privates P. Kineally, D. Lenaghan, W. Heffernan.

90TH REGIMENT — Colour-Sergeant C. Sanderson; Corporal H. Hill; Privates J. Alexander, J. Lawless, T. Bayley, J. Goldsmith, M. Whelan; Bugler E. Flaxman.

93RD REGIMENT — Colour-Sergeant A. Knox; Sergeants J. Kiddie, A. Crabtree; Lance-Corporal W. M'Kenzie; Privates J. Cobb, J. Forbes, J. Leslie, J. Davidson, P. M'Kay.

95TH REGIMENT — Sergeant N. Ormond; Corporals S. Webb, J. Linn; Privates W. Harris, J. English, P. Gallagher, J. Jacques, P. Dooley, J. Cody.

97TH REGIMENT — Colour-Sergeant F. Wedgeworth; Sergeants P. Donellan, W. Newmann, Corporal A. Curran; Privates H. Jackson, J. Cotterill, P. M'Miltry, W. Fitzgerald.

RIFLE BRIGADE — Sergeant-Majors J. Waller, R. Cornelius; Colour-Sergeants C. Munro, D. Fisher, J. Hicks; Sergeants T. Burge, J. Harrywood; Corporal J. Bradshaw; Privates C. Dencer, M. Benn, M. M'Cormick, C. Frough, W. Eagle, J. King, P. M'Cann, H. Bailey, T. Davis, J. Green, B. M'Mahon.

1B LIST OF THE RECIPIENTS OF THE SARDINIAN WAR MEDAL FOR THE CRIMEA—all engraved by E. Nash, a Royal Mint sub-contractor, the medals having been struck in Turin.

GENERAL OFFICERS — General Sir G. Brown, Lieutenant-General Sir R. England; Major-Generals Sir H. Bentinck, Lord Rokeby, Sir J. Scarlett, Sir H. Jones, Sir W. Eyre, J. Dupuis.

STAFF — Lieutenant-Colonels Hon. Adrian Hope, E. B. Hamley; Brevet Lieutenant-Colonels G. W. Mayow, Hon. L. Curzon, K. D. Mackenzie, Hugh Smith, J. E. Thackwell, R. L. Ross, L. Shadwell, A. M. Cathcart, J. V. Kirkland; Brevet-Majors V. Wing, E. Fellowes, J. Hackett, A. P. S. Wortley, Hon. G. Elliott, W. Faussett, A. C. Snodgrass, Hon. W. Colville, A. Garrett, F. A. Thesiger, R. Luard, R. L. Pearson, F. Hammersley, C. W. St. Clair; Major A. Pitcairn; Captains A. Ponsonby, H. C. Jervoise, Hon. C. J. Keith, R. Swire, C. E. Mansfield, R. G. Ellison, W. Earle, H. H. Day, G. M. Stopford.

4TH DRAGOON GUARDS — Lieutenant-Colonel T. W. M'Mahon; Brevet Lieutenant-Colonel W. C. Forrest; Brevet-Major F. R. Forster; Assistant-Surgeon W. Cattell; Troop Sergeant-Major J. Evans; Lance-Sergeant J. Gamble.

1ST DRAGOONS — Colonel J. Yorke; Captain G. Campbell; Sergeant J. Hill.

2ND DRAGOONS — Colonel H. D. Griffith, Captain G. Buchanan; Sergeant-Major J. Wilson.

4TH LIGHT DRAGOONS — Colonel Lord George Paget; Brevet Lieutenant-Colonel A. Lowe; Brevet-Major R. Portal; Troop Sergeant-Major W. Waterson.

6TH DRAGOONS — Captain E. D. Hunt, Trumpeter J. Hardy.

8TH HUSSARS — Lieutenant-Colonel R. De Salis; Brevet-Major E. Tomkinson; Trumpeter W. Wilson.

10TH HUSSARS — Colonel W. Parlby.

11TH HUSSARS — Lieutenant and Adjutant J. Yates; Sergeant R. Davis.

12TH LANCERS — Major T. G. A. Oakes.

13TH LIGHT DRAGOONS — Captain P. S. Smith; Corporal W. Gardiner.

17TH LANCERS — Colonel J. Lawrenson; Cornet J. Duncan; Sergeant A. Ranson.

ROYAL ARTILLERY — Brevet Lieutenant-Colonels J. C. Fortescue, C. H. Morris, S. E. Gordon, Hon. E. T. Gage, C. S. Henry, H. J. Thomas; Major F. B. Ward; Brevet-Majors P. G. Pipon, G. L. Tupper, C. H. Ingilby, H. P. Yates, J. F. Pennycuick, A. C. Hawkins, G. Shaw, E. Mowbray, W. Barry, J. Mitchell, G. Henry, J. Sinclair, L. Penn, E. Taddy, P. L'Estrange, R. Champion, W. Andrews, W. Le Mesurier; Lieutenants B. Humphrey, Sir J. Campbell, E. Ward, F. Anley, C. Browne, H. Maule, C. Roberts; Staff-Surgeon W. Perry; Assistant-Surgeon E. Bowen; Troop Sergeant-Major J. Beardsley; Company Sergeant-Major J. Hamilton; Sergeants J. Hamilton, S. Ewing, D. Dowling, G. Symonds, M. Hunter; Bombardiers D. Cambridge, W. Ramsey, H. Collier; Gunners and Drivers E. O'Brien, J. M'Garry, T. Arthur, J. Barrett, J. Death.

ROYAL ENGINEERS — Colonels J. W. Gordon, F. E. Chapman; Lieutenant-Colonels E. Stanton, J. Manners Browne; Majors H. W. Montague, F. C. Hassard, C. B. Ewart, F. H. De Vere; Lieutenants W. O. Lennon, A. Leary, F. E. Pratt; Corporal W. Baker; Privates A. M'Caughey, W. Tumble.

GRENADIER GUARDS — Colonel C. W. Ridley; Lieutenant-Colonel Lord Arthur Hay; Captains C. N. Sturt, H. W. Verschoyle, R. W. Hamilton; Colour-Sergeant R. Minor; Private T. Sharpe.

COLDSTREAM GUARDS — Lieutenant-Colonels C. W. Strong, Lord A. FitzRoy; Brevet-Majors P. Crawley, Sir James Dunlop, J. A. Connolly; Sergeant G. Haynes; Lance-Sergeant F. File.

SCOTS FUSILIER GUARDS — Colonel E. Forestier Walker; Brevet-Majors Hon. W. Coke, Hon. A. E. Frazer; Captains S. J. Blane, J. Scott; Sergeants J. McBain, J. Stewart.

1ST REGIMENT — Lieutenant-Colonel A. Montgomery; Brevet Lieutenant-Colonels Hon. C. D. Plunkett, F. G. Urquhart; Major W. J. Gillum; Captains W. F. Rudd, W. Cookworthy; Lieutenant F. H. Hope; Sergeant-Major R. Henshall; Colour-Sergeant W. M'Dowell; Private G. Woodhouse.

3RD REGIMENT — Colonel C. Van Straubenzee; Brevet-Major G. Ambrose; Private J. Fahey.

4TH REGIMENT — Lieutenant-Colonel J. J. Hort; Captain A. J. Sykes; Lieutenant J. Howley; Sergeant J. M'Ardell; Private T. Scannells.

7TH REGIMENT — Lieutenant-Colonel R. Y. Shipley; Brevet Lieutenant-Colonel J. R. Heyland; Brevet-Major H. R. Hibbert; Lieutenant W. Hope; Privates W. Barrack, J. M'Guire.

9TH REGIMENT — Lieutenant-Colonel F. D. Lister; Captain W. Nugent; Sergeant P. Donohue.

14TH REGIMENT — Colonel M. Barlow; Brevet Lieutenant-Colonel Sir J. E. Alexander; Brevet-Major W. C. Trevor; Captain J. G. Maycock; Sergeant W. Hopkins.

18TH REGIMENT — Lieutenant-Colonel J. C. Kennedy; Brevet Lieutenant-Colonel F. S. Call; Lieutenant T. D. Baker; Private J. Weir.

19TH REGIMENT — Lieutenant-Colonel R. Warden; Captains H. T. Uniacke, G. A. Warburton; Lieutenant and Adjutant T. Thompson; Sergeant J. Sherlock; Private J. Halloran.

20TH REGIMENT — Colonel F. Horn; Major W. P. Radcliffe; Captain C. E. Parkinson; Lieutenant H. B. Vaughan; Colour-Sergeant J. Whybrow; Private P. Rowe.

21ST REGIMENT — Colonel C. R. Sackville; Brevet-Major G. Boldero; Captains H. King, R. Stephens, S. H. Clerke; Sergeant-Major W. Fowler; Colour-Sergeant R. Ellis.

23RD REGIMENT — Colonel D. Lysons; Major F. E. Drewe; Captain S. C. Millett; Lieutenant L. O'Connor; Corporals E. Luby, T. Symonds.

28TH REGIMENT — Colonel F. Adams; Lieutenant-Colonel R. Baumgartner; Brevet Lieutenant-Colonel E. Hallewell; Major T. Maunsell; Captains S. A. Messiter, T. L. Bell; Corporal J. M'Loughlin; Private W. Gleeson.

30TH REGIMENT — Lieutenant-Colonel J. Mauleverer; Brevet Lieutenant-Colonel T. Pakenham; Major R. Dillon; Lieutenant and Adjutant G. Sanders; Sergeant T. Shaw; Private J. Andrews.

31ST REGIMENT — Colonel G. Staunton.

33RD REGIMENT — Lieutenant-Colonel G. V. Mundy; Brevet Lieutenant-Colonel J. E. Collings; Captain A. B. Wallis; Lieutenant R. H. De Montmorencey; Assistant-Surgeon T. Clarke; Privates P. Leary, J. Bond.

34TH REGIMENT — Brevet Lieutenant-Colonel J. Simpson; Brevet-Major J. Jordan; Lieutenants A. W. Boyce, F. Peel; Colour-Sergeant J. Pratt; Corporal D. Coughlan.

38TH REGIMENT — Lieutenant-Colonel J. P. Sparkes; Brevet Lieutenant-Colonel W. J. Loftus; Lieutenants C. W. Gaynor, A. J. Ewen; Privates P. McGuire, T. Reynolds.

39TH REGIMENT — Major T. W. Hudson; Lieutenant and Adjutant T. W. Bennett; Private J. M'Cluskey.

41ST REGIMENT — Lieutenant-Colonel R. Pratt; Majors G. Skipworth. H. S. Bush; Captain G. Peddie; Corporal W. Crawford; Private P. Collins.

42ND REGIMENT — Colonel D. A. Cameron; Lieutenant-Colonel A. Cameron; Captains H. Montgomery, Sir Peter Halkett; Colour-Sergeant D. Dalgleish; Private E. M'Millan.

44TH REGIMENT — Colonel Hon. A. A. Spencer; Lieutenant-Colonel C. W. Staveley; Brevet Lieutenant-Colonel W. M'Mahon; Brevet-Major W. Fletcher; Captain R. Baillie; Lieutenant W. A. Wood; Privates W. Doole, W. Woodgate.

46TH REGIMENT – Colonel Sir Robert Garrett; Brevet Lieutenant-Colonel C. F. Campbell; Captains N. Dunscombe, G. H. Knapp; Colour-Sergeant P. Cullen; Private P. Flinn.

47TH REGIMENT – Lieutenant-Colonel R. T. Farren; Brevet Lieutenant-Colonels J. Villiers, J. H. Lowndes; Captains Hon. B. M. Ward, H. J. Buchanan; Sergeant W. Grant; Private E. M'Mahon.

48TH REGIMENT – Captain W. H. Cairnes; Sergeant R. Batlin.

49TH REGIMENT – Lieutenant-Colonels J. T. Grant, J. H. King; Captains G. K. Chatfield, W. Young; Surgeon J. Davis; Sergeant-Major R. Holden; Private J. Gibbons.

50TH REGIMENT – Colonel R. Waddy; Lieutenant-Colonel J. L. Wilson; Brevet Lieutenant-Colonel H. E. Weare; Major E. G. Hibbert; Lieutenants M. G. Clarke, J. Lamb; Privates A. O'Leary, T. Reghan.

55TH REGIMENT – Colonel C. Warren; Lieutenant-Colonel A. Capel Cure; Lieutenants W. B. Johnson, J. Scott; Sergeant J. Meara; Lance-Sergeant J. O'Donnell.

57TH REGIMENT – Lieutenant-Colonel J. A. Street; Brevet-Major G. J. Forsyth; Lieutenant A. F. Slade; Drummer M. Norton; Private J. Healy.

62ND REGIMENT – Colonel C. Trollope; Lieutenant-Colonel W. L. Ingall; Brevet-Major C. Cooch; Captain G. H. Wilkinson; Sergeant J. Warren; Private J. Farrell.

63RD REGIMENT – Lieutenant-Colonel Hon. R. A. Dalzell; Lieutenant-Colonel C. E. Fairclough; Captain F. T. Paterson; Private P. Ceaton.

68TH REGIMENT – Colonel H. Smith; Lieutenant-Colonel G. Macbeath; Lieutenant S. Grace; Lieutenant F. Saunderson; Privates S. Burrows, J. Magner.

71ST REGIMENT – Captains F. J. Halkett, J. O. Wemyss; Privates H. Gourley, J. Cathcart.

72ND REGIMENT – Lieutenant-Colonel Parke.

77TH REGIMENT – Brevet Lieutenant-Colonel G. H. Willis; Captain R. Willington; Assistant-Surgeons R. Burton, A. Humfrey; Sergeant R. Bushell; Lance-Corporal G. Brown.

79TH REGIMENT – Lieutenant-Colonels J. Douglas, R. C. Taylor; Brevet Lieutenant-Colonel R. Clephane; Captain H. H. Stevenson; Quarter-Master R. Jameson; Sergeant J. Anderson; Private W. Campbell.

88TH REGIMENT – Colonel H. Shirley; Lieutenant-Colonels G. V. Maxwell, E. Vesey Brown; Brevet-Majors T. Gore, E. Maynard; Captain J. E. Riley; Lieutenant G. Priestly; Privates J. Sullivan, W. Durwoode.

89TH REGIMENT – Lieutenant-Colonel C. Egerton; Majors R. B. Hawley, L. Skynner; Corporal P. Scott.

90TH REGIMENT – Brevet Lieutenant-Colonel T. Smith; Brevet-Major J. Perrin; Captain J. H. Wade; Sergeant Major A. Kirkland; Private W. Smith.

93RD REGIMENT – Lieutenant-Colonel W. B. Ainslie; Brevet Lieutenant-Colonel J. A. Ewart; Captain J. Dalzell; Lieutenant R. A. Cooper; Colour-Sergeant G. Allan; Lance-Corporal J. Robertson.

95TH REGIMENT – Lieutenant-Colonel A. T. Hayland; Brevet-Majors J. A. Raines, A. J. Macdonald; Captain B. C. Boothby; Colour-Sergeant F. Cluney; Private J. Keenan.

97TH REGIMENT – Major F. Burton; Captain G. H. Ware; Lieutenant C. H. Brown; Sergeants W. Kemmy, W. Moore.

RIFLE BRIGADE – Colonel W. S. Norcott; Lieutenant-Colonels A. H. Horsford, A. Macdonell; Brevet Lieutenant-Colonels C. J. Woodford, Lord Alexander Russell; Brevet-Major Hon. James Stuart; Lieutenants G. R. Saunders, F. W. Freemantle, J. C. Moore; Sergeant J. Cherry; Corporals J. Rudling, T. Tarrant; Private E. Tarvish.

ROYAL NAVY — Rear Admirals Sir J. Lushington, Hon. Henry Keppel; Captains W. Peel, V.C., T. S. Brock, W. Moorsom, J. J. Kennedy; Commanders R. B. Oldfield, H. J. Raby, F. W. Gough, E. Hardinge, H.S.H. Prince Victor of Hohenlohe; Lieutenants W. N. Hewett, V.C., J. C. Evered, A. J. Kennedy, J. E. Hunter, G. C. Sinclair; Midshipman C. A. Hayward; Surgeons D. J. Duigan, G. Mason; Engineer G. Murdoch; Assistant-Paymaster M. G. Autey; Gunners R. Rowe, G. G. Dunlop; Boatswains W. Cruys, J. Sheppard, V.C., J. Sullivan V.C.; Carpenter J. Casey; Petty Officers J. Murdock, T. Dunning; Chief Gunner's Mate J. Cleverly.

ROYAL MARINES — Colonel T. Hurdle; Brevet-Colonel T. Holloway; Lieutenant-Colonel W. F. Hopkins; Brevet Lieutenant-Colonel G. Alexander; Brevet-Majors W. H. March, G. B. Payne; Captains H. Timpson, C. J. Ellis; 1st Lieutenants A. Douglas, R.M.A., H. J. Jull, R.M.A., A. Wolrige, C. J. Napier; Sergeant-Major G. White; Colour-Sergeants E. Richards, T. Hatch, R.M.A.; Sergeant J. Prettyjohn, V.C.; Gunner J. Bull, R.M.A.; Privates J. Perry, J. Tozer, J. Hucknall.

2 ANGLO-BOER WAR MEDAL, 1899—1902

One side	The Arms of the Transvaal composed with a lion, sentry and wagon on a circular shield with an anchor in the centre. Around the circumference is the inscription "ANGLO-BOERE OORLOG 1899—1902".
Other side	The Arms of the Orange Free State composed of a tree, lion, cattle and a wagon, together with the inscription "VRYHEID GEDULD EN MOED IMMIGRATIE" (Freedom, Patience and Courage, Immigration). Around the circumference is the inscription "ANGLO-BOERE OORLOG 1899-1902".
Size	1.45 in. diameter in silver.
Ribbon	1·25 in. Reading from the left, green and yellow, with three narrow central stripes of red, white and blue when the medal is worn by a Transvaaler. Yellow and green with central stripes of blue, white and red when worn by a Freestater although this is probably a sentiment that has developed over the years.
Suspension	By a plain, straight, non-swivelling suspender.
Naming	The recipient's name is engraved on the edge of the medal.
No. of bars issued	Nil.

On 21st December, 1920, the Government of the Union of South Africa authorized the award of 13,956 medals to all ranks of the Boer forces who had distinguished themselves in the Anglo-Boer War, 1899—1902.

The medal has no obverse and reverse in the generally accepted sense, as it fulfils two functions according to the way it is worn. If the Transvaal side is showing, then the green edge of the ribbon is worn towards the centre of the breast. When the medal is worn by a Freestater the other side of the piece is exposed and the yellow edge of the ribbon worn towards the centre.

4 ANGLO-BOER WAR WOUND RIBBON, 1899—1902

Particulars	1·25 in. wide. A central 1/8 in wide white stripe divides those of green and yellow. On one edge is a 1/8 in. wide stripe of deep orange; on the other a similar one of dark blue.

(Obverse)   (Reverse)

Varia 5. The Imperial East Africa Company's Medal, 1900-1903.
"The Reward of Bravery"

(Obverse)   (Reverse

Varia 6. The Sultan of Zanzibar's Medal.

To face page 392

(Obverse)

(Reverse)

Varia 11. The King's Medal for Service in the Cause of Freedom, 1939-45.
(Reduced)

(Obverse)

(Reverse)

Varia 15. The United Nations Service Medal, 1950-

This ribbon, authorized by the same Warrant as the last medal, could be worn by members of the Boer Forces who had been wounded in the Boer War.

When worn by a Transvaaler the deep orange border stripe is worn inwards, followed by those of green, white, yellow and deep blue as previously described.

When worn by a Freestater the deep blue edge is worn towards the centre.

There is no medal to the ribbon.

4 MEDAL FOR THE DEFENCE OF OOKIEP, 4th April—4th May, 1902

Obverse	A miner standing with his legs crossed, holding a shovel in his right hand, with his left resting on a small four-wheeled mine truck. In the background is a hill, behind which the sun is rising. The whole is surrounded by the inscription, "THE CAPE COPPER COMPANY LIMITED". In the centre, at the bottom, is the date "1888".
Reverse	The whole of the reverse is taken up by the following inscription which occupies thirteen lines of capital lettering: PRESENTED TO THE OFFICERS, NON-COMMISSIONED OFFICERS AND MEN OF THE GARRISON OF OOKIEP IN RECOGNITION OF THEIR GALLANT DEFENCE OF THE TOWN UNDER LT. COL. SHELTON, D.S.O., AGAINST A GREATLY SUPERIOR FORCE OF BOERS APRIL 4TH TO MAY 4TH 1902". The medal has a raised rim as found on the Long Service Medals awarded during the reign of Queen Victoria.
Size	1·4 in. diameter.
Ribbon	1·5 in. wide. Dark brown with a central green stripe, ·5 in. wide.
Suspension	By means of a floreated suspender identically the same as those fitted to Indian General Service Medals. The pin on which the suspender swivels is fixed direct to the piece—*i.e.* there are no claws over the raised rim.
Naming	In indented capitals.
No. of bars issued	Nil

Ookiep, in Namaqualand, lay about seventy-five miles inland on a light railway from Port Nolloth and was the centre of the Cape Copper Mining Company. Lieutenant-Colonel Shelton, 3rd West Surrey Regiment, was in command of all the forces in the district with his H.Q. in Ookiep and small garrisons at Concordia, Nalabeep and Springbok. When Smuts invaded the district the garrison at Nalabeep retired on Ookiep; that at Concordia surrendered without offering any opposition to him, whilst that at Springbok surrendered to Maritz.

Major Dean, the Company's manager, prepared the town for defence and erected a perimeter of blockhouses. The garrison consisted of 661 half-castes, 206 European miners, 44 men of the 9th Warwickshire Militia and 12 men of the Cape Garrison Artillery who manned the 9-pdr. and Maxim gun. The total strength was 923 officers and men.

Major Edwards was placed in command of the outer, whilst Major Dean commanded the inner defences; Captain Freeland was C.R.A.; Captain Macdonald, Intelligence Officer, with Lieutenant Meyrick looking after the plate-layers and half-castes.

The garrison was relieved by a force dispatched by sea from Cape Town under the Command of Colonel Cooper, though the immediate relief was carried out by a column of this force composed of 5th Lancers (109) 116th and 118th Companies Imperial Yeomanry (170); one squadron Cape Police and two guns of the 44th Battalion, all under command of Colonel Callwell.

The medal, awarded in silver to officers, (and very rare) in bronze to other ranks, was probably allowed to be worn in uniform.

5 IMPERIAL BRITISH EAST AFRICA COMPANY'S MEDAL 1900—03

Obverse	The arms of the Company, being a crowned rayed sun in the centre with a scroll below containing the Company's motto "LIGHT AND LIBERTY" with an arabic inscription "THE REWARD OF BRAVERY" and surrounding "THE IMPERIAL BRITISH EAST AFRICA COMPANY".
Reverse	Plain except for a wreath of lotus flowers.
Size	1·55 in.
Riband	Plain blue.
Suspension	A swivelling scroll suspender although occasionally the medal is seen with a ring suspender.
Designer	?
Naming	Engraved on the edge.
No. of bars issued	Nil.
Recipients	A roll is not in existence but it is known that the following received silver medals: Sir Frederick Jackson, K.C.M.G., C.B.; Lord Lugard; Mr. S. Bagge (the last survivor of Lord Lugard's expedition who died in 1950 at the age of 91); Pte. M. Hicks.

It is with regret that no historical detail concerning the award of this medal is available.

The Company received its charter on 3rd September, 1888, and was wound up on 30th October, 1895. It is thought that the medals were awarded to those members of the Company who took part in the expeditions for which the East and West Africa Medal with bars for "Witu 1890", "Witu August 1893" and/or "Juba River 1893" was given. We have seen the medal in groups in which the East and Central Africa Medal was included.

6 THE SULTAN OF ZANZIBAR'S MEDAL

Obverse	An almost full-face bust of the Sultan, surrounded by an Arabic inscription which reads, "EL SEYYID HAMDI BIN THWAIN, SULTAN OF ZANZIBAR, 1313".
Reverse	The same inscription in four lines occupying the whole field.
Size	1·4 in. diameter.
Ribbon	1·25 in. wide, plain bright scarlet.
Suspension	By a straight, swivelling suspender.
Naming	In crudely impressed block capitals.
No. of bars issued	Four were issued for Pumwani, Jongeni, Takaungu and Mwele. The wording is in Arabic.

The medal illustrated was awarded to a member of the 3 King's African Rifles, but one cannot identify the expedition, or expeditions, for which the Sultan made the award.

This medal must not be confused with the Order of the Brilliant Star of Zanzibar which was instituted by Barghash Seyyid, the second Sultan, in 1875.

Awarded to the force raised by Lieut. Lloyd-Mathew, R.N., under the Sultan. The Naval Lieut. was promoted to Brigadier General which is probably a record regarding promotion.

7 ALLIED SUBJECTS MEDALS

After the 1914—18 war, His Majesty King George V approved of the awarding of 133 silver and 573 bronze medals to those who had risked their lives behind the enemy's lines in assisting British soldiers and airmen.

The medals, which are circular, were designed by Mr. C. L. J. Doman, R.B.S. The head of the King is on the obverse, whilst the reverse depicts a very fine figure of Humanity standing over a steel-helmeted and seated British soldier in the act of offering him a cup of water. In the background are shown the ruins of war. The method of suspension is the same as that for the Victory Medal 1914—18. The ribbon has a central blue stripe, and then, reading outwards towards each edge, are those of broad yellow, narrow black, narrow white with broad red stripes at both outside edges.

The medals were only awarded, as far as is known, to French and Belgian civilians and are very rarely seen.

8 H.M.A.S. SYDNEY — S.M.S. EMDEN MEDAL

On the outbreak of the First World War on 4th August, 1914, a few German warships were away from their home ports. The most individually famous of these was the light cruiser *Emden*, which by brilliant tactical handling and clever camouflage and that modicum of luck which is seldom denied a bold commander, enabled Captain von Muller to enter Penang Roads, on 30th September, sink the old Russian gunboat *Jemchug*, shell the shore installations and then escape.

For some while after this her whereabouts were unknown. Her end was brought about as follows.

About seven hundred miles to the south-west of Sumatra is a small group of islands known as the Cocos or Keeling Islands. On one of these lone British possessions there was a wireless station. The *Emden* anchored off shore and sent a landing party to demolish the transmitter, but the chief operator had his suspicions aroused and managed to get off some sort of a message before the party arrived. This message was picked up by H.M.A.S. *Sydney*, which immediately altered course and steamed at full speed for the islands. On arrival her 6-inch guns soon reduced the *Emden* to a shambles and forced her to surrender. When she was boarded by the crew of the *Sydney* a quantity of Mexican dollars was found which, if memory serves me aright, had been obtained in China before the outbreak of the war.

1,000 of these dollars were mounted as medals and given to the crew of H.M.A.S. *Sydney* to commemorate the engagement, whilst 996 were sold to the general public to defray the cost of this free distribution. The medal consists, therefore, of a Mexican dollar piece on which a Crown has been fitted and the words "9TH NOV., 1914, H.M.A.S. SYDNEY — S.M.S. EMDEN" added. In addition Capt. Glossop of H.M.A.S. *Sydney* was given a $20 U.S. gold piece, another being kept at the Navy Office in Melbourne.

These medals, which were really only mementoes, were not allowed to be worn in uniform.

9 CHINA 1926

Though several decorations and Mentions in Dispatches were awarded for service at Wanhsien on the Yangtse River on 5th September, 1926, and subsequent days, no medal or bar was awarded for service in China during the troubles out there during that year.

The ships concerned at Wanhsien were H.M.S. *Cockchafer*, *Kiawo* and *Widgeon*, whilst S.S. *Wanhsien* and *Wantung* also figured prominently.

10 THE ITALO-ABYSSINIAN WAR

During the Italo-Abyssinian War a detachment of three British and four Indian Officers and about eighty-five other ranks of the 5th/14th Punjab Regiment furnished a Legation Guard at Addis Ababa, the capital of Abyssinia.

For their splendid services after the Abyssinian forces left the capital until the Italians took over the British community gave every member of the Legation Guard a die-struck silver medal, the particulars of which are as follows:

Obverse	Plain, except for the inscription round the circumference, "PRESENTED TO THE BRITISH LEGATION GUARD". In the centre the inscription continues "BY THE BRITISH COMMUNITIES AT ADDIS ABABA TO COMMEMORATE SERVICES RENDERED 2ND TO 6TH MAY 1936".
Reverse	A native inscription at the top and bottom. Between them is the recipient's name. Though the abbreviation "No." appears, the number is not given.
Size	2 in. diameter.
Ribbon	None.
Suspension	A small ring, 3/8 in. diameter, passes through a fitting on the piece.
Naming	In large engraved block capitals.
No. of bars issued	None.

This is not a campaign medal, so that it is not allowed to be worn in uniform, which must not detract from the fact that it was earned by a display of discipline and quiet efficiency that evoked praise from all who saw these fine Sikhs maintaining order between October, 1935, and December, 1936, though the actual rioting only lasted a few days.

11 THE KING'S MEDALS FOR SERVICE AND COURAGE IN THE CAUSE OF FREEDOM

For Service

A silver medal with the above title was sanctioned for award to civilians of foreign nationality for furtherance of the interests of the British Commonwealth in the Allied cause during the 1939—45 War.

The obverse bears the crowned effigy of King George VI. The reverse, designed by T. H. Paget, depicts a knight in armour, just returned from combat with a broken lance, receiving refreshment from an allegorical female figure.

Suspension is by means of a ring which is connected to the piece by a claw identical to that of the Defence Medal (No. 112).

It is estimated that 3,000 of these medals, which are 1·42 in. in diameter, were struck.

The ribbon, which is 1·25 in. wide, is white with a central red stripe 1/8 in. wide. A quarter of an inch on either side of this red stripe are two more of the same width of dark blue.

For Courage

Another medal, known as the King's Medal for Courage in the Cause of Freedom, was instituted to recognize acts of courage by civilians of foreign nationality during the 1939—45 war.

The medal, which is of silver 1·42 in. in diameter, was modelled and designed by Mr. W. H. Gardner. The obverse bears the crowned effigy of King George VI. The reverse bears the title within a chain.

The ribbon, which is 1·25 in. wide, is white with red stripes at the edges. In the centre are two dark blue stripes each 1/10 in. wide and 1/16 in. apart.

12 INDIAN OVERSEAS BADGE (3rd September, 1939—2nd September, 1945)

Obverse	A laurel wreath surmounted by a crown and crossed swords. Across the centre are the words "OVERSEAS SERVICE".
Reverse	Perfectly plain except for the brooch fastenings.
Size	1·5 in. diameter.
Naming	Awarded unnamed.
Composition	Dark bronze.

This circular badge, which is thicker in the centre than at the edges, is of poor quality, but has a most ingenious idea for ensuring that the brooch pin does not come undone which is worthy of a place on the most expensive jewellery.

The various orders published concerning its award make most confusing reading, but the gist of them is to convey that the badge was for award to all Viceroy's commissioned officers, Indian other ranks, enrolled and unenrolled non-combatants, unenrolled civilians, etc., who served overseas from India beyond the Eastern Frontier, or in the 14th Army. One order states that eligibility consisted of being borne on the strength of a unit serving overseas, which must have been difficult for an unenrolled non-combatant, but, of course, they do things differently out East. An order also states that the receipt of the badge must be entered in the recipient's Army Book 64, which was, one presumes, only issued to unenrolled non-combatants who kept their weapons clean.

The final order states that the badge is to be worn on the centre of the left breast pocket below the button by those who received neither Campaign Stars nor Defence Medal, and adds a warning that any abuse would render the wearer liable to a term of imprisonment extending to five years or a fine, or both.

13 THE INDIAN INDEPENDENCE MEDAL, 1948

Obverse	A representation of the Imperial Crown and Asoka's Chakra surrounded by the inscription "GEORGIVS VI D: G: BRITT: OMN: REX: FID: DEF:".
Reverse	The three lions of Asoka as depicted on Asoka's Pillar at Sarnath with the inscriptions "INDIAN INDEPENDENCE" and "15TH AUGUST, 1947".
Size	1·42 in. diameter.
Ribbon	1·25 in. wide, of three equal stripes of saffron, white, and green. The saffron is to the left when facing the wearer.
Suspension	By a straight suspender.

Naming	Issued unnamed.
No. of bars issued	Nil.
Composition	Cupro-nickel.

This medal, sanctioned by Royal Warrant dated 21st July, 1948, was awarded by the Government of the Dominion of India to certain British personnel who were serving with the Armed Forces of the Dominion on 1st January, 1948, including those on leave at that date pending retirement, but who had volunteered and were serving with the Indian Forces between 15th August, 1947, and 1st January, 1948.

The object of the medal was to reward those who were serving with the Indian Forces on Independence Day (15th August, 1947) and volunteered to serve on for the period stated.

Gurkas and members of the various Armed Forces of the Ruling Princess acceded to the Dominion of India by the 1st January, 1948, were also eligible for the award.

The medal, whose order of precedence comes immediately after the bronze Royal Victorian Medal, is the fourth junior of all British awards.

Asoka, whose lions are depicted on the reverse of the medal, was Emperor of India from about 268-226 B.C. with an empire that extended from the Himalayas to Southern India and included what is now Afghanistan. On the death of his father he massacred his brothers and seized the throne. As soon as he felt secure he adopted Buddhism and had edicts carved on pillars and rocks in different parts of the country propounding the morality of the subject!

To those whose memories are not too short, and especially to those in India at the time, this medal will recall the dreadful inter-religious and inter-racial massacres that took place in many parts of the country as soon as partition was declared.

India's idea of what independence means was brutally illustrated on Sunday, the 17th December, 1961, when she made a sudden invasion of the small Portuguese possession of Goa that had been in existence without causing any trouble since about 1510. This followed similar actions in Hyderabad and Kashmir.

14 THE PAKISTAN INDEPENDENCE MEDAL, 1950

Obverse	The Royal Cypher, G.R.VI, surmounted by the Imperial Crown with encircling legend "GEORGIVS VI. D.G. BR. OMN REX".
Reverse	The Pakistan Flag within a wreath, with an inscription above and below.
Size	1·45 in. diameter.
Ribbon	1·3 in. wide. Dark green with 1/8 in. central white stripe.
Suspension	By means of a straight non-swivelling suspender, with a rose in the centre of the arched claw.
Naming	Awarded unnamed.
No. of bars issued	Nil.
Composition	Cupro-nickel.

This medal, the particulars of which regarding qualifying service and eligibility were not published till Pakistan Army Order 73 of 1950, was awarded to full-time personnel of the Armed Forces, who had opted for service in Pakistan, who were serving on 15th August, 1947, either in Pakistan, India, or any other country

398

and subsequently became members of the Armed Forces of Pakistan. Personnel on leave on that date were not eligible unless they were recalled for further service before their release leave expired.

The following categories were also eligible for the award:

(a) All British personnel who were serving in the Navy, Army and Air Force of Pakistan, or India, on 1st January, 1948, who volunteered for, and subsequently served with, these three services.

(b) Enrolled boys of the late Indian Army, who were serving in either India or Pakistan on 15th August, 1947, providing they were 16 years of age or over on that date.

(c) Personnel of the Bahawalpur State Forces who were serving on a full time engagement on the day of the accession of the State to Pakistan.

The precedence of this medal is exactly the same as that of the Indian Independence Medal, *i.e.* immediately after the bronze Victorian Medal. The two, obviously, could not be obtained by the same individual.

15 THE UNITED NATIONS KOREA SERVICE MEDAL (27th June, 1950—   )

Obverse	The United Nations Emblem.
Reverse	Perfectly plain except for the inscription "FOR SERVICE IN DEFENCE OF THE PRINCIPLES OF THE CHARTER OF THE UNITED NATIONS" in five lines.
Size	1·4 in. diameter.
Ribbon	1·25 in. wide, with nine blue and eight white stripes.
Suspension	By a straight, non-swivelling suspender.
Naming	Awarded unnamed.
No. of bars issued	One — Korea.
Composition	Bronze.

The suggestions for the awarding of this medal came from the Philippine delegation in December, 1950. The authority for its award to United Kingdom and Commonwealth Forces was published on 6th November, 1951.

The names of all units of the United Nations Forces eligible for the award of the bar "KOREA" appear in General Orders published by the United Nations Commander-in-Chief and include all who rendered service whether combatant or non-combatant. The latter category includes the hospital units supplied by certain nations.

The regulations made by the different nations whose units qualified are not known, but those for the United Kingdom and Commonwealth Forces are as follows:

For all the Services the qualifying period was one day, except for visits of inspection which, either continuous or in aggregate, had to total thirty days.

Certain civilians whose organizations were certified by the Commander-in-Chief as having supported military operations were also eligible.

International Red Cross personnel engaged for service under the United Nations Commander-in-Chief with any United Nations relief team in Korea were, strange to say, *not* eligible for this medal.

It should be noted that the qualifications for this medal are not the same as those for the Queen's Korea Medal, as service in Korea after the armistice does not qualify.

15A UNITED NATIONS MEDAL FOR SERVICE IN THE CONGO (10th July, 1960)

This medal which should be worn with British war medals in the order of the date of award, was and is to be given to members of United Kingdom forces and those of Nigeria, Sierra Leone, Ghana and Malaya who have completed 90 days service from 10th July, 1960.

Those whose service was curtailed on medical grounds will be eligible.

The medal is exactly the same as that illustrated facing page 395 (in 3rd edition). The ribbon is of United Nations blue flanked on each side by a narrow vertical white stripe.

15B UNITED NATIONS MEDAL FOR SERVICE IN CYPRUS (27th March, 1964)

Obverse   The United Nations emblem and letters "U.N.".

Reverse   The inscription "IN THE SERVICE OF PEACE".

Ribbon   United Nations blue with a central white stripe between those of dark blue.

This medal, sanctioned for awarding to U.K. troops by A.O. 56 of the 7th September, 1964, will be worn with British War Medals in the order of the date of award.

It will be awarded to all ranks of the three Services who have served in Cyprus with the United Nations Force (known as UNIFICYP) for 30 days in the island from the date shown to one to be decided later.

16 CAMPAIGN MEDALS TO WOMEN

If we assume that Jane Townsend received her Naval General Service Medal for being present at the Battle of Trafalgar, then this would constitute the first campaign medal awarded to a woman.

Four special Stars were awarded to ladies present during the Gwalior Campaign in 1843, as mentioned in the text on page 153.

The first general issue of a campaign medal to women acting as Nurses was that awarded for service in Egypt in 1882. There was no official authority in existence at the time for granting medals to women, but in view of their services at Alexandria, Ismailia and in the hospital ship *Carthage* it was decided that the Nurses employed should receive the campaign medal.

As a result of these awards the question of granting medals to the ladies who served in Natal during the Zulu War of 1879 either as Nurses or members of the Stafford House Aid Society was reconsidered. A War Office Committee had previously decided they were ineligible for medals, but, as will be seen by the table that follows, the ruling was rescinded.

The first Army Order dealing with the subject of the award of medals to Nurses and Nursing Sisters was No. 94 of 1901, which authorized the grant of the Queen's South Africa Medal. Army Order, No. 195 of the same year stated that the terms "Nurses" and "Nursing Sisters" applied only to those appointed as such and to the staffs of local charitable institutions in South Africa which were recognized by the military authorities and used by them for the care of the sick and wounded.

After the conclusion of the South African War, 1899–1902, the following regulations were published concerning the awarding of Campaign Medals to women:

(Obverse) (Reverse)

Varia 13. The Indian Independence Medal, 1948.

(Obverse) (Reverse)

Varia 14. The Pakistan Independence Medal, 1950.

(1) That the conditions laid down in Army Order 19 of 1901 be adhered to.

(2) That only duties performed by women which could not be done by Army personnel would count.

(3) That Nurses appointed to Hospital Ships at a base should be eligible.

(4) That Nurses employed on transports not used as hospital ships would be ineligible.

(5) That under no circumstances would Nurses be eligible for bars to their medals.

The fact that medals were awarded with bars on the first possible occasion should be noted.

The following table gives the number of campaign medals awarded to women by the British Government up to, but excluding, the first World War.*

Campaign	Numbers awarded Medals	Bars	Description of Medals and Bar
Zulu War, 1879	14	14	South Africa Medal, 1877—9. with bar "1879"
Egyptian War, 1882	17	Nil	Egyptian Medal, 1882 design.
Egyptian War, 1885** . . .	12	12	Egyptian Medal, 1882 design, with bar "Suakin 1885".
Egyptian War, 1885	—	1	"Suakin 1885". The medal was awarded for service in 1882.
Egyptian War, 1884—5 . . .	4	6	Egyptian Medal, 1882 design, with bar "The Nile 1884—85".
Egyptian War, 1888	2	2	Gemaizah, 1888.
Benin	3	3	East and West Africa bar "Benin 1897".
Ashanti War, 1896***. . . .	3	Nil	The bronze Ashanti Star.
East and Central Africa, bar Uganda 1897—8	8	8	All were members of the Church Missionary Soc. including Miss G. H. Bird.
China, 1900 (Boxer Rebellion)	15	Nil	The China Medal, 1900.
Ashanti War, 1900	6	Nil	The Ashanti Medal, 1900. This number includes a medal awarded to a native nurse.
South African War, 1899—1902	2,706	Nil	The Queen's Medal, 1899—1902.
South African War, 1899—1902	587	Nil	The King's Medal, 1901—02.
Nyasland Rising	4	4	The Africa General Service Medal, 1902—1920 with bar "Nyasaland 1915".
India	36	36	Various I.G.S. 1906 bars.

*We acknowledge the kindness of the Hon. Secretary of the Society for Army Historical Research in allowing us to quote the figures from an article by the late Lieutenant-Colonel J. H. Leslie in the Journal, Vol. 1, No. 6, December, 1922.

**At least two were awarded for service on the hospital ship Ganges.

*** At least two were awarded for service on the hospital ship Coromandel.

17 MINIATURE MEDALS

Miniature medals were not mentioned in official correspondence until 1873, though they were worn soon after the Battle of Waterloo.

There is no uniformity as to size, but ¾ in. in diameter has seemed to be the general rule from about the mid-19th century.

Except for the lack of historical interest in the piece, I get—and so do, or would, others—great pleasure from miniature medals which have the unquestionable advantages of occupying little space and a whole collection costing possibly only a fraction of two or three rare full-sized medals. The collector has almost no fluctuations in value to worry about, and any more recent medal he may want can be obtained at short notice and not, as is so often the case with the others, only after some important sale. However early miniatures in good condition are bcoming more difficult to obtain. The beginner need have no expert knowledge. A good book giving accurate particulars of the bars and ribbons is the only essential to start with. The rest can follow.

Finally, one can say from practical experience that miniature medals are an *excellent* means of assisting in teaching history and geography to children (of all ages). They learn to associate battles with campaigns, campaigns with geographical locations. If ports of disembarkation, rivers crossed, etc., are introduced, it is extraordinary how interest is aroused and knowledge unconsciously assimilated. The interest in history and geography, and often in medals too, remains.

18 DISCHARGE BADGE (1915—18)

This badge was given to discharged personnel of the Fighting Services to wear on their lapels to show that they had been honourably discharged on account of wounds or other causes due to military service.

It was of silver, 1·35 in. diameter, hollow in the centre except for the Royal Cypher surmounted by the Imperial Crown. On the band which surrounded this was "FOR KING AND EMPIRE" in the top half, and "SERVICES RENDERED" around the bottom half.

The method of attachment was by means of a horizontal wire safety-pin with the usual hinge and catch.

19 WEARING OF MEDALS

When medals are worn, or mounted on a brooch, they should all be of exactly the same length. The ribbon should be 1¼ in. long, unless the number of bars makes it necessary to have it longer, in which case no official length is stated.

The group shall be arranged so that the lower edges, or the lowest point of a star, are in line.

20 LOSS OF MEDALS

Orders, decorations and medals lost by serving personnel as a result of the exigencies of the service may be replaced free.

Campaign medals will not be replaced after the death of the recipient.

Retired personnel may have their awards replaced on payment, but such replacement will not be made until after two months have elapsed from the date of application to the appropriate authority.

All medals replaced are now impressed "Replacement".

INDIAN ARMY RANKS AND BRITISH EQUIVALENTS

One must preface these remarks with the reminder that they refer to the period prior to the 15th August, 1947.

Cavalry	Infantry
Risaldar Major	Subadar-Major
Risaldar	Subadar
Jemadar	Jemadar

The above were senior Indian officers to whom there were no British equivalents. They excerised command similar to a British captain or subaltern, but the most junior British officer ranked senior to them all.

Cavalry	Infantry	British Equivalent
Duffadar-Major	Havildar-Major	Regimental Sergeant-Major
Quartermaster Duffadar	Quartermaster Havildar	Regimental Quartermaster Sergeant
Duffadar	Havildar	Sergeant
Lance-Duffadar	Naik	Corporal
	Lance-Naik	Lance-Corporal
Sowar	Sepoy	Private

There were the ranks of Tindal and Khalassi (corrupted to Lascar) in the artillery.

The spellings of the Indian ranks altered with the years. In the official orders of about the 1790's one finds the words Soubadar, Jemidar, Naick, etc. When so many different spellings occur in official records, it is impossible in this space to list all variations.

In the British Infantry regiments stationed in India the head man of the followers was known as the Kotwal. The other followers, together with their duties, were:

Bhisti	Water carrier	Mehta	Sweeper
Dhobi	Washerman	Syce (or Sais)	Groom
Khidwatgar	Table servant		

The Indian regiments had another follower known as a Langri. He was a cook.

The word "bearer" is, of course, connected with the palanquin or palke. This was a sort of sedan chair about 8 feet long, 4 feet wide, and 4 feet high, roofed in and fitted with blinds and furnished with cushions or a mattress. It was carried by four hammals, or bearers, two at each end, who held the handles or poles fitted to each side.

When the palanquins were abolished the term "bearer" was retained, indicating a personal servant. The term "hammal" was used in the Bombay Presidency to denote a personal servant.

The ambulances used dhoolies, or stretchers, and those who carried them were known as dhoolie-bearers. They, of course, were entitled to a campaign medal for active service so that there were different employments covered by the term "bearer".

GLOSSARY OF SOME OF THE MEDICAL UNITS

MS	Medical Staff
MSC	Medical Staff Corps
AHC	Army Hospital Corps
AMD	Army Medical Department
AMS	Army Medical Staff
OMD	Ordnance Medical Department
HCC	Hospital Conveyance Corps
AC	Ambulance Corps
NVAC	Natal Voluntary Ambulance Corps
CVBC	Cape Volunteer Bearer Corps
IYB	Imperial Yeomanry Bearer Corps
IYH	Imperial Yeomanry Hospital
IHC	Indian Hospital Corps
IMD	Indian Medical Department
LSMD	Indian Subordinate Medical Department
MSMD	Madras Subordinate Hospital Department
MANHC	Madras Army Native Hospital Corps
ANHC	Army Native Hospital Corps
BANHC	Bengal Army Native Hospital Corps
NFH	Native Field Hospital
BFH	British Field Hospital
BMD	Bengal Medical Department
CMSC	Cape Medical Staff Corps
NMC	Natal Medical Corps
EAAMC	East African Army Medical Corps
Br Coy	Bearer Company
	also
Mil MSC	Militia Medical Staff Corps
Vol MSC	Volunteer Medical Staff Corps
RAMC V	RAMC Volunteers
RAMC Mil	RAMC Militia
	and
CAMC	(R) Canadian, N.Z., Australian AMC *et al.*, as well as types of units, e.g.
CCS	Casualty Clearing Station
(Para) Fd Amb.	Parachute Field Ambulance
Cav. Fd Amb.	Cavalary Field Ambulance

LIST OF REGIMENTS AND CORPS, 1970

WITH AUTHORISED ABBREVIATIONS

Arranged Alphabetically with notes regarding the Division of which they now form a part.

	Abbreviation
The Argyll and Sutherland Highlanders (Princess Louise's) — *Scottish Division*	A. & H.S.
Army Air Corps	A.A.C.
Army Catering Corps	A.C.C.
Army Physical Training Corps	A.P.T.C.
The Black Watch (Royal Highland Regiment) — *Scottish Division*	B.W.
The Blues and Royals (Royal Horse Guards and 1st Dragoons) — *Household Cavalry*	R.H.G./D.
The Cameronians (Scottish Rifles) — *Scottish Division* . . .	Cameronians
3rd Carabiniers (Prince of Wales's Dragoon Guards) — *R.A.C.*	3 D.G.
The Cheshire Regiment — *Prince of Wales's Division*	Cheshire
Coldstream Guards — *Guard's Division*	Coldm. Gds.
Corps of Royal Electrical and Mechanical Engineers	R.E.M.E.
Corps of Royal Engineers	R.E.
Corps of Royal Military Police	R.M.P.
The Devonshire and Dorset Regiment — *Prince of Wales's Division*	D. & D.
The Duke of Edinburgh's Royal Regiment (Berkshire and Wiltshire) — *Prince of Wales's Division*	D.E.R.R.
The Duke of Wellington's Regiment (West Riding — *King's Division*	D.W.R.
General Service Corps	G.S.C.
The Gloucestershire Regiment — *Prince of Wales's Division* . .	Glosters
The Gordon Highlanders — *Scottish Division*	Gordons
The Green Howards (Alexandra, Princess of Wales Own Yorkshire Regiment) — *King's Division*	Green Howards
Grenadier Guards — *Guards Division*	Gren. Gds.
Gurkha Engineers — *Bde. of Gurkhas*	Gurkha Engrs.
2nd King Edward VII's Own Gurkha Rifles (The Sirmoor Rifles) —*Bde. of Gurkhas*	2 G.R.
6th Queen Elizabeth's Own Gurkha Rifles — *Bde. of Gurkhas*	6 G.R.
7th Duke of Edinburgh's Own Gurkha Rifles — *Bde. of Gurkhas*	7 G.R.
10th Princess Mary's Own Gurkha Rifles — *Bde. of Gurkhas*	10 G.R.
Gurkha Signals — *Bde. of Gurkhas*	Gurkha Sigs.
Gurkha Transport Regiment — *Bde. of Gurkhas*	G.T.R.
Intelligence Corps	Int. Corps.
Irish Guards — *Guards Division*	I.G.
14th/20th King's Hussars — *R.A.C.*	14/20 H.
The King's Own Royal Border Regiments — *King's Division* . .	Kings Own Border
The King's Own Scottish Borderers — *Scottish Division* . . .	K.O.S.B.
The King's Regiment — *King's Divisision*	King's
15th/19th The King's Royal Hussars — *R.A.C.*	15/19 H.
The Lancashire Regiment (Prince of Wales Volunteers) — *King's Division*	Lan. R. (P.W.V.)
17th/21st Lancers	17/21 L.
The Life Guards — *Household Cavalry* . ◦	L.G.
The Light Infantry — *Light Division*	L.I.
The Loyal Regiment (North Lancashire) — *King's Division* . .	Loyals

	Abbreviation
Military Provost Staff Corps	M.P.S.C.
Officers Training Corps	O.T.C.
The Parachute Regiment	Para.
The Prince of Wales's Own Regiment of Yorkshire — *King's Division*	P.W.O.
Queen Alexandra's Royal Army Nursing Corps	Q.A.R.A.N.C.
1st The Queen's Dragoon Guards — *R.A.C.*	Q.D.G.
Queen's Own Highlanders (Seaforth and Camerons) — *Scottish Division*	Q.O. Hldrs.
The Queen's Own Hussars — *R.A.C.*	Q.O.H.
The Queen's Regiment — *Queen's Division*	Queens
The Queen's Royal Irish Hussars — *R.A.C.*	Q.R.I.H.
16th/5th The Queen's Royal Lancers — *R.A.C.*	16/5 L.
The Royal Anglian Regiment — *Queen's Division*	R. Anglian
Royal Armoured Corps	R.A.C.
Royal Army Chaplain's Department	R.A.Ch.D.
Royal Army Dental Corps	R.A.D.C.
Royal Army Education Corps.	R.A.E.C.
Royal Army Medical Corps	·R.A.M.C.
Royal Army Ordnance Corps	R.A.O.C.
Royal Army Pay Corps	R.A.P.C.
Royal Army Veterinary Corps	R.A.V.C.
Royal Corps of Signals	R. Signals
Royal Corps of Transport	R.C.T.
4th/7th Royal Dragoon Guards — *R.A.C.*	4/7 D.G.
The Royal Green Jackets — *Light Division*	R.G.J.
The Royal Hampshire Regiment — *Prince of Wales's Division* .	R. Hamps.
The Royal Highland Fusiliers (Princess Margaret's Own Glasgow and Ayrshire Regiment) — *Scottish Division*	R.H.F.
Royal Horse Artillery	R.H.A.
The Royal Hussars (Prince of Wales's Own) — *R.A.C.* . . .	R.H.
13th/18th Royal Hussars (Queen Mary's Own) — *R.A.C.* . . .	13/18 H.
5th Royal Inniskilling Dragoon Guards — *R.A.C.*	5 Innis. D.G.
The Royal Irish Rangers (27th [Inniskilling] 83rd and 87th) — *King's Division*	R. Irish
9th/12th Royal Lancers (Prince of Wales's) — *R.A.C.*	9/12 L.
Royal Malta Artillery	R.M.A.
Royal Pioneer Corps	R.P.C.
Royal Regiment of Artillery	R.A.
The Royal Regiment of Fusiliers — *Queen's Division* . . .	R.R.F.
The Royal Regiment of Wales — *Prince of Wales's Division* . .	R.R.W.
The Royal Scots (The Royal Regiment) — *Scottish Division* . .	R.S.
The Royal Scots Greys (2nd Dragoons) — *R.A.C.*	Scots Greys
Royal Tank Regiment — *R.A.C.*	R.T.R.
The Royal Welch Fusiliers — *Prince of Wales's Division* . .	R.W.F.
Scots Guards — *Guards Division*	S.G.
The Sherwood Foresters (Nottinghamshire and Derbyshire Regiment) — *Prince of Wales Division*	Foresters
Small Arms School Corps	S.A.S.C.
Special Air Service Regiment	S.A.S.
The Staffordshire Regiment (The Prince of Wales's) — *Prince of Wales Division*	Staffords
Welsh Guards — *Guards Division*	W.G.
Women's Royal Army Corps	W.R.A.C.

		Abbreviation
The Worcestershire Regiment — *Prince of Wales's Division*	. .	Worc. R.
The York and Lancaster Regiment — *Kings Division*	. . . .	Y. & I.

T. & A.V.R. UNITS

1. THE TITLES OF WHICH DIFFER FROM THOSE OF REGULAR UNITS

	Abbreviation
The Honourable Artillery Company.	H.A.C.
51st Highland Volunteers — *Scottish Division*	51 Highland
Lancastrian Volunteers — *King's Division*	Lancastrian
Light Infantry Volunteers — *Light Division*	L.I.V.
52nd Lowland Volunteers — *Scottish Division*	52 Lowland
Mercian Volunteers — *Prince of Wales's Division*	Mercian
4th Bn. R. Irish Rangers	R.I.R.
Royal Monmouthshire Royal Engineers (Militia)	R. Mon. R.E.(M)
The Royal Yeomanry Regiment (V) — *R.A.C.*	R.Y.R.
Welsh Volunteers — *Prince of Wales's Division*	Welsh
Wessex Volunteers — *Prince of Wales's Division*	Wessex
Yorkshire Volunteers — *King's Division*	Yorks.

2. THESE YEOMANRY AND INFANTRY EXIST IN CADRE FORM

3rd (Territorial) Battalion The Argyll and Sutherland Highlanders (Princess Louise's) — *Scottish Division*	3 A. and S.H.
The Ayrshire (Earl of Carrick's Own) Yeomanry — *R.A.C.* . .	AYR. Yeo
The Bedfordshire and Herfordshire Regiment — *Queen's Division*	Bedfs. Herts.
3rd (Territorial) Battalion The Black Watch (Royal Highland Regiment) — *Scottish Division*	3 B.W.
4th Battalion The Border Regiment — *King's Division*	4 Border
The Buckinghamshire Regiment — *Light Division*	Bucks.
6th/7th (Territorial) Battalion The Cameronians (Scottish Rifles) — *Scottish Division*	6/7 Cameronians
The 4th/7th Battalion The Cheshire Regiment — *Prince of Wales's Division*	4/7 Cheshire
The Cheshire Yeomanry (Earl of Chester's) — *R.A.C.*	Cheshire Yeo.
The Dorset Territorials — *Prince of Wales's Division*	Dorset
The Duke of Cornwall's Light Infantry — *Light Division* . . .	D.C.L.I.
The Duke of Lancaster's Own Yeomanry (Royal Tank Regiment) — *R.S.C.*	D.L.O.Y. (R.T.R.)
The West Riding Battalion The Duke of Wellington's Regiment — *King's Division*	W. Riding
The 6th/8th Battalion The Durham Light Infantry — *Light Division*	6/8 D.L.I.
4th Battalion The East Lancashire Regiment — *King's Division* .	4 E. Lan. R.
The Essex Regiment — *Queen's Division*	Essex
3rd (Territorial) Battalion The Gordon Highlanders — *Scottish Division*	3 Gordons
The Green Howards Territorial — *King's Division*	Green Howards
The Hampshire and Isle of Wight Territorials — *Prince of Wales's Division*	Hamps. and I.O.W.
The Highland Yeomanrry — *R.A.C.*	Highland Yeo.
Inns of Court and City Yeomanry — *R.A.C.*	I.C. and C.Y.

	Abbreviation
4th/5th Battalion The King's Own Royal Regiment — *King's Division*	4/5 Kings Own
4th/5th (Territorial) Battalion The King's Own Scottish Borderers — *Scottish Division*	4/5 K.O.S.B.
The 4th Battalion The King's Own Yorkshire Light Infantry — *Light Division*	4 K.O.Y.L.I.
The King's Shropshire and Herefordshire Light Infantry — *Light Division*	K.S. and Hereford L.I.
The Leeds Rifles — *King's Division*	Leeds Rifles
The Leicestershire and Derbyshire (Prince Albert's Own) Yeomanry — *R.A.C.*	L.D.Y.
The London Scottish — *Scottish Division*	Lond. Scot.
8th/9th Battalion The Manchester Regiment (Ardwick and Ashton) — *King's Division*	8/9 Manch.
The Northamptonshire Regiment — *Queen's Division*	Northamptons
North Irish Horse — *R.A.C.*	N.I.H.
The Northumberland Hussars — *R.A.C.*	N.H.
The Oxfordshire Territorials — *Light Division*	Oxford
3rd Battalion The Prince of Wales's Own Regiment of Yorkshire — *King's Division*	3 P.W.O.
3rd (Territorial) Battalion Queen's Own Highlanders (Seaforth and Camerons) — *Scottish Division*	3 Q.O. Hldrs.
The Queen's Own Lowland Yeomanry — *R.A.C.*	L.Y.
The Queen's Own Warwickshire and Worcester Yeomanry — *R.A.C.*	W.W.Y.
The Queen's Own Yorkshire Yeomanry — *R.A.C.*	Yorks. Yeo.
7th Battalion The Queen's Regiment (East Kent) — *Queen's Division*	7 Queens
10th Battalion The Queen's Regiment (Middlesex) — *Queen's Division*	10 Queens
6th Battalion The Queen's Regiment (Queen's Surreys) — *Queen's Division*	6 Queens
9th Battalion The Queen's Regiment (Royal Sussex) — *Queen's Division*	9 Queens
8th Battalion The Queen's Regiment (West Kent) — *Queen's Division*	8 Queens
The Royal Berkshire Territorials — *Prince of Wales's Division*	Berks.
The Royal Devon Yeomanry/1st Rifle Volunteers — *R.A.C.*	Devon
The Royal Gloucestershire Hussars — *R.A.C.*	R.G.H.
Royal Green Jackets London — *Light Division*	R.G.J. Lond.
3rd (Territorial) Battalion The Royal Highland Fusiliers (Princess Margaret's Own Glasgow and Ayrshire Regiment) — *Scottish Division*	3 R.H.F.
5th Battalion The Royal Inniskilling Fusiliers (Royal Irish Rangers) — *King's Division*	5 Inniskillings (R.I.R.)
7th Battalion The Royal Irish Fusiliers (Royal Irish Rangers) — *King's Division*	7 R.IR.F. (R.I.R.)
The Royal Leicestershire Regiment — *Queen's Division*	R. Leicesters.
The Royal Lincolnshire Regiment — *Queen's Division*	R. Lincolns
The Royal Norfolk Regiment — *Queen's Division*	R. Norfolk
The 4th/5th/6th Battalion The Royal Northumberland Fusiliers — *Queen's Division*	4/5/6/ R.N.F.
7th Battalion The Royal Northumberland Fusiliers — *Queen's Division*	7 R.N.F.

	Abbreviation
8th/9th (Territorial) Battalion the Royal Scots (The Royal Regiment) — *Scottish Division*	8/9 R.S.
6th Battalion The Royal Ulster Rifles (Royal Irish Rangers) — *King's Division*	6 R.U.R. R.I.R.
The 4th Battalion The Royal Welch Fusiliers — *Prince of Wales's Division*	4 R.W.F.
The 6th/7th Battalion The Royal Welch Fusiliers — *Prince of Wales's Division*	6/7 H.W.F.
The Royal Wiltshire Yeomanry (Prince of Wales's Own) — *R.A.C.*	R. Wilts. Yeo.
The Nottinghamshire Battalion (Territorial) The Sherwood Foresters (Nottinghamshire and Derbyshire Regiment) — *The Prince of Wales's Division*	Notts. Foresters.
The Sherwood Rangers Yeomanry — *R.A.C.*	S.R.Y.
The Shropshire Yeomanry — *R.A.C.*	Shrops. Yeo.
The Somerset Yeomanry and Light Infantry — *Light Division* .	S.Y. and L.I.
The Monmouth Battalion The South Wales Borderers — *Prince of Wales's Division*	Mon.
5th/6th Battalion The Staffordshire Regiment (The Prince of Wales's) — *Prince of Wales's Division*	5/6 Staffords.
The Staffordshire Yeomanry (Queen's Own Royal Regiment) — *R.A.C.*	Staffs. Yeo.
The Suffolk and Cambridgeshire Regiment — *Queen's Division* .	S.C.
The 4th Battalion The Welch Regiment — *Prince of Wales's Division*	4 Welch
The 5th/6th Battalion The Welch Regiment — *Prince of Wales's Division*	5/6 Welch
The Wiltshire Regiment — *Prince of Wales's Division*	Wilts.
The Hallamshire Battalion, The Hallams York and Lancaster Regiment — *King's Division*	Hallams

PRECEDENCE OF CORPS, ETC.

1. The Life Guards and the Blues and Royals.
2. Royal Horse Artillery.
3. Royal Armoured Corps.
4. Royal Regiment of Artillery (Royal Horse Artillery excepted).
5. Corps of Royal Engineers.
6. Royal Corps of Signals.
7. Regiments of Foot Guards.
8. Regiments of Infantry.
9. Special Air Service Regiment.
10. Army Air Corps.
11. Royal Malta Artillery.
12. Royal Army Chaplain's Department.
13. Royal Corps of Transport.
14. Royal Army Medical Corps.
15. Royal Army Ordnance Corps.
16. Corps of Royal Electrical and Mechanical Engineers.
17. Corps of Royal Military Police.
18. Royal Army Pay Corps.
19. Royal Army Veterinary Corps.
20. Small Arms School Corps.

21. Military Provost Staff Corps.
22. Royal Army Educational Corps.
23. Royal Army Dental Corps.
24. Royal Pioneer Corps.
25. Intelligence Corps.
26. Army Physical Training Corps.
27. Army Catering Corps.
28. General Service Corps.
29. Queen Alexandra's Royal Army Nursing Corps.
30. Women's Royal Army Corps.
31. Royal Monmouthshire Engineers (Militia) (Territorial and Army Volunteer Reserve.
32. The Honourable Artillery Company (Territorial and Army Volunteer Reserve).
33. Territorial and Army Volunteer Reserve (other than 31 and 32 above).
34. Ulster Defence Regiment.
35. The Home Guard.

PRECEDENCE OF INFANTRY REGIMENTS

The Royal Scots (The Royal Regiment).
The Queen's Regiment.
The King's Own Royal Border Regiment.
The Royal Regiment of Fusiliers.
The King's Regiment.
The Royal Anglian Regiment.
The Devonshire and Dorset Regiment.
The Light Infantry.
The Prince of Wales's Own Regiment of Yorkshire.
The Green Howards (Alexandra, Princess of Wales's Own Yorkshire Regiment).
The Royal Highland Fusiliers (Princess Margaret's Own Glasgow and Ayrshire Regiment).
The Cheshire Regiment.
The Royal Welch Fusiliers.
The Royal Regiment of Wales.
The King's Own Scottish Borderers.
The Cameronians (Scottish Rifles).
The Royal Irish Rangers (27th [Inniskilling] 83rd and 87th.).
The Gloucestershire Regiment.
The Worcestershire Regiment.
The Lancashire Regiment (Prince of Wales's Volunteers).
The Duke of Wellington's Regiment (The Prince of Wales's).
The Royal Hampshire Regiment.
The Staffordshire Regiment (The Prince of Wales's).
The Black Watch (Royal Highland Regiment).
The Sherwood Foresters (Nottinghamshire and Derbyshire Regiment).
The Loyal Regiment (North Lancashire).
The Duke of Edinburgh's Royal Regiment (Berkshire and Wiltshire).
The York and Lancaster Regiment.
Queen's Own Highlanders (Seaforth and Camerons).
The Gordon Highlanders.
The Argyll and Sutherland Highlanders (Princess Louise's).
The Parachute Regiment.
The Brigade of Gurkhas.
The Royal Green Jackets.

CAVALRY AND INFANTRY REGIMENTS OF THE BRITISH ARMY

CAVALARY REGIMENTS*

TITLE	DATE OF RAISING	
First Life Guards	1661 }	Originally composed of three troops: The King's Own, The Duke of York's and Duke of Albemarle's. The latter duke, as Lord Monk, commanded our fleet at Dunkirk in 1666.
Second Life Guards	1661 }	
Royal Horse Guards (The Blues) . .	1661	Originally known as the Oxford Blues.
The First (King's) Dragoon Guards .	1685	Originally known as the Queen's Regiment of Horse.
The Second Dragoon Guards (Queen's Bays) .	1685	Originally raised in 1682 by the Earl of Peterborough.
The Third (Prince of Wales's) Dragoon Guards .	1685	Raised by the Earl of Plymouth and originally styled the Fourth Horse.
The Fourth (Royal Irish) Dragoon Guards .	1685	Originally known as Arran's Cuirassiers, after their founder.
The Fifth (Princess Charlotte of Wales's) Dragoon Guards	1685	Raised by the Earl of Shrewsbury. Fought at the Battle of the Boyne, 1st July, 1690, as Coy's Horse.
The Sixth Dragoon Guards (Carabiniers) . .	1685	Originally the Ninth Horse which, under Colonel Lumley, captured the Duke of Monmouth on 8th July, 1685.
The Seventh (The Princess Royal's) Dragoon Guards	1688	Now amalgamated with the 4th Dragoon Guards. Their original title was The Tenth Horse, raised in 1688.
The First (Royal) Dragoons . . .	1684	Originally the Earl of Peterborough's Tangier Horse, raised in 1661.
The Second Dragoons (The Royal Scots Greys) .	1681	They were included in the Army in 1690.
The Third (The King's Own) Hussars . .	1685	Prior to 1861 they were known as the Third (King's Own) Light Dragoons.
The Fourth (The Queen's Own) Hussars . .	1685	Raised originally as Princess Anne of Denmark's Dragoons on 17th July, 1685.

*The list that follows is now obsolete, as regiments have been amalgamated and given new titles. For instance the Seaforth and Cameron Highlanders, after amalgamation, are known as Queen's Own Highlanders (Seaforth and Camerons) — See the preceeding 1970 list.

TITLE	DATE OF RAISING	
The Fifth (Royal Irish) Lancers	1858	Now amalgamated with the 16th Lancers. First constituted in 1690 and disbanded in 1798, reconstituted in 1858.
The Sixth (Inniskilling) Dragoons	1689	Joined the Army establishment in 1690.
The Seventh (The Queen's Own) Hussars	1690	Disbanded and re-formed in 1714. At one time known as The Queen's Own Regiment of Dragoons.
The Eighth (The King's Royal Irish) Hussars	1693	Raised from Irish Protestants by Colonel Henry Cunningham.
The Ninth (The Queen's Royal) Lancers	1715	Originally styled Wynne's Dragoons.
The Tenth (The Prince of Wales's Own Royal) Hussars.	1715	It was first engaged at Falkirk, where the Young Pretender defeated the Royal Forces on 17th June, 1746.
The Eleventh (Prince Albert's Own) Hussars	1715	Originally known as Honeywood's Dragoons.
The Twelfth (The Prince of Wales's) Royal Lancers	1715	The Duke of Wellington served in this regiment from 1788-91.
The Thirteenth Hussars	1715	Originally raised in 1697, but disbanded soon afterwards. Now amalgamated with the 18th Hussars.
The Fourteenth (The King's) Hussars	1715	Now amalgamated with the 20th Hussars.
The Fifteenth (The King's) Hussars	1759	Now amalgamated with the 19th Hussars.
The Sixteenth (The Queen's) Hussars	1759	Now amalgamated with the 5th Lancers.
The Seventeenth The Duke of Cambridge's Own) Lancers	1579	The "Death or Glory Boys," originated in Hertfordshire. Now amalgamated with 21st Lancers.
The Eighteenth (Victoria Mary, Princess of Wales's Own) Hussars	1858	Originally raised in Ireland in 1759 by the Earl of Drogheda. Now amalgamated with the 13th Hussars.
The Nineteenth (Queen Alexandra's Own Royal) Hussars	1781	Now amalgamated with the 15th. Raised in 1781 as the 23rd Dragoons and took number of 19th in 1783.
The Twentieth Hussars	1791	Now amalgamated with the 14th Hussars. They have their origin in the 20th Inniskilling Light Dragoons formed in 1759.
The Twenty-first (Empress of India's Own) Lancers	1874	Originally the Empress of India's Bengal European Cavalry. They were, until 1897, known as the Twenty-first Hussars.

BRIGADE OF GUARDS

TITLE	DATE OF RAISING	
First Foot Guards, Grenadier Guards	1656	Title of Grenadiers granted 29th July, 1815, after defeat of French Grenadiers at Waterloo. John Churchill, later Duke of Marlborough, was appointed to the Regiment about 1687. Originally raised by Lord Wentworth as escort to Charles II during his exile in Flanders in 1656. Amalgamated with Russel's Regiment and styled the King's Regiment of Foot Guards in 1665. The grenade from which they take their name was first introduced in 1677. The Grenadiers formed No. 1 Company.
Second Foot Guards, Coldstream Guards	1673	Lord Monk started from Coldstream when he marched to overthrow Parliament and reinstate the Monarchy. At the head of the Coldstream he entered London on 2nd February, 1660. On the accession of Charles II the whole army was disbanded except the Lord General's Regiment, which paraded and laid down their arms for the Government and took them up again for the Sovereign. They were constituted The Queen's Regiment by Royal Warrant of March, 1673, and to rank after the First Foot Guards.
Third Foot Guards, Scots Guards	1662	There is insufficient evidence to connect the early highland bands which attempted to reinstate Charles II and were defeated by Cromwell at Dunbar on 3rd September, 1650, and Worcester, 3rd September, 1651, with the present Scots Guards. As the prisoners at Worcester were sold to America as slaves I think the year 1662, when the Earl of Linlithgow was appointed as the first Colonel, is more likely to be correct. King William IV styled them the Scots Fusilier Guards in 1831, but Queen Victoria in 1877 regranted them their former title.
Fourth Foot Guards, Irish Guards	1901	The regiment was raised by Queen Victoria, who appointed Lord Roberts to be their first Colonel.
Fifth Foot Guards, Welsh Guards	1915	They were raised from Welshmen of the Brigade of Guards by King George V. Their first Colonel was the Prince of Wales.

413

1	1st and 2nd Bns. The Royal Scots (The Royal Regt.)	1st (The Royal Scots)	1633 —	It is impossible to trace earlier authenticated history. Scots formed bodyguards to the Kings of Sweden and France in the ninth century. The Scots Brigade after the Battle of Nordlingen, 27th August, 1634, appear to have joined up with John Hepburn's Scots and became known as Le Regiment de Douglas, then Dumbarton's Regiment, and they remained on the continent until 1661. The title of "The Royal Regiment" was granted them by Charles II in 1684. Their first service in conjunction with English regiments was at Steenkirk on 24th July, 1692.
2	1st and 2nd Bns. The Queen's Royal Regt.	2nd (The Queen's Royal)	1661	The title of The Queen's was granted in 1662 and title of Royal in 1703. A 2nd Bn. was formed in 1794. The present 2nd Bn. dates from 1857.
3	The Buffs (The Royal East Kent Regt.)	3rd (East Kent) (The Buffs)	1665	As the Regiment of Holland they saw much service in Holland before joining the Army establishment. They were later known as Prince George of Denmark's Regiment of Foot, and then Churchill's Regiment (the Duke of Marlborough's brother being their Colonel). The name Buff was derived from the colour of their facings.
4	1st and 2nd Bns. The King's Own RoyalRegt.	4th (The King's Own Royal)	1680	In 1684 their title was Her Royal Highness the Duchess of York and Albany's Regiment, which was changed to that of The Queen's Regiment of Foot. At the capture of Gibraltar in 1704 they were acting as Marines. The title of the King's Own was given them by George I on parade at Windsor in 1715.

*The titles in this column are those which the regiments held *immediately* preceding the adoption of their present territorial ones in 1881.

NO.	PRESENT TITLE	FORMER TITLE	DATE OF FORMATION	OTHER BT. NO.	
5	1st and 2nd Bns. The Royal Northumberland Fusiliers	5th (Northumberland) Fusiliers)	1685	—	This was the date of their establishment, though one can trace their existence before this. They were, for instance, the Irish portion of the British Legion in Holland.
6	1st and 2nd Bns. The Royal Warwickshire Regt.	6th (Royal 1st Warwickshire)	1685	—	They formed part of the forces in Holland before this date, being originally raised in 1673 for service with Sir Walter Vane.
7	1st and 2nd Bns. The Royal Fusiliers, City of London Regt.	7th (Royal Fusiliers)	1685	—	It seems almost, if not quite, impossible to trace any organized forces which could be constituted as the forerunners of this regiment, which obtained its present title as the result of the amalgamation of several units then in existence. They formed part of the famous Fusilier Brigade at Albuera, where Soult was defeated, on 16th May, 1811.
8	1st and 2nd Bns. The King's Regt.	8th (The King's)	1685	—	Their first title was The Princesse Anne of Denmark's Regiment. It was not until after the Battle of Sheriff Muir, on 13th November, 1715, that George I granted them the title of The King's and granted the Horse of Hanover as their badge.
9	1st and 2nd Bns. The Royal Norfolk Regt.	9th (East Norfolk)	1685	—	Strange to say, the regiment was originally raised in Gloucestershire. The original 2nd Bn. was disbanded in 1815 and re-formed in 1858.
10	1st and 2nd Bns. The Royal Lincolnshire Regt.	10th (North Lincolnshire)	1685	—	They were originally formed from the garrison of Plymouth. The first record of them in action that I can trace was at Steinkirk on 24th July, 1692.
11	1st and 2nd Bns. The Devonshire Regt.	11th (North Devonshire)	1685	—	The second battalion was raised in 1756, later to become the 64th, which number was later turned over to the North Staffs Regiment.
12	1st and 2nd Bns. The Suffolk Regt.	12th (East Suffolk)	1685	—	They were, before this, garrison troops at Windsor Castle.
13	1st and 2nd Bns. The Somerset Light Infantry (Prince Albert's)	13th (1st Somersetshire) Prince Albert's	1685	—	They fought at the Battle of the Boyne in 1690 and in Holland, under Marlborough, in 1701.

No.	Regiment		Year		Notes
14	1st and 2nd Bns. The West Yorkshire Regt. (The Prince of Wales's Own)	14th (Buckinghamshire) (The Prince of Wales's Own)	1685	—	They were raised in the neighbourhood of Canterbury by Sir George Hales.
15	1st and 2nd Bns. The East Yorkshire Regt. (The Duke of York's Own)	15th (Yorkshire East Riding)	1685	—	Originally raised in Nottinghamshire.
16	The Bedfordshire and Hertfordshire Regt.	16th (The Bedfordshire)	1688	—	Their first service was at Walcourt.
17	The Royal Leicestershire Regt.	17th (Leicestershire)	1688	—	Their first service was in the Netherlands in 1694.
18	1st and 2nd Bns. The Royal Irish Regt.	18th (The Royal Irish)	1684	—	They were disbanded on 31st July, 1922.
19	1st and 2nd Bns. The Green Howards (Alexandra, Princess of Wales's Own Yorkshire Regt.)	19th (1st Yorkshire North Riding) (Princess of Wales's Own)	1688		Raised originally in Devonshire. At one time (about 1737) this regiment and the East Kent Regiment were both commanded by Colonels of the name of Howard. To distinguish them, the common practice being to call the regiment after its colonel, they were known as the Green Howards and the Buff Howards.
20	1st and 2nd Bns. The Lancashire Fusiliers	20th (The East Devonshire)	1688*	—	They were garrison troops on St. Helena and supplied the funeral party for Napoleon on 5th May, 1821.
21	1st and 2nd Bns. The Royal Scots Fusiliers	21st (Royal Scots Fusiliers)	1678	—	They joined the establishment in 1688. Their first service was at Bothwell Bridge, 22nd June, 1679.
22	1st and 2nd Bns. The Cheshire Regt.	22nd (The Cheshire)	1689	—	The regiment was raised by Henry, Duke of Norfolk, for service in Ireland.
23	1st and 2nd Bns. The Royal Welch Fusiliers	23rd (Royal Welsh Fusiliers)	1689	—	Their first service was at the Battle of the Boyne, 1st July, 1690.
24	1st and 2nd Bns. The South Wales Borderers	24th (The 2nd Warwickshire)	1689	—	The regiment was raised in Ireland.
25	1st and 2nd Bns. The King's Own Scottish Borderers	25th (The King's Own Scottish Borderers)	1688*	—	They were raised in Edinburgh by the Earl of Leven. The title "Scottish" was not added until 1877.

*Some historians quote 1689.

NO.	PRESENT TITLE	FORMER TITLE	DATE OF FORMATION	OTHER BT. NO.	
26	1st Bn. The Cameronians (Scottish Rifles)	26th (The Cameronians)	1689	90	They were raised from Covenanters. Their first service was at Dunkeld, under Lord Angus.
27	1st Bt. The Royal Inniskilling Fusiliers	27th (Inniskilling)	1689	108	Their badge commemorates the Defence of Inniskilling.
28	1st Bn. The Gloucestershire Regt.	28th (North Gloucestershire)	1694	61	They first saw service in Holland at Huy.
29	1st Bn. The Worcestershire Regt.	29th (Worcestershire)	1694	36	They were present at the Battle of the Glorious First of June and in 1909 were awarded a Naval crown superscribed 1st June, 1794.
30	1st Bn. The East Lancashire Regt.	30th (The Cambridgeshire)	1702	59	Originally raised by Colonel Sanderson as Marines and served as such until 1814. Their first service was at the Capture of Gibraltar in 1704.
31	1st Bn. The East Surrey Regt.	31st (The Huntingdonshire)	1702	70	They were originally raised by Colonel George Villiers as Marines. They joined the establishment as infantry in 1715.
32	1st Bn. The Duke of Cornwall's Light Infantry	32nd (Cornwall) Light Infantry	1702	46	They were originally raised as Marines. They became the Cornwall Regiment in 1782 and Light Infantry in 1858.
33	1st Bn. The Duke of Wellington's Regt. (West Riding)	33rd (Duke of Wellingtons)	1702	76	They assumed their present title and motto on the Duke's death in 1852.
34	1st Bn. The Border Regt.	34th (The Cumberland)	1702	55	The regiment was originally raised in Essex and Norfolk.
35	1st Bn. The Royal Sussex Regt.	35th (Royal Sussex)	1701	107	Raised in Ireland. It was placed on the establishment in 1702 "for sea service".
36	2nd Bn. The Worcestershire Regt.	36th (Herefordshire)	1702	29	Originally raised in Ireland by Lord Charlemont, and served as Marines.
37	1st Bn. The Royal Hampshire Regt.	37th (North Hampshire)	1702	67	Their first service was at Schellengeberg under Marlborough.
38	1st Bn. The South Staffordshire Regt.	38th (1st Staffordshire)	1705	80	Raised in Lichfield and went to the West Indies in 1707, where it served for over fifty years.

No.	Regiment	Date	Old No.	Notes
39	1st Bn. The Dorsetshire Regt.	1702	54	Originally raised in Ireland and were the only British regiment present at Plassey in 1757. Their present title dates from 1804.
40	1st Bn. The South Lancashire Regt. The Prince of Wales's Volunteers	1717	82	They were formed from companies raised in the West Indies and America. Their first service was at Louisburg, 27th July, 1758.
41	1st Bn. The Welch Regt.	1719	69	Their first title, The Regiment of Royal Invalids, is probably derived from the fact that they were originally formed from old veterans. They bear unique honours for Detroit and Miami on their Colours. They served in America throughout the Peninsular War.
42	1st Bn. The Black Watch* (Royal Highland Regt.)	1729	73	Their first foreign service was at Fontenoy, 30th April, 1745.
43	1st Bn. The Oxfordshire and Buckinghamshire Light Infantry	1741	52	They first served overseas in Minorca in 1742, but their first active service was with General Wolfe at Quebec in 1759. They became Light Infantry in 1803.
44	1st Bn. The Essex Regt.	1741	56	Their first active service was in America.
45	1st Bn. The Sherwood Foresters. (Nottinghamshire and Derbyshire Regt.)	1748	94	Originally a regiment of Marines formed in 1740 and disbanded in 1748. The present 45th, the old 56th, was formed in 1748; In 1778 it was stationed in Nottinghamshire and joined with the Nottinghamshire Militia, from which it obtained its present title.
46	2nd Bn. The Duke of Cornwall's Light Infantry	1741	32	This battalion was the old 57th, raised in 1741.
47	1st Bn. The Loyal Regt. (North Lancashire)	1740	81	Their first service was at Louisburg in 1758, then at Quebec, 1759.
48	1st Bn. The Northamptonshire Regt.	1740	58	Their first active service was probably at the defeat of the Duke of Cumberland, at Laffeldt, 2nd July, 1747. It appears doubtful whether they were at Fontenoy in 1745.

*Mentions of Independent Companies of Foot date as far back as 1667 (some say 1633). They are mentioned in General Wade's orders of 1725.

NO.	PRESENT TITLE	FORMER TITLE	DATE OF FORMATION	OTHER BT. NO.	
49	1st Bn. The Royal Berkshire Regt. (Princess Charlotte of Wales)	49th (Princess Charlotte of Wales's)	1743	66	The regiment was formed from details of the 22nd Foot in the West Indies. They received their present number in 1748. They served at Copenhagen in 1801 as Marines.
50	1st Bn. The Queen's Own Royal West Kent Regt.	50th (The Queen's Own)	1741	97	First known as the 7th Marines and disbanded in 1748. Re-formed in America in 1755. Their first service was at the attack on Rochefort, 20th September, 1757.
51	1st Bn. The King's Own Yorkshire Light Infantry	51st (2nd Yorkshire Wdst Riding)	1755	105	Their first service was with General Mordaunt's expedition against Oleron and Rochefort in September, 1757,
52	2nd Bn. The Oxfordshire and Buckinghamshire Light Infantry	52nd (Oxfordshire) (Light Infantry)	1775	43	First saw service at Bunker's Hill on 17th June, 1775. On their return home they were styled the Oxfordshire Light Regiment.
53	1st Bn. The King's Shropshire Light Infantry	53rd (Shropshire)	1755	85	Their first foreign service was in Gibraltar and then in Canada.
54	2nd Bn. The Dorsetshire Regt.	54th (West Norfolk)	1755	39	Its first service was garrison duty in Gibraltar. It then served in America.
55	2nd Bn. The Border Regt.	55th (Westmorland)	1755	34	It received its present number in 1757. Its first active service was in America.
56	2nd Bn. The Essex Regt.	56th (West Essex)	1755	44	Their first action was at Moro, in Cuba, on 30th July, 1762. They are the only regiment to bear this battle honour.
q					
57	1st Bn. The Middlesex Regt. (The Duke of Cambridge's Own)	57th (West Middlesex)	1755	77	Their first active service was at Brooklyn in 1776 They had previously done garrison duty in Gibraltar, the Balearic Islands and Ireland.
58	2nd Bn. The Northamptonshire Regt.	58th (Rutlandshire)	1755	48	Their first service was at Louisburg in 1758, and then at Quebec in 1759.
59	2nd Bn. The East Lancashire Regt.	59th (2nd Nottinghamshire)	1755	30	Their first service was at Bunker's Hill, 17th June, 1775.
60	The King's Royal Rifle Corps	60th (The King's Royal Rifle Corps)	1755	—	Their first service was at Charlestown, though their first Honour is for Louisburg, 1758.

61	2nd Bn. The Gloucestershire Regt.	1758	28	They were formed from the 2nd Bn. of the Buffs. Their first service was in Martinique.
62	1st Bn. The Wiltshire Regt. (Duke of Edinburgh's)	1756	99	Their first service was as Marines under Admiral Boscawen when they arrived on 8th June, 1758, at Jabaru's Bay to assist in the capture of Louisburg in 1758.
63	1st Bn. The Manchester Regt.	1756	96	Raised from the 2nd Bn. of the 8th Foot, they first served in Martinique in 1759.
64	1st Bn. The North Stafford-shire Regt. (The Prince of Wales's)	1756	98	Raised from the 2nd Bn. of the 11th Foot, it first saw active service in Martinique in 1762. It does not carry this battle honour.
65	1st Bn. The York and Lan-caster Regt.	1756	84	Originally the 2nd Bn. of the 12th Foot they first saw active service at Guadaloupe in 1759.
66	2nd Bn. The Royal Berkshire Regt.	1755	49	Originally the 2nd Bn. 19th Foot, they became the 66th Foot in 1758. Their first foreign service was in Jamaica.
67	2nd Bn. The Royal Hamp-shire Regt.	1756	37	Originally the 2nd Bn. of the 20th Foot. It received its present number in 1758.
68	1st Bn. The Durham Light Infantry	1756	106	Formed from the 2nd Bn. Welch Fusiliers they first served at Cherbourg.
69	2nd Bn. The Welch Regt.	1758	41	Raised in Lincolnshire and first saw service in America. A detachment under Lieutenant Chas. Pierson served on H.M.S. *Captain* with Nelson at St. Vincent.
70	2nd Bn. The East Surrey Regt.	1756	31	At one time styled the Glasgow Lowland Regiment.
71	1st Bn. The Highland Light Infantry (City of Glasgow Regt.)	1777	74	It was originally the 73rd Regiment, receiving its present number in 1786. First saw service in India in 1780.
72	1st Bn. The Seaforth High-landers (Ross-shire Buffs, The Duke of Albany's)	1778	78	Raised by Lord Seaforth. They first saw active service in India under General Stuart at the Siege of Cuddalore in 1783.
73	2nd Bn. The Black Watch (Royal Highlander Regt.)	1780	42	Their first service was in India against Tippoo Hyder Ali and Tippoo Sahib.

NO.	PRESENT TITLE	FORMER TITLE	DATE OF FORMATION	OTHER BT. NO.	
74	2nd Bn. The Highland Light Infantry	74th (Highlanders)	1787	71	Their first service was against Tippoo Sahib in 1791.
75	1st Bn. The Gordon Highlanders	75th (Stirlingshire)	1787	92	Raised by Colonel Robert Abercromby and embodied at Stirling in June, 1788. They first saw service in India, where they distinguished themselves at Seringapatam in 1799.
76	2nd Bn. The Duke of Wellington's Regt.	76th Foot	1787	33	The cost of raising this battalion was borne by the East India Company.
77	2nd Bn. The Middlesex Regt.	77th (East Middlesex) (The Duke of Cambridge's Own)	1787	57	This Battalion saw almost continuous service in India from 1788-1807.
78	2nd Bn. The Seaforth Highlanders	78th (Highland) (Ross-shire Buffs)	1793	72	Originally raised in 1756 by Lord Seaforth, they became the 78th Highlanders in 1793. Their first active service was in the Netherlands in 1794.
79	1st and 2nd Bns. The Queen's Own Cameron Highlanders	79th (Queen's Own Cameron Highlanders)	1793	—	Founded by Sir Alan Cameron, the regiment first saw active service in Holland in 1799.
80	2nd Bn. The South Staffordshire Regt.	80th (Staffordshire Volunteers)	1793	38	They first saw active service in the Netherlands under the Duke of York in 1794.
81	2nd Bn. The Loyal Regt.	81st (Loyal Lincoln Volunteers)	1793	47	This Battalion was raised in Lincoln and first saw active service in South Africa in 1799.
82	2nd Bn. The South Lancashire Regiment	82nd (The Price of Wales's Volunteers)	1793	40	They first saw service at St. Domingo and later at Copenhagen.
83*	1st Bn. The Royal Ulster Rifles	83rd (County Dublin)	1793	86	They first saw service in the Maroon Rebellion on the island of Jamaica in 1795.
84	2nd Bn. The York and Lancaster Regt.	84th (York and Lancaster)	1793	65	They first served in India. On their return they took part in the Expedition to Flushing in 1809.
85	2nd Bn. The King's Shropshire Light Infantry	85th (Bucks Volunteers) (King's Light Infantry)	1793	53	Fought in Holland in 1794 and 1799. Trained as Light Infantry in 1808 and fought in Holland as such in 1809.

*The 83rd and 86th Foot were linked in 1881 as the Royal Irish Rifles and subsequently, on the formation of the Irish Republic in 1921, became the Royal Ulster Rifles.

86	2nd Bn. The Royal Ulster Rifles	86th (Royal County Down)	1793	83	They served as Marines 1795-96 and then went to the Cape of Good Hope. Their first active military service was in Egypt in 1801.
87	1st Bn. The Royal Irish Fusiliers (Princess Victoria's)	87th (Royal Irish Fusiliers)	1793	89	Their first service was at Bergen in 1799. They fought at Montevideo on 3rd February, 1807, which fact is recorded on their Colours. They also fought at Buenos Aires on 5th July, 1807.
88	1st Bn. The Connaught Rangers	88th (Connaught Rangers)	1793	94	First saw active service at Alost in 1794. They were disbanded in 1922.
89	2nd Bn. The Royal Irish Fusiliers	89th (Princess Victoria's)	1793	87	Their first service was in Holland. They were present in Ireland at Lake's defeat of the rebels at Vinegar Hill on 21st June, 1798.
90	2nd Bn. The Cameronians	90th (Perthshire Volunteers Light Infantry)	1794	26	They were raised by Mr. Thomas Graham. Their first service was at Isle de Dieu and Quiberon in 1795.
91	1st Bn. The Argyll and Sutherland Highlanders (Princess Louise's)	91st (Princess Louise's Argyllshire Highlanders)	1794	93	Their first service was at Cape Town in 1795.
92	2nd Bn. The Gordon Highlanders	92nd (Gordon Highlanders)	1794	75	Raised by the Marquis of Huntly, later Duke of Gordon.
93	2nd Bn. The Argyll and Sutherland Highlanders	93rd (Sutherland Highlanders)	1800	91	Originally known as the Sutherland Fencibles, they first served in Ireland and then at Cape of Good Hope in 1806.
94	2nd Bn. The Connaught Rangers	94th Regiment of Foot	1824	88	The original Scots Brigade, designated the 94th in 1803, was disbanded in 1818. In 1824 it was re-formed as the 2nd Bn. The Connaught Rangers and again disbanded on 31st July, 1922.
95	2nd Bn. The Sherwood Foresters	95th (Derbyshire)	1824	45	The present 95th is the sixth Regiment to be so numbered. The fourth 95th was that which served in the Peninsular War, and is now the Rifle Brigade.
96	2nd Bn. The Manchester Regt.	96th Regiment of Foot	1824	63	Their first active service was in New Zealand in 1845 after serving eleven years in America.

NO.	PRESENT TITLE	FORMER TITLE	DATE OF FORMATION	OTHER BT. NO.	
97	2nd Bn. The Queen's Own Royal West Kent Regt.	97th (The Earl of Ulster's)	1824	50	This is the fifth regiment to bear this number. Its first active service was in the Crimean War.
98	2nd Bn. The North Stafford-shire Regt.	98th (Prince of Wales's)	1824	64	They are the sixth regiment to bear this number. They served in South Africa and then in the China War of 1840-42.
99	2nd Bn. The Wiltshire Regt.	99th (Duke of Edin-burgh's) (Lanark-shire)	1824	62	They were raised in Scotland. Their first active service was in New Zealand in 1845.
100	1st Bn. The Prince of Wales's Leinster Regt. (Royal Canadians)	100th (Prince of Wales's Royal Canadian)	1858	109	They were the sixth regiment to bear this number The honour for Niagara was earned by the fourth. They were disbanded on 31st July, 1922.
101	1st Bn. The Royal Munster Fusiliers	101st (Royal Bengal Fusiliers) (First Royal Bengal Fusiliers)*	1756	104	They joined the establishment in 1861, having seen considerable service in India before this. They were disbanded on 31st July, 1922.
102	1st Bn. The Royal Dublin Fusiliers	102nd (Royal Madras Fusiliers) (First Madras European Regt.)*	1748	103	Originated as the garrison of Fort George in the East India Company's service.
103	2nd Bn. The Royal Dublin Fusiliers	103rd (Royal Bombay Fusiliers) (First Bombay Fusiliers)*	1661	102	Bombay was included in the marriage dowry of Catherine of Portugal to Charles II in 1666. In 1668 it was rented to the East India Company for "ten golden sovereigns per annum." The British troops elected to serve the Company and so formed the 1st European Regiment, afterwards known as the Bombay Fusiliers.
104	2nd Bn. The Royal Munster Fusiliers	104th (Bengal Fusiliers) (Second Bengal Fusi-liers)*	1859	101	Their history is practically the same as that of the 101st. They were disbanded on 31st July, 1922.

*These are the titles held by the regiments before they joined the Home Establishment.

105	2nd Bn. The King's Own Yorkshire Light Infantry	105th (Madras Light Infantry) (Second Madras European Light Infantry)*	1826	51	They joined the establishment in 1861, but did not returned to England until 1874, having seen service in India and Burma.
106	2nd Bn. The Durham Light Infantry	106th (Bombay Light Infantry) (Second Bombay European Regt.)*	1826	68	They joined the establishement in 1861 after much service with the East India Company.
107	2nd Bn. The Royal Sussex Regt.	107th (Bengal Infantry) (Third Bengal European Infantry)†	1854	35	First saw service in the Mutiny and did not reach England until 1875.
108	2nd Bn. The Royal Inniskilling Fusiliers	108th (Madras Infantry) (Third Madras European Regt.)*	—†	27	Joined the establishment in 1861 after much service with the East India Company.
109	2nd Bn. The Prince of Wales's Leinster Regiment (Royal Canadians).	109th (Bombay Infantry)	1853	100	They joined the Army establishment in 1861 and were disbanded on 31st July, 1922.
—	The Rifle Brigade (Prince Consort's Own)	Rifle Brigade (Prince Consort's Own)	1800	–	The Rifle Brigade takes precedence after the 91st and was, until 1818, the 95th. Their title signifies their *raison d'être* in that they were formed to use the then newly introduced rifle. In 1800 they were formed from details of the 21st, 23rd, 25th, 27th, 29th, 49th, 55th, 69th, 71st, 72nd, 79th, 85th, and 92nd Regiments. They were embarked as a possible landing force at Copenhagen in 1801.

*These are the titles held by the regiments before they joined the Home Establishment.

†This is the third regiment to bear the number 108. The first was raised in 1760, the second in 1794. When, in 1861, the H.E.I. Company's regiments were transferred to the Crown this regiment was known as Her Majesty's 108th (Madras Infantry) Regiment. It assumed its present title on coming to England in 1874.

IDENTICAL OBVERSES

It is interesting to note how often the same obverses have been used for campaign medals. We give below ten examples of where this has been done up to 1945.

1. Diademed head of Queen Victoria and legend "VICTORIA REGINA".

   No. 36   Military General Service Medal. It also bears the date 1848.
   No. 40   Naval General Service Medal. It also bears the date 1848.
   No. 44   Army of India Medal.
   No. 47   Candahar, Ghuznee and Cabul Medals (rare striking).
   No. 50   First China War Medal.
   No. 51   Scinde Campaign Medal.
   No. 53   Sutlej Campaign Medal.
   No. 54   Punjab Campaign Medal.
   No. 55   South Africa Medal (1834—53).
   No. 56   Baltic Medal.
   No. 57   Crimean War Medal. It also bears the date 1854.
   No. 58   Indian Mutiny Medal.
   No. 59   Second China War Medal.
   No. 64   South Africa Medal for the Zulu and Basuto Wars (1877—79).
   No. 71   India General Service Medal, 1854.

2. Small veiled bust of Queen Victoria.

   No. 60   New Zealand Medal   Only the busts are the same.
   No. 61   Abyssinian Medal

3. The veiled bust of Queen Victoria and legend "VICTORIA REGINA ET IMPERATRIX".

   No. 62   Canada General Service Medal.
   No. 80   India Medal 1895.

4. Diademed head of Queen Victoria wearing a veil and legend "VICTORIA REGINA".

   No. 63   Ashantee War Medal.
   No. 67   North West Canada Medal.
   No. 68   Egyptian Medal.
   No. 76   Central Africa Medal.
   No. 78   East and West Africa Medal.

5. The half-length figure of Queen Victoria wearing a small crown and veil and holding a sceptre in her right hand. There is also the legend "VICTORIA REGINA ET IMPERATRIX".

   No. 77   East and Central Africa Medal.
   No. 81   Queen's Sudan Medal.

6. The bust of Queen Victoria, who is wearing a small crown and a veil. There is also the legend "VICTORIA REGINA ET IMPERATRIX".

   No. 79   Third China War Medal.
   No. 84   Queen's South Africa Medal.
   No. 85   Queen's Mediterranean Medal.

7. The bust of King Edward VII in Field Marshal' uniform and the legend "EDWARDVS VII REX IMPERATOR".

No. 80   India Medal, 1895, second issue.
No. 86   King's South Africa Medal.
No. 93   Africa General Service Medal.

It should be noted that the obverse of the medal for the Ashanti War of 1900 is not exactly the same as these. though at first glance it would appear to be so.

8. The bust of King Edward VII in Field-Marshal's uniform and the legend "EDWARDVS VII KAISER-I-HIND".

No. 89   Tibet medal.
No. 100   India General Service Medal, 1908, first striking.

9. The coinage head of King George V and the legend "GEORGIVS V BRITT; OMN REX ET IND: IMP:"

No. 96   British War Medal, 1914—20.
No. 97   Mercantile Marine War Medal 1914—18.
No. 99   Territorial Force War Medal, 1914—18.
No. 102   First striking of the General Service Medal (Army and Royal Air Force) 1918—.

10. The crowned coinage of King George VI and the legend "GEORGIVS VI D: G: BR: OMN: REX ET INDIAE IMP:"

No. 101   Second striking of the Naval General Service Medal.
No. 102   Second striking of the General Service Medal (Army and Royal Air Force).
No. 103   India General Service Medal, 1936.
No. 113   The War Medal, 1939—45.
No. 114   The India Service Medal, 1939—45.
No. 117   The Australia Service Medal, 1939—45.

GLOSSARY

Bars	These are additions to the medal with the names of the campaigns or service thereon, such as Somaliland 1902—04, or designating the actions in which the recipient took part, for instance Mooltan, Goojerat. In many cases the year or years of service involved is on the bar, as is seen on the medal for South Africa, which bears bars 1878, 1878—9. 1877—8—9 amongst others. Many medals were issued without any bars and yet represent considerable service, such as those for the New Zealand campaigns. It is, however, usual for these medals to have the date thereon. In many cases medals were issued to those who were present in the theatre of operations, but who took no part in the battles for which bars were awarded, such as the Indian Mutiny, and Afghan War of 1878—80. In a few cases, the bars are affixed to the ribbon, and not to the piece; an example of this is the bar for the 1914 Star. Bars are of different patterns: (1) Plain rectangular, thin, or wide; (2) Fishtail as used on the China, 1860, and Indian Mutiny Medals. The bars for the Crimean War Medal are of unique design.
Classic Head	See Coinage Head.
Clasp	This is an alternative term for bar, though sometimes used to designate the suspender (*quod vide*).
Claw	This is the fitting on the piece which joins it to the suspender.
Coinage Head	This is the Sovereign's head as used on coins. In the case of service medals it is generally crowned when used in the reign of King George VI.
Condition	The terms in common use are: (1) Mint, to mean that the medal is in absolutely perfect order; (2) Very fine denotes very slight wear; (3) Fine, which means that the medal has been worn and probably has a few minor blemishes. Opinions vary considerably as to the condition of a medal and consequently these expressions are unreliable.
Ears	These are the fittings at both ends of the bars to enable subsequent bars to be fitted; in many cases they are hidden by roses.
Edge	The outside circumference of the piece which usually bears the recipient's name, etc.
Embossed	This means that the wording or matter referred to is raised, such as the recipient's name on the reverse of the Abyssinian Medals issued to Europeans.
Engraved	This means that the inscription of such matter as is found on the edge, such as the particulars of the recipient, is engraved.
Exergue	The space below the horizontal line on the reverse.
Group	A group of medals awarded to one recipient.
Impressed	This means that the particulars on the edge have been impressed.
Indented	This means that the particulars on the edge have been indented. The terms impressed and indented are synonymous.

Obverse*	The side of the piece which usually bears the Sovereign's head. There are, however, many medals which bear other heads, such as those awarded for Waterloo, the Sarawak Long Service Medal, etc.
Piece	This is the lower circular, or octagonal part of the medal.
Rarity	This is an extremely controversial subject. It is probably fair to judge rarity by the number of times a medal is found mentioned in catalogues of sales, or to be seen in collections, rather than by the numbers said to have been issued.
Re-engraved	A re-engraved medal is one that has had the recipient's name and other particulars filed off the edge. In the majority of cases the renaming was done either because the original rank, name or unit was incorrect or because the medal had been used as a replacement piece.
Reverse	The opposite to obverse. This generally bears a design or inscription, and sometimes both.
Rim	The raised part of the edge which prevents damage to the piece when it is laid flat.
Rosettes	These, as their names suggest, are small circular roses placed at the top end of the bars of all the Indian medals, except those for Afghanistan 1878–80. The only occasion on which they have been used with medals fitted with straight suspenders is in the case of the British North Borneo Company's silver and bronze medals for Tambunan.
Set	A complete collection of all the combinations of bars that were issued for one campaign or with any particular medal. For instance, one might obtain all the bars awarded for service in the Peninsular War. This would mean obtaining only twenty-one of the twenty-nine bars awarded with the Military General Service Medal. To obtain every combination of bars awarded for a medal, or for some campaigns, is so extremely difficult that the term is more generally used to denote a collection which includes at least one or more of every bar awarded for the campaign or medal referred to.
Suspender	This is the fitting which takes the ribbon and joins on to the claw either rigidly, or in such a way as to enable the piece to be swivelled. It is either plain and straight or ornate. The pieces of some medals are suspended by a ring connecting the ribbon directly with the piece, such as the Turkish Crimean Medal. Again on some medals, such as that for Central Africa, the ribbon passes through a ring which is capable of being swivelled on the usual type of claw.
Verification	When a medal is stated to have been verified it should mean that the recipient's name is on the medal roll and that the bars on the medal agree with those given against the man's name.

---

* The earliest naval and military Long Service Medals bore no head. In such cases the side with a design is usually considered to be the obverse. A good way to distinguish between the obverse and the reverse is to remember the slang expression "nob" for head, *i.e.* the 'nobverse' or 'obverse' is the side with the head.

BIBLIOGRAPHY

BIDDULPH, Major H., R.E.: "Indian War Medals." The Royal Engineers Institute.

CARTER, THOMAS: "Medals of the British Army." Groombridge & Sons, Paternoster Row.

CHAPMAN, F. SPENCER: "Northern Lights." Chatto & Windus, 40-42 William IV Street, London W.C.2.

CHURCHILL, WINSTON: "The River War." Longmans & Co., 6 Clifford Street, London, W.1.

CLOWES, SIR WILLIAM LAIRD: "The Royal Navy." Sampson Low, Marston & Co., St Dunstan's House, Fetter Lane, London, E.C.

DORLING, Captain TAPRELL, D.S.O., R.N.: "Ribbons and Medals." George Philip & Son, Ltd., 32 Fleet Street, London, E.C.4.

GEARY, Sir W. N., BART: "Nigeria Under British Rule." Methuen & Co., 36 Essex Street, London, E.C.

HAYES, J. GORDON: "Antarctica." The Richard Press, London.

HEADLAM, Sir JOHN, Major-General, K.B.E., C.B., D.S.O., R.A.: "The History of the Royal Artillery."

HIBBARD, M.G.: "Queen's South Africa Medal, Single Bars"

HIBBARD, M.G.: "Military Commemorative Medals of the South African war 1899-1902"

IRWIN, D. HASTINGS: "War Medals and Decorations." H. Upcott Gill, 170 Strand, London, W.C.

HUTCHINSON, Colonel H. D.: "Tirah, 1897-98." Macmillan & Co., St. Martin's Street, London, W.C.2.

JAMES, WILLIAM: "The Naval History of Great Britain." Richard Bentley, New Burlington Street.

JARDINE, D., O.B.E.,: "Mad Mullah of Somaliland." Herbert Jenkins, Ltd., 3 York Street, St. James's, London, S.W.

JOHNSON, Dr. STANLEY C.: "The Medal Collector." Herbert Jenkins, Ltd., 3 York Street, St. James's, London, S.W.

LOW, C.R.: "Her Majesty's Navy." J. S. Virtue & Co., Ltd., 274 City Road, London.

MAWSON, SIR DOUGLAS: "Home of the Blizzard." Hodder & Stoughton, St. Paul's House, Warwick Square, London, E.C.

MAYO, J. H.: "Medals and Decorations of the British Army and Navy." Archibald Constable & Co., 2 Whitehall Gardens, London.

NORMAN, C. B.: "Battle Honours of the British Army." John Murray, Albermarle Street, London, W.

PAGET, Lieut-Colonel W. H., and MASON, Lieut. A. H.: "Record of Expeditions against the North West Frontier Tribes." 1884 Edition.

POULSOM, Major N.: "The White Ribbon." B. A. Seaby Ltd.

RICHARDS, WALTER: "Her Majesty's Army." J. S. Virtue & Co., Ltd., 274 City Road, London.

RUTTER, OWEN: "British North Borneo." Constable & Co., 10 Orange Street, London, W.C.2.

STEWARD, W. AUGUSTUS: "A.B.C. of War Medals." Stanley, Paul & Co., 31 Essex Street, London, W.C.2.

TANCRED, GEORGE: "Historical Record of Medals and Honorary Distinctions." Spink & Son, 7 King Street, St. James's, London, S.W.

"The Times" History of the War in South Africa, 1900-1902. Sampson Low, Marston & Co., Ltd., 25 Gilbert Street, W.1.

The Geographical Journal. The Royal Geographical Society, Kensington Gore, London, S.W.7.

The Polar Record. The Scott Polar Research Institute, Cambridge.
Army Historical Research Society Journal, Whitehall, London.
"Official History of The Somaliland Campaign, 1901-04." H.M. Stationery Office.
Royal United Service Institution Magazine. The Royal United Service Institution,
  Whitehall, London.

INDEX

(Italic type indicates bars and clasps for battles, campaigns, expeditions and naval engagements)